T0190413

Enterprise Architecture Function

Ingo Arnold

Enterprise Architecture Function

A Pattern Language for Planning,
Design and Execution

 Springer

Ingo Arnold
Riehen, Switzerland

ISBN 978-3-030-84588-9   ISBN 978-3-030-84589-6   (eBook)
https://doi.org/10.1007/978-3-030-84589-6

This Springer imprint is published by the registered company Springer Nature Switzerland AG.
The registered company address is: Gewerbestrasse 11, 6330 Cham, Switzerland

For my family, my loved ones and for my wonderful sons Jonas and Luis who followed their father's path into computer science.

Preface

Architecture Has Become All-Pervasive in the Twenty-First Century

The topics of *architecture* in general and *enterprise architecture* in particular have become ubiquitous in the twenty-first century. The networked universal computing machine (*the world computer*) has directly or indirectly permeated virtually every aspect of our lives, transforming *the way we cooperate, partner, create, and run businesses and plan, implement, and provide goods and services. What were originally distinguished as* business *and* technology *are merging and constituting a common* business model *backbone that is neither distinguishable in form nor in essence.* At the same time, we find that dealing with, if not mastering, complexity has become the central challenge for modern enterprises. Successfully planning, designing, and operating business models today is increasingly synonymous with establishing and evolving their digital means and building materials. In summary, business ecosystems have gained significantly in potential through digital means on the one hand but have also become inherently more complex on the other—both in their breadth (*many touchpoints*) and in their depth (*complex touchpoints*). Architecture has become ever-present because of its enormous relevance for the enterprise-wide planning, construction, and operation of digital material constituting digitalized services and means.[1] Job titles on business cards include *enterprise*

---

[1] In terms of digital means, the industry delineates two terms that sound very similar but have important differences in their conception: *digitalization* and *digitization*. Gartner, for example, defines digitalization in its IT Glossary as follows: "Digitalization is the use of digital technologies to change a business model and provide new revenue and value-producing opportunities; it is the process of moving to a digital business." Similarly, definitions of digitization have been proposed, with Gartner defining the term in their IT Glossary as follows: "Digitization is the process of changing from analogue to digital form, also known as digital enablement. Said another way, digitization takes an analogue process and changes it to a digital form without any different-in-kind changes to the process itself" (Gartner Glossary 2020).

architecture, *architecture management*, *business*, and *domain architecture*, or *enterprise solution architecture*. Architects participate in steering board meetings, contribute to strategic decision-making, create roadmaps, identify consolidation opportunities, or identify systematic shortcomings from a perspective that goes beyond individual services. Although the term *enterprise architecture* is so commonly used, a closer look reveals that architects, strategists, portfolio managers, project managers, and other stakeholders lack a common understanding of its conception.

At the Same Time Architecture Is Interpreted in Lots of Different Ways

For some, *enterprise architecture* is an architecture super-discipline that encompasses all other disciplines, like domain, solution, security, or data architecture; for others, it is a framework or tool; for still others, it is part of the corporate police department trying to make the good work of others hurt; for many, *enterprise architecture* may be a binder of drawings geared to help a manager convince others that he is in charge and in control and that his yard is in beautiful order. In its practical use, the term *enterprise architecture* covers quite a wide field—that is, it is not uniformly defined or understood.

My Own Architecture Journey

I have spent my entire professional life in the architecture arena. While practically designing and delivering concrete solutions caught my initial attention, over time I broadened my perspective of architecture as a strategic planning and governance discipline. Ten years ago, I wrote a book on *solution architecture* with three friends (Vogel et al. 2011). The goal of the book was to strike a good balance between the aspects of holistic orientation, theoretical substance, and practical guidance—a consolidation of our architecture experiences at that time. When we thought about writing the book, the topic of solution architecture lacked a holistic framework that established a common, unified terminology and described architecture in a differentiated way. We had all been intuitively searching for a framework that covered the essential solution architecture dimensions for a long time. Throughout our professional lives and educational journeys, each of us had developed our architecture understanding from individual insights. With the book we wrote, we finally reached the point where we reconciled our individual insights and finally merged them into a common architecture orientation framework that became the core of our book.

Ten years have passed since then, and I decided it was the right time to summarize my experience in the field of *enterprise architecture* and write the book you are holding in your hands. However, there is a difference between the situation of solution architecture in 2011 and the topic of enterprise architecture in 2021. In the area of solution architecture, a framework gap existed, and we suffered from lacking an orientation model that was timeless, agnostic to technology, and that provided a sustainable reference beyond temporary architecture trends. In the area of enterprise architecture, the situation today is almost exactly the other way around. Numerous enterprise architecture frameworks claim to cover the topic in whole or in part, and an enormous amount of effort has been and is being expended to not only create the corresponding paperwork but to build an entire industry on it.

Initially I Was Enthusiastic About Enterprise Architecture Frameworks...

When I started my journey into enterprise architecture, I found that there were already several frameworks. They included definitions of what architecture means, suggested view models, development processes, roles and responsibilities, artifacts, and nomenclatures for modeling and more. I considered myself fortunate to be able to build on proven practices, most of which were offered in a comprehensive, unique package. These frameworks impressed me a lot—not only but also because of their sheer size, emphasis on inherent structures, and the list of prominent companies that have contributed to them and claim to use them themselves. And I was not alone. Academic and non-academic publications, enterprise architecture experts and consultants, architecture tool and platform vendors, and practitioners in the field—basically everyone I met or everything I read (a few exceptions included)—sang one song in unison: "Enterprise architecture frameworks have everything you need—just do it."

Since an *enterprise architecture function*[2] has full responsibility for the governance and execution of the architecture within an enterprise, corresponding

---

[2]Enterprise architecture functions establish architecture capabilities organizationally—they are socio-technical systems that realize architecture disciplines by integrating their full breadth and depth into an enterprise-wide operating model.

frameworks are basically blueprints that identify all aspects that a well-designed architecture function generally needs to consider.

When I speak of *enterprise architecture frameworks* here, I am not thinking of Zachman,[3] *The Open Group Architecture Framework*[4] (TOGAF), or ArchiMate[5] in the narrowest possible sense—i.e., not in the sense that their cores are released by respective consortia and then eke out a quiet existence on bookshelves or on their official websites. A complementary (yet essential) addition to *naked* TOGAF or ArchiMate is a vast commercial ecosystem, an ecosystem that includes consulting services; tons of publications, books, tools, and platforms that feed respective tool vendors; and an architecture certification industry. In addition, there are countless architecture practitioners who have gone to the trouble of acquiring certifications—and who want something in return for the investment they have made. Finally, those practitioners whose frustration with using such frameworks increased over time also remain stabilizing factors. While frustrated practitioners, on the one hand, have painfully learned that an architecture framework is not "all you need" and that it is not enough to "just do it," these practitioners, on the other hand, have also learned how useful the authoritative power of dropping framework names can be in the pursuit of their own personal agendas.

...Until I Realized a Widely Spread Misconception

When I first started my enterprise architecture journey, I quickly climbed the learning curve thanks to these frameworks, delighted in what my colleagues had to say, and happily joined in the enterprise architecture song myself. I trusted in the wisdom of crowds. However, despite my initial enthusiasm, I painfully realized over the years that the claim of frameworks to be all you need is false. There were simply too many disappointments, frustrations, and merely declared successes (which were in fact failures) to continue to ignore the evidence of a significant gap between the

---

[3] The Zachman Framework proposes a basic enterprise architecture schema that provides a structured approach to holistically viewing and defining an enterprise's architecture. The basic scheme distinguishes two dimensions that introduce the intersection of two classifications. While the first classification distinguishes the primitive interrogatives what, how, when, who, where, and why, the second classification is derived from the philosophical concept of reification (i.e., from the process of transforming an abstract idea into its instantiation and vice versa).

[4] The Open Group Architecture Framework (TOGAF). TOGAF proposes an approach to design, plan, implement, and govern enterprise architecture. It describes a generic method for developing architectures. TOGAF suggests a common vocabulary, a generic information model, an adaptable role model, general architecture artifacts, and tooling.

[5] ArchiMate is an open and independent modeling standard for enterprise architectures that supports the description, analysis, and presentation of architecture within and between architectures. ArchiMate is an open group standard and is based on fundamental architectural concepts defined by the IEEE (i.e., IEEE 1471).

frameworks themselves and their successful operationalization in a specific business context.

Do not get me wrong. Enterprise architecture frameworks are extremely useful in many ways. They do a good job of aggregating architecture best practices, generic knowledge, and reference material and making them compactly available to the architecture community. The fact that frameworks exist and are widely accepted sends a silent, albeit clear, message to all: do not reinvent the wheel where proven practices exist. While it is naïve to recklessly ignore best practices, believing that an architecture practice or framework is in itself a *solution* that is fit for purpose in a concrete environment without adaptation is similarly naïve.

When I reached the peak of my frustration curve, I took stock of *what* I saw going wrong frequently when using architecture frameworks. Next, I analyzed *why* this was happening. At a very high level, the *what* can be traced to one, surprisingly common, misconception: the extremely unfounded expectation that a generic solution will completely satisfy the requirements of a specific problem. Generic solutions such as architecture frameworks propose generic best practices, techniques, and other responses to appropriately generic problems. However, concrete problems must be addressed by concrete solutions. Where concrete problems differ, concrete solutions differ as well.

When I wanted to understand *why* this is such a widespread misconception, I found it due to a paradox: The impressive amount of material that frameworks contain, their apparent completeness, supposed comprehensiveness, as well as their structuredness, loudly confirmed by a huge commercial ecosystem, give the strong impression that this is *all you ever need* and that you *do not need to do or adapt anything else.* I have seen architects with years of experience naively (i.e., 1:1) adopt generic framework practices for their concrete solutions. The real paradox is that the richer the framework, the worse it is applied. It is the heightened version of the well-known "a fool with a tool is still a fool" aphorism: "a fool with a tool is an armed fool"—armed in the sense that the fool has successfully immunized himself against the insight of being a fool in the first place.

Problems in Operationalizing Enterprise Architecture Frameworks

Obviously, the naive use of generic reference models almost inevitably leads to suboptimal concrete solutions. To better understand this phenomenon, I have held generic frameworks against concrete architecture function designs over the past 10 years and analyzed frequently observed, or experienced, shortcomings or even complete failures. Here, it did not matter whether it was an initial function design or an evolution to improve its fitness. Based on the analysis, I narrowed down those aspects that disproportionately determine success versus failure. It is imperative that these be designed correctly and therefore deserve our undivided attention—so let me give you specifics on some of the misconceptions.

For example, when adopting frameworks, architecture functions do not consider the complete service lifecycle as equally relevant. Enterprise architecture frameworks tend to overemphasize planning aspects (*plan*) while at the same time underemphasizing their contribution to continuous service improvement (*build* and *run*). Another faulty notion to which architecture functions succumb under overwhelming framework impression is to focus too much on the internal makeup of a function (*white-box perspective*) without considering the expectations of their actual stakeholders (*black-box perspective*). Frameworks also largely conceal their concrete establishment in the form of an organizational capability. As a result, they lack references to *evolutionary fitness* as an important design maxim for architecture functions. This in turn leads to regular organization restarts, which undermines trust and acceptance. To give another example, frameworks seem taxonomically complete at first glance. Accordingly, architecture functions often expend little or no effort in creating a company-specific, stringent, and unambiguous conceptual as well as terminological foundation. This inevitably creates a relevant gap in understanding since the central conceptions of each business are simultaneously subsets and supersets of a respective framework glossary. Architecture functions pay the price for this bitterly and yet at the same time almost unnoticeably: in the form of inefficient, ineffective, and mostly never-ending debates, which in turn lead to suboptimal decisions and their protracted consequences. Furthermore, the frameworks often lack references to differentiations that are important in practice. For example, many frameworks do not give any indication of the *architecture levels*[6] to be differentiated in a company or do not adequately separate the *perform mandates* of an architecture organization from its *governance*[7] *mandates*. This, in turn, leads to imprecise organizational boundaries. As a final example of the inadequate adoption of frameworks by architecture functions, consider the inconsistent and disconnected definition of practices, like *architecture methods*, *view models*, *patterns*, *principles*, and *roadmaps*. These are often implemented incompletely, vaguely, and thus inconsistently and are isolated from each other, which leaves their potentials insufficiently exploited.

Aim of This Book

The blurred line between critical and semi-critical success factors in frameworks showed that we do not need larger or more frameworks but that the central gap appears where the concrete design of enterprise architecture functions is concerned. For this reason, I have placed the architecture function at the center of consideration.

---

[6]See the *Architecture Level* pattern in this book's pattern catalog (Chap. 6).
[7]See the *Architecture Governance* pattern in this book's pattern catalog.

In other words, I make it a first-class citizen and view the topics of architecture and frameworks through the ocular of their organizational incarnation.

Specifically, my book proposes how to design an architecture function so that it ultimately meets the expectations of the business for effectively developing, delivering, as well as operating digitalized services. My book will further outline what roles, services and processes, elaboration and reference methods, disciplines, or artifacts an architecture function is responsible for. It will make tangible to you the overall value proposition of an architecture function, as well as introduce an enterprise operating model into which architecture integrates as an organizational capability. In doing so, I do not reduce the term *architecture function* to the realm of IT but remain largely agnostic in the objective as well as normative portions of my book—agnostic regarding the nature of the contributions (e.g., business versus IT), the process models and attitudes employed (e.g., agile, waterfall, DevOps), the size of the enterprise, and other determining factors.

When an enterprise architecture framework is a blueprint for the subject of enterprise architecture, then my book is a blueprint for an architecture function enabling a digitalized business in the twenty-first century.

In any book, beyond *what* is to be described, the way in which (*how*) it presents its content and offers guidance and orientation accordingly is significant. For my book, the challenge was, on the one hand, to capture the full breadth and depth of the topic of architecture function design and, on the other hand, not to reduce the multifaceted nature of the theme to an oversimplified formula or a monodimensional set of function building blocks. In addition to typical framework content, establishing organizational capabilities is not only about the methods, roles, activities, artifacts, and responsibilities of an architecture discipline but also about its capacity, funding, mandate, engagement model, or adequate organizational embedding in a surrounding operating model, to name just a few examples. Because my book, unlike frameworks, claims to literally generate an architecture function design tailored to its context, I decided to use a pattern language regarding the *how* of my book. I deliberately chose a pattern language and patterns because they have a high degree of familiarity among architects, scale well, but also have the flexibility to accommodate design-determining factors of very different kinds in a single design proposal.

I encourage all readers to follow the navigational structures of my book closely. These structures allow you to fully grasp an architecture function in its holism and plasticity and thus to plan, design, and ultimately operate it accordingly. You will further round out and condense your understanding of what is presented in a pattern by following its references to associated patterns. In this way, you iteratively increase your understanding of architecture functions in general and develop a fully customized design for your own architecture function in particular.

Overall, this book is an expression of my desire for a work that meaningfully structures the design of an enterprise architecture function while providing hands-on guidance for practitioners. In particular, the book is independent of any particular enterprise architecture framework, mindset, tool, or platform—thus timeless in that regard. It belongs to that group of foundational works that provide you with a stable and future-proof reference that transcends current or future trends in enterprise architecture schools. Writing this book demanded an intensive and in-depth examination of the subject of architecture beyond the usually isolated considerations of individual aspects. During the time I planned, designed, and wrote this book, I learned a great deal and steadily broadened my own perspective and experience. On the one hand, I drew on my own experience; on the other hand, I discussed with many enterprise architects and with colleagues in my network who held and still hold senior architecture positions in a variety of multinational companies and across many industries. I also had challenging conversations with students and people freshly entering the field of architecture. All these exchanges helped me to look at the subject from many different, new, and fresh angles. As a result of these fruitful debates, I gained valuable knowledge and a deeper understanding regarding the design and operation of an enterprise architecture function.

What you hold in your hands is my approach of organizing and explaining architecture from the perspective of an architecture function, putting it on a solid conceptual foundation and merging it into a pattern language. I sincerely hope that this book will help you build and evolve your own specific architecture function, customized to the needs of your business. You are most welcome to share your experiences, successes, as well as failures, or just questions, with me. Please let me know where my book has been of great help to you. But please also be sure to let me know where you have unanswered design questions even after reading the book. I am extremely curious to hear from you about how you fared on your own personal architecture function journey.

Riehen, Switzerland   Ingo Arnold

References

Vogel, Oliver, Ingo Arnold, Arif Chugtai, Timo Kehrer, *Software Architecture: A Comprehensive Framework and Guide for Practitioners*, Springer-Verlag, Berlin, 2011

Gartner, *Gartner Glossary*, https://www.gartner.com/en/information-technology/glossary, 2020

Contents

1 Introduction 1
   1.1   Starting Position 1
   1.2   Aims of the Book 10
   1.3   Architecture 14
   1.4   Enterprise Architecture 18
   1.5   Enterprise Architecture Function 20
   1.6   Pattern Language 21
   1.7   Reader Guide 23
       1.7.1   Book Architecture 23
       1.7.2   Target Audience 26
       1.7.3   Chapter Overview 28
       1.7.4   Chapters in Detail 28
   Further Reading 30

2 Architecture Function Pattern Language 31
   2.1   Overview 31
   2.2   Pattern 32
   2.3   Pattern Catalog 36
   2.4   Pattern Language 36
   2.5   Architecture Function Pattern Language 41
       2.5.1   Architecture Function Pattern Topology 43
       2.5.2   Architecture Function Pattern Catalog 47
       2.5.3   Architecture Function Pattern Ontology 49
   2.6   Architecture Function Pattern Language Adoption 50
   Further Reading 54

3 Architecture Function: Context 57
   3.1   Overview 57
   3.2   Business Model 59
   3.3   Operating Model 60
   3.4   Value Chain 62

3.5   Organization   64
3.6   Digitalization   68
3.7   Service   74
3.8   Enterprise   75
        3.8.1   Enterprise Organization   76
        3.8.2   Enterprise Value Chain   77
Further Reading   92

4   Architecture Function: Challenge   95
4.1   Overview   95
4.2   Architecture Function   97
        4.2.1   Architecture Function Vision and Mission   98
        4.2.2   Architecture Function Organization   99
        4.2.3   Architecture Function Engagement Model   100
        4.2.4   Architecture Function Communication   101
        4.2.5   Architecture Function Governance   102
        4.2.6   Architecture Function Roadmap   103
        4.2.7   Architecture Function Apparatus   103
4.3   Architecture Function Services   104
        4.3.1   All Value Streams   106
        4.3.2   Service Planning Value Stream   109
        4.3.3   Service Building Value Stream   114
        4.3.4   Service Running Value Stream   116
4.4   Architecture Function Qualities   118
        4.4.1   Architecture Function Usability   119
        4.4.2   Architecture Function Elasticity   120
        4.4.3   Architecture Function Evolvability   121
        4.4.4   Architecture Function Reliability   122
Further Reading   123

5   Architecture Function: Constitution   125
5.1   Overview   125
5.2   Architecture Function   127
        5.2.1   Architecture Function Vision and Mission   128
        5.2.2   Architecture Function Organization   131
        5.2.3   Architecture Function Engagement Model   135
        5.2.4   Architecture Function Communication   137
        5.2.5   Architecture Function Governance   138
        5.2.6   Architecture Function Roadmap   140
        5.2.7   Architecture Function Apparatus   142
5.3   Architecture Function Services   143
        5.3.1   All Value Streams   145
        5.3.2   Service Planning Value Stream   152
        5.3.3   Service Building Value Stream   173
        5.3.4   Service Running Value Stream   181

    5.4   Architecture Function Qualities 184
          5.4.1   Architecture Function Usability 185
          5.4.2   Architecture Function Elasticity 187
          5.4.3   Architecture Function Evolvability 188
          5.4.4   Architecture Function Reliability 190
    Further Reading 192

6   Pattern Catalog 193
    6.1   Overview 193
    6.2   Architecture Organization 195
          6.2.1   Organizational Replication 195
          6.2.2   Learning Organization 203
          6.2.3   Architecture Maturity 207
          6.2.4   Architecture Capacity 218
          6.2.5   Architecture Role 222
          6.2.6   Architecture Ownership 231
          6.2.7   Architecture Funding 237
          6.2.8   Architecture Sourcing 241
    6.3   Architecture Engagement Model 249
          6.3.1   Architecture SPOC 250
    6.4   Architecture Discipline 254
          6.4.1   Enterprise Architecture Discipline 254
          6.4.2   Domain Architecture Discipline 260
          6.4.3   Solution Architecture Discipline 264
    6.5   Architecture Governance 267
          6.5.1   Architecture Governance 268
          6.5.2   Managed Architecture Evolution 274
          6.5.3   Architecture Policy 281
          6.5.4   Architecture Calendar 286
          6.5.5   Domain-Organization Agnosticism 290
          6.5.6   Decommissioning Reward 294
          6.5.7   Architecture Decision 299
          6.5.8   Architecture Traceability 304
    6.6   Architecture Communication 308
          6.6.1   Architecture Language 309
          6.6.2   Domain Taxonomy 318
          6.6.3   Architecture Innovation 325
    6.7   Architecture Objective 329
          6.7.1   Need to Know 329
          6.7.2   Architecture Mandate 334
    6.8   Architecture Asset 341
          6.8.1   Architecture Demarcation 342
          6.8.2   Architecture Asset 346
          6.8.3   Landscape Asset 353

		6.8.4	Off-the-Shelf Solution	362
6.9		Architecture Elaboration		366
	6.9.1	Architecture Significance	367
	6.9.2	Architecture Level	373
	6.9.3	Architecture Condition	377
	6.9.4	Architecture Alternative	385
	6.9.5	Architecture Approach	393
	6.9.6	Business Versus Technical	400
	6.9.7	Architecture Artifact	405
	6.9.8	Baseline Architecture Versus Target Architecture	411
6.10		Architecture Apparatus	415
	6.10.1	Your Own Architecture Methodology	416
	6.10.2	Architecture Methodology Adapter	424
	6.10.3	Your Own Architecture View Model	430
	6.10.4	Domain Architecture Methodology	444
	6.10.5	Solution Architecture Methodology	450
	6.10.6	Architecture Assessment Methodology	462
	6.10.7	Reference Architecture Methodology	470
	6.10.8	Architecture Roadmap Methodology	479
	6.10.9	Architecture Pattern Methodology	489
	6.10.10	Architecture Principle	501
	6.10.11	Your own Architecture Platform	504
Further Reading			513

Index 517

About the Author

Ingo Arnold shaped the *enterprise architecture function* of a global Fortune 50s in the pharmaceutical industry and held a variety of architecture management positions over the course of 25 years. In addition to his roles in industry, Ingo is an assistant professor at universities in Switzerland and formerly in Germany, sharing his insights and experiences with several generations of computer science students. As the author of books on solution architecture, Ingo covers virtually the entire architecture spectrum of modern enterprises. Finally, Ingo is a well-known speaker at conferences, where he gives talks to international audiences on topics such as architecture management, governance, enterprise, solution, and security architecture.

List of Abbreviations

AADL	Architecture Analysis and Design Language
ABB	Architecture Building Block
ACID	Atomicity, Concurrency, Isolation, Durability
ADL	Architecture Description Language
ATAM	Architecture Trade-off Analysis Method
ATM	Automatic Teller Machine
BLOB	Binary Large Object
BPMN	Business Process Model and Notation
CAPEX	Capital Expenditure
CMM	Capability Maturity Model
CMS/CMDB	Configuration Management System or Database
COBIT	Control Objectives for Information and Related Technologies
CoP	Community of Practice
CSI	Continual Service Improvement
DoD	Definition of Done
DSL	Domain-Specific Language
EAM	Enterprise Architecture Management
ERP	Enterprise Resource Planning
GIOP	General Inter-ORB Protocol
I18N	Internationalization
IAM	Identity and Access Management
IEEE	Institute of Electrical and Electronics Engineers
IoC	Inversion of Control
IoT	Internet of Things
IT4IT	IT for IT
ITIL	Information Technology Infrastructure Library
KPI	Key Performance Indicator
MDA	Model-Driven Architecture
MIB	Management Information Base
ML	Machine Learning
NFR	Non-functional Requirement

OODBMS	Object-Oriented Database Management Systems
Open CA	Open Certified Architect
OPEX	Operational Expenditure
ORM	Object-Relational Mapping
PaaS	Platform as a Service
QAS	Quality Attribute Scenarios
RACI	Responsible, Accountable, Consulted, Informed
RDBMS	Relational Database Management System
RMI	Remote Method Invocation
ROI	Return on Invest
RPC	Remote Procedure Call
SaaS	Software as a Service
SEI	Software Engineering Institute
SLA	Service-Level Agreement
SPOC	Single Point of Contact
SWOT	Strengths, Weaknesses, Opportunities, Threats
TCO	Total Cost of Ownership
TOGAF	The Open Group Architecture Framework
UML	Unified Modeling Language

Chapter 1
Introduction

Abstract This chapter positions the topic of enterprise architecture and focuses on the architecture function as an organizational capability. It explains the starting position and the goals of this book and introduces key concepts that are further explored throughout it. The chapter concludes with an overview of the intended audience, the internal architecture of the book itself, and the contributions of each chapter. After reading this chapter, you will know how enterprise architecture, domain architecture, and solution architecture are differentiated from each other and how they holistically combine in an architecture function to form an overall organizational capability. You will know the intent of this book and how to use it to critically reflect on the architecture function in your organization, plan its construction or renewal, design and implement it, and ultimately operate it effectively.

1.1 Starting Position

Business in the Twenty-First Century
We find ourselves in extremely turbulent times of fundamental transformations encompassing all habitats and areas of life. In the twenty-first century, humanity is confronted on the one hand with the consequences of its rapid growth and its short-sighted overharvesting of the globe. It is therefore facing Herculean tasks in areas such as food, water, climate, energy, or biodiversity as well as crises and coordination processes around these, which demand a dizzying speed of adaptation from their societies. At the same time, we have at our disposal impressive technologies and the innovative power of a global knowledge community that has reached a level of organization and interconnectedness that is unique in the history of mankind.

Beyond impressive innovations in areas such as bio- and neurotechnology, energy, aerospace, or agrotechnology, the universal computing machine (i.e., the computer in all its shapes, sizes, and areas of application) connected to the world-wide web has become a fundamental game changer, catalyzing virtually all other technical and non-technical areas of life.

The networked universal computing machine (i.e., the world computer) has directly or indirectly penetrated virtually all of our spheres of life and work and, in just a few decades, has very fundamentally changed how we network socially, acquire and impart knowledge, optimize ourselves medically, plan vacations, travel and orient ourselves in the world, organize mobility, meet new partners, entertain ourselves, or participate in social discourse and political processes. And, of course, the world computer, and the plethora of specific applications and information we constructed on its basis, has changed the way we cooperate, join forces, start and run businesses, and plan, create, and provide goods and services. At the same time, the world computer has changed how we demand goods and services and use them in cumulative value creation processes to further refine them into our own services. It allows us to completely rethink the hitherto valid axiomatic basis of economic models and confronts us with questionings of fundamental premises concerning our legal norms—questioning that seemed unthinkable to us since the times of the *ius civile*,[1] simply because technically impossible. The networked universal computing machine has stripped traditional business models of their premises virtually overnight, thus depriving business of its foundation. It has changed our demands as well as our demand-satisfaction rituals so fundamentally that long-practiced social processes and traditions have lost their meaning or been replaced by entirely new models of demand-satisfaction at a speed that is nothing short of breathtaking. In a nutshell, transformative technologies, directly or indirectly catalyzed by the world computer in just a few decades, have led to upheavals of established business and operating models and the disappearance of entire industries but also to new social habits, rituals, and needs as well as models of demand-satisfaction that we would never have dared to dream of before. As special and worthy of consideration as each of the transformation phenomena outlined here may be, in our observations, reflections, and discussions today, we use the term *digitization* to refer, grosso modo,[2] to our ability to completely rethink long entrenched premises, beliefs, and social as well as business rituals and processes.

Enterprises are increasingly relying on *digital means*[3] as elementary foundations of their business models. As a result, companies in certain industries (e.g., finance, insurance, entertainment and music, telecommunications) have successively

---

[1] *Ius civile*. Even though Roman law was initially a body of law that arose from many years of practice without written laws, so-called customary law, very early on ancient Rome created a universally applicable set of rules that has gone down in history as *ius civile*. In the *ius civile*, fundamental legal concepts and goods were defined and regulated, which still influence our legal norms today (e.g., property conception, commercial law, rights to political participation).

[2] *Grosso modo* is an adverbial locution whose etymological roots are in Latin "grossus" (*approximately*) and "modus" (*way, method*). In English, *grosso modo* mostly enters in the meaning of *roughly, approximately*, or *coarse*.

[3] In terms of *digital means*, the industry clearly delineates two terms that sound very similar but have important differences in their conception: digitalization and digitization. Gartner, for example, defines digitalization in its IT Glossary as: "Digitalization is the use of digital technologies to change a business model and provide new revenue and value-producing opportunities; it is the process of moving to a digital business." Similarly, definitions of digitization have been proposed, with Gartner defining the term in their IT Glossary as follows: "Digitization is the process of changing from analogue to digital form, also known as digital enablement. Said another way,

transformed their originally analog business models into digitalized ones. New technologies (or innovations regarding the use of technologies) are emerging at an increasingly rapid pace, enabling business model transformations on an unprecedented scale and disruptiveness, turning established analog business models upside down, and replacing traditional players in a market with new and innovative entrepreneurs. You are certainly familiar with these famous examples where analog business models have been replaced by digitalized ones that function in a fundamentally different way. For example, in that, digital business and operating models have decoupled from space and time, where analog ones are still tied to them: "Facebook, the world's most popular media owner, creates no content. Alibaba, the most valuable retailer, has no inventory. And Airbnb, the world's largest accommodation provider, owns no real estate" (Goodwin 2015).

Svyatoslav Kotusev observes in *The Practice of Enterprise Architecture* (Kotusev 2018) that with the steady growth, use, and proliferation of digital means, organizations are transforming into socio-technical systems, where a clear demarcation between business and business-enabling digital technology is increasingly blurring or disappearing. What was originally distinguished as business and technology are merging and constituting a common backbone of business models that is neither distinguishable in form nor in essence. From this perspective, we can already view most of today's enterprises as socio-technical systems that ultimately form a carefully tuned conglomerate of organization and people, processes for shaping efficient and effective cooperation, and digital means and technologies united by common enterprise goals and mission.

A brief look at the anatomy of digitized, socio-technical systems reveals their potential. However, this consideration also gives an impression of the inherent complexity of socio-technical systems, with which enterprises must find a creative and novel way of dealing. The digitization of socio-technical systems initially implies that elementary means and tools (*resources*) are increasingly based on data and networked computers that manage and utilize this data. On the one hand, these resources are used as components in services; on the other hand, they are building blocks in a value chain for planning, designing, implementing, deploying, and operating these services. The fact that resources in an enterprise are increasingly digitized and flow into virtually all the essential building blocks of the enterprise value chain digitalizes (directly or indirectly) the entire cooperative system—i.e., the functions and disciplines (*organization*), *processes*, *services*, and *service offerings*. An effect of the digital material of all building blocks that should not be underestimated is that they can be replicated virtually infinitely often and quickly and are flexibly adaptable and highly scalable, with marginal costs close to zero and negligible space-time expansion. The digital material of modern enterprise building blocks travels across digital networks, enabling both duplication and teleportation of digital and semi-digital building blocks in a matter of seconds (Fig. 1.1).

---

digitization takes an analogue process and changes it to a digital form without any different-in-kind changes to the process itself" (Gartner Glossary 2020).

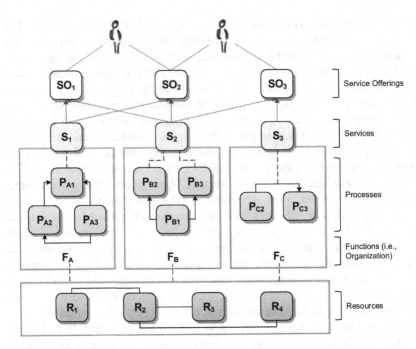

Fig. 1.1 Digitized business in the twenty-first century

Putting all this together, we can say that differentiation between business and IT has (meanwhile) become artificial at least if not obsolete altogether. At the same time, we note that dealing with, if not mastering, complexity has become the central challenge for enterprises in the twenty-first century.

Challenges for Enterprises in the Twenty-First Century
In *Collaborative Enterprise Architecture: Enriching EA with Lean, Agile, and Enterprise 2.0 Practices*, Stefan Bente, Uwe Bombosch, and Shailendra Langade (Bente et al. 2012) state that complexity in enterprises results from a combination of opportunities and challenges that can be directly or indirectly attributed to the phenomenon of advancing digitization. Whether changes in the business context, such as government regulation, mergers, and acquisitions, or whether new business models or changes in the range of enterprise resources used to run the business (e.g., new technologies, retirement, replacement or consolidation of resources, or supplier changes), these are all complexity drivers in modern enterprises. In addition, there are other drivers and challenges, such as ensuring unconditional quality with respect to all of the above resources, for example, their evolutionary fitness, where they need to be easily adapted to changing business contexts (i.e., modifiability, adaptability), or their reliability, where adequate scalability, availability, performance, or security must be ensured. But also an efficient and effective engineering discipline for

digitized resources increases the complexity compared to the analog pendant, because—unlike in traditional engineering disciplines—important material of digital resources is model and thus language. Moreover, the engineering of a product does not end (anymore) with its delivery—rather, the engineering continues while the resources remain in use. While in traditional engineering disciplines the requirement to turn a car into an anesthetic gun by flipping a switch leads to sheer horror on the engineering side, such requirements are at least conceivable in the case of systems whose building blocks are digital in nature and thus data-based. Another complexity driver is the segregation of business as well as globalized, cooperative processes, which leads to a segregation of resources in central enterprise structures as well as on the level of their change vehicles (e.g., projects). In particular, segregation undermines desired synergies and economies of scale. Also, the fact that actual assets (e.g., information) often take a back seat to pseudo-assets (e.g., applications), or are scattered across them, often leads to fundamental misconceptions in the sense of confusion between ends and means. In summary, it can be said that business ecosystems have experienced significant growth in potential as a result of digital materials on the one hand but have also become inherently more complex on the other—both in their breadth (i.e., *many touchpoints* in processes organized on the basis of the division of labor) and in their depth (i.e., *complex touchpoints*).

Potential of Architecture to Address Enterprise Challenges
In the course of this introductory chapter, I will further elaborate on the distinction between enterprise, domain, and solution architecture. In addition, throughout the book, I will distinguish between architecture as a subject, architecture as a discipline, and architecture as an organizational capability (i.e., architecture function). At the same time, however, I will ignore such distinctions where they do not contribute to understanding, or subsume them under the term *architecture*.

In summary, we can say that architecture makes significant contributions in the areas of enterprise strategic development (e.g., through contributions to strategy formulation or strategic alignment of the enterprise), strategic planning (e.g., through architecture baseline, target and roadmap development, or transformation planning), enterprise portfolio management (e.g., through contributions to investment planning, prioritization, risk, time, and resource planning), as well as in the areas of solution lifecycle, project, and service development (e.g., through contributions to project and service management, service architecture and design, implementation, and operations). If we shorten this view to the essentials of architecture, then architecture is both a portfolio and planning discipline as well as a transformation and implementation discipline.

For example, the architecture discipline addresses the impact of change initiatives on applications in an enterprise, the realization of organizational capabilities through applications, or the optimal support of enterprise services through applications. Other examples of architecture contributions include planning and implementing services based on processes; analyzing the impact of decommissioning[4] or changing applications, services, or platforms; and analyzing the propagation of errors across systems. Architecture is also concerned with identifying optimization potentials in the operational assets (i.e., landscape assets) of a company—for example, gaps or redundancies in services with regard to their support of an enterprise business model. Finally, architecture contributes to reducing complexity, identifying and resolving overlapping responsibilities, and ensuring that landscape assets[5] such as services, applications, and platforms comply with regulatory constraints.

The successful orientation, design, and operation of business models today is increasingly synonymous with the establishment and evolution of their digital means and building materials, enabling the adaptation and evolution of modern business models to ever-changing environmental conditions. This new blurring of the distinction between a business model and the digital means on the basis of which it is realized requires a disciplined and systematic approach to planning, developing, delivering, and operating enterprise services. Architecture is a cornerstone discipline here, ensuring both intelligent decision-making and sustainable implementation. It increases both the effectiveness and efficiency of planning, developing, and operating enterprise services. Architecture achieves this by providing the transparency needed to make the right decisions, translate decisions into quality solutions, and to deploy those solutions correctly. Furthermore, the architecture identifies risks and proposes remedial actions; promotes the reuse of intellectual, conceptual, and physical assets to reduce redundancy and exploit synergies in the enterprise; and adequately balances conflicting expectations of time-to-market versus quality requirements. Architecture establishes effective communication between business implementation and business-enabling disciplines, like the information technology discipline. In this respect, it acts as a change agent on a journey that transforms an enterprise from a state of being overwhelmed by complexity to a rationally organized state that enables it to respond efficiently and effectively to the challenges of a digitized world. The contributions of the architecture discipline presented here demonstrate its invaluable importance to the effective operation of modern enterprises.

When Architecture Fails to Fully Leverage and Contribute Its Potential
While the importance of architecture and its potential contributions are apparent on the one hand, it is by no means certain that they will be recognized and brought to full fruition in every organization. Thus, an inadequate understanding or definition of architecture leads to an unclear architecture mandate and to reducing architecture to a purely technical discipline, without recognizing that the architecture discipline could make equivalent contributions to business domains. Furthermore, an insufficiently developed understanding leads to architecture learning and standardization taking place in silos, without architecture being understood as a holistic discipline. In

---

[4] See the *Decommissioning Reward* pattern in this book's pattern catalog (Chap. 6).
[5] See the *Landscape Asset* pattern in this book's pattern catalog.

summary, in such enterprises architecture is misinterpreted as having no impact on the business, leading to this potential being left untapped. Another common problem in enterprises is an ineffective or completely absent architecture organization. That is, architecture understanding and skills are either non-existent, underdeveloped, or lack traction to drive appropriate change. Other symptoms include the lack of a systematic approach to driving and approving architecture decisions, inconsistent tool base and metrics, and unilaterally balanced incentive systems.

A culture of firefighting replaces serious planning when there is a lack of alignment between business and information technology departments. Holistic, transversal, and fully integrated architecture plans are either not developed or do not have the buy-in of relevant parties. In such organizations, a focus on short-term success at the expense of sustained pursuit of longer-term plans can be observed, as well as an uncontrolled proliferation of redundant enterprise assets and processes. Architecture organizations must succeed in demonstrating that architecture costs and investments are distinctly linked to business outcomes. Here it is particularly important to monetize both—costs and benefits—not just in the short term but in the medium and long term. Both costs and benefits should consider monetized risk, architecture debt[6] and solution complexity, as well as architecture development, operations, and maintenance.

According to Bente (Bente et al. 2012), there are four deficiencies that result from an insufficiently established enterprise architecture capacity[7]: architecture does not achieve an adequate impact (e.g., reducing complexity or making enterprise operations more cost- and resource-efficient), architecture does not fully exploit its contribution potential (e.g., architecture contributions from strategy through to operations), architecture fails to evolve with an ever-changing business ecosystem, and architecture fails to address the enterprise as a whole. In addition, Carsten Sensler and Thomas Grimm (Sensler and Grimm 2015) describe in *Business Enterprise Architecture: Praxishandbuch zur digitalen Transformation in Unternehmen* prerequisites for a successful enterprise architecture, which—if they are missing—lead to architecture not unfolding its full potential. As prerequisites, Sensler and Grimm see recognition of a problem that requires substantial improvement, such as enterprise transformation (i.e., organizational will), sufficient leadership support and resources to address the problem (i.e., feasibility), and a master plan that appropriately describes the desired transformation goal (i.e., vision and plan).

Exploiting the Potential of Architecture
So the million-dollar question that arises from the above deficit considerations is: how can we ensure that architecture fully realizes its potential to effectively make valuable business contributions in an enterprise? The short answer is that effective

---

[6]Architecture debt (also known as technical or design debt) is a concept that reflects the cost of future rework. In other words, costs incurred by choosing a simple solution now rather than an approach that is more resilient to rework in the future. In other words, costs incurred today to avoid rework costs in the future.

[7]See the *Architecture Capacity* pattern in this book's pattern catalog (Chap. 6).

architecture is achieved by embedding it as an organizational capability in an enterprise operating model. However, what is an enterprise operating model? In simple terms, an operating model defines and standardizes the cooperation within and between enterprise functions with the goal of optimizing them in both efficiency and effectiveness.[8] An operating model typically standardizes enterprise processes, roles, and responsibilities (i.e., disciplines), information that is exchanged across processes, and means (i.e., resources) to facilitate cross-process collaboration, coordination, and information exchange (Fig. 1.2).

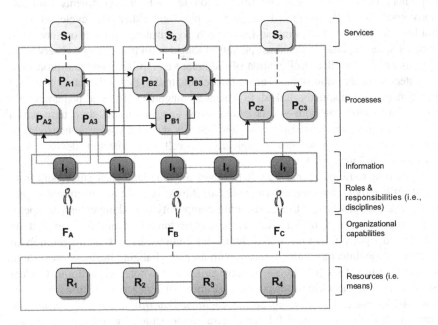

Fig. 1.2 Operation model anatomy

But how is architecture practically embedded as an organizational capability in an enterprise-wide operating model? The short answer here is by establishing an enterprise architecture function and integrating it with other enterprise functions. But how is this achieved in a meaningful way? Enterprise architecture as a topic has a high degree of maturity and is well developed. Many standardized resources exist, such as architecture frameworks, consulting services, or platforms and tools. Thus, standardized enterprise architecture frameworks provide comprehensive guidance. They define core concepts and recommend practices for planning, developing, maintaining, and executing architecture. Also they offer a variety of components

---

[8]Efficiency versus effectiveness. Something is effective to the extent that it achieves an intended result. In contrast, something is efficient to the extent that it achieves something with minimal use of resources. It is possible to be effective without being efficient and vice versa.

such as generic architecture view models, artifacts, processes, principles, or maturity metrics.[9] The genericity of architecture frameworks requires their adaptation to concrete problems, which means that they are helpful heuristics—but no off-the-shelf solutions. An example of such a framework is the Zachman Framework for Enterprise Architectures,[10] which is named after its founder John Zachman and is one of the first frameworks in the field of enterprise architecture. Another framework is called TOGAF,[11] which is an industry- and vendor-neutral as well as community-based framework maintained by the Open Group.

The question that arises is whether these architecture resources already represent an effective architecture function in a concrete enterprise context or allow an immediate derivation of it. Generic architecture resources such as enterprise architecture frameworks represent architecture as a topic in a structured and generic way (i.e., at the class level) and are thus immensely useful—but not yet guarantees of success. Successful architecture is always enterprise-specific, i.e., a function of the organization's industry, geographic distribution, work culture, or business model. This in turn means that generic architecture resources such as frameworks must always be adapted. Therefore, it is best to think of architecture frameworks and other resources as a loose collection of best practices proposed by experienced architects for practitioners. If you pick and choose from an architecture framework what makes sense to you in your particular context and for your particular purpose, then you use the framework as intended. However, if you understand an architecture framework as something you should read to the letter or follow in an all-or-nothing manner, you are misinterpreting it. For selecting context-appropriate practices, techniques, and approaches from a framework, you must first learn and know the entire framework very well—only then will you have enough context to understand the components of the framework and use them deliberately. However, to realize the full potential of architecture, a framework must first be tailored to the needs of a particular organization and embedded in the organization's particular operating model. Ultimately, a key success factor of architecture is the degree to which collaboration between the architecture and its stakeholders is brought to life. Thus, to practically embed architecture in an enterprise operating model, an enterprise architecture function (i.e., architecture function) must be established and mandated—i.e., the generic architecture potential must be concretely offered and brought into an operating

---

[9] See the *Architecture Maturity* pattern in this book's pattern catalog (Chap. 6).

[10] The Zachman Framework proposes a basic enterprise architecture schema that provides a structured approach to holistically viewing and defining an enterprise's architecture. The basic scheme distinguishes two dimensions that introduce the intersection of two classifications. While the first classification distinguishes the primitive interrogatives what, how, when, who, where, and why, the second classification is derived from the philosophical concept of reification (i.e., from the process of transforming an abstract idea into its instantiation and vice versa).

[11] The Open Group Architecture Framework (TOGAF). TOGAF proposes an approach to design, plan, implement, and govern enterprise architecture. It describes a generic method for developing architectures. TOGAF suggests a common vocabulary, a generic information model, an adaptable role model, general architecture artifacts, and tooling.

model through the organizational capability of an architecture function. This means that an architecture function is the organizational entity for effectively embedding and operationalizing the architecture discipline in an enterprise.

When an enterprise fails to exploit its architecture potential, it is often because architecture functions do not adequately integrate the architecture discipline into the operating model. The background to this is the misunderstanding that a generic architecture discipline (e.g., in the form of generic frameworks) is already considered a complete or at least sufficient solution to a concrete organizational problem. This misunderstanding is based on a, intentionally or not, misleading suggestion of generic architecture resources, such as frameworks, literature, consulting services, or tools: the suggestion of their immediately operationalizable completeness. The need for as well as the process of instantiating generic frameworks into a well-designed architecture function is only marginally—in any case insufficiently—described in publications and resources.

1.2 Aims of the Book

Motivation
In a nutshell, closing the gap between generic architecture frameworks and an appropriately instantiated architecture function is the central motivation for writing this book. As invaluable as the potential of the architecture discipline is for addressing increasingly pressing challenges of our century, only an architecture function that is precisely integrated into the enterprise operating model will practically realize that potential.

My book therefore positions itself at the intersection of generic architecture resources and practices on the one hand and an enterprise-specific architecture function on the other. In the words of a software architect, one could say that this book provides a model-driven generator[12] of architecture functions. The generator (i.e., my book) presupposes general frameworks, tools, and practices and assists you in generating an architecture function that is optimally embedded in your enterprise operating model. The model underlying my book considers other discipline-specific enterprise organizations, an enterprise value chain, and enterprise services representing the company's market offering as environmental premises. As premises for the application of my book, I consider your desire to concretely establish, or renovate, an architecture function and integrate it into your operating model in such a

---

[12]Model-driven architecture (MDA) is a forward engineering approach in which executable or semi-executable artifacts are generated from abstract, human-made architectural models (e.g., class diagrams). MDA tools are used to develop, interpret, compare, align, measure, verify or transform models and metamodels. Generator-based architecture approaches very generally decouple solution specifications from their physical generation. They increase domain specificity and the degree of abstraction of the models that architects use to represent a solution. Generators receive architecture models as inputs and create artifacts at the source level or related physical structures as outputs.

way that it makes purposeful contributions along the entire value chain. In summary, this book provides you with a method to plan, develop, validate, or evolve the design of your architecture function so that it fully meets your organization's needs. By the way, where enterprise architecture, or the architecture discipline as a whole, is demystified from mystical fogs, this is an unsought but thoroughly enjoyable side effect of my book (Fig. 1.3).

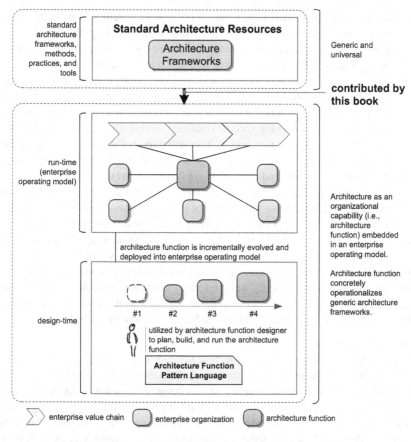

Fig. 1.3 Architecture functions operationalize universal architecture concepts

The *place to stand*[13] or angle I have chosen to leverage the vast and often confusing subject of architecture is the architecture function. With this book, I propose a generic method for planning, building, and operating an architecture function that it is embedded in an operating model and works with other business organizations to achieve set business goals along the value chain. In this respect, my book offers you a way not only to think about the value potential of architecture but also to tap this potential in your company in a concrete manner.

You will benefit from this book in two ways. First, it will provide you with a structured overview and orientation to the subject of architecture from an architecture function perspective. You will gain orientation regarding the problem of inadequate architecture function designs, the dimensions that span and structure this topic, and basic architecture function concepts and ontologies.

Second, the book will guide you through the process of planning, building, and operating your own architecture organization based on a generic architecture function blueprint. The blueprint presents itself in the form of a pattern language that provides a structured means for navigating, contextualizing, combining, and composing the architecture function patterns it provides. You will plan, build, and evolve an architecture function that ideally addresses your organization's needs by using the pattern language to navigate, adapt, and concretely apply its patterns to your situation.

Coherence, completeness, and consistency are among the overarching design goals for the architecture function patterns, the pattern language, and the architecture function design process the language inherently represents. The pattern language achieves *coherence* by maintaining a balance between partitioning the architecture function for structuring purposes and representing it as a whole in terms of its collaboration with other enterprise organizations. It achieves *completeness* in the sense that patterns inspire broadly while referring to further literature for details that go into depth. *Consistency* is achieved in the sense that essential concepts are always defined in relation and distinction to each other, establishing ontological holism.

Subject of the Book

The core subject of this book is *architecture function design*, while the *architecture function pattern language* serves as the vehicle through which the design process is offered. Hence, the architecture function and its design is the *what* of my book, while the pattern language is the *how* in terms of implementation. The language is generic and expressive enough to support a wide variety of concrete architecture function designs. At the same time, it is specific enough to guide you concretely through your own function's design and accompany you in its further evolution. The pattern language is easy to understand, navigate, and apply. Its patterns are intended to inspire you in your design efforts. They provide you with critical design considerations and suggestions and invite you to engage in deeper design thinking along suggested schemas. The level of detail in the patterns is kept rather coarse, as some patterns, or the themes they outline, are themselves worth an entire book. Like other patterns,

---

[13] Archimedes of Syracuse (c. 287 B.C. probably in Syracuse; † 212 B.C. ibid.) was a Greek mathematician, physicist, and engineer. He is considered one of the most important mathematicians of antiquity. Archimedes is credited with the quote "Give me a place to stand and with a lever I will move the whole world" (Wikipedia Archimedes 2020b).

architecture function patterns are largely context-agnostic, so they can be reused, combined, and applied in a wide variety of business environments and situations.

Beyond a collection of architecture function patterns, the pattern language includes a pattern catalog listing the patterns, a pattern topology, and a pattern ontology. The *architecture function pattern topology* represents the structure of the architecture function design process, enabling meaningful navigation, selection, and application of patterns. At the top level, the topology distinguishes between the context, challenge, and constitution segments. The *context* segment subdivides the enterprise context within which an architecture function operates. For example, enterprise services, enterprise organizations, or the enterprise value chain and the value streams into which it is divided. The *challenge* segment looks at the architecture function from the outside and outlines recurring challenges it faces. It distinguishes the three sub-segments of architecture function, building blocks, architecture functional services, and architecture functional qualities, to explore and present challenges in a structured way. Finally, the *constitution* segment white box zooms into the architecture function and proposes approaches[14] to respond to the challenges that architecture functions repeatedly face. The *architecture function pattern catalogue* contains 48 patterns assigned to 9 pattern groups, which cluster the patterns thematically. Finally, the *architecture function pattern ontology* clarifies essential concepts necessary for understanding as well as applying the patterns. I have chosen not to concentrate the ontology in a single chapter in this book, nor to formalize it heavily, but to present the definition of the essential concepts where they first matter. In this respect, the ontology is spread across the pattern topology and the patterns in the catalog.

Uniqueness of the Book
The special feature, or uniqueness, of my book is that the broad topic of architecture (as a discipline) is looked at with fresh eyes—virtually through the eyes and from the perspective of an architecture function. The advantage of this approach is not to present the value potential of architecture (as a discipline) but to suggest a concrete procedure for practically harvesting this value potential in your enterprise.

Further Features of the Book
Other special features of my book are that I consider the three disciplines, enterprise, domain, and solution architecture, as inseparable parts of the topic of enterprise architecture in general and enterprise architecture function in particular. The book, its structuring parts, essential concepts, patterns, and procedures for establishing an architecture function are a mixture of my own experience and empiricism, a broad knowledge base in all three architecture disciplines, and standing on the shoulders of architecture giants.[15] My book offers you both a conceptual and a practical perspective and follows a systematic, coherent, and user-friendly approach to provide you

---

[14] See the *Architecture Approach* pattern in this book's pattern catalog (Chap. 6).

[15] While the allegory first appears in Bernard of Chartres around 1120 (cited by John of Salisbury in his work *Metalogicon*), Isaac Newton also used the metaphor of the dwarf standing on the shoulders of giants ("If I have looked further, it is because I stand on the shoulders of giants.") in a letter to Robert Hooke in 1676. Isaac Newton thus determines the relationship of a respective current state of knowledge to the achievements of earlier knowledge creators.

with a generative tool to improve your own architecture function. The approaches and tools you will find in this book are agnostic to factors that vary widely in concrete contexts to enhance its usefulness and broad applicability. The book is agnostic to a specific enterprise organization, business model, or industry; to enterprise or service size and scope; to service, application, or platform archetype; or to process model attitudes such as Agile[16] or DevOps.[17] The goal of my book is to strike a good balance and a middle ground—that is, to be neither too detailed nor too simplistic. I adopt a *miles wide and inches deep* approach—thus shifting detailed discussions to existing literature, industry frameworks, or other proven practices. Finally, I place my book in the context of existing literature and refer to publications or ideas where appropriate.

Success Criteria for This Book
I will consider myself successful if you can successfully transfer the architecture function design suggestions outlined in this book to establish an architecture function perfectly suited to your organization—thus achieve your enterprise architecture goals both effectively and efficiently.

1.3 Architecture

Classic Architecture
Before going into more detail about the three architecture disciplines that this book brings together, I take a look at classical architecture, whose starting point is the design of structures, buildings, cities, and similar urban conglomerates. In *Software Architecture: A Comprehensive Framework and Guide for Practitioners* (Vogel, Arnold et al. 2011), we show that classical architecture is perceived as both an art and a science, concerned with the design and construction of buildings, and thus the entire process, from planning to realization. Classical architecture is concerned with the ordering structure of parts of an intended whole. Thereby, architecture pursues an *architecture purpose*, which, with the help of given *architecture means* (e.g.,

---

[16] Agile, in the field of software development and similar process models, refers to agile practices the collaboration of self-organizing and cross-functional teams and their customers and end-users in the context of both requirements discovery and solution development. Agile practices generally advocate adaptive planning, evolutionary development, early delivery, and continuous improvement. They encourage flexible responses to change (Wikipedia Agile 2020a). Agile methods trace their roots to a set of principles known as the Agile Software Development Manifesto (Agile Manifesto 2020).

[17] DevOps describes an approach to improving collaboration between the development and operation of, for example, services. DevOps is a portmanteau of the terms *development* and *operations*. DevOps is intended to enable improved collaboration between the areas of development, operations, quality assurance, and business departments by means of common incentives, processes, and tools (Wikipedia DevOps 2020c).

building material, tools, techniques, and methods[18]), strives to address *architecture conditions*[19] (e.g., the desire for functional, inexpensive living space). The classical concept of architecture combines both the systematic process of architecture planning, design, and realization and the outcome of that architecture process. In other words, classical architecture includes both the architecture development process and the developed design of buildings or cities (Fig. 1.4).

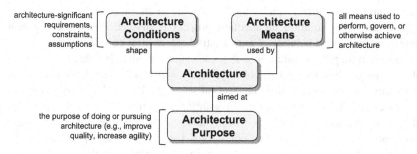

Fig. 1.4 Classic architecture as a starting point

By extending classical architecture from urban conglomerates to systems more broadly, I generalize the concept of architecture. With this generalized ambition, architecture is concerned with the formal description of systems or with detailed plans of systems at the building block level—ultimately with the goal of precisely guiding and directing the process of system development. Architecture thus defines the structure and orderly arrangement of the building blocks (i.e., parts) of a system (i.e., whole), their interrelationships, and the principles and guidelines that govern their design and evolution[20] over time (Perroud and Inversini 2013) (Fig. 1.5).

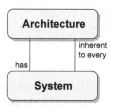

Fig. 1.5 System and architecture

---

[18] See all patterns included in the *Architecture Apparatus* group in this book's pattern catalog (Chap. 6).

[19] See the *Architecture Condition* pattern in this book's pattern catalog.

[20] See the *Managed Architecture Evolution* pattern in this book's pattern catalog.

From Classic Architecture to Solution Architecture

The term *solution architecture* complements the concept of *solution*, which in turn implies another concept—the concept of the *problem* to which a solution responds. While problems are discrepancies between a desired (i.e., future) state and an undesired (i.e., present) state, solutions are sought and established to address corresponding problems. Thus, the term *solution architecture* implies a situation in which a system is understood as a solution to a given problem, and the architecture of that system is consequently understood as a solution architecture.

Essentially, the solution architecture process is divided into three segments: context, problem, and solution. *Context* introduces central concepts and categories. A *problem* anticipates a solution in that each problem already inherently spans its solution space. Thus, the problem of wayfinding, which is formulated in the question "Do I turn left or right at this intersection to get to Rome?" already completely anticipates the limited set of possible solutions: "turn left" or "turn right." The solution architecture process is specifically about identifying the architecture-significant[21] portions in given problem conditions. Once context and problem are well understood, the design for an adequate solution is derived from these. *Solutions* are thus about making important design decisions. The sum of all significant design decisions for a system that is a solution to a problem in a given context is called the solution architecture (Fig. 1.6).

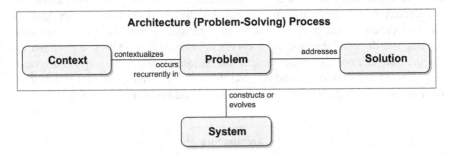

Fig. 1.6 The process of solution architecture

However, the question remains as to what constitutes design decisions that significantly shape a solution and what aspects of a system they affect. Here there are two types of decisions: decisions concerning the static arrangement and partitioning of subsystems (i.e., $subsystem_1$, ..., $subsystem_4$) that constitute the system as a whole (i.e., static structure) and decisions about the way the subsystems interact (i.e., dynamic structure) in order to realize a desired property from a teleological[22] system perspective—thus, to adequately address identified problematic aspects (Fig. 1.7).

---

[21] See the *Architecture-Significance* pattern in this book's pattern catalog (Chap. 6).

[22] Teleological system concept. The term *teleological system* deals with a system's function and behavior as observed from the outside (external behavior). The teleological systems perspective is useful when using a system.

Fig. 1.7 Static versus
dynamic system structure

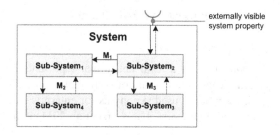

Domain Architecture

Where solution architecture is concerned with finding solutions and improving concrete systems, domain architecture asks which problems are the most pressing and, from a higher-level, strategic perspective, justify a search for solutions against the background of scarce resources, such as time, budget, or personnel. Domains are areas of interest that are defined and institutionalized by architecture functions in order to break down the entire enterprise into architecturally digestible parts. Architecture domains enable architects to coherently consider, plan, or pursue a topic of enterprise interest. Architects communicate and discuss together within a domain, relying on domain-specific[23] language[24] and jargon. *World, sphere, universe of discourse* (Dietz 2006), or *large system* (Murer et al. 2010) is used synonymously for the term *domain*.

Domain architecture provides maximum overview and transparency to identify relevant deficits and improvement potentials in a domain—ultimately, to enable optimal decision-making. Domain architects capture the current state of their domain (i.e., baseline architecture), desired future target states (i.e., target architecture), and the domain's development planning (i.e., domain architecture roadmap). In addition, domain architects create and use reference assets, such as architecture patterns, principles, or reference architectures, to provide solution architects with guardrails along their solution design efforts.

---

[23] See the *Domain Taxonomy* pattern in this book's pattern catalog (Chap. 6).

[24] See the *Architecture Language* pattern in this book's pattern catalog.

1.4   Enterprise Architecture

Enterprise

An *enterprise* is a legal entity that represents an association of actors, whether natural, legal, or a mixture of both, that cooperatively and concertedly pursue a set goal. Commonly used synonyms for enterprise are *company*, *corporation*, or *business*. Marc Lankhorst (Lankhorst et al. 2011) defines *enterprise* as:

> Enterprise is any collection of organizations that has a common set of goals and/or a single bottom line. Enterprise architecture is a coherent whole of principles, methods, and models that are used in the design and realization of an enterprise's organizational structure, business processes, information systems, and infrastructure.

Enterprise Architecture

Enterprise architecture is architecture at the enterprise level.[25] Enterprise architecture relates information from formerly unrelated domains to obtain a holistic view of the enterprise. It ensures vertical (e.g., from strategic to operational, from coarse-grained to fine-grained) and horizontal (e.g., from planning through building to the running enterprise services) alignment across enterprise information viewpoints. Enterprise architecture maintains a baseline architecture[26] perspective representing the current state of the enterprise. It also proposes target architecture[27] states in the light of strategic forces an enterprise must absorb. For example, the major change in an enterprise's business model is a strategic force. Enterprise architecture can also be viewed as a master plan facilitating the convergence of diverging forces toward a strategic transformation target, like a targeted business model or a targeted operating model (Schekkerman 2004).

Enterprise architecture is an amorphous concept in the sense that a wide range of enterprise architecture perceptions and definitions exist. Three of the more prominent enterprise architecture perceptions are accentuated below. In the *design business* segment, enterprise architecture takes a top-down approach and starts with the business model and drivers, identifying gaps between business goals and existing capabilities and capacities. In the *align business and IT* segment, enterprise architecture does not review fundamental decisions regarding the business model but focuses on gaps in terms of suboptimal execution. It looks at the business model through the lens of IT-based means and seeks to improve them in terms of optimizing their business alignment. In the *design IT* segment, enterprise architecture takes a bottom-up approach, focusing on technological innovation, standardization, consolidation, and cost reduction. Ultimately, IT seeks to meet business expectations (i.e.,

---

[25] See the *Architecture Level* pattern in this book's pattern catalog (Chap. 6).

[26] Baseline architecture describes the current architecture state—for example, the architecture state of a domain or an enterprise.

[27] Target architecture describes the desired future state of an architecture developed for a domain or an enterprise. There can be several future states developed as a roadmap to highlight the evolution of the architecture toward a strategically desired target state.

IT does not challenge business expectations) by making its contribution more effective and efficient. The *operational* planning horizon is short (i.e., less than 1 year), while *tactical* planning is a medium-term projection (i.e., between 1 and 3 years), and the *strategic* perspective extends substantially beyond the 3-year horizon. Enterprise architecture functions, with a mandate for *enterprise IT architecture*, are expected to lead the process of planning and designing an organization's IT capabilities to address predetermined business objectives. An *enterprise alignment architecture* mandate expects enterprise architecture functions to promote coherence across different disciplines and departments (e.g., strategic planning, demand management, operations). Finally, an *enterprise business architecture* mandate expects architecture functions to view the enterprise as a system in its entirety and help it evolve successfully within its ecosystem (Fig. 1.8).

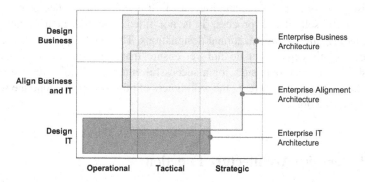

Fig. 1.8 Enterprise architecture coordinate system

Enterprise architecture can be viewed, on the one hand, as a super-discipline that connects the solution and domain architecture disciplines and ensures their alignment and common direction. In addition, enterprise architecture can be understood as a super-domain—i.e., as the root domain or domain of all domains of an enterprise.

In this book, I position enterprise architecture as both a super-discipline (i.e., combination of solution and domain architecture disciplines) and a super-domain (i.e., domain of all enterprise domains). The *enterprise architecture function* (i.e., *architecture function* for short) is the central perspective on enterprise architecture and thus responsible for serving all architecture-oriented needs in the enterprise. This means that the architecture function covers the entire enterprise value chain (i.e., from strategic planning to the operation of digitized services), is responsible for the architecture of enterprise services, and addresses needs across all levels of granularity and planning horizons. In summary, the enterprise architecture understanding that underlies my book encompasses the disciplines of domain and solution architecture.

The enterprise architecture discipline is responsible for planning, elaborating, describing, and validating the architecture of systems at different levels of granularity (i.e., enterprise, domain, and solution level). In addition, it supports the architecture needs along the entire enterprise value chain—i.e., the elaboration of service, application and platform architectures, the development and use of reference architectures, validations and assessments, communication and moderation of architecture dialogs, the creation and further development of artifacts, as well as the use of architecture platforms, methods, and tools.

It is often helpful to explain not only what something is but also what it is not. Therefore, in addition to the positive criteria mentioned above, I will conclude with a few examples of what enterprise architecture is not. For example, enterprise architecture is not to be confused with an architecture framework or a corresponding certificate (e.g., TOGAF). Enterprise architecture is also not an exclusively technical[28] discipline or a specific technology stack. It is not solely a state or result of a process—but itself also a process. It is not filled with life in a company by corresponding titles or organizational designations. The newly appointed enterprise architect and his department do not yet ensure that the required competence is established or that prerequisites for a successful enterprise architecture discipline are fulfilled in the company (e.g., the willingness of other actors to cooperate with an architecture function).

1.5   Enterprise Architecture Function

In short, a *function* represents the organizational capabilities of a business organization—that is, the contributions that an organization makes to the functioning of a business whole. A description of an organizational structure highlights the structural characteristics of the organization (e.g., division, federation, reporting lines). The functional decomposition of the same organization typically emphasizes the capabilities that an organizational unit contributes to collaborating across all units within an enterprise. The *enterprise architecture function* organizationally realizes the enterprise architecture discipline by integrating its full breadth and depth into the enterprise operating model. Depending on enterprise size, industry, and architecture mandate,[29] an architecture function can be quite large and appropriately substructured. It may include special decision[30]-making bodies that coordinate governance[31] processes within, but also outside, the architecture organization. It

---

[28] See the *Business versus Technical* pattern in this book's pattern catalog (Chap. 6).

[29] See the *Architecture Mandate* pattern in this book's pattern catalog.

[30] See the *Architecture Decision* pattern in this book's pattern catalog.

[31] See the *Architecture Governance* pattern in this book's pattern catalog.

is quite common (though not required) for all architects in a company to be organizationally combined in its architecture function. Architecture functions pursue a structured approach to creating, evolving, and leveraging the enterprise architecture discipline to help their organization achieve its operational, tactical, as well as strategic ambitions. Since architecture functions are one among many other organizational functions, they must be integrated with these to realize their full potential and make all demanded contributions. Furthermore, an architecture function is a socio-technical system embedded in the overall socio-technical system of the enterprise. This is why the term *architecture* has an extended meaning compared to architecture in the context of purely technical systems. Architecture functions deal not only with enterprise services of a technical nature but also with social aspects, such as organizational processes, political dynamics, corporate culture, and similar soft factors in the enterprise.

Note that instead of using *enterprise architecture function*, I refer predominantly to the shorter *architecture function* to refer to the organizational architecture capability in this book. In the literature, architecture functions are alternatively referred to as *enterprise architecture management* (EAM).

1.6   Pattern Language

While, in my book, I focus on the design of an architecture function in terms of content, I have chosen *pattern language* as a methodological means of implementing and describing the design process.

The concept of pattern languages was introduced by architect Christopher Alexander and popularized by his famous book *A Pattern Language* in 1977 (Alexander et al. 1977). Pattern languages are organized, navigable, and coherent sets of patterns. Each pattern generalizes a recurring problem as well as the core of a corresponding solution design. Pattern languages, in a sense, superimpose themselves on their patterns and show their users ways to successively derive their own solution designs from offered patterns and the relationships between them. The desired design results from the adaptation of many patterns, applying them one by one to incrementally generate a solution. The contribution of a pattern language is to guide the designer through the patterns in such a way that he recognizes the patterns that are relevant for the next design increment. Pattern languages thus support demand-driven navigation and guidance through their patterns. While a single pattern addresses single problem and solution aspects, pattern languages and their patterns address complex problem and solution compositions.

A pattern language is sometimes compared to a spoken language. Just as words must have grammatical and semantic relationships to each other to make a spoken language useful, design patterns must be related to each other to make up a pattern language. Pattern relationships that make up a language give an architect many additional clues. For example, each problem aspect that an architect considers at the beginning of a solution journey is related to other problem aspects. The first pattern an architect visits gives him valuable solution clues. At the same time, this first pattern points the architect to typically related problem aspects for which other patterns exist. A pattern language emphasizes the relationships that inherently exist between patterns. The main purpose of a pattern language is to help navigate patterns to raise awareness and enable architects to solve composite problems, that is, problems that cannot be solved by a single architecture pattern alone. Moreover, a pattern language promotes the recognition of relationships between patterns belonging to different architecture domains, thus supporting interdisciplinary architectural thinking. A pattern language inherently or explicitly brings in its own super perspective and context. In this respect, it may well be viewed as a pattern itself—a pattern composed of patterns. Moreover, a single pattern can be referenced by multiple languages, which themselves serve different navigational and orientational needs.

Architects using a pattern language begin elaborating their design by finding a pattern that fits an initial part of their overall problem. Once the initial pattern is found and the first part of an overall solution design is elaborated, the pattern language points the architect to patterns that are associated with the initial pattern—thus with other potentially legitimate aspects of the given overall problem. Navigating and viewing this initial set of associated patterns provides the architect with more useful clues for the next round of associated patterns and so on. The subset or network of patterns associated with the initial problem part can get very large very quickly. This makes pattern languages powerful tools in the study of larger problems and the design of complex and overarching solutions. Note that language partitions are introduced as structures that group patterns with commonalities. Furthermore, pattern languages are highly scalable. Adding patterns over time does not break existing relationships but adds to them (Fig. 1.9).

Fig. 1.9 Pattern language

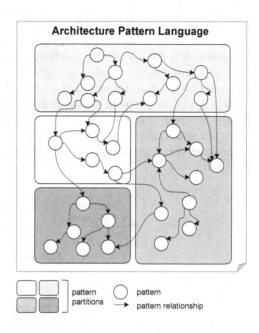

In his book *A Pattern Language*, Christopher Alexander emphasizes the generative nature of a pattern language. The idea is that when a pattern is applied in
generating a desired solution, a new context automatically emerges—a context in
which other patterns of the pattern language can be applied. It is like asking a question
and getting an answer that automatically generates new questions on your end. You
iterate over a series of questions and answers that converge to more and better
insights. Pattern languages are applied in a similarly incremental and convergent
way. Each pattern you pick up, each associated pattern you consciously consider from
there, helps you traverse your problem space more completely. Ultimately, a pattern
language, viewed as a whole, guides you incrementally to a more holistic solution.

Like all pattern languages, the *architecture function pattern language* in this book
has the above-mentioned characteristics of pattern languages. It thus provides you
with a generic yet flexibly adaptable design process for planning, developing,
validating, and operating your architecture function.

1.7   Reader Guide

1.7.1   Book Architecture

What could be more natural in a book written about architecture and the architecture
process to subject the design of the book itself to architecture development

principles? I have picked up this very idea, which is why my book assumes a situation in which a concrete enterprise has either already experienced its needs and constraints for an effective architecture discipline or is planning to do so (*enterprise conditions*). Another prerequisite I assume is a basic familiarity with enterprise architecture (*architecture means*). If, in addition to basic architecture knowledge, other means or an architecture function already exist, that is all the better—however, it is not an inevitable prerequisite. The functions my book provides you with are to construct or evolve your *architecture function*. Inputs in this process are the enterprise conditions and architecture means of your enterprise (Fig. 1.10).

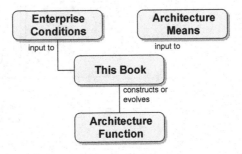

Fig. 1.10 Teleological system perspective on this book

While the functional contribution of the book application process is thus very roughly clarified, the internal building blocks of my book (which I view as a system) and their arrangement need to be further elaborated, specifically the building blocks of context, problem, and solution, their interrelationships, and their respective details and internal arrangement. The *problem* building block, for example, has to explain the generic requirements to which architecture functions are basically exposed, while the *solution* building block has to show variable design approaches that you can follow for the construction of your own architecture function. In summary, this consideration results in the well-known pattern triad as a schema (i.e., context, problem, solution). I have made this my overarching book topology, which is also reflected in the table of contents (Fig. 1.11).

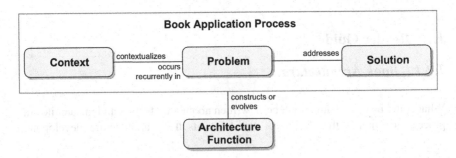

Fig. 1.11 Process of applying this book

In order to provide orientation and structure to the discussion of architecture function design, I have selected three essential schema dimensions that mirror the pattern triad of context, problem, and solution. This schema enables successive and incremental elaboration of an architecture function design without running the risk of losing sight of a holistic perspective. I refer to this scheme by the term *architecture function pattern topology*. In this topology, *architecture function context* highlights considerations of the enterprise context, in which architecture functions operate—for example, enterprise value chain and enterprise organizations. *Architecture function challenge* (i.e., the problem part of the pattern triad) discusses foundational expectations of enterprises for their architecture functions. The challenge view takes the outside perspective of other enterprise organizations—viewing the architecture function as a black box. Here, in addition to the expectations for the individual architecture function components, the expectations for the contributions of the architecture services and the qualitative requirements for architecture functions are elaborated. By the way, you can consider expectations for architecture function services as functional requirements and qualitative expectations as non-functional requirements. Finally, *architecture function constitution* (i.e., the solution part of the pattern triad) takes a white-box perspective and zooms into the individual building blocks, services, or quality attributes of an architecture function to propose and discuss their pattern-based designs (Fig. 1.12).

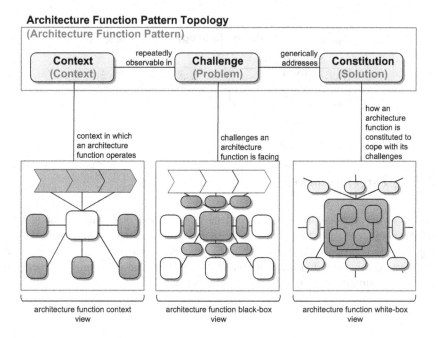

Fig. 1.12 Architecture function pattern topology

In addition to the high-level structuring *pattern topology*, there are aspects that run throughout the book. For example, many architecture and associated concepts are defined and introduced across the book. Taken together, these definitions add up to the distributed *pattern ontology* and thus establish a conceptual platform upon which all further design considerations are based. Finally, there is the *pattern catalog*, which lists all architecture function patterns in an essentially linear fashion and arranges them into coherent groups. The individual patterns offer design considerations, inspirations, and suggestions and are referenced extensively within the pattern topology. The three building blocks, pattern ontology, pattern topology, and pattern catalog, together form the architecture *function pattern language* (Fig. 1.13).

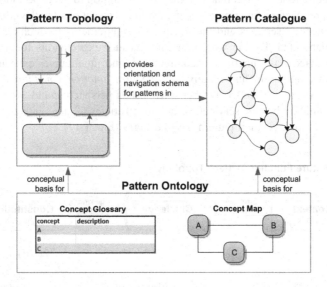

Fig. 1.13   Pattern language = architecture of this book

1.7.2   Target Audience

The book is intended for a broad readership, including enterprise, domain, and solution architects, educators and learners, and anyone else interested in understanding the value proposition, responsibilities, outcomes, methods, and practices of architecture functions and thus, of course, to all those interested in the subject of enterprise, domain, and solution architecture per se.

In addition, the book is aimed at readers who want to understand how an architecture function should be embedded in an organization to ensure efficient and effective development of digitized services and products—ultimately, anyone interested in understanding, planning, developing, and operating an ideal architecture function design.

My book does not assume sophisticated prior theoretical knowledge or practical experience with enterprise, domain, or solution architecture—although an understanding of operational issues that an architecture function addresses is beneficial. It introduces the basic concepts and theories needed to understand the pattern language presented and the patterns it summarizes and to apply them in your own organization. In addition, literature is referenced to help you further explore important concepts. However, a general understanding of socio-technical systems, organizational dynamics, economic concerns, or solutions based on digital building materials will certainly not hurt the reader either.

The answer potential offered by this book is as comprehensive as you are able to create pattern permutations and adapt them to your business context—in other words, the answer space that the book opens up is virtually infinite. However, to give you a concrete impression of the answers you can hope to find in this book, I present a few questions that my book addresses. For example, if you want to understand why architecture (i.e., the potential it offers) and architecture functions (i.e., exploiting these architecture potentials concretely for you) are so important, you will be able to learn this in my book. Furthermore, you will understand the context in which architecture functions operate, what are essential context components, and how you appropriately consider this context when designing your architecture organization. You will learn what cooperative relationships exist between an architecture function and other business organizations—that is, what cooperative expectations are placed on architecture functions from the outside. You will also understand the contributions that architecture functions make along an enterprise value chain—from early strategic and portfolio planning through detailed planning, design, and implementation and into operations. You will get a concrete overview of the service offering that architecture functions provide but also of service-independent quality expectations that enterprises have of architecture functions. You will learn about the different architecture disciplines[32] and roles[33] and understand how they differentiate but also how they cooperate to jointly make the contributions of an architecture function. You will get a sense of the dimensions that span the architecture space—whether the different levels of architecture abstraction and granularity, the differentiation between govern versus perform architecture or solution archetypes, and how architecture contributions differ depending on them. Besides common architecture tools and platforms, you will get a comprehensive overview of architecture methods, practices, and view models. The overview will

---

[32] See the *Enterprise, Domain,* and *Solution Architecture Discipline* pattern in this book's pattern catalog (Chap. 6).

[33] See the *Architecture Role* pattern in this book's pattern catalog.

help you understand how enterprise, domain, and solution architecture are planned, developed, and validated as well as how reference architecture assets[34] (e.g., patterns and principles) are used to evolve architecture in a controlled manner. Finally, you will learn fundamental abstractions, concepts, and terms that underlie sound and unambiguous architecture discussions and design considerations.

1.7.3   Chapter Overview

I will give you an overview of the chapters and content of the book, before I introduce the individual chapters in a little more detail, below (Table 1.1).

Table 1.1 Chapter overview

No.	Chapter	Contents
1	Introduction	Motivation, introduction into basic concepts and book architecture, target audience
2	Architecture Function Pattern Language	Patterns and pattern language (topology, catalog, ontology), language application
3	Architecture Function: Context	Business and operating model, value chain, enterprise organizations, service, digitalization, generic context schema
4.	Architecture Function: Challenge	Architecture function black-box perspective, building blocks, services, and qualities expectations
5	Architecture Function: Constitution	Architecture function white-box perspective, building blocks, services, and qualities designs, pointers to patterns in catalog
6	Pattern Catalog	Architecture pattern groups, 48 architecture function patterns, pointers between patterns

1.7.4   Chapters in Detail

Chapter 1: Introduction
This chapter explains the starting position and objectives of this book and introduces key concepts that will be explained further in subsequent chapters. It points out the special feature of this book to elaborate the topic of enterprise architecture from the perspective of an architecture function. The chapter introduces the architecture of the book itself and concludes with an overview of the target audience as well as the contributions of each chapter. You should read this chapter to know the intent of this book and to understand how you can use it to critically reflect, establish, or evolve your architecture function.

---

[34] See the *Architecture Asset* pattern in this book's pattern catalog.

Chapter 2: Architecture Function Pattern Language

This chapter introduces the concepts of pattern, pattern catalog, pattern topology, and ontology. It goes on to explain how these concepts are combined to form a pattern language for planning, designing, and operating an architecture function. The chapter concludes with an overview of how the pattern language in this book is applied to design, develop, and operate a concrete architecture function for a given enterprise situation. You should read this chapter to understand how this book *works*, how the other chapters fit together to form a pattern language, and how you can use this language to construct or evolve your own architecture function.

Chapter 3: Architecture Function—Context

In this chapter, contextual concepts are introduced. These concepts are crucial for understanding the challenges that an architecture function faces. They are also important for understanding the solution approaches used to address these challenges—for example, concepts such as business model, operating model, digitization, or service. The chapter also presents a generic schema for the business organizations and value chain. The generic schema enables a structured discussion of the challenges each architecture function faces as well as the proven approaches to address them. You should read this chapter to get an overview of the environmental conditions in which architecture functions meet expectations and make their contributions.

Chapter 4: Architecture Function—Challenge

This chapter looks at an architecture function from a black-box perspective. It outlines the expectations and requirements that companies place on architecture organizations by looking at an ideal-typical architecture function from the outside. The chapter discusses the building blocks of an architecture function, the services that an architecture function provides along the enterprise value chain, and the quality attributes that enterprises expect from their functions in the twenty-first century. You should read this chapter to gain an understanding of the outside perspective on architecture functions—ultimately, to create that perspective for your own function as completely as possible yourself.

Chapter 5: Architecture Function—Constitution

This chapter shifts from a black-box perspective to a white-box perspective and outlines the generic design of an architecture function. The design describes how it realizes functional and quality-related requirements, in turn intensively referencing patterns in the pattern catalog. Functional requirements are realized by architecture services, while the realization of non-functional requirements is represented by quality attribute scenarios. You should read this chapter while critically reflecting, constructing, or evolving your architecture function. You follow the design hints in this chapter, which in turn point to patterns in the pattern catalog.

Chapter 6: Pattern Catalog

This chapter introduces the pattern catalog, which contains a total of 48 architecture function patterns. The patterns in this catalog guide you in designing and embedding your architecture function in your enterprise. They suggest designs for collaboration between the architecture function and enterprise organizations, as well as for the elaboration and development of enterprise services along the enterprise value chain. In addition, the patterns recommend designs for integrating your architecture apparatus into the enterprise apparatus and aligning architecture governance with enterprise governance. You can read this chapter by diving selectively into patterns that interest you on the fly. However, you will get references to patterns from the previous chapters even if you do not go directly to this chapter. So if you follow those references, which you should, you will inevitably learn about the patterns in this pattern catalog sooner or later. Each of the patterns presents, for one aspect of an overarching design, the challenge that architecture functions face and makes a proposal to adequately address that challenge—examples of particular aspects addressed by individual patterns are *architecture funding, sourcing, ownership, roadmap, mandate, methodology, organizational replication*, or *architecture levels*. The catalog divides the 48 patterns into the 9 pattern groups: *architecture organization, architecture objective, architecture disciplines, architecture engagement model, communication, architecture governance, architecture elaboration, architecture asset*, and *architecture apparatus*.

Further Reading

Agile Manifesto, *Agile Manifesto Principles*, http://agilemanifesto.org/principles.html, 2020
Alexander, Christopher; Ishikawa, Sara; Silverstein, Murray; Jacobson, Max; Fiksdahl-King, Ingrid; Angel, Shlomo, *A Pattern Language*, Oxford University Press, 1977
Bente, Stefan; Bombosch, Uwe; Langade, Shailendra, *Collaborative Enterprise Architecture - Enriching EA with Lean, Agile, and Enterprise 2.0 Practices*, Elsevier, London, 2012
Dietz, Jan, and Enterprise Ontology. 2006. *Theory and Methodology*. Berlin Heidelberg: Springer Science & Business Media.
Gartner, Gartner Glossary, https://www.gartner.com/en/information-technology/glossary, 2020
Goodwin, Tom; *The battle is for the customer interface*; https://techcrunch.com/2015/03/03/in-the-age-of-disintermediation-the-battle-is-all-for-the-customer-interface/, 2015
Kotusev, Svyatoslav. 2018. *The Practice of Enterprise Architecture*. Melbourne, Australia: SK Publishing.
Lankhorst, Marc, Enterprise Architecture at Work, Springer-Verlag, Berlin Heidelberg, 2011
Lankhorst, Marc. 2017. *Enterprise Architecture at Work*. Berlin Heidelberg: Springer-Verlag.
Murer, Stephan; Bonati, Bruno; Furrer, Frank, *Managed Evolution – A Strategy for Very Large Information Systems*, Springer Science & Business Media, Berlin Heidelberg, 2010
Perroud, Thierry; Inversini, Reto, *Enterprise Architecture Patterns*, Springer-Verlag, Berlin Heidelberg, 2013
Schekkerman, Jaap. 2004. *How to Survive in the Jungle of Enterprise Architecture Frameworks – Creating or Choosing an Enterprise Architecture Framework*. Victoria: Trafford Publishing.
Sensler, Carsten, Grimm, Dr. Thomas, *Business Enterprise Architecture – Praxishandbuch zur digitalen Transformation in Unternehmen*, Entwickler.press, Unterhaching, 2015
Vogel, Oliver; Arnold, Ingo; Chugtai, Arif; Kehrer, Timo, *Software Architecture: A Comprehensive Framework and Guide for Practitioners*, Springer-Verlag, Berlin Heidelberg, 2011
Wikipedia, *Agile*, https://en.wikipedia.org/wiki/Agile_software_development#The_Agile_Manifesto, 2020a
———, *Archimedes*, https://en.wikipedia.org/wiki/Archimedes, 2020b
———, *DevOps*, https://en.wikipedia.org/wiki/DevOps, 2020c

Chapter 2
Architecture Function Pattern Language

Abstract This chapter introduces the concepts of pattern, pattern catalog, and pattern language. It explains how I use and combine these concepts to design a pattern language for planning, designing, and executing an architecture function. The chapter concludes with an overview of how to apply the pattern language of this book to design, evolve, and operate an actual architecture function in your own organization.

2.1 Overview

The subject of architecture is multifaceted and multiperspective. Architecture frameworks overwhelm us by their sheer magnitude and the many dimensions they encompass. They offer us hundreds of architecture concepts, roles, artifacts, principles, guidelines, or processes. On top of that, new architecture trends and approaches are constantly emerging to keep pace with rapidly changing business models, be it due to a global pandemic or a universal trend toward digitalization. In this tangled web of architectural contexts and challenges, architectural frameworks and hypes, and the resulting terminological Babylon,[1] it is easy to lose sight of the big picture. Without sufficient architecture orientation, you run the risk of no longer being able to meaningfully distinguish the architecturally relevant from the irrelevant.

At the same time, architecture orientation is crucial. It is crucial to know the current state of the art, to evaluate emerging architecture approaches, and to develop your own architecture awareness. Quoting Archimedes of Syracuse (c. 287 BC–c.

---

[1] In the *Old Testament*, the story of the Tower of Babel is told. In this parable, the tower building project is judged as an attempt by mankind to equal God. Because of this self-conceit, God brings the building of the tower to a bloodless halt by causing a confusion of languages. This forces the abandonment of the project because of insurmountable communication difficulties and scatters the builders of it for the same reason over the whole earth. The *Babylonian confusion of languages* has found its way into common usage as a figure of speech—as a symbol for the clash of several languages.

212 BC), a Greek mathematician, philosopher, scientist, and engineer, we see how much emphasis he placed on a clarified position:

> Give me a place to stand, and I shall move the world.

Our *place* to stand or chosen perspective on the vast and often confusing subject of architecture is the architecture function. While the entire book outlines in detail a generic method for planning, building, and operating an architecture function, this chapter provides you with an overview of the method's schema, its core building blocks, and essential concepts with which you should be familiar. Adapting the method offers you a path not only to *reflect on the value potential of architecture* but to *concretely leverage that potential* in your organization.

While Sects. 2.2, 2.3, and 2.4 lay the foundation, Sect. 2.5 introduces the goals, schema, building blocks, and application of the architecture function pattern language.

2.2 Pattern

Pattern is a pivotal concept in this book, and I want to take a broader view before we look more closely at patterns in the context of architecture and pattern languages. Patterns are all around us, from the people we meet to the repetitive patterns we find in nature and daily routine. Humans have used patterns from the beginning to explain and orient themselves in the complex world around them. A pattern abstracts and generalizes a concrete phenomenon so that it represents a whole class of concrete phenomena. To recognize a pattern is to recognize commonalities among concrete phenomena. As a means of abstraction, a pattern is an excellent vehicle for documenting and exchanging know-how and expertise. Patterns provide a common vocabulary, language, and protocol that resolves or mitigates ambiguities in exchanges between communicating parties. Patterns also provide us with guidance and inform us of the potential consequences of their use. They help us cope with the overwhelming complexity of signals streaming through our senses as our cognitive system aggregates the isolated signal points into a dense set of information (i.e., patterns representing phenomena in the real world). Patterns also help us efficiently learn and memorize new phenomena we encounter. They give us the confidence that a situation we have mastered in the past can be mastered again by bringing a proven pattern to bear. But while patterns are concrete means for orientation in the world, concrete means also for adaptation of solution approaches to recurring problems, patterns remain heuristic.

From a problem-solving perspective, each pattern is a recipe that describes what one must do to create the solution that the pattern prescribes. Part of what leads us to choose a solution is recognizing competing alternative solutions. Patterns make such solutions and the criteria for selecting them explicit. They are powerful means for efficiently finding, discussing, and deciding effective solutions, while at the same time no pattern is ever *the solution*. Problems recur, and so do their corresponding responses. By generalizing the context, problem, and associated solution, we obtain a reusable solution pattern—that is, a highly efficient and effective solution blueprint.

The *stairs pattern* is an example to illustrate the basic pattern idea to visualize the ways in which patterns can be used and referenced in real life. The context in which stairs are planned, discussed, and referenced is *house construction*. In this context, the recurring need (*problem*) that the stairs pattern addresses is that of a person who wants to negotiate the height between floors while walking upright. The proven *solution* suggested by the stairs pattern is one in which the total height is divided into blocks of equal size, in which the blocks are arranged as shown, and in which a passageway is left open at the top floor such that a person can pass through (Fig. 2.1).

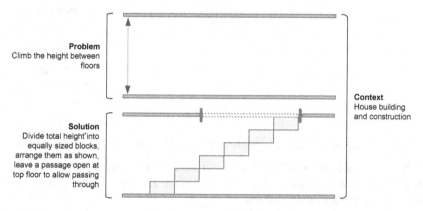

Fig. 2.1 The stairs pattern

Patterns have become famous through Christopher Alexander's book *A Pattern Language* (Alexander 1979). Alexander presented patterns of urban architecture. He defines a pattern as a description of a proven architecture approach associated with a recurring problem in the urban context. His book is the first *architecture best practice* summary in more than 2000 years, when Marcus Vitruvius Pollio (c. 80–70 BC, after c. 15 BC), commonly known as Vitruvius, published his multivolume work *De Architectura: Libri Decem* (Vitruvius 2013).

In the early 1990s, Christopher Alexander's work was adapted to the domain of software development by Erich Gamma, Richard Helm, Ralph Johnson, and John Vlissides—known as the Gang of Four (GoF)—in their book *Design Patterns: Elements of Reusable Object-Oriented Software* (Gamma et al. 1994).

Since then, many more pattern contributions have emerged that adapt patterns and pattern language as a methodological technique for analyzing and representing classes of solution designs for associated classes of problems, for example, patterns for the analysis of domains (Fowler 1997), patterns for domain-driven design (Evans 2004), or patterns for enterprise architecture management (Matthes et al. 2015).

While there are many differences between the domains for which authors have published pattern books or papers, there is also a fundamental commonality. As the least common denominator, all pattern publications share the basic pattern triad scheme as introduced by Christopher Alexander (Fig. 2.2):

Fig. 2.2 Pattern triad schema

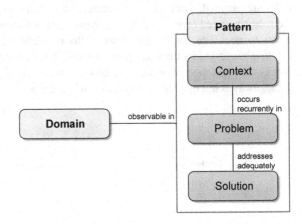

A pattern is a proven solution to a problem that recurringly arises within a defined context.

Frank Buschmann, Kevlin Henney, and Douglas C. Schmidt define pattern in *Pattern-Oriented Software Architecture, Volume 5: On Patterns and Pattern Languages* (Buschmann et al. 2007) as:

> A pattern describes a particular recurring design problem that arises in specific design contexts and presents a well-proven solution for the problem. The solution is specified by describing the roles of its constituent participants, their responsibilities and relationships and the ways in which they collaborate.

Patterns outline the common characteristics of problem-solving phenomena by generalizing their context, problem, and associated solution. In addition, patterns involve variations in their generalization of context, problem, and solution, for example, structural versus behavioral variations or variations in the degree of abstraction of patterns (e.g., design patterns versus architecture patterns). This implies that patterns must be concretized and translated when they are adapted to establish concrete solutions in response to correspondingly concrete problems. Using the example of two granite houses, a traditional construction method in the Swiss canton of Ticino, you can nicely see how the previously discussed stairs pattern can be physically realized in very different ways. While both staircases are equally derived from the stairs pattern, their concrete constructions differ significantly (Fig. 2.3).

Fig. 2.3 Stairs pattern applied

Beyond prescribing context, problem, and solution state, inherent in a pattern is the process of its own application—that is, a pattern is always both a thing and a process. Patterns enable the complete reasoning cycle, from initial orientation (i.e., context) through reflection and understanding of the challenge at hand (i.e., problem) to an adequate approach to resolving the challenging forces (i.e., solution).

Patterns must be made available in such a way that they can be practically found and applied. Therefore, they must be documented in a structured way, maintained, evolved, promoted, and made publicly available. In addition to making patterns available, architects must be trained in the handling and application of patterns. The use and implementation of patterns must be learned and practiced. Finally, patterns are disseminated and made publicly available through pattern catalogs and pattern languages.

As an aside, the term *pattern* also appears in a context where algorithms are shaped by the patterns contained in vast amounts of data. A machine learning[2] solution based on an artificial neural network[3] design adjusts its own algorithm (i.e., the shape and weighting of the neural network) based on the massive amount of training and correction data presented to it. Once the algorithm is sufficiently trained, it is shaped such to implement the targeted function and can be used to produce acceptable approximate results in response to real (i.e., untrained) data inputs. By analogy, shaping the algorithm by extracting the pattern inherent in the training data

---

[2]Machine learning (ML) refers to a genre of computer algorithms that are initially established, or continuously improved, through experience and by the use of data. Machine learning is a subfield of artificial intelligence. Machine learning algorithms build a statistical model based on sample data (i.e., training data) to make predictions or decisions without being explicitly programmed to do so.

[3]An artificial neural network is a network of artificial neurons. Artificial neural networks, like artificial neurons, have a biological model. They are contrasted with natural neural networks, representing a network of neurons in the nervous system of a living being. Artificial neural networks provide an elementary design approach for algorithms of the machine learning genre.

is analogous to creating an architecture pattern. Consequently, using the algorithm after final shaping is analogous to adapting the pattern and generating a concrete solution.

2.3 Pattern Catalog

A *pattern catalog* is simply an organized grouping and collection of patterns. The distinguishing criteria by which the collection is assembled determine the catalogue's purpose. For example, an *enterprise pattern catalog* may list all patterns in an enterprise that are endorsed by the architecture function, with membership in the catalog based simply on the *endorsed by architecture* criterion. Membership in the catalog may also be based on a pattern's membership in a particular domain. For example, a *security pattern catalog* contains all patterns in the enterprise that belong to the security domain. Finally, catalog membership can be based on the level of abstraction at which each pattern exists. For example, a *design pattern catalog* contains all patterns that propose detailed designs, while an *architecture pattern catalog* contains only patterns proposing conceptual designs.

Pattern catalogs can be unstructured or structured. They may be implemented simply as an aggregated document into which the pattern descriptions have been copied, or as luxuriously as a digital document repository with complex filtering, search, and lifecycle management capabilities.

2.4 Pattern Language

When Christopher Alexander published *The Timeless Way of Building* (Alexander 1979), he not only promoted the notion of pattern as a powerful technique for capturing proven architecture practice but also introduced the notion of *pattern language*, which he likened to ordinary language in terms of its expressive and constructive power:

> The people can shape buildings for themselves, and have done it for centuries, by using languages which I call pattern languages. A pattern language gives each person who uses it, the power to create an infinite variety of new and unique buildings, just as his ordinary language gives him the power to create an invite variety of sentences.

While an ordinary language like English or German allows us to create an infinite variety of word combinations called sentences, a pattern language is a system that allows its users to create an infinite variety of *context-problem-solution* triples.

Just as there are natural relationships between related problems, similarly natural relationships exist between patterns. For any reasonably complex real-world problem, a single pattern is often not enough to suggest a complete solution. You need to find and apply associated patterns (and associated patterns of associated patterns and so on) to deal with the many facets of the real-world problem in their entirety. This is where pattern languages come into play. While an individual pattern describes a solution to a single problem, a pattern language is a collection of semantically related patterns spanning a larger solution space. The solution space addressed by a pattern language is appropriately oriented toward complex and interrelated problems.

Let me introduce *balustrade* and *roofing* as complementary patterns to stairs. The *balustrade* problem is one where a person is not protected from falling off a deck, while a waist-high enclosure around the deck adequately solves the problem. The *roofing* problem is one where something can fall from above and hit a person, while the solution is a large enough shield mounted so that it fully protects the person upward (Fig. 2.4).

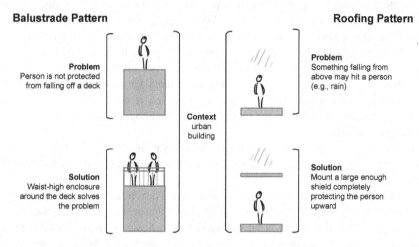

Fig. 2.4   Balustrade and roofing patterns

Whereas in a pattern catalog *stairs*, *roofing*, and *balustrade* are associated only by the common attribute of *catalog membership*, a pattern language with stairs, roofing, and balustrade transcends catalogs by semantically linking its patterns to one another.

For example, when an architect uses the language of *stairs*, *balustrade*, and *roofing* patterns in the context of designing an entire building, an architect may first consider the problem of overcoming the height between floors. In this way, the architect first finds the stairs pattern. By studying the stairs pattern, the same architect may recognize that stairs above a certain height expose their users to the risk of falling. Fortunately, the pattern language suggests an associated pattern (*balustrade*) to solve the particular problem of falling. The stairs pattern points the architect to another associated pattern (*roofing*). Since the planning of the new building is still in its infancy, the architect has not yet considered protection from anything that might fall from above. However, by explicitly referencing the stairs pattern, the architect recognizes that at a later date, a staircase is indeed planned for the exterior of the building. This will be a moment when roofing comes in handy and will address the problem of protecting the stairs users from bad weather conditions, such as rain (Fig. 2.5).

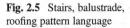

Fig. 2.5 Stairs, balustrade,
roofing pattern language

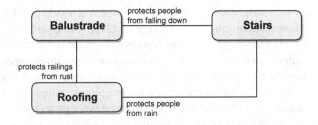

The above example of the *stairs*, *balustrade*, and *roofing* demonstrates the value of a pattern language. A pattern language provides solutions to problems that none of its individual patterns entirely address. For example, the *stairs*, *balustrade*, and *roofing* language points the architect to an associated pattern (i.e., *balustrade*) so that the architect combines stairs and balustrade. This results in the combination of the stairs (i.e., height to be climbed) and balustrade (i.e., protecting the person from falling off the stairs) patterns. Finally, the pattern language alerted the architect to a need that he had not yet even recognized. However, it was in fact relevant: the roofing for stairs mounted on the outside of the building when large parts of the building are erected.

Similar to a complex system being broken down into smaller but interrelated parts, a pattern language, viewed as a system of patterns, is broken down into related patterns.

In his book *A Pattern Language*, Christopher Alexander also emphasizes the generative nature of a pattern language. The idea is that when a pattern is applied in generating a desired solution, a new context automatically emerges—a context in which other patterns of the pattern language can be applied. It is like asking a question and getting an answer that automatically generates new questions on your end. You iterate over a series of questions and answers that converge to more and better insights. Pattern languages are applied in a similarly incremental and convergent way. Each pattern you pick up, each associated pattern you consciously consider from there, helps you traverse your problem space more completely. Ultimately, pattern language, viewed as a whole, guides you incrementally to a more holistic solution.

Pattern languages are domain-specific languages. This means that a pattern language makes domain-specific concepts inherently contextual to the patterns it contains and references. This allows pattern languages to consult you in deciding which pattern to apply and when. Each pattern you apply adds an increment to the solution you are building—that is, it changes its state. After a pattern is applied, the pattern description immediately advises you of its associated patterns. The pattern description explains when and why you should consider the patterns it references. These relationships are called pattern sequences. Pattern sequences in a language significantly reduce the number of all possible pattern combinations to those combinations that work. Ultimately, a pattern language makes its patterns navigable and makes you conscious of this navigability when you are searching for a solution. In a nutshell, a pattern language is a network of semantically related patterns that define a system for solving related problems in a particular problem domain.

Whether you want to design a building, a computer system, or an architecture function, use an appropriate pattern language as a tool to generate your desired design in an incremental, systematic, and guided manner. The algorithm of applying a pattern language to a complex problem to generate a corresponding solution design is comparatively simple and highly repetitive. For example, knowing your problem, you start (*1*) traversing the patterns in the language to find an initial match (P_1). Applying pattern P_1 produces an initial design increment (*#1*). Once you have applied P_1, its description draws your attention to an associated pattern (P_2) that might be worth considering. You decide that it is indeed worth considering and apply P_2, evolving (*2*) your initial design increment (*#2*). Next, you consider patterns P_3 and P_4, both of which are associated with pattern P_2. You recognize that both patterns are considerable extensions in the context of the complex problem you are trying to solve—so you apply them (*#3*). This leads to your next increment version (*#3*). P_4 has no other patterns associated with it. However, P_3 has one final hint that you find very useful (P_5). So, you follow P_3's advice and apply P_5, which leads to the final increment version of your design (*#4*) (Fig. 2.6).

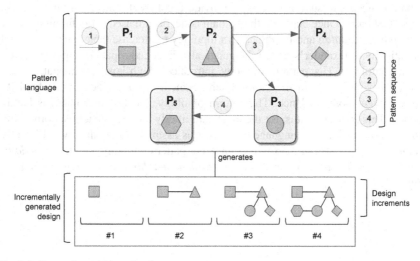

Fig. 2.6 Pattern language application

Like other complex systems, pattern languages need to evolve to accommodate changes in an ever-evolving environment. Unlike other complex systems, gradual evolvability is automatically built in by the inherently loosely coupled design[4] of pattern languages. Adding a new pattern does not interrupt pattern language utilization or application. At most, the addition of a pattern results in minor changes in the descriptions of those patterns with which the new pattern is meaningfully associated. A new pattern, in turn, may relate to patterns that already exist in the language. However, the disruptive potential of extending or modifying a pattern language is negligible from the user's point of view.

Pattern languages can become overwhelming when they contain many patterns. Complex pattern languages often additionally contain one or more pattern topologies. A *pattern topology* introduces an additional layer of order and orientation into a pattern language to improve its usability. A pattern topology represents a navigation scheme that overlays the patterns in the language. Pattern topologies are thus above the level at which direct navigation between patterns is based on pattern sequences. For a semantically sophisticated domain, a pattern language usually also encompasses a concisely defined conceptual basis. The more metaphysical a domain is in nature, the more urgent a clarified conceptual basis becomes. I refer to this part of a pattern language as a *pattern ontology*. A pattern ontology defines and relates domain concepts in such a way as to provide a coherent, consistent, and concise conceptual basis. Once clarified, the domain concepts are used for defining *patterns* in the *pattern catalog* and for the pattern topology to increase their conciseness and unambiguity. Alexander's pattern language also included a pattern topology and a pattern ontology. His pattern topology introduced high-level segmentation into *cities*, *buildings*, and *constructions*. Each segment is subdivided in his book to provide even more guidance. The pattern ontology, on the other hand, is barely noticed. This is because it is, for the most part, utterly identical to terms, norms, and protocols of the English language—that is, it is assumed to be already sufficiently established. Examples of Alexander's inherent pattern ontology are the terms *door*, *window*, *arcade*, *room*, *floor*, *building*, *garden*, *neighborhood*, *street*, or *square* (Fig. 2.7).

---

[4]Loose coupling between components means that connected components have little or no knowledge of each other's definitions, while tight coupling is the exact opposite.

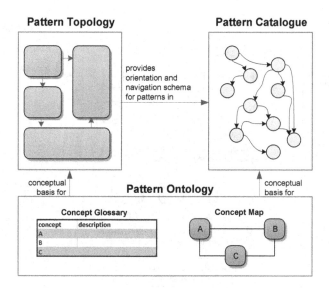

Fig. 2.7   Pattern language, topology, and ontology

2.5   Architecture Function Pattern Language

The aim of this book is to equip you with a systematics with which you can plan, build, and operate your architecture function. In other words, the systematics is a generic design blueprint for architecture functions in the form of a *pattern language*. The *architecture function pattern language* views your *architecture function* as a complex system that you incrementally plan, design, build, and deploy in your enterprise operating model. The *enterprise operating model* is the context within which your architecture function contributes to the *enterprise value chain* by collaborating with other *enterprise organizations*—ultimately aiming to support your enterprise achieve its operational and strategic objectives. In applying the architecture function pattern language, you reflect on the specific context of the enterprise operating model and the particular challenges your architecture function faces. Finally, the architecture function pattern language supports you in succes- sively developing your concrete architecture function design according to your situation. For your architecture function development, the pattern language is a tool that helps you navigate, contextualize, combine, and apply the patterns it contains. The individual patterns are organized and separately defined in the pattern catalog—itself a part of the architecture function pattern language (Fig. 2.8).

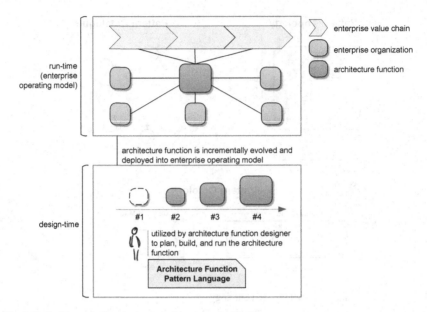

Fig. 2.8 Architecture function pattern language application

The architecture function pattern language includes a pattern topology and a pattern ontology, as well as patterns in a pattern catalog. It is generic and expressive enough to support a wide variety of concrete architecture function designs. At the same time, it is specific enough to guide you concretely through your own architecture function design and accompany you in its further evolution. The architecture function pattern language is easy to understand, navigate, and apply. Its patterns are intended to inspire you in your design efforts. The patterns provide you with critical design considerations and suggestions and invite you to engage in deeper design thinking along suggested schemas. The level of detail in the patterns is kept rather coarse, as some patterns, or the themes they outline, are themselves worth an entire book. Like other patterns, architecture function patterns are largely context-agnostic, so they can be reused, combined, and applied in a wide variety of contexts (Fig. 2.9).

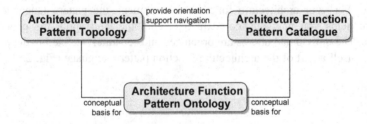

Fig. 2.9 Architecture function pattern language building blocks

I outline the scheme of the architecture function pattern topology and its relationship to the other chapters of this book in Sect. 2.5.1. I then give an overview of
the architecture pattern catalog structure and the patterns it contains in Sect. 2.5.2.
Section 2.5.3 introduces the architecture function pattern ontology and explains how
essential concepts, as well as their relationships, are defined and illustrated throughout the book. Finally, Sect. 2.6 proposes use cases for the concrete application of the
architecture function pattern language.

2.5.1   Architecture Function Pattern Topology

Alexander used *cities*, *houses*, and *constructions* as the overarching segmentation for
his pattern language. I use the pattern triad of *context*, *problem*, and *solution* as the
top-level segmentation scheme for the architecture function pattern language.
Choosing the pattern triad as a top-level schema makes the architecture function
pattern language a super-pattern, a pattern of patterns that recursively decomposes an
architecture function context, problem, and solution into its pattern parts, which in
turn adopt the same generic solution scheme (i.e., context, problem, solution). The
pattern triad underscores the book's goal of providing a practical solution approach
for planning, building, and executing an architecture function.

The top-level structure of the *architecture function pattern topology* allows us to
consider the design of the architecture function as a recurring design *problem*, discuss it,
and present proven *solutions* to it. The distinctive feature of the architecture function's
solution segment is that its participants, their responsibilities and relationships, and the
way they work together are themselves patterns—patterns in the *architecture function
pattern catalog*. While I have adopted the semantics of the pattern triad in its entirety, I
have made a terminological adjustment due to the organizational nature of architecture
functions. While I retain the term *context*, I use *challenge* instead of *problem* and
replace *solution* with the term *constitution* (Fig. 2.10).

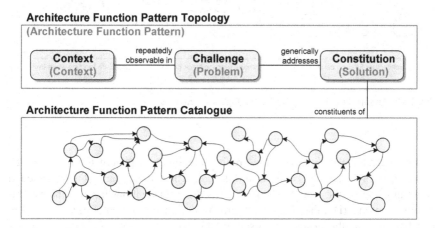

Fig. 2.10 Pattern triad adopted for architecture function pattern topology

The architecture function pattern topology segments *context*, *challenge*, and *constitution*, each introduce their own substructures. The *context* segment subdivides the enterprise context within which an architecture function operates, for example, enterprise services, enterprise organizations, or the enterprise value chain and the value streams into which it is partitioned. The *challenge* segment looks at the architecture function from the outside and outlines recurring challenges it faces. The challenge segment distinguishes the three sub-segments of architecture function, i.e., building blocks, architecture function services, and architecture function qualities, to explore and present the challenges in a structured way. Finally, the *constitution* segment white box zooms into the architecture function and proposes approaches to respond to the challenges that architecture functions face repeatedly. It adopts the structure in which the challenges were presented—thus also knows the sub-segment architecture function building blocks, services, and qualities. The suggested designs in the constitution sub-segments are based on architecture function patterns in the pattern catalog (Fig. 2.11).

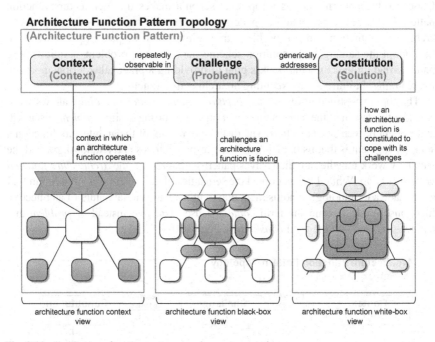

Fig. 2.11 Architecture function pattern topology segmentation

You may have noticed that the architecture function pattern topology can be found again in the table of contents of this book. The *context* segment is presented in detail in Chap. 3, the recurring expectations that organizations have of their architecture functions (i.e., the *challenge* segment of the pattern topology) are presented in Chap. 4, and the design proposal suitable to address the challenges (i.e. the *solution* segment) is found in Chap. 5.

Architecture Function Pattern Topology: Context

Understanding the context within which a system is placed is a prerequisite for comprehending the challenges it faces and the constitution it chooses to address them. Chapter 3 explains crucial concepts such as *business model* and *operating model*. A generic *enterprise value chain* is then presented in a separate subchapter. The enterprise value chain is further subdivided into four enterprise value streams. It provides a schematic canvas to explore the cooperative relationships between the *architecture function* and other *enterprise organizations* that collectively contribute to *enterprise services* lifecycle management (Fig. 2.12).

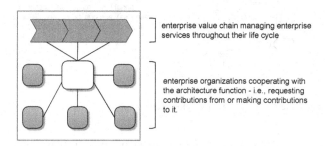

Fig. 2.12 Architecture function pattern topology: context

The enterprise value chain breaks down into the *service planning, service building, service running,* and *service delivering* value streams. At the end of *service planning*, the enterprise knows which projects need to be financed in order to evolve the service portfolio so that it meets the agreed service demands. At the end of *service building*, new services have been established or further evolved, tested, and deployed. At the end of the *service delivering* value stream, customer expectations have been met while services are monitored and kept vital during *service running*. The value streams schema permeates the entire pattern topology—and thus spans Chaps. 3, 4, and 5 (Fig. 2.13).

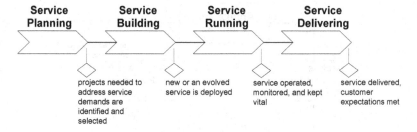

Fig. 2.13 Architecture function pattern topology: context subschema

Architecture Function Pattern Topology: Challenge
Chapter 3 outlines the environment in which architecture functions operate. It
introduces a generic schema of the enterprise value chain and equally generic
enterprise organizations. Chapter 4 relates to Chap. 3 but shifts its focus to specifying the recurring challenges that architecture functions must meet in their enterprise
context (Fig. 2.14).

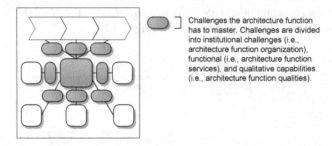

Fig. 2.14 Architecture function pattern topology: challenge

Chapter 4 is divided into the *building blocks* of an architecture function, architecture function *services*, and architecture function *qualities*. Before an architecture
function can ensure the qualitative provision of the architecture services required by
an enterprise, it must be established and institutionalized. This is covered in *architecture function organization* (Sect. 4.2). Regularly requested architecture contributions are presented as architecture function service specifications. Think of the
architecture function service specifications as the functional requirements that architecture functions must meet on a recurring basis. The enterprise value chain canvas is
used to position architecture function services where they make their initial contributions from a lifecycle perspective. Architecture services are specified in *architecture function services* (Sect. 4.3). Finally, recurring qualitative expectations for
architecture functions are specified in *architecture function qualities* (Sect. 4.4)
(Fig. 2.15).

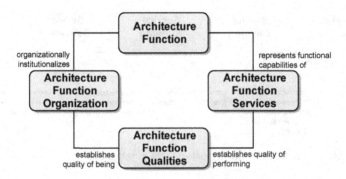

Fig. 2.15 Architecture function pattern topology: challenge subschema

Architecture Function Pattern Topology: Constitution

While Chap. 4 takes a black-box perspective on an architecture function and describes expectations for it, Chap. 5 takes a white-box view and proposes a design for constituting an architecture function that addresses the challenges presented (Fig. 2.16).

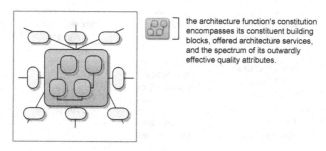

the architecture function's constitution encompasses its constituent building blocks, offered architecture services, and the spectrum of its outwardly effective quality attributes.

Fig. 2.16   Architecture function pattern topology: constitution

Chapter 5 adopts exactly the same substructure as Chap. 4. It is divided into architecture function organization (Sect. 5.2), architecture function services (Sect. 5.3), and architecture function qualities (Sect. 5.4). However, where Chap. 4 specifies expectations for an architecture function, Chap. 5 suggests designs to meet them.

For their part, the designs proposed by Chap. 5 rely heavily on the architecture function patterns in the pattern catalog. Patterns are referenced by name and identified by specific formatting, with the pattern references embedded directly in the design descriptions.

2.5.2   Architecture Function Pattern Catalog

The *architecture function pattern catalog* in this book contains 48 architecture function patterns and is fully *implemented*, if you wish, by Chap. 6. It is subdivided into nine pattern groups. The architecture pattern groups *architecture organization*, *architecture disciplines*, *architecture engagement model*, and *communication* discuss fundamental and constituent architecture function considerations. Furthermore, they suggest ways of shaping the cooperation between the architecture function and other enterprise organizations. *Architecture governance* patterns deal with the design of architecture control and monitoring as well as embedding an architecture function into the enterprise governance ecosystem. The patterns in the *architecture objective*, *architecture elaboration*, and *architecture asset* groups focus on the design and further evolution of the architecture of both landscape assets and structural assets (i.e., domains). Patterns in these groups primarily contribute to planning, building, and running the enterprise value chain and enterprise services. Finally, *architecture apparatus* patterns suggest the design of the architecture apparatus and its integration with the surrounding enterprise methodologies and platforms (Fig. 2.17).

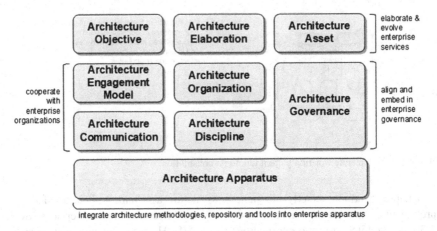

Fig. 2.17   Architecture function pattern catalog: pattern groups

However, the architecture function pattern catalog does not provide any further features for finding, filtering, or navigating patterns beyond the pattern groupings shown above. It merely lists patterns in order.

Each pattern in the catalog offers its particular design considerations, suggestions, and inspirations—contributing a specific design part to the holistic design of an entire architecture function. Each pattern also suggests associated patterns in its descriptions and contextualizes them accordingly. By navigating through the associated patterns, you surf pattern sequences.

The descriptions of the architecture function patterns in the pattern catalog aim to be informative, descriptive, and inspiring. To this end, they are formulated in a relatively informal manner. However, for all its informality, each pattern description contains the same essential components. It has a descriptive *name* that corresponds to the name of the pattern catalog chapter. For naming patterns, I chose noun phrases that compactly indicate an aspect relevant to the architecture function. Pattern names are thus easily embedded in ordinary sentences or in conversation with others. Pattern *context* is introduced by the description surrounding a pattern reference, for example, from other patterns in the catalog or by design suggestions in Chap. 5. The *problem* section of a pattern description follows the chapter heading and is highlighted in bold. It summarizes the challenges and problems that architecture functions repeatedly face. Finally, the *solution* section of a pattern description is divided into ontology and design, with both aspects flowing into each other. The *ontology* section begins a pattern description and compactly introduces concepts that are essential for understanding the pattern and its design propositions. This is followed by the design section of the corresponding pattern, which guides you through concrete design considerations and suggestions with respect to the architecture function aspect explored in the pattern. References to other patterns complement the design suggestions (Fig. 2.18).

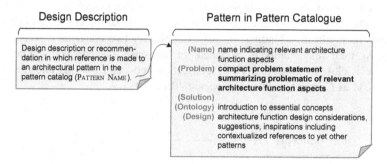

Fig. 2.18 Pattern description

The architecture function patterns in the pattern catalog are intentionally lightweight, thought-provoking, and inspirational—rather than heavyweight, imperative, and prescriptive. They are intended to accompany an iterative design process in which an architecture function gradually emerges. The emphasis of architecture function patterns is on the breadth (rather than the depth) of architecture function design.

2.5.3 Architecture Function Pattern Ontology

I have chosen neither to concentrate the *architecture function pattern ontology* in a single chapter in this book nor to formalize it strongly but to present the definition of essential concepts where they first matter.

Since many architecture concepts gain clarification and contour primarily by delineating them from one another rather than by isolated, prose-centric definitions alone, I supplement textual definitions by illustrating concepts on the basis of concept maps. A *concept map* is a technique for visualizing terms (i.e., in the sense of symbols referring to concepts) and their interrelationships in the form of a graph. Concept maps are a means for graphical representation of information as well as for mental ordering and reflection. The elements for concept map representation are *boxes*, *connecting lines*, and *line labels*. The boxes represent essential concepts (i.e., in the form of terms). The connecting lines between concepts symbolize the relationships between them. The labels of connecting lines define and qualify the relationship. A distinction is made between *status indicating* (i.e., *static*) and *transformation indicating* (i.e., *dynamic*) relationships. Examples for status indicating relationships are *consists of* (i.e., part-whole relation), *corresponds to* (i.e., synonymous relation), or *is a* (i.e., generalization-specialization relation). Examples of transformation indicating relationships are *leads to*, *changes*, *causes*, *requires*, *increases*, or *decreases*.

I have refrained from showing the connecting lines directionally (i.e., via arrows). Instead, the proximity of a connecting line label to one of the connected concepts indicates its predicative binding. In this example, for two concepts *Concept_A* and *Concept_B*, their relationality is indicated. In this case, the connecting line label *relates to* is close to *Concept_A*. Thus, the relation between *Concept_A* and *Concept_B* can be read as *Concept_A relates to Concept_B* (Fig. 2.19).

Fig. 2.19 Concept maps

You will find corresponding concept maps for relational clarification of important concepts to supplement prosaic definitions throughout the book—but especially in the architecture function pattern descriptions. The set of all definitions together constitutes the *architecture function pattern ontology* on the basis of which the *architecture function pattern language* and its components are defined in this book.

Last but not least, two patterns in the pattern catalog deal with the topic of linguistic, conceptual, and terminological foundations, ontologies, and meta-languages. So delve further into the topic of ontology by visiting the ARCHITECTURE LANGUAGE and ARCHITECTURE TAXONOMY patterns in the *architecture function pattern catalog* (Chap. 6).

2.6 Architecture Function Pattern Language Adoption

Adopting the architecture function pattern language means using it to achieve a defined goal more efficiently and effectively. This, in turn, means that the concrete goal you want to achieve determines how best to customize the architecture function pattern language. Your goal might be to learn about architecture. For example, to learn what tasks architecture functions perform in modern enterprises. Another goal might be to review the completeness of your existing architecture function's vision, maybe because you planned and established it 5 years ago and now want to check if it still fits or you just want to dive into a specific area or discipline that is part of an architecture function. In this case, the best way to match the architecture function pattern language to the architecture function is to briefly consult the pattern topology for guidance and then dive right into your architecture area of interest.

Despite the wide variety of ways to apply the architecture function pattern language, the process of planning, building, and executing your architecture function represents the most comprehensive approach to its application. This use case spans all components of the pattern language. I explain this process in more detail because other application scenarios are either true subsets or minor variations of it (Fig. 2.20).

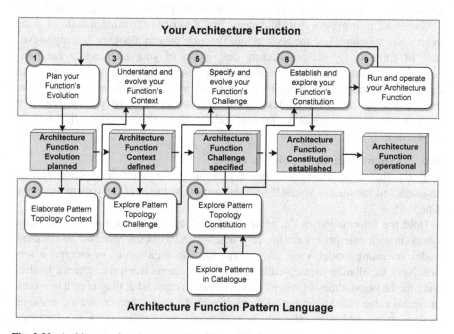

Fig. 2.20   Architecture function pattern language adoption

Precondition: Prepare Architecture Function Pattern Language Adoption

Note that the pattern language application process starts from a situation in which you are either planning to establish an entirely new architecture function or to evolve one that already exists in your enterprise. Pattern language application basically means that you use the pattern language as a tool to create or evolve your architecture function. Of course, you are not creating a living function. What you are creating is a holistic clarified specification of one. A specification such that you can take further action to concretize your architecture function.

Also, note that despite the sequential impression I give of the pattern language application process (e.g., due to the numbering of the individual steps), the process must be applied again and again in an evolutionary manner. Finally, familiarize yourself with the architecture function pattern language so that you can use and apply it most efficiently and effectively in your environment.

Step 1: Plan Your Architecture Function's Evolution
Before you start applying the architecture function pattern language, you need to clarify and understand where you currently stand and what you aspire to achieve with the evolution of your architecture function. You may be able to derive this from an architecture function roadmap you maintain and continually feed with opportunities and spaces for architecture function improvement. It may also be that you are starting from scratch and have not yet established an architecture function at all. Another example is that you want to fundamentally renovate your existing architecture function to boost its maturity—so the evolution you are targeting is significant.

Gather all information that documents and describes the current state of your architecture function. Use the architecture function pattern topology as a high-level table of contents for the architecture description of your architecture function. Compile all information collected today about your architecture function into the architecture description. The pattern topology scheme in the architecture description ensures that you keep the context, challenge, and structure of your architecture function in mind throughout the process and that you systematically reflect on and document it.

Step 2: Explore Pattern Topology Context
At this point at the latest, you should pick up the architecture function pattern language and familiarize yourself with the context segment of the pattern topology (Chap. 3).

Hold the information in the context segment against the architecture function context in your enterprise. Familiarize yourself with basic concepts, such as business model, operating model, value chain, organization, digitization, or enterprise service. Next, familiarize yourself with the proposed generic enterprise schema. Understand the responsibilities of enterprise organizations and what they contribute to an enterprise value chain. Familiarize yourself with the value streams and value stages into which an enterprise value chain is decomposed. Review the key milestones along the value chain and the enterprise artifacts that reflect progress along the lifecycle in managing enterprise services (Sect. 3.8).

Step 3: Understand and Evolve Your Architecture Function's Context
In the previous step, you familiarized yourself with the pattern topology context. In this step, you develop an understanding of your own enterprise context by deriving your own view in part from references to the pattern topology context segment.

Your concrete situation will not differ significantly from the generic schema suggested by the pattern topology context segment. However, you may want to go far beyond the generic schema and capture variations and other specifics of your enterprise in more detail. For example, your enterprise may have not just one business strategy organization but five such organizations—one in each of your five business units. In this case, flesh out the generic organization (i.e., named *business strategy organization* in the pattern topology context) to capture the five organizations as they exist in your enterprise. The roles and responsibilities of all five organizations, including their expectations of an architecture function, do not fundamentally change. Therefore, your five concrete organizations can inherit characteristics of the generic organization in pattern topology context. Similarly, you may decompose your value chain into value streams differently, or you may name your value streams, value stages, enterprise organizations, or artifacts otherwise.

At the end of this step, you will have clarified all the relevant facets of the context in which your architecture function is placed and have captured everything in the context chapter of your architecture function description.

Step 4: Explore Pattern Topology Challenge

Again, as in step 2, you pick up the architecture function pattern language. But this time, familiarize yourself with the challenge segment of the pattern topology (Chap. 4).

You will soon hold the information in the pattern topology against your architecture function (i.e., in step 5). However, for now, you will explore and capture the challenges that the architecture function faces in your organization.

To prepare for the next step, familiarize yourself with the proposed schema of generic architecture function challenges. Understand the institutional challenges of an architecture function, such as the architecture function vision and mission, organization, engagement model, communication, governance, roadmap, or apparatus (Sect. 4.2). Next, understand the set of generic architecture function services that are needed to make the architecture contributions that other organizations along the enterprise value chain expect from you. These might include *assess architecture*, *elaborate domain architecture*, or *determine architecture relevance* services (Sect. 4.3). Finally, familiarize yourself with generic quality attributes expected of the architecture function, for example, architecture function *usability*, *elasticity*, *evolvability*, or *reliability* (Sect. 4.4).

Step 5: Specify and Evolve Your Architecture Function's Challenge

In the previous step, you have familiarized yourself with the challenge segment of the pattern topology. In this step, you capture your own challenges, which you can derive at least in part from the challenge segment of the pattern topology and the generic challenges outlined there.

Again, as in step 3, your concrete situation will not differ significantly from the generic challenges described in the pattern topology's challenge segment. However, the generic challenges will not suffice to reflect your concrete situation. Therefore, you need to capture your concrete requirements in a way that adequately reflects both your institutional requirements and your architecture service- and quality-oriented requirements. At the end of this step, you have clarified the concrete challenges that your architecture function must address, and you have captured them in the challenges chapter of your architecture function description.

Step 6: Explore Pattern Topology Constitution

As in steps 2 and 4, you will return to the architecture function pattern language, where you familiarize yourself with the pattern topology constitution segment (Chap. 5).

Like before, familiarize yourself with the proposed design of a generic architecture function presented in the pattern topology's constitution segment (Chap. 5).

This chapter mirrors the structure of the challenge chapter (Chap. 4). Thus, in Sect. 5.2 you will find the proposal for the institutional design of an architecture function, in Sect. 5.3 the generic design for architecture services, and in Sect. 5.4 the generic design proposal for architecture function qualities. The generic designs themselves rely heavily on references to architecture function patterns in the pattern catalog. You follow the references (step 7), consider the patterns, and return to step 6 to further familiarize yourself with a proposed design.

Step 7: Explore Patterns in Pattern Catalog

While you were studying the design in the constitution segment and thinking about how to adapt the design to your specific needs, you followed a pattern reference that led you here—to an architecture function pattern in the pattern catalog.

Familiarize yourself with the pattern as a whole, considering the design context of the reference that led you here. Follow any other references to yet other architecture function patterns in the pattern catalog as you deem them valuable. Gather any insights you have gained from examining this pattern as well as related patterns. Incorporate your findings back into your design considerations in step 6. Continue alternating between step 6 and step 7 until you have become familiar with all the related patterns.

Step 8: Establish and Evolve Your Architecture Function's Constitution

By switching back and forth between steps 6 and 7, you have become familiar with the proposed designs in the pattern topology's constitution segment and with the architecture function patterns as they were associated with the designs you studied in step 6.

In this step, you will capture the concrete design you have derived from considering the generic designs in steps 6 and 7. Although you will benefit massively from the design considerations, inspirations, and suggestions, you still need to make your own concrete and detailed design decisions.

At the end of this step, you have clarified how your architecture function needs to be constituted to meet the challenges it faces in your enterprise context.

Step 9: Run and Operate Your Architecture Function

As your architecture function is executed and operated, you will identify where it needs further improvement once it is established, for example, through a new architecture service or changes to the architecture engagement model. This means returning to step 1 when you decide it is time to mature and evolve your architecture function.

Further Reading

Alexander, Christopher. 1979. *The Timeless Way of Building*. New York: Oxford University Press.
Alexander, Christopher, Sara Ishikawa, Murray Silverstein, Max Jacobson, Ingrid Fiksdahl-King, and Shlomo Angel. 1977. *A Pattern Language*. Oxford University Press.

Buschmann, Frank, Kevlin Henney, and Douglas C. Schmidt. 2007. *Pattern-Oriented Software Architecture Vol. 5, On Patterns and Pattern Languages*. West Sussex: Wiley.

Evans, Eric. 2004. *Domain-driven Design - Tackling Complexity in the Heart of Software*. Boston: Addison-Wesley Professional.

Fowler, Martin. 1997. *Analysis Patterns - Reusable Object Models*. Boston: Addison-Wesley Professional.

Gamma, Erich, Richard Helm, Ralph Johnson, and John Vlissides. 1994. *Design Patterns - Elements of Reusable Object-Oriented Software*. Amsterdam: Pearson Education.

Matthes, Florian, Aleatrati Khosroshahi, Pouya, Matheus Hauder, and Alexander Schneider. 2015. *Enterprise Architecture Management Pattern Catalogue, Software Engineering for Business Information Systems (sebis)*. Technische Universität München.

Pollio, Marcus Vitruvius. 2013. *De Architectura – Libri Decem*. Amsterdam: Elsevier.

Chapter 3
Architecture Function: Context

Abstract This chapter introduces contextual concepts. These concepts are crucial for understanding the challenges an architecture function faces. They are also essential for understanding the solution approaches used to address them—for example, concepts such as business model, operating model, digitalization, or service. The chapter also introduces a generic schema for business organization and value chain. The generic business organization and value chain enables a structured discussion of the challenges each architecture function faces (Chap. 4) and the proven approaches to address them (Chap. 5).

3.1 Overview

To understand the constitution (*solution*) of a system, one must understand its *context*. You also need a solid idea of the challenges (*problem*) that the system is supposed to address in that context. In this book, I consider an architecture function as a system and present its generic design in the style of a pattern. It remains your responsibility in your enterprise to instantiate the generic design for your own architecture function. As explained in Chap. 2, patterns capture proven designs for recurring problems in particular contexts. Therefore, my book proposes an architecture function design that is composed of the *context* in which architecture functions operate, the *challenges* they repeatedly face, and an idealized *constitution* to adequately address the challenges.

This chapter introduces contextual concepts, which Chap. 4 takes up to present recurring challenges architecture functions need to address. Finally, Chap. 5 introduces a generic design for constituting an architecture function. It explains in detail, with reference to patterns in the pattern catalog of this book, how an architecture function meets the expectations of the enterprise (Fig. 3.1).

© The Author(s), under exclusive license to Springer Nature Switzerland AG 2022
I. Arnold, *Enterprise Architecture Function*,
https://doi.org/10.1007/978-3-030-84589-6_3

Architecture Function Pattern Topology

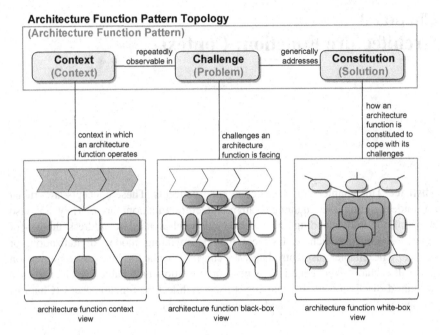

Fig. 3.1 Architecture function pattern (context)

Architecture functions are embedded in enterprises. In this context, every enterprise has a *business model* and an *operating model* to optimally pursue its business goals. Digitization, another crucial concept, has a strong influence on modern enterprises, their business, and operating models. Digitization affects both the services an enterprise offers its customers and the value chains through which it plans, designs, builds, and operates the services it offers on the market. Business and operating models encompass the concepts of *enterprise value chain*, *enterprise organization*, and *enterprise service*. I refer to these concepts throughout and repeatedly in this book to provide a structured discussion of the overall challenges and design of architecture functions in modern enterprises (Fig. 3.2).

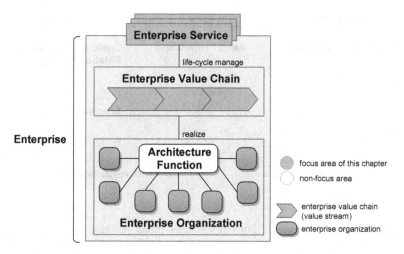

Fig. 3.2 Architecture function context

3.2   Business Model

Business models capture the anatomy of how business is conducted—quoting from *Business Model Generation* (Osterwalder et al. 2010):

> A business model describes the rationale of how an organization creates, delivers, and captures value, in economic, social, cultural, or other contexts.

Concrete business models can differ considerably. Alexander Osterwalder et al. propose the *business model canvas* as a general template for discussing, elaborating, and documenting business models. The *business model canvas* presents a schema to help enterprises examine and describe the back-end and front-end components of a business and its value proposition. The *back-end* is where value is created, while the *front-end* demands and consumes the created value. *Partners* are the external organizations that provide critical inputs to the business—for example, raw materials, supplies, or services, like IT services. Activities are the steps that the business performs to deliver its value proposition. *Activities* are performed by or based on the enterprise's resources. *Resources* are the assets of the enterprise, such as employees, technology, or buildings. The *value proposition* refers to what a company offers its customers or beneficiaries, usually in the form of services or products. While *customer segments* distinguish different consumer groups, *customer relationships* describe how customers are acquired and retained. *Channels* are the means by which the enterprise communicates with its customers. *Cost structure* captures the financial view of the resources used, while *revenue streams* represent how the enterprise makes money (Fig. 3.3).

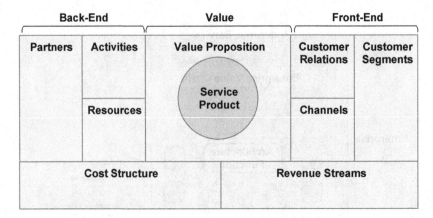

Fig. 3.3 Business model canvas (© 2010 www.strategyzer.com, reprinted with permission)

3.3 Operating Model

An *operating model* is an inherent part of any business model and fits into their back-end. An operating model specifies and captures how the inner workings of an organization are designed to deliver value to its customers. It describes how an organization collaborates—but limits itself to the essentials of organizational coop-eration. Similar to the business model canvas, there is also an *operating model canvas*. David Campbell, Mikel Gutierrez, and Mark Lancelott, in *Operating Model Canvas* (2017), propose a corresponding template, tools and techniques, and a variety of possible applications. The standard components of the operating model canvas are suppliers, locations, organization, information, management system, and the value chain. *Suppliers* are synonymous with partners in the business model canvas. *Locations, organization,* and *information* are synonymous with *resources*. *Locations* determine where work is performed and what resources are needed at each location. *Organization* describes the organizational structure and *who* performs *which* activities in the value chain. *Information* represents the data and the technical means to create, modify, find, retrieve, or archive the data underlying the activities of the operating model. *Management system* refers to all the means used by manage-ment to plan, build, and operate the business. The *value delivery chain* describes the steps required to deliver the value proposition and corresponds to the *activities* in the business model canvas. *Activities* are captured in the form of processes that explain precisely how work is performed and by whom (Fig. 3.4).

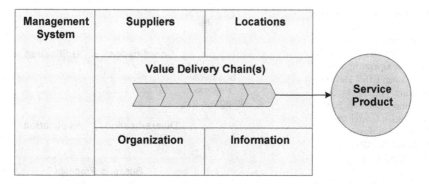

Fig. 3.4 Operating model canvas (© 2017 Van Haren Publishing BV, reprinted with permission)

Similar to business models, many differences exist between specific operating models. Campbell, Gutierrez, and Lancelott illustrate the *operating model canvas* by discussing how it is applied in different industries and fictional enterprises, for example, a fast fashion store, a strategic consulting firm, a trade publisher of management books, or an asset finance company.

In *Forget Strategy: Focus IT on Your Operating Model* (Ross 2005), Jeanne Ross proposes a coordinate system that distinguishes four types of operating models. Her scheme differentiates operating models along their degree of *business process integration* and their degree of *business process standardization*. An operating model in the *coordination* quadrant is characterized by a low degree of business process standardization because the business units are relatively unique. At the same time, however, business units share critical concepts, such as similar customers, suppliers, services, or partners. This indicates a high degree of shared information and transactions. An operating model in the *replication* quadrant is qualified the other way around. In this operating model, the level of standardized business processes is high, while the ability to benefit from shared information is low. Business units in this type of operating model have many activity-oriented commonalities but cannot benefit from shared customer, partner, product, or similar business information. Operating models in the *unification* quadrant combine a high level of standardized business processes with a similarly high level of information that can be shared between business units. You often find this operating model in commodity markets. Finally, *diversification* operating models combine a low level of business process standardization with a low level of shareable information. From a business perspective, business units perform their own unique business processes and share no or minimal information with other units. Opportunities to leverage economies of scale are limited to sharing business-agnostic (i.e., technical) systems (Fig. 3.5).

Fig. 3.5 Operating model
diversification (based on a
figure from J. W. Ross,
"Forget Strategy: Focus IT
on Your Operating Model,"
MIT Sloan CISR Research
Briefing Vol. V, No. 3C,
December 2005. © 2005
MIT Sloan Center for
Information Systems
Research (CISR), reprinted
with permission)

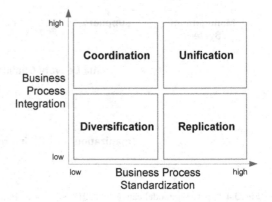

Comprehensive operating model descriptions must cover all components of the
operating model canvas and must be sufficiently detailed. Although the business
model front-end is not included in an operating model description, it must be well
understood regardless. For example, to design an operating model, you need to
understand the targeted customer segments and how they will benefit from your
value proposition. You also need to understand where and how your customers wish
to be served and how your enterprise's engagements generate revenue. Operating
model design decisions are long-term decisions that affect the structure of the
business organization, which means they also affect the design of the architecture
function.

3.4   Value Chain

A *value chain*, according to Michael Porter (1985), is a set of activities that an
enterprise in a particular industry performs to deliver a valuable product (i.e., goods
or services) to the marketplace. While an enterprise is both a collection of activities
and a set of resources and capabilities, activities are what enterprises do and what
defines the relevant resources and capabilities. A value chain views an organization
as a set of processes at different levels of process aggregation. It also views an
organization as a system that is decomposed into subsystems, with each subsystem
having its inputs, transformation processes, and outputs. Input consumption, output
generation, and input-to-output transformation involve the acquisition, management,
and consumption of resources and how an organization does this affects its cost
scheme and profit. Porter distinguishes five primary and four supporting activity
groups, with primary activities contributing significantly to value creation, while
supporting activities increase the efficiency and effectiveness of primary activities.
Porter counts *inbound logistics, operations, outbound logistics, marketing and sales*,
and *services* among the primary activity groups. Supporting activity groups include

enterprise infrastructure, human resource management, technology, and *procurement,* according to Porter.

The term virtual value chain was coined in 1995 by Jeffrey Rayport and John Sviokla (1995) to complement Porter's original definition. Virtual value chains describe the distribution of information services and their value contributions throughout the enterprise as they complement the physical value chain parts.

Porter suggests clustering value chain activities into activity groups to establish a high-level overview of the significant value contributors. At the next level of detail, activities are sorted along value stages. *Value stages* are arranged such that the desired overall outcome is achieved incrementally by passing its increments sequentially through all stages. Each value stage represents a series of activities that consume inputs from the preceding stage and produce outputs for the succeeding stage. However, do not overinterpret the sequential arrangement of value stages. The actual flow that incremental work takes through value chain stages may deviate from an idealized unidirectional and sequential flow. Preconditions are formulated as quality gates for inputs, while postconditions guarantee a defined output quality for the successor of a value chain stage. A value stage is still a relatively coarse-grained set of activities. Processes define the detailed flows through activities performed by individual actors (Fig. 3.6).

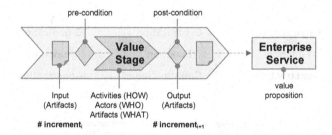

Fig. 3.6 Value chain stage

Process Model

Wikipedia defines a process (Wikipedia 2020b) as a series of activities that interact to produce a result, where the activities can be one time or recurring, or periodic. A *process model* (Wikipedia 2020c) groups similar processes into an overarching classification scheme. It is a description of a process at the type level, while a corresponding process is an instantiation of its process model. Process models prescribe how activities must or should be performed, while processes represent what actually happens. Process models assume specific contexts (e.g., industry), have a purpose (e.g., validating an artifact to ensure its quality), and must be customized for each application.

You will find collections of process models as components in standard methodologies such as ITIL[1] or COBIT.[2] A *methodology* defines approaches to accomplish something with a defined set of disciplines, roles, processes, deliverables, policies, and attitudes. Methodologies are typically focused on solving recurring problems, are containers of solution-oriented tools and techniques, and prescribe or suggest attitudes. For example, you adopt an agile attitude when you accept uncertainty and repeatedly perform a process to incrementally evolve its outcome to completion.

3.5 Organization

The Merriam-Webster Dictionary defines *organization* as an administrative and functional structure, such as a business or a political party (Merriam-Webster Dictionary 2020), while other definitions add the social facet (i.e., humans as actors) or the purpose an organization pursues as essential characteristics. If one considers an organization as a system, as suggested by J. Dietz (2006), its function (i.e., teleological system concept[3]) is realized through its construction (i.e., ontological system concept[4]). This means that the constitution of an organization may be based in part on the use of the function of another organization (Fig. 3.7).

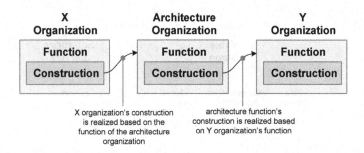

Fig. 3.7 Organization function and construction

---

[1] ITIL (Information Technology Infrastructure Library) is an IT service management methodology. ITIL describes processes, procedures, tasks, roles, work products, and checklists that are neither organization- nor technology-specific and represent a blueprint for implementing ITSM in enterprises.

[2] COBIT (Control Objectives for Information and Related Technologies) defines several general processes and an elementary maturity model for IT management. COBIT was specially developed to help companies comply with laws in an agile way.

[3] Teleological system concept. The term *teleological system* deals with a system's function and behavior as observed from the outside (external behavior). The teleological system's perspective is useful when using a system.

[4] Ontological system concept. The ontological system view deals with a system's mechanics as observed inside the system (internal behavior). It also distinguishes the concept of aggregate from the concept of system. Concepts, aggregate, and system are collections of objects. However, in aggregates, the elements are not held together by interaction bonds, whereas in systems, they are. A system, therefore, has unity and integrity. Both properties are lacking in aggregates.

While a value chain proposes groups of activities, an organization groups actors that perform activities. An organization has an associated scope of responsibility that describes the activities that an organization performs on a recurring basis. The scope of responsibility also includes artifacts as activity inputs and outputs. Organizational responsibility can be further structured, for example, along the stages of the value chain, a capability model, geographic areas, or enterprise service segments (Fig. 3.8).

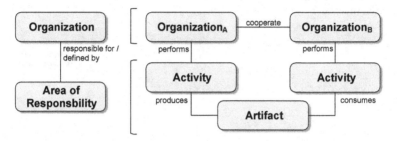

Fig. 3.8 Organization and area of responsibility

Organization Model

An *organizational model* defines how organizations are structured and how activities, coordination, and supervision are directed toward achieving organizational goals (Wikipedia 2020a). Different *organizational structuring schemes* fit different organizational conditions, constraints, or goals, are influenced by their environment, and suggest different approaches to sharing power between superiors and subordinates.

As characterized by Max Weber (1948), *bureaucratic organizations* have a strictly hierarchical structure with rigid processes in terms of decision-making authority and information passing through all organizational levels from top to bottom. Bureaucratic organizations tend to inhibit creativity and innovation and discourage necessary adaptations to changing environmental conditions (Fig. 3.9).

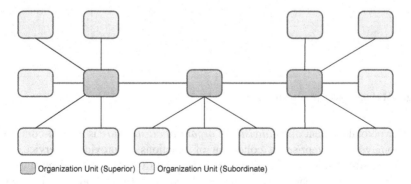

Fig. 3.9 Bureaucratic organization structure

In *post-bureaucratic organizations*, as described by Charles Heckscher in *The Post-Bureaucratic Organization* (Heckscher 1994), decision-making favors dialog and consensus over authority and command and principles over procedural policies. Decision-making is a horizontal rather than a strictly vertical process and is favored by cooperatives, nonprofits, or community organizations. Post-bureaucratic organizations tend to encourage participation and empower their members (Fig. 3.10).

Fig. 3.10 Post-bureaucratic organization structure

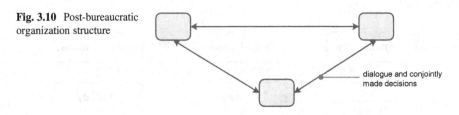

Functional organizational structures group people according to functions that are required to achieve the organization's goals. Examples of functions include *procurement, production, accounting*, or *human resources*. A functional organizational structure promotes specialization, which leads to operational efficiency and effectiveness. However, function-oriented specialization tends to undermine latent communication between functions, which unintentionally impairs an organization's ability to adapt to changes in the marketplace. Function orientation can foster a territorial attitude and an unwillingness to collaborate beyond the boundaries of one's function. Functional organizations are best suited as producers of commodity services (Fig. 3.11).

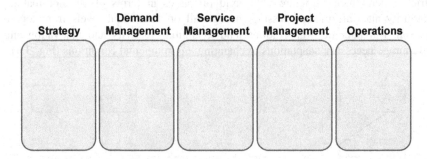

Fig. 3.11 Functional organization structure

The pivotal element of the *divisional organization structure* is the self-contained division, which comprises a collection of functions to provide a service. The divisional structure grants each division autonomy over its costs and revenues so that divisional performance can be measured and rewarded individually. This tends to increase the motivation, loyalty, and morale of divisional employees. Weaknesses of the divisional structure are harmful rivalries between divisions and superfluous resources and costs due to redundant divisional investments (Fig. 3.12).

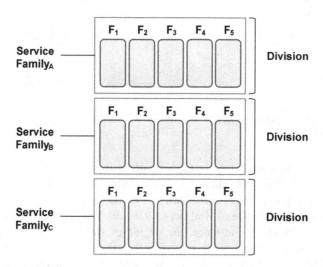

Fig. 3.12 Divisional organization structure

Matrix organizations group employees by function and service at the same time. For example, an enterprise offers two service families (*service family_A* and *service family_B*) and distinguishes between the functions of *research and development*, *production*, and *sales*. Using the matrix organization structure, this enterprise would organize itself as follows. There would be one department for each function and one department for each service family. The three function-oriented departments would support the two service family-oriented departments in their respective areas of expertise. For example, the production function (*production department*) would support both service family departments with respect to their production needs. One sub-department would provide production services to service family_A (*production for service family_A department*), and one would provide services to service family_B (*production for service family_B department*). A matrix organization aims to reduce the strictly vertical orientation of functional organizations in favor of a more horizontal and lateral structure, thereby promoting the dissemination of information across functional boundaries. However, matrices can be confusing in terms of power distribution in conflict situations. The extended version of a matrix organization is the multinational design of global enterprises. Their organizational scheme is a three-dimensional matrix that coordinates among functions, service families, and geographies (Fig. 3.13).

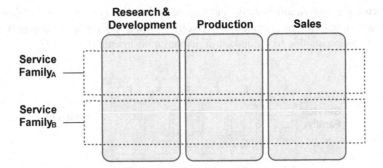

Fig. 3.13 Matrix organization structure

In the real world, companies adapt hybrids of the above stereotypical organization models. There are a host of other aspects that determine the cooperative dynamics and impact of a specific organization design. For example, Henry Mintzberg in *The Structuring of Organizations* (Mintzberg 1979) distinguishes six mechanisms of coordination of work, for instance, the degree of standardized work processes, standardized inputs, outputs, skills, norms, or the extent to which direct supervision is practiced in an organization. Other facets of concrete organization design include the degree of centralization versus federation of power, the distinction between operating and support organizations, hierarchical depth, or the degree of information exchange between organizational units.

3.6   Digitalization

Digitalization is not just another buzzword but a topic that will fundamentally change almost all areas of life. For example, digitalization is fundamentally changing the way we conduct business. However, before we look at the terms *digital system*, *digital business*, and *digital enterprise*, it is essential to define the basic terms *digital*, *digitized*, and *digitalized*, which are not always sufficiently delineated. Several definitions of *digitalization* have been proposed. Gartner, for example, defines digitalization in its IT Glossary (Gartner Glossary 2020) as:

> Digitalization is the use of digital technologies to change a business model and provide new revenue and value-producing opportunities; it is the process of moving to a digital business.

Similarly, definitions of *digitization* have been proposed, with Gartner defining the term in their IT Glossary as follows:

> Digitization is the process of changing from analogue to digital form, also known as digital enablement. Said another way, digitization takes an analogue process and changes it to a digital form without any different-in-kind changes to the process itself.

Digitization refers to the creation of digital representations of non-digital objects or processes, for example, scanning a paper document and processing it in its digitized form. Digitization is about converting a non-digital original into a corresponding digital representation. It is foundational and connects a non-digital, analogue world with its digitized counterpart. That is what we have been doing since the 1960s. *Digitalization* cannot happen without digitization. While digitization is the transformation from analogue to digital, digitalization uses digitized processes, data, tools, and technologies to transform the way businesses and their customers interact and create entirely new forms of digital revenue streams. While digitization refers to the optimization of originally analogue processes, digitalization aims to fundamentally change entire business models.

If we take the word at face value, *digitized* means that something has undergone a digital transformation or conversion. For example, an object O has been digitized from its original analogue form ($O_{analogue}$) to the digitized representation of O ($O_{digitized}$). However, there may also be non-analogue and purely digital objects, for which the term *digitized* would confusingly suggest an analogue-to-digital conversion. Therefore, I take an agnostic perspective on any preceding transformation steps and refer to objects based on digital building material as $O_{digital}$ in this chapter. This is in contrast to $O_{analogue}$, where the building material of O is analogous.

Digital building material enables two types of components: data and functions. Functions are themselves encoded in the form of digital data, whereby data defining functions in turn becomes executable data. Functions can refer to data, where this data encodes information. Digital technology enables elementary manipulation of digital building material—i.e., functions and data. For example, the manipulation of data by creating, changing, reading, deleting, or displaying digital data from functions (Fig. 3.14).

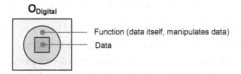

Fig. 3.14 Digital building material

While the analogue and digital representations of an object can be seen as merely two forms of the same basic thing, at the same time, there are crucial differences. While the building material of $O_{analogue}$ is the molecules of the physical world and the basic constituent structures filling space and time, the building material of $O_{digital}$ is the bits and bytes and the molecules of the digital world made possible by universal digital machines. Interactions or interdependencies between $O_{analogue}$ and other analogous objects are constrained by the laws of nature and other constraints of the analogue world. At the same time, $O_{digital}$ is far less subject to such restrictions. While $O_{analogue}$ cannot be teleported, $O_{digital}$ can by sending itself digitally to another computational node. Moreover, while duplicating $O_{digital}$ can be done in (almost) no time and at marginal cost, duplicating $O_{analogue}$ is relatively expensive in terms of time, space, and cost. Fundamental modification or adaptation of $O_{analogue}$ to environmental changes may be impossible due to its fixed, immutable form, while the mutable form of $O_{digital}$ makes it inherently more modifiable. $O_{digital}$ offers additional advantages over $O_{analogue}$. For example, $O_{digital}$ is automatically introspectable and composable to a degree that $O_{analogue}$ is not. $O_{digital}$ can change its purpose, shape, and interaction relationships with other objects in a very flexible way, whereas $O_{analogue}$ is bound to a fixed shape (Fig. 3.15).

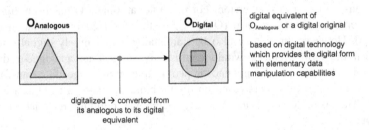

Fig. 3.15 Analogous versus digital

Digital System

Etymologically, the term *system* is borrowed from the Latin *systēma*, meaning *overall concept consisting of several parts or members*. Merriam-Webster (2020) defines a system as:

> A system is a group of interacting or interrelated entities that form a unified whole.

The notion of system is adapted in many disciplines. However, *systems theory* is the discipline that fundamentally studies the nature and essence of systems. It defines a system as a coherent whole of interconnected and interdependent parts. A system exists in a context and is affected by its environment. It is defined by its structure and has a purpose that it pursues through its functioning. Systems have properties that cannot be observed at the level of their parts but emerge from their interactions—a property called *emergence*.

A *digital system* is a system that is either based on parts whose building material is digital or that orchestrates its structure and the interaction of its parts digitally. This means that a digital system is based in whole or in part on digital building material. To the extent a digital system is based on digital parts, it can be duplicated at marginal spatial and temporal cost by sending its parts over digital networks. It can be fundamentally modified or spontaneously adapted to environmental changes because its digital parts are malleable. A digital system is reflective, introspective, and formable so that it can be learned from and flexibly combined with other digital systems to constitute new system entireties (Fig. 3.16).

Fig. 3.16 Digital system

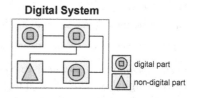

Digital systems, viewed generically, have a common anatomy and properties. The interaction potential of the parts of a system emerges from its static structure. The static system structure thus determines the functional and state-related potentials of a system. The dynamic structure of a system is a subset of its static structure, the subset implemented to realize its functions and states. It results from the interaction relations of the system parts. Modifiability, and thus system composability, results from the fact that a system allows changes to its dynamic system structure. This means that the dynamic structure enables system modifiability as a capability. To modify a system means to change its dynamic structure. There are a wide range of design approaches for realizing system modifiability and composability—for example, metaprogramming,[5] interpreters,[6] or generator-based architecture approaches.[7] Finally, system composability enables the flexible creation of new digital systems from existing ones (Fig. 3.17).

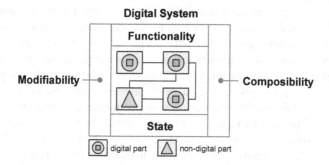

Fig. 3.17 Digital system characteristics

---

[5]Metaprogramming is a programming technique in which computer programs treat other programs as data. A metaprogramming-based program reads, generates, transforms, or interprets another program.

[6]Interpreters are built into systems to enable powerful customization hooks via which one can massively optimize the off-the-shelf capabilities of a system. Interpreters require programming skills. However, they offer programmable access to the off-the-shelf system's object model—and thus push the limits of adaptation toward the respective programmers' ambition and imagination.

[7]Generator-based architecture approaches decouple solution specifications from their physical generation. They increase domain specificity and the degree of abstraction of the models that architects use to represent a solution. Generators receive architectural models as inputs and create artifacts at the source level or related physical structures as outputs.

Digital Business

Gartner defines *digital business* in its IT Glossary (Gartner Glossary 2020):

> The creation of new business designs by blurring the digital and physical worlds.

I call a *business* a *digital business* if its business model is based (in whole or in large part) on digital systems. According to this definition, almost all of today's businesses are digital businesses. Inputs from suppliers, organizational or informational resources, and many other aspects on which a value chain is based or which it generates itself are—at least in part—digital in nature. I have deliberately decided against demanding *transformative potential* as a *digital business characteristic*. After all, such potential may only become visible and thus recognizable in retrospect. However, the degree of digitization of businesses (i.e., the degree to which their business models are based on digital systems) is continuously evolving and inevitably leads to strategic adjustments of business models over time.

In *Exploring Strategic Change*, Julia Balogun and Veronica Hailey (2008) propose four types of strategic change along their *nature* and *extent of change*. Regarding the nature of change, Julia Balogun and Veronica Hailey distinguish *incremental* from *Big Bang* changes, while regarding the extent of change, they distinguish *realignment*-oriented from *transformational* changes. The authors refer to incremental changes in the realignment segment as *adaptive* change in contrast to changes in the transformation segment, which they call *evolution*. Big Bang changes in the realignment segment are called *reconstruction*, in the transformation segment *revolution*. *Adaptive* change is compatible with a current paradigm—that is, it is based on established beliefs and assumptions. Change occurs incrementally through phased initiatives designed to gradually adapt the way the enterprise operates. *Reconstructive* change does not change an established paradigm either. However, reconstructive changes do not aim to transform an organization but to optimize what it is already doing. *Evolutionary* changes are transformative but are implemented incrementally, while *revolutionary* changes are both transformative and disruptive.

The increasingly digital nature of systems is influencing today's enterprises and their business models on many levels. *Digital services* become easily modifiable and adaptable to a constantly changing environment. They become reusable, composable, or replicable—at marginal spatial and temporal cost. Because they are introspective, digital services become internally illuminable and measurable throughout their entire lifespan, which significantly increases transparency. Transparency, in turn, optimizes the planning, building, and operation of digital services as well as their continuous improvement. Finally, digital services increase usability through their adaptability to customer needs. Digital value chains can be tracked and monitored because their transactional states can be automatically introspected. As a result, *digital value chains* greatly increase their evolutionary fitness, efficiency, and effectiveness. Enterprises improve their profitability by digitally transforming their business models on the basis of digital systems.

Digital Enterprise

A *digital enterprise* is an enterprise that operates a digital business. An *enterprise organization* constitutes a digital enterprise and establishes an *enterprise value chain*. It plans, builds, and operates *enterprise services* which it provides to its customer base (Fig. 3.18).

Fig. 3.18   Digital enterprise

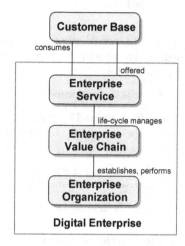

This book assumes a digital enterprise as the context to examine and propose the generic design of an architecture function. In non-digital enterprises, architecture functions plan and design the means to produce and offer primarily analogue enterprise services or products. In contrast, in a digital enterprise, the architecture function plans, designs, and evolves the architecture of digital services, the digital value chain, and the resources and means to implement both the digital value chain and the services offered.

The expanded scope that architecture functions occupy in digital enterprises inevitably arises from the substantially different nature of digital systems and their significant impact on entire business models. What Kevin Kelly explores and describes in *The inevitable: Understanding the 12 Technology Forces that Will Shape Our Future* (Kelly 2016) requires significantly increased architecture attention, not just to isolated digital systems but to the digital enterprise as a whole. Meandering, ever-changing, ever-emerging digital system, as we have established today and will continue to establish over time, is one of the 12 forces Kevin Kelly calls *becoming*. Another inevitable force he calls cognifying. By *cognifying*, Kelly refers to the phenomenon of a digitally permeated world and our ability to relate to that world with an extrinsic cognitive force that enables us to gain insights detached from human bias. By *flowing*, Kevin refers to a world in which everything, non-digital and digital means, is either absorbed into or rendered as an information stream. Kevin describes each of the 12 technological forces in his book as an aspect of a digitally pervasive, emergent future, confronting digital enterprises as well as societies with a complexity that requires an architecture discipline to resolve the complexity through holistic order, reflection, and creativity.

3.7 Service

Service, like *architecture*, is an amorphous, controversial, and poorly defined term, which may be why the Merriam-Webster Dictionary (2020) defines service rather rudimentarily:

> Service is the work performed by one that serves.

The Infrastructure IT Library[8] (ITIL) emphasizes in its glossary (ITIL Glossary 2020) the possibility of delegating cost and ownership, motivating service utilization:

> Service is a means of delivering value to customers by facilitating outcomes customers want to achieve without the ownership of specific costs and risks.

IT service is defined in the ITIL Glossary as a service provided by an IT service provider that includes both technological and non-technological means—ultimately as a *socio-technical system*:

> IT Service is a service provided by an IT service provider. An IT service is made up of a combination of information technology, people, and processes. A customer-facing IT service directly supports the business processes of one or more customers and its service level targets should be defined in a service level agreement. Other IT services, called supporting services, are not directly used by the business but are required by the service provider to deliver customer-facing services.

Although not explicitly mentioned in the above service definitions, other attempts to define service emphasize the intangible or ephemeral nature of service. Such definitions propose terms such as *product* or *good* to delineate tangible from intangible (*service*) value propositions. I am aware that there is a fine line between *intangible services* and *tangible products*. However, this line is blurring, evaporating, or becoming marginalized in many of today's digitized value propositions. For example, when you visit a bike store and buy a navigation device, it is about more than just buying a product (i.e., the navigation device). It is also about a set of intangibles (i.e., services). The bike store mechanics mount the device on your bike and connect it to the manufacturer's map and location service backbone (a configuration service), which you will soon be using extensively as you navigate new terrain. The mechanics in the store will also explain how to best use the navigation device or preinstall great mountain bike trails in your area (a training and consultancy service). In

---

[8]ITIL (Information Technology Infrastructure Library) is an IT service management methodology. ITIL describes processes, procedures, tasks, roles, work products, and checklists that are neither organization- nor technology-specific and represent a blueprint for implementing ITSM in enterprises.

addition, the navigation device provides information for other devices you may want to connect (a functional expansion service), for example, a portable fitness device that calculates the calories you have burned on your trips from the kilometers you have ridden.

To resolve the distinction between tangible versus intangible and technical versus socio-technical value propositions, I introduce the concept of *enterprise service*. In my book, the term *enterprise service* removes the often significant distinction between product and service. While an enterprise service can be both a purely tangible product and an exclusively intangible service, in many cases it is a combination of both. Furthermore, by introducing the term *enterprise service*, I remove the distinction between analogue and digital. Enterprise services can include digital systems, analogue systems, and any combination thereof. Finally, there are connections between the analogue systems, the digital systems, and between both types of systems in an enterprise service. This means that an enterprise service is itself a digital system. Enterprises services are the value vehicles that digital enterprises put in their storefronts to meet the needs of their customers (Fig. 3.19).

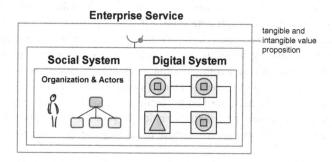

Fig. 3.19 Enterprise service

3.8 Enterprise

In what follows, I present a generic organization and value chain schema that serves as an orientation framework and guide through this book. Both the organization and value chain schema provide a frame of reference that contextualizes the constitution and contributions of an architecture function. I refer to the generic organization and value chain schema as the *enterprise organization* and *enterprise value chain*. At the heart of the enterprise value chain is the planning, building, delivering, and running (i.e., operating) of enterprise services and other critical architecture assets,[9] for

---

[9] See the *Architecture Asset* pattern in this book's pattern catalog (Chap. 6).

example, landscape assets[10] such as services, applications, platforms, or information. The enterprise value chain is inspired by IT4IT[11] (Open Group IT4IT 2020), an Open Group methodology that proposes a value chain-based operating model for managing the IT business. Generic enterprise organizations and artifacts through which they collaborate are both embedded in the enterprise value chain. They are described in this chapter, where they each make their main contributions.

3.8.1 Enterprise Organization

A generic enterprise organization schema is presented in Sect. 3.8.2. I will introduce the name of an organization, its area of responsibility, and the artifacts it exchanges with others to make its key contributions to the enterprise value chain. While the value chain stages and artifacts explain *what* is contributed to the lifecycle of an enterprise service, organizations clarify *who* is responsible.

I do not presuppose any particular organizational model for the generic schema of enterprise organization. One of the few assumptions I make is that enterprise organizations cooperate through enterprise artifacts. However, the generic organization schema is agnostic with respect to the distinction between operating and support organizations, agnostic also with respect to the degree of organizational centralization, organizational depth, distribution of power, process standardization, or the extent of information sharing among organizational functions. Individual enterprise organizations are described by outlining their responsibilities, including the artifacts they consume and their activities to produce corresponding artifact outputs. Enterprise artifacts are described by explaining their purpose and key characteristics (Fig. 3.20).

Fig. 3.20 Enterprise organization interaction

Enterprise organizations, their embeddedness in the value chain, and their cooperative relationships provide us with a generalized operating model as a generic frame of reference. The contributions of an architecture function, which are examined and highlighted in this book, are motivated and explained by the generic frame

---

[10] See the *Landscape Asset* pattern in this book's pattern catalog.

[11] IT4IT is a vendor-neutral reference architecture for managing the business of IT. It consists of a formal IT operating model based on the value chain concept that once revolutionized manufacturing. The IT4IT value chain consists of four value streams, namely, plan, build, run, and deliver. Via a reference architecture, IT4IT proposes essential services, functionality, and information based on which IT4IT value chains can be realized.

of reference. To this end, the generalized operating model explains *who* (enterprise organization) contributes *what* (enterprise artifact), *when*, and *under what* circumstances (enterprise value stage) to achieve the overall business objectives (enterprise service).

3.8.2   Enterprise Value Chain

The *enterprise value chain* can be decomposed into four enterprise value streams. An *enterprise value stream* provides a schema for exploring and explaining the contributions of architecture functions. Enterprise value streams are long-lived, coarse-grained groups of activities that are disaggregated into and chain *enterprise value stages*.

> **Phase Versus Stage**
> *The IEEE Recommended Practice for Architecture Description of Software-Intensive Systems* (IEEE 2000) distinguishes between phase and stage. A *phase* is a period in a lifecycle during which activities are performed to achieve the goals of that phase. A *stage* is a point within the lifecycle of an entity that refers to the state of its description or realization. Stages refer to the progress of an entity and the achievement of milestones.

Enterprise value stages are geared to the evolution of enterprise artifacts—ultimately, the incremental evolution of a company's enterprise services. Value stages represent what is contributed along a lifecycle of enterprise services. A value stage ends with an *enterprise value stage milestone*, where the milestone both specifies and controls the achievement of the targeted progress. Progress manifests itself in the form of *enterprise artifacts*, for example, a solution architecture description, a signed architecture mandate[12] document, or an architecture decision made. At the end of the day, progress manifests itself in the form of established or evolved enterprise services. *Enterprise organizations* (*who*) perform acts and cooperate through enterprise artifacts to collectively execute an enterprise value stage (Fig. 3.21).

---

[12] See the *Architecture Mandate* pattern in this book's pattern catalog (Chap. 6).

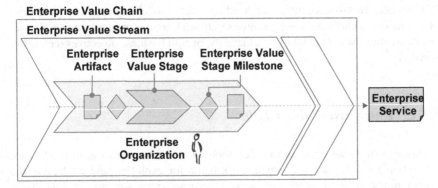

Fig. 3.21 Enterprise value chain schema

Enterprise value chains are the engines that underlie the planning, building, and operation of enterprise services. However, an enterprise service may itself be the host for an entire value chain, for example, a knowledge-intensive service such as an *architecture training service*. The provision of architecture training includes planning, building, and running the training and is thus itself arranged along a value delivery chain (Fig. 3.22).

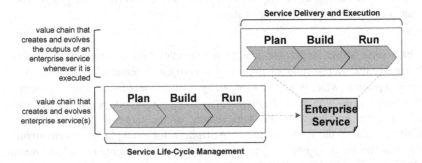

Fig. 3.22 Service delivery value chain

The enterprise value chain comprises the streams *service planning*, *service building*, *service running*, and *service delivering*. At the end of *service planning*, we know what projects are needed to develop the service portfolio to meet the enterprise's service requirements. At the end of *service building*, new services are built, tested, and deployed. At the end of *service delivering*, customer expectations are met, while services are monitored and kept vital during *service running* (Fig. 3.23).

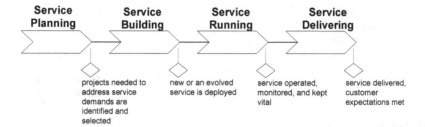

Fig. 3.23 Enterprise value chain

3.8.2.1   Service Planning Value Stream

The *service planning value stream* is divided into the service strategy, service demand, service portfolio, and project portfolio stages. The goal of the *service strategy stage* is an endorsed service strategy, while service demand is defined and endorsed at the end of the *service demand stage*. In the *service portfolio stage*, new services or changes to the existing service portfolio are determined to meet service demand. At the end of the *project portfolio stage*, the projects required to implement the service portfolio changes are proposed and endorsed. Service planning is performed on a continuous or periodic basis. Its ultimate goal is a portfolio of endorsed projects that represent the changes needed to maintain the overall fitness of the organization (Fig. 3.24).

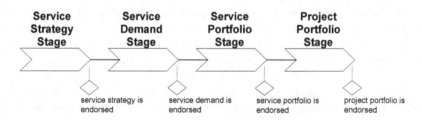

Fig. 3.24 Service planning value stream

Service Strategy Stage

The *service strategy stage* clarifies *why* an enterprise strategically needs which services (*what*) in order to achieve a competitive edge over its rivals. Furthermore, it is clarified what the identified services specifically offer (*how*) and *whom* they address. A service strategy may distinguish different strategic horizons for different planning perspectives, for example, a 3-year planning horizon for a single service versus a 5-year planning perspective for all services in a particular architecture domain. The *business strategy organization* evolves the *business strategy* artifact based on market and industry trends or market expansions that the business is planning. The *service strategy organization* uses the business strategy to create the *service strategy* output and clarify which services are required to support the business strategy (Fig. 3.25).

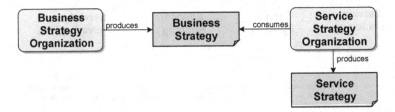

Fig. 3.25 Service strategy stage

The *business strategy organization* is responsible for the creation and further development of the *business strategy artifact*. Based on a segmented organizational model, multiple business strategy organizations may coexist, for example, in a divisional organization structure. The following artifacts are business strategy inputs: an *enterprise vision*, which clarifies *why* an enterprise exists and what its values are; an *enterprise mission*, which explains *what* an enterprise wants to achieve; and an *enterprise strategy*, which describes *how* it will pursue its goals. The main purpose of a business strategy is to envision what the business will look like in 3–5 years, who its customers will be, and what customer needs the business wants to address by that time. Furthermore, a business strategy clarifies the markets in which the enterprise intends to operate or the expertise required to successfully implement the business strategy plan. A business strategy includes internal and external strengths and weaknesses. These include, for example, employees, their skills and attitudes, products, their quality and price, operational and financial performance, and market reputation. However, a business strategy also includes external factors such as market trends, regulatory requirements, or the pace of technological change and innovation.

The *service strategy organization* is responsible for creating and refining the service *strategy artifact* to clarify customers' medium- to long-term service needs. A service strategy organization takes business strategy as input and examines other available inputs, such as emerging technology trends, to develop the service strategy artifact. The primary purpose of the service strategy is to capture medium- to long-term customer needs and answer strategic service questions, for example, questions such as what enterprise services should be provided, whom, and why or how are services best positioned in a competitive market. Other examples of service questions include what are the critical criteria for a successful service offering, its delivery, its operation, as well as its evolution or how are resources best allocated to ensure sufficient capacity across the entire portfolio of enterprise services.

Robert Mack and Ned Frey, in *Six Building Blocks for Creating Real IT Strategies* (Mack and Frey 2002), propose a model for mapping business strategies to service strategies. Mack and Frey postulate that a business strategy takes a vision or goal and narrows down the options for achieving that goal. As an approach to bounding the options, they suggest abstract fields for strategic decision-making. For instance, they suggest *geography*, which is about expansion and international distribution of the enterprise. They also introduce *governance*, which deals with who makes decisions and how decisions are made. In Mack and Frey's model, *future* is concerned with how far the enterprise's planning horizon should be, while *legacy enterprise resource(s)* is concerned with the degree to which an enterprise is willing to make drastic changes as opposed to taking a more conservative stance. *Virtual* measures the degree to which service providers, suppliers, and partners are involved and integrated, while *customer* expresses the degree to which customers are integrated into the enterprise processes. Finally, *funding* is about who finances the necessary investments.

The service strategy is established by mapping the business imperatives in the business strategy to five service strategy components, which I have adapted slightly from the model presented by Mack and Frey. The *service* component deals with all enterprise services, while the *applications* attribute refers to the application portfolio, individual applications, their capabilities, and how they support enterprise services. *Platform* refers to the platforms, technologies, and infrastructures needed to implement applications or enterprise services. *Information*, on the other hand, refers to information needed to implement the business strategy. *Integration* refers to the means by which all other components are connected or behave as a unit. Finally, *sourcing*[13] encompasses internal and external actors as well as rules and guidelines in their selection (Fig. 3.26).

Business Strategy vs. Service Strategy Mapping

		Service Strategy					
		Services	Applications	Platforms	Information	Integration	Sourcing
Business Strategy	Geography						
	Governance						
	Future						
	Legacy						
	Virtual						
	Customer						
	Funding						

Fig. 3.26 Mapping business against service strategy

Service Demand Stage

Service demand represents the need that an enterprise plans to meet by adding, adjusting, or removing services, for example, new customer needs that are not covered by current services or deficiencies in an existing service that will be addressed through modification. The ultimate goal of the service demand stage is to fully map the enterprise's service needs in the service demand portfolio. Portfolio stands for a grouping of things, which is why an enterprise demand portfolio refers to a grouping of demands. Inputs to the service demand stage are derived from *service strategy* or *business demand* or obtained from other sources, such as service

---

[13] See the *Architecture Sourcing* pattern in this book's pattern catalog (Chap. 6).

managers. Different types of service demands are distinguished, for example, enhanced service functionality, improved service quality, increased service efficiency, or scaled service capacity. For new service demands, costs, risks, and impacts of changes are investigated and estimated. As a result, the *service demand organization* delivers a prioritized *service demand portfolio* that is agreed with and supported by all stakeholders, including the architecture function (Fig. 3.27).

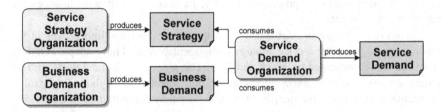

Fig. 3.27   Service demand stage

The *business demand organization* is responsible for surveying, collecting, and understanding business needs, for example, needs such as enhanced service functionality, improved service quality, or increased service efficiency. Business demand is surveyed, captured, consolidated, evaluated, and regularly exchanged with the *service demand organization* via *business demand artifacts*.

The *service demand organization* is responsible for reflecting business demand and service strategy inputs in the *service demand portfolio*, where demands from different channels are collected, discussed, and prioritized. Service demand may lead to new services, enhanced service functionality, or improved service quality (e.g., performance, usability, or security). Service demand may also lead to decommissioning or consolidation of services. Service demands result from new customer needs, the need to mitigate risks, dealing with constraints (e.g., limited budget), or changing regulations (e.g., Safe Harbor Act[14]).

Service Portfolio Stage
During the *service portfolio stage*, the *service portfolio organization* updates the *service portfolio* and reflects changes in the service demand portfolio. Portfolio management is generally about doing the right thing. So this is about identifying and prioritizing the right services to respond to changes in the service demand portfolio. New services are added, and existing services are adjusted or removed from the portfolio to reflect changes in demand. Service attributes such as service-level agreements, benefits, service costs, risk, service lifecycle status, or business criticality are updated. The architecture function elaborates an initial service architecture vision, which is another outcome of this stage. The service portfolio organization aligns the service portfolio with all relevant stakeholders (Fig. 3.28).

---

[14] Safe Harbor Act is a decision of the European Commission in the field of data protection law from 2000. The decision was intended to enable companies to transfer personal data from a European Union country to the USA in accordance with the European Data Protection Directive.

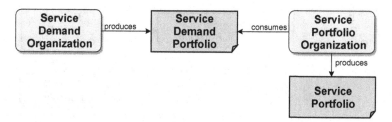

Fig. 3.28 Service portfolio stage

The *service portfolio organization* moderates discussion, development, and prioritization with other responsible and affected stakeholders. A *service portfolio* provides an overview of all enterprise services—past, current, and planned. It ensures that each service is reviewed and sufficiently described to guarantee that information, critical to service delivery and support, is shared with all related processes. Service interdependencies are captured and seriously considered—especially with respect to service priority segments (e.g., operational necessity, business criticality). A service portfolio provides answers to a variety of questions from different stakeholder groups, for example, who does the service offering reach, what is the value proposition of the service, what other services depend on a service, or how can the efficiency of the service be further improved? The architecture function analyzes the impact of significant service changes. The primary goal of this analysis is to anticipate impending ripple effects and understand how they can be mitigated. For example, a planned change to an existing service may result in adjustments to two dependent services, if the planned change threatens the operational stability of those services. The architecture function develops an initial vision that anticipates the future design of the service architecture at a relatively early stage. Without such initial, rudimentary, architecture vision, there would be no evidence base for anticipating the complexity, cost, or duration of a planned service change.

Project Portfolio Stage

A *project portfolio* is a collection of projects. The projects in this collection are described so that similarities and differences can be identified, and projects can be compared, ranked, and prioritized. The *project portfolio organization* ensures that the project portfolio reflects changes in the service portfolio in a timely manner. For example, let us say a new service was recently added to the service portfolio. In this case, a new project is added to the project portfolio to design, build, and implement the new service. The insights derived from the service architecture vision are necessary inputs in the creation of the new project in the portfolio. The ultimate goal of the project portfolio stage is a prioritized set of projects that are technically and capacity feasible, affordable, and suitable to achieve the organization's tactical and strategic goals (Fig. 3.29).

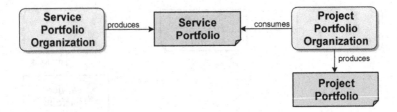

Fig. 3.29   Project portfolio stage

Not all services in a service portfolio can be pursued simultaneously; some may not be pursued at all. Enterprises may have an appetite for far more services than their resource or funding capacity justify. The *project portfolio organization* facilitates a selection process in which stakeholders agree on a subset of projects to maximize the enterprise's bottom line while respecting budgetary constraints. The project portfolio organization balances an enterprise's hunger for services with available resources and capacity and brings a pinch of realism to planning processes. Once all *project proposals* are created and projects are prioritized in the project portfolio, budgets and resources are allocated, and timelines are set. At this stage, project proposals are still a draft. A project's business value, risks, and assumptions, costs, schedule, deliverables, required skills and resources, project manager, key stakeholders, or dependent services and projects are provisionally captured. Once a project proposal is approved, a *service plan* is created from it. The service plan accompanies the project execution phase and outlines the details of project implementation.

3.8.2.2   Service Building Value Stream

The *service building value stream* is divided into the service plan, service architecture, service implementation, and service deployment stages. While a plan for the introduction of a new service is created in the *service planning stage*, the architecture design of the service is elaborated and endorsed in the *service architecture stage*. In the *service implementation stage*, the proposed design is physically realized, validated, and endorsed. The finalized service is deployed in the operational environment in the *service deployment stage*. The ultimate goal of the service building value stream is to deploy a new or evolved service or to consolidate and decommission[15] services that have become obsolete (Fig. 3.30).

---

[15] See the *Decommissioning Reward* pattern in this book's pattern catalog (Chap. 6).

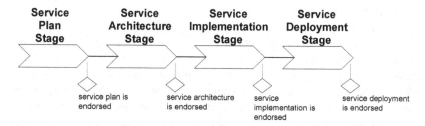

Fig. 3.30 Service building value stream

Service Plan Stage

In the *service plan stage*, the *service plan organization* creates the *service plan*, which defines the phased introduction or evolution of the envisioned service. The service plan defines the required skills and resources and refines the input from the initial project proposal. It clarifies the steps to be taken by a team and defines the phased rollout and the authorities that sign off on milestones. The service plan outlines roles and responsibilities, anticipated risks, and their mitigation and derives the required efforts and realistic timelines. Ultimately, the plan charts the path from gaining a holistic understanding of what needs to be addressed to developing the design of an adequate service. The project portfolio and the corresponding service architecture vision are inputs to the service plan stage. The architecture function determines which domains will be affected by the envisioned service and identifies the leading domain of each project. It summarizes the affected and leading domains, the roles and responsibilities, and the agreed architecture deliverables, resources, and timelines in an architecture mandate (Fig. 3.31).

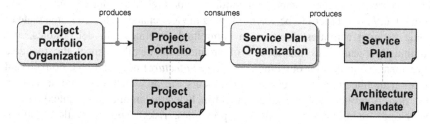

Fig. 3.31 Service plan stage

The *service plan organization* is responsible for transforming an initial project proposal into a sound *service plan*. The service plan ensures that the process of creating, evolving, or decommissioning a service is a systematic endeavor. The familiar project disciplines strongly support the service plan organization—for example, project management, business analysis, solution architecture, technical expertise, quality management, testing, and validation. The architecture function creates an *architecture mandate*, which it derives from the service plan to clarify the architecture responsibilities.

Service Architecture Stage

In the *service architecture stage*, the *service architecture organization* creates an architecture blueprint (*service architecture*) for the envisioned service. Service plan, architecture mandate, and early architecture vision are critical inputs to the service architecture stage. The architecture organization determines relevant roadmaps, landscapes, or reference assets from the affected domains. In addition to understanding the context, architects identify the architecture-significant[16] requirements of the service and incrementally derive adequate design responses, which they continuously synthesize into a holistic architecture design. Architects explore alternatives,[17] develop detailed architecture descriptions, communicate, and align decisions[18] with relevant stakeholders and regularly validate architectural progress. The result of the service architecture stage is a service architecture that can be implemented in the service implementation stage (Fig. 3.32).

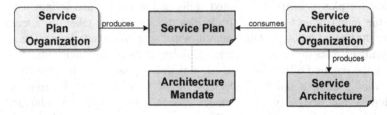

Fig. 3.32 Service architecture stage

The *service architecture organization* is a role[19] that the architecture function takes on in an enterprise. It develops a sound architecture design for a service (*service architecture*) that evolves gradually over the transformation effort (*project*). The service architecture organization requires a comprehensive understanding of the context and the problem to be solved. It uses the associated architecture mandate to guide its own activities, focuses on committed timelines and deliverables, and continually recalibrates the level[20] of architectural detail to meet the mandate agreements. The desired outcome (*service architecture*) may combine domain and solution architecture[21] aspects and documents the architecture of the service in question. A service architecture document includes the architecture context, conditions (e.g., requirements, constraints, principles, risks), and a detailed solution architecture description. The service architecture organization further ensures

---

[16] See the *Architecture-Significance* pattern in this book's pattern catalog (Chap. 6).

[17] See the *Architecture Alternatives* pattern in this book's pattern catalog.

[18] See the *Architecture Decision* pattern in this book's pattern catalog.

[19] See the *Architecture Role* pattern in this book's pattern catalog.

[20] See the *Architecture Level* pattern in this book's pattern catalog.

[21] See the *Domain Architecture Discipline* and *Solution Architecture Discipline* patterns in this book's pattern catalog.

traceability between the architecture conditions[22] and the solution architecture responses, conformance to the architecture mandate, and conformance to the domain and reference architecture.

Service Implementation Stage

The *service implementation stage* includes all aspects pertaining to the physical realization and validation of the targeted service. The *service implementation organization* takes the service architecture from the service architecture stage and gradually transforms it into a corresponding *service implementation design*. The service implementation organization, supported by architects, translates the service architecture into software and hardware specifications, physical database schemas, configurations, or deployment descriptors and creates prototypes to finally validate the service implementation. The result of this stage is a service implementation that physically implements the service architecture and is successfully validated in its test environment (Fig. 3.33).

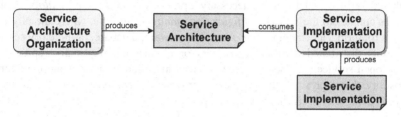

Fig. 3.33 Service implementation stage

The *service implementation organization* works closely with the service architecture organization to ensure that the physical implementation respects the design of its conceptual predecessor (*service architecture*). Alternatively, the service implementation organization cites reasons to deviate from the architecturally specified design—for example, unforeseen technical problems in realizing the envisioned service architecture. While the service architecture addresses the conceptual design of a service, the associated service implementation documents the physical design details—for example, hardware and software specifications.

Service Deployment Stage

The goal of the *service deployment stage* is the successfully deployed service—i.e., a service that is deployed in the enterprise's operating environment and ready to serve its customers. Apart from the physical handover, the service deployment stage resembles a clean-up campaign. The deployed service is registered in knowledge, change, and configuration management, its release plan is updated, and training begins. Demand, service, and project portfolios are updated to reflect recent changes. Finally, the provisioned service is advertised publicly via service catalogs (Fig. 3.34).

---

[22] See the *Architecture Condition* pattern in this book's pattern catalog.

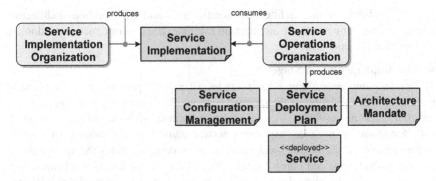

Fig. 3.34 Service deployment stage

The *service operations organization* works closely with the service architecture and service implementation organizations to ensure sustainable operation of the deployed service and to make necessary updates to the *service catalog*. It also ensures updates to the *service configuration management base*, where the physical service footprints are captured, for example, software, database, or directory service footprints distributed across data centers or clouds that physically represent a provisioned service. The service configuration management base is an operational repository that represents the physically provisioned components in the form of data—making them searchable and relatable.

3.8.2.3 Service Running Value Stream

The *service running value stream* is divided into service monitoring and detection, service diagnosis, and service problem resolution. It is a continuous stream that runs in parallel with the service planning, creation, and delivery streams. The service running value stream ensures timely responses to operational anomalies, defects, or inefficiencies observed in deployed enterprise services. *Service monitoring and detection* is a continuous stage that provides ongoing monitoring of service vitality. Service diagnostics is a stage that is switched on only in case of a problematic event. The *service diagnostics stage* diagnoses the root cause of the event. The *service problem resolution stage* takes the analysis of its predecessor (*service diagnosis stage*) as input and repairs or otherwise fixes the detected problem so that the service subsequently returns to a normal operating state (Fig. 3.35).

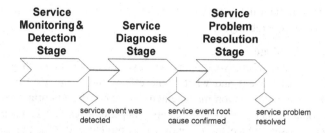

Fig. 3.35 Service running value stream

Service Monitoring and Detection Stage

The *service monitoring and detection stage* ensures continuous monitoring of the deployed services to detect operational anomalies in a timely manner. Service configuration management is an essential input to the monitoring and detection stage in order to correctly correlate related events. The primary goal of this stage is to detect problematic events, identify impacted services, alert service diagnostics, and equip them with appropriate event details (Fig. 3.36).

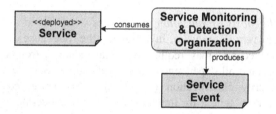

Fig. 3.36 Service monitoring and detection stage

The *service monitoring and detection organization* works closely with the service operations organization and monitors all *deployed services* in their production environment to detect anomalies. Among other information sources, it uses the service configuration management base for detected *service events*. Events that require detailed analysis and timely resolution are forwarded to the service diagnostics organization for further investigation, such as a database running out of storage. Events that can be easily remediated are fixed immediately, and the service returns to normal operation. For example, a crashed service is recovered by an application restart performed by the service monitoring and detection organization. Events may also indicate service gaps. For example, an application signals health problems to a monitoring agent, but does not disclose specific problem details. The service monitoring and detection organization enters a requirement into the application's requirements list (e.g., "enrich the health problem report with additional application fitness data"). The requirement list is considered in the next revision of the application to further improve its operability.

Service Diagnosis Stage
The goal of the *service diagnosis stage* is to analyze and understand (diagnose) what caused a problematic event and what ripple effects the event itself has on other assets. The service configuration management base provides important information about operational dependencies—for example, dependencies between services and other landscape assets. Once the diagnosis is complete and both the causes and impacts are fully understood, the service problem resolution stage is activated to resolve the problem (Fig. 3.37).

Fig. 3.37 Service diagnosis stage

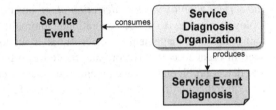

The *service diagnosis organization* investigates what caused a *service event* to create the *service event diagnostics*. Investigating the root cause of a service event can be very involved and may require significant support from the architecture function to understand all dependencies and implications. Service event diagnosis encompasses severity classification (e.g., *simple, recurring, complex*), impact assessment (e.g., the potential for impact is assessed as moderate, while the likelihood of impact occurring is assessed as very likely), affected services or landscape assets, and other event details needed by the service problem resolution organization.

Service Problem Resolution Stage
In the *service problem resolution stage*, a solution is sought to avoid, fix, or work around the identified problem. A detailed analysis of the problem, potential impact, and associated risks is performed to derive and elaborate an optimal conceptual as well as physical resolution. The desired end state of this stage is a successfully restored service (Fig. 3.38).

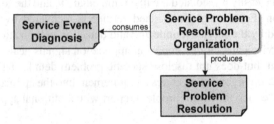

Fig. 3.38 Service problem resolution stage

The *service problem resolution organization* investigates and elaborates approaches to resolve or otherwise overcome a diagnosed service event. The ultimate goal is to return a service to normal operating status. For complex service problem solutions, the architecture function proposes architecture approaches that help mitigate or transform the problem. Problem solutions that result in conceptual or physical service changes are documented in the appropriate artifacts. For example, solution architecture documentation is adjusted in an architecture repository, and the service configuration management base is updated to reflect the service changes.

3.8.2.4   Service Delivery Value Stream

The *service delivery value stream* includes service publication, service subscription, service fulfillment, and service measurement. It is a continuous stream, similar to the service running stream. The service delivering value stream deals with consumer requests and their fulfillment. This stream is not examined in detail because the architecture function is minimally involved (Fig. 3.39).

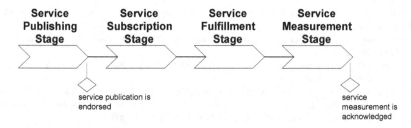

Fig. 3.39   Service delivering value stream

Service Publishing Stage

In the *service publishing stage*, services are published via catalogs to make them broadly requestable by their target consumer groups. A service catalog makes services navigable and allows consumers to tag, search, and request them. A service is fully described by its attributes. These include, for example, service name, service hours, service-level agreements and similar obligations, service release, or details about how the service is billed. Other attributes support searching and filtering of services in a corresponding catalog view, for example, service type (e.g., business versus technical[23] service), geolocation, or popularity ratings that express customer satisfaction.

---

[23] See the *Business versus Technical* pattern in this book's pattern catalog (Chap. 6).

Service Subscription Stage

In the *service subscription stage*, service consumers search for, find, and subscribe to the services they are interested in. The billing of services also takes place in the service subscription stage.

Service Fulfillment Stage

In the *service fulfillment stage*, services are delivered in accordance with the service-level agreements. Service desks support customers with questions or problems during service fulfillment.

Service Measurement Stage

Finally, in the *service measurement stage*, service usage is continuously measured and surveyed. Service key performance indicators[24] (KPI) provide valuable insights into the performance of individual services so that targeted optimization can be conducted. KPIs are essential to ensure continuous service improvement[25] (CSI).

Further Reading

Balogun, Julia, and Hope Veronica Hailey. 2008. *Exploring Strategic Change*. Amsterdam: Pearson Education.

Campbell, Andrew, Mikel Gutierrez, and Mark Lancelott. 2017. *Operating Model Canvas*. Van Haren Publishing.

Dietz, Jan. 2006. *Enterprise Ontology: Theory and Methodology*. Berlin, Heidelberg: Springer Science & Business Media.

Gartner, *Gartner Glossary*, https://www.gartner.com/en/information-technology/glossary, 2020

IEEE Computer Society, *IEEE Recommended Practice for Architecture Description of Software-Intensive Systems*, IEEE std. IEEE – pp. 1472-2000, New York, 2000

ITIL *Glossary and Abbreviations*, https://www.axelos.com/corporate/media/files/glossaries/itil_2011_glossary_gb-v1-0.pdf, 2020

Heckscher, Charles. 1994. *The Post-Bureaucratic Organization*. Sage Publications.

Kelly, Kevin. 2016. *The inevitable – Understanding the 12 Technology Forces that will shape our future*. New York: Penguin.

Mack, Robert and Ned Frey, *Six Building Blocks for Creating Real IT Strategies*, Gartner Group, Report R 17-3607, 2002

Merriam-Webster, *Merriam-Webster Dictionary*, https://www.merriam-webster.com/dictionary, 2020

Mintzberg, Henry. 1979. *The Structuring of Organizations: A Synthesis of the Research*. Prentice-Hall.

The Open Group, *IT4IT™*, https://www.opengroup.org/it4it, 2020

Osterwalder, Alexander, Yves Pigneur, Alan Smith, and 470 practitioners from 45 countries, *Business Model Generation*, self-published, 2010

Porter, Michael. 1985. *Competitive Advantage*. New York: Free Press.

---

[24] Key Performance Indicators (KPI) measure and indicate the performance of an organization or activity based on an underlying performance measurement metric.

[25] Continual Service Improvement (CSI) uses quality management methods to learn from past successes and failures to improve IT services and processes.

Rayport, Jeffrey, and John Sviokla. 1995. *Exploiting the virtual value chain.* Harvard Business Review.

Ross, Jeanne, and Forget Strategy. 2005. *Focus IT on your Operating Model.* MIT CISR Research Briefing V (3C).

Weber, Max. 1948. *Essays in Sociology, translated, edited and with an introduction by H.* London: H. Gerth and C. W. Mills.

Wikipedia, *Organization Structures,* https://en.wikipedia.org/wiki/Organizational_structure, 2020a
———, *Process,* https://en.wikipedia.org/wiki/Process, 2020b
———, *Process Modelling,* https://en.wikipedia.org/wiki/Process_modeling, 2020c

Chapter 4
Architecture Function: Challenge

Abstract While the previous chapter (Chap. 3) introduced contextual concepts such as a generic enterprise organization or enterprise value chain, this chapter takes a black-box perspective on an architecture function. It outlines the expectations and requirements that enterprises have for architecture functions by looking at an idealized function from the outside. It discusses the building blocks of an architecture function, the services it provides along the enterprise value chain, and the quality attributes that enterprises expect from their architecture functions in the twenty-first century. The next chapter (Chap. 5) continues the structures introduced here and proposes a generic design of an architecture function. To this end, the generic design outlines proposals for the realization of the constituent building blocks, the implementation of the functional offering (services), and the approach to realizing the quality attributes of an architecture function.

4.1 Overview

Chapter 3 introduced enterprise concepts that define the environment in which architecture functions operate. It introduced generic enterprise organizations and their collaborative relationships along a correspondingly generic enterprise value chain. In this chapter, I refer to these concepts to describe the challenges that architecture functions face—ultimately, the challenges that any architecture organization must address. While this chapter takes a black-box perspective on an architecture function and describes the expectations (*requirements*) for it, the next chapter takes a look behind the scenes of the architecture organization. Chapter 5 takes a white-box perspective and proposes a generic function design that addresses the requirements presented here (Fig. 4.1).

© The Author(s), under exclusive license to Springer Nature Switzerland AG 2022
I. Arnold, *Enterprise Architecture Function*,
https://doi.org/10.1007/978-3-030-84589-6_4

Architecture Function Pattern Topology

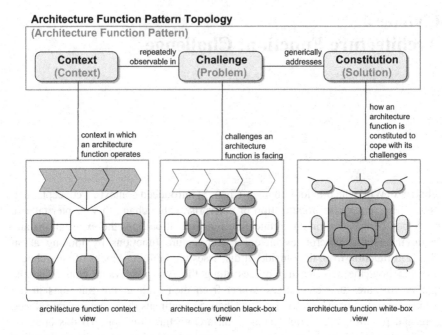

Fig. 4.1 Architecture function pattern (challenge)

An architecture function makes direct contributions to an enterprise value chain, such as endorsing its service portfolio—for example, an architecture assessment of an unstable service and a refactoring proposal to improve its operational stability. However, an architecture function also makes indirect contributions to the value chain. For example, it provides an enterprise organization with information, such as an architecture roadmap, that the organization needs to make its own contribution to the value chain. Architecture functions provide services for contributions that are regularly requested by other organizations, while contributions to the value chain typically manifest as enterprise artifacts. In addition to offering contributions per se, an architecture organization must ensure that these contributions are informative, consistent, reliable, and repeatable, in other words, of high quality. The bottom line for an architecture function is to demonstrate that the value of the services it provides permanently exceeds the cost of maintaining them (Fig. 4.2).

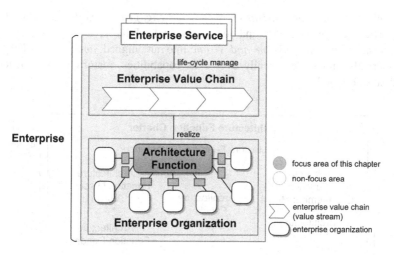

Fig. 4.2 Architecture function challenge

An architecture organization must be established before it can offer its services, ensure their qualitative delivery, or guarantee its own evolutionary fitness. In Sect. 4.2, I explore what is required to initially establish an architecture function or, alternatively, to evolve an existing one. I then address what an enterprise expects from an architecture organization by looking at it from the outside. For regularly requested contributions, I propose architecture service specifications, for example, services such as *solution architecture development, architecture relevance checking,* or *architecture alternatives development.* Service specifications are equivalent to functional requirements that architecture functions must meet. In Sect. 4.3, the division of the enterprise value chain into architecture value streams is used as a schema to contextualize service specifications. Qualitative expectations of an architecture function are outlined and specified in Sect. 4.4, for example, quality expectations such as its usability, availability, or evolvability.

4.2   Architecture Function

Before an architecture function can contribute to the achievement of enterprise goals, it must be established, embedded in the operating model, aligned with the value chain, integrated with other organizations, and equipped with an *architecture function apparatus.* Establishing or evolving an existing function encompasses many aspects and touches on many facets, which are summarized in an *architecture function charter.* It must be organized and staffed (*architecture function organization*). It needs a sound understanding of how to govern (*architecture function governance*), communicate (*architecture function communication*), and interact with other organizations (*architecture function engagement model*) to support the enterprise achieve its short- and long-term goals. Finally, it must translate the *architecture function mission and vision* into an aligned *function roadmap* to transparently and systematically evolve its capabilities, maturity,[1] and capacity[2] over time (Fig. 4.3).

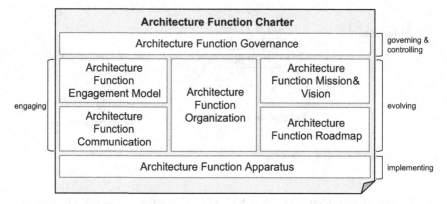

Fig. 4.3 Architecture function charter

4.2.1 *Architecture Function Vision and Mission*

> A *vision* is a thought, concept, or object formed by the imagination. (Merriam-Webster Dictionary 2020)

Vision statements aim to inspire an idealistic future for an organization or enterprise. They provide an entry point to envision a future state and are intended to inspire their members to turn that future vision into reality. An architecture function can use a vision as a tool to articulate what an ideal future state looks and feels like. Organizations next derive their *mission* from a vision, with their mission not so much to inspire as to help implement.

> A *mission* is a specific task with which a person or a group is charged. (Merriam-Webster Dictionary 2020)

---

[1] See the *Architecture Maturity* pattern in this book's pattern catalog (Chap. 6).

[2] See the *Architecture Capacity* pattern in this book's pattern catalog.

Patrick Hull (2013) suggests that an organization's *mission statement* must answer four questions. It answers the question "what do we do?" by clearly articulating what the organization does. A mission answers the question "how do we do it?" by outlining a plan that shows how the organization will achieve what it strives to do. Further, a good mission statement answers the question "who are we doing this for?" by identifying precisely who the target audiences are. Finally, it shows how the target audiences will benefit by answering the fourth question, "what value do we bring?"

While vision statements are motivational precursors to mission statements and explain *why* an organization exists, a mission describes its overarching goal (*what*) and *who* benefits from the organization pursuing its objective. A mission may also include other aspects of a universal or fundamental nature, for example, a foundational value system, ethical standards, contributions to society, or the desired organizational state of an enterprise. This could be an example of the mission statement of an architecture function: "Providing architecture services to support the full lifecycle of enterprise services at minimal cost."

A mission statement establishes an overarching direction—helping an architecture function more appropriately deal with orientation challenges when making strategic decisions. A mission also provides a clear articulation of the architecture function's primary purpose, which helps eliminate ambiguity and allows stakeholders to consciously agree or disagree with the function's mandate (Fig. 4.4).

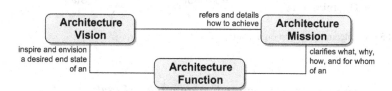

Fig. 4.4 Architecture vision and mission

4.2.2 Architecture Function Organization

Architecture function organizations are a pivotal element[3] in meeting the expectations that enterprises have of architecture. An architecture organization is a vehicle that establishes the baseline for all architecture capabilities an enterprise requires. Architecture organizations must harmonize with surrounding *enterprise organizations*. This means that an architecture organization must be aligned with the power distribution, organizational depth, or geographic spread of an enterprise. It must scale up and down to flexibly accommodate the enterprise's need for architecture contributions. It must provide architecture skills at the required competency levels. It

---

[3] See the *Organizational Replication* pattern in this book's pattern catalog (Chap. 6).

must also group skills into coarser-grained architecture roles[4] and disciplines.[5] Together, the roles form an *architecture role model* that must be aligned with an overarching enterprise role model. Once a role model is defined, funds are needed to recruit and staff the defined roles (*architecture staff*). Despite available funding,[6] recruitment can be difficult because good architects are a scarce resource. Ongoing training and development programs are required to maintain the skills base and retain high performing architects. Once established, an architecture organization does not stand still—it is constantly evolving. It also includes components that tend to be more formally defined than others due to labor laws and the fact that they are legal entities (Fig. 4.5).

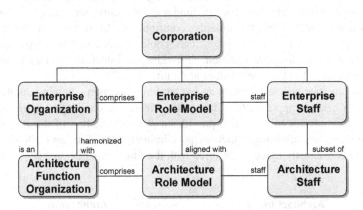

Fig. 4.5 Architecture function organization

4.2.3 Architecture Function Engagement Model

Defining and staffing an architecture organization does not yet actively engage any architect. An *enterprise organization* needs to be guided by the contributions it offers. It also needs to understand how someone can reach and engage the architecture organization, for example, through *architecture services* listed in a *service catalog*. An enterprise organization needs to know what contributions it can expect from an architect and, in turn, what inputs it owes an architect in specific *value chain* contexts. An *engagement model* clarifies all of this—it is thus an essential component of the architecture function. Section 4.3 proposes generic architecture service specifications and thus describes the functional shell of a generic *engagement model* (Fig. 4.6).

---

[4] See the *Architecture Role* pattern in this book's pattern catalog (Chap. 6).

[5] See the *Enterprise Architecture Discipline*, *Domain Architecture Discipline*, and *Solution Architecture Discipline* patterns in this book's pattern catalog.

[6] See the *Architecture Funding* pattern in this book's pattern catalog.

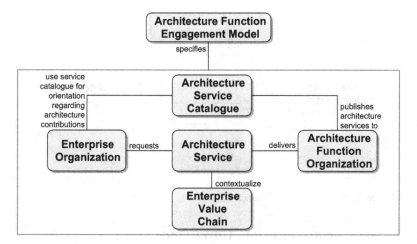

Fig. 4.6 Architecture function engagement model

4.2.4 Architecture Function Communication

Communication and language[7] are the ultimate means of building any human interaction; a shared understanding, value base, and communication protocols are their concretization. To fulfill their mission and contribute appropriately, architecture functions must understand and be understood by other *enterprise organizations*, which requires a common language and shared concepts. These form the basis for mutual understanding and thus a prerequisite for trust. Architecture functions establish *architecture ontologies* for this purpose. An ontology clarifies the meaning of both basic concepts and domain-specific abstractions[8] of an enterprise's essential domains. Architecture ontologies enable efficient and effective information exchange between architects and non-architecture organizations. Architecture is an abstract and amorphous subject, so communication of the architecture function deserves the highest attention and should be a cornerstone in the engagement model (Fig. 4.7).

---

[7] See the *Architecture Language* pattern in this book's pattern catalog (Chap. 6).

[8] See the *Domain Taxonomy* pattern in this book's pattern catalog.

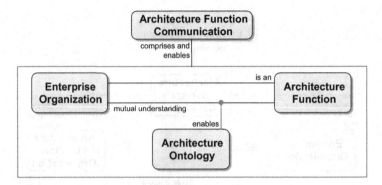

Fig. 4.7 Architecture function communication

4.2.5   Architecture Function Governance

For complex social systems, such as large and geographically dispersed international corporations, common ethics, rules, and policies are required to operate in a coordinated, well-organized, and aligned manner. Governance, in its broadest sense, is the act of steering as well as overseeing and monitoring the direction of something, such as the directional control of an enterprise. Architecture functions establish governance[9] (*architecture function governance*) to define architecture ethics, rules, and policies and to monitor the enterprise's compliance with those policies. They must tune governance granularity so that effectiveness and scalability are not sacrificed on the altar of strong organizational countercurrents. Architecture organizations must also regularly reflect on whether their governance interventions are achieving the desired effects and continuously evolve their governance accordingly (Fig. 4.8).

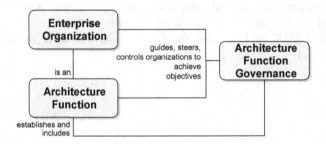

Fig. 4.8 Architecture function governance

---

[9] See the *Architecture Governance* pattern in this book's pattern catalog (Chap. 6).

4.2.6   Architecture Function Roadmap

A roadmap is a detailed plan used to guide progress toward a desired target state. An architecture organization needs a roadmap (*architecture function roadmap*) to plan and guide its evolution from a current state (*architecture function baseline*) to the desired target state[10] (*architecture function target*). For example, an architecture organization uses a roadmap to improve its maturity level, close service gaps, or overcome scalability deficiencies and chronic undercapacity. Ultimately, the roadmap guides an architecture function on the path to its vision. Architecture functions need a roadmap as an informative and prescriptive tool that ensures planned states are understood, agreed upon, and aligned with all stakeholders. A roadmap enables functions to achieve their desired future state in a planned and systematic way (Fig. 4.9).

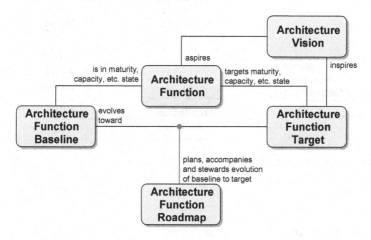

Fig. 4.9   Architecture function roadmap

4.2.7   Architecture Function Apparatus

Apparatuses are means (e.g., tools, methodologies, or techniques) by which something can be performed and achieved more effectively and efficiently. An *architecture function apparatus* underpins the processes that an architecture function performs and the artifacts[11] that it maintains and continuously creates. In addition to boosting the productivity of the architecture function, an apparatus also comprises

---

[10] See the *Baseline Architecture versus Target Architecture* pattern in this book's pattern catalog (Chap. 6).

[11] See the *Architecture Artifact* pattern in this book's pattern catalog.

methodologies. An *architecture methodology*[12] increases the systematicity and repeatability of architecture development in an organization. It promotes deliberate and coordinated interaction, standardized procedures, and organizational economies of scale—ultimately, an attitude of repeating rather than reinventing. Apparatuses must be aligned with the defined *role model*. For example, an *architecture role model* is implemented in a platform[13] to enforce access rights when architects perform activities in a corresponding tool base (Fig. 4.10).

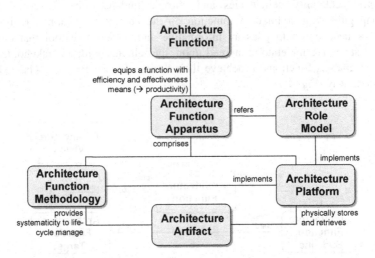

Fig. 4.10   Architecture function apparatus

4.3   Architecture Function Services

Architecture function services are the workhorses of an engagement model (Sect. 4.2.3). They express the contributions an architecture organization offers in a tangible and retrievable way, for example, through a service catalog. An architecture service specifies an interaction protocol that structures the cooperation between enterprise organizations and the architecture function.

Architecture services are the externally visible and retrievable capabilities that an architecture organization exposes to other organizations. Service-oriented architecture function designs are driven by the demands of the business (Bente et al. 2012). A service-oriented organization design standardizes interorganizational touchpoints, thereby increasing the reusability and repeatability of organizational capabilities.

---

[12] See the *Your own Architecture Methodology* pattern in this book's pattern catalog.

[13] See the *Your own Architecture Platform* pattern in this book's pattern catalog (Chap. 6).

Service-oriented designs also separate the offerings that an architecture organization makes externally from how they are realized internally. This decoupling enables greater flexibility and evolvability of architecture services. While the service interface in a service catalog does not change but remains stable externally, its implementation can evolve independently.

This chapter presents a generic set of services as perceived by customers of the architecture function. It thus takes a black-box perspective (requirements perspective) on architecture services. The focus of the service descriptions in this chapter is on *what* an architecture function brings to the table. Section 5.3 picks up the thread where it leaves off here and switches to the white-box perspective of each architecture service—i.e., it zooms into the internal design of that service to describe *how* it is generically realized. The schema for the enterprise value chain, streams, and stages introduced in Sect. 3.8.2 structures the present chapter and provides a corresponding context for each service presented (Fig. 4.11).

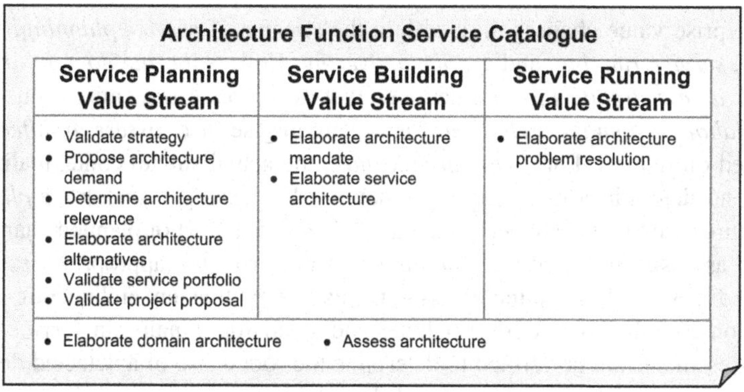

Architecture Function Service Catalogue		
Service Planning Value Stream	**Service Building Value Stream**	**Service Running Value Stream**
• Validate strategy • Propose architecture demand • Determine architecture relevance • Elaborate architecture alternatives • Validate service portfolio • Validate project proposal	• Elaborate architecture mandate • Elaborate service architecture	• Elaborate architecture problem resolution
• Elaborate domain architecture	• Assess architecture	

Fig. 4.11 Architecture service catalog

The service descriptions in this chapter are kept compact and close to the respective service catalog entries. The goal of the service descriptions in this chapter is to clarify which requirements and expectations the architecture services primarily address. Note, however, that certain aspects are hidden behind the service names, such as the scope or level[14] of granularity at which a service operates. For example, the service *determine architecture relevance*, when applied at the solution level, determines relevance to the architectural elaboration of an application or platform. In contrast, the same service, when applied at the domain level, determines relevance to the architectural elaboration or investigation of an entire domain. In addition to

---

[14] See the *Architecture Level* pattern in this book's pattern catalog (Chap. 6).

service *name* and *purpose*, service descriptions include the *trigger* (i.e., what initiates a service request), the *inputs* (i.e., the information and artifacts required by the architecture organization to execute the service), and the *outputs* (i.e., the information returned and the state reached upon successful execution of the service) (Fig. 4.12).

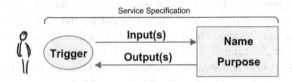

Fig. 4.12 Architecture service description

4.3.1 All Value Streams

The enterprise value chain is divided into the streams of *service planning*, *service building*, *service running*, and *service delivering*. Both *elaborate domain architecture* and *assess architecture* are services that accompany the entire value chain. While *elaborate domain architecture* is an ongoing service, *assess architecture* is performed on request. For *assess architecture*, the actual stream contextualizes the service and determines its execution semantics. For example, in *service planning*, architecture assessments are performed to analyze the impact of planned changes. In contrast, assessments in *service building* aim to verify the appropriateness of an elaborated design. For example, assessments verify that an architecture-revised application complies with design policies and standards. Finally, in *service operations*, assessments are performed to determine the root cause of a detected defect so that the defect can be promptly repaired (Fig. 4.13).

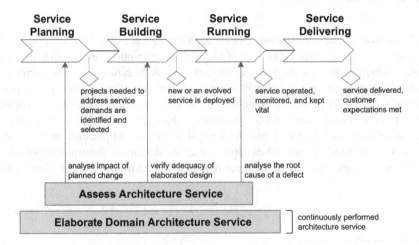

Fig. 4.13 Enterprise value chain architecture services

4.3.1.1   Assess Architecture

Purpose An assessment[15] validates the outcome of an architecture elaboration activity. The early vision of a design serves as input to assessments performed in the service planning stream. This assessment variant analyzes the impacts of the anticipated design change to determine whether its continued pursuit will benefit the business more than it costs. Investigating opportunities to increase efficiency is another assessment event in the service planning stream, such as investigating consolidation opportunities around landscape assets[16] in a domain. In the context of the service building stream, architecture assessments analyze fully elaborated designs, for example, a recently elaborated application design. An assessment validates the appropriateness of the proposed design against given evaluation criteria—for example, the appropriateness of a landscape asset, such as an application, with respect to its security or performance approaches. In the service running stream, assessments analyze the architecture description of assets that exhibit defects. Here, the goal of assessments is to quickly determine the root cause of the defect and develop a solution to the problem. For example, the architecture of an application that crashes repeatedly during normal operation is examined to find the root cause and then propose a fix.

Trigger An assessment is triggered by the interest in anticipating the impact of a planned change in *service planning*. In contrast, in *service building*, it is triggered by the desire to review a recently developed design for appropriateness. In *service operations*, detected asset defects trigger an architecture assessment.

Inputs Important inputs for an assessment are the *assessment drivers*, *architecture drivers*, and *architecture descriptions*. In the service running stream, documentation of a detected defect completes the input list. *Assessment drivers* represent and specify the goal of an assessment—for example, the goal of analyzing a detected defect and proposing a solution. *Architecture drivers* describe the goals of the assessed asset itself—for example, the goal of a platform to meet high scalability requirements or be particularly reliable. Finally, *architecture descriptions* are the artifacts that an assessment team tangibly uses to understand both the current and planned architecture states—for example, the baseline and target architecture descriptions of a new enterprise platform.

Outputs The main output of an assessment is the *architecture assessment report*. If the report includes recommendations, corresponding architecture descriptions complement the report.

---

[15] See the *Architecture Assessment Methodology* pattern in this book's pattern catalog (Chap. 6).

[16] See the *Landscape Asset* pattern in this book's pattern catalog.

4.3.1.2   Elaborate Domain Architecture

Purpose Elaborate domain architecture[17] is an architecture lifecycle service, which means that it is a continuously performed activity. Domain architecture elaboration begins with the birth of a domain and ends with its demise. Generally speaking, a domain delineates an area of interest in the world. In architecture, a domain constitutes a frame around a particular area of interest. Architects can refer to the area by name and discuss matters within it based on a common conceptual foundation. The *elaborate domain architecture* service accompanies the entire lifecycle of all architecture assets[18] (e.g., landscape assets such as services or applications) within a domain—i.e., their planning, building, running, and decommissioning stages. As part of the service, a domain architect creates baseline and target architecture overviews, a roadmap,[19] and reference assets[20] within a domain. In performing the service, an architect may also take a solution architecture perspective on an entire domain by viewing it as a coarse-grained solution. Finally, domain architects perform assessments by validating compliance with domain policies. A domain description comprises descriptions of the domain's baseline and target architectures, a domain roadmap, reference assets associated with the domain, and a solution architecture depiction of the domain. Other architecture services extensively utilize domain descriptions. For example, *elaborate service architecture* uses domain baseline architecture descriptions to obtain an overview of the landscape assets that a new service may use. To give another example, *validate service portfolio* ensures that service prioritization is aligned with domain architecture roadmaps.

Trigger Domain architecture elaboration begins with the birth of a domain and usually leads to an extension of the architecture function by a newly commissioned domain architect.

Inputs The inputs are diverse and range from domain-specific strategy and planning artifacts to analyst reports or market studies to forecasts about emerging technologies. Due to the continuous nature of the service, its outputs are recycled as inputs in its next iteration.

Outputs The key outputs of the *elaborate domain architecture* service are the domain baseline and target architecture descriptions; the domain roadmap; the associated reference assets, such as architecture patterns; the domain's solution architecture depiction; and the domain-related assessment reports.

---

[17] See the *Domain Architecture Methodology* pattern in this book's pattern catalog (Chap. 6).

[18] See the *Architecture Asset* pattern in this book's pattern catalog.

[19] See the *Architecture Roadmap Methodology* pattern in this book's pattern catalog.

[20] See the *Reference Architecture Methodology* pattern in this book's pattern catalog.

4.3.2   Service Planning Value Stream

The *service planning value stream* is broken down into the service strategy, service demand, service portfolio, and project portfolio stages. In the *service strategy stage*, the architecture service *validate strategy* ensures that design considerations are adequately addressed by the business and the service strategy. In the *service demand stage*, the *propose architecture demand* service contributes the demands deemed relevant by the architecture function. The *determine architecture relevance* service derives architecture relevance from the significance[21] of an expected change, while the *elaborate architecture alternatives* service explores alternative approaches to achieve a defined objective. The *validate service portfolio* service helps to finally endorse an appropriate portfolio. By performing this service, the architecture organization confirms that it has investigated the architectural value, impact, cost, and risk of the endorsed portfolio and that its capacity is sufficient to support the envisioned changes. Finally, the *validate project proposal* service ensures that architecture is adequately represented in an appropriate project proposal (Fig. 4.14).

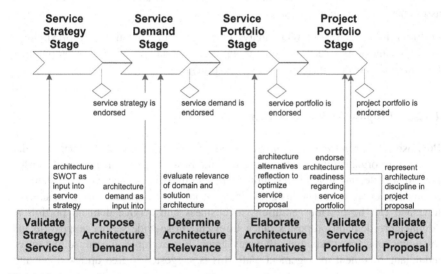

Fig. 4.14   Service planning value stream architecture services

---

[21] See the *Architecture-Significance* pattern in this book's pattern catalog (Chap. 6).

4.3.2.1   Validate Strategy

Purpose The *validate strategy service* ensures and endorses that architecture considerations are adequately considered by the business and service strategy. It leverages enterprise-level architecture descriptions and plans and provides input to business and service strategy SWOT[22] analyses, for example. The service compares emerging technologies, architecture patterns, and business models with the business and service strategy and explores innovative approaches[23] to achieve strategic business goals more efficiently and effectively.

Trigger Business and service strategy revisions are recurring events—therefore, *validate strategy* is usually triggered by a synchronized architecture calendar event.[24] However, the service can also be initiated ad hoc by a service requester. For example, a sudden technological breakthrough requires an immediate revision of the service strategy of the entire enterprise or selected architecture domains.

Inputs Primary inputs are the current business and service strategies at the enterprise or domain level. Internally, the architecture organization uses other inputs for this service—for example, a domain's baseline or target architecture description, its assessment reports, and roadmap.

Outputs Key output is a SWOT analysis the architecture function performed. Sign-off of business and service strategy inputs might be an additional output that formally validates the business or domain strategies.

4.3.2.2   Propose Architecture Demand

Purpose The *propose architecture demand* service contributes the demand that the architecture organization deems relevant to the business or service demand portfolios. An architecture function has intimate insight into the mechanical underpinnings of business operations. The insights it gains from this perspective accumulate over time and can be precious additions to business and service demand portfolios. Architecture demand proposals range from enterprise-wide service improvements to suggestions for substantial efficiency gains. For example, the consolidation of redundant document management platforms is suggested to free up resources and

---

[22] SWOT analysis (i.e., an acronym for strengths, weaknesses, opportunities, and threats) is used to position and develop a strategy for enterprises and other organizations. Opportunities and threats represent external factors. Opportunities are, for example, possibilities to win customers through new or improved services. In contrast, threats are recognized risks. For example, identified opportunities may be threatened by more attractive competitor offerings or by emerging technology. In view of the external factors (i.e., opportunities and threats), enterprises consider their own measures to respond to these factors. Own measures cannot ignore the enterprise's intrinsic strengths and weaknesses.

[23] See the *Architecture Innovation* pattern in this book's pattern catalog (Chap. 6).

[24] See the *Architecture Calendar* pattern in this book's pattern catalog.

thereby permanently reduce operating expenses (OPEX[25]). An architecture function also proposes demands that reflect its own needs, such as additions or changes to its own set of services, for example, adding an architecture assessment service to its service portfolio because it has been identified as a gap. Another example of an architecture-centric demand is a required change to architecture function building blocks, such as its organizational structure, engagement model, or apparatus.

Trigger Business and service demand portfolio revisions are recurring events— hence the *propose architecture demand* service is typically triggered by a synchronized architecture calendar event. However, the service might also be performed without an external trigger if the architecture function spontaneously deems a demand addition appropriate.

Inputs No inputs are required to perform this service.

Outputs Outputs are demands that the architecture organization considers relevant business or service demand complements. Sign-off of the business and service demand portfolios might be a complementary output that formally endorses them by the architecture function.

4.3.2.3 Determine Architecture Relevance

Purpose Architecture functions increase their productivity to the extent that they succeed in focusing their efforts on relevant contributions. This ability relieves them of avoidable effort. For a targeted activity, the *determine architecture relevance* service evaluates whether the required effort is wisely invested or whether it is wiser to forgo the architecture engagement altogether. For a planned activity or modification, this service estimates whether it deserves special architectural attention. For example, the plan is to replace an existing collaboration platform, running in the enterprise's own data center, with a cloud-based collaboration platform. For this plan, the *determine architecture relevance* service checks whether the planned change is architecturally relevant, in other words, whether the architecture function needs to be involved. *Determine architecture relevance* uses heuristics to distinguish between relevant and non-relevant engagements to avoid two types of efficiency mistakes: ignoring a task that, unrecognized, was actually highly relevant and engaging in a task that was incorrectly classified as architecturally important.

Trigger Focusing the *determine architecture relevance* service on business and service demands makes it possible to anticipate their complexity and thus supports demand organizations in obtaining signals for necessary efforts and investments at an early stage. While the *determine architecture relevance* service is already

---

[25] Operational expenditure (OPEX) is the ongoing costs of reliably operating existing assets, while capital expenditure (CAPEX) is the money an organization spends creating, buying, or evolving assets.

triggered during the discussion of business and service demands, it comes into play at the latest during the discussion of project portfolio entries. Here, it provides valuable input for identifying project risks or determining project budgets and, if necessary, booking the required capacities with the architecture function before the project begins.

Inputs Primary inputs are the demand or portfolio entries for which this service is to check architecture relevance—for example, business demand for a new enterprise service desired by the company's customers.

Outputs The banal result of this service is the appraisal of architectural relevance or non-relevance for a given input. Beyond the yes-no portion, the service provides a rationale for its appraisal and further details about the breadth and depth of further architecture involvement.

4.3.2.4 Elaborate Architecture Alternatives

Purpose Alternative solutions[26] exist for almost any problem at any level of granularity or detail. The *elaborate architecture alternatives* service explores and elaborates alternative design approaches to a given condition[27] and proposes the architecturally preferred approach.[28] In service planning, the service produces high-level design sketches of alternative approaches to realizing a given overall problem. That is, the service elaborates architecture options for addressing given conditions at the level of an overall solution. During service building, the service is repeatedly employed to explore alternative approaches for partial solutions. For example, the service explores different approaches for a solution that requires transactional consistency across multiple persistence systems. To this end, the service examines the alternatives *database replication*[29] and *external transaction processing monitor*[30] and, after checking the degree of fulfillment of each alternative, recommends the architecture approach based on *database replication*.

---

[26] See the *Architecture Alternative* pattern in this book's pattern catalog (Chap. 6).

[27] See the *Architecture Condition* pattern in this book's pattern catalog.

[28] See the *Architecture Approach* pattern in this book's pattern catalog (Chap. 6).

[29] Database replication is supported by modern database management systems (i.e., DBMS) and enables synchronization between physically distributed data stores that form a logically unified entirety. A replication mechanism ensures that updates sent to one of several database replicas are synchronized with all others. The mechanism also resolves synchronization collisions when the same database record is modified simultaneously in different database replicas.

[30] Transaction processing monitor (TP monitor) is a control program monitoring data transfer between multiple persistence systems. A TP monitor ensures that a transaction is either fully processed or that appropriate action is taken in the event of an error (e.g., rollback of the entire transaction to restore a system to its previous state). TP monitors ensure ACID principles (i.e., atomicity, consistency, isolation, durability) for monitored transactions.

Trigger Focusing the *elaborate architecture alternatives* service on business and service demands explores options to address them. This helps portfolio organizations openly discuss a wide range of accentuated options and select the most optimal architecture approach among them. Business and service demands, service portfolio, and project portfolio revisions are recurring events, so the *elaborate architecture alternatives* service is usually triggered by a synchronized architecture calendar event in the service planning value stream. In the service building stream, the *elaborate architecture alternatives* service is repeatedly triggered by situations where architects find it beneficial to overcome their own conditioning in addressing partial solutions.

Inputs For *service planning*, the inputs are the demand or portfolio entries and their conditions for which the *elaborate architecture alternatives* service is to explore alternative design approaches. In *service building*, the inputs are the architecture description elaborated so far, an optimization metric, and the conditions for which the service shall propose alternative architecture approaches.

Outputs Outputs are the studied alternatives elaborated to an agreed level of detail, a preferred alternative, and supplementary information supporting the architecture proposal. Note that each investigated alternative is an early draft of a complete architecture description.

4.3.2.5   Validate Service Portfolio

Purpose By performing the *validate service portfolio* service, the architecture organization confirms that it has examined the architecture value, impact, cost, and risk of the portfolio and that the architecture capacity is sufficient to support the planned changes. The architecture function also documents its support and alignment by formally endorsing the service portfolio.

Trigger Service portfolio revisions are recurring events—so *validate service portfolio* is typically triggered by a synchronized architecture calendar event.

Inputs The primary input is a service portfolio—for example, an enterprise or domain-level service portfolio. Note that architecture-relevant services include both architecture alternatives and an early architecture description in their service portfolio entries. Internally, the architecture organization utilizes additional inputs— for example, a domain baseline and target architecture or an architecture roadmap.

Outputs The output is an updated service portfolio that reflects the architecture function's input on the value, impact, cost, and risk of each service. Sign-off of the service portfolio is an additional output which is formally endorsed by the architecture function.

4.3.2.6   Validate Project Proposal

Purpose The *validate project proposal* service reviews a given project plan and ensures that the architecture organization is adequately involved and included in the project proposal. Based on previous contributions (e.g., elaborating alternatives and recommending the architecturally preferred alternative), this service contributes the architecture function's view to the business value, skills and resources, cost, schedules, and risk segments of the project proposal. The architecture function books the planned resources and capacities and ensures their availability at the start of the project. It documents its support and approval by formally endorsing the project proposal.

Trigger Project portfolio revisions are recurring events—thus, *validate project proposal* is triggered by a synchronized architecture calendar event. However, the service may also be triggered outside the regular project portfolio review cycle by an ad hoc project proposal.

Inputs The primary input is the project proposal. Internally, the architecture function utilizes further inputs, such as a domain baseline architecture, to examine dependent landscape assets and the likelihood that they will be affected by the project.

Outputs The output is an updated project proposal reflecting the inputs of the architecture function. Another side effect of providing this service is pre-booked architecture resources. By signing off on the project proposal, the architecture function formally confirms it.

4.3.3   Service Building Value Stream

The *service building value stream* is divided into the service plan, service architecture, service implementation, and service deployment stages. In the *service plan stage*, the *elaborate architecture mandate* service creates a mandate that specifies the relevant architecture obligations of a project. The service also ensures that the key parties involved formally endorse the mandate. In the *service architecture stage*, *elaborate service architecture* takes an architecture mandate as input and ensures that the mandated goal is pursued and the appropriate outcome is achieved. *Elaborate service architecture* also accompanies the physical implementation, testing, and delivery of the design. Finally, the service validates and endorses that the implementation design is within an acceptable design corridor (Fig. 4.15).

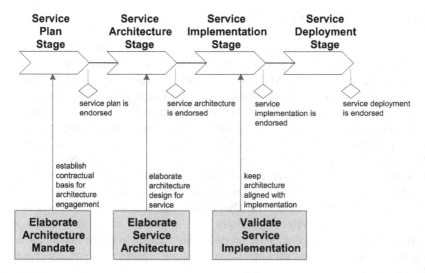

Fig. 4.15 Service building value stream architecture services

4.3.3.1 Elaborate Architecture Mandate

Purpose The *elaborate architecture mandate* service creates a mandate[31] that sets out the architecture commitments of a project. The service ensures that the mandate is formally agreed upon by the key parties involved. The main purpose of an architecture mandate is to clarify and specify design tasks, timelines, and deliverables. However, it also serves as a contractual basis between the architecture function and other organizations. A mandate accompanies inherently complex architecture endeavors, in other words, endeavors that are not sufficiently detailed by a simple service contract but necessarily require a more detailed specification of exactly what architectural contributions are expected.

Trigger Architecture mandates are a preliminary stage for elaborating the service architecture within projects. Therefore, project initiation usually triggers the *elaborate architecture mandate* service.

Inputs Typical inputs are the project proposal, the architecture portion contained therein, and pre-booked architecture resources and other capacities. However, the elaboration of a mandate may also be requested ad hoc.

Outputs The main output is a newly created or updated mandate that is signed off jointly by the project lead, the architecture function, and other project responsible parties.

---

[31] See the *Architecture Mandate* pattern in this book's pattern catalog (Chap. 6).

4.3.3.2   Elaborate Service Architecture

Purpose   *Elaborate service architecture*[32] takes an architecture mandate as input
and elaborates the design of an aspired asset so that the mandated output is delivered.
Although the name of the service indicates that architecture elaboration is limited to
assets of type *service*, the actual asset type for which a design is developed is
determined by the architecture mandate. The asset may be an enterprise service, an
application, a platform, or even a domain. The architects performing the service
interact intensively with other disciplines over several iterations to elaborate
the mandated design. They examine the context of the desired solution, explore
the problem at hand (e.g., requirements, constraints, risks), and continuously evolve
the design. Architecture design, physical implementation, testing, and deployment
seamlessly transition in iterations. This means that this service encompasses the
service architecture, service implementation, and *service deployment stages* and
fully accompanies the evolution of the architecture design to its physical implementation. The service also ensures that the architecture organization formally endorses
the implemented design.

Trigger   *Elaborate service architecture* is usually triggered during project initiation
and requires an architecture mandate as input.

Inputs   Minimal inputs are an architecture mandate and the early architecture vision
initially created by the *elaborate architecture alternatives* service. Additional inputs
include information about the context of the targeted solution, requirements it must
meet, or constraints it must cope with. Internally, the architecture organization uses
additional inputs to this service. These include descriptions of the domain architecture or reference assets, such as architecture patterns.[33]

Outputs   The main output is the newly created or evolved architecture design of the
targeted asset.

4.3.4   Service Running Value Stream

The *service running value stream* is subdivided into the *service monitoring and
detection, service diagnosis*, and *service problem resolution stages*. The *elaborate
architecture problem resolution* service analyzes the cause of a detected defect in the
service problem resolution stage. It suggests an architecture approach that is suited to
remedy or at least mitigate the defect (Fig. 4.16).

---

[32] See the *Solution Architecture Methodology* pattern in this book's pattern catalog (Chap. 6).

[33] See the *Architecture Pattern Methodology* pattern in this book's pattern catalog (Chap. 6).

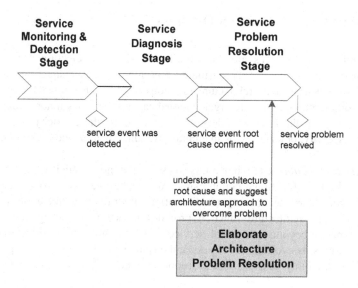

Fig. 4.16 Service running value stream

4.3.4.1   Elaborate Architecture Problem Resolution

Purpose The *elaborate architecture problem resolution* service analyzes the cause of a detected error and proposes an architecture approach that is suitable for overcoming or at least mitigating the defect. Think of this service as an adaptation or shrunken version of *elaborate service architecture*—shrunk in the sense that the architectural intervention is not intentional (e.g., to increase the feature set of a service) but is seen as unavoidable to overcome operational problems.

Trigger A problem detected in the operational environment of an architecture asset triggers *elaborate architecture problem resolution*. Sufficient capacity is critical for architects to execute the service immediately when the trigger is pulled.

Inputs The input is the observed problem, which contains all defect details collected by the operations organization. Internally, the architecture function uses the architecture descriptions of the faulty asset—for example, its solution architecture description and descriptions of any dependent assets, such as upstream or downstream applications or platforms.

Outputs Output is a description of the root cause of the problem and the proposed architecture approach to overcome it.

4.4   Architecture Function Qualities

While architecture services are the workhorses of an architecture organization
engagement model, the quality attributes presented in this chapter are equally
essential for ensuring that architecture functions meet organizational expectations
over the long term. Qualities are organizational capabilities that cannot be explicitly
requested (e.g., in the form of a service) but determine the elasticity, scalability,
reliability, security, or usability of an architecture function as a whole or the services
it provides.

Architecture qualities are inherently present, but not explicitly tangible and
available like their functional counterparts. Architecture services provide an overview of *what* an architecture organization offers. Examining architecture qualities
reveals *how* an architecture function provides its service offering and *how* it
addresses needs beyond individual services. For example, how an architecture
function ensures its evolutionary fitness and ensures that it can evolve its portfolio
of services smoothly and without disruption to the services it has previously
provided.

This chapter proposes a generic set of qualities. The focus for their descriptions is
on *what* an architecture function offers in terms of quality capabilities. Section 5.4
picks up the thread where it leaves off here and zooms into the white-box perspective
of each architecture quality to describe *how* it is ideally realized and implemented
(Fig. 4.17).

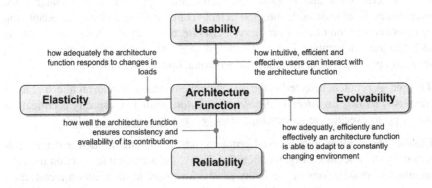

Fig. 4.17 Architecture function qualities

4.4.1 Architecture Function Usability

The Institute of Electrical and Electronics Engineers (IEEE) defines *usability* as (IEEE 2000):

> *Usability* is the ease with which an actor can learn to operate, prepare inputs for, and interpret outputs of a system.

Architecture function usability is the ease with which anyone interacting with it can *orient* themselves to the capabilities offered, learn and *understand* the particular value proposition, engage with the architecture function, actively *utilize* its offerings, and provide *feedback* or share thoughts with it. Architecture function usability also includes how architects understand their roles and responsibilities and comprehend their own processes, methods, and platforms. Usability significantly impacts the utilization, acceptance, and performance of all services that the architecture function offers. The truth about usability is brutal but simple. An offering that is not usable is a dysfunctional offering.

Ease of orientation, understanding, utilization, and feedback concern the corresponding learnability, efficiency, memorability, and satisfaction. *Learnability* is a measure of how intuitive and easy it is for an external actor to learn about the options for interacting with the architecture function and understand its offerings. For architects, learnability denotes the steepness with which an architect climbs the learning curve. *Efficiency* indicates the degree of productivity that external actors achieve when interacting with the architecture function. At the same time, *memorability* measures how easy it is for casual actors to remember the interaction protocols through which they interact with the architecture function. *Satisfaction*, finally, determines the comfort level of actors when interacting with the architecture function. Satisfying experiences build trust and increase the attractiveness of an offering (Fig. 4.18).

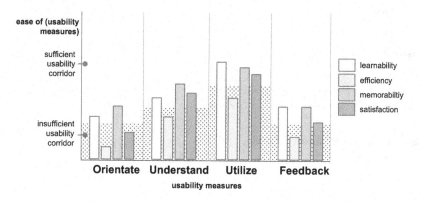

Fig. 4.18 Architecture function usability

4.4.2   Architecture Function Elasticity

The Merriam-Webster Dictionary (2020) defines elasticity as:

> The quality or state of being elastic, such as the quality of being adaptable, or the responsiveness of a dependent variable to changes in influencing factors.

Occasionally, *elasticity* and *scalability* are used interchangeably, and looking up *scalability* yields:

> Scalability is the capable of being easily expanded or upgraded in response to changing demand.

Architecture function elasticity is its ability to accommodate heavier (*area of exceptionally high demand*) or lighter (*area of exceptionally low demand*) loads in terms of demand for service requests or similar contributions. Elasticity is the property of an architecture function to handle an exceptionally high or low workload by increasing or decreasing capacity in a non-disruptive, efficient, and gradual manner. Architecture capacity is a prerequisite for an architecture function to satisfy stakeholder expectations regarding quantity, quality, and timeliness. Architecture functions aim to minimize both overcapacity and undercapacity, as both lead to avoidable costs. In particular, they aim to keep capacity within a reasonably *adequate performance corridor* (Fig. 4.19).

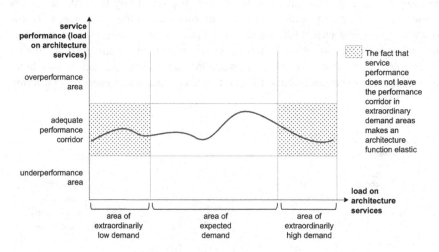

Fig. 4.19 Architecture function elasticity

4.4.3 Architecture Function Evolvability

In his seminal work *On the Origin of Species* (Darwin 1859), Charles Darwin established the theory of evolution based on the hypothesis that individuals of a species are not identical, characteristics are passed from generation to generation, more offspring are born than can survive, and only the survivors of competition for resources reproduce—that is, survive. The Merriam-Webster Dictionary (2020) defines *evolution* as:

> A process of change in a certain direction. A process of continuous change from a lower, simpler, or worse to a higher, more complex, or better state.

Evolvability[34] is the ease with which a system can be modified to improve relevant attributes or otherwise adapt[35] to a constantly changing environment. In the extreme case, evolvability means that a system can be modified for use in applications other than those for which it was originally designed.

Architecture function evolvability is its ability to absorb changes in the enterprise (e.g., new architecture services) with negligible or no disruption and continue to help the business achieve its strategic objectives. Hesham El-Rewini distinguishes different dimensions along which systems evolve. Suppose the dimensions referred to by El-Rewini in *Advanced Computer Architecture and Parallel Processing* (El-Rewini and Abd-El-Barr 2005) are generously applied to an architecture function context. In this case, three particular manifestations of evolvability emerge: organizational, service, and apparatus evolvability. *Organizational evolvability* is the ability of an architecture function to change its organizational scheme or geographic spread to absorb changes in the environment. For example, the architecture function is changed to reflect a newly created business unit (e.g., as a result of a corporate acquisition). *Service evolvability* is the ability of a function to expand, reduce, or otherwise significantly change its service offering without disrupting existing activities, for example, in response to new types of demands for the architecture function, or when substantially different service levels are required for existing services because regulations have changed. *Apparatus evolvability* is the ability to change or extend architecture methodologies, view models,[36] or platforms while sustaining an integrated experience (Fig. 4.20).

---

[34] See the *Managed Architecture Evolution* pattern in this book's pattern catalog (Chap. 6).

[35] See the *Architecture Methodology Adapter* pattern in this book's pattern catalog.

[36] See the *Your own Architecture View Model* pattern in this book's pattern catalog.

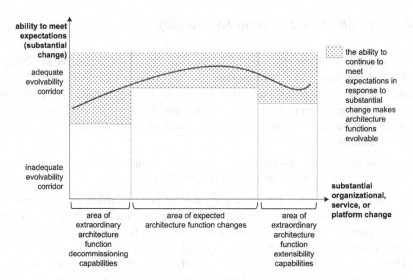

Fig. 4.20 Architecture function evolvability

4.4.4 Architecture Function Reliability

The Merriam-Webster Dictionary (2020) defines *reliable* as "yielding the same result on successive trials," and Wikipedia (2020) clarifies that:

> Reliability of a system emphasizes the ability of the system to function without failure— under stated conditions.

Architecture function reliability is a measure of its ability to maintain its states *consistently* and *effectively*. *Effectiveness* ensures that activities leave the desired footprints in reality. For a minimum level of effectiveness, architecture functions must execute services according to their service-level agreements (SLA[37]) using ACID[38] principles familiar from transaction processing. *Consistency* is its ability to ensure that state transitions are performed only between valid states. An architecture function specifies its valid states by prescribing appropriate policies. The state of an

---

[37] Service-level agreements (SLA) are commitments between service provider and service consumer. Particular aspects of a service are formally agreed in an SLA contract, for example, service availability, service response time, mean time to repair, or mean time between failures.

[38] ACID is short for atomicity, concurrency, isolation, and durability and refers to a set of properties designed to guarantee the validity of database transactions despite errors, power failures, or other mishaps. Atomicity guarantees that each transaction is treated as a single unit that either completely succeeds or entirely fails. Consistency ensures that transactions can only move a database from one valid state to another. Isolation ensures that concurrent execution of transactions leaves a database in the same state as if the transactions were sequentially executed. Durability ensures that once a transaction is committed, it remains committed even in the event of a system failure.

architecture function is determined by the set of processes, methodologies, roles, artifacts, platforms, and information currently in place and in use, for example, solution architecture descriptions of applications or architecture patterns that guide architects through platform customization in the enterprise security domain (Fig. 4.21).

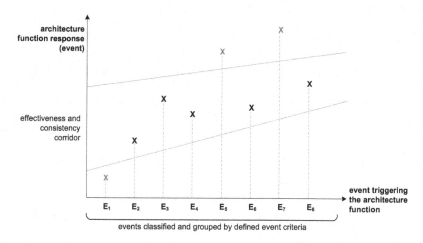

Fig. 4.21 Architecture function reliability

Further Reading

Bente, Stefan, Uwe Bombosch, and Shailendra Langade. 2012. *Collaborative Enterprise Architecture - Enriching EA with Lean, Agile, and Enterprise 2.0 Practices.* London: Elsevier.

Darwin, Charles. 1859. *On the Origin of Species.* London: John Murray.

El-Rewini, Hesham, and Mostafa Abd-El-Barr. 2005. *Advanced Computer Architecture and Parallel Processing.* New York: John Wiley & Sons.

Hull, Patrick, *Answer 4 Questions to Get a Great Mission Statement,* https://www.forbes.com/sites/patrickhull/2013/01/10/answer-4.questions-to-get-a-great-mission-statement/, Forbes, Forbes Media, 2013

IEEE Computer Society, *IEEE Recommended Practice for Architecture Description of Software-Intensive Systems,* IEEE std. IEEE – pp. 1472-2000, New York, 2000

Merriam-Webster, *Merriam-Webster Dictionary,* https://www.merriam-webster.com/dictionary, 2020

Wikipedia, *Reliability Engineering,* https://en.wikipedia.org/wiki/Reliability_engineering, 2020

Chapter 5
Architecture Function: Constitution

Abstract While Chap. 3 introduced contextual concepts such as a generic enterprise organization or an enterprise value chain, Chap. 4 looked at an architecture function from the outside (via a black-box perspective) and introduced its constituent, functional, and quality-related requirements. The present chapter switches from the black-box perspective (Chap. 4) to the white-box perspective and outlines the generic design of an architecture function. The generic design describes how it realizes the constituent, functional, and quality-related requirements for architecture functions, in turn referencing patterns in the pattern catalog (Chap. 6).

5.1 Overview

Chapter 3 introduced enterprise concepts that define the environment in which architecture functions operate. It introduced generic enterprise organizations and their collaborative relationships along a generic value chain. Chapter 4 related to these concepts and described the challenges that architecture functions fundamentally and recurrently face in a similarly generic manner. While Chap. 4 took a black-box perspective on an architecture function and described expectations for it, the present chapter takes a white-box view. It proposes a generic design of an architecture function that realizes the requirements from Chap. 4 (Fig. 5.1).

Architecture Function Pattern Topology

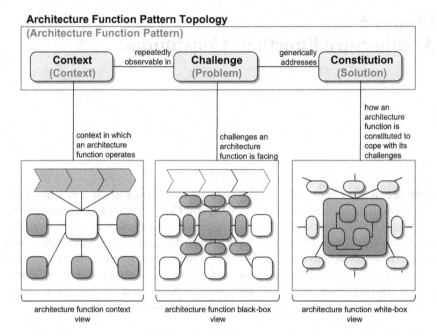

Fig. 5.1 Architecture function pattern (constitution)

The description of the architecture function design encompasses its core building blocks (Sect. 5.2), such as its organization, its engagement model, or its roadmap. Furthermore, the design includes the services (Sect. 5.3) and the qualities (Sect. 5.4) of a generic architecture function. For example, the design approach of an *assess architecture* service (Sect. 5.3.1.1) proposes a fundamental algorithmic schema for that service. Each of the proposed design approaches represents a solution aimed at addressing the expectations described in Chap. 4. The architecture function design descriptions are predominantly in plain text and refer intensively to the patterns in Chap. 6 (Fig. 5.2).

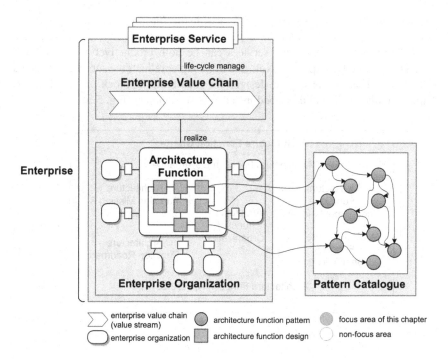

Fig. 5.2 Architecture pattern catalog reference

Note that references to patterns in the pattern catalog are usually placed at the end of a paragraph in parentheses and are specially formatted. For example, this text excerpt ORGANIZATIONAL REPLICATION refers to a pattern of the same name in Chap. 6. Follow the reference to a pattern, taking into account the notes made in the paragraph. In other words, read the pattern referenced at the end of the section in the context of the hints and details given in the paragraph. Note further that in each of the patterns referenced in this chapter, you will get similar references to other patterns. Follow these references in the same way, using paragraphs of each pattern description to contextualize a pattern referenced there.

5.2   Architecture Function

Section 4.2 provided an overview of the building blocks that make up an architecture function charter. For each building block, the challenges that need to be addressed were presented. An architecture function must be organizationally established and staffed (*architecture function organization*). It needs a sound understanding of how to guide, communicate, and interact with other organizations (*architecture function governance, architecture function engagement model,* and *architecture function communication*). It must also translate its mission (*architecture function mission and vision*) into an aligned *architecture function roadmap*. Finally, an *architecture function apparatus* ensures that services can be both productively delivered and efficiently captured and queried. Note that this chapter reflects the subsection schema of Sect. 4.2. That is, the generic designs for each building block proposed in this chapter are discussed and described in separate subchapters (Fig. 5.3).

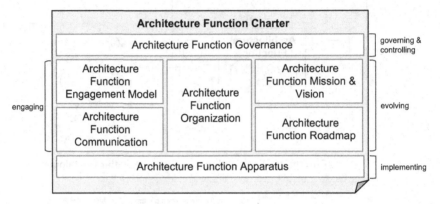

Fig. 5.3   Architecture function charter

At the end of your adaptation process, compile your own architecture function building blocks into an *architecture function charter*. Function charters are summarized descriptions of the function state, aspiration, and formal mandate. Design and position your function charter as a holistic manifesto for authorizing and mandating your enterprise's architecture function. Therefore, ensure that all relevant stakeholders formally approve and sign off on your function charter. In this way, you will fulfill a key requirement for making the expected contributions: well-coordinated collaboration between your architecture function and other enterprise organizations (**ARCHITECTURE MANDATE**).

5.2.1   Architecture Function Vision and Mission

Refer to your given enterprise context, and make sure to have the *vision and mission* of the next higher authority in your organization at hand. Use this as a reference point when creating a new *vision and mission* statement for the architecture function or thinking about evolving one that already exists. For example, refer to your IT department's *vision and mission* statement. An overarching *vision and mission* provides a framework and direction regarding the one you want to review, shape, or evolve. Note that the process of thinking and reflecting on *vision and mission* is a value in itself and is already halfway there for you. Avoid unproductive distractions, such as an early focus on wordsmithing. Instead, start with a rough draft and continually refine it. Coordinate your *vision and mission* statement with all key stakeholders and ensure that the *vision and mission* of the architecture function is formally signed off and supported at the end of each evolution.

Your initial step on the journey of *vision and mission* creation is to imagine and sketch an idealized future state of your function, ideal in the sense that this state harmonizes with the desired vision of your next higher authority or your enterprise as a whole. Detach from your current state—both in terms of the architecture function and the enterprise. Think of this step as a thought experiment, and mentally prepare yourself to imagine the idealized state of the architecture function from the other end. Describe the ideal future state by its attributes or properties, or by the contributions your function makes to help the enterprise achieve its goals in the future. Clarify *where* the architecture organization ought to be in the future and *why*. Next, describe *what* it contributes, *how*, and to *whom*, to accomplish the desired state transformation (Fig. 5.4).

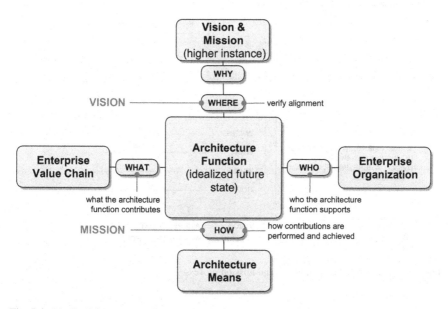

Fig. 5.4 Idealized future state of your architecture function

Start with *where* the idealized future state of your function lies so that it fits into the visions and missions of higher-level organizations. Next, consider your idealized *what*—that is, what you want your function to contribute and achieve for your business, for example, what additional services the architecture function should deliver and at what quality (e.g., transparency or agility). From the *what*, you derive *who* will benefit from the contributions you will make. Finally, consider and outline *how* your function will deliver the *what* and to *whom*. Once you have dreamed and described the future state of your function and confirmed alignment with its framing conditions, distill what you have identified as the *where*, *what*, *who*, and *how* into one simple statement each. The *where* and *what* are components of your *vision*, while the *what*, the *who*, and the *how* are mission components (Fig. 5.5).

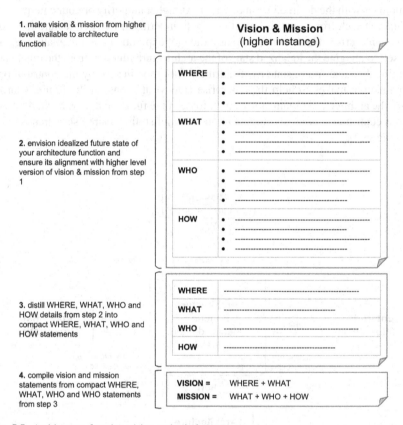

Fig. 5.5 Architecture function vision and mission process

Aside from the high-level process outlined above, consider the following heuristics for *vision and mission* statements. The first principle you apply is to *avoid waste*. Vision and mission statements are extreme distillates. Therefore, use the process of creating them to think about what is essential, not incidental, to your function. Clarify what your function should focus on and strive for. Another maxim preached by Agile is to *favor evolution over revolution*—so *avoid over-perfection*. Instead, consider the process of periodically reviewing the *vision and mission* of your function as a valuable check on your ambitions and aspirations and an opportunity to adjust direction where indicated. *Vision and mission* represent the primary focus of the architecture organization—so align your function's strategy and organizational goals with them.

5.2.2 Architecture Function Organization

An *architecture function organization* consists of an organizational chart, a role model, and staff who perform the roles through their competencies and skills. To realize the full potential of your function, it needs to be properly anchored in the enterprise organization. Ensure efficient and effective architecture practices by aligning the organization of your function with the needs and dynamics of the enterprise operating model, and ensure that it is fully embedded. The degree to which the interaction between an architecture function and its enterprise organization truly comes to life is an indicator of its effectiveness. An organization chart depicts the structural characteristics of an organization—for example, organizational structure, reporting system, committees, or the distribution of authority and power. Depending on its size, scope, and mandate, your function may be quite large, in which case it is deeply structured. Your architecture function typically includes committees, not visible on your organization chart, to which it delegates particular tasks and decisions. The *enterprise architecture board* of an entire company, the *technical architecture board* of all technical domains, or the *security architecture board* of the security domain are examples of such architecture committees.

Pay attention to the phenomenon that socio-technical systems (e.g., business organizations) replicate their internal structures, their motivations and tensions, or their conflicts into the technical systems they use or produce. Anticipate and mentally simulate how design decisions to be made for an organization replicate into the systems that organization uses or produces. If you agree with the simulation result, make the decision as intended. If the simulated outcome is unacceptable, adjust your organizational design decisions until you are satisfied with the projected system-level results (ORGANIZATIONAL REPLICATION).

Decide how your organization is organizationally embedded in the enterprise organization. An architecture organization can vary in size, embeddedness, or anchoring in an enterprise organizational schema. The approaches outlined here are complementary options that you can combine to design your function. An architecture function represented in the *corporate strategy* organization (1) oversees the entire enterprise. By taking a comprehensive view of the strengths, weaknesses, opportunities, and threats of the enterprise as a whole, the architecture function can holistically evaluate emerging technologies and their potential. Involving the architecture organization in *portfolio planning* (2) gives it authority over investment and disinvestment decisions across portfolio responsibilities of other disciplines and thus across all portfolios of the enterprise, for example, *service portfolio, application portfolio, platform portfolio, information portfolio,* or *project portfolio.* Thus, an architecture function can Pareto[1]-optimize enterprise domains and landscapes by, for example, promoting consolidation programs to reduce redundancies and free up operating costs. Architecture organizations anchored in *program management* (3) enable not only the making but also the enforcement and operationalization of portfolio decisions. An architecture function anchored in program management is well positioned to ensure that portfolio decisions are followed through to physical implementation. Embedding a subset of the architecture function into *corporate platforms and operations* (4) may complement the options discussed above. In this case, a subset of the overall function is specifically responsible for optimizing the portfolio of shared platforms and ensuring their reliable operation—for example, infrastructure and shared platform services. The final scenario is when each *business unit* (5) plans, builds, and runs its own replica of an architecture organization. This scenario must be combined with either the *corporate strategy* (1) or *portfolio planning* (2) approach so that a corporate architecture function ensures alignment across the entire enterprise (Fig. 5.6).

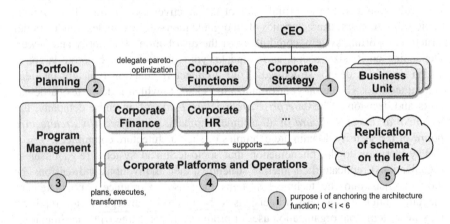

Fig. 5.6 Embedding the architecture function in an enterprise organization

Differentiate varying degrees of membership to architecture groups. In this model, the *core architecture group* is comparatively small and concentrates decision-making power, while the extended architecture group can be five to ten times larger. However, the *extended architecture group* often has no, or minimal, decision-making power compared to the group of core architects. Both the core and extended architecture groups are usually part of the formal organization. In contrast, the *architecture community group* may well span beyond pure architects and include

---

[1] Pareto optimum is an optimum at which no preference criterion can be better without at least one individual or preference criterion being worse off. The concept is named after Vilfredo Pareto (1848–1923), who used it to research economics.

anyone with a passion or responsibility for architecture. Despite its informal nature, a well-functioning community offers attractive potential for innovation. It can also increase the elasticity of an architecture function by serving as a pool of resources that can be developed and promoted to the extended architecture group on relatively short notice. This is an exciting option for managing peak loads by flexibly ramping up and down the capacity of your function on short notice (ARCHITECTURE CAPACITY) (Fig. 5.7).

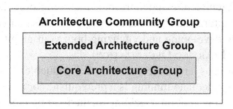

Fig. 5.7 Architecture group belonging

Design your architecture role model to reliably deliver the services and qualities required to support your enterprise value chain. The specific design of your role model will depend on numerous factors, such as your decision on an organization scheme, distribution of power, or your considerations about the size of a core versus an extended architecture group. Regardless of how you specifically design your role model, you should group similar roles into architecture disciplines to increase efficiency in recruitment, assignment, and development (ARCHITECTURE ROLE, ENTERPRISE ARCHITECTURE DISCIPLINE, DOMAIN ARCHITECTURE DISCIPLINE, SOLUTION ARCHITECTURE DISCIPLINE).

Align and associate your architecture role and discipline model to the different levels of oversight, and scale your enterprise organization distinguishes. For example, distinguish one enterprise level, two domain levels, and two solution levels vertically from each other. The higher-level domain level distinguishes between business and technical domains, while the higher-level solution level differentiates large or significant solution assets from relatively insignificant ones. In addition to organizational levels and areas of responsibility, you should consider the nature and composition of your enterprise assets and the relationships between them in your organization design. For example, the ability to clearly delineate an architecture asset is a prerequisite for assigning ownership or other types of attention between a role and an asset. Your architecture organization must reflect asset delineation—at a minimum, it must reflect the logic inherent in delineating your architecture domains (ARCHITECTURE LEVEL, ARCHITECTURE DEMARCATION, ARCHITECTURE ASSET).

Another essential facet of organization design is the coupling between organizations and domains. An organization takes ownership and lifecycle responsibility for a domain. A perfect organization design optimally handles the challenges an organization faces today. Organizational designs change frequently in response to their ever-changing environment, for example, when new regulations are enacted or new competitors enter the market. The high frequency of organizational change contrasts with the low frequency of change regarding the schema of architecture domains. The schema of a domain represents the abstract structures of a topic of enterprise interest, so it changes less frequently and fundamentally over time. Therefore, the looser you make the link between organizations and their associated domains, the more independently organizations and domains can evolve at their own pace (ARCHITECTURE OWNERSHIP, DOMAIN-ORGANIZATION AGNOSTICISM).

Transform your architecture function into a learning organization. Ensure that you systematically capture and share the collective insights that your architects gain, thereby continuously developing and vitalizing both your architects and your organization as a whole (LEARNING ORGANIZATION).

Architecture functions are expected to make valuable contributions to their businesses. However, adequate funding is a prerequisite for an architecture function to make the expected contribution. Deciding on the funding model is one of the most critical decisions an organization must make. For example, prefer a *cost center funding model* if the contributions of your function cannot be easily linked to business results. In contrast, architecture functions managed as *profit centers* are driven and shaped by the demands of other enterprise organizations. Profit center-based functions will therefore primarily make contributions that are deemed valuable by individual enterprise organizations. As a result, architecture contributions that are nonetheless valuable from a cross-organizational perspective are not demanded, not recognized, and thus not made (ARCHITECTURE FUNDING).

Make versus delegate is another important design decision you need to make at the organizational level. While an architecture function ensures that the services provided are of the promised quality, you must decide whether service delivery is in the hands of your own architects (*make*) or delegated (*delegate*) and provided by a similarly competent and capable external architecture party. In other words, you must make architecture sourcing decisions for each of the branches of your organization (ARCHITECTURE SOURCING).

Regularly review the design of your architecture organization to ensure that it is evolving appropriately within an environment of ever-changing conditions. Derive criteria from your vision, mission, and strategy that are suitable for defining an evolution corridor. An evolution corridor allows you to consider, for individual architecture decisions, whether the corridor covers them (i.e., whether the decision can be made) or is already outside of it (i.e., whether the decision must be discarded). The criteria enable objective dialogues about whether a discussed organizational change and its system-level consequences are still inside or already outside an evolutionary corridor (ARCHITECTURE CONDITION, MANAGED ARCHITECTURE EVOLUTION).

5.2.3 Architecture Function Engagement Model

Defining and staffing an architecture function does not automatically result in any architect being actively involved in enterprise processes. An *architecture function engagement model* informs everyone in the enterprise about the various possibilities to engage with the architecture organization as well as how to specifically engage.

Define your engagement model by clarifying the details of the building blocks it is composed of. Define who can engage with the architecture function, for example, the entire business organization, a limited subset of it, or the architects within the architecture organization. Next, define the types of engagements your function needs to support. Derive this set of engagements from the contributions you expect to make along the enterprise value chain. For each engagement type (*engagement event*), define whether it is explicitly or implicitly triggered and how it is performed, including its inputs and outputs. Finally, define the *engagement interfaces* your function should support to efficiently handle corresponding events (Fig. 5.8).

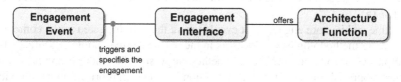

Fig. 5.8 Architecture function engagement model building blocks

Start with *what* your function needs to support. Derive the *what* from the contributions expected along your enterprise value chain. Specify the identified contribution requirements in terms of *engagement event types*. For example, give every event type a *name*, describe its *purpose*, and clarify which *source* emits signals *triggering* the event and the associated *inputs* and *outputs* (Fig. 5.9).

Fig. 5.9 Engagement event

Engagement Event

Name:	
Purpose:	
Trigger:	{explicit, implicit}
Source:	{human actor, system, rule}
Input(s):	
Output(s):	

Define architecture services as responses to each specified type of engagement event. Use the services suggested in Sect. 5.3 as a starting point. However, tailor the proposed generic services to your particular situation or add services you do not find in my generic service portfolio but still need in your organization, for example, a service that seeks landscape decommissioning opportunities (**DECOMMISSIONING REWARD**).

Define which *source* can trigger which engagement event. For example, the service portfolio organization can trigger the *review architecture event* associated with the *assess architecture* service in the architecture function's service catalog. Specify the *inputs* required to perform the service and clarify the *outputs* produced by its execution. A service can be explicitly requested, for example, by a service portfolio manager. Make all services that can be ordered by human actors requestable in your service catalog. At a minimum, set up an architecture calendar for your function so that you can regularly schedule required service launches by automatically firing corresponding engagement events. For example, schedule an annual *review and endorse service portfolio event* in your architecture calendar to recurrently trigger the associated *validate service portfolio* service (**ARCHITECTURE CALENDAR**).

Define architecture engagement events where they are triggered in the context of performing methodologies or processes in the respective methodology artifacts. For example, your solution architecture methodology specifies that an architect must request approval for an elaborated solution by the appropriate domain review committee. In this way, ensure that contributions are systematically requested and delivered accordingly. Increase or amplify the effect of automatically solicited architecture contributions by similarly integrating events directly into your architecture platform. For example, have an *assess architecture* event triggered when a released model is changed in your modeling platform (**YOUR OWN ARCHITECTURE METHODOLOGY, YOUR OWN ARCHITECTURE PLATFORM**).

Finally, establish a *single point of contact* (SPOC) as a one-stop shop for your architecture function. An architecture SPOC acts as a façade[2] for the function's organizational units that provide services or otherwise handle incoming requests. As a result, an architecture SPOC takes the guesswork out of telling function customers which part of the organization is responsible for a particular contribution. A SPOC greatly improves the ergonomics and usability of interacting with your function. It also serves as a central point of contact for services—especially services not yet available in your function's portfolio. In other words, an architecture SPOC can be seen as a catch-all service. Also, offer your customers the opportunity to direct comments, ideas, or unmet expectations to an appropriate feedback channel in your SPOC organization (**ARCHITECTURE SPOC**).

---

[2]Façade, organizational facade. A facade is a function that serves as a front-facing organization and masks a more complex underlying organizational structure. Facades improve the usability of the organization scheme they mask. They serve as an intervention point for improving the interaction between architecture functions and business organizations.

5.2.4 Architecture Function Communication

Communication and language are the ultimate means on which any human interaction is built; common concepts and protocols are its concrete. Communication permeates every action in the enterprise—whether coordination, performance, or decision-making. Yet, despite its importance, a great deal of communication takes place inattentively or even unconsciously. The building block *architecture function communication* is dedicated to maintaining or improving conscious communication and is thus a central prerequisite for appropriate architecture contributions.

Make communication a separate chapter in your architecture charter. Assign accountability for communication to the leadership of the architecture function, and assign personal communication responsibilities to all architects for their areas of responsibility to minimize the risks and associated costs of miscommunication. For example, include communication-oriented objectives in your role descriptions as well as your architects' incentive plans. Prohibit questioning or continually re-discussing established conceptualizations. In contrast, value design descriptions that comprehensively refer to, e.g., standardized domain concepts (**ARCHITECTURE ROLE, ARCHITECTURE OWNERSHIP**).

Establish communication channels through which you can reach all relevant stakeholder groups and interact with them reciprocally, for example, architecture webinars, community wikis, or chatbots for frequently asked architecture questions. Pre-register all architects for your communication channels, but let other interested parties subscribe as well. Push relevant information into the channels regularly, and assign individuals responsible for following up on each incoming message or conversation. Delegate responsibility for ensuring responsiveness overseeing all communication channels between enterprise organizations and your architecture SPOC (**ARCHITECTURE** SPOC).

Tailor the *what, why,* and *how* of your communication to the targeted stakeholder groups. This means that the *what, why,* and *how* of communication are a function of the *who*. When communicating with non-architecture stakeholders, focus on the *why*[3] and only address the *what* or *how* if it is essential.

Communicate general information about the architecture function regularly. For example, publish the monthly function scorecard via an architecture newsletter. Use calendars to ensure regularity in your communications. Make your calendar itself publicly available to provide insight into the architecture schedule. Consider opening a calendar to *write operations* so that scheduling requests can be communicated

---

[3] Start with why (Sinek 2009). In his inspiring TED Talk, Sinek points out that people are inspired by a sense of purpose (i.e., the why) and that this should come first in communication, even before the how and the what. Sinek calls this triad the golden circle. In the innermost circle is the why. This circle represents people's motives or purposes. In the next circle is the how, which represents people's processes or methods. Finally, in the outermost circle is the what, which represents results or outcomes. For experts, the way from the outside to the inside is acceptable—for non-expert communities, good communication leads from the inside to the outside. In other words, good communication starts with the why.

directly to the architecture function through the calendar. Schedule regular communication events, for example, a monthly exchange of the entire architecture community where an open discussion of project successes and failures can take place (ARCHITECTURE CALENDAR).

Establish a foundation of commonly clarified and fundamental architecture concepts within and outside your function. A shared understanding of crucial concepts is an essential prerequisite for any function. It enables an organization to accomplish its mission, while a lack of common conceptual ground inevitably leads to miscommunication—and ultimately to dysfunctionality (ARCHITECTURE LANGUAGE).

Similar to the common language described above, you should clarify and define common concepts for each domain in your enterprise. The set of common concepts in a domain and the relationships between those concepts are called a domain taxonomy. Think of a *domain taxonomy* as a knowledge model that clarifies the basic abstractions that exist in a respective domain. A domain taxonomy equips architects with a normalized, domain-specific language that enables efficient and effective communication within a domain. An architecture language can be thought of as a domain taxonomy for the domain of architecture (DOMAIN TAXONOMY).

5.2.5 Architecture Function Governance

In addition to the architecture organization, its engagement model, and orderly communication, you need a common set of ethics, rules, and policies so that complex social systems can operate in a coordinated, organized, and well-aligned manner. *Architecture governance* is a branch of the *architecture function* and an integral part of *enterprise governance*. Architecture governance provides direction to ensure that the architecture function fulfills its responsibilities to support alignment and maximize or protect business value (1). It implements controls to steer all architecture activities toward the specified direction based on processes, policies, guidelines, reference architecture assets, or methodologies (2). Finally, architecture governance ensures that all contributions are made in accordance with the specified rules and policies (3) (Fig. 5.10).

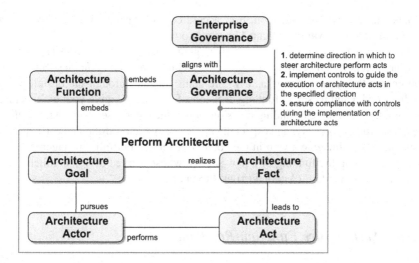

Fig. 5.10 Architecture governance

Begin by establishing the directions and goals toward which governance should direct all *architecture perform acts*. One direction might be to ensure that design documentation exists for every enterprise application. Another example of a direction is the goal of ensuring that new services are added to the enterprise service portfolio only with the approval of the architecture function. Capture the identified goals and directions in the form of policies and be sure to maintain and evolve your policies over time to keep them current and fresh (**Architecture Policy**).

Next, for each goal, determine which architecture control is best suited to ensure the practical tracking of direction in the day-to-day operations of your function. Architecture governance permeates all building blocks of the architecture function— for example, its organization, engagement model, and services or apparatus. Each building block provides its own types of controls and governance capabilities, which you may consider. For example, you can further decompose the organization building block into architecture boards, which you assign the task of directing and controlling design activities within their areas of responsibility. A *security architecture governance board* is tasked with steering design activities within the security domain, while an *architecture methodology governance board* is tasked with the controlled evolution of methodologies and frameworks (**Architecture Governance**).

Introduce controls via architecture methodologies to embed governance mechanisms into your architects' daily lives, to give them traction. For instance, embed pattern conformance testing as a mandatory checkpoint in your enterprise's solution architecture methodology. By systematically embedding this checkpoint, you ensure that every design adopts mandatory architecture security patterns when implementing user authentication, user access control, or a certified authorization system (**YOUR OWN ARCHITECTURE METHODOLOGY**).

You ensure that your control mechanism gains traction in the day-to-day lives of your architects by embedding controls into architecture methodologies. Similarly, you ensure that your function as a whole gains traction through the design of its funding model and its say in funding decisions. For example, give your architecture function the right to veto funding decisions along the enterprise value chain. Define these veto rights precisely, and especially enable vetoes at portfolio and early design decision stages. Imagine a veto in the context of service portfolio management, for example, vetoing the funding of a new service whose aspired design conflicts with an architecture standard (**ARCHITECTURE FUNDING**).

5.2.6   Architecture Function Roadmap

A roadmap is a detailed plan used to guide progress toward a desired target state. With an *architecture function roadmap*, an architecture organization can systematically evolve from a current state (*architecture function baseline*) to a desired future state (*architecture function target*). View the architecture organization as an architecture asset, and apply roadmap practices to create and evolve its future plan. An architecture function roadmap views the architecture organization as a system itself. It is an informative and prescriptive tool that you use to ensure that the planned states of your function are understood, deliberately agreed upon, and aligned. It also ensures that progress toward the desired future function state can be tracked systematically and in accordance with the confirmed plan. Regularly validate and evolve your function roadmap as environmental conditions change (**BASELINE ARCHITECTURE VERSUS TARGET ARCHITECTURE**, **ARCHITECTURE ROADMAP METHODOLOGY**).

Reflect on the architecture function's baseline and a corresponding aspirational target in terms of maturity. A maturity model allows your function and its sponsors to regularly reflect on the steps you have taken toward set targets—for example, the goal of overcoming current deficiencies, such as the lack of offerings in the architecture service portfolio. If your maturity reflection shows that the steps you have taken are not appropriate to move your function forward in the desired direction, make any necessary adjustments to your function roadmap. Be sure to justify any roadmap adjustments with measured maturity evidence. Introduce key performance indicators[4] (KPIs) to quantify and systematically measure architecture maturity. For example, measure your function's contribution to enterprise goals by its business alignment (e.g., measured by operational plan and budget approval), by the value it delivers (e.g., measured by business performance), by its ability to manage costs

---

[4]Key Performance Indicators (KPIs) measure and indicate the performance of an organization or activity based on an underlying performance measurement metric.

(e.g., measured by achieving cost targets), or by its ability to manage risk (e.g., measured by internal audit results). To give another example, measure the level of customer focus of your architecture function by customer satisfaction (e.g., measured by survey scores) or cost competitiveness (e.g., measured by achieving cost targets). You may also measure the operational excellence of your function, for example, by the maturity of architecture processes and management (e.g., measured by the number of approved architectures that were successful, e.g., because they were reliable and modifiable) (ARCHITECTURE MATURITY).

Create a segment for each building block on the architecture function roadmap (i.e., architecture function organization, engagement model, services, qualities, communications, and apparatus). Further subdivide each building block segment into meaningful sub-segments. For example, subdivide the service segment into sub-segments along the enterprise value chain and form service clusters for the service planning, service building, and service running value streams. To give another example, divide architecture function qualities into *design time*, *runtime*, and *manage time* qualities. Runtime qualities, such as usability, tend to be qualities that can be optimized and changed in a timely manner. In contrast, design-time qualities, such as the architecture organization's evolvability, tend to require medium- to longer-term change efforts (Fig. 5.11).

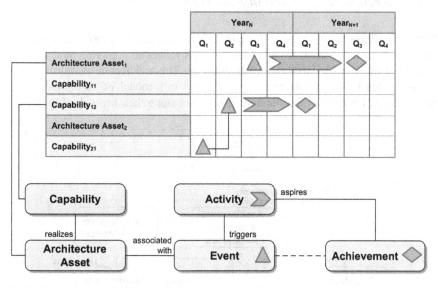

Fig. 5.11 Architecture function roadmap

Decompose the organization segment into the architecture levels as defined in your enterprise. This enables a differentiated discussion of organizational targets for each architecture level. Besides the levels, consider a complementary decomposition of the architecture organization along your enterprise's domain topology. Domain topology segmentation often borrows from architecture levels. Thus, viewed from the top down, an initial domain division may distinguish between business and technical domains, while a more finely granular domain division continues below (ARCHITECTURE LEVEL, DOMAIN TAXONOMY, BUSINESS VERSUS TECHNICAL).

Decompose the architecture apparatus segment into a sub-segment for your methodologies, which in turn is decomposed into your assessment methodology, reference architecture methodology, and solution and domain architecture elaboration methodologies. Also, decompose the architecture apparatus segment into a sub-segment for your reference assets, such as architecture patterns or principles. Finally, decompose the segment into sub-segments for your architecture platforms, such as an architecture repository or service portal (YOUR OWN ARCHITECTURE METHODOLOGY, REFERENCE ARCHITECTURE METHODOLOGY, YOUR OWN ARCHITECTURE PLATFORM).

5.2.7 Architecture Function Apparatus

The *architecture function apparatus* equips your function with tools for efficiency and effectiveness—increasing its productivity. It relates to your role model and is composed of your platform and methodologies. The architecture platform implements (at least in part) the methodologies and role model of your function. It physically stores your artifacts and manages them along their lifecycle (Fig. 5.12).

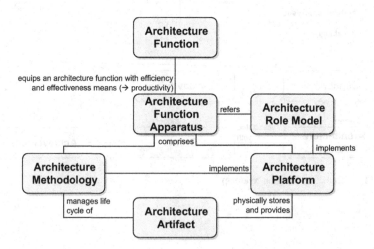

Fig. 5.12 Architecture function apparatus

Recognize that the architecture apparatus is itself an architecture asset. More specifically, it is a structural asset (*domain*) that deserves appropriate domain architecture attention in terms of lifecycle management. Consider assigning responsibility for the apparatus domain to the governance branch of your architecture function. In any case, be sure to combine responsibility for the architecture methodology with responsibility for the apparatus platforms to achieve a high degree of alignment and implementation coherence (ARCHITECTURE ASSET).

Appoint a domain architect for your apparatus who captures your current apparatus design in a corresponding baseline description. Next, the domain architect develops a feasible target architecture description against the backdrop of unmet needs in your enterprise. Finally, the architect reflects his or her planning in the apparatus roadmap, aligns it with the architecture function roadmap and other relevant stakeholders, and continues the lifecycle management of the apparatus domain (DOMAIN ARCHITECTURE METHODOLOGY).

Leverage the potential for rules and policies that an architecture function platform inherently provides by integrating and implementing essential controls of your governance framework into the apparatus platform, practices, and methodologies (ARCHITECTURE POLICY, ARCHITECTURE GOVERNANCE).

Implement critical parts of your architecture methodologies directly into your platform to increase the systematicity, repeatability, and traction of architecture governance and performance across the enterprise. This drives alignment, standardization, and economies of scale. Integrate your architecture platform with key partner platforms and systems. For example, integrate it with your portfolio management systems to ensure mutual alignment and consistency of the capabilities, services, applications, information, platforms, and technologies used across your organization. Consider integrating your architecture platform with systems that reflect the operational reality in your enterprise data centers or cloud platforms in the form of data—for example, configuration management bases or event logs (YOUR OWN ARCHITECTURE METHODOLOGY, YOUR OWN ARCHITECTURE PLATFORM).

5.3 Architecture Function Services

Section 4.3 presents a generic set of architecture services as they might be offered and exposed via an architecture service catalog (Fig. 5.13).

Architecture Function Service Catalogue		
Service Planning Value Stream	**Service Building Value Stream**	**Service Running Value Stream**
• Validate strategy • Propose architecture demand • Determine architecture relevance • Elaborate architecture alternatives • Validate service portfolio • Validate project proposal	• Elaborate architecture mandate • Elaborate service architecture	• Elaborate architecture problem resolution
• Elaborate domain architecture • Assess architecture		

Fig. 5.13 Architecture function service catalog

Section 4.3 described architecture services from a black-box perspective—i.e., it showed *what* an architecture function commonly contributes to an enterprise value chain and other enterprise organizations. This chapter zooms into the services presented in Sect. 4.3 and presents, for each service, the internal mechanism for realizing the service. Thus, this chapter depicts the generic algorithm of each service and *how* it reliably delivers promised outputs in response to the received inputs.

This chapter, similar to Sect. 5.2, mirrors the subchapter scheme of Sect. 4.3 so that the proposed design for each architecture service is discussed and described separately. In each of the following service descriptions, the service specification from Sect. 4.3 precedes the proposed service design to provide sufficient context. The service design describes in detail how a service realizes its contributions along the enterprise value chain. The service designs are generic in nature and accordingly outline general considerations of consumed inputs, processes, activities, methods, and platforms used to create and develop artifacts that the service delivers as outputs (Fig. 5.14).

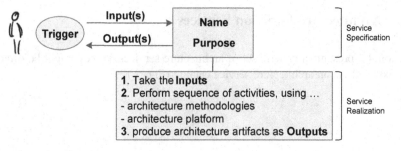

Fig. 5.14 Architecture service realization

5.3.1 All Value Streams

The enterprise value chain is divided into the streams of *service planning, building, running,* and *delivering.* Both *elaborate domain architecture* and *assess architecture* are services that accompany the entire enterprise value chain. While *elaborate domain architecture* is an ongoing service, *assess architecture* is performed on request. In *assess architecture,* the current stream contextualizes the service and determines its execution semantics. In *service planning, assess architecture* is performed to analyze the impact of planned changes, while in *service building,* assessments aim to verify the appropriateness of an elaborated architecture design. For example, assessments verify that a newly designed application complies with enterprise architecture standards. In *service running,* architecture assessments are performed to determine what caused a detected defect so that it can be fixed immediately (Fig. 5.15).

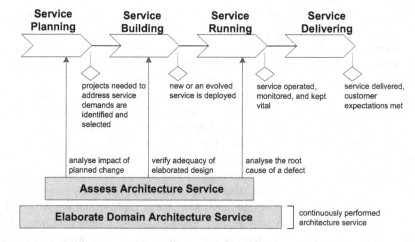

Fig. 5.15 Enterprise value chain architecture services

5.3.1.1 Assess Architecture

The *assess architecture* service, whose interface is specified in Sect. 4.3.1.1, validates the result of an architecture elaboration activity based on the assessment drivers, the architecture drivers, and the produced architecture description.

Before we take a closer look at the algorithm of this generic assess architecture service, a few primary considerations are essential. For example, if you have not already done so, you should derive your function's own assessment methodology from an appropriate architecture assessment methodology standard. Establishing and using your own assessment methodology will provide you with a systematic and repeatable approach to analyzing the designs of your enterprise assets along a metric that is objective but tailored to your enterprise. Your own assessment methodology is the workhorse upon which you will later perform concrete assessments (**YOUR OWN ARCHITECTURE METHODOLOGY, ARCHITECTURE ASSESSMENT METHODOLOGY**).

Design your assessment methodology such that it can be flexibly adapted to the contexts you intend to support. However, ensure that your methodology design remains open to adding further assessment contexts so that you can scale your methodology beyond the scenarios you originally supported. Therefore, design the core of your assessment method to be generic throughout, so that the application of the method is instantiated by selecting and applying an architecture assessment adapter to a particular validation scenario. For example, consider an assessment adapter for examining technical assets versus an adapter for evaluating business assets. While the consistency and coherence of information are the focus of business asset assessments, their shared use and thus runtime qualities such as scalability or availability are usually the focus of technical asset evaluations (**ARCHITECTURE METHODOLOGY ADAPTER**).

Next, create an initial set of adapters, with each adapter guiding an assessment team through the optimal application of the method in light of the supported assessment context. The *assess architecture* service supports three distinct assessment scenarios. Therefore, create at least three assessment adapters. Your first adapter (*new architecture asset adapter*) supports a scenario in which an assessment is performed to validate the architectural appropriateness of a new asset. The assessment adapter requires two inputs: the new asset's design description and the elaboration activity's mandate statement. Appropriateness is analyzed and reported in terms of the degree to which the proposed design deviates from the given mandate.

Your second assessment adapter (*existing architecture asset adapter*) supports a scenario where a change to an existing asset is planned. The assessment team is asked to validate the proposed design before the change is physically implemented. In this scenario, your assessment adapter steers the team through utilizing the assessment method such that the team anticipates the impact of the proposed change on the environment. Costly rollbacks of physically implemented architecture changes are a result of not performing such preemptive impact analysis.

Your third assessment adapter (*architecture asset defect adapter*) supports a scenario where defects or other operational deficiencies have been observed in an execution environment. The first goal is to understand what originally caused the observed defect (*root cause analysis*). The second goal is to make a refactoring proposal that is suitable to fix the observed defects, or at least mitigate their undesired effects (Fig. 5.16).

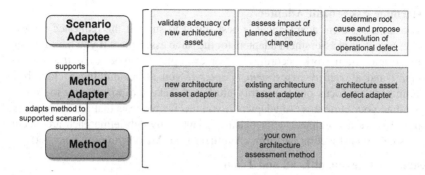

Fig. 5.16 Architecture assessment method adapters

Request Assessment

Initiate the *assess architecture* service in response to an assessment request received from an *assessment requester*. Verify the adequacy of the *assessment inputs* received, check feasibility, and agree on roles and responsibilities on both sides of the service (Fig. 5.17).

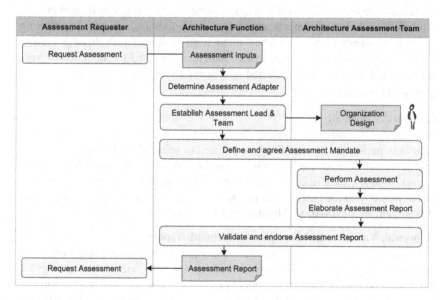

Fig. 5.17 Assess architecture process

Determine Assessment Adapter

Select an assessment adapter that is best suited to support the requested scenario. Combine multiple assessment adapters for the same assessment if you have designed your adapter framework accordingly. For example, combine a *cloud assessment adapter* and a *security assessment adapter* if you are examining a cloud-based solution with a focus on its security attributes. Take the opportunity to consider extending your current set of adapters if you receive requests that are not supported today. Evolve and enhance your existing adapters by debriefing each architecture assessment your function performs (**ARCHITECTURE METHODOLOGY ADAPTER**).

Establish Assessment Lead and Team

Appoint an assessment lead and establish an assessment team. Ensure that the agreed-upon roles are also assumed on the requester's side. Ensure everyone involved in performing the assessment—requester and assessment team—is familiar with the assessment method itself. Include an appropriate training offering in your training program. Provide tailored training on the architecture assessment method and its adapters to your architecture and non-architecture community (**LEARNING ORGANIZATION**).

Define and Agree Assessment Mandate

Create a concrete mandate for assessments with fuzzy expectations. The purpose of an architecture assessment mandate is to enable and encourage sufficient clarification before formal commitments are made—i.e., before assessments are performed. Assessment mandates help an assessment team continually calibrate its altitude during the engagement. In other words, mandates are used to continuously verify that assessments are being conducted in a manner that meets expectations (**ARCHITECTURE MANDATE**).

Perform Assessment

Next, the *architecture assessment team* performs the assessment. The assessment method is performed by iteratively applying the selected adapters, increasing the level of detail to meet the assessment mandate. Assessments are labor-intensive, interaction-heavy undertakings. Therefore, make sure that you have sufficient free capacity—both on the part of your function and on the part of the assessment client (**ARCHITECTURE ASSESSMENT METHODOLOGY, ARCHITECTURE CAPACITY**).

Elaborate, Validate, and Endorse Assessment Report

The assessment team compiles the observations, findings, and recommendations into an assessment report (*elaborate assessment report*). The *assessment report* is validated and endorsed within the architecture function before it is released and communicated to the requestor (*receive assessment report*) (**ARCHITECTURE GOVERNANCE**).

5.3.1.2 Elaborate Domain Architecture

The *elaborate domain architecture* service, whose interface is specified in Sect. 4.3. 1.2, accompanies the entire lifecycle of all assets within a domain—i.e., their planning, building, running, and decommissioning stages. The service continuously evolves baseline and target architecture overviews, an architecture roadmap, and reference assets for the respective domains. Domain architecture descriptions are used extensively by other services.

Establish your own domain architecture methodology to underpin the *elaborate domain architecture* service with a systematic and repeatable approach to holistic lifecycle management of all assets within a domain. Domain methodologies are super-methodologies. They include or refer to solution architecture and reference architecture methodologies, as well as assessment methodologies. A solution methodology applied to an architecture domain considers the domain as a coarse-grained solution. When applying the solution perspective, a domain architect views landscape assets and domains as black boxes to examine the coarse-grained dependencies between them. Both the baseline and target architecture of a domain are depicted by applying the coarse-grained solution perspective. Reference architecture methods equip domains with reference assets, such as architecture patterns, or principles. Finally, assessment methodologies are used in a domain architecture context to evaluate and validate domain-level changes at the respective lifecycle stages (YOUR OWN ARCHITECTURE METHODOLOGY, DOMAIN ARCHITECTURE METHODOLOGY).

Design your domain methodology to be flexible for different types of domains with appropriate method adapters. Support core domains such as *finance, purchasing*, or *human resources* and cross-cutting domains such as *security, performance*, or *usability* with respective adapters. However, ensure that your domain methodology design remains open to adding more contexts via appropriate adapters to scale your methodology beyond the originally supported scenarios. Therefore, design the core of your methodology generically so that it can be instantiated into a specific method for a specific domain by selecting and applying an appropriate adapter. Early on, define at least one adapter for business and one for technical domains (ARCHITECTURE METHODOLOGY ADAPTER, BUSINESS VERSUS TECHNICAL).

Elaborate domain architecture is an architecture lifecycle service. This means that the service is continuously performed—a perpetual activity. However, before the service can be continually performed (*continuous lifecycle management phase*), a new domain must first be born (*initiation phase*) (Fig. 5.18).

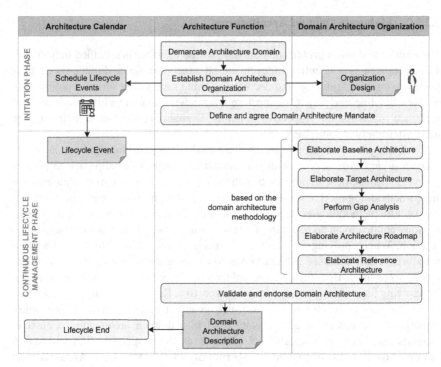

Fig. 5.18 Elaborate domain architecture process

Demarcate Architecture Domain

Define a new architecture domain by determining its scope and boundaries, its inherent assets, and its relationships to other domains. In architecture, a domain provides a boundary around an area of interest so that architects can refer to the area by name and discuss related matters based on a common conceptual foundation. You determine relationships to other domains based on relationships between assets that cross domain boundaries. Aggregation relationships, typically based on architecture levels, are another category of relationships that exist between domains and delineate them from one another (**ARCHITECTURE DEMARCATION, ARCHITECTURE LEVEL**).

Establish Domain Architecture Organization

Appoint a domain architect, or establish a new *domain architecture organization*. Familiarize the domain organization with the enterprise, domain, and solution architecture disciplines. Ensure that everyone involved in performing domain architecture activities is knowledgeable about relevant processes, methodologies, view models, rules, and policies (**ENTERPRISE ARCHITECTURE DISCIPLINE, DOMAIN ARCHITECTURE DISCIPLINE, SOLUTION ARCHITECTURE DISCIPLINE**).

Establish domain-specific *calendars* to *schedule lifecycle events* for each domain. A calendar automatically notifies architects of appropriate calendar events and triggers architecture activities along the lifecycle stages of a domain (*continuous lifecycle management phase*) (**ARCHITECTURE CALENDAR**).

Define and Agree Domain Architecture Mandate

Define and agree on a specific mandate with the domain architecture organization. A domain architecture mandate clarifies the mission, vision, and organization of the new domain, its inherent assets, its horizontal and vertical boundaries, and its associated domains. Align the mandate with an *architecture function charter* as described in Sect. 5.2. Mandates help domain architecture organizations understand how their area of responsibility is embedded in the surrounding domains—and ultimately how their domain is embedded in the overall enterprise. This enables domain organizations to anticipate both outbound and inbound impacts of domain changes and thus carefully monitor their dependency hotspots (**ARCHITECTURE MANDATE**).

The *domain architecture organization* launches new lifecycles in response to *lifecycle events* it receives via *calendars*. Domain architects use the solution methodology to capture or evolve a domain baseline architecture and elaborate a corresponding next target architecture version. Solution architects who apply the solution methodology to landscape assets have a vital interest in dynamic architecture views, which they use to explore and illustrate how a solution design realizes requirements through elaborated architecture approaches. In contrast, domain architects who apply solution perspectives to their domains focus primarily on static viewpoints. Their main interest is the inventory of assets in their domain and their interdependencies. However, for coarse-grained or cross-domain use cases, domain architects also apply dynamic solution viewpoints (**SOLUTION ARCHITECTURE METHODOLOGY**).

Elaborate Baseline and Target Architecture

The domain architecture organization uses the target architecture description from the previous lifecycle as input to the development of the domain baseline architecture in this iteration (*elaborate baseline architecture*). New business and service demands, emerging trends and technologies, and other aspects that have arisen in the interim are incorporated into the development of the target architecture to reflect the latest domain demands and constraints (*elaborate target architecture*) (**BASELINE ARCHITECTURE VERSUS TARGET ARCHITECTURE**).

Perform Gap Analysis

Architects perform a fit-gap analysis to determine the relevant delta between the baseline and target architectures of their domain. In particular, they focus on known gaps and deficiencies, new demands, risks, and constraints, such as government regulations. They think about emerging technologies and the opportunities they present for their domain. They also think about technologies that are nearing end-of-life and can be dismantled or decommissioned. The collected insights from the fit-gap analysis activity are incorporated into the update of the architecture conditions inventory (**ARCHITECTURE CONDITION, DECOMMISSIONING REWARD**).

Elaborate Architecture Roadmap
The architecture conditions from the previous activity and the updated target architecture are the principal inputs for updating and evolving the domain roadmap. An architecture roadmap captures planned states or anticipated future events related to assets or other aspects of architecture concern. The domain organization updates a roadmap to track recent changes to a baseline or target architecture. Changes are reflected such that roadmap states or events are added as new steps toward the aspired end state. Synchronicity between an updated roadmap and the roadmaps of the other domains is verified and ensured for each change. The finalized roadmap is formally endorsed and serves as an architecture governance vehicle. Architecture functions thereby ensure that the evolution of a domain's assets takes place within the boundaries defined by its roadmap (MANAGED ARCHITECTURE EVOLUTION, ARCHITECTURE ROADMAP METHODOLOGY).

Elaborate Reference Architecture
Throughout the lifecycle of their domains, architects discover good and bad practices, misunderstandings, missing guidance, or confusing guidelines. For example, the good intent of a shared platform may be hindered by the lack of a rule clarifying how the platform must be adopted. An architect has one intended and potentially many undesirable architecture approaches in mind for consumers using the shared platform. The domain architect's intended approach ensures that the shared platform reaches its full potential. In contrast, the unintended approaches prevent the platform from reaching its full potential and adequately serving its purpose. These and similar concerns lead architects to create reference assets to bridge the rule and prescription gap. Typical examples of reference assets include architecture patterns, principles, tactics, or styles. Reference assets can be specific to a single domain, but they can also be shared across many domains (ARCHITECTURE APPROACH, REFERENCE ARCHITECTURE METHODOLOGY).

Validate and Endorse Domain Architecture
Finally, the architecture function validates the developed domain architecture with the responsible architecture organization and formally endorses it (ARCHITECTURE GOVERNANCE).

5.3.2   Service Planning Value Stream

The *service planning value stream* is broken down into the service strategy, service demand, service portfolio, and project portfolio stages. In the *service strategy stage*, the service *validate strategy* ensures that architecture considerations are adequately addressed by the business and service strategy. In the *service demand stage*, the service *propose architecture demand* contributes demands that are deemed relevant by the architecture function. The *determine architecture relevance* service derives architecture relevance from the design significance of a proposed change, while the *elaborate architecture alternatives* service explores alternative approaches to achieve a specified objective. The *validate service portfolio* service contributes to the final endorsement of a corresponding portfolio. By performing this service, the architecture function confirms that it has investigated the value, impact, cost, and risk of the endorsed portfolio and that its capacity is sufficient to support the envisioned changes. Finally, the *validate project proposal* service ensures that the architecture disciplines are adequately included in an appropriate project proposal (Fig. 5.19).

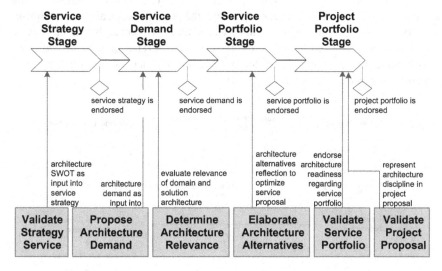

Fig. 5.19 Service planning value stream architecture services

5.3.2.1   Validate Strategy

The *validate strategy* service, whose interface is specified in Sect. 4.3.2.1, ensures that business and service strategy organizations adequately address architecture considerations. It considers emerging technologies or patterns in light of given strategic goals and develops proposals to achieve strategic objectives more efficiently and effectively.

As a preliminary reflection, consider institutionalizing architectural innovation to regularly gather innovative ideas[5] as input for revising business and service strategy. Motivate your architects to look for new and inspiring concepts. Inspiring ideas can

---

[5] Ideation is the creative process of generating, developing, evaluating, and communicating new ideas. An idea is a fundamental thought element and can be concrete or abstract. Ideation encompasses all stages of a thought cycle, from innovation and discovery to development and realization. Ideation can be carried out as a process by individuals or groups of people, in an organized or unorganized manner, planned or spontaneous.

be entirely new to the world, a unique combination of existing ideas, or simply brand new to your enterprise. An inspiring idea can be technical in nature—for example, a highly efficient way of technically transferring data between two computing nodes. It can be business in nature—for example, a new approach to conducting business, processing payments, or an entirely new method of creating business value. It can also be methodological in nature, e.g., a new and more efficient way for evaluating and exploring applications (ARCHITECTURE INNOVATION).

Establish Business and Service Strategy Lifecycle

A lifecycle event (*business and service strategy lifecycle event*) launches *validate strategy* to synchronize service execution with the periodic renewal of an enterprise-wide or domain-specific business and service strategy. However, before the service can expect synchronized launches, the *business and service strategy organization* must initiate the outer lifecycle of the *validate strategy* service (*establish business and service strategy lifecycle*) (Fig. 5.20).

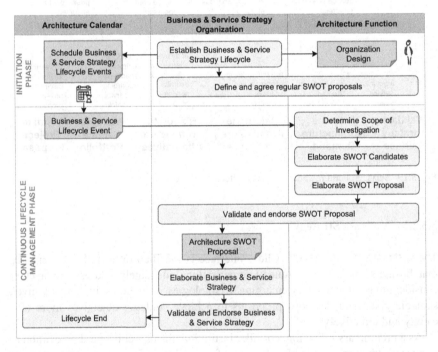

Fig. 5.20 Validate strategy process

Define and Agree on Regular SWOT Proposals

Establish a cooperation agreement with the business and service strategy organization that specifies the time required for the architecture function to prepare and deliver its strategy input. This is the lead time by which launching events must be received by the architecture function and scheduled accordingly as recurring dates in the *architecture calendar*. Clarify the types or forms of input that both the business and service strategy organizations wish to receive from the architecture function to maximize the collaboration's efficiency and effectiveness from the outset, for example, as an *architecture SWOT[6] proposal* (**Architecture Calendar**).

Determine Scope of Investigation

Define the exact scope of strategy validation associated with a scheduled event. For example, an enterprise federates its business and service strategy definition across multiple business domains. Accordingly, multiple *validate strategy lifecycle events* are scheduled in the architecture calendar—one per business domain. Each event is directed to a domain organization and sets the horizontal validation scope to the corresponding domain. Specify the extent to which strategic architecture contributions are made to clarify the vertical scope of *validate strategy lifecycle events* along different levels of granularity and planning horizons (**Architecture Level**).

In the context of architecture governance, your function has defined evolution corridors within which the evolution of assets must always take place. An evolution corridor is a guardrail typically defined at the domain level (i.e., for large systems). It measurably defines thresholds that asset modifications must not leave or exceed. Verify that the foreseeable impact of a given business and service strategy is within defined evolution corridors. Where the impact of business and service strategies is expected to move outside the corridor boundaries, verify that the defined evolution corridors still adequately represent the direction of your organization. Adjust evolution corridors if you recognize that they are no longer appropriate (**Managed Architecture Evolution**).

Elaborate SWOT Candidates

Examine the architecture descriptions of the domains in scope to identify strengths, weaknesses, opportunities, and threats. Consider *strengths* and *weaknesses* to be internal to the organization, while *opportunities* and *threats* represent external factors and circumstances. The strengths and weaknesses of internal aspects change less frequently and radically. Therefore, maintain the strengths and weaknesses of your function as a continuous artifact and as context-agnostic as possible. Consider this view when planning the evolution of your architecture function. Low flexibility in adapting capacity to volatile demand is an example of an architecture function

---

[6]SWOT analysis (i.e., an acronym for strengths, weaknesses, opportunities, and threats) is used to position and develop a strategy for enterprises and other organizations. Opportunities and threats represent external factors. Opportunities are, for example, possibilities to win customers through new or improved services. In contrast, threats are recognized risks. For example, identified opportunities may be threatened by more attractive competitor offerings or by emerging technology. In view of the external factors (i.e., opportunities and threats), enterprises consider their own measures to respond to these factors. Own measures cannot ignore the enterprise's intrinsic strengths and weaknesses.

weakness, while high competency in microservices-based architectures[7] could be an architecture function strength. External aspects (i.e., opportunities and threats) develop more spontaneously in the short term and therefore need to be reviewed regularly. An emerging new storage technology that enables exceptionally secure management of big data is an example of a design opportunity. In contrast, an emerging change in the licensing model of an intensively used technology in the enterprise may qualify as a threat. In particular, also review recent updates to domain-level roadmaps to identify weaknesses, opportunities, or threats as they are often implicit in the roadmaps (DOMAIN ARCHITECTURE METHODOLOGY, ARCHITECTURE ROADMAP METHODOLOGY).

Review the domain baseline architectures to identify current strengths. However, also take a fresh look at the differences between domain baselines and targets, as these may not yet be reflected in all domain roadmaps. Distill further weaknesses, opportunities, and threats from the identified differences. Pay particular attention to landscape assets with promising business potential, such as emerging technologies that fundamentally disrupt existing solution approaches (BASELINE ARCHITECTURE VERSUS TARGET ARCHITECTURE, LANDSCAPE ASSET).

Review architecture patterns to identify strategic opportunities. Before patterned solutions emerge, often recurring problems can be identified. Capture emerging problems in the problem chapter of a new pattern, even if an adequate solution design has not yet been determined. Consult such semi-finished patterns to identify threats but also to think about opportunities. For example, a recurring need arises in an organization for access protection in databases at the field level. This recurring problem could already be captured in a corresponding pattern, without an associated solution design already existing (ARCHITECTURE PATTERN METHODOLOGY).

Also, develop opportunity candidates by considering strategic cost reduction measures. In particular, think about reducing landscape complexity, for example, by consolidating redundant solutions or decommissioning those that are obsolete or no longer needed (DECOMMISSIONING REWARD).

Utilize the strategic angle to overcome organizational conditioning and systematically think about alternatives to SWOT candidates or impacts. Always consider doing nothing as a possible response to SWOT challenges, and identify both opportunities and risks of this response to derive opportunity costs from them and incorporate these into strategic decisions. For example, always discuss both investment and disinvestment as equally valid alternatives for addressing a given challenge (ARCHITECTURE ALTERNATIVE).

Elaborate SWOT Proposal

Anticipate the consequences and implications of the SWOT candidates studied that are relevant to the strategic perspective by examining the solution architecture of a

---

[7]Microservices are fine-grained, context-agnostic functions or function endpoints. Microservices are requested and delivered via lightweight protocols. Applications are established as loosely coupled microservices.

domain from a helicopter perspective. Set a timeframe (*timebox*) for elaborating the domain's solution architecture, and focus your investigation on strategic impacts, implications, and consequences. At the end, summarize all insights gained in the SWOT proposal (**SOLUTION ARCHITECTURE METHODOLOGY**).

Validate and Endorse SWOT Proposal
Finally, compile your SWOT proposal in the agreed form. Discuss, validate, and endorse it jointly with the *business and service strategy organization*. The endorsed *architecture SWOT proposal* is your function's contribution to the business and service strategy revision (*elaborate business and service strategy*) (**ARCHITECTURE GOVERNANCE**).

5.3.2.2 Propose Architecture Demand

The *propose architecture demand* service, whose interface is specified in Sect. 4.3. 2.2, proposes demands the architecture function deems relevant to the business and service demand portfolio. Typically, this is demand that other enterprise organizations have not yet identified. An architecture function also proposes demands that specifically reflect its own needs, such as additions or changes to its own set of services (*architecture service demands*).

Establish Business and Service Demand Lifecycle
Like the *validate strategy* service, the *propose architecture demand* service is launched by a lifecycle event (*business and service demand lifecycle event*). This synchronizes service execution with the regular renewal of enterprise-wide or domain-specific business and service demand. However, before the service can expect synchronized launches, the *business and service demand organization* must initiate the *propose architecture demand* service's outer lifecycle event (*establish business and service demand lifecycle*) (Fig. 5.21).

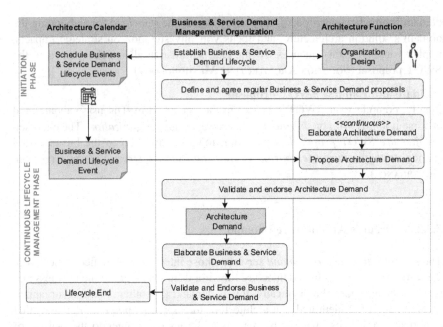

Fig. 5.21 Propose architecture demand process

Define and Agree Regular Business and Service Demand Proposals
Establish a collaboration agreement between the architecture function and the business and service demand organization, which specifies the time for preparation and submission of the proposed demand. This is the lead time by which the triggering event must be received—i.e., scheduled as a recurring event on your *architecture calendar*. Clarify the types or forms of input that both the business and service demand organizations wish to receive from your function to maximize the efficiency and effectiveness of the collaboration from the outset—for example, an *architecture demand form* to capture demand owners, rationale, and details (ARCHITECTURE CALENDAR).

Elaborate Architecture Demand
Collect architecture demand continuously and independently of demand triggers you receive from your calendar. Create in your own architecture platform the ability to physically manage your demand portfolio. Assign contribution rights to the architect and non-architect community in your enterprise to openly and broadly collect demand candidates. Alternatively, connect your architecture tool base to an external demand management system. In either case, ensure that demand management and domain architecture elaboration are tightly integrated. In particular, grant domain architects rights in your platform for the final selection of demands as well as demand prioritization (YOUR OWN ARCHITECTURE PLATFORM).

Use the three areas that constitute an architecture function as a high-level orientation to systematically search and collect your own demand, for example, the building blocks of an architecture function, such as its organization, engagement model, or apparatus. Something within each of your function building blocks might merit further development that you reflect as a new demand in your architecture demand portfolio. Another building block area is your architecture services. Here you may identify the addition, modification, or removal of a service as a new demand. Lastly, there is the architecture function qualities area, where a required qualitative improvement may result in a new demand, for example, the demand for an architecture service portal to improve the usability of the architecture organization.

Collect your architecture asset-specific demands separately within each asset category. For example, assets, such as services, applications, or platforms, form architecture landscapes. For the landscape asset category, focus on the assets that underpin your function—for example, applications, information, and technologies that implement your architecture platform. Methodological assets are another asset category where renovating an existing methodology or introducing a new one is considered a new methodological demand. Also, consider the demand for reference assets, for example, demand for new patterns or modification of architecture styles or principles (ARCHITECTURE ASSET, ARCHITECTURE PATTERN METHODOLOGY, ARCHITECTURE PRINCIPLE).

Exploit your function roadmap to derive architecture needs and translate timely roadmap entries into new demand. Also, analyze the differences and gaps between your function's baseline and target architecture, focusing on differences that overlap in time with the next demand lifecycle. Translate the discovered gaps into new demands accordingly (ARCHITECTURE ROADMAP METHODOLOGY, BASELINE ARCHITECTURE VERSUS TARGET ARCHITECTURE).

Also, take a fresh look at anything that became obsolete or would benefit from streamlining, for example, an architecture policy that has proven ineffective or even counterproductive. Think about removing anything that is not needed or negatively impacts the efficiency of your function—think about it as an also valid variant of new demand (DECOMMISSIONING REWARD).

Propose Architecture Demand
Keep an eye on the maturity level your function is aiming for and know your architecture maturity metrics and derived KPIs. Prioritize your demands before assembling and proposing them in response to a business and service demand lifecycle event. Calculate the priority of an architecture demand from the degree to which it contributes to the maturity of your function (ARCHITECTURE MATURITY).

Validate and Endorse Architecture Demand
Next, the architecture function validates the proposed demand with the business and service demand management organization and formally endorses it. The endorsed demand (*architecture demand*) is your input for the elaboration of the business and service demand portfolio (*elaborate business and service demand*) (ARCHITECTURE GOVERNANCE).

5.3.2.3   Determine Architecture Relevance

The *determine architecture relevance* service, whose interface is specified in Sect. 4. 3.2.3, checks how reasonable it is to consider an architecture activity and its associated effort for a defined context and task. The service evaluates whether the effort is wisely invested or whether it makes more sense to refrain from considering the activity altogether. For business demands, service demands, or planned projects, the service evaluates the complexity of their further pursuit and recommends the degree of meaningful architectural involvement.

Perform *determine architecture relevance* in response to a relevance request (*request architecture relevance report*) that you receive from an *architecture relevance requester* (Fig. 5.22).

Fig. 5.22 Determine architecture relevance process

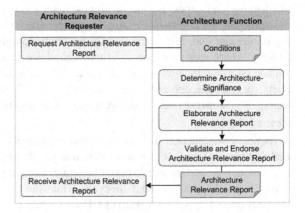

This service helps requesters distinguish between relevant and irrelevant areas of architecture concern and engagement—that is, between relevant and irrelevant design effort and investment. Note that the *architecture relevance requester* is just a role, which means that anyone, including architects, can initiate a relevance check by stepping into this role. Also, note that this service provides only a checkpoint. So do not confuse checking relevance with deciding to pursue further architecture activities. When in doubt, the decision to pursue further architecture investments is made independently of a prior relevance determination.

Before you engage and begin performing the service, critically question the question. Your relevance check looks at a task, or a set of conditions, to decide how relevant architecture contributions are to their pursuit. That is, you first check with the requestor to see if the conditions posed are clear, complete, and correct.

Also, more importantly, test whether the given conditions really represent the actual problem and do not mislead to a supposed representation of what is at stake (NEED TO KNOW).

Determine Architecture Significance

Your goal is to anticipate the degree of architecture involvement required to adequately address the given set of conditions. Addressing conditions adequately means solving the problem represented in terms of conditions. A solution that solves a problem absorbs the conditions that define that problem. A distinction is made between different types of conditions. Requirements and principles express a concrete desire—for example, the desire for a new feature in an application. Constraints are conditions that are not desired but also cannot be ignored. For example, the lack of a Python developer on the team can be considered a skills constraint. Your goal is to anticipate the degree of architecture involvement (*architecture relevance*) while having a set of *conditions* in hand. The conditions you have received as input represent a *problem* that your requestor is trying to solve. A *design* that has yet to be found represents a *solution* to that problem. The *architecture design* is a subset of the overall design of a solution. It is the set of architecturally significant design decisions, where significance is measured by the cost of change. In other words, architecture design is the subset of an overall design that cannot be readily changed. Consequently, *architecture conditions* are those conditions that lead to the architecture design. Put differently, the overall design, once found, satisfies all given conditions, while the architecture design satisfies all architecture conditions (Fig. 5.23) (ARCHITECTURE-SIGNIFICANCE).

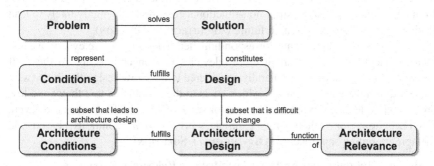

Fig. 5.23 Architecture relevance reasoning

Apply the following reasoning to determine architecture relevance. Anticipate a design given the conditions you received as input to this service. Next, anticipate the design parts that you consider architecturally significant (*architecture design*). That is, the design parts that will take a lot of effort to change once they are decided and implemented. If the architecture design portion is huge or otherwise highly critical, conclude that architecture involvement is urgently needed to address the conditions at hand. For these design portions, you must track and trace how the given conditions are addressed by respective design approaches (**ARCHITECTURE TRACEABILITY**).

While the above reasoning is logical, anticipating a solution design based on a set of conditions is not as straightforward as it may sound at first glance. Anticipating a solution design without serious elaboration carries the risk of an incorrect design extrapolation—and thus the risk of drawing incorrect conclusions about the relevance of architecture involvement. However, this fuzziness and the associated risks cannot be avoided. Nor is there any other metric that can easily determine whether a set of given conditions will definitely lead to architecturally significant decisions in a corresponding design (**ARCHITECTURE CONDITION**).

You have limited time to anticipate a solution design that emerges from the given conditions, i.e., one that takes these conditions into account and solves them. Therefore, use heuristics to pragmatically approximate your estimate. For example, estimate the complexity of an architecture approach to satisfy given conditions based on the number of conditions the approach accommodates. If an architecture approach hosts multiple conditions simultaneously, its modification will inevitably have a greater impact than changing an approach that hosts only a single condition. In addition, architecture approaches that accommodate multiple conditions simultaneously must compromise more often—in other words, these are architecture trade-off points[8] (**ARCHITECTURE APPROACH**).

Consider other heuristics such as the importance of the stakeholder group from which a condition emanates (e.g., the business criticality of the stakeholder group), the degree to which a condition is exceptional (e.g., a first-timer condition), or the degree of uncertainty associated with a given condition (e.g., the likelihood that a condition will change frequently). Another excellent heuristic is to test a condition for its non-functional nature since non-functional conditions are highly likely to lead to significant design decisions in future (**ARCHITECTURE DECISION**).

Avoid misconceptions and corresponding heuristics in your relevance assessment. Typical examples of architecture relevance misconceptions are off-the-shelf solutions. Such solutions are generally considered to have low design flexibility with respect to fundamental decisions, which leads to the conclusion that they have low architecture relevance. What may be true for some off-the-shelf solutions is a severe misconception for others—for example, off-the-shelf solutions based on metaprogramming[9] approaches (**OFF-THE-SHELF SOLUTION**).

Elaborate, Validate, and Endorse Architecture Relevance Report

Compile your relevance considerations along with your final assessment (i.e., architecture relevant vs. irrelevant) into an *architecture relevance report*. The report is validated and endorsed within the architecture function before being delivered and

---

[8] Architecture trade-off points are the basis for sensitivity points. Typical trade-offs exist between usability and security or between modifiability and performance attributes.

[9] Metaprogramming is a programming technique in which computer programs treat other programs as data. A metaprogramming-based program reads, generates, transforms, or interprets another program.

communicated to the requestor (*receive architecture relevance report*) (ARCHITEC-TURE GOVERNANCE).

5.3.2.4 Elaborate Architecture Alternatives

The elaborate architecture alternatives service, whose interface is specified in Sect. 4. 3.2.4, explores and elaborates alternative design approaches for given conditions and recommends a preferred alternative. In the service planning stream, this service produces high-level architecture sketches of alternative approaches for the design of an overall solution. The goal is to provide demand management, service management, or project portfolio management organizations with accentuated solution alternatives so that they have a choice. The service is repeatedly used to design sub-designs of an end-to-end service architecture in the service building stream. The goal here is to find optimal design approaches for parts of an overall solution design. In general, however, the service devises alternative approaches in response to a set of architecture conditions.

Perform architecture alternative elaboration in response to an alternative elaboration request (*request architecture alternative elaboration*) you receive from a respective requester (*architecture alternatives requestor*) (Fig. 5.24).

Fig. 5.24 Elaborate architecture alternatives process

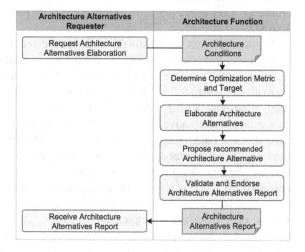

Alternative solutions exist for almost every problem. Both individuals and organizations, like your function, tend to stagnate in their own conditioning unless countermeasures are taken to overcome this tendency. This tendency puts your function at risk of unconsciously excluding potentially promising architecture approaches by favoring familiar but suboptimal designs. Elevate exploring alternative approaches to known problems to a maxim to counteract this tendency. Remember that *architecture alternatives requester* is only a role. This means that anyone at any time, including architects, can think about alternatives or initiate a request for alternatives elaboration (**ARCHITECTURE ROLE**).

Note also that the service allows the enterprise to explicitly request alternative solution approaches from the architecture function—alternative approaches that respond to the same set of architecture conditions. However, even if the service suggests multiple approaches and recommends one over all others, it ends with delivering an *architecture alternatives report*. This means that the service does not prescribe a final solution design for the given set of conditions and context but merely recommends it.

As with *determine architecture relevance*, you are well-advised to question the question before using this service and beginning execution. In other words, test the given conditions together with the requester to confirm they are clear, complete, and correct. Also, seriously verify that the given conditions match the mental image of the problem as your requester has it in mind. Systematically searching and developing alternative solutions is costly, so a mature understanding of the underlying problem is an essential prerequisite for successfully performing this service (**NEED TO KNOW**).

Consider context and distinguish alternative requests in the *service planning value stream* from those you receive in the *service building value stream*. In service planning, requestors are primarily interested in understanding the full range of alternative options for the solution as a whole. However, they do not expect detailed solution designs. Rather, what they expect are high-level architecture sketches for each explored alternative. These sketches are used to understand the opportunities, dependencies, risks, costs, or benefit profile of each alternative—which is ultimately used to make an informed portfolio decision. In the context of service building value streams, the high-level architecture approach is already in place. Requesters are interested in exploring alternative approaches for smaller parts within the overarching design, for example, an optimal architecture approach for persistence of conversational data to bridge interrupted user sessions. Calibrate granularity and level of detail to view landscape assets and domains as architecture building blocks in a service planning context. Zoom into landscape assets and their internal designs to explore alternative approaches in a service building context (**ARCHITECTURE LEVEL**).

Determine Optimization Metric and Target

Derive a performance metric from the architecture conditions and an optimization target shared with you by the requestor. The performance metric may include performance criteria such as *complete satisfaction of all architecture conditions*, *zero deviation from enterprise standards*, *maximum acceptable cost is C_{MAX}*, or *maximum acceptable time to build the desired solution is T_{MAX}.* Select as the optimal alternative from the set of alternatives developed the one that satisfies the performance metric Pareto[10] maximal (**ARCHITECTURE ALTERNATIVE**).

Elaborate Architecture Alternatives

Develop promising alternatives using your architecture expertise, experience, and creativity. The performance metric you developed earlier provides a framework within which you should seek and cover the full range of alternative approaches. Use the metric to focus your elaboration on relevant performance criteria. For example, gather cost information for building block variants if *maximum cost* is among the criteria for selecting the preferred alternative. Place the elaboration of each design alternative in a timeframe to evenly distribute your capacity and attention among them, and apply a mile-wide and inch-deep approach to their further exploration. However, use your solution methodology as systematic to ensure that your approach is both solution-focused and methodologically compatible with your organization's practices (**SOLUTION ARCHITECTURE METHODOLOGY**).

Propose Recommended Architecture Alternative

Create an *architecture alternatives report* based on a schema that you derive from the specified performance metric. Once you have elaborated all examined alternatives to the defined level of detail, summarize them in the report and compare and evaluate them. Rank alternatives studied according to the optimization goal you received from the requestor, and mark either one or a combination of several alternatives as your preferred, i.e., recommended and proposed, alternative option (Fig. 5.25).

Architecture Alternatives Summary

Optimization Target	Minimize Cost		Maximize Architecture Condition Coverage	Minimize Dependencies
Measurement Metric	CAPEX	OPEX	% coverage	# dependencies
Architecture Alternative $_1$	100	500	80%	12
Architecture Alternative $_2$	80	250	70%	10
Architecture Alternative $_3$	50	200	75%	9
Architecture Alternative $_4$	45	300	50%	11
Architecture Alternative $_5$	60	400	650%	8
Architecture Alternative $_6$	70	450	75%	14

performance metric   preferred architecture alternative

Fig. 5.25 Architecture alternatives report

---

[10]Pareto optimum is an optimum at which no preference criterion can be better without at least one individual or preference criterion being worse off. The concept is named after Vilfredo Pareto (1848–1923), who used it to research economics.

Validate and Endorse Architecture Alternatives Report
Validate and approve the report within the architecture function before forwarding it to
the proposer (*receive architecture alternatives report*) (**ARCHITECTURE GOVERNANCE**).

5.3.2.5   Validate Service Portfolio

By performing the *validate service portfolio* service, whose interface is specified in
Sect. 4.3.2.5, the architecture function confirms that it has examined the value,
impact, cost, and risk of the endorsed portfolio and that it confirms its capacity as
sufficient to support the planned changes. The architecture function also documents
its support and alignment by formally endorsing the service portfolio.

A lifecycle event (*service portfolio lifecycle event*) launches *validate service
portfolio* to synchronize service execution with the periodic renewal of an
enterprise-wide or domain-specific service portfolio. However, before the service
can expect synchronized launches, the *service portfolio organization* must initiate
the outer lifecycle of the *service* (*establish service portfolio lifecycle*) (Fig. 5.26).

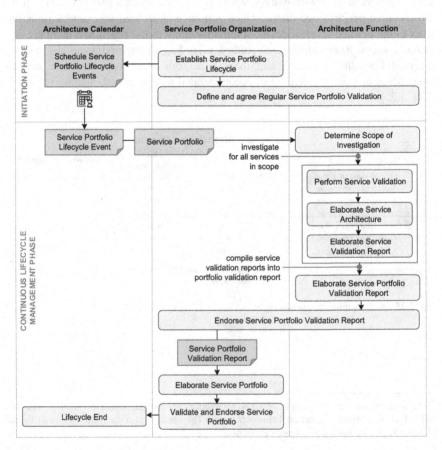

Fig. 5.26 Validate service portfolio process

Define and Agree Regular Service Portfolio Validation
Establish a collaboration agreement with the service portfolio organization that specifies the time required for architecture functions to prepare and submit their service portfolio input. This is the lead time by which a launching event must be received—i.e., scheduled as a recurring date in the *architecture calendar*. Clarify the types or forms of input the service portfolio organization wishes to receive from the architecture function to maximize the efficiency and effectiveness of the collaboration, for example, a *service portfolio validation report* that includes individual validation reports for each architecturally validated service in the portfolio (ARCHITECTURE CALENDAR).

Determine Scope of Investigation
Define the exact scope of portfolio validation associated with a scheduled event. For example, an enterprise federates service portfolios across multiple business domains. Accordingly, multiple *service portfolio lifecycle events* could be scheduled in the architecture calendar—one per business domain. Each event is directed to a domain organization and sets the horizontal validation scope to the corresponding domain. Set the scope of strategic architecture contributions to clarify their vertical scope along architecture levels (ARCHITECTURE LEVEL).

Perform Service Validation
Next, iterate across the entire service portfolio. For each service, investigate and validate the architectural impacts of pursuing it further, for example, the environmental impact of deploying the service, the associated architecture risks, or the design capacity required to deploy the service. Capture the findings in a *service validation report* (ARCHITECTURE TRACEABILITY) (Fig. 5.27).

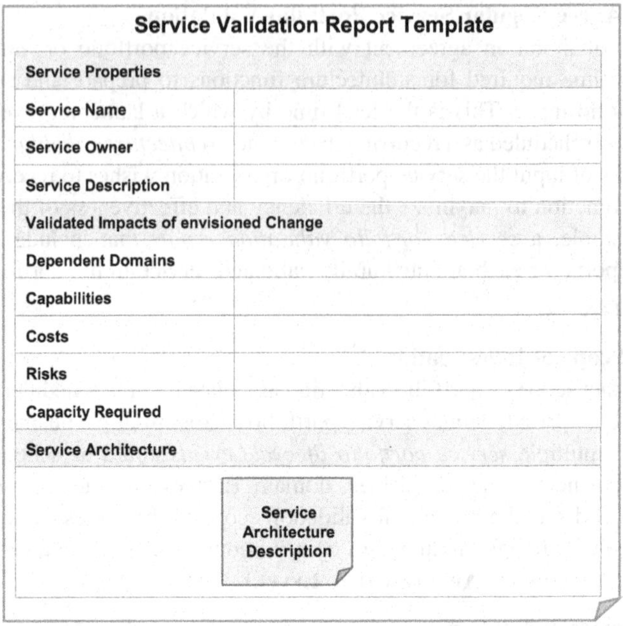

Service Validation Report Template	
Service Properties	
Service Name	
Service Owner	
Service Description	
Validated Impacts of envisioned Change	
Dependent Domains	
Capabilities	
Costs	
Risks	
Capacity Required	
Service Architecture	

Service
Architecture
Description

Fig. 5.27 Service validation report

Examine the dependencies and impacts that a change to the service could cause
by consulting the architecture descriptions of all affected domains. A shared service
that is used by many services and whose availability is critical to the operational
stability of dependent services deserves your undivided attention. You must ensure
that a change to this service does not cause outages of other services. If in doubt, you
must establish a parallel service to serve dependent consumers while you complete
the rebuild (DOMAIN ARCHITECTURE METHODOLOGY).

Elaborate Service Architecture

Elaborate a high-level *solution architecture vision* for each service in the portfolio.
Here, of course, pick up on the existing ones from previous alternative elaboration
activities and evolve them accordingly. Even if it is still only a very thin high-level
sketch, a solution architecture description for each service enhances portfolio management by providing holistically grounded input to portfolio decision-making.

Include your solution description in the service architecture section of the service validation report (SOLUTION ARCHITECTURE METHODOLOGY).

Elaborate Service Validation Report

At the end of each iteration, you summarize your individual service findings, including the respective service architecture descriptions in a service validation report. The validation report provides an overview of the architecture assessments for an entire service portfolio as well as further architecture details for each individual service (Fig. 5.28).

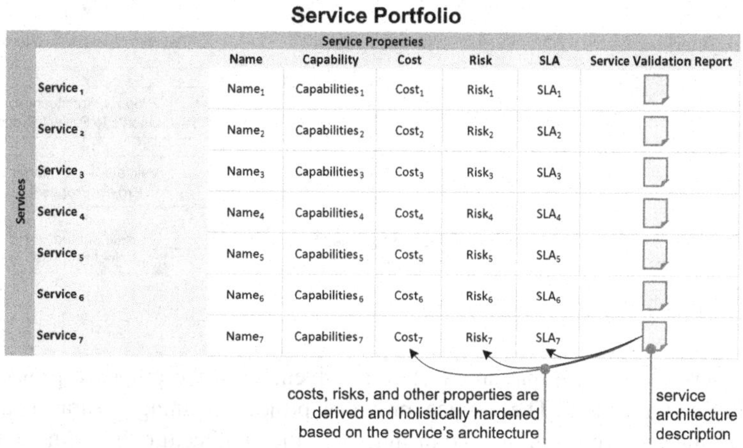

Service Portfolio

		Service Properties				Service Validation Report
	Name	Capability	Cost	Risk	SLA	
Service$_1$	Name$_1$	Capabilities$_1$	Cost$_1$	Risk$_1$	SLA$_1$	
Service$_2$	Name$_2$	Capabilities$_2$	Cost$_2$	Risk$_2$	SLA$_2$	
Service$_3$	Name$_3$	Capabilities$_3$	Cost$_3$	Risk$_3$	SLA$_3$	
Service$_4$	Name$_4$	Capabilities$_4$	Cost$_4$	Risk$_4$	SLA$_4$	
Service$_5$	Name$_5$	Capabilities$_5$	Cost$_5$	Risk$_5$	SLA$_5$	
Service$_6$	Name$_6$	Capabilities$_6$	Cost$_6$	Risk$_6$	SLA$_6$	
Service$_7$	Name$_7$	Capabilities$_7$	Cost$_7$	Risk$_7$	SLA$_7$	

costs, risks, and other properties are derived and holistically hardened based on the service's architecture

service architecture description

Fig. 5.28 Service portfolio

Evaluate and Endorse Service Portfolio Validation

Discuss, validate, and endorse the service portfolio validation report together with the service portfolio organization. The validated report (*service portfolio validation report*) is the architecture function input to the service portfolio revision (*elaborate service portfolio*) (ARCHITECTURE GOVERNANCE).

5.3.2.6 Validate Project Proposal

The *validate project proposal* service, whose interface is specified in Sect. 4.3.2.6, ensures that the architecture discipline is adequately represented and included in project proposals. It contributes the architecture function's view of the business value, required skills, and resources, costs and schedules, and risk segments of the project proposal. The architecture function secures the required resources and capacity and documents its readiness to support the project by formally endorsing the project proposal.

Request Validation of Project Proposal

Perform the *validate project proposal* service in response to a corresponding project validation request you receive from a *project proposal requester* (Fig. 5.29).

Fig. 5.29 Validate project
proposal process

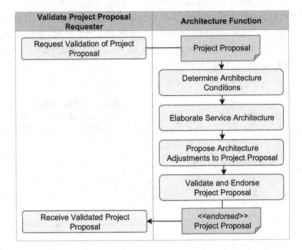

This service assumes that architecture involvement in the proposed project has been deemed relevant. The service provides project planning assurance at the proposal stage by verifying and confirming that the architecture discipline is sufficiently represented in the proposed project charter. The service receives the project proposal as input in the form of a project charter. The project charter may already contain an assessment of the architecture relevance (*architecture relevance report*), an early architecture vision from the service portfolio, and a list of rejected solution alternatives (*architecture alternatives report*) (Fig. 5.30).

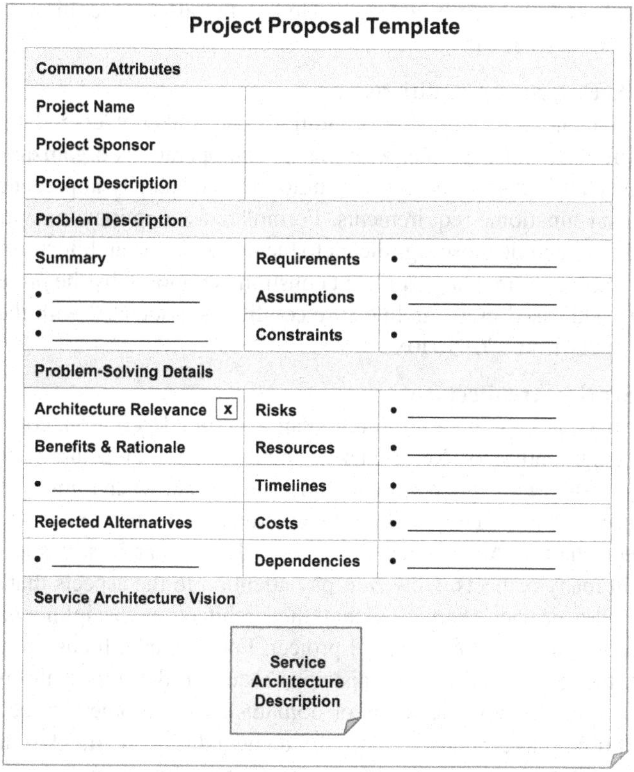

Project Proposal Template

Common Attributes		
Project Name		
Project Sponsor		
Project Description		

Problem Description		
Summary	Requirements	• _____
• _____	Assumptions	• _____
• _____		
• _____	Constraints	• _____

Problem-Solving Details		
Architecture Relevance [x]	Risks	• _____
Benefits & Rationale	Resources	• _____
• _____	Timelines	• _____
Rejected Alternatives	Costs	• _____
• _____	Dependencies	• _____

Service Architecture Vision

Service
Architecture
Description

Fig. 5.30 Project charter

Check whether the architecture insights gained and captured so far are still up-to-date, complete, and accurate, as many months may have passed since this information was last updated. In particular, check to what extent the given problem has changed in the meantime before executing the service. In other words, you initially focus on the architecture conditions as captured in the early version of the solution design (i.e., as contained in the project charter). Verify that the architecture conditions are still valid—i.e., that they still adequately represent the understanding of the problem that has since been established. Update the affected architecture artifacts accordingly (NEED TO KNOW).

Determine Architecture Conditions
Confirm completeness of architecture conditions with stakeholders in later phases of the service lifecycle, for example, with the service operations organization. Ensure that the quality attributes of the target solution are adequately appreciated through appropriate non-functional requirements. Formulate assumptions to capture known uncertainties and include those significant to the design in the architecture conditions collection. Finally, ensure that significant constraints imposed by the project are also appropriately addressed in the architecture conditions associated with the proposed project (ARCHITECTURE CONDITION).

Elaborate Service Architecture
Next, perform a quick run over the solution architecture description, considering the recently updated conditions. Refer back to the solution architecture version that is available as a result of the quick run you performed earlier when running the *validate service portfolio* service. You can find the architecture description as an addendum to the project charter. Accept that the design description is still superficial and incomplete in many respects. However, pay attention to the aspects that impact the attributes of the project charter so that the architecture discipline is fully and accurately represented in the proposed project. For example, focus on architecture risk or cost, the competencies and capacities required, the impact the project will have on assets (e.g., landscape assets or domains), and on other projects. If architecture conditions have changed more fundamentally since the last update, the established architecture vision should be reconsidered, for example, by considering alternatives to design approaches that address changed or newly introduced conditions (SOLUTION ARCHITECTURE METHODOLOGY, ARCHITECTURE ALTERNATIVE).

Pay attention to the impact of organizational forces on architecture outcomes. Sociotechnical systems, such as project organizations, tend to replicate their internal structures, dynamics, or conflicts into the technical systems they use or produce. Anticipate how the design of the project organization will affect the architecture design of a targeted solution. Propose appropriate adjustments to the project organization to mitigate undesirable replication effects. For example, make vendors of a technology that is an essential basis of the envisioned solution contractually co-responsible for feasibility testing of project requirements. In this way, you can counter the risk of vendors retreating to the technology level and not feeling responsible for delivering a solution at the application level. Further build appropriate responsibilities and reporting structures into the project organizations (ORGANIZATIONAL REPLICATION).

Propose Architecture Adjustments to Project Proposal

Propose adjustments to the project charter to reflect the latest findings. For example, propose the inclusion of cloud architecture expertise because a flat OPEX[11] scheme was recently introduced as a constraint.

Create an architecture mandate when the architecture discipline is intensely involved in a project and project success depends significantly on accurately delivered architecture contributions. Dedicated mandates increase the predictability, accuracy, and verifiability with which architecture contributions are delivered in a project context. Explicit mandates are therefore an effective means of mitigating the risk of design-related over- and under-delivery (ARCHITECTURE MANDATE).

Validate and Endorse Project Proposal

Finally, discuss, validate, and endorse the project proposal together with the project manager and other relevant project stakeholders. The architecturally adjusted project charter (*project proposal*) is your contribution to *receive validated project proposal* (ARCHITECTURE GOVERNANCE).

5.3.3 Service Building Value Stream

The *service building value stream* is divided into the service plan, service architecture, service implementation, and service deployment stages. In the *service plan stage*, the *elaborate architecture mandate* service creates a mandate that details the commitments of the architecture function to a client. The service also ensures that the critical parties involved formally sign off on the mandate. In the *service architecture stage*, *elaborate service architecture* receives an architecture mandate as input and ensures the agreed output is created. *Elaborate service architecture* accompanies the process of physically implementing, testing, and deploying the architecture design until it finally validates the implementation design and confirms that it is within an acceptable design corridor (Fig. 5.31).

---

[11] Capital expenditure (CAPEX) is the money an organization spends creating, buying, or evolving assets, while operational expenditure (OPEX) is the ongoing costs of reliably operating existing assets.

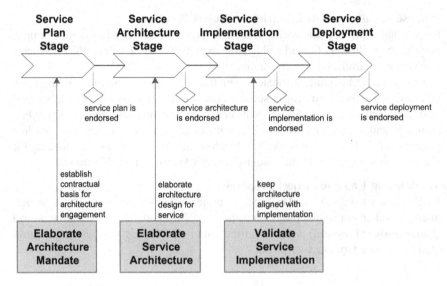

Fig. 5.31 Service building value stream architecture services

5.3.3.1 Elaborate Architecture Mandate

The *elaborate architecture mandate* service, whose interface is specified in Sect. 4.3. 3.1, creates a mandate that defines the contributions that the architecture function makes to a customer in a binding manner. The mandate formally clarifies, specifies, and agrees upon the tasks, schedules, and deliverables expected of the architecture function.

Request Elaboration of Architecture Mandate

Perform the *elaborate architecture mandate* service in response to a mandate elaboration request received from a respective requester (*architecture mandate requester*) (Fig. 5.32).

Fig. 5.32 Elaborate
architecture mandate
process

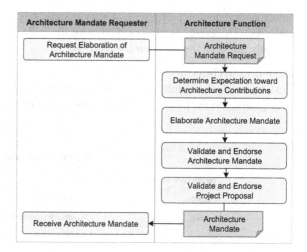

Some collaboration between the architecture function and other functions along the enterprise value chain is lightweight and informal. Other collaborations are heavyweight but pre-formalized—for example, collaboration via architecture services whose interfaces structure and formalize the interaction. Still other collaborations are neither lightweight nor predefined and require explicit clarification of architecture expectations and the commitments an architecture function makes to meet them. Architecture mandates target situations where expectations for contributions are neither trivial nor predefined. A mandate fills this specification gap by clarifying, capturing, and formally agreeing on the scope, objective, deliverables, resources, and schedule of an expected contribution. Note that a mandate must also be created in advance for some predefined services, for example, when the expected deliverables require clarification beyond a simple service interface signature, as in the case of architecture development of a sophisticated service (*elaborate service architecture*) (**ARCHITECTURE MANDATE**).

Determine the Expectation for Architecture Contributions

As always, before you can respond to a request, you must understand exactly what is expected of you. In other words, you need to review and determine whether the contributions a requestor expects via a mandate match the requestor's actual expectations. For example, have the client first formulate the *mandate purpose* in terms of simple, straightforward questions—questions to which the client wishes to receive answers through your contributions. Keep in mind that optimally pursuing a wrong goal is usually a bigger mistake than suboptimally pursuing a right goal—right or wrong goal in the sense that a wrong goal is pursued when the mandate describes an objective that does not represent, or very inaccurately represents, the client's actual objective. Therefore, as always, first critically reflect on the given task—that is, critically question the question (NEED TO KNOW).

Elaborate Architecture Mandate

Next, elaborate the architecture mandate with the requestor by exploring, discussing, and agreeing on the properties and sections of the mandate in detail (Fig. 5.33).

Architecture Mandate Template

Common Attributes			
Requester		Lead Architect	
Purpose		Architecture Domain	
Objective		Scope	

Resources						
Name	First Name	Role	Competency	Cost	Capacity	Availability

Deliverables				
Name	Artifact Type	Methodology	Platform	Date

Requester: __________ Lead Architect: __________

Fig. 5.33 Architecture mandate

In addition to the properties that are captured for all types of mutual agreements, such as date, time, requester name and address, or signature fields, an architecture mandate includes specific attributes. Use the schema presented below as a template for mandate artifacts in your enterprise (Table 5.1).

Table 5.1 Architecture mandate scheme

Attribute name	Attribute description
Purpose (*why*)	Description of the overarching goal an applicant is pursuing, for example, improving the reliability of an enterprise service, functionally extending an application, or saving costs by consolidating redundant platforms
Objective (*what*)	Summarize the contributions expected from the architecture function. For example, elaborate on a refactoring approach to improve the reliability of an enterprise service Use simple and unambiguous language for this summary. Capture the mandated objective in the form of questions to be answered by the expected contributions
Scope	Clarify the boundary between *in-scope* and *out-of-scope*, distinguishing between horizontal and vertical scoping. In horizontal scoping, you define the in-scope assets at the same levels (**Architecture Demarcation**) In contrast, in vertical scoping, you define the in-scope architecture levels for the mandated engagement (**Architecture Level**)
Resources (*who*)	Summary of architecture roles and resources. By specifying the roles, the mandate clarifies the necessary responsibilities and competencies to ensure that the architecture contribution can be delivered professionally (**Architecture Role**) By allocating resources and their required capacities, the mandate ensures that the contribution can be delivered effectively (**Architecture Capacity**)
Deliverables (*what details*)	Detailed specification of the outcomes expected from the architecture contribution in the form of artifacts and deliverables (**Architecture Artifact**)
Timelines (*when*)	Specifying dates by which agreed architecture artifacts must have reached a defined level of maturity. For greater timing flexibility, you can also grant timeframes for artifact delivery. Link milestones to specified dates and deadlines. For milestones, clarify what type of artifact verification guarantees that a desired state could actually be achieved. Performing a specific architecture assessment is an example of artifact verification
Means (*how*) *Methodology and platform*	Clarification of methodologies, frameworks, and other means that will be used to produce the mandated contribution, for example, your particular architecture methods and view models as you plan to use them in the mandated engagement (**Your own Architecture Methodology, Your own Architecture View Model**)
Cost (*how much*)	Estimate the costs incurred in performing the engagement. Architecture costs can be both internally generated and tied to architecture service providers. Service provider-based delegation models usually allow more precise cost breakdowns, as corresponding services and prices are contractually defined (**Architecture Sourcing, Architecture Funding**)

Validate and Endorse Architecture Mandate

Finally, validate and endorse the architecture mandate jointly with all relevant parties and share it with the *mandate requestor* (**Architecture Governance**).

5.3.3.2   Elaborate Service Architecture

Elaborate service architecture, whose interface is specified in Sect. 4.3.3.2, elaborates the architecture design of an asset in accordance with the mandate received as an input. The architecture of the asset is elaborated over multiple iterations, with seamless activities for design, physical asset implementation, testing, and deployment. This service spans the service architecture, implementation, and deployment stages. It accompanies the elaboration of the service architecture through to its physical implementation.

Establish your own solution architecture methodology to underpin this service with a systematic and repeatable approach to holistically develop a solution in response to a problem. Solution methodologies standardize the elaboration of designs and hence the standardization of architecture descriptions. A solution methodology includes both an architecture development process and a view model. While the solution architecture development process suggests a sequence of activities, the view model suggests *what* needs to be captured and *how* and when solution architects perform the process (**Your own Architecture Methodology, Solution Architecture Methodology**).

Design your solution methodology to be flexible to the solution archetypes you wish to support, for example, an archetype for a *data-centric solution*, an archetype for *distributed applications*, or one for *highly secure solutions*. Choose an extensible design for your method so that solution architecture adapters can be added flexibly over time. In other words, design the core of your solution methodology in an archetype-agnostic manner so that it can be instantiated for a particular solution scenario by selecting and applying an appropriate method adapter. Create an initial set of adapters for the most common solution archetypes in your organization. Once an adapter is selected, it guides a service architecture team through the optimal application of your solution methodology. Finally, design your solution architecture method and associated adapter framework so that complementary adapters can be jointly applied. For example, adapters for *data-centric solutions* and *distributed applications* are used in combination to guide architects through the architecture development of a data-centric distributed application (**Architecture Methodology Adapter**).

Create adapters for solutions that provide business capabilities rather than solutions that provide technical capabilities. Solutions that provide business capabilities tend to be more tightly bound to their contexts because of their business semantics. This is in contrast to technical solutions that are more loosely tied to their contexts, which makes them inherently reusable. Also, create an adapter for solutions that rely heavily on off-the-shelf building blocks. Create this adapter as a counterweight to the common misconception that design decisions made when deploying off-the-shelf solutions are considered superfluous (**Business versus Technical, Off-the-shelf Solution**).

Request Elaboration of Service Architecture

Perform *elaborate service architecture* in response to an elaboration request you receive from a *service architecture requester* (Fig. 5.34).

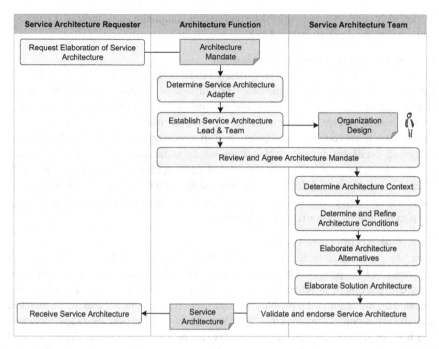

Fig. 5.34 Elaborate service architecture process

Determine Service Architecture Adapter

Select a solution architecture adapter that is best suited to support the requested scenario. Combine multiple adapters if you have designed your adapter framework accordingly. Take the opportunity to consider extending your current adapter set when you receive solution elaboration requests that are not supported today. Also, evolve your existing adapters by debriefing each solution architecture elaboration that your architecture function has performed to identify new solution archetype variations (**ARCHITECTURE METHODOLOGY ADAPTER**).

Establish Service Architecture Lead and Team

Appoint a service architecture lead and establish a *service architecture team*. Familiarize the service architecture team with the solution architecture discipline to ensure everyone involved in performing respective design activities is aware of the relevant processes, methodologies, view models, or governance policies (**SOLUTION ARCHITECTURE DISCIPLINE**).

Ensure that the agreed roles are understood and taken on both the requester side and the architecture function side. In particular, ensure efficient and effective collaboration between the service architecture team and a team of peers on the requester side. For example, provide architecture training to familiarize all involved parties with your organization's basic architecture language and concepts (LEARNING ORGANIZATION, ARCHITECTURE LANGUAGE).

Review and Agree Architecture Mandate
The service architecture team reviews the mandate received as input and clarifies any vagueness or unrealistic expectations. The purpose of the mandate is to sufficiently clarify expectations before formal elaboration commitments are made—in other words, before service architectures are developed. Mandates also help a service architecture team continuously review and, if necessary, adjust the level of granularity and detail during service development. In addition, mandates alert a service architecture team to deadlines and expected deliverables and help the team verify when a corresponding deliverable has been sufficiently developed. Put differently, mandates are used to continuously verify that architecture deliverables meet agreed-upon expectations (ARCHITECTURE MANDATE).

Determine Architecture Context
Next, the service architecture team begins elaborating the architecture by examining the context of the proposed service. The team consults domain architecture descriptions of the domain in which the service resides, as well as related domains. The baseline architecture is the primary artifact used. The architects seek to understand how the given context impacts their problem-solving efforts (*inbound dependencies*) and how its solution may affect the context in the future (*outbound dependencies*) (DOMAIN ARCHITECTURE METHODOLOGY, BASELINE ARCHITECTURE VERSUS TARGET ARCHITECTURE).

Determine and Refine Architecture Conditions
Once the context is clear, the team reviews the architecture conditions in the mandate to verify and further refine them. More than ever, it is essential to draw a clear line between the actual problem to be solved and a merely assumed version of it (NEED TO KNOW).

At the end of revising architecture conditions, the team knows its focus—and thus entry points for developing architecture approaches to carry the weight of respective conditions. A key focus in the revision of existing conditions is the distinction between architecturally significant and insignificant conditions. Another focus is on linking conditions and architecture approaches that address them. Architects take care to make the corresponding links mutually traceable (ARCHITECTURE CONDITION, ARCHITECTURE-SIGNIFICANCE, ARCHITECTURE TRACEABILITY).

Elaborate Architecture Alternatives
During solution discovery, it can be a valuable investment for the architecture team to explore alternative approaches to the same architecture condition, for example, finding an optimal architecture approach for granting limited access to technical system agents impersonating human users. Of course, exploring alternatives is an extra effort and comes with additional costs. However, in a world that is changing so rapidly, it is not entirely unreasonable to expect the discovery of a new and better approach to a known problem than the one that worked well 2 years ago. In this

respect, very often, the benefits of exploring alternatives outweigh the additional costs incurred (ARCHITECTURE ALTERNATIVE).

Elaborate Solution Architecture
The architecture team pursues the elaboration of the solution design using the solution architecture methodology and selected adapters. The team uses the given mandate to constantly check and confirm that their progress remains within the desired solution corridor. Of course, the architects pick up the existing solution architecture description that has emerged from the previous activities on the service portfolio and project proposal. Depending on the agile attitude, the architecture, design, and implementation teams collaborate intensively to incrementally build the solution from high-level to detailed design to physical implementation (SOLUTION ARCHITECTURE METHODOLOGY).

For the solution development process, architects consult reference assets to increase the efficiency and effectiveness of elaboration, improve the quality of the architecture, or ensure the conformance of their design approaches to domain architecture maxims. For example, a solution architect adopts the hub-and-spoke[12] architecture style to avoid combinatorial explosion of a fully connected graph of nodes and to achieve a linear growth pattern when more nodes need to be added (ARCHITECTURE PATTERN METHODOLOGY).

Solution architects inherently encode architecture decisions in the designs they create. However, explicitly documenting major architecture decisions in the solution artifacts makes them tangible and enables collaborative decision-making and formal validation of architecture decisions with implications beyond individual design approaches (ARCHITECTURE DECISION).

Validate and Endorse Service Architecture
Solution development, accompanied by an agreed mandate, ends when the architecture function formally certifies mandate fulfillment. To do this, use your architecture assessment methodology in combination with assessment method adapters for solution architecture milestones. After formal validation, the architecture function delivers the *service architecture* to the respective requester (*receive service architecture*) (ARCHITECTURE ASSESSMENT METHODOLOGY, ARCHITECTURE GOVERNANCE).

5.3.4   Service Running Value Stream

The *service running value stream* is divided into the service monitoring and detection, diagnosis, and problem resolution stages. In the *service problem resolution stage*, the *elaborate architecture problem resolution* service analyzes the cause of a detected defect and proposes an architecture approach that is suited for correcting or at least mitigating the defect (Fig. 5.35).

---

[12] Hub-and-spoke is an integration architecture style favoring communication via applications and a central hub over direct communication between applications.

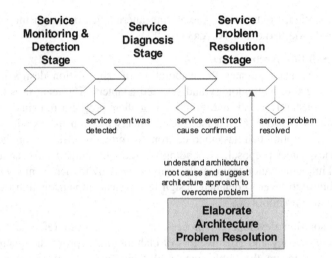

Fig. 5.35   Service running value stream

5.3.4.1   Elaborate Architecture Problem Resolution

The *elaborate architecture problem resolution* service, whose interface is specified in Sect. 4.3.4.1, analyzes the cause of a detected defect and proposes an architecture approach that is suitable for correcting or at least mitigating the error. This service can be thought of as an adaptation or shrunken version of *elaborate service architecture*. A shrunken version in the sense that in *elaborate architecture problem resolution*, the architecture intervention is not desired but is seen as unavoidable to overcome operational problems. The amount of error analysis and fixing is also usually smaller than in full architecture development or refactoring.

Request Architecture Problem Resolution
Perform an *elaborate architecture problem resolution* in response to an appropriate request received from an *architecture problem resolution requester* (Fig. 5.36).

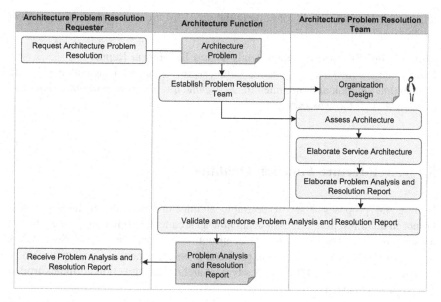

Fig. 5.36 Elaborate architecture problem resolution

Establish Architecture Problem Resolution Lead and Team

As mentioned earlier, this service is a highly compressed combination of the *assess architecture* and *elaborate service architecture* services. Rapid resolution of issues detected during the operation of an asset is a crucial success factor. Appoint an architecture problem resolution lead and establish a team as soon as you receive an identified problem as input.

Assess and Elaborate Service Architecture

The architecture team runs an accelerated version of the *assess architecture* service. It uses the received problem (i.e., symptoms of the defect) and the architecture descriptions associated with the affected asset as input to the assessment. The goal of the assessment is to analyze, approximate, and ideally identify the root cause of the defect (**ARCHITECTURE ASSESSMENT METHODOLOGY**).

Next, the problem-solving team initiates an accelerated version of *elaborate service architecture* using the insights from the assessment. Remember that *elaborate service architecture* makes heavy use of your solution methodology. Therefore, consider including a *problem resolution adapter* in the adapter framework that complements your methodology to optimize its application for this particular scenario (**ARCHITECTURE METHODOLOGY ADAPTER**).

Elaborate Problem Analysis and Resolution Report

The results of the architecture assessment (i.e., the issue causing the operational problem) and the subsequent architecture elaboration (i.e., the approach to refactoring the architecture for solving the problem) are summarized in a *problem analysis and resolution report*.

Validate and Endorse Problem Analysis and Resolution Report
Finally, the *problem analysis and resolution report* is validated and endorsed by the architecture function and submitted to the *architecture problem resolution requester* (ARCHITECTURE GOVERNANCE).

5.4   Architecture Function Qualities

Section 4.4 proposes a set of desirable architecture function qualities. For the proposed qualities, it describes in detail *how* an architecture function should perform its services or make other types of contributions. At the same time, Sect. 4.4 is limited to describing the black-box perspective on corresponding quality attributes. In other words, the chapter describes typical architecture function attributes from a requirement perspective (Fig. 5.37).

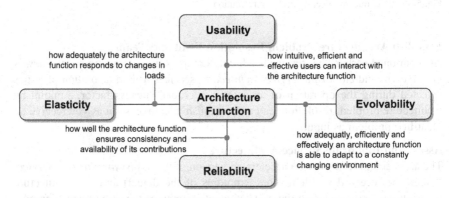

Fig. 5.37   Architecture function qualities

The present chapter discusses the quality attributes presented in Sect. 4.4 and explores approaches to their realization and achievement. Similar to Sects. 5.2 and 5.3, the present chapter mirrors the subsection scheme of Sect. 4.4. Following this subchapter scheme, I also discuss and describe separately the proposed design for each architecture function quality below.

5.4.1 Architecture Function Usability

Architecture function usability is the ease with which anyone interacting with the architecture function can *orient* themselves about the capabilities offered, learn and *understand* the particular value proposition, engage with the architecture function, actively *utilize* its offerings, and provide *feedback* or share thoughts with it. In Sect. 4.4.1, a usability schema was presented that consists of four segments: *orientation*, *understanding*, *utilization*, and *feedback*. *Learnability*, *efficiency*, *memorability*, and *satisfaction* are measures within each of the segments by which overall usability is determined (Fig. 5.38).

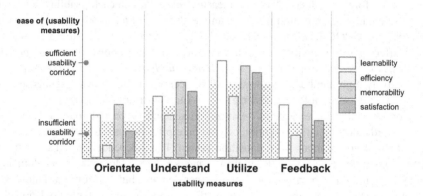

Fig. 5.38 Architecture function usability

Architecture function *learnability* is a measure of how intuitive it is for an external actor to navigate, learn how to interact with, and understand the offerings of an architecture function. For architects, learnability determines the steepness of the learning curve they must climb. Architecture function *efficiency* indicates how smooth and productive the interaction experiences are that internal and external stakeholders have when interacting with the architecture function, for example, when they learn about offered services, when they understand the service semantics, or when they request a particular architecture service. *Memorability* measures how easy it is for casual actors to remember the protocols of interacting with the architecture function. Finally, *satisfaction* determines the comfort level of actors in interacting with the architecture function. A satisfactory experience builds trust and increases the attractiveness of the architecture organization.

Establish an architecture single point of contact (*architecture SPOC*) for your function. An architecture SPOC provides the ability to interact with the architecture organization at any time, despite other guidance you may provide, like an architecture function portal or service catalog. This convenience in interacting with the architecture organization lowers the barrier for requests to reach it and ensures that you do not inadvertently miss important requests. A SPOC improves *understanding* by tuning into the language or request handling of different stakeholder groups. It improves *feedback* gathering by encouraging all requestors to share their views on the appropriateness and quality of the architecture contributions they receive. A SPOC also improves *orientation* by routing underspecified requests to the appropriate response point in the architecture function. Finally, SPOCs recognize patterns of interaction between requestors and the architecture function. You improve efficiency of your function by establishing standardized offerings associated with frequent request patterns that are recognized by your SPOC (**ARCHITECTURE SPOC**).

Make architecture function usability a prominent norm in your maturity metric. Efficiency culminates learnability, memorability, and satisfaction in a meaningful way. Therefore, introduce a KPI that measures efficiency in each usability segment (e.g., orientation, understanding), for example, the ratio of *the number of requests an architecture SPOC received unnecessarily* (i.e., unnecessarily because a standardized offering was available in the architecture service catalog) to *the number of requests an architecture SPOC received that actually required SPOC intervention*. A relatively high number of requests a SPOC received unnecessarily signals spaces to improve orientation for requester groups (**ARCHITECTURE MATURITY**).

Loosely link your enterprise organization schema to your domain schema. In other words, decouple the evolution of your enterprise organization design from the evolution of your domain decomposition design. The independence and stability of your domain architecture model improves *memorability*. Moreover, your domains are pivotal reference points—not only for other domains but also for your landscape assets, reference assets, or architecture platforms. So, the more stable your domain model is, the less often fundamental clean-ups are required. This directly improves the orientation, understanding, and usage *efficiency* of your architecture function (**DOMAIN-ORGANIZATION AGNOSTICISM**).

Define common architecture concepts and communicate them openly to improve *learnability*, *efficiency*, and *memorability* across all usage segments. A common concept base avoids or at least reduces miscommunication and misunderstandings. Similarly, introduce and evolve domain-specific languages to meet the specific communication needs of particular stakeholder groups. Explaining domain-specific concepts underscores the need for a common conceptual foundation. It also makes clear that a common conceptual basis is neither automatic nor necessarily trivial (**ARCHITECTURE LANGUAGE, DOMAIN ARCHITECTURE TAXONOMY**).

Establish pattern languages within and across your domains. Pattern languages complement domain architecture taxonomies. While taxonomies clarify concepts, patterns are activatable concepts that architects use practically in their solution efforts. While pattern languages, like domain taxonomies, improve *orientation* and *understanding*, their particular emphasis is on application and supporting the production of design (**ARCHITECTURE PATTERN METHODOLOGY**).

A seemingly small and innocent ingredient to greatly increase the efficiency of your function is the practice of questioning questions. Pursue only critically reflected goals while strictly avoiding the pursuit of presumptive goals. For example, task your SPOC to critically reflect on all incoming requests before initiating further activities. Assigning your SPOC to not only critically reflect on all incoming requests but also to review the requests for their architecture relevance (i.e., whether the request is misaddressed to the architecture function) will increase its *efficiency* (NEED TO KNOW, ARCHITECTURE-SIGNIFICANCE).

5.4.2 Architecture Function Elasticity

Architecture function elasticity is the ability of an architecture function to accommodate heavier loads (*area of extraordinarily high demand*) or lighter loads (*area of extraordinarily low demand*) in terms of demand for service requests or similar contributions.

In Sect. 4.4.2, an elasticity coordinate system for architecture functions was presented. The coordinate system explains elasticity as the ability of an architecture function to keep service performance within a predefined and deemed appropriate performance corridor—even in situations with exceptionally low or high service demand (Fig. 5.39).

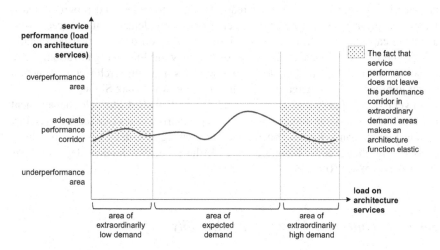

Fig. 5.39 Architecture function elasticity

Extraordinary demands are what their name implies: unusual, out of the ordinary, or even strange—in either case, they surprise an architecture function when they arise. One of the most potent buffers to compensate for them is the resilience and flexibility of your architects. Their hard and soft skills, expertise, and experience, coupled with a positive *can-do attitude*, are the critical ingredients to cushion the negative impact of surprising demands. Give your architects room to develop effective strategies for dealing with unusual challenges. Anchor this space in both architects' role descriptions and their annual incentive goals, for example, challenges related to unusual urgency with which solutions are expected, challenges related to overcoming dilemmas or trade-off situations, or challenges related to rapidly emerging disruptive technologies (**ARCHITECTURE ROLE**).

Establish architecture demand forecasting as a discipline within your function. Demand forecasting is not an exact science. However, it helps catch surprise spikes by giving you early warning of foreseeable demand in the future. It allows you to anticipate situations where forecasted demand is scraping against the maximum capacity of your architecture function. This allows you to take appropriate countermeasures at an early stage (**ARCHITECTURE CAPACITY**).

Supplement your pool of internal resources with an externally sourced pool of architects. The goal is to reduce both ramp-up and ramp-down times when demand spikes or fluctuations hit your function out of the blue. An external pool of architects can be more flexibly defined and operated. Contract design with your sourcing provider is an important architecture decision in this context. For example, the architects in the pool need not be named resources if the sourcing partner has many great architects under contract and can guarantee adequate talent whenever you need it. This can also give your function elasticity in terms of access to rare skills and competencies that you would never build internally (**ARCHITECTURE SOURCING**).

Prioritize and rank each request your function receives by relevance, and maintain an overview of currently processed requests, their priorities, and progress status. Defer low-priority tasks when you receive or expect demands that exceed your available capacity. Catch up on low-priority tasks when demand is exceptionally low. Centralize the management of priorities in your SPOC organization. Also, empower your SPOC to bundle similar requests that the architecture function might jointly handle to increase its throughput (**ARCHITECTURE SPOC**).

Leverage the opportunity to go beyond your established lifecycle management norm and clean up your domains and landscapes during times of exceptionally low architecture demand. Reduce operational or architectural debt[13] by continuously encouraging the decommissioning of superfluous and redundant legacy assets (**DECOMMISSIONING REWARD**).

5.4.3 Architecture Function Evolvability

Architecture function evolvability is the ability of a function to absorb changes in the enterprise (e.g., through the introduction of new services) with negligible or no disruption. In other words, evolvability is the ability of an architecture function to sustainably support the enterprise in achieving its strategic goals in a constantly changing environment.

In Sect. 4.4.3, the evolvability of an architecture function was presented as its ability to uninterruptedly meet enterprise expectations despite fundamental changes in its own constitution, the services it provides, or its quality attributes (Fig. 5.40).

---

[13] Architectural (technical) debt describes the phenomenon of inadequate system design that achieves short-term benefits at the expense of long-term gradual deterioration in system agility.

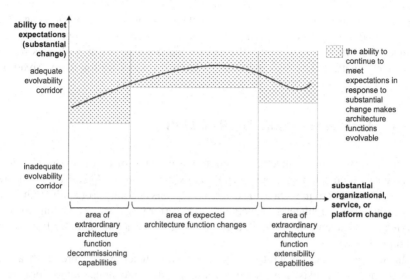

Fig. 5.40 Architecture function evolvability

Align the top-level organization schema of your architecture function with the schema of your enterprise's domains. You can assume that changes to the organization schema of the architecture function are rare due to the usually low frequency of domain model changes. Critically reflect on all organizational structure decisions below the top decomposition level, especially with respect to the expected frequency of change, for example, organizational structures that affect the geographic distribution of your company or the division of labor along the enterprise's value chain. By linking your top-level organizational schema to a domain decomposition approach that naturally reflects your overarching business model, you gain the evolvability you need to absorb unwanted changes over time (DOMAIN-ORGANIZATION AGNOSTICISM).

Consider your function as a system in its own right, and accompany the evolution of your function as you accompany the evolution of other systems. Define separate evolution corridors for its building blocks (e.g., *architecture function organization*, *engagement model*, or *governance*), services, and qualities. For example, define a corridor for the function engagement model that clearly delineates what is acceptable as the function evolves. A delineation example would be a principle that dictates that architecture engagement must always be possible via self-service, SPOC, and calendar events (MANAGED ARCHITECTURE EVOLUTION).

Supplement your architecture methodologies with an adapter framework to boost their adaptability and extensibility. For example, let us say that *elaborate service architecture* is a service in your current service catalog, but it does not yet support the design of mobile solutions. However, *mobile applications* are a new solution archetype for which your function has recently been frequently asked to provide design support. With an adapter framework that complements your solution methodology, you enable smooth service evolution of *elaborate service architecture* simply by adding a *mobile application adapter*. Both the service foundation and other adapters remain completely unaffected by this modification (ARCHITECTURE METHODOLOGY ADAPTER).

5.4.4 Architecture Function Reliability

The reliability of an architecture function is a measure of its ability to *effectively* maintain its own states in a permanently *consistent* manner. *Effectiveness* ensures that architecture activities leave the desired footprints in reality. For a minimum level of effectiveness, architecture functions must perform services according to their service-level agreements (SLA[14]), applying ACID[15] principles familiar from transaction processing.

In Sect. 4.4.4, the reliability of the architecture function was presented as the effectiveness and consistency with which it responds to incoming requests or events. Recurring, identical events reliably lead to identical results as long as the triggering events lie within a corridor defined by the architecture function (Fig. 5.41).

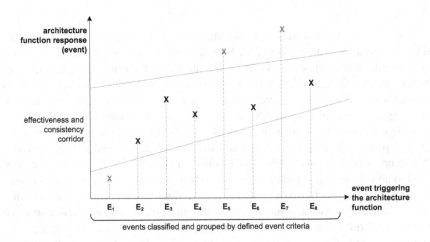

Fig. 5.41 Architecture function reliability

---

[14] Service-level agreements (SLA) are commitments between service provider and service consumer. Particular aspects of a service are formally agreed in an SLA contract, for example, service availability, service response time, mean time to repair, or mean time between failures.

[15] ACID is short for atomicity, concurrency, isolation, and durability and refers to a set of properties designed to guarantee the validity of database transactions despite errors, power failures, or other mishaps. Atomicity guarantees that each transaction is treated as a single unit that either completely succeeds or entirely fails. Consistency ensures that transactions can only move a database from one valid state to another. Isolation ensures that concurrent execution of transactions leaves a database in the same state as if the transactions were sequentially executed. Durability ensures that once a transaction is committed, it remains committed even in the event of a system failure.

Measurability and corresponding performance metrics are common prerequisites for specifying and verifying how reliably a delivery was performed. Hence, ensure that appropriate controls measure all architecture requests and associated responses. Inject controls at the points where request-response handshakes occur. For example, the architecture SPOC performs a control by measuring the time it takes for an architecture service to deliver its outcomes in response to a given request (ARCHITECTURE SPOC, ARCHITECTURE MATURITY).

Require explicit mandates for all non-standard architecture contributions whose inherent complexity justifies the effort to create a mandate. Mandates make both the expectations of the architecture function and its responses measurable and are therefore a prerequisite for the reliability verification of sophisticated architecture assignments. Further ensure that both organizational and personal accountabilities in the mandate are transparently defined, understood, and practiced by both the architecture function and other organizations. A strong sense of personal accountability is half the battle for your function's reliability (ARCHITECTURE MANDATE, ARCHITECTURE OWNERSHIP).

Critically reflect on the right level of architectural granularity, formality, and engagement to ensure you are truly creating the desired effects. The danger is that you will lose traction and disconnect from the real world if you take a bird's eye view with too little on-site engagement. The flip side of this coin is that you will get lost in distracting details of the actual architecture task. Therefore, carefully determine an appropriate altitude at which to engage to achieve the desired effects. Subsequently, pay strict attention to compliance with the defined level of granularity (ARCHITECTURE LEVEL).

Architecture policies, their relevance, adherence, and enforcement are crucial to your function to ensure that you really bring about the desired effects on the ground. Defining architecture policies too rigidly or enforcing rules without compromise puts you at risk of losing credibility. You also need to avoid situations where architecture policies are followed just for the sake of following them. Such situations defeat their purpose. Finally, inadequate policies may lead to bottlenecks in decision-making processes, for which you in turn pay credibility costs. On the other hand, if compliance with policies is perceived as *nice to do* rather than *must do*, your function will be pushed around. Therefore, design your policies so that you neither become a *no-cost advisor* nor a *must-do auditor*. In either case, you will not achieve the desired effects to the extent necessary (ARCHITECTURE GOVERNANCE).

Finally, in architecture planning, you should strike a balance between too long-term and too short-term a perspective to achieve the desired reliability and effectiveness of the architecture function. If you overemphasize long-term planning, short-term needs will be neglected, and you will lose touch with reality. Such planning risks unrealistic speculation, and you will be perceived by others as sitting in an ivory tower. However, if your planning activities are too narrow and short term, you run the risk that your strategic planning will degenerate into a flood of architecture change requests. In the worst case, the business wish list will be labeled a *strategy*, and you will miss your major contribution of abstracting business demands into a holistically thought-out vision of the future (**ARCHITECTURE ROADMAP METHODOLOGY**).

Further Reading

Sinek, Simon, *Start with why – how great leaders inspire action*, https://www.ted.com/talks/simon_sinek_how_great_leaders_inspire_action, 2009

Chapter 6
Pattern Catalog

Abstract The 48 patterns in this pattern catalog chapter are intensively referenced in Chap. 5, in which a generic design describes how the constituent, functional, as well as quality-related requirements for architecture functions are implemented. Each of the patterns presents, for one aspect of an overarching design, the challenge that architecture functions face and makes a proposal to adequately address that challenge—examples of particular aspects addressed by individual patterns are *architecture funding, sourcing, ownership, roadmap, mandate,* or *methodology.* The catalog divides the 48 patterns into 9 pattern groups of *architecture organization, architecture objective, architecture disciplines, architecture engagement model,* and *communication, architecture governance, architecture elaboration, architecture asset,* and *architecture apparatus.*

6.1 Overview

The architecture function patterns in this catalog guide you in designing and embedding the architecture function into your enterprise. The patterns suggest designs for the cooperation between architecture function and enterprise organizations as well as for the elaboration and evolution of enterprise services along the enterprise value chain. Further, the patterns recommend designs for integrating your architecture apparatus into the enterprise apparatus and aligning architecture governance with enterprise governance (Fig. 6.1).

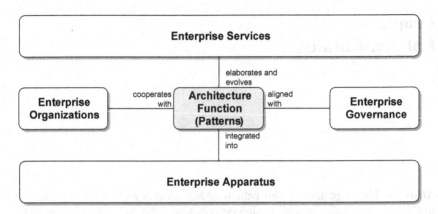

Fig. 6.1 Architecture function pattern catalog overview

In more detail, the architecture function pattern catalog is divided into nine pattern groups. The patterns in the *architecture objective*, *architecture elaboration*, and *architecture asset* groups focus on the design and further evolution of the architecture of landscape assets and structural assets (i.e., domains). Patterns in these groups primarily contribute to planning, building, and running the enterprise value chain and enterprise services. The architecture pattern groups *architecture organization*, *architecture disciplines*, *architecture engagement model*, and *communication* discuss fundamental and constituent architecture function considerations. Furthermore, they suggest ways of shaping the cooperation between the architecture function and other enterprise organizations. *Architecture governance* patterns deal with the design of architecture control and monitoring as well as embedding an architecture function into the enterprise governance ecosystem. Finally, *architecture apparatus* patterns suggest the design of the architecture apparatus and its integration with the surrounding enterprise methodologies and platforms (Fig. 6.2).

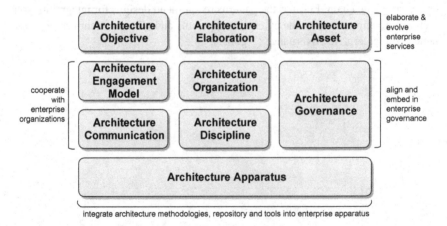

Fig. 6.2 Architecture function pattern catalog: pattern groups

6.2 Architecture Organization

The *architecture organization* patterns all make suggestions about the architecture function organization design. The *organizational replication* pattern points out the strong impact that organization design decisions have on resulting system design. The *learning organization* pattern recommends embedding architectural learning in the organization design. The *architecture funding* pattern contributes considerations for financing an architecture function, while the *architecture capacity* pattern makes recommendations for avoiding both function over- and undercapacity. The *architecture maturity* pattern suggests measures for determining and achieving desired maturity levels. The *architecture role* pattern distinguishes the architecture function's primary areas of responsibility and recommends a rudimentary role model. The *architecture ownership* pattern links ownership and accountability to the establishment or evolution of architecture functions, while the *architecture sourcing* pattern suggests criteria along which architecture contributions should be handled internally versus delegated.

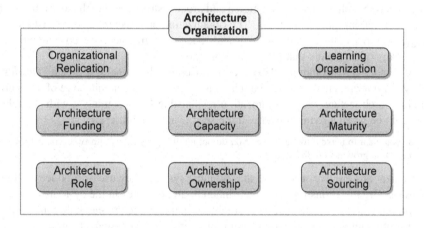

6.2.1 Organizational Replication

Socio-technical systems, such as enterprise organizations, tend to replicate their internal structures, incoherence, or conflicts in technical systems—systems that they use and produce. The technical systems can be enterprise services that are offered to customers and internal systems such as applications or platforms that are used to implement services. A deficiency or defect at the technical system level inevitably results from the conflict inherent in the socio-technical system generating the technical system. Overcoming the deficiency of a technical system, therefore, begins with healing conflicts at the level of social systems.

An *organization* is an administrative and functional structure (such as a business or a political party). (Merriam-Webster Dictionary 2020)

Melvin Conway researched and described the phenomenon of organizational replication already in 1968 (Conway 1968):

> Any organization that designs a system will inevitably produce a design whose structure is a copy of the organization's communication structure. The very act of organizing a design team means that certain design decisions have already been made, explicitly or otherwise. Given any design team organization, there is a class of design alternatives which cannot be effectively pursued by such an organization because the necessary communication paths do not exist.

Think of a *system* as anything from a transportation vehicle to a recommendation for a social challenge to a dishwasher or a computer program. *Communication structures* are the intended, motivating, but also destructive forces inherent in organizations. People establish and run enterprises. We all have our individual goals, interests, preferences, beliefs, personalities, attitudes, and priorities. All of these factors have a massive impact on how we work together or compete, how we see or value contributions, or how we make decisions.

We can say that the architecture of a system is already anticipated in the architecture of the organization responsible for its design. The architecture of an organization includes its organizational and process structures and the distribution of decision-making powers to them. The organization architecture also consists of an organization's culture, value system and incentive agreements, deep convictions, and many other factors that motivate people to act.

Christopher Alexander (1979) presents a compelling analogy in *The Timeless Way of Building*. He compares the relationship between the architecture of a system and the architecture of the organization responsible for designing it with the relationship between a living flower and the seed from which it grew:

> If you want to make a living flower, you do not build it physically, with tweezers, cell by cell. You grow it from the seed.

Organizations are like seeds, and the technical systems they use or produce are like flowers. Organizations replicate their inherent architectures in the systems they use or produce, which means that their organizational architecture inevitably influences and significantly shapes the architecture of their technical systems (Fig. 6.3).

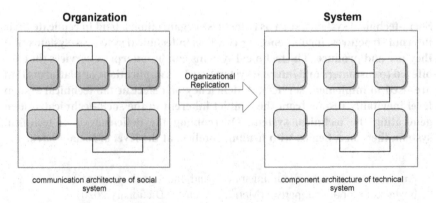

Fig. 6.3 Organizational replication phenomenon

Organizational Replication Example

Scenario 1

A company comprises the three divisions *business unit A*, *business unit B*, and *business unit C*. Their business models are similar, with each operating in its own regional market. The business units have relatively large budgetary autonomy to optimally adapt to their markets' regional conditions. Business unit A has to cope with the smallest budget, while business unit C is the unit with the largest financial capacity. Business unit B is positioned between A and C in budget terms. At the same time, all markets are extremely demanding and dynamic, requiring specialized and regularly adjusted business capabilities. The business capabilities in all business units are provided by *business services*, while business services, in turn, are based on *technical services* (Fig. 6.4).

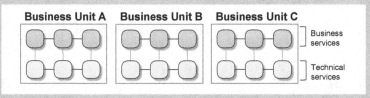

Fig. 6.4 Organizational replication example: scenario 1

Assume no countermeasures are taken to influence or mitigate organizational replication. In this case the organizational forces described above affect all business and technical services—both within individual business units and at the enterprise level. The need for specialized business capabilities likely leads to correspondingly specialized business services. Specialized business services, in turn, place high demands on the services upon which they operate, requiring highly specialized and individualized technical services accordingly. The demand for highly specialized business and technical services tends to lead to more systems than are actually needed. The reason for this is that generalized services cover a broader spectrum of requirements, which is why, in principle, a smaller number of generalized services would address a proportionally larger number of requirements. The organizational forces outlined above also lead to less adaptable services. Specialized services are optimized in terms of their specialization, which contrasts to generalization and an associated need for adaptability. High service specialization coupled with correspondingly low adaptability leads to increased redundancy both within business units and at the enterprise level. The increased redundancy ultimately causes an inefficiently high investment and operating cost profile, which may

(continued)

be acceptable in the short term, but is highly undesirable in the long term (Fig. 6.5).

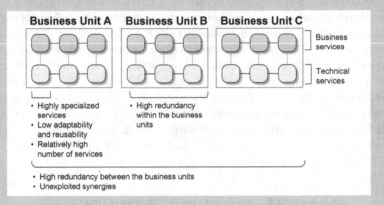

Fig. 6.5 Organizational replication example: scenario 1 consequences

Scenario 2

In a slightly modified scenario, the company has decided to leave sovereignty over business services with the business units, but to bundle technical services centrally in a separate organizational unit (*TC provider*). The part of the autonomous business unit budgets used for technical services is transferred to *TC provider* to supply it with the required funds. TC provider is operated as a cost center.[1] This means that although TC provider manages its costs, it does not have to achieve its own revenues in order to operate successfully. In this scenario, TC provider will pay close attention to adhering to its budget framework—in other words, it will be highly cost-conscious. The technical services offered exclusively by TC provider will be more generalized than the individualized technical services in the previous scenario. Technical services will also tend to strive for shared-use or multi-tenancy[2] models to achieve synergies across many service consumers. While technical service adaptability will increase, their individually optimized support for business services will be

(continued)

---

[1]Cost center is an organization within a business to which costs can be allocated. It is an organization that does not contribute directly but incurs costs to the business. The cost center manager is not accountable for the business's profitability and investment decisions but responsible for some of its costs.

[2]Multi-tenancy design is an approach in which a single physical solution serves multiple clients (i.e., tenant). Systems adopting a multi-tenancy architecture provide physically shared resources, while ensuring logically separated and tenant-specific spaces. Multi-tenant architectures are designed to provide each tenant with a dedicated share of a physical instance, where such share includes data, configuration, user administration, and tenant-specific functional as well as non-functional properties.

reduced compared to scenario 1. Assuming that business units have the necessary budgets, they will establish their own technical services whenever decision-makers consider this essential for their business success. At the same time, business units that cannot afford additional investments in establishing and operating their own highly specialized technical services will suffer from the *Pareto*[3]-optimized TC provider offering (Fig. 6.6).

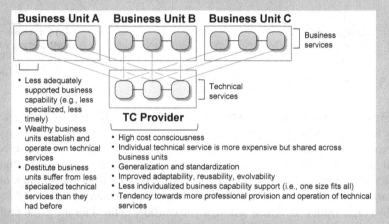

Fig. 6.6 Organizational replication example: scenario 2 consequences

Both scenarios outlined in this example demonstrate the likely medium-term impact of forces at the social system level (i.e., organizational architecture) on the architecture of technical systems (i.e., system architecture).

Architecture Function and Organizational Replication
Ensure that organizational forces are systematically considered in all architecture assignments. Consider organizational replication when designing your architecture function, policies, or methods by incorporating the necessary awareness into them. Also, consider the phenomenon when designing contracts with sourcing vendors and when considering other organizational forces with a tendency to replicate into your architecture assets (Fig. 6.7).

---

[3]Pareto optimum is an optimum at which no preference criterion can be better without at least one individual or preference criterion being worse off. The concept is named after Vilfredo Pareto (1848–1923), who used it to research economics.

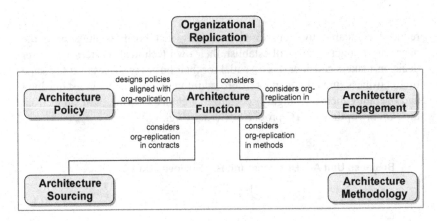

Fig. 6.7 Architecture function and organizational replication

First and foremost, acknowledge the phenomenon itself. Acknowledge the tendency for organizations to replicate their own architectures into the systems they use or produce. For example, when you join a project, anticipate the system architecture as it results from the architecture of the project organization, assuming that no countermeasures are taken (*system architecture emerging from organization architecture*). Next, mentally separate yourself from the architecture you derived from the project organization and create a design you consider optimal for the given problem (*ideal system architecture*). Carefully calibrate the abstraction level at which you reflect on both designs—the design resulting from the project organization versus the system architecture—you deem ideal for the given situation. It does not make sense to anticipate detailed designs if you only have a grainy view of the organizational workforce, such as a project organization chart. Avoid overdevelopment in favor of capturing the overarching design traits along which the system architecture is most likely to arise. If your ideal system architecture matches the system architecture emerging from the organizational architecture, you are done. Otherwise, either consider increasing the intersection or live with the deviation as an acceptable optimum (Fig. 6.8).

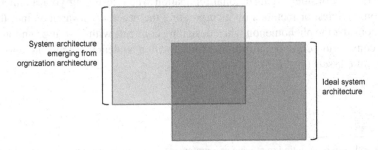

Fig. 6.8 Organizationally replicated system architecture versus ideal system architecture

Suppose you cannot accept the incongruity between the *system architecture emerging from organizational architecture* and the *ideal system architecture*. In this case, you can adapt the organization (e.g., by changing the project organization structure, renegotiating delivery dates, or expanding architectural involvement in the project). Alternatively, you can view organizational replication as a force inevitably impacting system architecture and consider this force accordingly in elaborating your system design.

If you purchase architecture services through external architecture service providers, organizational replication results largely from the design of your sourcing contract. If your procurement contract, for example, makes the *number of designed services* a performance indicator or if it makes *development of new service* a billable service, you have to expect that unnecessarily many and unnecessarily small services with a correspondingly large number of interfaces will arise. These will significantly increase the complexity of your landscape over time (**ARCHITECTURE SOURCING**) (Fig. 6.9).

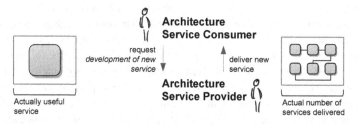

Fig. 6.9 Organizational replication reflecting contract design

Money rules the world, and your architecture funding model similarly shapes the architecture of your systems. For example, an architecture organization set up as a profit center[4] would like to satisfy its customers by paying close attention to their individual needs. Collective needs individual customers never raise are not considered by the architecture organization. In contrast, an architecture organization operated as a cost center will not seek to satisfy all individual customer needs, but rather optimize its contributions to customers as a collective. Therefore, consider monetary motivators in particular. Accompany the development of architecture by intervening in monetary flows or corresponding financial decisions in your enterprise (**ARCHITECTURE FUNDING**).

Make your architects personally responsible for the architecture assets they own or develop. An architecture asset receives undivided attention from an architect who

---

[4]Profit center is an organization within a business expected to make an identifiable contribution to business profits due to which it calculates profits or losses separately. The profit center manager is held accountable for both revenue and costs—thus for profits.

is responsible for its management. Your architects' attention will naturally affect your domain and landscape asset designs. Therefore, establish an ownership design in such a way that it produces the desired system architecture when it replicates naturally along its organizational forces (ARCHITECTURE ASSET, ARCHITECTURE OWNERSHIP).

Be authentic and honest. Avoid setting architecture standards and guidelines that differ massively from your enterprise's value system. Periodically evaluate standards, policies, or methods to ensure they are still realistic and feasible. For example, do not demand sophisticated architecture development and description via respective policies if development in your enterprise tends to take place under heavy time pressure or if your architects are otherwise overburdened to meet your quality expectations. Either work to fix the root causes of such problems or adjust your governance framework to stop trying to do what you have identified as unfeasible (ARCHITECTURE POLICY, ARCHITECTURE GOVERNANCE).

Organizational replication is a phenomenon you can observe at all levels of architecture. At the enterprise level, for example, you can anticipate the architecture of enterprise systems by examining the design of the enterprise operating model. At the domain level, you examine the structures of your domain organizations in order to anticipate the architecture of your domains. At the solution level, you explore the structures of projects or operationally responsible organizations to predict your landscape asset designs—for example, the design of a new application. The enterprise's organizational structure is replicated in your enterprise system architecture. The architecture of your systems at the domain level (e.g., the security domain is viewed as a system) results from your enterprise and your domain organizational structures. Ultimately, the architecture of your systems at the solution level (e.g., services, applications, or platforms) results from your domain and project organization structures (ARCHITECTURE LEVEL) (Fig. 6.10).

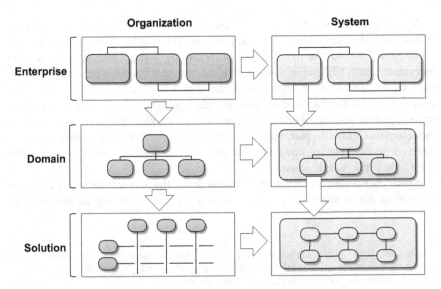

Fig. 6.10 Organizational replication and architecture levels

It is difficult to overestimate the architectural implications of organizational replication. Therefore, incorporate countermeasures or other balancing forces into your most foundational architecture means. Capture, for example, known organizational forces, their typical effects on system design, and suitable countermeasures in the form of architecture patterns and guidelines, or embed them in your architecture methods (YOUR OWN ARCHITECTURE METHODOLOGY, ARCHITECTURE PATTERN METHODOLOGY).

The entirety of your enterprise organizations realizes both business and domain disciplines. Your business organizations both execute strategic business planning (i.e., business strategy) and operate the business on a daily basis (i.e., business operations). In contrast, your domain organizations manage both logical and physical domain architectures and associated architecture assets for all domains in the enterprise. While *business strategy* and *logical domain architecture* are strategic organizations, *business operations* and *physical domain architecture* are tactical organizations. Emphasize organizational proximity between the business disciplines on the one hand and the domain organizations on the other, if your enterprise operates in a volatile business environment. The loose connection between domain and business disciplines leads to comparatively generic domain designs. This improves your ability to absorb change, which strengthens your competitive position in highly dynamic business environments. On the other hand, if your business environment is relatively stable and you gain a competitive advantage by optimizing operational efficiency, then you emphasize organizational proximity between the strategic disciplines (i.e., *business strategy* and *logical domain architecture*) on the one hand and the operational disciplines (i.e., *business operations* and *physical domain architecture*) on the other. Tight integration between the business operations and physical domain architecture organizations will result in a landscape design that is optimized to support your current business needs, which is your primary focus because business conditions rarely change (DOMAIN-ORGANIZATION AGNOSTICISM).

In the signature process, for each architecture mandate submitted, check whether it conflicts with the organizational force field. Expand the signature panel to include representatives of the organizations that are in conflict (directly or indirectly) with the architecture goal that the mandate specifies. Accept mandate adjustments to the extent that they represent non-negotiable positions for the signatories. This will ensure that architecture mandates are not decided for futile missions and against an existing force field in your organization (ARCHITECTURE MANDATE).

6.2.2   Learning Organization

Organizations must continuously learn to respond to evolving challenges and keep pace with other environmental changes. An architecture function that does not consciously reflect on new knowledge and experiences and uses them to improve its services, methods, and processes misses a golden opportunity to continuously improve itself.

Learning is the act or experience of one that learns, it is the knowledge or skill acquired by instruction or study. (Merriam-Webster Dictionary 2020)

As the saying goes, *change is the only constant*, and change is the rule, not the exception, in the twenty-first century. As the world changes, so do business models—a reality companies constantly face. While new challenges and framing conditions call established solution approaches into question, corresponding adjustments require flexibility and a company's high willingness to learn.

Peter Senge (2010) and colleagues coined the term *learning organization* in 1990. They defined a learning organization as one that enables its members to learn and continuously change in order to maintain or increase its competitiveness. Peter Senge et al., in their research, differentiated five disciplines of a learning organization:

- *Systems thinking* is a skill that learning organizations establish when they think systematically and measurably about their company's performance.
- *Personal mastery* strongly presupposes each individual's will to learn, reflect critically on the status quo, question it, and become personally involved.
- *Mental models* refer to the conscious and unconscious collective assumptions, beliefs, and ideas that determine how individuals perceive the world—what they can observe and imagine (and what they cannot).
- *Shared vision* describes the phenomenon of a common identity between people in a learning organization with the aim of intersubjective coordination and orientation.
- *Team learning* is the accumulation of individual learning and aims to reconcile individual experimentation with supra-individual coordination and networking.

The advantages of learning architecture organizations are apparent. Learning organizations improve their organizational vitality. By welcoming and encouraging a continuous stream of new experiences, insights, but also irritations, learning keeps architecture organizations dynamic and improves their ability to absorb change. A learning organization improves its innovative strength, as learning and innovation are two sides of the same coin. An architecture organization encouraging its architects to learn continuously will inevitably create an innovative environment. It also improves organizational efficiency since sharing and reusing individually gained knowledge creates learning synergies throughout the company.

Architecture Function and Learning Organization

Set up your architecture function to continuously adapt to a fast-paced and ever-changing environment by embracing Peter Senge's five disciplines of a learning organization. Include learning objectives in your architecture role definitions. Systematically capture the knowledge gained in reference assets (e.g., architecture patterns) so that they can be shared with other architects via an architecture platform. Make fundamental concepts and categories available to the architecture community via an architecture language and domain taxonomies. Optimize your methods so that architects are systematically reminded of capturing individual findings and share them with peers (Fig. 6.11).

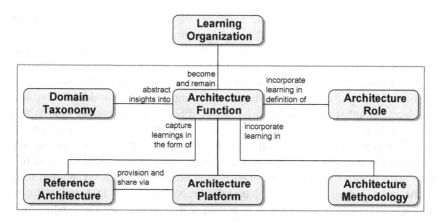

Fig. 6.11 Architecture function and learning organization

Include individual and organizational learning responsibilities in your architecture role model. For example, make domain architects responsible for explaining essential domain concepts to a broad architecture community via training courses. At the same time, require all architecture roles to capture, generalize, and share lessons learned and accept training offers from others (**ARCHITECTURE ROLE**).

Establish a positive culture of failure to stimulate architectural experimentation. Give your architects time and space to explore new territory. Set up an architecture laboratory, for example, or finance experimental prototypes together with interested parties outside of the architecture function, for example, business units or suppliers. Determine the capacity you need to ensure adequate bandwidth for research, learning, and experimentation, and provide that capacity with an appropriate mandate and funding (**ARCHITECTURE CAPACITY, ARCHITECTURE FUNDING**).

Establish a common, overarching, and clear vision and mission statement and commit all architects to aligning with it. For example, clarify and capture the primary purpose, goals, and objectives of your architecture function. Distinguish between what is essential to your success and what is not—short, medium, and long term. Clarify which architecture assets deserve maximum attention as opposed to comparatively less critical assets. For example, clarify which architecture services are vital instead of services that are just *nice to have*. Summarize this in your function's vision and mission statement as your *shared vision* (**ARCHITECTURE ASSET**).

Team learning is the natural accumulation of people who gain, capture, and share knowledge. Improve team learning by rotating architects through an architecture SPOC organization. The SPOC is the hinge between the architecture function and your customers—therefore crucial to get an overview of the what, why, who, and how of your function (**ARCHITECTURE SPOC**).

Encourage your architects to step out of their comfort zones and openly discuss their ideas both inside and outside the enterprise. Invite them to verify ideas across other functions and disciplines. Host and attend collaborative formats such as webinars or conferences to generate, exchange, and test ideas. Conduct architecture ideation sessions that systematize the process of promoting and collecting innovative ideas. Schedule recurring ideation sessions via your calendar to regularly poll your architects for inspiring ideas (**ARCHITECTURE INNOVATION**).

Our *mental models* enable and limit our ability to perceive the world. Your architects' ability to create outstanding designs, find innovative solutions to business problems, or otherwise crack tough nuts is limited by the mental models they maintain for a given domain. This means that your architects' mental models enable or hinder your architecture function in fulfilling its mandate. Turn their partially unconscious mental models into explicit domain taxonomies to gain control over how your architecture community perceives a domain. Domain taxonomies make unconscious mental models tangible and relatable. They are an excellent fix for misunderstandings by establishing important abstractions, categories, and relationships between them within a given domain at the linguistic level (**ARCHITECTURE LANGUAGE, DOMAIN TAXONOMY**).

Encourage your architects to question questions and appreciate the personal commitment of your architects. Ensure that excellent expertise coupled with the right attitude is valued in architecture roles, yearly objectives, or personal development plans to foster *personal mastery* (**NEED TO KNOW**).

Systematically incorporate debriefing points and retrospectives into your architecture methodologies, processes, and view models to promote a reflective learning attitude (i.e., *systems thinking*). For example, include a *lessons learned* step in your solution architecture methodology as a final activity at the end of a problem-solving endeavor. Make this step mandatory and provide means to share individual lessons learned with a broad architecture community (**YOUR OWN ARCHITECTURE METHODOLOGY**).

Promote and use reference assets intensively. Accumulate the knowledge of individual architects and share it with all architects in your organization. Generalize specific findings to make them widely available. The generalization makes the knowledge of individual architects reusable for many in your enterprise. For example, an architect designs an authentication approach for a particular application and then generalizes the chosen approach via a security architecture pattern. The new pattern summarizes what was learned individually in a reusable and replicable fashion. In future, other architects in the enterprise will noticeably benefit from the individual architect's learning by using the new security pattern and applying it as part of their problem-solving efforts (**ARCHITECTURE PATTERN METHODOLOGY**).

Anonymize valuable architectural artifacts and treat them as intellectual property—such as guidelines or white papers that architects have created in a project. Classify the anonymized artifacts comprehensively so that your architects can easily find them and link them to their tasks. For example, set up a portal for intellectual property and encourage your architects to use the portal's resources and encourage them to contribute their own insights to the portal. At the same time, promote the intensive use of portal contributions made by others (**YOUR OWN ARCHITECTURE PLATFORM**).

Use the structures and contents of this book to establish the basis for diverse learning curricula in your company, for example, the pattern *language topology* and patterns of this book. Lay multiple learning paths (i.e., each path is a separate curriculum) across your learning base in such a way that you can offer training and education along roles, disciplines, domains, and other dimensions relevant in your enterprise.

6.2.3   Architecture Maturity

An architectural value proposition remains unclear when the extent to which architecture meets company expectations cannot be articulated or quantified. Architecture functions must provide indisputable evidence of their contributions to justify investments in them. An architecture function that fails to meet the expectations of the business loses its raison d'être. A function that cannot determine or communicate its degree of maturity is immature.

Maturity is the quality or state of being mature, which is having attained a final or desired state. (Merriam-Webster Dictionary 2020)

Merriam-Webster defines maturity or maturation as the process of reaching a desired end state. The normative question of what should be desired remains open, however.

A *norm* is a principle of right action serving to guide, control, or regulate proper and acceptable behavior. (Merriam-Webster Dictionary 2020)

A utilitarian perspective assumes corporate norms as inherent in strategic corporate goals. A company's strategic goals are the main reasons for its existence, for example, selling the cheapest cars in the world. Secondary goals are inwardly directed and derived from the primary goals, for example, reducing the budget of the IT department to lower the production costs of cars. While primary goals represent the corporate purpose, secondary goals serve the corporate purpose indirectly by being the means to achieve the purpose.

Architecture Function and Architecture Maturity
Architecture functions align their degree of maturity to optimally support their companies. Maturity models are critical for them to achieve the desired maturity level as planned. Architecture-related maturity models are differentiated by architecture level. Their quantifiability is ensured by KPIs, pervading methods, and platforms. Architecture functions delegate the definition and adoption of maturity models to their governance branches (**ARCHITECTURE GOVERNANCE**) (Fig. 6.12).

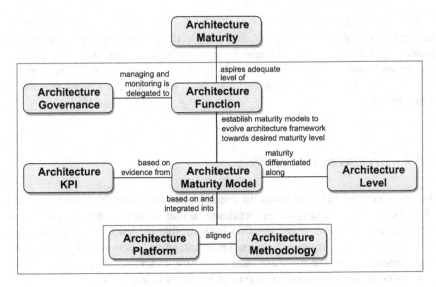

Fig. 6.12 Architecture function and architecture maturity

Architecture Maturity Model

Architecture functions have *architecture goals* that are derived from corporate goals (*enterprise goal*). Architecture norms are inherent in the architecture goals. Once defined, architecture goals are periodically reviewed to ensure that they remain consistent with the corporate goals. Architecture functions execute *architecture acts*, which lead to *architecture facts* that in turn fulfill *architecture goals*. Essential aspects of facts are systematically measured using performance indicators (*architecture KPI*[5]). Architecture maturity metrics indicate the extent to which architecture facts deviate from architecture goals. This degree of deviation determines the maturity level of an architecture function (Fig. 6.13).

---

[5] Key performance indicators (KPIs) measure and indicate the performance of an organization or activity based on an underlying performance measurement metric.

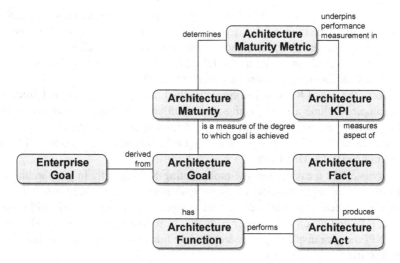

Fig. 6.13 Architecture maturity metamodel

Distinguish two types of *deviation* between *facts* and *goals* from a purely *quantitative* perspective: too few facts or too many facts. For example, introducing too many architecture guidelines can lead to inadequately followed guidelines. In another example, an architecture function elaborates a solution as an answer to a problem. The function may over- or under-analyze the problem and design an architecture solution that is too detailed or too abstract.

Maturity metrics are also *normative* metrics that distinguish mature from immature facts. They guide architects on right and wrong. Even if maturity metrics exist, architects must be able to measure the effects (*architecture facts*) of architecture contributions (*architecture acts*) against them. Architecture facts must be measurable so that architects can assess and further improve them. Without measurement, their maturity can neither be determined nor enhanced. A healthy measurement culture is therefore crucial for architecture functions—or, to put it with Galileo Galilei:[6]

Measure what is measurable and make measurable what is not so.

Architecture Key Performance Indicators (KPIs)

Introduce maturity metrics and KPIs to measure architecture facts. KPIs enable the quantification and qualification of the contributions made by your function. They measure architecture effectiveness and the degree of achievement of set goals. KPI definitions clarify *what* is being measured, *how* and *why* it is being measured, and by *whom* it is being measured. They refer to architecture assets and measure aspects relevant to the performance evaluation of these, for example, measuring aspects of

---

[6]Galileo Galilei (1564–1642).

landscape assets (e.g., the number of patterns adopted for the design of an application), structural assets (e.g., the degree of service portfolio changes adhering to domain roadmap planning), reference assets (e.g., degree of adopting a particular pattern in solution design), and methodological assets (e.g., the number of received method advancement suggestions) (**ARCHITECTURE ASSET**).

Enforce the use of KPIs by incorporating them into your methods and processes. For example, include a *retrospective activity* in your solution architecture method and encourage architects to suggest method improvements. Capture the feedback you receive in a *number of received method advancement suggestions* KPI (**YOUR OWN ARCHITECTURE METHODOLOGY**).

Automate KPI measurement by implementing KPIs directly in your architecture platform. For example, provide a form in your architecture portal to collect method improvement ideas. Automatically update and publish a corresponding KPI on your platform depending on the number of method improvements received. This gives you a KPI monitor displaying your architecture function's health in real time (**YOUR OWN ARCHITECTURE PLATFORM**).

Clarify the purpose each KPI serves by linking it to the goals it supports. Points of reference are the goal KPI matrices suggested in the EAM KPI Catalog (Matthes et al. KPI 2011). Goal KPI matrices also help you determine the KPI priority, which you can derive from the priority of supported goals (Fig. 6.14).

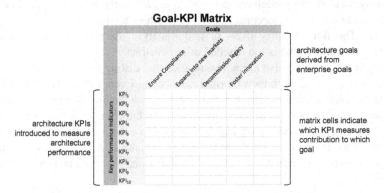

Fig. 6.14 Goal KPI matrix

Design your KPIs so that you can determine and improve the degree to which your architecture function effectively supports your company's goals, for example, the extent to which architecture services meet your enterprise needs. Let us look at some examples of incorporating KPIs into your architecture function's services. For example, you can measure the *number of requests* your function handled in a given period, as well as the *customer satisfaction* you received for the service delivery. You can measure the *ratio of services delivered in accordance with service-level agreements (SLA[7])* or *service availability*. Yet other examples are the *number of service improvements* delivered, *number of received service escalations,* or the *number of contributions not in the service catalog.* Measure the desired effects—not their causes, for example, the *total cost savings due to options proposed by the architecture function,* or *efficiency improvements (monetized) of architecture services.*

Correlate complementary KPIs to get summary insights without introducing additional metrics. For example, an architecture function could differentiate between measurement points distributed horizontally along the enterprise value chain (classification, *value chain KPI*) and vertically across architecture levels (classification, *architecture levels KPI*). The function defines KPI_{S2} as a value chain KPI that measures the effectiveness of architecture processes executed in the building stream. KPI_{L4} and KPI_{L5} are defined as level KPIs, with KPI_{L4} measuring the adequacy of the domain architecture and KPI_{L5} measuring the quality of a delivered solution architecture. The combination of KPI_{S2} and KPI_{L4} may indicate that the architecture process's poor performance in the build phase correlates with unsatisfactory domain architecture results. The combination of KPI_{S2} and KPI_{L5} may indicate a similar correlation between the appropriateness of the architecture process and the quality of architecture at the solution level (**ARCHITECTURE LEVEL**) (Fig. 6.15).

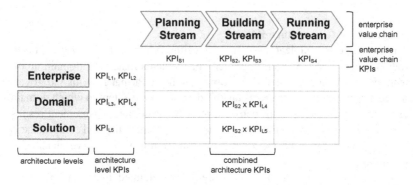

Fig. 6.15 Combined architecture KPIs

---

[7]Service-level agreements (SLA) are commitments between service provider and service consumer. Particular aspects of a service are formally agreed in an SLA contract, for example, service availability, service response time, mean time to repair, or mean time between failures.

Adopt the attribute schema below as a basic template for your architecture KPI definitions (Table 6.1).

Table 6.1 KPI definition template

Attribute name	Attribute description
KPI abstract	Summary of a KPI's *what*, *why*, *who*, and *how*
KPI owner	Defines the party (*who*) responsible for evolving, measuring, and communicating the KPI
KPI stakeholder	Defines the parties that are interested in viewing the measured KPI results
KPI frequency	Defines *when* and *how* often measurements are taken
KPI observed object	Defines the measured object (*what*), for example, an architecture asset or process
KPI measuring	Defines *how* KPI measuring is carried out, for example: "divide the number of *satisfactory customer feedback received* by the number of all *service requests executed*"
KPI target value	Defines the desired value, which acts as a constant. The value is not calculated or updated when the KPI is applied
KPI measured value	A variable that records the measurement result. The attribute is recalculated every time the KPI is applied
KPI evaluation	Interpretation of the difference between the measured KPI value and the KPI target value. The attribute is recalculated every time the KPI is applied
KPI escalation	Defines when and how a measurement result is escalated as a result of the KPI evaluation
KPI status	Lifecycle status of the KPI (e.g., active, inactive)

Let us look at an example of how an architecture function has defined a KPI to review and ensure appropriate use of the domain architecture methodology.

Architecture Governance KPI

The governance organization of an architecture function (*KPI owner*) plans to regularly measure the extent to which engagements match the domain architecture methodology. It defines a corresponding KPI that informs the governance organization and the KPI stakeholders about the extent to which domain architecture methods are correctly adopted. Suppose the measurement results indicate poor method conformance. In this case, domain method compliance is made a personal goal by the architecture function in its incentive plans (*KPI escalation*).

The frequency of the KPI measurement is defined quarterly (*KPI frequency*). Domain architecture descriptions are the objects observed by the KPI (*KPI observed objects*), the measurement of which is defined as a two-phase process (*KPI measuring*). In the first phase, all descriptions of the

(continued)

domain architecture are reviewed, and the test results are rated as either *poor*, *fair*, or *good*, while in the second phase, the average of the tests is calculated.

The *KPI target value* is defined as the interval [*fair*, *good*], while the *KPI measured value* in this example was determined to be *fair*.

The performed KPI delivered satisfactory results, as the value *fair* is within the *KPI target value* interval (*KPI evaluation*). Therefore, no escalations (*KPI escalations*) need to be triggered. Otherwise, the architecture function would have taken countermeasures to increase method compliance (Fig. 6.16).

Domain Architecture Methodology KPI	
KPI abstract	Measure indicates degree to which architecture engagements conformed to domain architecture methodology during measurement period 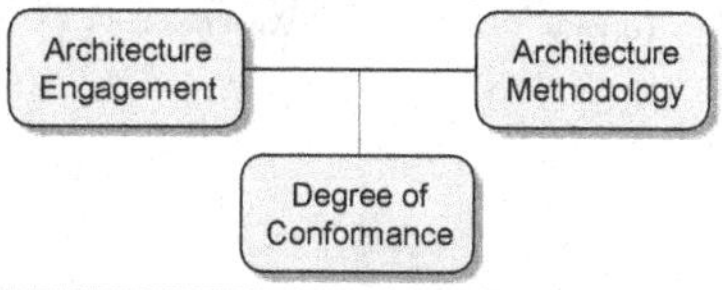
KPI owner	Architecture governance organization
KPI stakeholder	Architecture function
KPI frequency	Quarterly
KPI observed object	Domain architecture description

KPI measuring	I. For all architecture descriptions (AD) AD$_i$ do
	   1. assess AD$_i$
	   2. classify method-conformance (poor, fair, good)
	   3. confirm with all architects
	 II. Create distribution over all AD$_i$ assessments

KPI target value	Arithmetic mean over all AD$_i$ is in [fair, good]
KPI measured value	Fair
KPI evaluation	Ok. However, room for improvement identified
KPI escalation	Make domain method adherence a pivotal objective in all architects' incentive plans

Fig. 6.16 *KPI example*

Consolidate KPIs into *architecture scorecards*.[8] Architecture scorecards provide an overview of architecture organizations' performance by displaying the mission and vision, contributions made, and architecture maturity indicators over a period of time (Fig. 6.17).

---

[8] Scorecard (also: balanced scorecard) is a performance management tool in the form of a semiformal report that managers use to track the execution of activities and monitor these actions' consequences.

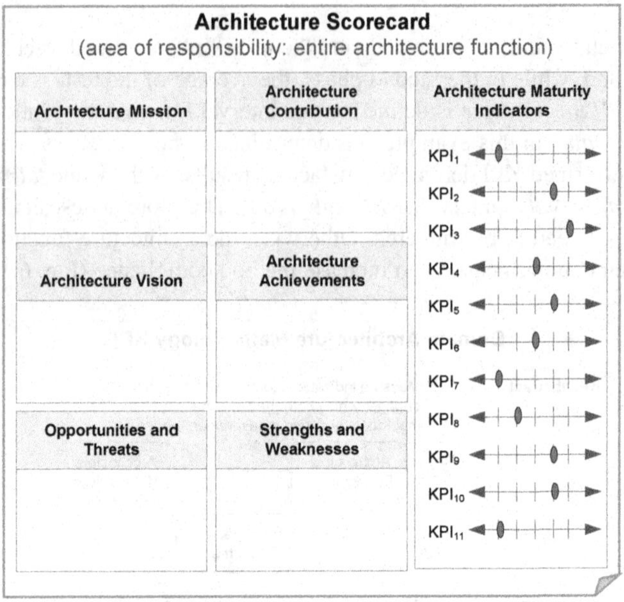

Fig. 6.17 Architecture scorecard template

Use the *radar-chart method* (Keller 2017) to display maturity assessment results using a qualitative metric and relate these to the desired results. Radar-charts support architecture functions in systematically understanding and closing the gaps between their currently measured (*measured today*) and their desired performance (*plan 2022, plan 2023*) (Fig. 6.18).

Fig. 6.18 Architecture
radar-chart

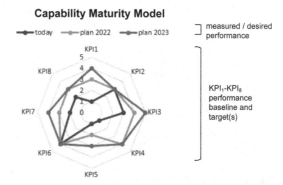

Measuring architecture maturity is associated with costs. Therefore, carefully measure only those aspects that help your company achieve its goals. Derive architecture goals from your business objectives. Next, derive KPIs from a prioritized set of architecture goals. Before deciding on a final set of KPIs, assess their feasibility. A KPI is feasible if its regular measurement is realistic and reasonable in terms of its cost-benefit ratio. For example, it is pointless to introduce a KPI if it is unrealistic to address the problems it signals (**ARCHITECTURE FUNDING**, **ARCHITECTURE CAPACITY**).

Architecture Maturity Model

Equip your function with an *architecture maturity model*. Architecture maturity models have a long history and are derived from capability maturity models developed by the Software Engineering Institute (SEI) in the 1990s. The first software engineering and development capability maturity model (CMM) was published in 1990. Organizations use capability maturity models to gain control over and improve their organizational processes. You use capability maturity models to determine the maturity level baseline of your architecture function so that you can systematically plan improvements to achieve your desired maturity state. Capability maturity models include *capabilities* (i.e., capability$_1$), *maturity levels* (i.e., L_1), and *maturity criteria*. Maturity criteria define criteria that must be met for a particular capability to be considered mature (e.g., C_{11}) (Fig. 6.19).

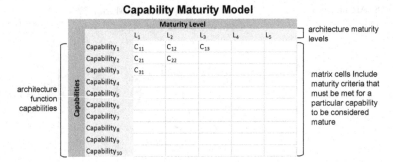

Fig. 6.19 Capability maturity model

The IT Governance Institute (2020) suggested criteria (e.g., for organizations, policies, and processes) when it introduced the *COBIT 4.1 maturity model*. Although COBIT[9] was not explicitly defined for architecture functions, it is still fully applicable to architecture as a whole (Table 6.2).

Table 6.2 COBIT maturity levels

Attribute name	Attribute description
(0) *None*	No governance process. The organization does not even realize that a problem needs to be fixed
(1) *Initial*	It is recognized that governance issues exist and that they need to be addressed. Isolated ad hoc actions are taken to alleviate governance issues
(2) *Repeatable but intuitive*	There is an awareness of governance issues. Governance activities and performance indicators that include planning, deployment, and monitoring processes are under development. Specific processes are identified for improvement
(3) *Defined*	The importance of governance is understood and communicated by the management organization. The procedures are standardized and documented
(4) *Managed and measurable*	The understanding of governance issues at all levels is fully established. Responsibilities are defined (SLAs) and monitored (KPIs). The duties are clear, and the process responsibility is fully defined. Processes and governance controls are built into the achievement of business goals and strategies
(5) *Optimized*	Governance issues and corresponding solutions are fully anticipated. Training and communication are established throughout the organization. Processes are operated at an industry best-practice maturity level, and continuous process improvement measures have been taken. Organizations, employees, and processes can flexibly adapt to changing environmental conditions

---

[9]COBIT (control objectives for information and related technologies) defines several general processes and an elementary maturity model for IT management. It was specially developed to help companies comply with laws in an agile way.

Define your function's maturity model by specifying architecture services and other valuable contributions you regularly make along the architecture levels. Use the COBIT definitions for maturity level (horizontal axis) as a starting point. Next, define the architecture capability criteria in the maturity model cells. Base your criteria specifications on architecture processes (*acts*), successes (*facts*), and KPIs. For example, on the vertical axis, the maturity model lists the capabilities *determine architecture relevance* and *elaborate solution architecture*. The maturity criterion L_3 (EA-C$_3$) requires that *a solution architecture methodology is established and documented*. The L_5 maturity criterion (EA-C$_5$) is *all architects fully adopt solution architecture methodology in the organization, architecture training is established, and the method is continuously improved, anticipating future method demand*. Group architecture services and functions according to the architecture levels differentiated in your enterprise (e.g., *solution architecture, domain architecture, enterprise architecture*). Aggregate and average maturity for each architecture level (ARCHITECTURE LEVEL) (Fig. 6.20).

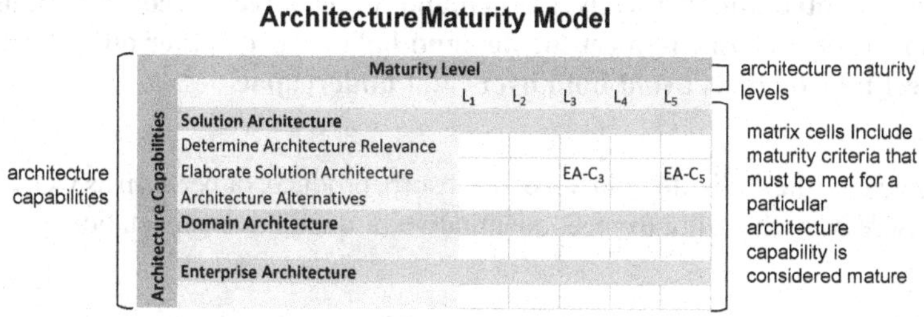

Fig. 6.20   Architecture maturity model

Regular maturity measurement is important to correctly assess development trends and take corrective action when needed. Therefore, ensure that the measurement, consolidation, and communication of the architecture maturity are performed regularly by including appropriate reminders in your architecture calendar (ARCHITECTURE CALENDAR).

Put the most essential of all maturity considerations at the beginning of any architecture activity: a critical reflection on the given task and the question of its relevance, correctness, and completeness. In other words, make sure that your architects always critically question themselves and others regarding the goal of an action—that is, that they do not accept questions unquestioningly. Avoiding superfluous contributions and their consequences is arguably one of the greatest contributors to organizational maturity (NEED TO KNOW).

Another seemingly banal but often not even rudimentarily established prerequisite for maturity is a clearly established common architectural vocabulary. Language is the basis for any coordinated action and cooperation—regardless of whether problems, goals, or measures for achieving them are discussed and coordinated. Thus, ensure that a common linguistic base for fundamental concepts is established in your organization—both with respect to fundamental and domain-specific concepts (ARCHITECTURE LANGUAGE, DOMAIN TAXONOMY).

The bottom line is that the maturity of a system, such as an application, a domain, or a methodology, is a function of the extent to which someone is held responsible for that system. A strong and intrinsic sense of responsibility cannot be replaced by any extrinsic system of order, like policies, rules, or guidelines (ARCHITECTURE OWNERSHIP).

6.2.4 Architecture Capacity

Sufficient capacity is a prerequisite for an architecture function to meet its stakeholders' expectations and to provide architecture services or make other necessary contributions. Ideally, the demand for architecture contributions and the capacities available to meet the demand balance each other out. Therefore, architecture functions avoid both over- and undercapacities.

> *Capacity* is the ability to hold, receive, absorb, produce, or perform as well as a measure of such ability to meet quantitative or qualitative expectation.

Architecture capacity is the ability of an architecture function to meet stakeholder expectations quantitatively, qualitatively, and promptly.

Architecture capacity management ensures that architecture demands are reliably met by providing the required capacity. Demand for architecture fluctuates over time, as does demand for architecture services. Architecture capacity management anticipates future demand to provide sufficient capacity, for example, by surveying customers to accurately forecast future demand. Capacity management derives from the forecasts *what* architecture services and resources (*who*) will be needed and to what extent (*how much*) to meet the forecasted demand. When an architecture service is effectively requested, capacity management reviews the capacity required to perform the request satisfactorily. It allocates the required resources, calculates the cost, and finally commits to delivery. Capacity management distinguishes demand and associated capacity in terms of specificity. Forecasted demand can only vaguely anticipate specific deliverables or exact delivery dates, while a concrete architecture service request concretely specifies expected outcomes.

Architecture Function and Architecture Capacity
Architecture capacity includes, for example, organizational capacity or platform capacity. Architecture functions perform their capacity management in such a way that both overcapacity and undercapacity are avoided. Overcapacity is a situation where the available capacity outweighs the demand for architecture services.

Overcapacity means that the potential for valuable contributions is unnecessarily funded. In times of undercapacity, service requests cannot be processed due to insufficiently qualified or available architecture resources. If overcapacity is a frequent occurrence in your enterprise, you should remove irrelevant services, or lower the quality level at which you guarantee service delivery. If undercapacity is the more common phenomenon, you should consider architecture sourcing to cope with demand volatility (**ARCHITECTURE SOURCING**) (Fig. 6.21).

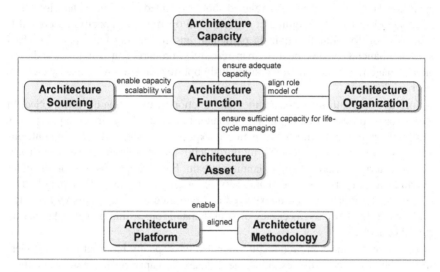

Fig. 6.21 Architecture function and architecture capacity

Optimize architecture capacity by improving the productivity of the architecture function, what you achieve best in the area of cognitive performance (i.e., brainwork) through education. For example, continuously develop the capabilities of your architects through training, coaching, and other means of a learning organization to improve the quality and adaptability of their contributions—ultimately to increase the efficiency and effectiveness of your architecture function (**LEARNING ORGANIZATION**).

Negotiate expectations or service guarantees and reduce them partially if you suffer from capacity constraints and need to overcome them. For example, an architecture function agrees with the customer of an *elaborate architecture* service that only an initial draft[10] will be created instead of a fully developed design. Furthermore, the function discusses that the focus in the design should be on

---

[10] Architectural draft is an initial architectural design that provides an early basis for reflection and discussion but is expressly unfinished and requires further evolution.

identifying architecture conditions and considering architecture alternatives (**ARCHI-
TECTURE CONDITION, ARCHITECTURE ALTERNATIVES**).

Distinguish between constituent and operational capacity. Research has shown
that only 20% of the total cost of ownership[11] (TCO) is the cost of initially setting up
a system. In comparison, 80% of the total cost of ownership is the cost of maintenance, development, and operation of a corresponding system. Your function is a
system—a system consisting of organization, services, assets, and platforms, among
other things. So when in doubt, focus your attention on optimizing your function's
operational capacity and be more relaxed about expended constituent capacity. Once
you have identified the required constituent and operational capacity, ensure sufficient funding for your function. In particular, ensure funding for support services
such as financial management, human resources, procurement, sourcing, and supplier management that help you continuously optimize operational capacity (**ARCHI-
TECTURE FUNDING**).

Improve the maturity of the architecture function by expecting the unexpected. In
other words, prepare for exceptional demand. For example, a strategic program is
launched where the architecture function is expected to make a significant contribution. Improve demand forecasting by introducing the appropriate checkpoints early
in your enterprise value chain's planning stream. For example, include architecture
demand checkpoints in your demand, service, or project portfolio. Introduce KPIs[12]
measuring the ratio between unexpected and expected demands. This will provide
evidence of the predictive accuracy of your demand forecasting process (**ARCHITEC-
TURE MATURITY**).

Note that advances in architecture increase the capacity required for their operation. Therefore, carefully examine the increase in capacity that will result from
respective advancement. For example, an architecture function plans to introduce a
policy (e.g., that every cross-domain interface requires the enterprise architecture's
approval). The architecture function estimates that the new policy will significantly
increase the number of approvals required. The capacity to approve interfaces
between domains will also need to be increased to avoid project delays. Calculate
the future capacity required by a planned policy rollout or change and make approval
of planned policy changes contingent on available capacity (**ARCHITECTURE POLICY**).

It may seem counterintuitive, but removing an architecture asset (e.g., application, platform, or service) that has expired can easily outweigh the positive effects of
adding new assets. Therefore, allocate and provision capacity not only for expanding
your asset portfolios but also for reducing them and thus decommissioning assets
(**DECOMMISSIONING REWARD**).

---

[11] Total cost of ownership (TCO) is a financial metric that helps cost bearers determine the direct
and indirect costs of a product or service. The key figure is used in full cost accounting and is a long-
term cost indicator.

[12] Key performance indicators (KPIs) measure and indicate the performance of an organization or
activity based on an underlying performance measurement metric.

Tie architecture mandate and capacity management processes together, closely. Include a capacity checkpoint and corresponding form fields in your architecture mandate template to ensure that capacity is checked before commitments are officially made—that is, before a mandate is finally signed (ARCHITECTURE MANDATE).

Avoid the mistake that is made far too often and do not focus your efforts on a single lifecycle phase or a few select asset types. Instead, ensure sufficient capacity to support the entire lifecycle of all asset types adequately. For example, support the planning, building, and running of services, applications, platforms, architecture methods and processes, and reference assets such as architecture roadmaps or patterns (LANDSCAPE ASSET, YOUR OWN ARCHITECTURE METHODOLOGY, REFERENCE ARCHITECTURE METHODOLOGY).

Keep your capacity profile low by promoting reusability. Reusability comes at a cost, but extra effort usually pays off. For example, *business unit A* uses an application that *business unit B* created. Business unit B's application design supports the logical separation of multiple tenants[13] that can be individually adapted. In this way, business unit A can seamlessly use the application that B created. In another example of reusability, A has devised an architecture pattern that B reuses when designing a new service (ARCHITECTURE PATTERN METHODOLOGY).

Similarly, allocate capacity to build and evolve an architecture platform that gives you visibility and holistic landscape perspectives, ultimately enabling you to deliver architecture services productively. Do not underestimate the capacity required to establish and maintain a platform that meets your needs. You need to design it, implement it, and integrate it with other systems, and you need to operate and evolve it over time. At the same time, do not underestimate the productivity gains you can expect from a well-designed platform for making your contributions (YOUR OWN ARCHITECTURE PLATFORM).

Increase the level of automation of your architecture function to optimize the capacity you need to meet the given demands. Use a SPOC organization to identify frequently recurring demands—thus to identify automation potentials. Make sure that all (not yet) standardized architecture requests have to be placed with your SPOC before they are processed. This way, the SPOC organization recognizes frequent request patterns and thus corresponding automation and optimization potentials (ARCHITECTURE SPOC).

---

[13]Multi-tenancy design is an approach in which a single physical solution serves multiple clients (i.e., tenant). Systems adopting a multi-tenancy architecture provide physically shared resources, while ensuring logically separated and tenant-specific spaces. Multi-tenant architectures are designed to provide each tenant with a dedicated share of a physical instance, where such share includes data, configuration, user administration, and tenant-specific functional as well as non-functional properties.

6.2.5   Architecture Role

Architects assume alternating responsibilities in an area of diverse architecture engagements. An architecture role is a specification of competencies, responsibilities, and authorizations independent of the people assuming the role. Architecture role models enable capability and capacity planning by decoupling role definitions from currently available competencies. They help align the development or recruitment of architectural skills with future demands. Roles make the definition of methods and processes, ownership structures, or guidelines independent of competencies as they exist in the organization today.

> An *actor* is one that acts, or one that takes an active part. (Merriam-Webster Dictionary 2020)

Actors are those who act—they are the active parts of a company. The actors carry out coordination and production acts. A subject or a group of subjects who perform actions is called an actor. The actor concept can be extended beyond humans to nonhuman actors. For example, we can consider a clinical thermometer emitting temperature events as an actor.

> A *role* is a character assigned or assumed or a function or part performed, especially in a particular operation. (Merriam-Webster Dictionary 2020)

While the term actor emphasizes presence and action orientation, the term role has a slightly more distant connotation. A role defines privileges, responsibilities, liabilities, or authorizations that an actor who takes on the role inevitably inherits and performs. Architecture roles are at the heart of your functional design. The totality of all architecture roles gives an overview of the totality of all architecture coordination and production acts that your organization has committed to carry out. It inherently defines your architecture value proposition.

Architecture Function and Architecture Role
Derive your function's role model from the architecture needs of your enterprise. For example, derive roles from the services required for architecture-related support to the enterprise value chain. Define roles considering their responsibilities, liabilities, authorizations, competencies, and attitudes, and ensure that the role model is practically adopted (Fig. 6.22).

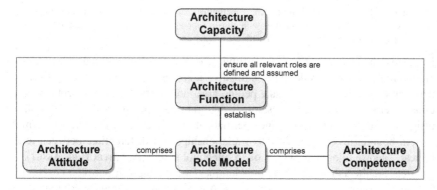

Fig. 6.22   Architecture function and architecture role

Naturally born architects share fundamental competencies and attitudes—regardless of a particular role they take on at a particular point in time. Often, if not always, the importance of the attitude toward architecture outweighs the importance of related book knowledge. For example, suppose two architects are asked to come up with a solution. A bug-prone system that keeps crashing needs to be healed. The system's codebase is not available, so fixing the bug by making changes to the code is not an option. A pilot study proposes creating a corrective component that monitors the unstable system and automatically restarts it when a failure is detected. The tech-savvy architect, lacking an ideal architectural attitude, delves deeply into the technical details of heartbeat protocols, management information bases (MIBs[14]), watchdogging,[15] and daemon[16] processes and comes back with an armada of impressive design models. However, the other architect, who is endowed with a reflective mindset and architectural stance, tries to clarify the problem before going in search of a solution. For example, he asks the following questions: What is the fault-prone system's remaining lifetime, and how much effort is justified for the healing component? Can the component determine the correct reboot and recovery of the unstable system beyond doubt, and if so, how? Can we reuse or customize components from a systems management platform instead of building the monitoring component from scratch? Great architects value questions at least as much as answers. They carefully consider directions before heading toward solutions (**Need to Know**).

In his opus *De Architectura—libri Decem*, Marcus Vitruvius Pollio[17] described well what makes a great architect (Vitruvius 2013):

---

[14] Management information base (MIB) is a database used to manage the entities in a communication network. MIBs are also queried by monitoring agents.

[15] Watchdog is a computerized timer that one uses to detect and correct system malfunctions. Watchdogs are utilized to facilitate automatic recovery from system crashes that occur infrequently or temporarily.

[16] Daemon process is a program that runs as a background process and is not directly controlled by an interactive user.

[17] Marcus Vitruvius Pollio (Vitruvius) was a Roman author, architect, and civil and military engineer in the first century BC. He suggested that buildings should have the three attributes: firmitas (strength), utilitas (utility), and venustas (beauty).

A man of letters, a skilled draftsman, a mathematician, familiar with historical studies, a diligent of philosophy, acquainted with music, not ignorant of medicine, earned in the response of juris consultis, familiar with astronomy and astronomical calculations.

If we trust the analysis of Marcus Vitruvius, we can say that rationality, knowledge orientation, creativity, reflexivity, curiosity, eagerness to learn, and team spirit are personal characteristics that make people great architects. Great architects are genuine system thinkers. They consciously take on many perspectives to gain holistic insights. Great architects conduct permanent relevance checks. They determine system boundaries and cross-system relationships and differentiate between teleological[18] and ontological[19] views of architectural assets (ARCHITECTURE ASSET).

Great architects use abstraction techniques and distinguish between conceptual, logical, and physical system perspectives. A great architect begins every journey by asking *why*, followed by *what, when, how,* and *by whom.* For example, when an architect is asked to tackle a proposed solution, he discusses and captures rationale (*why*), expected deliverables (*what*), schedules (*when*), approaches (*how*), and skills and capacities (*who*) in an architecture mandate. He formally discusses and agrees the mandate with stakeholders and sponsors. Next, he formulates a *definition of done*[20] based on quantifiable criteria for each of the agreed deliverables before elaborating the solution architecture (ARCHITECTURE MANDATE).

Great architects are efficiently organized realists who continuously think about the practical feasibility of their ideas, plans, and designs. They are immune to naïve and superficial concepts such as *tool = solution.* They communicate unambiguously and professionally and are cautious listeners who seek a holistic understanding of a given topic. A great architect articulates architectural facts with the intended audience in mind. He accurately recognizes ambiguities and ensures that they are quickly resolved. On the one hand, a great architect maintains a questioning and skeptical attitude; on the other hand, he is able to formulate discovered potential for improvement with a positive twist (ARCHITECTURE LANGUAGE).

You cannot easily measure attitudes, and there are no certificates (or diplomas) attesting reasonable attitude toward architecture. However, the right attitude is half the battle in becoming a great architect and is therefore of immanent importance. If you ever observe inadequate attitudes, check motivation. An architect, for example,

---

[18]Teleological system concept. The term teleological system deals with a system's function and behavior as observed from the outside (external behavior). The teleological system's perspective is useful when using a system.

[19]Ontological system concept. The ontological system view deals with a system's mechanics as observed inside the system (internal behavior). It also distinguishes the concept of *aggregate* from the concept of *system.* Both concepts, aggregate and system, are collections of objects. However, in aggregates, the elements are not held together by interaction bonds, whereas in systems, they are. A system, therefore, has unity and integrity. Both properties are lacking in aggregates.

[20]The definition of done (DoD) is an Agile and Scrum terminology. However, it is a much broader concept for determining an exit criterion for a work product or activity. A definition of done must be created individually for each task. The DoD specifies criteria that can be held against the task's progress to recognize the achievement of the desired end state and to end the task.

fears the loss of skills because he has to deal with backward-looking topics in the context of his assignments. Perhaps an architect is also demoralized because he is frequently confronted with non-architectural conflicts for which he lacks the mandate and thus the necessary authorization within the company. Non-architectural problems such as organizational-territorial conflicts are ubiquitous in large organizations. Individually appropriate attitudes can also be eroded by the inadequate collective attitude of an organization. Heike Bruch and Bernd Vogel (2009) describe the phenomenon of *organizational energy* and how it relates to the overall success of a company:

> Research results show that an essential cause for the differences between enterprises transforming successfully and those which are overstrained by their transformation necessities is the enterprise's degree of organizational energy.

Productive energy is ideal for cooperative efforts to achieve common goals. People are collectively excited, attentive, and focused on their work. *Comfortable energy* is characterized by a high level of satisfaction and collective and individual identification with the status quo. The highest risk for this energy state is a trend toward complacency—especially in companies that have enjoyed long-term success. *Resigned phlegm* leads to mentally withdrawn individuals or individuals who are indifferent to an enterprise's challenges and goals. The resulting organizational energy is low, and the ability to improve, innovate, or perform is limited. After all, *corrosive energy* can arise at any time and any level of a company. For example, corrosive energy arose in a company that halved its workforce in a major organizational transformation. As a result, the company observes a high level of anger and distrust in this state of energy. The worst part about this energy state is that it is challenging to leave (Fig. 6.23).

Fig. 6.23 Organizational energy (© 2009 Springer Science & Business Media, reprinted with permission)

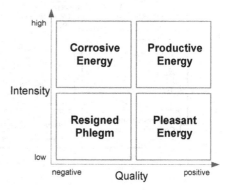

Architecture Role Model

Establish an architecture role and competency model for your function once you have addressed attitude. Equip your enterprise with all the skills it needs to accomplish its mission by establishing sufficiently diverse architecture roles. Highly specialized roles can vary significantly. However, they also always have common characteristics. For example, all roles refer to a common set of architecture methodologies or platforms practiced in an enterprise. While you demand selected roles to define, maintain, and further develop methods, you expect all architects to respect and adequately practice the defined methods and processes. For example, all architects contribute to demand management, project management, quality, and risk management by adhering to process guidelines and policies. Other expectations you have for all architects include their ability to work with architecture platforms, validate architecture results, and communicate appropriately. Identify the portion of responsibilities, liabilities, and authorizations that overlap between different role definitions and capture that portion in a role from which all others inherit.[21] Once the common aspects are clarified, focus your attention on specialized roles complementing your basic architecture role definitions. A distinction is made between different types of specialized roles, for example, roles with subject matter orientation, landscape asset orientation, governance orientation, or discipline orientation (Fig. 6.24).

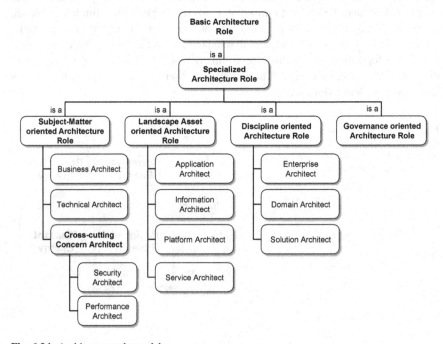

Fig. 6.24 Architecture role model

---

[21] Role inheritance defines an inheritance relationship between roles. A role on a lower hierarchy level, which is derived from a role on a level above, completely inherits the responsibilities of this role. An inheriting role specializes in an inherited role, while an inherited role generalizes an inheriting role.

Subject matter roles embrace roles that focus on business domains (*business architect*). Business architects specialize in their particular business domains (e.g., procurement, retail, or banking). They are knowledgeable about business models, major business concepts, processes, services, applications, or business patterns. They are also familiar with business domains associated with theirs. The group of subject matter roles also embraces roles that focus on technical domains (*technical architect*). Technical architects specialize in technical areas such as data warehouses[22] or IoT[23] and have the relevant technical architecture knowledge. They know important technical concepts, services, applications and platforms, and technical patterns and are familiar with related or dependent technical domains. Finally, subject matter roles embrace roles that focus on cross-cutting themes, for example, security-oriented (*security architect*), performance-oriented (*performance architect*), or availability-oriented (*availability architect*) roles.

Another notable class of roles is the group of landscape asset-oriented architecture roles. A landscape asset-oriented role focuses on a specific type of landscape asset. For example, an *information architect* role deals with conceptual, logical, and physical information entities or models representing data at rest, data in use, and data in transit.[24] Accordingly, *application architects* and *platform architects* assume responsibility for applications and platforms, while *service architects* deal with the orderly arrangement of socio-technical components making up the services (LANDSCAPE ASSET).

Next comes the class of discipline-oriented roles that correspond to the three architectural disciplines: *enterprise architect, domain architect,* and *solution architect*. While enterprise architects view the enterprise as a whole and accordingly take coarse, strategic perspectives, domain architects take on a similar role with regard to their respective domains. Enterprise and domain architects deal with overarching and portfolio-related issues. In contrast, solution architects plan and design landscape assets such as services or applications to solve particular problems (SOLUTION ARCHITECTURE DISCIPLINE, DOMAIN ARCHITECTURE DISCIPLINE, ENTERPRISE ARCHITECTURE DISCIPLINE).

Governance-oriented architecture roles are often indirectly defined by incorporating their responsibilities, liabilities, and authorizations into other roles. For

---

[22] Data warehouse is a central repository for data from various operational sources in a company. Data warehouses store and aggregate both current and historical data. Data warehouses are used for data analysis and reporting and are core components of business intelligence.

[23] Internet of things (IoT) refers to the network of physical objects (i.e., "things") in which digital operating systems, sensors, or algorithms are embedded or which connect and exchange with other systems via the Internet.

[24] Data at rest, data in use, and data in transit distinguish the three states of digital data. *Data at rest* refers to data permanently stored on computer data warehouses. Data at rest includes both structured and unstructured data. *Data in use* refers to data stored in a non-persistent state—for example, in the random access memory (RAM) of a compute node. *Data in transit* refers to data that flows between compute nodes over a network. A distinction is made for the data whether it flows over a public and untrusted network such as the Internet or whether it flows within the boundaries of a private network (e.g., corporate LAN).

example, a domain architect role defines that individuals assuming the role are responsible for reviewing and approving assets whose changes are likely to impact their domains. Review and approval in this example are governance responsibilities. However, they are not grouped together in a dedicated governance role but instead combined in a domain architecture role (**Architecture Governance**).

Architecture Competence

Architecture roles specify competencies and experience, which are prerequisites for an architect to fill a role adequately. Competencies range from technical to business skills, from expertise to experience, and from soft to hard skills. Competences range from those that your enterprise has today to those that you lack and need to develop. Retain the skills you have today and develop those you need to keep pace with future demand. For example, adopt off-the-shelf architecture training and certification programs or competency benchmarking frameworks to efficiently maintain and develop your function's competencies. One example is the Open Group's[25] Open Certified Architect (Open CA) program (Open Group Open CA 2020a). However, your function has unique competency needs beyond the general competencies covered by Open CA. Develop your own architecture training material to complement the standard training programs. For example, develop training courses to explain how your solution architecture method can be combined with other frameworks in your enterprise.

Rotate jobs to develop new skills based on expertise available in other parts of the organization. For example, you can expand your pool of architecture experts by encouraging business and technical specialists (e.g., business analysts or software developers) who have an affinity for architecture to advance into architecture positions in your organization. Conversely, you can introduce your architects to the enterprise value chain from new perspectives by offering them opportunities for positions outside of architecture, for example, in business strategy, demand management, or service portfolio management. Every new experience will further round out exposed experts. Use this opportunity as a comparatively cheap, synergistic, and effective approach for developing architecture competencies. Set up architecture communities of practice[26] (CoP) for areas that are of increasing architectural interest to your company. For example, an architecture function initiates an *IoT community of practice* because of the recent increase in sensor-based, ubiquitous computing solutions in the enterprise. Another powerful and mutually enriching technique for developing your architects is coaching. Reward coaching-coachee arrangements or other forms of semiformal knowledge sharing (**Learning Organization**).

Reward architects who recognize, capture, and share individually gained insights with others. Also, reward architects who reuse shared knowledge or develop it over

---

[25] The Open Group is an industry consortium whose aim is to achieve business goals by providing open, vendor-neutral, methodological, and technological standards and certifications.

[26] Community of Practice (CoP) describes a group of people who share a concern or interest, organize themselves, and, through regular interaction, strive to increase their knowledge or improve the results of their actions.

time. For example, reward architects who capture recurring architecture conditions as requirement patterns and share them with others. Requirement patterns generalize specific requirements or constraints. They explain which questions a requirement raises—questions that you should answer as part of specifying a requirement. They point out potential pitfalls that you regularly stumble upon when describing a requirement, and they suggest requirement variations. A requirement pattern increases the quality and productivity when creating and validating requirements (Withall 2007). For example, an architect creates a requirement pattern for the interface between systems. The pattern helps other architects create qualitative, inter-system interface specifications more efficiently and effectively based on the proven requirements design that the pattern provides (**ARCHITECTURE PATTERN METHODOLOGY**).

Architects need to aim for and maintain a level of abstraction above that of implementation teams to reduce the risk of getting lost in the overwhelming details of physical problems. On the other hand, architects must analyze and understand these details as needed; otherwise, they cannot guide, monitor, or discuss with the implementation experts. Position domain-specific languages at the intersection of competencies to provide common conceptual and terminological ground between architecture and implementation disciplines (**DOMAIN TAXONOMY**) (Fig. 6.25).

Fig. 6.25 Competence intersection

Architecture Role Definition

A competence metric is a prerequisite for defining architecture roles. Define a competence metric to distinguish competency maturity levels (e.g., basic, trained, advisory, senior) (**ARCHITECTURE MATURITY**) (Table 6.3).

Table 6.3 Competence metric

Competence level name	Competence level description
Basic	Entry-level or beginner knowledge
Trained	Educational knowledge (reading and listening knowledge)
Experienced	Working knowledge under supervision
Advisory	In-depth knowledge. Ability to act as an advisor to other architects
Senior	Well-rounded architectural expert who chairs the governing bodies of architecture, is recognized in his domain, and regularly publishes articles or speaks at conferences. Someone who drives the state of architecture in your company

Create role definitions reflecting the resource requirements of your architecture function. Define roles by combining architectural competencies and competency metrics in your role descriptions. For example, list the competency areas relevant to your function (e.g., *soft skills*, *basic architecture* knowledge, *landscape asset orientation*) and distinguish specific competencies within them (e.g., *application architecture* under *landscape orientation*). For all concrete competencies, describe the minimum maturity level this competency must have for a defined role. In the example proposed here, the cross marking is limited to a competence indication that is binary (i.e., competence level present or not). Of course, you can always go beyond a simple *yes or no* and specify further criteria in the cross points between competence and competence level (Fig. 6.26).

Security Domain Architect Role

Name	Security Domain Architect
Experience	> 5 years
Architecture Ownership	Security Domain

	Basic	Trained	Advisory	Senior
Soft Skills				
Architectural Attitude	x			
Communication	x			
Team-Minded	x			
Basic Architecture				
Architecture Methods			x	
Architecture Processes	x			
Architecture Platforms			x	
Subject-Matter Orientation				
Business			x	
Cross-Cutting Concern			x	
Landscape Orientation				
Service			x	
Application			x	
Platform				x
Information			x	
Technology				x
Governance Orientation				
Assess Architecture				x
Architecture Policies				x
Discipline Orientation				
Enterprise Architecture			x	
Domain Architecture				x
Solution Architecture	x			

Fig. 6.26 Architecture role definition

Use your role definitions to create job profiles, recruit staff, identify training needs, and calculate existing as well as future architecture capabilities. Also, utilize your role definitions to regularly reflect and decide which roles are strategic versus which should be outsourced. Create definitions for all (i.e., internal and external) roles to ensure role model consistency. Use role definitions for internal roles as a blueprint for job profiles you post on job portals and via which you recruit your internal workforce. Use role definitions for external roles to select your sourcing partner and define the competencies, responsibilities, and liabilities that your partner's architects must meet (**ARCHITECTURE CAPACITY, ARCHITECTURE SOURCING**).

In your role model, distinguish roles that align with your logical (i.e., more durable and sustainable) organizational scheme from roles that relate to your physical organization as it exists here and now. In other words, design part of your role model agnostically in terms of your physical organization. Within your methods and view models, refer to logical roles (i.e., roles that align with the logical organization schema) to decouple methodology changes from organizational changes (**DOMAIN-ORGANIZATION AGNOSTICISM, YOUR OWN ARCHITECTURE METHODOLOGY**).

6.2.6   Architecture Ownership

Planning, designing, and operating architecture assets are demanding and therefore deserve the utmost attention. Architecture activities and their results only unfold their potential if architecture organizations take full responsibility for them.

> *Ownership* is the state or fact of exclusive rights and control over property, which may be any asset, including an object, or intellectual property. (Wikipedia Ownership 2020a)

While Wikipedia emphasizes the rights and controls an owner has over something, the concept of ownership has a complementary connotation in architecture. Ownership includes both the right to an object and obligations concerning an object. Architecture ownership regards the relationship between an architecture organization and an architecture task or asset. The peculiarity of architecture ownership is that an architecture organization takes full responsibility for architecture decisions regarding tasks or assets.

Responsibility assignment matrices differentiate ownership semantics. RACI[27] is an example of a responsibility assignment matrix that distinguishes four

---

[27]RACI is a responsibility assignment matrix that specifies the participation of different roles in completing tasks, deliverables, or services. RACI is an acronym derived from responsibilities: responsible, accountable, consulted, and informed.

responsibilities: responsible, accountable, consulted, and informed. *Responsible* means that an architect is specifically and practically charged with developing an architecture asset or implementing an architecture activity. For example, architect A_1 is charged with the specific development of asset X and architect A_4 with the execution of activity Y. *Accountable* means that an architect is responsible for the result of an activity or an asset's condition without necessarily having been involved with their own concrete contributions. For example, architect A_2 is accountable for approving asset X. At the same time, A_3 is accountable for overseeing activity Y. Architects are *consulted* whose advice is sought as a contribution to an asset or activity. For example, the advice of architect A_3 is sought as a contribution to asset X. At the same time, A_2 contributes to the execution of task Y. Finally, actors on the distribution lists of an architecture task or an asset are *informed* when status changes occur. For example, architect A_4 is informed of the change in status of asset X, while A_1 is informed of the execution of task Y (Fig. 6.27).

	type of ownership			
owned object	R	A	C	I
architecture asset X	A_1	A_2	A_3	A_4
architecture task Y	A_4	A_3	A_2	A_1

$A_i :=$ Architect$_i$

Fig. 6.27 Responsibility assignment matrix

Ownership of assets is complemented by ownership of artifacts, particularly in the case of intangible assets. An architect who owns an intangible asset inevitably has responsibility for related architecture artifacts. For example, a solution architect who architecturally owns an application is responsible for the architecture descriptions associated with the application. A simple ownership semantics only distinguishes the duality of ownership and non-ownership. In the area of methods, there are also complementary ownership relationships between methods and the artifacts or assets created by these methods. For example, one architect has full responsibility for a reference architecture method (e.g., the architecture pattern method). In contrast, another architect owns an asset (e.g., a particular architecture pattern) created by the architecture pattern method. While owning a methodology involves periodically conducting surveys to continuously improve the methodology, owning a reference asset may make a respective architect responsible for monitoring the compliant use of the reference asset by other architects (**ARCHITECTURE ASSET**) (Fig. 6.28).

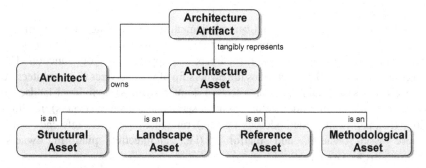

Fig. 6.28 Architecture ownership

Architecture assets are represented tangibly by appropriately owned artifacts. For example, a solution architecture description (i.e., artifact) represents an application's architecture. In contrast, a solution architecture methodology description (i.e., artifact) represents a methodology asset. To give you another example, a domain architecture description represents the actual architecture of a domain. Domain architecture descriptions may contain other artifacts such as architecture patterns, roadmaps, or principles, which themselves represent assets of their own (**ARCHITECTURE ARTIFACT**).

Architecture Function and Architecture Ownership

Architecture functions use the concept of ownership as a means to delegate and control responsibility for planning, building, or executing assets over their lifetime. Your function assigns ownership to individual architects or groups of architects. For example, domain development ownership is assigned to a domain architect. Delegate the definition of architecture ownership matrices to the governance branch of your function. Differentiate ownership vertically across architecture levels. Differentiate ownership horizontally across architecture roles and capture the details of ownership in your role definitions. Architecture assets are not the only objects owned. Similarly, manage and assign ownership for architecture activities. For example, a domain architecture role assigns ownership of a particular review and approval decision to a domain architect (Fig. 6.29).

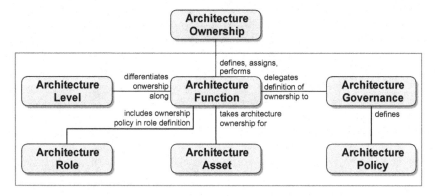

Fig. 6.29 Architecture function and architecture ownership

Architecture Governance

Make architecture ownership a central element in your architecture governance framework. At a minimum, your architecture governance framework specifies the organization's ownership structure, roadmap, and apparatus of your function. The governance framework also clarifies the ownership of your services (i.e., architecture service owners), domains (i.e., architecture domain owners), individual landscape assets (e.g., application architecture owners, service architecture owners), methodology (i.e., architecture methodology owners), reference assets (i.e., reference architecture asset owners), and platforms (i.e., architecture platform owners) (**ARCHITECTURE GOVERNANCE**).

Define your ownership policies with *separation of powers* principles in mind— for example, separate ownership of lifecycle-related asset decisions from responsibility for asset lifecycle management. For example, an organization responsible for the architecture of an application (i.e., owner of an architecture asset) suggests an enhancement to meet new requirements. A domain architect owns the decision to approve or reject the proposed application architecture (i.e., owner of an architecture lifecycle decision) (**ARCHITECTURE POLICY**).

Avoid frequent changes once you have assigned ownership for an asset to an individual architect or an architecture organization. Your architects identify with the assets they own. The longer architecture ownership relationships last, the more durable they are, and the more your architects will take genuine charge of the vitality of owned assets. Hold individual architects personally accountable for their owned assets and emphasize respective ownership in their incentive plans. Create and manage ownership matrices to uniquely assign asset ownership to individual architects. For example, the role R_1 assumes responsibility for concretely performing domain architecture tasks, while R_2 accountably performs architecture reviews on domain architectures proposed by R_1. The architects *Jonas* and *Luis*, who perform R_1, are responsible for *domain$_A$* (*Luis*) and *domain$_B$* (*Jonas*). In contrast, *Lea*, who takes on R_2, accountably owns all three domains (**ARCHITECTURE ROLE**) (Fig. 6.30).

	Architecture Role R_1		Architecture Role R_2
	Architect (Luis)	Architect (Jonas)	Architect (Lea)
Domain	R		A
Domain$_A$	R		A
Domain$_B$		R	A
Domain$_C$		R	A
Landscape Asset	A		C
Landscape Asset$_1$		A	C
Landscape Asset$_2$	A		C
Landscape Asset$_3$		A	C
Architecture Methodology	R		A
Architecture Method$_1$		R	A
Architecture Method$_2$	R		A
Methodology Asset	A		C
Methodology Asset$_1$		A	C
Methodology Asset$_2$		A	C

who

how

what

Fig. 6.30 Architecture ownership matrix

Ensure organizational alignment and vertically consolidate ownership by defining ownership hierarchies between your architecture levels. In ownership hierarchies, owners at higher levels assume overall responsibility or responsibility for more granular assets. For example, a domain architect owns an architecture domain. Hence, he also particularly owns the domain-specific relationships between landscape assets in the domain (**ARCHITECTURE LEVEL**).

Utilize ownership matrices beyond your architecture governance framework. A comprehensive ownership matrix is the *who-is-who* of your architecture function. At a glance, you can see who you can architecturally talk to when questions arise, or decisions are pending. Make sure your architecture SPOC uses ownership matrices as a routing table and guidance on responsibilities (**ARCHITECTURE SPOC**).

Note that the notion of ownership can evoke territorial mindsets and a hostile attitude toward sharing, but also toward reuse of architecture assets. Mitigate territorial stance by rewarding reuse and penalizing the re-creation of existing assets (**DECOMMISSIONING REWARD**).

Mitigate narrow mindsets by preferring ownership of an abstract whole to ownership of a concrete part. For example, assign ownership to an entire domain rather than a particular application. Architecture domains are less predetermined and, therefore, more abstract and malleable than individual landscape assets. For this reason, domain perspectives encourage a more open mindset and inspire architects to

think more independently and innovatively about their areas of responsibility
(**ARCHITECTURE INNOVATION**).

Assigning ownership becomes difficult when designated assets are inherently
ambiguous and their demarcation is unclear. For example, *architecture domain$_A$*
contains three landscape assets (*application$_1$, information$_1$, service$_1$*), while *architecture domain$_B$* includes *information$_1$, service$_1$*, and *platform$_2$*. What does this
mean from an ownership point of view? Is *service$_1$* jointly owned by the architects
of *domain$_A$* and *domain$_B$*, so they must agree on any changes to *service$_1$*? Or can
domain$_A$ override decisions made by the architect of *domain$_B$*? Ownership sounds
simple at first glance but becomes tricky when owned assets cannot be sufficiently
delineated. Therefore, avoid and resolve demarcation ambiguity for your architecture assets (**ARCHITECTURE DEMARCATION**) (Fig. 6.31).

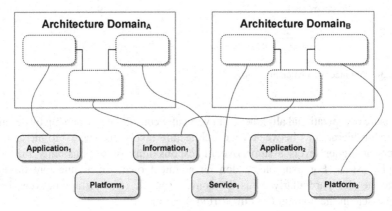

Fig. 6.31 Architecture ownership and demarcation

Finally, assign architecture ownership to off-the-shelf assets in your enterprise.
Architecture decisions, which are an inherent part of an off-the-shelf asset, are
practically made with the purchase decision. The off-the-shelf asset's vendor has
taken such architecture decisions. However, you almost always make complementary architecture decisions when you adapt an off-the-shelf asset to meet your needs
and embed it in your enterprise environment. For example, an architecture function
introduces a data exchange interface between two off-the-shelf assets, such as
application$_A$ and *application$_B$*. The interface introduces a new context for each
application. *Application$_A$* thus becomes the context for *application$_B$* and vice
versa. The interface couples both applications. Each application's future development requires special architecture attention and can no longer be done independently
of the other application. For this reason, assigning architecture ownership for the
interface is essential (**OFF-THE-SHELF SOLUTION**).

6.2.7 Architecture Funding

Architecture functions only unfold their potential under the premise of solid financing and funding. Achieving desired and valuable results requires a willingness to make the necessary investments. Establishing and delivering reliable architecture services that achieve the desired effects requires adequate funding of the necessary means and resources. While architecture functions must avoid inadequate funding, two types of unsatisfactory funding exist: underfunding and overfunding. Architecture functions are underfunded when their reasonable funding needs exceed available funding capacity. They are overfunded if the value of the results they produce could have been achieved with less financial investment than was actually made.

> *Funding* is a sum of money or other resources whose principal or interest is set apart for a specific objective. (Merriam-Webster Dictionary 2020)

There is no such thing as a free lunch—and architecture is no exception. Architects must be hired, tools purchased, or facilities rented before architecture functions can profitably return their contributions. Valuable returns require both initial and ongoing investments. While adequate funding is not spectacular, inadequate funding undermines an architecture organization's ability to fulfill its mission to the point of dysfunction.

Architecture functions are supposed to make the contributions their enterprises expect. For example, an enterprise expects its architecture function to design a specific business application. In this example, the application design costs can be related to the application's value from a business perspective so that funding can be measurably justified. Consider another example in which an architect plans to replace multiple similar platforms with a single one to reduce the total cost of ownership. In this example, an architecture function contributes to the profitability of the business by eliminating redundancy. Such indirect contributions to business results tend to require a more nuanced justification for funding. While architecture contributions to the longevity of assets are crucial, the returns on investment (i.e., ROI[28]) are primarily realized over the long term.

Architecture Function and Architecture Funding

Architecture funding is a prerequisite for your function to contribute as expected. Funding is the cost side of your cost-benefit ratio. Funding needs depend on both the quantitative and qualitative architecture requirements of your enterprise. Justify funding the architecture function by effectively delivering the desired benefit and reporting on its delivery if the benefit is not sufficiently obvious. Adjust architecture funding to suit

---

[28] Return on investment (ROI) depicts the ratio between the outcome of an investment and the associated investment over a defined period of time. The ROI indicates the performance of an investment in terms of its profitability.

your architecture levels. Prefer, for example, *profit center*[29] at the solution level and *cost center*[30] as the funding model at the domain and enterprise levels (Fig. 6.32).

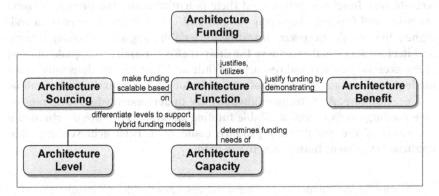

Fig. 6.32 Architecture function and architecture funding

Cost Center Versus Profit Center

From a high-level perspective, cost centers and profit centers are very different financing approaches. Choose the *cost center* funding model if the majority of your contributions are not readily associated with business results. Choose the *profit center* funding model if you want your function to be responsible for its contributions as well as its own bookkeeping, income, and costs.

The *cost center* is an entity (e.g., organizational unit) to which you assign costs. It does not make a measurable monetary contribution to business results, but it does make a measurable monetary contribution to business costs, for example, costs for designing a business service. *Human resources, finance,* and *IT* are enterprise organizations that often adopt a cost center model. A cost center has a clear focus on efficiency and effectiveness. Let us look at an example: an architecture function adopts cost center as its funding model. Due to bad business, the enterprise decides to completely dismantle the architecture organization. What is the effect of the dismantling? Since effectively needed architecture activities are no longer performed, the removed architecture function either leaves a painful gap or the remaining organizations carry out the architecture activities redundantly on their own account to fill the gap created. Either way, there is a hidden cost that negatively impacts the profitability of the entire enterprise.

---

[29] Profit center is an organization within a business expected to make an identifiable contribution to business profits due to which it calculates profits or losses separately. The profit center manager is held accountable for both revenue and costs—thus for profits.

[30] Cost center is an organization within a business to which costs can be allocated. It is an organization that does not contribute directly but incurs costs to the business. The cost center manager is not accountable for the business's profitability and investment decisions but responsible for some of its costs.

Unlike cost centers, *profit centers* are treated as a *business within a business*. Managing profit centers is like running an independent business. Profit center managers take responsibility for both their costs and their revenues. They calculate profits and losses separately and are fully responsible for their profit center. While cost centers only make a measurable contribution to the cost side of your enterprise's cost-income equation, profit centers make a quantifiable contribution to both sides, costs and revenues. Cost centers are driven by the predominant goal of minimizing costs, while profit centers seek to maximize profit. You can communicate architecture contributions more easily and naturally if your function adopts the profit center as a funding model since the profit center's performance measurement reflects that of the entire business.

An architecture organization adopting the cost center model has more autonomy in its investments, divestments, or service decisions. Other enterprise organizations rarely request dedicated technological innovations, research into promising concepts, or make comparable investments in unrecognized potential. For investments that are either indirect or pay no dividends in the short term, organizations need greater budgetary autonomy. Choose a cost center-based funding model if your architecture function is primarily expected to support strategic and collective corporate interests.

Balance your architecture function meaningfully in terms of funding by considering a hybrid model. On the one hand, address collective and long-term corporate interests that are rarely directly requested via service requests. On the other hand, address requests that are made directly, repeatedly, and individually by other organizations (e.g., via architecture service requests). Select the preferred architecture delivery model based on the optimization scale and investment amortization horizon dimensions. Prefer the profit center model for architecture contributions tending to short-term and individual demand satisfaction while favoring a cost center model for rather community-oriented or long-term contributions (Fig. 6.33).

Fig. 6.33 Cost center versus profit center model

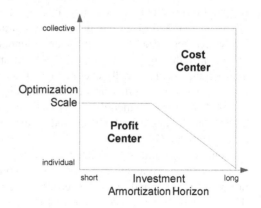

Prefer *profit center* for architecture services you delegate to an external architecture service provider. Consider delegating those services to external architecture service providers, which aim to meet short-term individual demand. The commercial principles inherent in a delegated sourcing approach naturally favor the profit center funding model (**ARCHITECTURE SOURCING**).

Also favor *profit center* to discipline service consumers and reduce avoidable service requests. Architecture capacity is an expensive resource you do not want to waste on low-value contributions. Steer highly individual interests or inquiries to profit center-based organizations. Conversely, finance the capacity for the basic operation of your architecture function and support of collective business interests by adopting a cost center-based funding model (**ARCHITECTURE CAPACITY**).

In principle, prefer a cost center-based model to address collective interests. Prefer a profit center model to address the individual interests of other organizations. Use a hybrid financing approach by combining both models and linking them to specific architecture levels and disciplines. Adopt the profit center model at the solution level, while organizations at domain or enterprise level tend to adopt cost center-based models. At the solution level, you can largely leave it up to the market to determine which applications, platforms, and services are desired and financed by other enterprise organizations. On the other hand, domain architects regularly perform domain- and enterprise-level activities that no enterprise organization will ever request individually, for example, portfolio analysis, architecture roadmap planning, or performing architecture assessments as a means of quality assurance. Domain and enterprise architects perform their deliberations in the collective interest of the enterprise. They identify systematic deficiencies, redundancies, or consolidation opportunities. For this reason, domain- and enterprise-level organizations tend to be financed through a cost center-based funding model (**ARCHITECTURE LEVEL**).

Note an architecture organization adopting a profit center model is primarily shaped by business organization demands. This means that business demand shapes the architecture service offering. As a result, services that are rarely needed receive marginal or no attention. Collective interests are neglected if they are not individually expressed and given purchasing power. For example, an architecture function rarely receives requests to consolidate redundant applications despite a collective interest in reducing costs. To take another example, the governance branch of an architecture function hardly ever receives requests to verify compliance with standards (e.g., to verify that an application only uses technologies that have been declared enterprise standards). This is despite the fact that there is a collective interest in avoiding complexity caused by uncontrolled proliferation of applications (**ARCHITECTURE GOVERNANCE**).

Communicate indirect architecture contributions by equating cost avoidance and cost reduction with architectural benefits. Communicate these as architecture function contributions and show the cost-benefit ratio you have achieved to justify funding costs. For example, equate the operating costs of a decommissioned landscape asset to the revenue generated by your function (**DECOMMISSIONING REWARD**).

Justify funding measurably by insisting on dedicated mandates whenever you conduct architecture engagements. Correlate the anticipated costs in your architecture mandate artifacts with the targeted and monetized business outcomes. For example, an architecture function adopts the cost center model. It requests an architecture mandate for all tasks longer than 5 days and captures the desired business outcomes and corresponding costs. At the end of a funding period, the function can justify its costs because it has quantified and systematically captured them. It finally holds the accumulated business results against the accumulated architecture costs (ARCHITECTURE MANDATE).

6.2.8 Architecture Sourcing

Architecture is complex, and architects cover a wide range of architecture contributions and assets. Among its noblest tasks an architecture function enables its enterprise to achieve its strategic goals. Architecture functions making low-value, high-volume contributions at the expense of undelivered high-value services make their businesses neither efficient nor effective. A clear delineation between architecture services giving their enterprise a competitive edge and those that do not is a prerequisite for delegating lower-value services to architecture service providers.

> *Delegation* is the act of empowering to act for another. (Merriam-Webster Dictionary 2020)

From the outside, an architecture function adds value by executing services to address business requirements. For example, a service portfolio organization asks the architecture function to support portfolio prioritization. The architecture function accepts the request and examines options for service consolidation. In its response, it suggests marking two services as *consolidate* and setting their *lifecycle priority status* to a low value. The rationale behind this is that both assets are likely to be decommissioned once the enterprise consolidates as suggested by the architecture function (Fig. 6.34).

Fig. 6.34 Architecture contributions via architecture services

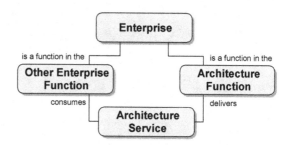

The black-box view depicts *that* an architecture function delivers services in response to requests. However, the black-box view leaves open *how* service delivery is handled and organized internally to the architecture function. The architecture function either delivers a service itself (*make*) or delegates service delivery (*delegate*) to a competent and capable party outside the enterprise. Whenever you take *make versus delegate* decisions, evaluate whether your function has a qualitative advantage over commercial service providers and how strategic respective services are for your enterprise. Focus your function on strategically important services that require high-quality delivery. Consider delegating the delivery of the remaining services to external service providers (Fig. 6.35).

Fig. 6.35 Architecture sourcing—make or delegate (© 2011 based on a figure from Prof. Dr. Stephen Tallman, reprinted with permission)

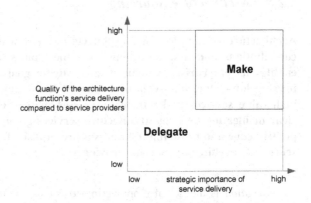

Beware, delegation does not mean that there is nothing left to do on your part—delegation is development, not dumping. When delegating a service to an expert (*most experienced*), all you need to do is clarify *why* (i.e., context and goal), while experts know exactly *what* to do and *how*. When delegating a service to a novice (*least experienced*), you need to guide the novice all the way through the *why*, *what*, and *how*. While beginners become experts over time, your intensive supervision and accompaniment is required in the early stages and will only gradually diminish (Fig. 6.36).

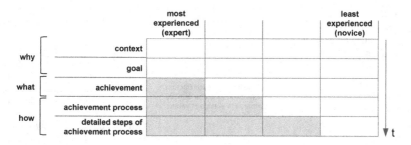

Fig. 6.36 Delegation model

Architecture Function and Architecture Sourcing

Determine your delegable architecture services and evaluate service providers before selecting and establishing a partner relationship. Integrate your sourcing partner or partners into your architecture function and align them with your organization. Design your relationship based on a sourcing agreement that defines mutual adherence to architecture policies, the use of platforms and tools, adoption of reference assets such as patterns, or the compliant use of architecture methodologies (Figs. 6.32 and 6.37).

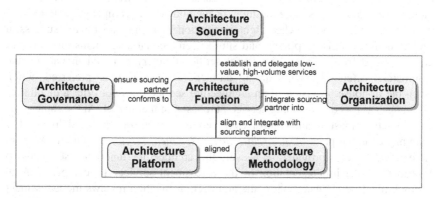

Fig. 6.37 Architecture function and architecture sourcing

Architecture Making, Buying, or Outsourcing

The *make-buy-outsourcing matrix* (Tallman 2011) describes three options for the procurement of architecture services—i.e., three options for taking a differentiated *make versus delegate* decision. The criterion for your decision is, on the one hand, the extent to which your function makes more adequate quality contributions than service providers in the market. On the other hand, you consult the strategic importance of architecture contributions when deciding on make versus buy versus outsourcing (Fig. 6.38).

Fig. 6.38 Make-buy-outsourcing matrix (© 2011 Prof. Stephen Tallman, reprinted with permission)

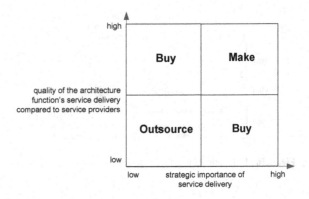

Make is a suitable approach for services your function plans, develops, and delivers from the ground up—without any outside support or assistance. You guarantee the capacity to design, deliver, and operate architecture services in the make quadrant by employing and retaining your own architecture experts over the long term.

You are adopting a hybrid approach for developing and delivering services in the *buy* quadrants. Services in the buy quadrants are partially based on your own contributions and in other parts on purchased services. Architecture service providers adapt to the work style, attitude, or methods of the company that consumes their services, especially when tight integration is a prerequisite for successful service delivery. Service pricing and similar commercial agreements on your part are simplified by the fact that internal service delivery is based in part on the commercial offers of your sourcing partners. Buying is your preferred option when the in-house provision of an architecture service does not offer a qualitative advantage over a corresponding service purchased in the market. At the same time, your function must retain control over certain aspects of service delivery. For example, essential parts of an *architecture assessment service* are purchased from an external service provider. However, the architecture function also needs to contribute to the implementation of the assessment service. To comply with an internal quality assurance policy, the architecture function reviews the assessment outcome and recommendation before passing it on to the service requester. Ensure that architecture policy conformance is legally binding in all sourcing contracts in order to propagate your rules and attitudes beyond the perimeter of your organization (ARCHITECTURE POLICY).

The *outsourcing* quadrant is reserved for services that are fully delegated to external service providers. Outsourcing means that your architecture function has little or no control over service delivery. However, do not underestimate the control you have over the design of an outsourced service. The contract between you and the sourcing partner establishes framing conditions that constrain the design of any service that falls under the wing of the contract. Treat outsourcing contracts as significant architecture assets (**ARCHITECTURE SIGNIFICANCE**).

Architecture Sourcing Models

Strategic sourcing models combine relationship and economic models. Relationship models define how enterprises formally control service providers, while an economic model prescribes the management of relationship economics (Keith et al. 2015) (Fig. 6.39).

Relationship Model	Sourcing Model	Economic Model
Transactional Contract	Basic Provider Model	Transaction-based
	Approved Provider Model	
Relational Contract	Preferred Provider Model	Output-based
	Performance-based Model	
	Vested Provider Model	Outcome-based
	Shared Services Model	
Vertical Integration	Equity Partnership	

Fig. 6.39 Sourcing business models (© 2015 Springer Science & Business Media, reprinted with permission)

Basic provider models assume that prices for services can be calculated per unit (e.g., per activity or per hour). They are suitable for standardized or standardizable services. Prefer this model if you aim to purchase services at the lowest possible cost. For example, an architecture function wants to equip its architects with a *TOGAF basic certificate* and therefore buys TOGAF training at a fixed price. A fixed price means that a firm price has to be paid for each training course.

Approved provider models extend the basic model. Architecture functions leverage volume discounts with selected suppliers and sign corresponding master agreements. Suppliers are selected because they can demonstrate performance in their area of expertise. For example, an architecture function enters into a master agreement with an established TOGAF training provider. The framework agreement specifies a package of ten TOGAF training courses that can be definitely ordered with a lead time of 3 weeks.

Preferred provider models include longer-term contractual commitments. They are often exclusive providers who offer streamlined purchasing processes. For example, an architecture function contracts for architecture training with a single provider who becomes the function's preferred provider for all types of architecture training (e.g., TOGAF,[31] ArchiMate,[32] or UML[33] training).

Performance-based models transfer responsibility and risk to the service provider. Providers in this model are paid for performance and are expected to provide services at contractually agreed service levels. For example, a service provider offers an *architecture platform* service. The service offering includes an architecture repository and associated modeling tools as a basis for the implementation of architecture processes. The provider guarantees 98% service availability.[34]

Vested provider models are highly collaborative. They assume that both sides of the agreement are equally committed to the success of the other. Vested provider models are long-term relationships that foster joint innovation and share risk fairly. They are aimed at achieving an effective business result. For example, an architecture function agrees with a vested provider that the number of enterprise applications must remain constant. In this example, both the architecture function and the provider have a shared interest in retiring assets for newly introduced ones. After the first year, the vested provider proposes an application decommissioning service. The service idea is to make application removal attractive to owners by offering a convenient path to application decommissioning (**DECOMMISSIONING REWARD**).

Shared services models are adopted by companies that set up their own internal suppliers. While the internal supplier organization plans, designs, and delivers services, their consumption is charged to the other enterprise organizations. Service prices are regularly benchmarked against external market prices. For example, an architecture function provides a *root cause analysis* service internally. It puts a price tag on the service and charges other organizations for service consumption.

Equity partnership is legally binding through formal structures such as acquisitions, joint ventures, or subsidiaries. In this model, an enterprise invests directly in building capabilities together with a suitable partner. Equity partnerships are highly collaborative. However, they are comparatively expensive and require a carefully calibrated architecture governance framework to achieve effective cooperation on essential matters through aligned practices (**ARCHITECTURE GOVERNANCE**).

---

[31] The Open Group Architecture Framework (TOGAF). TOGAF proposes an approach to design, plan, implement, and govern enterprise architecture. It describes a generic method for developing architectures. TOGAF suggests a common vocabulary, a generic information model, an adaptable role model, general architecture artifacts, and tooling.

[32] ArchiMate is an open and independent modeling standard for enterprise architectures that supports the description, analysis, and presentation of architecture within and between architectures. It is an Open Group standard and is based on fundamental architectural concepts defined by the IEEE (i.e., IEEE 1471).

[33] Unified Modeling Language (UML) is a universal modeling language that provides a standard approach to modeling and visualizing system design. Note that the concept of system is not limited to IT system. UML supports the expression and modeling of dynamic and static perspectives, individual building blocks, and their relationships (OMG UML 2020a).

[34] Service availability is a function of agreed service time (T_{ast}) and measured downtime (T_{dt}) as $x = \frac{T_{ast} - T_{dt}}{T_{ast}} \cdot 100$. If T_{ast} is 100 h and T_{dt} is 2 h, then the service is 98% available. $x = \frac{100-2}{100} \cdot 100 = 98\%$.

Architecture functions involving external partners must manage two relationships regardless of which delegation model they have chosen. On the one hand, they must communicate with service consumers in the enterprise, understand their needs and priorities, and anticipate their future demands. On the other hand, architecture functions must select and manage sourcing partners and monitor service provisioning. Architecture functions can tolerate direct interactions between external sourcing providers and internal consumers. However, they are still responsible for monitoring service quality, receiving escalations, and resolving issues that arise. Architecture functions must also manage supplier contracts (Fig. 6.40).

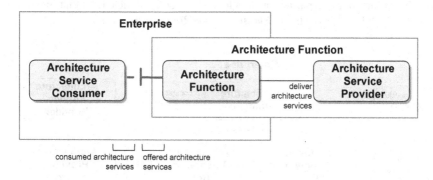

Fig. 6.40 Architecture sourcing and relationship management

Beware, the design of contracts with sourcing providers affects the design of delegated architecture services. Therefore, over time, the design of sourcing contracts will replicate the design of architecture services into the design of your architecture assets. A service contract, for example, lists an *architecture elaboration* service. The service is offered at a fixed price without considering different degrees of complexity in given assignments. This means that the appropriate elaboration of an architecture, which is more time-consuming for more complex problems, is not rewarded contractually. An intelligent service provider will therefore probably decompose complex problems into several less complex subproblems before submitting corresponding offers. The service provider will then apply the *architecture elaboration* service to all subproblems individually to increase revenues. Performing the *architecture elaboration* service on many subproblems will likely lead to many relatively small landscape assets (e.g., applications) with many dependencies between them—resulting in an unnecessarily fragmented solution landscape (ORGA-NIZATIONAL REPLICATION).

Optimize your architecture capacity for designing and deploying low-value services by delegating such services to sourcing partners. Also, use sourcing partners to respond flexibly to significant fluctuations in demand. For example, an architecture function covers normal operations with its own capacity and delegates peak demand to architecture service providers (ARCHITECTURE CAPACITY).

Distinguish between architecture roles assuming responsibilities within your function and those on the side of your service provider. Introduce roles in your function that bridge (*architecture integration role*) between internal (*architecture function*) and external (*architecture service provider*) areas of responsibility. Be aware that if you over-outsource, you may have difficulty retaining or attracting highly skilled architectural personnel. For example, an architecture function sources 100% of its services from external partners. The only task retained by the architecture function is to administer and monitor contract performance. The architecture function will have difficulty retaining good architecture staff. At the same time, good architects will still be needed when contract design changes are due, to monitor the quality of the sourcing partner or to detect architectural deficiencies that inevitably arise in a landscape over time (**Architecture Role**) (Fig. 6.41).

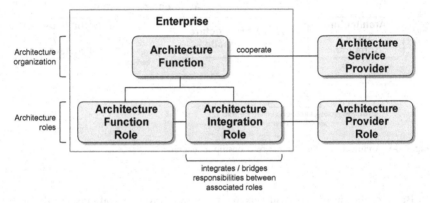

Fig. 6.41 Architecture integration role

Service providers may use their own architecture methods, tools, and platforms in the outsourcing model, making the model more flexible. Methodology disruption, however, leads to additional handshaking overhead when services are invoked or service results are received. You may need to provide additional information to your service provider so that they can meet their obligations. Additionally, you may need to support a reverse process for their service outputs to be usable by your enterprise. Service outsourcing means that the provision of architecture services is completely delegated to external partners. This inevitably extends contractual agreements to your architecture assets. Design your contracts to avoid contract changes when outsourced services need to be enhanced or supplemented. In other words, design delegated services with *design for change principles*[35] in mind. For example, contractually specify that the *architecture elaboration* service must always be

---

[35]Design for change principles improve the modifiability and expandability of a system, for example, loose coupling, information hiding, separation of concerns, or inversion of control.

combined with an architecture adapter. Further, specify that you can add new adapters to the solution architecture method at any time. In this way, you avoid changes to the architecture elaboration service as new solution archetypes emerge (e.g., cloud-based off-the-shelf solutions). If this is the case, add a *cloud-based off-the-shelf adapter* to your solutioning method and avoid changing the design of the elaboration service (MANAGED ARCHITECTURE EVOLUTION, ARCHITECTURE METHODOLOGY ADAPTER).

Be aware of the additional burden delegated architecture services place on architecture traceability. For example, an application adopts a security pattern for its design—the application's solution architecture description points to the adopted pattern. However, the pattern is managed by your security architecture provider, which uses an internal platform to store and develop their pattern artifacts. Minimize coupling and reduce media breaks related to traceability by softly linking[36] to supplier resources within your internally managed architecture artifacts (ARCHITECTURE TRACEABILITY, ARCHITECTURE ARTIFACT).

Architecture sourcing can significantly broaden as well as deepen your competency base. It can encourage innovation and refresh your architecture resources more regularly than you can achieve in-house. Include incentives for service improvement in your provider contracts to inspire more innovative than *working by the book* attitudes (ARCHITECTURE INNOVATION).

6.3 Architecture Engagement Model

While many patterns contribute to improving the interaction with an architecture function, I have chosen to list only the architecture SPOC[37] pattern in the *architecture engagement* model pattern group. The *architecture SPOC* pattern proposes a complement to an architecture organization design in which a SPOC organization acts as a façade[38] to optimize the interaction between the architecture function and its customers.

---

[36] Soft links consist of an outer and an inner representation of the link target. The external representation can be a name, the internal representation a technically resolvable address. Naming services implement a soft link approach technically.

[37] SPOC, abbreviation for single point of contact.

[38] Facade, organizational facade. A facade is a function that serves as a front-facing organization and masks a more complex underlying organizational structure. Facades improve the usability of the organization scheme they mask. They serve as an intervention point for improving the interaction between architecture functions and business organizations.

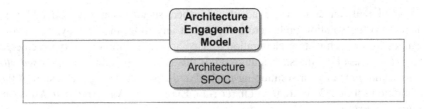

6.3.1   Architecture SPOC

Architecture value propositions remain unclear to anyone unfamiliar with the architecture function and the services it provides. Disorientation leads to unexploited architecture potential or exploited architectural non-potential. Both types of disorientation lead to considerable opportunity costs due to untapped architectural value propositions.

> A *contact* is a person serving as a go-between, messenger, connection, or source of special information. (Merriam-Webster Dictionary 2020)

A *single point of contact (SPOC)* is an engagement concept where all inquiries to an organization are routed through a single funnel. This funnel is a person or a group of people who receives the inquiries and efficiently routes them to the correct department in the organization. In this sense, a SPOC is an organizational capability whose function is analogous to the function of a routing table used for mediating communications in technical systems. As a potential customer of an organization, you turn to its SPOC for information about the *why*, *what*, *who*, and *how* of the organization's value proposition.

Accordingly, an *architecture single point of contact (architecture SPOC)* is an organizational capability that acts as a funnel to route customer requests to the architecture function in order to improve the efficiency of its external communication.

The cooperation between organizations is based on two premises. First premise: the requesting organization ($organization_R$) is aware of the providing organization ($organization_P$)—aware in the sense that $organization_R$ knows of the existence of $organization_P$. Second premise: $organization_R$ knows the services it can request from $organization_P$ and understands why it makes sense to request which service. Finally, $organization_R$ understands *how* to correctly request a desired service and *who* can be contacted with questions or problems (Fig. 6.42).

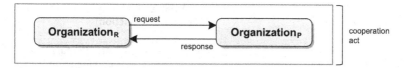

Fig. 6.42 Cooperation between organizations

Architecture Function and Architecture SPOC

Architecture functions establish SPOCs as a funnel to manage and optimize communication between architecture and other enterprise organizations. Architecture SPOCs save capacity by mitigating the wasteful effects of miscommunication. They make valuable contributions to matching supply with demand by observing the actual patterns of architecture engagement and utilizing them to create and provide relevant services. An architecture SPOC optimally adapts communication to the respective stakeholder groups and improves expectation management by enhancing awareness of the correct request and delivery of architecture services (Fig. 6.43).

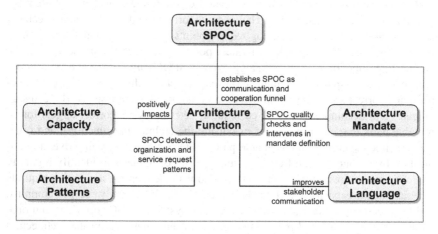

Fig. 6.43 Architecture function and architecture SPOC

Architecture SPOCs serve as one-stop shops[39] for their functions. They act as facades[40] toward particular groups within the architecture function—groups that deliver services or otherwise cope with respective requests. They improve usability, increase transparency, and ensure consistency of communication and collaboration measures between enterprise organizations and the architecture function (Fig. 6.44).

---

[39] One-stop shop is a business that offers various services. This means customers get everything they need at a single stop, giving them the convenience of meeting multiple needs in a single location.

[40] Facade, organizational facade. A facade is a function that serves as a front-facing organization and masks a more complex underlying organizational structure. Facades improve the usability of the organization scheme they mask. They serve as an intervention point for improving the interaction between architecture functions and business organizations.

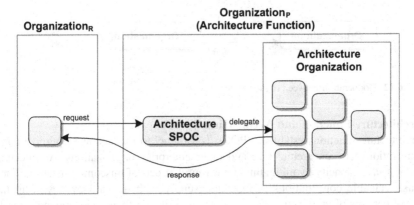

Fig. 6.44 Architecture SPOC

Architecture SPOCs broker request-response communications between architecture and enterprise organizations. They receive formal or informal as well as catalog and non-catalog requests. A catalog request points to a previously defined publicly offered response. For example, a request points to an architecture service in the architecture function's service catalog. While SPOCs *may* intervene in catalog-related request-response communication (e.g., to check their relevance, completeness, and correctness), they *must* intervene in non-catalog requests. A SPOC disaggregates and decomposes a received request, determines the correct targets for its routable parts (e.g., a group inside or outside the architecture function), and organizes ad hoc support for non-routable parts. SPOCs significantly improve communication by monitoring the frequency and priority of requests to identify regularly recurring request-response patterns. They also validate, correct, and enrich requests and validate the capacity to respond to requests. A SPOC formally accepts, commits, and logs each request (e.g., based on a ticketing system). SPOCs prioritize and rank requests by relevance and route them to service providers within the architecture organization. Once delegated, they track, trace, and manage requests throughout their lifecycle and update and communicate the status of requests on a regular basis. Finally, SPOCs measure request-response performance, conduct customer satisfaction surveys, and close as well as archive requests, once they are delivered.

Implement your architecture SPOC as a dedicated organization and link it to your enterprise's service desk ecosystem. SPOCs, like other organizations, are socio-technical systems. They utilize technical means to increase their efficiency and effectiveness. For example, an architecture SPOC decides to offload standardizable communication traits to chatbots. SPOCs inevitably observe and learn about request-response patterns and can convert them into corresponding request-response routing tables. These routing tables essentially describe the mechanics of your architecture function as a service delivery organization. They represent the *who-is-who*[41] of your function. Use them as input to your optimization considerations (e.g., organizational optimization) (**ORGANIZATIONAL REPLICATION**).

Encourage your architecture SPOC to increase the level of request-response standardization by suggesting predefined responses. Empower your SPOC to process straightforward requests themselves, relieving the burden on the architecture function. Your SPOC will inevitably be exposed to the request-response patterns contained in requests. By systematically evaluating these patterns, your SPOC can identify gaps in your architecture service portfolio and make appropriate suggestions for improving your service offering. Request-response patterns also improve your SPOC's understanding of how architecture demand is distributed across your supply (i.e., across offered architecture services). This helps your function improve both your service prioritization and capacity planning (**ARCHITECTURE CAPACITY**).

Position your SPOC as a quality gateway for all communication between architecture and enterprise organizations. Ensure open, honest, and transparent communication. Communicate strengths and opportunities as well as weaknesses and threats. Optimize language and protocols and adapt them to your stakeholder groups. Continually evolve your architecture and domain-specific languages by leveraging your SPOC's access to customer trends, demands, and customer jargon (**ARCHITECTURE LANGUAGE, DOMAIN TAXONOMY**).

Develop the holistic profile of your architects by rotating them through your SPOC organization. They will learn the breadth of architecture offerings you make and gain valuable insight into the variety of customer groups your function interacts with (**ARCHITECTURE ROLE**).

Add value to your SPOC by making it an innovation hub. On the one hand, this makes it a first port of call for innovative ideas that are brought to your architecture function. On the other hand, an attentive SPOC can identify potential for innovation in exceptional customer inquiries and flag them as innovation candidates. Finally, you can assign your SPOC to launch ideation campaigns and maintain corresponding calendar reminders (**ARCHITECTURE INNOVATION, ARCHITECTURE CALENDAR**).

Architecture SPOCs are facades for their architecture functions. This particularly applies to requests that are not standardized via architecture services. Thus, SPOCs are ideal checkpoints for the relevance or significance of given architecture requests. Every request to the architecture function that is recognized as irrelevant early on increases its efficiency. For this, however, a SPOC needs an architecture-significance-related set of criteria that it can apply to given queries without involving further architecture competencies and resources (**ARCHITECTURE SIGNIFICANCE**).

Once the significance of a request has been identified, SPOCs consider whether further processing requires an explicit architecture mandate or is simple enough to be

---

[41] Who-is-who (also: who's who) is the title of publications that generally contain prominent people in a country. However, it is always adopted to denote a group of distinguished entities in a referenced area or context.

routed immediately to the appropriate department within the architecture function. If a dedicated mandate is required, the SPOC starts the mandate creation process, pre-fills the template with the already collected data, and accompanies the mandate creation until it is finally signed. From this moment on, the responsibility for mandate fulfillment passes to the signing parties (ARCHITECTURE MANDATE).

6.4   Architecture Discipline

Architecture is a people business, and architecture functions comprise three disciplines, aggregating roles, responsibilities, and capabilities. The *enterprise architecture discipline* pattern recommends the design of roles and responsibilities in enterprise architecture and identifies this discipline as a super-discipline to domain and solution architecture. The *domain architecture discipline* pattern focuses on the domain as a structural asset or large system, while the *solution architecture discipline* pattern introduces a solution perspective on landscape assets such as services, applications, platforms, information, or technologies. The discipline patterns complement each other and together form the discipline base of the architecture function.

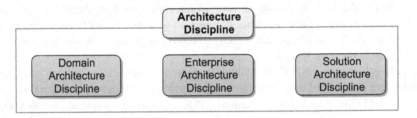

6.4.1   Enterprise Architecture Discipline

Attitudes, principles, methods and framing conditions, tools and techniques, skills, and resources that enable enterprises architecturally in their entirety are collectively regarded as enterprise architecture discipline. Enterprises lacking a solidly established enterprise architecture discipline lack a systematic approach to architecture planning and decision-making at the enterprise level.

Discipline designates a field of study, a rule or system of rules governing conduct or activity. (Merriam-Webster Dictionary 2020)

  Architecture is the art or science of building, a method or style of building, or an architectural work product. (Merriam-Webster Dictionary 2020)

Architecture is both a process and the result of a process. Architecting is the process of systematically converting uncertainty into certainty. It is a process in which a solution systematically emerges in response to a problem. Architecting may start chaotically[42] and continues until an adequate solution has fully emerged.

Architecture is a process that inevitably involves two systems (Dietz 2006): the *using system* (teleological system concept[43]) and the *object system* (ontological system concept[44]). While object systems are the systems to be designed, the using systems consume the functions that object systems provide. Architecture, therefore, involves two distinct activities and perspectives: requirements elicitation and devising specifications. Requirements elicitation begins with the construction of the using system and ends where the object system's functionality begins. Devising specifications begins with the functionality of the object system and ends with its construction. Constructional architects have to bridge the mental gap between function and construction (Fig. 6.45).

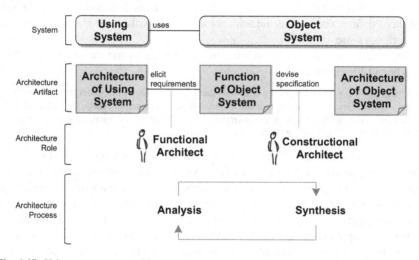

Fig. 6.45 Using system versus object system

---

[42] Chaos in the early stages of architectural development is a healthy indication that a problem is being viewed from many perspectives.

[43] Teleological system concept. The term teleological system deals with a system's function and behavior as observed from the outside (external behavior). The teleological system's perspective is useful when using a system.

[44] Ontological system concept. The ontological system view deals with a system's mechanics as observed inside the system (internal behavior). It also distinguishes the concept of *aggregate* from the concept of *system*. Both concepts, aggregate and system, are collections of objects. However, in aggregates, the elements are not held together by interaction bonds, whereas in systems, they are. A system, therefore, has unity and integrity. Both properties are lacking in aggregates.

Architecture is a process of alternating analysis and synthesis steps. While analysis steps help to better understand the problem, the solution emerges from synthesis steps. Architecture is not a waterfall but an iterative and evolutionary process. Eliciting requirements and devising specifications take place incrementally. Designing a system is a continuous stream in which white-box mechanisms are deduced from corresponding black-box perspectives such that each inner model can be completely derived from the previous (outer) model.

The IEEE Computer Society defines *architecture* as the result of a process (IEEE 2000):

> The fundamental organization of a system embodied in its components, their relationships to each other and the environment, and the principles governing its design and evolution.

We can relate architecture (as a result) and architecting (as a process). If we think of architecture as the essence of a system, then architecting is the elimination of everything nonessential. Len Fehskens (2008) defines *architecture* as those parts of an overall design that address all you essentially need and nothing you do not. Fehskens defines *essential* as the achievement of set goals at the maximum amount of work not done.

Enterprise architecture is architecture at the enterprise level, which Marc Lankhorst (2017) defines as:

> Enterprise is any collection of organizations that has a common set of goals and/or a single bottom line. Enterprise architecture is a coherent whole of principles, methods, and models that are used in the design and realization of an enterprise's organizational structure, business processes, information systems, and infrastructure.

Enterprise architecture relates information from formerly unrelated domains to obtain a holistic view of the enterprise. Enterprise architecture ensures vertical (e.g., from strategic to operational, from coarse-grained to fine-grained) and horizontal (e.g., from planning through building to the running enterprise services) alignment across enterprise information viewpoints. It maintains a baseline architecture[45] perspective representing the current state of the enterprise. It also proposes target architecture[46] states in light of strategic forces an enterprise must absorb. For example, the major change in an enterprise's business model is a strategic force. Enterprise architecture can also be viewed as a master plan facilitating the convergence of diverging forces toward a strategic transformation target, like a targeted business model or a targeted operating model (2004).

Architecture Function and Enterprise Architecture Discipline
Architecture functions establish and perform their enterprise architecture discipline as a super-discipline encompassing both solution and domain architecture

---

[45] Baseline architecture describes the current architecture state—for example, the architecture state of a domain or an enterprise.

[46] Target architecture describes the desired future state of an architecture developed for a domain or an enterprise. There can be several future states developed as a roadmap to highlight the evolution of the architecture toward a strategically desired target state.

disciplines. The enterprise architecture discipline typically hosts an enterprise-wide governance framework. The governance framework defines, evolves, and prescribes architecture methods, view models, and platforms, and it ensures conformance to guidelines and policies (Fig. 6.46).

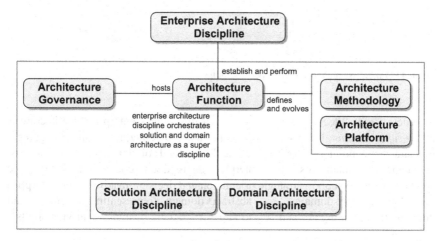

Fig. 6.46 Architecture function and enterprise architecture discipline

Architecture functions assume three basic responsibilities: a regulative, instructive, and informative responsibility (Greefhorst and Proper 2011). Their *regulative responsibility* makes architecture functions prescriptive. An architecture function determines how a system must become instead of describing how it has become. In assuming their *instructive responsibility*, architecture functions transform diffuse challenges into concrete designs. Architecture designs are instructive inputs for building physical systems. Thirdly, architecture functions have an *informative responsibility*, whose main purpose of which is to enable informed decisions along the entire value chain

Position your enterprise architecture as a *super-discipline* that oversees both the domain and solution disciplines and aligns them to ensure their effective cooperation. Domain and solution architecture disciplines make complementary contributions along an enterprise value chain. While domain architecture disciplines enable informed portfolio decisions (*do the right thing*), solution architecture disciplines ensure that portfolio decisions are professionally implemented by elaborating high-quality solution designs (*do the thing right*) (SOLUTION ARCHITECTURE DISCIPLINE, DOMAIN ARCHITECTURE DISCIPLINE) (Fig. 6.47).

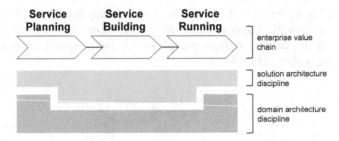

Fig. 6.47 Enterprise architecture as super-discipline

Enterprise architecture is not just a super-discipline—enterprise architecture is also a *super-domain*. It is the root domain of an entire enterprise—thus an aggregation and abstraction target for assets at the domain and solution levels (e.g., services, applications, or platforms). The enterprise aggregation process consolidates and abstracts assets to support strategic orientation and decision-making at the enterprise level. For example, $domain_{Enterprise}$ abstracts $domain_1$ (representing A_1 and A_2) and $domain_2$ (representing A_3 and A_4) to support strategic or transversal viewpoints[47] (Fig. 6.48).

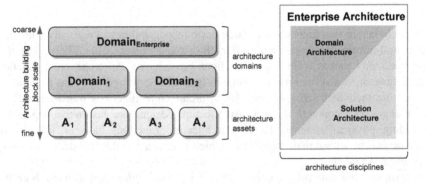

Fig. 6.48 Enterprise architecture as super-domain

Enterprise architecture addresses questions at the enterprise level, while domain and solution architecture provide their insights at the domain and solution level. The disciplines differ in terms of their underlying planning horizon. For example, the enterprise architecture discipline has a 5-year strategic planning perspective, while

---

[47] A transversal viewpoint is a viewpoint that is orthogonal to other viewpoints. Transversal viewpoints relate several perspectives to a common concern. For example, horizontal transversal viewpoints connect several architecture domains, while vertical transversal viewpoints enable navigation across architectural levels.

solution architecture usually has a planning horizon of 6–12 months (**ARCHITECTURE LEVEL**).

Beware of and avoid enterprise architecture myths and misconceptions. For example, avoid myths like *enterprise architecture is an architecture best practice compiled in a framework like TOGAF,*[48] *ArchiMate,*[49] *and Zachman,*[50] *the architecture of critical applications is enterprise architecture, enterprise architecture is the person titled "enterprise architect," or enterprise architecture is synonymous with technology standards.*

Establish your architecture governance framework at the enterprise level. Governance frameworks establish, control, and enforce the allocation of formal decision-making authority and the effective coordination of decision-making across the entire enterprise. However, scale your governance framework across domain and solution levels to ensure coherence and consistency in architecture decision-making (**ARCHITECTURE GOVERNANCE**).

Define your own methodology frameworks by adopting industry standards like TOGAF to your enterprise's specific needs. Tailor a given industry standard as much as necessary and as little as possible. Think of an architecture method as if it were a system itself. Gather your method requirements to understand what purpose your methodology should serve. Use the industry standards as if you were using patterns in system design. Once you have derived your own methodology, position it as your enterprise-level standard (**YOUR OWN ARCHITECTURE METHODOLOGY, YOUR OWN ARCHITECTURE VIEW MODEL**).

Consider the following architecture methods as essential components of your enterprise-level methodology framework: solution architecture elaboration method, domain architecture lifecycle method, architecture assessment method, reference architecture method, architecture roadmap method, and an architecture pattern method (**SOLUTION ARCHITECTURE METHODOLOGY, DOMAIN ARCHITECTURE METHODOLOGY, ARCHITECTURE ASSESSMENT METHODOLOGY, REFERENCE ARCHITECTURE METHODOLOGY, ARCHITECTURE ROADMAP METHODOLOGY, ARCHITECTURE PATTERN METHODOLOGY**).

---

[48] The Open Group Architecture Framework (TOGAF). TOGAF proposes an approach to design, plan, implement, and govern enterprise architecture. It describes a generic method for developing architectures. TOGAF suggests a common vocabulary, a generic information model, an adaptable role model, general architecture artifacts, and tooling.

[49] ArchiMate is an open and independent modeling standard for enterprise architectures that supports the description, analysis, and presentation of architecture within and between architectures. It is an Open Group standard and is based on fundamental architectural concepts defined by the IEEE (i.e., IEEE 1471).

[50] The Zachman Framework proposes a basic enterprise architecture schema that provides a structured approach to holistically viewing and defining an enterprise's architecture. The basic scheme distinguishes two dimensions that introduce the intersection of two classifications. While the first classification distinguishes the primitive interrogatives what, how, when, who, where, and why, the second classification is derived from the philosophical concept of reification (i.e., from the process of transforming an abstract idea into its instantiation and vice versa).

Establish a conceptual basis for the entire architecture function at the enterprise level—establish it in the form of an architecture language. Ensure that all relevant, fundamental concepts and terms are clarified by the language and actively adopted by both enterprise-wide methodologies, view models, and your architects (ARCHITECTURE LANGUAGE).

The enterprise architecture discipline is also an aggregate discipline in terms of architecture domains and assets—hence you need to ensure traceability across the intermediate aggregate levels (e.g., domains). Implement traceability as deeply as possible in your methodologies and architecture platforms. Consolidations across multiple aggregate levels must be repeatable according to fixed and easily understandable rules. Aim for a high degree of automation, which is best achieved by implementing consolidation rules in appropriate architecture platforms and tools. Assign the responsibility for establishing an enterprise-wide architecture platform, including the required modeling tools and traceability capabilities, to the enterprise architecture discipline in order to achieve maximum consistency of all architecture views and artifacts via the uniform use of a platform (ARCHITECTURE TRACEABILITY, YOUR OWN ARCHITECTURE PLATFORM).

6.4.2   Domain Architecture Discipline

Attitudes, principles, methods and framing conditions, tools and techniques, skills, and resources that enable the architecture lifecycle management of entire domains are collectively referred to as domain architecture discipline. Enterprises lacking a well-established domain architecture discipline lack a systematic approach to architecture planning and decision-making at the domain level.

> A *domain* is a sphere of knowledge, influence, or activity. (Merriam-Webster Dictionary 2020)

Domains are areas of interest. Domains can be defined and delineated in both very formal and totally informal ways. Scientific areas such as *mathematics* or *epistemological philosophy* are examples of highly institutionalized domains, while practicing a sport such as *bouldering with friends* is a comparatively informal domain. There may be a domain-specific language or jargon as well as relationships between domains. For example, the domains Swiss, German, French, Italian, and Austrian Alps all refer to a geographic domain called Alps. Domains establish common languages, protocols, or rituals. They contain common value systems and enable coherent action by providing intersubjective frames of reference.

Architecture functions define and institutionalize domains to decompose the entire enterprise into architecturally digestible parts. Architecture domains enable architects to coherently view, plan, or pursue a topic of enterprise interest. They enable architects to focus and align on an area of enterprise interest without being paralyzed by the overwhelming complexity of the entire enterprise. Architects use domain names to refer to domains. They concertedly communicate and discuss within a domain basing their discussions on domain-specific language and jargon. *World, sphere, universe of discourse* (Dietz 2006), and *large system* (Murer et al. 2010) are used synonymously for the term domain (**DOMAIN TAXONOMY**).

Architecture domains serve the purpose of enabling architecture lifecycle management for an area of enterprise interest. Architecture functions need to draw the necessary attention to domain assets and delineate domains to assign ownership individually (**ARCHITECTURE OWNERSHIP**).

An architecture domain groups architecture assets. At the same time, an architecture domain is itself an architecture asset (Fig. 6.49).

Fig. 6.49 Architecture domain

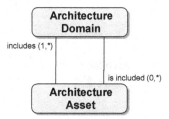

A domain, which is itself a whole, introduces context for its asset parts. This means that domains introduce their own contextualized views for their associated assets. This can lead to a domain abstracting a contained asset differently than another domain containing the same asset. Architecture domains containing the same architecture assets overlap and inevitably become related domains. For example, an application in the enterprise application portfolio is called *employee base*. However, the same application is regarded as *authoritative source* in the *security domain*, while the *human resources domain* names it *our most valuable asset*. Security and human resources are interrelated domains as both encompass the *employee base* asset. Ambiguity automatically arises when the same application is named differently in several domains. Mitigate ambiguity by ensuring consistent naming across all contexts and domains or by managing contextual references yourself as dedicated architecture assets.

While architecture lifecycle management is the primary perspective domain architects pursue, there is nothing preventing them from looking at an entire domain as a solution to an enterprise problem. This introduces the solution perspective to the domain architecture discipline. For example, an architecture function needs to understand how a domain's externally visible properties are implemented (e.g., a use case or a quality attribute at the domain level). In other words, at times, an architecture function needs to understand how the assets of a domain implement a domain-level use case. The *portfolio perspective*, which domain architects primarily use, is complemented by a *transformative perspective*, which is the primary perspective of the solution architecture discipline (SOLUTION ARCHITECTURE DISCIPLINE).

Architecture Function and Domain Architecture Discipline

Architecture functions establish and perform their domain disciplines with an emphasis on architecture lifecycle management. Domain architecture disciplines incorporate domain-specific languages to diminish ambiguity. They pay attention to a loosely coupled link between domain and organization structures. At the same time, they rigidly clarify ownership and architectural responsibility questions for domains and domain assets. They apply methodologies to ensure that domain assets are developed in accordance with enterprise standards (Fig. 6.50).

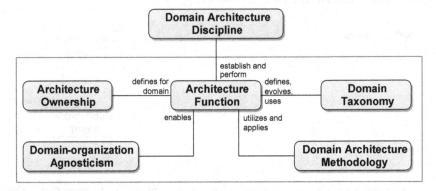

Fig. 6.50   Architecture function and domain architecture discipline

What the enterprise architecture discipline is to an overall enterprise domain, the domain architecture discipline is to a specific domain within the enterprise domain. Enterprise architecture is a *super-discipline*. It supervises all sub-domains and equips the architecture function with an enterprise-wide governance framework, methods, and platforms (ENTERPRISE ARCHITECTURE DISCIPLINE).

The domain architecture discipline focuses on the service planning value stream to ensure informed portfolio decisions (*do the right thing*). However, it accompanies the entire lifecycle and transformation of enterprise services. It cooperates intensively with the solution architecture discipline, to ensure that portfolio decisions are implemented professionally (*do the thing right*) (SOLUTION ARCHITECTURE DISCIPLINE).

Domain architecture becomes obligatory when planning, building, or running architecture assets confronts architects with complex systems. A system is complex if it consists of many building blocks and if there are many relationships between them or if it has many relationships to building blocks on its outside (Bente et al. 2012). For example, an enterprise domain includes many services, applications, platforms, technologies, and information assets. It also handles multiple business areas and regions. A complex situation like this cannot be designed or managed at the instance level. One can only manage such situations at a meta-level which Stefan Bente, Uwe Bombosch, and Shailendra Langade refer to as *architecture by maxims* (Bente et al. 2012). Domain architecture is primarily concerned with *why changes are needed* and *what is needed to pursue a desired change*. Domain architecture defines domain maxims and maintains baseline and target architecture viewpoints. Finally, domain architecture maintains architecture roadmaps. A domain roadmap suggests transformative steps to evolve a domain baseline architecture toward the desired target architecture.

Instantiate this list of questions stereotypically raised within the domain architecture discipline. Adapt and vary the questions for the specific domains (D) in your own enterprise:

- What are strategic, tactical, and operational requirements for domain D?
- Can we identify domain D opportunities to optimize business outcomes (e.g., new technologies, consolidation opportunities)?
- Can domain D threats jeopardize business outcomes (e.g., increase in business risk, building architecture indebtedness, and redundancy)?
- What is domain D's baseline architecture (BASELINE ARCHITECTURE VERSUS TARGET ARCHITECTURE)?
- What architecture demands and constraints determine domain D's target architecture (ARCHITECTURE SIGNIFICANCE, ARCHITECTURE CONDITION)?
- What plan ensures that domain D effectively evolves from its current baseline to its desired target architecture (ARCHITECTURE ROADMAP METHODOLOGY)?
- What reference assets are needed to ensure domain-compliant solutions during transformation steps (e.g., introducing a new service) in domain D (REFERENCE ARCHITECTURE METHODOLOGY)?
- Who has to know which architecture decisions need to be made in domain D to ensure alignment across D-dependent domains (ARCHITECTURE DECISION)?

Define processes for the compliant application of your domain methodology. Create adapters reflecting the diversity and particularities of your enterprise's domains such that you can complement your domain methodology and meaningfully guide your architects in method application. For example, differentiate between business and technical domains to support optimal method application via adapters (ARCHITECTURE METHODOLOGY ADAPTER, DOMAIN ARCHITECTURE METHODOLOGY, BUSINESS VERSUS TECHNICAL).

Define and evolve domain-specific reference assets to govern, guide, and control the solution architecture-like transformations of architecture assets at the domain level. For example, define principles or patterns and ensure that solution architects properly employ them (REFERENCE ARCHITECTURE METHODOLOGY).

Define processes for compliantly performing architecture assessments in your domains. Consider creating adapters for domain-specific needs so that you can take full advantage of the enterprise-wide assessment methodology at the domain level (ARCHITECTURE ASSESSMENT METHODOLOGY).

6.4.3 Solution Architecture Discipline

Professional attitudes, principles, methods and framing conditions, tools and techniques, skills, and resources that enable the planning, building, and running of architecture designs that respond to business problems are collectively referred to as solution architecture discipline. Enterprises lacking a coherently established solution architecture discipline lack a systematic approach to architecture planning and decision-making at the solution level.

> A solution is an answer to a problem. (Merriam-Webster Dictionary 2020)

The concept of *solution* implies another concept—the concept of *problem* to which a solution responds. While problems are discrepancies between a desired (future) state and an undesirable (present) state, solutions are sought and established to address corresponding problems.

Both problem and solution are abstract concepts that are mutually dependent. While a problem is represented by carefully formulated conditions such as requirements or constraints, a problem calls for a solution. A solution responds to an associated problem by providing capabilities that address the problem's conditions. A solution, in essence, is anything addressing a problem. Architecture assets are a common means of creating solutions in modern enterprise contexts (Fig. 6.51).

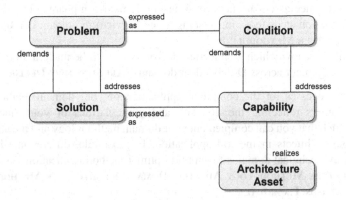

Fig. 6.51 Problem-solution dichotomy

Architecture assets realize capabilities (solution), and capabilities address conditions (problem). An asset (as a whole or in parts) realizes one or more capabilities. Conversely, a single capability can be realized jointly by multiple assets. Similarly, a capability addresses (in whole or in part) one or more conditions, which means that a single condition can also be addressed jointly by multiple capabilities (Fig. 6.52).

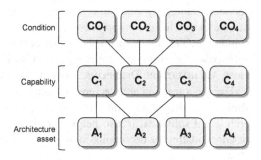

Fig. 6.52 Condition, capability, and landscape asset

Architecture Function and Solution Architecture Discipline

Architecture functions establish their solution architecture disciplines by viewing architecture assets (e.g., landscape assets, architecture domains) as responses to architecture conditions. Solution architecture disciplines apply methodologies to ensure solutions are designed in accordance with enterprise standards (Fig. 6.53).

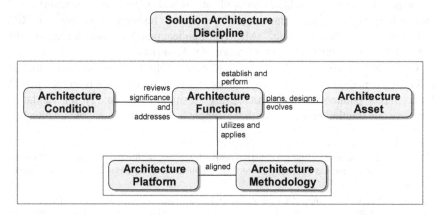

Fig. 6.53 Architecture function and solution architecture discipline

The solution architecture discipline is embedded in an enterprise-wide governance framework. It is equipped with methods and platforms by an overarching enterprise architecture discipline. In addition, the enterprise architecture discipline ensures that solution and domain architecture act in concert and establish artifacts that can be aggregated vertically. The solution architecture discipline focuses in particular on the service building value stream. However, it also contributes to service planning by examining alternative solutions and developing early visions of solution architecture approaches. While the main focus is on landscape assets, solution architecture is also suitable for developing domain or reference asset type solutions—for example, a reference asset such as an architecture pattern (ENTER-PRISE ARCHITECTURE DISCIPLINE, DOMAIN ARCHITECTURE DISCIPLINE).

Finally, a solution architecture discipline contributes to the service running value stream by diagnosing and remediating identified problems from previously architected solutions. It also helps determine the opportunities, risks, and impacts of consolidating or decommissioning existing landscape assets (DECOMMISSIONING REWARD).

Define processes for applying your solution methodology in a compliant manner. Create adapters that reflect the diversity and specifics of different asset archetypes in your organization to complement your solution methodology and increase efficiency and effectiveness of methodology application. For example, distinguish between landscape assets such as applications, services, or platforms on the one hand and structural assets such as domains on the other. In addition, differentiate further solution archetypes in the individual asset classes for which you create dedicated adapters, for example, an adapter for applications that implement a microservices[51] architecture style versus adapters for enterprise resource planning[52] (ERP), webshop,[53] or machine learning[54] (ML)-type applications (SOLUTION ARCHITECTURE METHODOLOGY, ARCHITECTURE METHODOLOGY ADAPTER).

Integrate into your solution processes pointers to methods of your domain architecture methodology at the appropriate decision, review, and reference points, for example, pointers to the architecture assessment methodology for validation steps in your solution process. Another example is a pointer to concrete architecture

---

[51] Microservices are fine-grained, context-agnostic functions or function endpoints. They are requested and delivered via lightweight protocols. Applications are established as loosely coupled microservices.

[52] Enterprise resource planning (ERP) is the integrated management of the most important business processes. An ERP system covers central functional areas shared by all companies, such as financial accounting, human resources, manufacturing, order fulfillment, supply chain management, or customer relationship management.

[53] A webshop enables online shopping as a form of electronic commerce that allows consumers to browse product catalogs and buy goods or services from a seller over the Internet using a web browser or a mobile application.

[54] Machine learning (ML) refers to a genre of computer algorithms that are initially established, or continuously improved, through experience and by the use of data. It is a subfield of artificial intelligence. Machine learning algorithms build a statistical model based on sample data (i.e., training data) to make predictions or decisions without being explicitly programmed to do so.

patterns that solution architects should consult to stay within the scope of recommended designs (DOMAIN ARCHITECTURE METHODOLOGY, ARCHITECTURE ASSESSMENT METHODOLOGY).

Instantiate this list of questions that are stereotypical of the solution architecture discipline. Adapt and vary the questions to concrete solutions (S) in your own enterprise:

- In what context does the problem arise that solution S must address?
- Which conditions (e.g., requirements, constraints, or assumptions) represent the problem that solution S must address?
- Which of these conditions are particularly significant from an architecture point of view (ARCHITECTURE SIGNIFICANCE)?
- What alternative architecture approaches are suitable for solution S to address the problem similarly well (ARCHITECTURE ALTERNATIVE)?
- Which architecture approach is the most promising and, therefore, the preferred alternative for solution S?
- What is the optimal architecture design for solution S (i.e., the desired target design for the preferred alternative) (ARCHITECTURE APPROACH)?
- How does solution S deal with each of its architecture-significant conditions (ARCHITECTURE TRACEABILITY)?
- What architecture decisions (inherent in the architecture of solution S) must be known and understood in order for the solution to be accepted by the responsible domain architects (ARCHITECTURE DECISION)?

6.5 Architecture Governance

The *architecture governance group's* patterns recommend approaches for shaping the guidance, direction, and control mandate of an architecture function. The *architecture governance* pattern differentiates govern from perform architecture responsibilities and sets a framework in which the other patterns make their contributions. The *managed architecture evolution* pattern recommends measures for the controlled evolution of the architecture function itself and of large systems, while the *architecture policy* pattern contributes to the definition of evolution corridors. The *architecture calendar* pattern recommends approaches for dealing with both plannable and planned architecture events. The *domain-organization agnosticism* pattern recommends domain-agnostic designs to decouple the differences in the pace of change between domain and organization structures. The *decommissioning reward* pattern draws attention to the end of life of systems in the enterprise and recommends actions to continuously landscape-cleanse superfluous assets and reduce corresponding operational debt. The *architecture decision* pattern differentiates significant types of architecture decisions, while the *architecture traceability* pattern helps an architecture function correlate architecture assets of different types and enables traceability from a problem to a corresponding solution perspective.

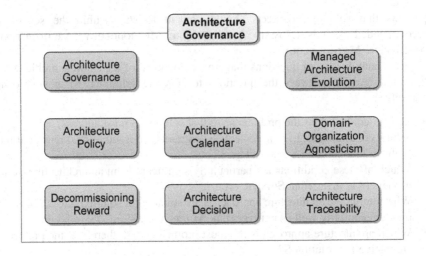

6.5.1   Architecture Governance

Enterprises expect their system architectures to reliably develop and adapt to a constantly changing environment. Architecture functions define architecture policies, guidelines, and processes to control and ensure enterprise architecture evolution stays within a predefined corridor.

> *Governance* is the act or process of governing or overseeing the control and direction of something (such as an organization). (Merriam-Webster Dictionary 2020)

Architecture governance is an integral part of corporate governance. It includes defining and implementing the processes, policies, and roles that enable an architecture function to fulfill its responsibilities for maximizing or protecting business value. Architecture governance is about assigning formal decision-making authority and coordinating and integrating architecture decisions across business and operating models (De Haes et al. 2020).

Governing architecture and performing architecture are two sides of the same coin. Performing architecture means that architects (*architecture actors*) pursue *architecture goals* by performing *architecture acts*. *Architecture acts* lead to *architecture facts* that accomplish aspired *architecture goals*. If performing architecture is about *perform actors* pursuing architecture goals, then governing architecture is about determining and prescribing the direction in which *perform actors* pursue their goals (Fig. 6.54).

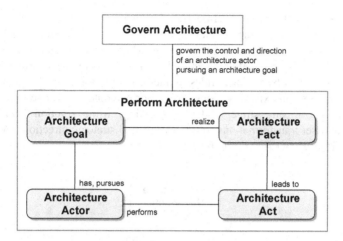

Fig. 6.54 Governing architecture versus performing architecture (overview)

Governing and performing architecture are closely interrelated. Performing architecture (inner quadrant) is oriented toward portfolio[55] or transformation[56] architecture. Governing architecture (outer quadrant) steers and controls perform architects regarding their contributions to the inner quadrant. Governing architecture means that architects direct, control, or review the transformational contributions of perform architects (Fig. 6.55).

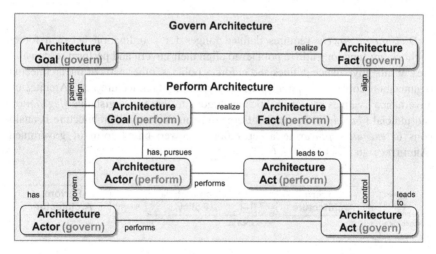

Fig. 6.55 Governing architecture versus performing architecture (detail)

---

[55] Portfolio architecture is the domain architecture discipline's main focus.

[56] Transformation architecture is the solution architecture discipline's main focus.

Architecture Function and Architecture Governance

Architecture functions define policies they embed in *methodologies* to make evolution a controlled and managed process (*managed architecture evolution*). Architecture governance ensures that architecture (*architecture decisions*) evolves within a corridor determined by policies, rules, guidelines, and processes. Different evolutionary corridors can exist at various levels. For example, enterprise-level policies frame and accompany strategic decision-making, while solution-level policies ensure that asset transformations follow established strategic directions (**MANAGED ARCHITECTURE EVOLUTION**) (Fig. 6.56).

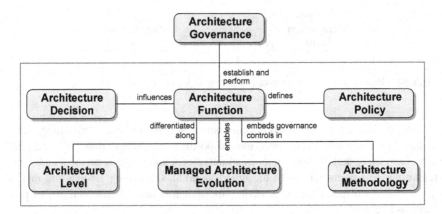

Fig. 6.56 Architecture function and architecture governance

Division of powers requires defined hinges for coordination between forces. Architecture functions utilize policies to align their govern and perform responsibilities. While governance defines and enforces policies, other parts of the architecture organization conform to policies when performing architecture acts. Architecture governance assumes responsibilities analogous to those of legislative (*legislature*) and judicial (*judiciary*) branches of government. Performing architecture is analogous to *executive power* in a separation-of-powers-based form of government (**ARCHITECTURE POLICY**) (Fig. 6.57).

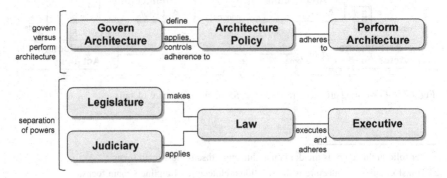

Fig. 6.57 Architecture and the division of powers

Architecture governance authorities measure policy compliance (and deviation from it) using measurement metrics. Governance is a continuous process that responds to events defined as policy triggers. For example, the request for elaborating a new service architecture triggers a policy that dictates the creation of an architecture mandate. The policy basically states that any service architecture development must be preceded by the precise definition of the development goal in the form of a mandate (**ARCHITECTURE MANDATE**).

Anticipate the designs that your architecture function aspires at the system level in the design of your governance organization. Minimize organizational blurring by ensuring that the various governance authorities are complementary in their areas of responsibility. Avoid overlapping responsibilities in your organizational design. For example, establish a central architecture board at the enterprise level to resolve escalations it receives from domain- or solution-level authorities. Assign a unique lead domain to all assets to resolve jurisdictional issues, especially when assets are part of multiple domains (**ORGANIZATIONAL REPLICATION**).

Include governance responsibilities and entitlements in the definition of architecture roles. Either define dedicated governance roles or create combined roles that merge govern and perform obligations. Few enterprise-level architects take roles exclusively containing governance responsibilities. Roles that combine govern and perform entitlements are prevalent at the domain level, while solution architects predominantly assume perform responsibilities (**ARCHITECTURE ROLE**).

Delegate *architecture governance organizations* the authority to make *governance decisions* as their pivotal activity. For example, an architecture function empowers its *security architecture board* to approve or disapprove security design decisions. Next, define an *architecture governance process* that structures and systematizes decision-making. The process clarifies what triggers decision-making, what policies are associated with what type of decision, and who (*governance authority*) is authorized to make a particular type of decision. A governance process can be informal and materialize in a governance body or amalgamate with an architecture methodology. Alternatively, governance processes may be comprehensively defined, formally mandated, and technically implemented to ensure compliance with them. For example, an architecture function defines, implements, and operates its governance process based on a business process management platform. This increases automatic compliance with the process and the policies defined within it. Finally, clarify the *architecture governance enforcement approach* that your function takes to ensure broad compliance with governance rules and policies. For example, an architecture function creates tollgates along the enterprise value chain. A tollgate may not be passed if the central governance group does not approve a proposed design. Let me give another example of an enforcement approach: an architecture function convinces its architects that compliance with policies is in their best interest. The architecture function regularly hosts training sessions and launches information campaigns explaining why and how architects benefit from adhering to policies. For example, the architecture function explains that by adhering to policies, architects can increase their individual efficiency over the entire course of an engagement and thus invest the time saved in their personal development or architectural education (**ARCHITECTURE DECISION**) (Fig. 6.58).

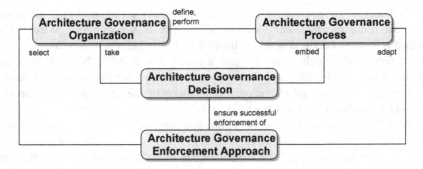

Fig. 6.58 Architecture governance decision

Distinguish governance decisions by the *type of asset* about which a decision is made, for example, asset portfolio decisions, landscape asset decisions, structural asset decisions, reference asset, and methodology asset decisions. Portfolio prioritization is an example of a portfolio decision, while refusing to approve an application architecture request is considered a landscape asset decision. Endorsing a new architecture pattern is deciding on a reference asset, while deciding to evolve the pattern method is a methodology-related governance decision. For example, you take a structural asset decision when you approve the request to introduce a new domain representing an area of growing architectural interest (e.g., introducing *machine learning* as a new domain). Define governance policies and decision criteria for each type of decision. For example, an architecture function specifies prioritization criteria that are contained in an architecture portfolio policy. When architects make portfolio decisions, they must adhere to portfolio policies and apply the prioritization criteria to all portfolio assets. This example's prioritization criterion specifies three attributes: architectural risk,[57] impact, and architectural technical debt.[58] The policy further specifies that, for example, landscape assets are given high priority when their architectural risk is *low*, when the impacts they cause are *minimal*, and if they *decrease* overall architectural debt (ARCHITECTURE ASSET).

Distinguish architecture governance decisions by the *type of rule* they define. For example, a standardization decision (e.g., approval of a new technology standard) defines a *zero deviation tolerance* rule. A business department requesting a database

---

[57] Architectural risk is the degree of a design's appropriateness in light of its desired functionality and in the face of unknowns. The unknowns bring uncertainty about the assumptions made as well as the decisions about those uncertainties. Risk is the result (e.g., the negative effect of desired but not accomplished functionality) of a particular uncertainty (e.g., technical unknowns) weighted with its probability.

[58] Architectural technical debt describes the phenomenon of inadequate system design that achieves short-term benefits at the expense of long-term gradual deterioration in system agility.

instance must accept *MySQL*[59] as a technical standard product if MySQL is defined as a mandatory *RDBMS*[60] *technology standard* in the enterprise.

Finally, differentiate governance decisions by their *intended purpose*. For example, governance decisions can be *detective* (e.g., architecture tollgates define checkpoints to systematically identify policy deviations), *preventative* (e.g., architecture patterns guide design designs to prevent poor solution outcomes), and *corrective* (e.g., architecture proposals are rejected with an indication of the corrective action required. Suggested corrective measures are used to support a targeted architecture refactoring).

Ensure your architecture function is set up to make governance decisions in a traceable and navigable manner across the enterprise value chain. While your function is solely responsible for particular governance decisions (e.g., deciding on the appropriateness of a proposed design), in other cases, you contribute the architectural perspective into overarching decision-making processes. Your function is involved in all enterprise-wide decisions. For example, it is involved in the prioritization, enrichment, risk, and impact assessment, advocation or rejection of business demands, service, or project portfolios (**ARCHITECTURE TRACEABILITY**).

Ensure your architecture function aligns governance decisions across all levels. Establish a central governance authority at the enterprise level. However, prefer a federated approach to governing architecture at the domain and solution level. The federated approach requires delegation of authority and responsibility and is and thus ultimately relies on mutual trust within the enterprise. Federated approaches pay off in increased scalability (**ARCHITECTURE LEVEL**).

Ensure that the intended governance impacts take hold. Regardless of the policies defined by your function, the desired outcomes will not take effect if your architects do not follow the established rules. Non-compliancy is not necessarily due to reluctance, ignorance, or unwillingness to comply. For example, an architect may not blissfully ignore rules or processes; the architect may simply not be aware of their existence. Another example is an enterprise that is exploring uncharted territory and finds that its governance processes do not adequately support the required exploratory approaches. To give you another example, an organization poisoned with mistrust at the social system level inevitably infects and undermines the seriousness of architecture policies, methods, and processes (**ORGANIZATIONAL REPLICATION**).

Communicate the value of governance rules clearly and regularly. Architects who expect personal benefits from complying will naturally conform to governance rules. *Hidden resistance* is more difficult to deal with. It can be observed as a behavioral pattern in very political and fearful environments. *Open refusal* is the most

---

[59] MySQL is among the most widespread relational database management systems (RDBMS) in the world. It is available as an open-source software as well as a commercial enterprise version for various operating systems.

[60] A relational database is a database for digital data management and is based on the relational calculus—a well-defined concept in mathematics. The associated database management system is called a relational database management system (i.e., RDBMS).

confrontational attitude. However, it can be dealt with better. You can discuss with the objecting party and either convince them or let them convince you. Increase the traction and impact of architecture governance by establishing Communities of Practice (CoP) or architecture guilds.[61] Architecture communities of practice are groups of architects who share a common interest in a particular domain. They meet informally and collaborate across organizational boundaries. Consider a *positive architecture pranger* as a technique to further promote governance traction. Use it to communicate and reward outstanding architecture contributions. Gain visibility into performance by systematically measuring contributions and policy compliance. Share measurement results widely and regularly to improve traction and maturity (ARCHITECTURE MATURITY).

Define governance rules that are cyclical and recurring, or those that you want to be alerted to, in architecture calendars. An example would be the *annual service portfolio review*, where the architecture function examines the planning of all services to approve it or recommend appropriate adjustments. Another example of recurring governance intervention is the annual determination of the architecture function's own demand, which must have entered the enterprise's demand planning by a certain date (ARCHITECTURE CALENDAR).

Fuse governance policies, rules, and guidelines with your architecture methods, view models, and platforms to ensure their inevitable, early, and automatic consideration. This is particularly effective in enterprises with a pronounced process orientation. For example, an architecture function has implemented an architecture evaluation checkpoint based on its platform so that the next process step can only be executed if the governance organization accepts the result of the check (YOUR OWN ARCHITECTURE METHODOLOGY, YOUR OWN ARCHITECTURE PLATFORM).

6.5.2   Managed Architecture Evolution

The only constant is change. In many areas of life, short-term goals tend to outpace longer-term aims. An architecture function is confronted with this phenomenon in two ways: by the evolution of architecture assets and by the evolution of its own function. The one-sided focus on functional advances that directly impact the evolution of architecture assets and the architecture function comes at the expense of their agility and sustainable changeability.

---

[61] Guild is a term from an Agile terminology. A guild is a community of members who share common interests. It consists of a group of people—regardless of their organizational affiliation. The purpose of a guild is to promote the exchange of knowledge, tools, insights, practices, or techniques among guild members (Business Architecture Guild 2016).

> *Evolution* is a process of change in a certain direction, a process of continuous change from a lower, simpler, or worse to a higher, more complex, or better state. (Merriam-Webster Dictionary 2020)

If evolution is a process to bring an object into a better state, both *better* and *object* require further clarification. While a normative metric is a prerequisite for clarifying the concept of *better*, the concept of *object* can range from something overly abstract, immaterial, or metaphysical to something very concrete, material, and rooted in the physical world.

Architecture Function and Managed Architecture Evolution

Architecture evolution aims to improve the state of an asset or other object of architectural interest. Architecture functions define normative metrics (*architecture maturity*) to plan and control the evolution of assets and sustain investments made over their entire lifespan. Architecture governance organizations define evolution corridors based on policies, rules, and guidelines to ensure that asset transformations remain within defined boundaries (**ARCHITECTURE POLICY**) (Fig. 6.59).

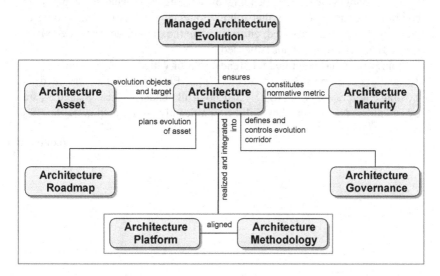

Fig. 6.59 Architecture function and managed architecture evolution

Architecture Evolution

Establish a maturity metric and utilize it to determine the maturity baseline of your assets. Apply fit-gap analysis techniques to determine the evolutionary path each of your assets should take. Consider applying other analytical frameworks to help guide you in areas of unexplored opportunity. For example, adopt the *Blue Ocean Strategy* (Kim and Mauborgne 2016) as an orientation framework for determining evolution direction. Blue Ocean Strategy encompasses the *four actions framework* that help address the trade-off between differentiation and low costs. Introduce architecture KPIs to regularly measure the degree of asset maturity and control asset progress (**Architecture Maturity**).

Blue Ocean Strategy: Four Actions Framework

Enterprise *A* plans to expand into an unexplored market. It analyzes and categorizes emerging trends in the new market—both upward and downward trends.

Enterprise *A* uses the *four actions framework* to analyze its service portfolio in light of the identified trends. Enterprise services that correspond to downtrends are classified as *reduce* (i.e., minor changes needed) or *eliminate* (i.e., massive changes needed) depending on the degree of change required. In contrast, enterprise services that follow uptrends are classified according to the degree of change required, either as *raise* (i.e., minor changes needed) or *create* (i.e., significant changes needed).

Enterprise *A* has identified ten trends, four of which are downward ($T_1 \ldots T_4$) and six are upward trends ($T_5 \ldots T_{10}$). Enterprise *A* has classified its existing enterprise services ($S_A \ldots S_G$) along all trends. Services S_A and S_B are classified as *eliminate* as they will be significantly adjusted soon. S_C and S_D

(continued)

are classified as *reduce* because both require minimal changes. S_E, S_F, and S_G require minimal changes to meet the T_5, T_6, and T_7 uptrend requirements—hence they are categorized as *raise*. Finally, three new services are required in the *create* category (Fig. 6.60).

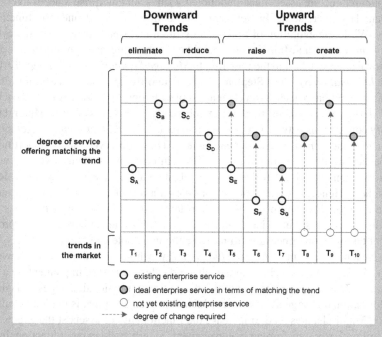

Fig. 6.60 Blue Ocean Strategy—four actions framework example

Use the *four actions framework* in your architecture function to determine the direction in which your assets ought to evolve. The framework distinguishes two axes, *degree of expansion* and *degree of change*, with scales between *high* and *low*. High degree of expansion and low degree of change defines the *raise*-segment, while the corresponding high degree of change defines the *create*-segment. A low degree of expansion and low degree of change is called *reduce* and correspondingly high degree of change is called *eliminate*. While *eliminate* suggests removing an asset (e.g., removing a service that supports a downward trend and requires extensive adjustments), *reduce* suggests limiting the investment and thus the effort required to evolve an asset. For example, an *architecture assessment* service that shows a downward trend but requires minimal changes can be operated at a reasonable level of effort via timeboxed[62] assessments. *Raise* suggests investments in an existing service based on an observed upward trend. At the same time, *create* justifies significant investment in a new service that is expected to grow with an observed upward trend.

Managed Evolution

Your architecture assets must undoubtedly suit your enterprise's needs over their lifespan. However, suitability encompasses both—functional and non-functional fitness. While the evolution of functionality often takes precedence over the evolution of an asset's non-functional capabilities, neglecting asset agility jeopardizes functional augmentation in the long run. In *Managed Evolution—A Strategy for Very Large Information Systems*, Stephan Murer, Bruno Bonati, and Frank Furrer (2010) examined what happens to assets that are subject to opportunistic evolution. By *very large information systems* they mean inherently complex systems. Murer et al. classify connections between interdependent parts as *functional, semantic, temporal, technical*, and *operational* dependencies. They observed that opportunistic approaches to the evolution of very large information systems overemphasize functional considerations at the expense of maintaining the large system's long-term fitness. Hence, opportunistic evolutionary approaches lead to complex systems whose functionality, optimized in the short term, erodes in the long term.

Murer et al. describe what happens if you follow an opportunistic approach without taking countermeasures to mitigate the inevitable evolutionary effects. The abscissa denotes architecture asset *functionality*, while the ordinate axis shows its agility. *Agility* is an asset characteristic that indicates the cost of implementing a *unit of change*. The arrows in the diagram indicate transformational changes. Imagine a transformational change as a major modification of an asset that is implemented in a project. Major changes tend to increase the functionality of assets at the expense of their agility. Early transformative engagements significantly expand functionality at a relatively low agility cost. However, this reverses over time resulting in minimal functionality expansion at disproportionately high agility costs. Murer identifies this phenomenon as inevitable if opportunistic evolutionary approaches are adopted without countermeasures being taken. At the end of the journey, the large information system is in a non-developable state. The actual state of the asset is significantly different from its desired state (*gap/deviation*) (Fig. 6.61).

---

[62] Timeboxing is a time management technique and an alternative to fixing scope. It assigns a fixed period of time, known as a timebox, during which scheduled activities are carried out. It is used as a form of mitigating the risk of overdoing inherently complex matters in light of a limited timeframe.

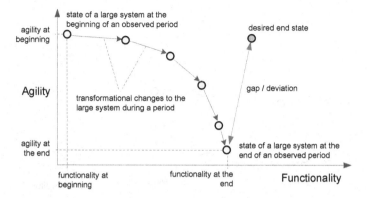

Fig. 6.61 System evolution coordinate system (© 2010 Springer Science & Business Media, reprinted with permission)

Murer et al. propose replacing the purely opportunistic approach with an evolutionary one to improve the undesirable long-term effects described above. Evolutionary approaches balance functionality and agility differently—thus, many transformative changes simultaneously increase functionality and agility. An evolutionary approach recognizes that greater agility enables functional advancement at lower cost and in less time. Evolutionary approaches require you to define evolution corridors and ensure that transformative changes stay within the defined corridor boundaries. Murer et al. distinguish three types of modifications. *Changes with a moderately upward sloping arrow* strike a balance between functional enhancement and architectural quality. While additional effort to develop an asset's agility may slow a change slightly, such slowing costs offset an attractive medium-term return on investment. *Changes with a downward sloping arrow* represent cases where functionality needs to be implemented urgently and the enterprise is willing to pay for the corresponding agility cost, for example, in the event of an overly urgent business need, such as losing customers to competitors, when functional service enhancements are not implemented. Finally, *modifications with a sharply upward sloping arrow* are specially designed to improve asset agility. For example, a project updates a technical module to the latest version because the current version is losing vendor support (Fig. 6.62).

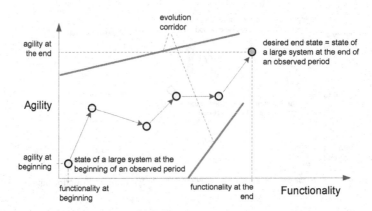

Fig. 6.62 System evolution coordinate system with evolution corridor (© 2010 Springer Science & Business Media, reprinted with permission)

Develop your function's approach to evolving asset portfolios based on three fundaments. First, *ensure strong management support*. Broadly aligned management is required to resolve disputes and arbitrate conflict, as large systems, and asset portfolios frequently cross organizational boundaries (ORGANIZATIONAL REPLICATION).

Next, specify criteria that define your evolutionary corridor. Choose quantifiable criteria to enable objective reflection and dialogue about transformational change. Select criteria that accompany the planning, building, and running of assets so you can unequivocally determine when corridor boundaries are crossed. Define criteria in the form of architecture policies, rules, or guidelines and consider implementing them in your methodologies. For example, define a policy and link it to a project portfolio tollgate. The architecture function performs the tollgate activity at the request of a project portfolio manager. The policy in this example requires an architect to review all project proposals above a certain threshold (e.g., all projects above a budget of one million euros) before approving the entire portfolio. It further requires that no approval be granted if the architecture portion of a project budget is less than 10% for solutions that are designated as shared platforms (ARCHITECTURE POLICY).

After all, you need a strong governance organization in your function. Architecture governance makes a significant contribution to asset portfolio decisions and the associated asset development. In particularly, it ensures that asset design and implementation remain within the defined evolution corridor (ARCHITECTURE GOVERNANCE).

Define policies to encourage the application of elementary *design for change principles*[63] when designing your assets at all architecture levels. The earlier and the deeper you build fundamental modifiability into your asset designs, the more smoothly they will evolve (**ARCHITECTURE PRINCIPLE**).

Optimize your architecture mandate artifacts to equally highlight functional and non-functional requirements. Architecture mandates are perfect for capturing functional and agility-oriented objectives for transformational changes before design elaboration gets underway. Mandates also accompany the further pursuit of transformational changes to ensure asset evolution remains within defined boundaries (**ARCHITECTURE MANDATE**).

Link your evolution corridors to asset roadmaps to ensure that roadmap events are systematically considered in asset evolution decisions. For example, during an architecture review of a project proposal, it turns out that the roadmap for the application transforming the project calls for a platform upgrade in the coming quarter. The platform upgrade is intended to bring the application up to date with the latest security technology. The information in the roadmap ensures that the platform upgrade is reflected in the project plan (**ARCHITECTURE ROADMAP METHODOLOGY**).

Finally, do not forget the last phase of your asset lifecycle: decommissioning. Oddly enough, dismantling an asset does neither increase its functionality nor its agility. However, decommissioning assets significantly reduces landscape costs and complexity. There is no longer a cost to operate the asset in the future.[64] In addition, most assets are part of one or more larger wholes. An asset you take out of service reduces the complexity of the assets to which it belongs or with which it is otherwise connected. Ultimately, you reduce complexity as well as demarcation issues by reducing the number of parts and connections in your landscapes (**DECOMMISSIONING REWARD, ARCHITECTURE DEMARCATION**).

6.5.3   Architecture Policy

Cooperation presupposes that all cooperating parties adhere to the rules, policies, regulations, and directives that serve as a reference for coordinated action. Lacking architecture policies as a binding framework for cooperation undermines effective collaboration within and outside the architecture function.

---

[63] Design for change principles improve the modifiability and expandability of a system, for example, loose coupling, information hiding, separation of concerns, or inversion of control.

[64] Capital expenditure (CAPEX) is the money an organization spends creating, buying, or evolving assets, while operational expenditure (OPEX) is the ongoing costs of reliably operating existing assets.

A *policy* is a deliberate system of principles to guide decisions and achieve rational outcomes. A policy is a statement of intent and is implemented as a procedure or protocol. (Wikipedia Policy 2020b)

An *architecture policy*, inspired by the Wikipedia definition, is a deliberate system of principles that guide architecture decisions and achieve rational, architecturally intended results.

Different types of policies exist—for example, architecture standards, principles, regulations, or guidelines. All architecture policies have in common that they are deliberately established. They expect policy-compliant behavior and steer architectural action and decision-making in intended directions or within a set of clearly defined framing conditions. For example, a technology standard expects strict conformance so that all applications within the scope of the standard base their implementations on that standard. To give another example, an architecture principle like *loose coupling*[65] expects a different type of conformance. The loose coupling principle expects a design to be elaborated in accordance with the principle. An architecture principle, therefore, neither prescribes technology nor a particular design. As an architect, you apply the loose coupling principle perfectly when, for example, you design an application to mediate the exchange of information with other applications via a MoM platform.[66] Similarly, you would apply the loose coupling principle if your information exchange design were based on an ETL approach.[67]

Associated conditions activate *architecture policies*. A *condition* specifies the circumstances under which a policy applies. Architecture policies also cause impacts. *Impact* is the intended effect of a compliantly applied policy. Policies define what compliance means by specifying *conformance criteria*. Finally, policies can define *sanctions* that are imposed in the event of noncompliance. For example, an architecture function establishes a pattern-related policy. The architecture function defines *proposal for a new pattern* as a *condition* of the policy. Pattern suggestions are transmitted, for example, via the *propose a new pattern* form in the architecture portal. The policy defines a *pattern {endorsed, rejected} decision* as the intended policy impact. Finally, the policy defines that a clearly specified *architecture authority must review a proposed pattern to approve or reject it* based on *conformance criteria* (Fig. 6.63).

---

[65] Loose coupling between components means that connected components have little or no knowledge of each other's definitions, while tight coupling is the exact opposite.

[66] MoM (message-oriented middleware) platforms are inter-system communication platforms that support mediation and exchange of information between distributed systems in the form of messages.

[67] ETL (extract, transform, load) refers to a generic design of a process divided into three phases. In the first phase (E), data is extracted from one or more source systems. In the second phase (T), the extracted data is transformed into the desired destination format. Finally, in the third phase (L), the transformed data is loaded into the corresponding target systems.

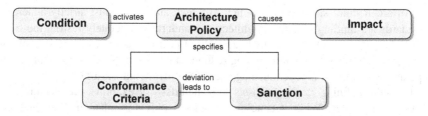

Fig. 6.63 Architecture policy

Adapt the following attribute schema and use it as a template for creating and evolving your own policy definitions. Note that policies are not necessarily captured in the form of the attribute schema shown. Rather, they are often fully integrated, or merged, into an architecture method. They are completely absorbed into the structure of a method or presented to architects in the form of decision points, tollgates, architecture patterns, or principles (Table 6.4).

Table 6.4 Architecture policy template

Attribute name	Attribute description
Policy name	Descriptive and uniquely identifying policy name
Policy actor(s)	Differentiate the policy owner (defines and develops the policy definition), the policy performer (expected to conform to the policy), and the policy governor (controls and ensures policy conformance)
Policy condition(s)	Circumstances in which the policy applies; what triggers the policy
Policy impact	Impacts caused by, or intended to be caused by, applying the policy
Policy conformance criteria	Criteria indicating what, in particular, conformity with the policy means. Conformity criteria describe, among other things, the rigor and stringency with which conformance with the policy is expected. For example, if the *rigor attribute* is set to *must*, the policy under consideration represents an *architecture standard*. If the *rigor attribute* is set to *consider*, a corresponding policy is directive in nature (i.e., a guideline). Finally, if a rigor attribute is read out as *should*, the policy corresponds to an architecture principle
Policy sanction	Defines *how* the KPI measurement is performed. For example: *divide the number of satisfactory customer feedback received by the number of all service requests executed*
Policy status	Policy lifecycle status (e.g., active, inactive)

Architecture Standard

> A *standard* is something set up and established by authority as a rule for the measure of quantity, weight, extent, value, or quality. (Merriam-Webster Dictionary 2020)

An architecture standard is a policy to which architects must strictly adhere—standards are binding policies. Architecture standards deliberately restrict the freedom of design. Standards are intended to limit cost and complexity by improving landscape interoperability, minimizing redundant investments, and optimizing asset operations as well as lifecycle management (**ARCHITECTURE ASSET**).

Consider defining reference assets as standards—for example, architecture patterns or principles. While technology standards only formulate implementation-related conditions, the standardization of patterns concretely guides the design-related approaches your architects choose for enterprise applications, services, or platforms. Define patterns as standards to induce architects such that they consider proven architecture approaches in their designs (**REFERENCE ARCHITECTURE METHODOLOGY**).

Define selected landscape assets as standards, e.g., services, applications, platforms, technologies, or information assets. For example, an architecture function declares technology T as a new technology standard. T limits architects' options in choosing technology stacks when they revise or evolve landscape assets. To give another example, the architecture function declares the service S as the new standard for capability C. Standardizing a service means that it must be utilized whenever the capability is needed. In this example, architects must use service S if they need capability C (**LANDSCAPE ASSET**).

Define architecture methodologies as standards. For example, declare your solution architecture methodology, inherent view model, model archetypes, and modeling nomenclatures as standards to ensure that all problem-solving applies the same systematic approach. Architects adhere to a methodology standard by applying the method completely and correctly (**YOUR OWN ARCHITECTURE METHODOLOGY**).

Architecture Function and Architecture Policy

Architecture functions delegate the definition, evolution, and enforcement of policies to their governance organizations. Architecture governance differentiates policies along levels and uses them to declare assets as standards. Architecture policies are integrated into methods and implemented on the basis of architecture platforms (*architecture apparatus*) (Fig. 6.64).

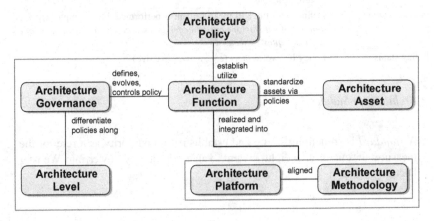

Fig. 6.64 Architecture function and architecture policy

Avoid reinventing the wheel; instead, adopt or expand industry frameworks and standards for policy definition, for example, the Open Group Architecture Framework (TOGAF[68]) or the metamodel standard for architecture descriptions (ISO/IEC/ IEEE 42010).

Place references to policies in close proximity to activities that you expect to be compliantly performed. For example, an architecture function manages patterns in a publicly accessible pattern catalog, where it declares some patterns as standards. The architecture function expects architects to apply patterns unconditionally if a standardized pattern fits a particular design problem. The architecture function includes a reference to the pattern catalog in its solution architecture methodology to ensure that architects systematically stumble upon the declared pattern standards when designing solutions. Implement policies either directly in your architecture platform or anchor references to policies in your platform (ARCHITECTURE PATTERN METHODOLOGY, YOUR OWN ARCHITECTURE PLATFORM).

Sharpen your role definitions and specify exactly which roles must define, evolve, own, enforce, or comply with which policies under which circumstances. Move the responsibility for policy conformance within role hierarchies to the highest sensible hierarchy level. For example, hold domain architects of security-sensitive domains accountable for strict compliance with security policies. Architecture roles that are subordinate to domain architects inherit their responsibility for policy compliance (ARCHITECTURE ROLE).

Do not tie conformance criteria to something that frequently changes, such as organizational structure, specific landscape assets, or individuals. If it cannot be avoided, introduce indirections, like smart pointers, to mitigate issues when changes occur. For example, the organizational structure of an enterprise frequently changes. The architecture function cannot completely avoid placing organizational references in its policy definitions. However, it can introduce a logical organization scheme to reduce the problem of organizational changes inevitably invalidating associated policies. The logical organization scheme provides policy definitions a reliable reference. At the same time, the architecture function can flexibly adapt them whenever changes need to be made to the physical organization (DOMAIN-ORGANIZATION AGNOSTICISM).

Ensure that architecture sourcing partners and service providers know your declared policies and similarly adhere to them. Make compliance with policies legally binding in your sourcing and service contracts. Encourage your sourcing partners to reflect the usefulness of your policies in their engagements. Incentivize them to submit suggestions for practical improvements to your policies. Sourcing partners have a more detached and, in some cases, more objective perspective on

---

[68] The Open Group Architecture Framework (TOGAF). TOGAF proposes an approach to design, plan, implement and govern enterprise architecture. It describes a generic method for developing architectures. TOGAF suggests a common vocabulary, a generic information model, an adaptable role model, general architecture artifacts, and tooling.

your architecture operations. Use their insights and viewpoints as a valuable resource (**ARCHITECTURE SOURCING**).

Beware, policy lifecycle management entails its own efforts and costs. Carefully balance the benefits you expect from demanding an architecture policy against the costs of defining, developing, and enforcing it over the long term. Calculate the expected efficiency[69] of the policy. For example, a policy is established to review the chosen architecture direction at an early tollgate. In the hypothetical case that a review is found to be *okay*, the checking costs could have been saved by omitting the architecture review in the first place. However, if a review had found that the chosen direction was inadequate, immediate action would have been taken to avoid future costs of resetting an incorrectly pursued solution from the start. Favor a few highly efficient policies over many that are inappropriate for optimizing your architecture function's capacity (**ARCHITECTURE CAPACITY**).

Guidelines are the lifeblood of any architecture governance organization. Ensure your governance organization pays as much attention to defining and managing lifecycle policies as it does to the compliant execution of architecture activities. Ensure that policy definition is based on quantifiable conformance criteria. Avoid unworkable, unenforceable, or other policies that are merely *wishful thinking* (**ARCHITECTURE GOVERNANCE**).

Position policies that affect the entire organization at the enterprise level, for example, enterprise architecture principles or methodologies. Domain-specific policies are positioned at the domain level—for example, a domain-specific architecture pattern. Very few policies may exist at the solution level, for example, a policy that prescribes a specific exchange format via which all applications within a domain must exchange data with one another (**ARCHITECTURE LEVEL**).

6.5.4 Architecture Calendar

Planning and scheduling architecture-relevant events and synchronizing organizational reactions are prerequisites for cooperative action, thus prerequisites for effectively supporting a company in pursuing its goals. An architecture function schedules events to synchronize coordinated reactions utilizing architecture calendars.

> A *calendar* is a system for fixing the beginning, length, and divisions of the civil year and arranging days and longer divisions of time (such as weeks and months) in a definite order. (Merriam-Webster Dictionary 2020)

---

[69] Efficiency is measured as the ratio of useful output to total input. It is expressed by the formula $= \frac{P}{C}$, where P is the amount of useful output produced per the amount C of resources consumed.

While a *calendar* is a system of chronologically[70] organized units of time[71] (e.g., hours, days, weeks, months), a *calendar event* is the designation of a single specific unit of time within a calendar.

Events are objects in time. They are uniquely identifiable particulars that, unlike universals, cannot be repeated at different times. A corresponding source (*event source*) triggers an event. Specific *event handling* may be required when an event occurs. For example, a crashed server is an emitter (*event source*) of a server outage event. Restarting the server (*event handling*) to resolve the failure is an *event response* (Fig. 6.65).

Fig. 6.65 Event

Architecture calendars are systems in which architects schedule events. Calendars emit events when they become due. Architecture events can be both one-time and recurring events. They can be planned and unplanned events, very serious or completely unproblematic. An enterprise can have several architecture calendars at the same time. Each calendar is tied to an architecturally relevant object. For example, the enterprise calendar of an architecture function is tied to the architecture organization as a whole. In contrast, a security-domain calendar is bound only to the security architecture domain (Fig. 6.66).

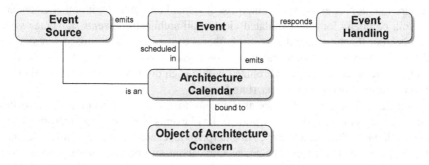

Fig. 6.66 Architecture calendar

---

[70] Chronology is the arrangement of events in their order of occurrence in time.

[71] Time is the indefinite continued progress of existence and events that occur in an apparently irreversible succession from the past, through the present, into the future (Wikipedia Time 2021).

Architecture Function and Architecture Calendar

Architecture functions establish and use architecture calendars to ensure synchronicity and collaborative action within and outside the architecture organization (*architecture governance*). Architecture calendars can be bound to assets so that events can be scheduled for individual assets. Calendars are referenced by architecture methods and implemented through platforms (*architecture apparatus*) (Fig. 6.67).

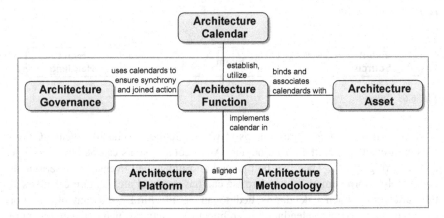

Fig. 6.67 Architecture function and architecture calendar

Establish an architecture calendar for your entire function. Position your architecture function calendar at the enterprise level and integrate it with other calendars in your company for a consolidated view of all architecture events. Leverage your architecture function calendar to ensure that activities are synchronized across your domains. Create individual calendars for each of your domains to ensure that architecture activities are synchronized within each domain and across its solution-level landscape assets (**ARCHITECTURE LEVEL**).

Utilize architecture calendars as a means to govern architecture. Reverse the enterprise-level consolidation of domain-level events by cascading enterprise-level events down to the domain level. An enterprise-level architecture function calendar, for example, synchronizes a calendar entry about an upcoming enterprise service portfolio review with all domain-level calendars to prepare domain architects that their contributions are due in a month's time. To give another example, an architecture function maintains recurring events in its enterprise-level calendar to remind the organization of regular hygiene measures—hygiene measures such as revising and refreshing architecture guidelines, reviewing patterns, or improving the usability of exposure points, e.g., by sprucing up the architecture portal. Use event information for chronological impact analysis. For example, two architecture events are defined in different domain calendars but refer to the same application. Both events require a change in the application's architecture, as described in their *event handling sections*. At the same time, they collide chronologically because their dates and times overlap. The governance organization uses this information to notify the affected domain architects of a possible conflict relating to the planned changes to the application (**ARCHITECTURE GOVERNANCE**).

Create and manage architecture calendars for individual architecture assets such as structural assets (e.g., domains) or landscape assets (e.g., services, applications, platforms, or information entities). Alternatively, you can link calendars to roadmaps as these anticipate and schedule events for their associated assets (**ARCHITECTURE ASSET, ARCHITECTURE ROADMAP METHODOLOGY**).

In addition, consider calendars to create and manage architecture mandates. In a calendar tied to a mandate that accompanies an engagement, enter project-specific review points, such as *completion of the analysis phase*, *achievement of alternatives development*, or *architectural readiness*. The engagement architecture team is then automatically alerted by the calendar to agreed review points (**ARCHITECTURE CALENDAR**).

Regularly review the maturity status of your architecture function in order to measure and reflect on its progress and, if necessary, decide on improvements and take measures to implement them. In particular, check the maturity level of your function in order to be able to counter deviations from your roadmap planning at an early stage. Also regularly review the ownership situation in your enterprise, as it changes gradually and continuously, and therefore schedule it as a recurring event in your organization's calendar. Identifying decommissioning opportunities is another activity you should conduct on a regular basis. On the one hand, ensure that you do not introduce new assets without eliminating existing ones. In addition, regularly, for example, every 2 years, examine your landscape asset portfolios for assets that have become obsolete or are about to become obsolete (i.e., that can be decommissioned) and approach their removal through dedicated programs (e.g., decommissioning projects) (**ARCHITECTURE MATURITY, ARCHITECTURE OWNERSHIP, DECOMMISSIONING REWARD**).

Adapt the following attribute schema and use it as a template for architecture events as you schedule them in your calendars. Examples of calendar events are annually recurring architecture contributions, such as submitting architecture demand reports, contributions to service, application, or project portfolio reviews, but also mandate, roadmap, domain, or landscape asset-specific events. Yet other possible calendar events are the exploration of decommissioning opportunities or the conduct of ideation processes to regularly unleash innovative potentials of the architecture function (Table 6.5).

Table 6.5 Architecture event template

Attribute name	Attribute description
Event name	Descriptive name that appears in calendar views
Event owner	Event owner is the person who scheduled the calendar event. Individuals or organizations are common sources of planned events
Event date and time	Date and time when the event is emitted by the calendar
Event target	Specification of who is alerted by an emitted event. Examples are email address, cell phone number, or executable targets that can be notified, for example, by remotely invoking a web service
Event handling	Instructions that describe how to process an architecture event properly or how to react to such an event. Prefer references to already existing reaction instructions and avoid copying instructions to avoid redundancy. For example, references point to policies or processes that explain how to handle a received event
Event status	Lifecycle status of the event (e.g., active, inactive, recurring)

6.5.5   Domain-Organization Agnosticism

Pivotal domain abstractions and structures, as well as cross-domain relationships, rarely change. Their purpose is to create order in a related area of architectural interests. In contrast, organizations are subject to frequent change, which makes their designs less stable. Tight coupling between domain schemas and organization structures forces unnecessary frequent adjustments of the domain schema in response to organizational changes—thus undermining the structuring and ordering purpose of architecture domains.

> *Agnosticism* describes a state of not taking a stand on something, especially not holding either of two usually strongly opposed positions. (Dictionary.Com 2020)

A *domain* is a sphere of knowledge and delineates an area of interest. Architecture functions define domains intending to decompose their enterprise as a whole into architecturally digestible parts. Architecture domains enable architects to coherently consider, plan, or pursue a topic of enterprise interest over the long term. They introduce domain-specific abstractions, categories, language, and jargon.

A logical domain schema (*domain schema (logical)*) abstracts from an infinite number of concrete schema instantiations (*domain schema (physical)*). For example, an enterprise domain schema mirrors the company's business model. At the same time, it does not reflect any of the concrete business model instantiations. A logical domain schema represents the generic and durable structures of a domain: subdomains, relationships between domains, or logical architecture assets as parts of a domain, which in turn abstract physical assets. For example, a *security architecture domain design* includes *reverse proxy* as a logical application asset, while concrete *reverse proxy instances* (i.e., technical reverse proxy software products) are not included. In domain schemas, physical assets are abstracted from their corresponding logical assets (Fig. 6.68).

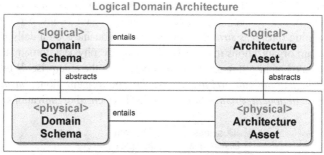

Fig. 6.68   Logical versus physical domain architecture

Logical domain architecture[72] strives to create a sustainable order based on a stable domain schema. In contrast, *physical domain architecture* changes more frequently in response to frequently changing business needs. Domain disciplines and business disciplines collaborate intensively. *Business disciplines* are aligned with the needs of the business (i.e., the pursuit of business goals) and are intended to directly support the enterprise. In contrast, *domain disciplines* are focused on domain transparency and manageability and therefore aim to support the business indirectly by providing orientation and making domains efficiently usable. While logical domain architecture supports the business in strategic planning (*business strategy*), physical domain architecture supports the business in execution (*business operations*) (Fig. 6.69).

Fig. 6.69 Business versus domain disciplines

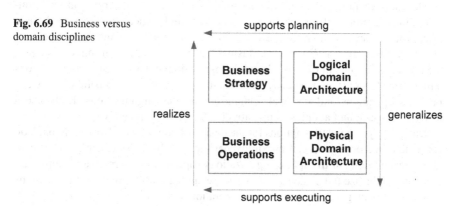

---

[72]Logical architecture versus physical architecture. A key difference between logical and physical architecture is that logical architecture's concern is to identify generic functions, components, and their interrelations. In contrast, physical architecture goes a step further and provides the details for implementing the logical architecture based on more concrete technologies or devices specified. The main purpose of logical architecture is to plan and communicate architecture (e.g., achieving consensus among architects). In contrast, the primary purpose of physical architecture is to implement solutions and make them available.

Ultimately, it is the set of specific enterprise organizations that carry out both business- and domain-related disciplines. Business organizations perform strategic business planning (*business strategy*) and operate the business on a daily basis (*operations*). Domain organizations manage both logical and physical domain architectures and the associated architecture assets for all domains in the enterprise. While *business strategy* and *logical domain architecture* are strategic organizations, *business operations* and *physical domain architecture* are tactically oriented organizations (Fig. 6.70).

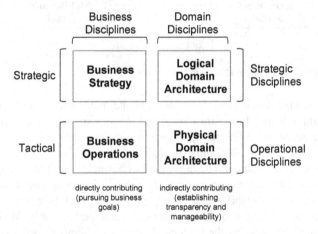

Fig. 6.70 Logical organizations

Design your physical organizations with the above logical organizational considerations in mind. Both the business strategy and logical architecture domain organizations are small in size. Both also take a strategic planning perspective. However, there are also differences. Business strategy organizations directly support their business in pursuit of its goals, while logical domain architecture organizations aim to provide order, transparency, and orientation. There are also parallels between business operations and physical domain architecture organizations. Both take a tactical approach and adopt a comparatively short-term perspective.

Basically, you have two options for the design of your physical organization. You can emphasize organizational proximity between the business discipline organizations and the domain discipline organizations (option 1). Alternatively (option 2), you can emphasize the closeness between the strategic disciplines or organizations versus close integration between the operational discipline organizations. Both options have their advantages and disadvantages.

Option 1: If your enterprise operates in a volatile[73] business environment, emphasize organizational proximity between business disciplines. Establish a close

---

[73] Volatility is a tendency to change quickly and unpredictably (Merriam-Webster Dictionary 2020). In the business context, it is primarily associated with market volatility (i.e., rapid fluctuations and changes in the market capitalization of companies, for example, due to substantially changing competitive situations) and thus treated as a condition that needs to be managed.

link between business strategy and business operations organizations and a similarly tight link between your logical and physical domain architecture organizations. Keep the links between business and domain discipline organizations relatively loose. The loose connection between domain and business disciplines leads to comparatively generic domain designs, which in turn improve your ability to absorb change.

Option 2: If your business environment is fairly stable and you are gaining a competitive advantage by optimizing operational efficiency, emphasize organizational proximity between the strategic disciplines on the one hand and the operational disciplines on the other hand. Establish a close connection between business strategy and logical domain architecture organizations and a similarly close connection between your business operations and physical domain architecture organizations. Keep the link between strategic and operational discipline organizations relatively loose. Tight integration of business operations and physical domain architecture organizations results in a landscape design that is optimized to support your current business needs.

In the physical design of your organization, be aware of the tendency of social systems to replicate their designs into the designs of technical systems they use or produce. The physical organization design of option 1 tends to result in a more generic technical system design that can be more easily adapted to changing conditions. However, the same design less optimally supports the specific needs the enterprise has here and now. In contrast, the physical organization design of option 2 tends to generate a technical system design that optimally meets today's business needs—but at the price of comparatively weak adaptability and a disproportionate proliferation of redundant solutions (ORGANIZATIONAL REPLICATION).

Optimize the design of your physical organization by distinguishing between business and technical domains. For example, adopt option 1 as the organizational pattern for your technical domain organizations, while you chose option 2 for the design of your business domain organizations. Option 1 for your technical domain organizations leads to a relatively generic design of your technical domains, which helps you absorb frequently changing technical requirements. At the same time, option 2 for your business domain organizations leads to a landscape design that optimally addresses your current business needs (BUSINESS VERSUS TECHNICAL).

Assign responsibility for logical assets (e.g., logical services, applications, platforms, technologies, and information) to your logical domain organizations while making your physical domain organizations responsible for planning and managing physical assets (e.g., physical services, applications, or platforms) (ARCHITECTURE ASSET, LANDSCAPE ASSET).

Distinguish between enduring architecture roles that align with your logical organizational scheme and ephemeral roles that relate to your current physical organization. By designing part of your role model as agnostic to your physical organization, you enable organization changes to be decoupled from methodologies, view models, or architecture policies in which roles are referenced. Another significant efficiency and evolution effect can be achieved by basing your architecture platform design exclusively on logical role definitions. The physical organization in an enterprise changes regularly. At the same time, physical role definitions are needed to regulate concrete responsibilities in organizations. Logical role references, however, save you from serious reengineering of architecture platforms that becomes necessary when platforms refer to physical roles (ARCHITECTURE ROLE).

6.5.6 Decommissioning Reward

Significant imbalance may exist between landscape investments and associated disinvestments. Architectural complexity arises from landscape investments permanently outweighing respective disinvestments. As a consequence, evolutionary fitness deteriorates, and funding for landscape assets steadily shifts from original to operational investments.

Decommissioning, to remove (something, such as a ship or a nuclear power plant) from service. (Merriam-Webster Dictionary 2020)

Obesity is a health problem for the human body as much as it is a problem for the body of landscape assets in a business. For the human body, obesity increases blood pressure, cholesterol levels, or blood sugar—the main causes of strokes and heart disease. For the human body obesity statistically shortens life expectancy. In enterprise landscapes, obesity[74] increases complexity and reduces transparency and modifiability—the main causes of operational inefficiencies, innovation backlog, or business crisis.[75] Overweight landscapes shorten the life of landscape assets and reduce profitability.

We monitor our body weight and aim to balance caloric intake (e.g., the quantity and quality of the food we eat) and the caloric expenditure (e.g., through physical or mental exercise) to avoid obesity in our personal lives. Obesity in our corporate landscapes follows the same basic pattern. If we add assets in the first place and rarely remove them, landscapes inevitably become overweight. Just as inevitably, funding is absorbed by the operation of landscapes and landscape assets. However, if we strike the right balance between adding and consolidating, retiring, or removing assets, we can avoid overfeeding landscapes. The undesirable effect of overfeeding is the growing complexity of landscapes, landscape assets, and their interdependencies (Fig. 6.71).

---

[74]Landscape obesity is a phenomenon where a landscape is overloaded with superfluous, redundant, or otherwise inadequate landscape assets. Landscape paralysis and the inability to evolve landscapes further are consequences of landscape overweight.

[75]Business crisis occurs when a problem seriously jeopardizes the stability of an enterprise or organization. Such a dilemma can either arise internally or be caused by external factors. If left unaddressed, it may permanently damage the business or cause it to fail. Business crises can result from financial, reputational, organizational, or natural threats. However, a business crisis can equally result from technological and complexity threats, for example, from paralyzed landscapes or landscape assets that cannot evolve with changing business requirements.

Fig. 6.71 Landscape complexity

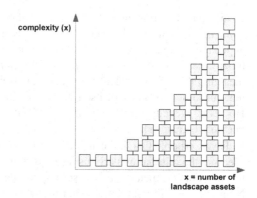

Architecture Function and Decommissioning Reward

Architecture functions delegate the measurement, promotion, or enforcement of decommissioning (*decommissioning reward*) of architecture assets to their governance organizations. Architecture governance establishes decommissioning controls and incentives (e.g., in the form of policies) and embeds them in the architecture apparatus (*architecture methods and platforms*) (Fig. 6.72).

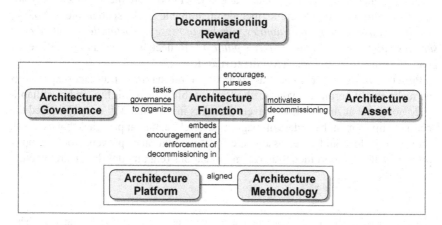

Fig. 6.72 Architecture function and decommissioning reward

Aim for flat growth curves for your landscapes and avoid the introduction of superfluous assets by rewarding the retirement of unneeded landscape assets and motivating asset reuse along the entire enterprise value chain. Use qualitative measures (i.e., beyond the purely quantitative) to assess the true weight new assets add to your landscapes and to mitigate overweight effects. For example, an architecture function uses a purely quantitative measure such as the *number of applications* to assess the weight of its landscapes. By applying this metric, a new application automatically adds landscape weight regardless of its potential to immobilize others. Consider *absorption of architecture capacity* as a qualitative and more meaningful metric for calculating landscape weight. For example, a new application that substitutes others will itself absorb a certain amount of architecture capacity. However, capacity is released for all applications that the new one replaces (**ARCHITECTURE CAPACITY**).

Favor criteria that indicate the impact of disproportionate landscape weight. Measure the criteria regularly using KPIs. For example, measure the ratio of capital to operational expenditure[76] to shift spending toward valuable asset investments. Note that each investment avoided today saves 20% of your costs, while over its lifetime you save 80% of total costs.[77] As another example, measure your business' return on asset investments[78] by distinguishing between short-term, medium-term, and long-term asset returns. To give yet another example, measure reuse to calculate avoided redundancy and associated opportunity cost. Incorporate the desired landscape weight into your architecture maturity metric (**ARCHITECTURE MATURITY**).

Promote landscape assets which, in particular, enable reusability, adaptability, or modifiability. Certain corporate cultures tend to foster territorial mindsets and hostile attitudes toward sharing with or reuse by others. Overcoming or mitigating such attitudes can save considerable costs in the long run and have an incredibly positive effect on the complexity, transparency, and profitability of your landscapes. Reward reuse and penalize recreation of landscape assets in your architects' incentive plans and role definitions. For example, include quantifiable goals, such as the *number of identified consolidation opportunities*, *number of reuse opportunities*, or *number of services supported by a new shared platform*. Reflect basic landscape efficiency goals in your role definitions (**ARCHITECTURE ROLE**).

Prescribe *design for change*[79] as an architectural maxim for all landscape assets and make sure it permeates your methods. Reusability, adaptability, and modifiability do not come at zero cost. However, the gains in modifiability usually exceed the necessary investment by orders of magnitude. Architecture approaches that establish modifiability for landscape assets are well known and proven, for example, approaches that support model-driven modifications (e.g., model-driven architecture

---

[76] Capital expenditure (CAPEX) is the money an organization spends creating, buying, or evolving assets, while operational expenditure (OPEX) is the ongoing costs of reliably operating existing assets.

[77] Total cost of ownership (TCO) includes the cost of acquiring and operating assets and the costs associated with evolving assets and dismantling them at the end of their life.

[78] Return on investment (ROI) depicts the ratio between the outcome of an investment and the associated investment over a defined period of time. The ROI indicates the performance of an investment in terms of its profitability.

[79] Design for change principles improve the modifiability and expandability of a system, for example, loose coupling, information hiding, separation of concerns, or inversion of control.

and generators[80]), decontextualized functions (e.g., microservices-based architectures[81]), comprehensive customizations (e.g., interpreters combined with object models[82]), or separation of technical and business concerns (e.g., aspect orientation[83]). Establish platforms that promote sharing and reuse of landscape assets, for example, a service directory through which you can actively share, promote, find, and utilize reusable services in your organization (YOUR OWN ARCHITECTURE METHODOLOGY).

Do not limit reusability to reusing landscape assets, but encourage creating, sharing, and reusing architecture designs within your enterprise and among your architects. Encourage, for example, the identification and capture of designs with high reusability potential through appropriate patterns and styles (ARCHITECTURE PATTERN METHODOLOGY),

In addition to motivating reusability, there are always opportunities to increase reuse in your architecture function by defining and enforcing policies, rules, or guidelines. For example, introduce a *tit for tat* policy so that for every asset introduced, at least one must be removed. In addition, drive the degree of reuse in your organization by establishing review hurdles along the enterprise value chain. Use these hurdles to check the extent to which reuse has taken place and demand that submitted designs be revised if they ignored respective reusability potential (ARCHITECTURE GOVERNANCE).

Encourage your function to constantly seek opportunities for reuse or consolidation across domain boundaries (horizontally) and architecture levels (vertically). Ensure reconciliation of interests among all affected stakeholders. For example, share recognition and credits with landscape asset owners whose assets are affected by a consolidation opportunity in a domain. Similarly, share credits with affected domain architects when an identified opportunity leads to a consolidation of assets in their domains (ARCHITECTURE DEMARCATION, ARCHITECTURE LEVEL).

Hold architects individually responsible for informing the architecture function of changes in an asset's synergy profile. For example, set *minimum utilization* thresholds for assets that support a sharing paradigm (e.g., a content management platform)

---

[80] Generator-based architecture approaches decouple solution specifications from their physical generation. They increase domain specificity and the degree of abstraction of the models that architects use to represent a solution. Generators receive architectural models as inputs and create artifacts at the source level or related physical structures as outputs.

[81] Microservices are fine-grained, context-agnostic functions or function endpoints. They are requested and delivered via lightweight protocols. Applications are established as loosely coupled microservices.

[82] Interpreters are built into systems to enable powerful customization hooks via which one can massively optimize the off-the-shelf capabilities of a system. Interpreters require programming skills. However, they offer programmable access to the off-the-shelf system's object model—and thus push the limits of adaptation toward the respective programmers' ambition and imagination.

[83] Aspect orientation is an architecture approach and technology that modularizes systems so that their secondary or supporting logic (technical aspects) is isolated from their primary logic (business aspects). In this way, technical and business concerns can be designed, developed, and optimized independently.

and require asset owners to notify the organization when usage falls below the set thresholds. Reduce service-level agreements (SLA[84]) for poorly synergized assets. For example, reduce the *service response time* of your *elaborate architecture problem resolution* service when a shared platform originally hosted 20 applications but now hosts only 1 application. Ensure that organizations that primarily benefit from the use of asset services bear the largest share of architecture and operating costs (**ARCHITECTURE OWNERSHIP**).

Consider shifting your company's focus on specific assets to other assets to unleash new options for decommissioning. Regardless of which assets you focus on today, they impose restraint on you regarding decommissioning. For example, if the *application* is your pivotal type of landscape asset today, the organization will undoubtedly welcome all new applications and regret all applications that have been decommissioned. But when you shift from applications as an asset focus to *information*, your organization's value system changes. Adding or removing applications is no longer the focus of corporate interest, making application decommissioning less of an issue. Ultimately, shifting the focus from applications to information unleashes opportunities for application retirement.

Money gets the mare going—and helps you get your landscapes back to a healthy weight state. Set cost and architecture funding targets to motivate healthy asset reductions financially. However, do not strip the thread either, and avoid both excessive and phony divestitures. An example of an excessive asset reduction is the dismantling of a globally used platform, which is now being rebuilt divisional, albeit on a smaller scale, thereby introducing new redundancies. A spurious reduction is, for example, consolidating four landscape assets by introducing a fifth asset to replace the four, while your asset count ends up being five, not one (**ARCHITECTURE FUNDING**).

Evaluate the impact of dismantling before making decisions about decommissioning. Retiring an asset implies ending the relationships it has with others. Decommissioning can easily lead to ripple effects that cause unjustifiable costs. Also, consider whether successful decommissioning of one asset streamlines further simplification of your landscapes, motivating decommissioning of other assets. If you do not already have asset migration or archiving services, consider adding them to your enterprise service portfolio (**ARCHITECTURE TRACEABILITY**).

Make decommissioning a critical activity in your contracts when delegating the entire lifecycle of landscape assets to external architecture service providers. Use specific insights from your sourcing partners into the services, applications, or platforms they manage to identify decommissioning opportunities. Ensure in your contracts that reducing complexity and thus removing assets that have become inadequate are significant motivators for your partners (**ARCHITECTURE SOURCING**).

---

[84] Service-level agreements (SLA) are commitments between service provider and service consumer. Particular aspects of a service are formally agreed in an SLA contract, for example, service availability, service response time, mean time to repair, or mean time between failures.

Integrate considerations of efficiency gains, or doing less, into your ideation and innovation process. Innovation or newness is often unconsciously associated with expansion or addition. However, redesigning something that already exists can also be legitimately understood as innovation—e.g., redesigning one platform allows three others to be decommissioned (**ARCHITECTURE INNOVATION**).

It often makes sense to look for asset reduction opportunities even without current expansion planning. Consider annual or biennial studies of decommissioning opportunities, rather than looking for such opportunities on an individual basis (e.g., a proposed transformation project for an application). Schedule corresponding recurring investigations in your architecture function calendar (**ARCHITECTURE CALENDAR**).

6.5.7 Architecture Decision

Architecture is the total of significant design decisions, where significant is measured by cost of change.[85] The ability to distinguish architecture from non-architecture decisions marks the fine line between efficient and inefficient architecture functions. As a consequence, delineating, documenting, and transparently sharing architecture decisions are crucial.

> A *decision* is a determination arrived at after consideration. (Merriam-Webster Dictionary 2020)

Significance is a measure of the cost of changing a design decision. Architecture decisions are significant design decisions—thus, decisions that are difficult to alter or undo later on. Architecture decisions are the significant portions of all design decisions constituting an architecture asset (**ARCHITECTURE SIGNIFICANCE**).

> **Architecture Decision Versus Design Decision**
> A building block of application$_A$ exposes a programmable object interface to which you bind via *Java RMI*[86] or *IIOP*.[87]
> The remote object class is called *ExRateCalculator*. The class publicly exposes a single method (*calculate*). The method signature entails parameters

(continued)

---

[85] Grady Booch (2009).

[86] Java remote method invocation (Java RMI) is the remoting protocol of the Java platform.

[87] GIOP (general inter-ORB protocol) is a protocol by which object request brokers (ORBs) communicate in CORBA (common object request broker architecture). The Internet inter-orb protocol (IIOP) is an implementation of GIOP for use over TCP/IP.

(*currencyFrom*, *currencyTo*, *amount*, and *date*), type of the method output (*float*), and type of an exception (*ExRateException*) thrown in case of dysfunction.

None of the above elements can be changed without causing a substantial impact to dependent objects—thus, all of the above are considered architecture-significant design. For example, changing the binding protocol from *Java RMI* to *.Net Remoting* will cause bind failures in components consuming the *calculate* function. Similarly, changing a single signature portion of the *calculate* method will equally break dependent components instantaneously.

However, the shape of the internal exchange rate algorithm encapsulated by the method interface can change without crashing dependent objects. Therefore, the design of the algorithm is architecturally insignificant (Fig. 6.73).

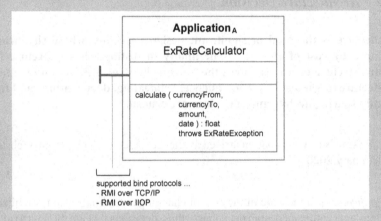

Fig. 6.73 Architecture decision versus design decision

Architecture Function and Architecture Decision

Architecture functions make and transparently share architecture decisions. *Architecture conditions* shape *architecture decisions*, which in turn are inherent in the designs of *architecture approaches* (i.e., micro-architectures). Architecture decisions are determinations differentiated by scale (*architecture level*). The architecture function delegates control over formal decision advocacy to its *governance* organization. Finally, architecture decisions are inherent in proven *pattern* designs (Fig. 6.74).

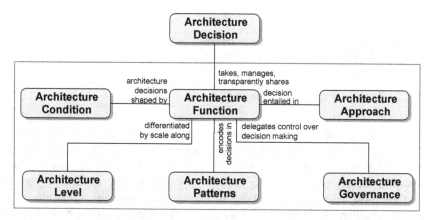

Fig. 6.74 Architecture function and architecture decision

While every decision in the design of a system is a design decision, architecture decisions are particular design decisions. Architecture decisions represent a subset of all design decisions—namely, the subset of essential design decisions. Similarly, we use the term architecture to refer to the essential design parts. While architecture approaches realize architecture conditions, their decisions are inherent in designs of architecture approaches (**ARCHITECTURE APPROACH**) (Fig. 6.75).

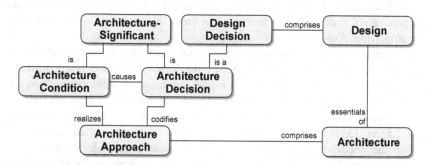

Fig. 6.75 Architecture decision

The IEEE[88] Computer Society suggests that *architecture rationales* justify *architecture decisions*, that architecture decisions both *raise* and *pertain* to corresponding *concerns*, and that dependencies exist between architecture decisions (IEEE 2000) (Fig. 6.76).

---

[88] The Institute of Electrical and Electronics Engineers (IEEE) is a professional association for electronic engineering and electrical engineering.

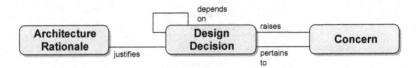

Fig. 6.76 Architecture decision as per the IEEE

An architecture decision is natively inherent and implicit in architecture design. The implicit nativeness of architecture decisions makes it necessary to extract them from the design and capture them explicitly. For example, an architecture function decides to loosely couple two applications (application₁ and application₂) via a MoM platform[89] design. Application₁ shares data with application₂ by placing a message entailing the data in a message queue. The queue mediates between both applications and informs application₂ about the new message. Application₂ retrieves the message from the queue via a messaging protocol, unfolds it, and extracts the data for further processing. Architecture decision-making is lightweight and soft as long as decisions are implicitly taken in an architecture design. For example, the architecture function decision adopts a message-based paradigm and uses a store-and-forward platform (i.e., MoM) to loosely couple both applications. However, implicit design decisions are not tangible—thus not referable by processes formally reviewing and endorsing decisions that have a broader impact. Explicitly captured decisions are a prerequisite also for sharing them transparently and preferably with others. Therefore, explicitly document architecture decisions so that the architecture function can formally review and discuss them, agree, or disagree with them (**ARCHITECTURE ARTIFACT**).

Standardize explicit capturing of architecture decisions in your enterprise by considering a basic set of attributes. Chose a memorable name and unique identifier (*Name/Id*) for every decision and refer to the architecture conditions (*architecture condition*) it addresses. Capture uncertainties in the context of taking decisions as assumptions (*assumptions*). Explain why the decision is relevant and essential (*motivation*). Outline alternative decision options (*alternatives*) to explain and support the decision finally made (*decision*). Provide a rationale for making the architecture decision (*justification*). Next, explain the implications (*implication*) and their likelihood and impact of materializing. Capture the scope of a decision (*scope*). For example, a decision may be limited to an organization (organizational scope) or may be time limited. Maintain decision state to enable its lifecycle management (*state*), for example, an architecture decision that has been considered and captured but not yet made (state, initial), a decision that has been made (state—decided), and a decision that has been endorsed or rejected by an appropriate decision authority (state—endorsed, rejected). Capture *costs* if they can be specifically associated with

---

[89]MoM (message-oriented middleware) platforms are inter-system communication platforms that support mediation and exchange of information between distributed systems in the form of messages.

a decision. Similarly, capture associated *risk*. Finally, capture dependencies and trade-offs between architecture decisions (*dependencies*). For example, a security decision contradicts a usability decision, and a global decision (e.g., at the enterprise level) overrides a local decision (e.g., at the solution level). To give another example, the architecture decision to *adopt hub-and-spoke*[90] *as architecture style for an application* is an upstream decision enabling the downstream decision to *adopt RPC*[91] *as the primary communication style for adapters (spokes)*. Enable traceability between architecture decisions, between decisions and their architecture approaches, and between architecture decisions and their associated conditions (**ARCHITECTURE TRACEABILITY**) (Fig. 6.77).

Architecture Decision Template	
Name / Id	
Architecture Condition	
Assumption(s)	
Motivation	
Alternative(s)	
Decision	
Justification	
Implication	
Scope	
State	
Cost	
Risk	
Dependencies	

Fig. 6.77 Architecture decision form

---

[90] Hub-and-spoke is an integration architecture style favoring communication via applications and a central hub over direct communication between applications.

[91] Remote procedure call (RPC) is a form of inter-process communication favoring a synchronous request-response paradigm.

Systematize the relation between decisions taken at different levels of architecture. For example, specify that architecture decisions made at any level constrain decision-making at all subordinate levels. To give a concrete example, an architecture function decides to favor *buying* solutions over *building* solutions. It positions the decision at the enterprise level. It further mandates that the enterprise architecture board must investigate, allow, and explicitly approve any deviation. In this example, domain or solution architects cannot negate or otherwise override enterprise architecture board decisions (ARCHITECTURE LEVEL).

Promote and establish patterns as they naturally encode enterprise, domain, or solution-wide architecture decisions. You are thus leveraging patterns as an effective means of automatically enforcing the decisions encoded in them—in other words, standardizing architecture decisions. Architects, in applying patterns, will inevitably repeat the decisions they contain in their own concrete designs (ARCHITECTURE PATTERN METHODOLOGY).

Specify precisely which architecture role is responsibly entitled to make which decisions based on *role-responsibility-decision* matrices. Ensure that your portfolio of architecture roles also includes architecture authorities and bodies, and in turn clarify for them which architecture authority is responsible for validating which types of decisions (ARCHITECTURE ROLE, ARCHITECTURE GOVERNANCE).

6.5.8 Architecture Traceability

Architecture functions review, recommend, and make decisions based on facts and methods of logical reasoning. They establish traceability between decisions and facts to provide rationale and achieve broad acceptance for the decision. Inadequate traceability weakens justification of the decisions made—thus weakening compliance with the architecture.

> *Tracing* means to follow or study out in detail or step by step. (Merriam-Webster Dictionary 2020)

Understanding decision rationality is a prerequisite for valuing architecture contributions. Architecture functions, therefore, ensure comprehension or reaffirmation of the rationality of decisions made by making them traceable to their facts. *Architecture traceability* means that there is a path that rationally derives an architecture-relevant *effect* from a corresponding *cause*—a path that is explicitly navigable. *Navigability* means there is documented evidence of cause and effect and that the effect is navigably referable to its cause (Fig. 6.78).

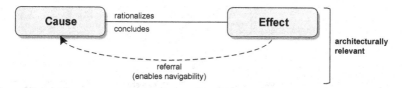

Fig. 6.78 Architecture traceability

Note an effect produced by a cause can be a cause of another effect. For example, a requirement for a new application specifies that users can place orders in a webshop. An architect creates a design in which a security perimeter separates the Internet webshop[92] from an intranet ordering system. The initial requirement led to the design decision (effect). However, the decision made leads to a new requirement. Orders received in the webshop need to be routed once and only once to the internal ordering system. The decision to separate the webshop from the internal ordering system became a cause for another effect. Cause and effect are relative concepts that intertwine to form a chain of reasoning (Fig. 6.79).

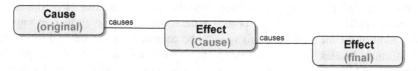

Fig. 6.79 Cause-effect chain

Architecture Function and Architecture Traceability

Architecture functions establish traceability between decisions and facts to provide a rationale for their decision-making. Holistic traceability provides a basis for improving *architecture maturity*. *Architecture approaches* are pivotal to traceability in connecting different dimensions (e.g., traceability between architecture decisions and conditions or between *architecture levels*). View models (*architecture apparatus*) inherently enable traceability through their viewpoint design (e.g., viewpoint relationships) (Fig. 6.80).

---

[92] A webshop enables online shopping as a form of electronic commerce that allows consumers to browse product catalogs and buy goods or services from a seller over the Internet using a web browser or a mobile application.

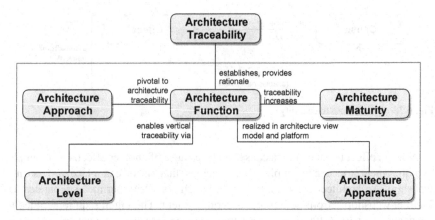

Fig. 6.80 Architecture function and architecture traceability

Understand what you need to know holistically—that is, how to rationally relate isolated insights to draw holistic conclusions. Ask yourself broad questions—that is, questions spanning multiple dimensions along the entire enterprise value chain. For instance: on what criteria do we base portfolio decision-making, like demand-, service-, application-, or project-portfolio decisions? To give further examples: what kind of architecture decisions need to be considered and approved by which architecture bodies, or which architecture decisions need to be explicitly documented? Derive your information needs from your questions—so information you need to answer your holistic questions. For example, project priority is a particular piece of information that is considered when making project portfolio decisions. Project priority is lowered in your enterprise when a project plans to evolve an application whose end of life is approaching (e.g., end of life is less than 2 years). Therefore, the architecture function includes end-of-life events in its application architecture roadmaps and ensures that roadmap events can be traced back to their root causes (e.g., business strategy decision, application technology, vendor end-of-life announcement). Traceability between project priority, architecture roadmap, and business strategy enables your organization to rationalize project prioritization at any time (NEED TO KNOW, ARCHITECTURE ROADMAP METHODOLOGY).

Address basic traceability needs through the design of your architecture view model. Traceability empowers architecture functions to perceive their enterprise architecture holistically. View models standardize architecture representation by explaining the *why*, *what*, *who*, *when*, and *how* of architecture manifestation. While view models entail viewpoints and relationships among them, a viewpoint specifies the particular insights it provides. A view model specifies how its viewpoints are navigated and combined to gain overarching insights. Predefined architecture view models (e.g., TOGAF content metamodel[93]) propose numerous viewpoints and relationships among them. Adopt them to your particular navigation and traceability needs (**Your own Architecture View Model**).

Relate the assets in your landscapes comprehensively to establish a solid base for architecture impact analysis. For example, relate applications to the services they support, platforms to the applications they host, applications to the technologies they apply, or information to the applications and services by which they are consumed or delivered. Analyze the impact of planned changes to landscape assets before making them to identify and mitigate risks. Mitigate risks by avoiding, reducing, or sharing them. Reduce risks by detecting and preventing them early (*preventative measures*) by reducing the frequency of risky events or mitigating their impact (*reactive measure*). Share risks by taking out insurance or outsourcing services and sharing some risks with sourcing partners. Accept a risk if the effort to mitigate it outweighs the gain (**Landscape Asset**).

Relate architecture-significant requirements to the business capabilities they represent in order to determine requirement priority. Further, relate your architecture approaches to the requirements they address. Architecture functions can ask exciting questions and support appropriate decisions if they systematically maintain a bidirectional link between business capabilities and architecture requirements and between architecture requirements and architecture approaches. An architecture function may ask: *what business capabilities are affected if this architecture approach (e.g., in a business application) is altered?* If the architecture approach simultaneously supports several critical capabilities, an architecture function will pay extra attention to mitigate the risk of undesired capability impacts (**Architecture Approach**).

Relate the solution architecture alternatives to the significant requirements they address and use the relationship information (i.e., navigation information) to select your preferred alternative. For example, prefer the architecture alternative that addresses selected requirements particularly well, addresses the most requirements, or involves the least number of trade-off decisions (**Architecture Alternative**).

Improve architecture maturity by providing traceable justification for recommendations, approvals, or objections. Expand architecture maturity to your partners by including traceability KPIs in your sourcing contracts. For example, consider a KPI that measures the number of architecture patterns referenced in your sourcing partners' designs (**Architecture Maturity, Architecture Sourcing**).

Assign ownership of traceability to the owner of the effect—not the owner of the producing cause. For example, it is the responsibility of a solution architect to point architecture-significant requirements to corresponding business demands (i.e., not the responsibility of the business demand owner) (**Architecture Ownership**).

---

[93] TOGAF content metamodel defines a set of entities that allow architectural concepts (e.g., logical versus physical applications, principles, requirements) to be captured, stored, filtered, queried, and represented consistently and traceably.

Establish traceability vertically and across architecture levels giving you a navigation path between enterprise, domain, and solution levels. This allows you, for example, to analyze the impact of a decision at the enterprise level on the solution level. It also enables aggregation across levels. For example, a domain architect can view all applications supporting a domain capability at the click of a button (**ARCHITECTURE LEVEL**).

Derive architecture significance from traceability observations. For example, a platform hosts five applications, three of which are highly business-critical. If an architecture function derives significance criteria from the number and risk profile of affected applications, it may flag architecture decisions made for the hosting platform as architecturally significant (**ARCHITECTURE SIGNIFICANCE**).

Identify decommissioning targets based on architecture traceability information. For example, an unused technology landscape asset is no longer applied by any application. The technology asset has become a dead link[94] that you can flag as decommissioning target (**DECOMMISSIONING REWARD**).

Beware, every traceable path poses an extra effort on your architecture function, in the short term. However, in the medium to long term, improved architecture maturity, increased transparency, and the ability to effectively rationalize architecture contributions will pay for the extra effort (**ARCHITECTURE CAPACITY**).

6.6   Architecture Communication

The *architecture communication* group patterns emphasize the importance of common conception, language, and norms if architecture functions are to make their contributions efficiently, effectively, and sustainably. While the *architecture language* pattern points to the clarification of elementary concepts and provides recommendations to address them, the *domain taxonomy pattern* complements these considerations with respect to domain-specific conceptualizations and vocabulary. The *architecture innovation pattern* supports you in making innovation a core part of your architecture function and thus extends established languages by a language of imagination.

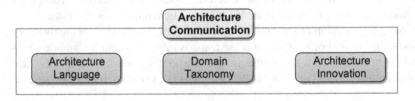

---

[94]Dead link is a hyperlink that pointed to an originally targeted resource while the resource was either relocated to a new address or became permanently unavailable or otherwise in the meantime.

6.6.1   Architecture Language

A common architecture language, understanding, and protocols are prerequisites for unambiguously communicating between architects and with other stakeholders. An insufficiently established common communication base leads, at least partially, to inadequate performance of architecture activities and failure to achieve desired outcomes.

> *Language* is a means of communicating ideas [...] by the use of conventionalized signs, sounds, gestures, or marks having understood meanings. (Merriam-Webster Dictionary 2020)

Communication is critical, and language is the raw material for communication—so, language is the foundation for alignment, cooperation, and joint action.

Meaning is pivotal to understanding language and communication. When communicating, we use *signs* as representations of objects and concepts. Signs enable us to communicate about *objects* and their meaning (*concept*)—even in the absence of objects. Objects are things we can perceive by observing their properties, like observing Ludwig Wittgenstein's shape. Signs represent objects, like the sign *Ludwig Wittgenstein* represents the person Ludwig Wittgenstein in written form. Signs and objects are both aspects of the objective realm. They could exist without a perceptive human mind. In contrast, *concept* is a subjective individual aspect. A concept is a mental image of an object in a human's mind, for example, my mental image of the person Ludwig Wittgenstein (Fig. 6.81).

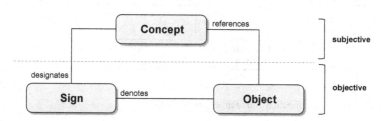

Fig. 6.81   Meaning triangle (semiotics)

Architecture languages, like any other language, both enable and constrain our imagination. Ludwig Wittgenstein, one of the twentieth century's most influential philosophers, summarized this in his *Tractatus Logico-Philosophicus* (Wittgenstein 1998):

> Whereof one cannot speak, thereof one must be silent.

Wittgenstein means that the inability to express a concept through a language inhibits our ability to imagine, recognize, or otherwise relate to that concept. He emphasizes the fundamental nature of language, including thinking about something while alone. What you cannot relate or refer through a language you cannot conceptualize—be it a problem or a solution to a problem.

Architecture Function and Architecture Language

Architecture functions establish an architecture language as a common conceptual foundation to enable essential communication and understanding between architects, various disciplines, and other stakeholders. While an architecture language provides a conceptual platform for domain-specific languages in the enterprise (*domain taxonomy*), it virtually dissolves into methodologies and view models (*architecture apparatus*) (Fig. 6.82).

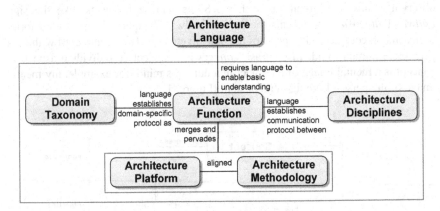

Fig. 6.82 Architecture function and architecture language

Architecture is inherently abstract—thus, architecture languages need to explicitly represent the respective abstraction. Common clarification of crucial concepts is essentially a prerequisite if architecture functions are to accomplish their mandates. An architecture language, which is appropriately established and adopted, mitigates the risk of miscommunication. It helps avoid both erroneous agreement and erroneous disagreement as two forms of communicative dysfunction (Fig. 6.83).

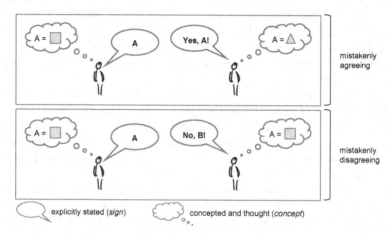

Fig. 6.83 Communication misconceptions

Architecture languages enable the communication, understanding, and discussion of ideas. They enable unambiguous, efficient, and effective communication between architects—on all issues of interest. For example, architecture language enables reflective discussion about the context, goals, and mandate of an architecture function. It underpins conversations about governance approach or required funding. Architects utilize architecture languages to discuss the appropriateness of a methodology, to agree on the adoption of a view model, or to conduct architecture activities collaboratively.

Searching for the term *architecture language* on the Internet, we receive numerous hits and a remarkable range of language connotations. Language classification spans semiformal architecture description languages (ADLs), analysis languages, or modeling languages. Architects use ADLs to represent the design of systems. They support the description of system building blocks, their externally visible properties, and their purposeful collaboration. ADL models may serve as inputs for the fully or semi-automated generation of physical designs in the form of code skeletons. While analysis languages describe problem spaces, ADLs are rooted in the solution space. ADLs vary in their support for particular system archetypes (e.g., ADLs for real-time, distributed, or mobile systems). ADLs that provide domain-specific abstractions are referred to as domain-specific language (DSL). Further, ADLs differ in their support of view models and viewpoints (e.g., functional viewpoint, operational viewpoint, information viewpoint), relationships between views (e.g., deployment viewpoint), model types, or modeling nomenclatures. Finally, ADLs differ in how they are embedded in an overarching methodology framework and process. ArchiMate[95] and AADL[96] are examples of architecture description languages.

This pattern interprets *architecture language* as a basic conceptual specification enabling an architecture function to conduct fundamental discussions about architecture issues. In this rudimentary sense, an architecture language specifies the meaning of fundamental architecture categories, concepts, and relationships among them. In other words, it is equivalent to an *architecture ontology*. Furthermore, this pattern is virtually the foundation for all other patterns in this catalog.

Architecture Ontology

In philosophy, an ontology determines the categories or highest kinds and how they form a system of categories that provides a holistic classification of all entities in a philosophical area of interest. Each academic discipline establishes ontologies to reduce ambiguity and improve common understanding. An architecture ontology includes a representation, formal naming, and definition of the categories, properties, and relations among important architectural concepts.

If an architecture ontology specifies the meaning of basic architecture categories, concepts, and relationships among them, what accounts for a basic architecture category or concept? The short answer is anything that architects exchange when they conduct a discussion about architecture. However, some architecture concepts are more, and some are less critical to your function to clarify and reduce ambiguity in your daily discussions. Therefore, focus your architecture function ontology on concepts that cause serious misunderstandings or repeatedly lead to endless and inefficient disputes between architects within your organization. For example, an architecture function and an independent design organization are always at odds over their responsibilities in helping their customers design new applications. Both the architecture function and the design organization claim responsibility for contributions that overlap. The endless dispute usually boils down to a controversial view of how architecture should be conceptualized differently from design. In this example, specifying the difference and the complementary relationship between both concepts (i.e., architecture versus design) can resolve ambiguity and thus end fruitless discussions.

While ontologies can be differently constructed and formulated, their main ingredients are *terms* representing *concepts*, *description* of their unique concept attributes, and the depiction of relationships between them. Relationship semantics

---

[95] ArchiMate is an open and independent modeling standard for enterprise architectures that supports the description, analysis, and presentation of architecture within and between architectures. It is an Open Group standard and is based on fundamental architectural concepts defined by the IEEE (i.e., IEEE 1471). ArchiMate particularly supports the description of architecture at the architecture domain level.

[96] Architecture analysis and design language (AADL) is an extensive and complete language intended for designing hardware and software aspects of a system.

may be expressed visually or simply annotated by descriptive text. Specify relationship direction and complement their cardinality to indicate relationship magnitude. Distinguish between various types of relationships, for example, generalization,[97] association,[98] or composition.[99] Finally, capture synonyms in your definitions and contextualize homonyms to clarify meaning.

Architecture Ontology: *Service* **Versus** *Application*
In an architecture function architects regularly argue about conceptual differences between *service* and *application*. The architecture function sets out to resolve these ambiguities by graphically depicting how service and application concepts relate.

Beyond clarifying the relationships between service and application, the function further details both concepts. For example, it specifies that a *service* is a socio-technical system that provides capabilities to its customers. Furthermore, it defines that services consume other services or utilize applications.

In contrast to a service, an *application* is a technical system that supports services through the capabilities it provides. The architecture function specifies for applications that they may utilize other applications (e.g., to exchange data between them). Finally, the architecture function distinguishes different types of applications, for example, by clarifying the categories of *web application, mobile application,* or *application embedded in a device* (Fig. 6.84).

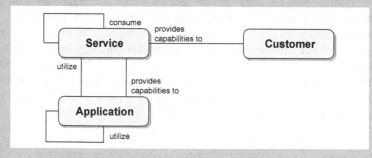

Fig. 6.84 Service versus application

(continued)

---

[97] Generalization of a concept is an extension of the concept to less-specific criteria. It is a foundational element of human reasoning. Generalizations posit the existence of a domain or set of elements and one or more common characteristics shared by those elements.

[98] Associations are simple referrals between concepts, where aggregations are a form of association that specifies a whole-part relationship between the aggregate (whole) and a component (part).

[99] Compositions are a form of aggregation with strong ownership and coincident lifetime as part of the whole.

The concepts of service and application defined in this way may be defined differently in another enterprise. For the architecture function presented here, however, this definition resolves otherwise inefficient discussions among architects.

In the example above, the architecture function defined *service* and *application* by basing its prose definitions on concepts, such as *system, technical, socio-technical, capability,* or *customer*. The architecture function may deem clarifying concepts such as *capability* or *technical,* referenced in the definitions, as critical to creating unambiguous specifications for application and service. Elaborating an ontology by focusing on relationships between concepts (rather than wordsmithing one ontology concept at the time) ensures a consistent and complementary overall ontology definition.

Perhaps you noticed something else in the example above. As mentioned in the *application* and *service* definitions, some concepts seem to exist at different ontological layers. For example, *system* and *capability* were mentioned in both prose definitions, which makes them seem fundamental to *application* and *service*. In contrast, *web application* and *mobile application* differentiate the application concept, making application ontologically fundamental to *web* and *mobile application*. Consider organizing your ontology comprehensively by differentiating ontological layers. Ontology concepts at any layer refer to concepts at the same layer recognizing the need to be horizontally differentiated. They operate at a similar semantic level within a multi-layered ontology. In contrast, a concept at a higher-level ontology layer relates to concepts below it such that it takes the abstractions below it as elementary language concepts. In other words, an ontology layer serves as a language for constituting the language at the next higher ontology layer—that is, as a meta-language to its object language above it. For example, the set of concepts and their relationships on *ontology layer 0* form a meta-language for constituting its object language (*ontology layer 1*). Ontology layer 1, in turn, is a meta-language for its object language *ontology layer 2* (Fig. 6.85).

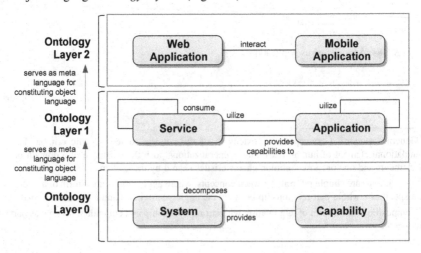

Fig. 6.85 Multi-layered ontology

Architecture Language as a Multi-layered Ontology

An architecture function created a multi-layered ontology as its formulation of a comprehensive language. The ontology comprises three language layers: *basic language, architecture language,* and *enterprise architecture language.* The basic language specifies abstractions that are considered elementary language concepts in the concept specifications of architecture language and enterprise architecture language. In other words, the basic language is a meta-language for its object languages: architecture and enterprise architecture language. The architecture language, in turn, is a meta-language for its object language: enterprise architecture language (Fig. 6.86).

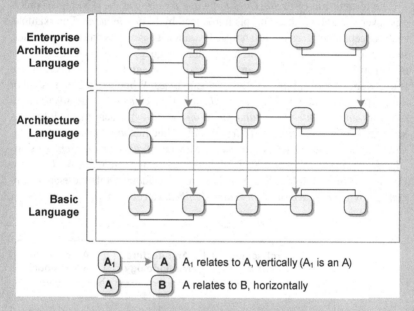

Fig. 6.86   Architecture language as multi-layered ontology

The architecture function introduced basic concepts in its multi-layered ontology's *basic language,* like *class* (synonym: *concept*), *object, property,* and *relationship.* Attentive readers may recognize the similarity between basic language concepts and the essential components of an ontology, generally speaking (Fig. 6.87).

(continued)

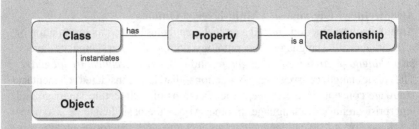

Fig. 6.87 Basic language

The formulation of *architecture language* concepts at the next higher ontology layer is based on the concepts introduced by *basic language*. For example,
each concept introduced by the architecture language is a class and has properties,
such as relationships. Also, each architecture language concept can be instantiated in such a way that objects are factorized. For example, the *architecture role*
is to govern or perform *architecture methodologies*. While methodologies are of
three types (*reference architecture methodology, architecture assessment methodology*, and *architecture elaboration methodology*), each methodology is
accompanied by an *architecture view model*. While methodologies create *architecture assets*, each asset is associated with an *architecture design*. Designs
address *architecture conditions* by inherently making *architecture decisions*.
Finally, architecture roles identify architecture conditions, while these are distinguished by their degree of *architecture significance* (Fig. 6.88).

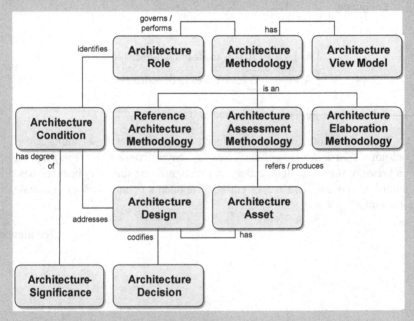

Fig. 6.88 Architecture language

(continued)

There is another ontology layer defined by the architecture function. *Enterprise architecture language* concepts are defined based on concepts introduced by the *architecture language*. For example, *enterprise architecture role*, *domain architecture role*, and *solution architecture role* differentiate the generalized *architecture role* concept. Similarly, *domain architecture methodology* and *solution architecture methodology* differentiate *architecture methodology* as introduced by the architecture language. Finally, *landscape asset*, *structural asset*, and *reference asset* differentiate the *architecture asset* (Fig. 6.89).

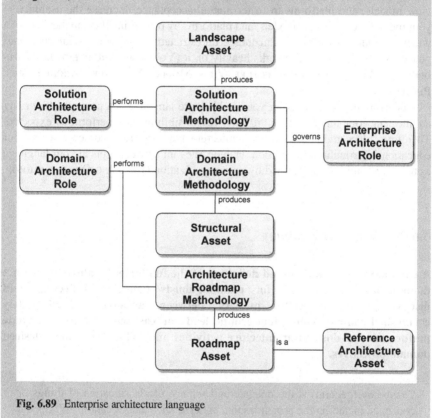

Fig. 6.89 Enterprise architecture language

Establish an architecture language that meets the needs of your enterprise. Consider creating your language in the form of a multi-layered ontology. Carefully delineate concepts that are crucial in your organization. Identify essential concepts by determining misunderstandings or other communication failures that repeatedly lead to inefficient disputes between your architects. Clarify how concepts relate to others as the first step in defining them. In other words, resist a comprehensive concept definition in prose as your first step. Your focus on delineating a concept sharpens its profile and fosters overall consistency in your architecture language. Be pragmatic in gathering and defining essential concepts. Avoid both over- and underspecification concepts. However, ensure you unambiguously define really critical concepts (NEED TO KNOW).

Coherently define domain-agnostic architecture concepts at the lower levels of a multi-layered ontology and define domain-specific concepts on its upper levels, accordingly. Establish domain-specific concepts as domain taxonomies to resolve terminological collisions by introducing the architecture domain as a namespace. Delegate the definition of domain taxonomies to the responsible domain architects to scale both the creation and evolution of your architecture function's overall language (DOMAIN TAXONOMY).

Ensure all essential language concepts are represented in your methodologies, view models, and platforms to foster mutual acceptance. Increase the usability of your methodologies, view models, and platforms by promoting them in the form of a widely introduced language. Encourage unrestricted use of your architecture language by basing your frameworks heavily on it (YOUR OWN ARCHITECTURE METHODOLOGY, YOUR OWN ARCHITECTURE VIEW MODEL, YOUR OWN ARCHITECTURE PLATFORM).

Understanding and speaking your architecture language is a prerequisite for any architect in your function to fulfill their responsibilities and perform as expected. Therefore, place training in your architecture language as a cornerstone in your educational curriculum. In addition, include relevant new concepts in your language as they are continuously learned by your organization (LEARNING ORGANIZATION).

6.6.2 Domain Taxonomy

A common understanding and definition of the fundamental abstractions in a domain are prerequisites for unambiguously detecting, reflecting, and discussing domain-specific matters between architects. Inadequately established common conceptual ground leads, at least partially, to inadequate performance of domain architecture activities and failure to achieve desired domain objectives.

> *Taxonomy* (general) is the practice and science of classification of things or concepts, including the principles that underlie such classification. (Wikipedia Taxonomy 2020c)

A *domain taxonomy* is a knowledge model that clarifies basic domain classifications and abstractions in a consistent and coherent manner. Domain taxonomies enable efficient communication among architects based on a domain-specific base language. While a *domain* delineates an area of interest in the *world*, a *domain taxonomy* represents a language of normalized abstractions and classification in a domain (Fig. 6.90).

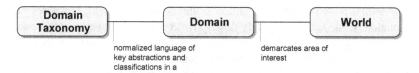

Fig. 6.90 World, domain, and domain taxonomy

Knowledge models are essential for orderly arranging and systematically evolving our thinking—or in the words of Thucydides (1981):

> A man who has the knowledge but lacks the power to clearly express it is no better off than if he never had any ideas at all.

Taxon[100] and relationships among taxa (*taxon relationship*) are the constituents of a domain taxonomy. A taxonomy conceptualizes its domain from a specific perspective pursuing a particular *intent*. A taxon refers to a crucial concept, abstraction, or classification in a domain. It can be textual or iconographic and can be related to other taxa. Examples of *taxon relationships* are generalization,[101] association,[102] or composition[103] (Fig. 6.91).

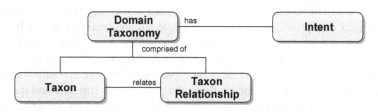

Fig. 6.91 Domain taxonomy constituents

> *Capability* is the quality, or state of being capable (also: ability). (Merriam-Webster Dictionary 2020)

---

[100]Taxonomy is the science of making a classification. Taxon represents a taxonomic group in a formal system of nomenclature. Taxa is the plural of taxon.

[101]Generalization of a concept is an extension of the concept to less-specific criteria. It is a foundational element of human reasoning.

[102]Associations are simple referrals between concepts, where aggregations are a form of association that specifies a whole-part relationship between the aggregate (whole) and a component (part).

[103]Compositions are a form of aggregation with strong ownership and coincident lifetime as part of the whole.

Capability, a well-established notion in the architecture field, has a normative connotation, while *taxon* is a purely descriptive concept. However, the difference in meaning diminishes where enterprise vocabularies are formed based on capabilities that relate very different architecture building blocks, like services, applications, platforms, information, and architecture conditions, roadmaps, or patterns.

A capability specifies *what* something of enterprise interest (e.g., an application) can, should, or does do. Capability does not indicate *how*, *why*, or *where* this is provided by *whom*. *What* something, like an enterprise, provides remains relatively stable over time. By contrast, *why* or *how* an enterprise provides what it provides, or *who* in the enterprise is responsible, changes more frequently. Architecture functions standardize enterprise vocabularies based on capabilities to differentiate the *what* from the *why*, *how*, or *who*.

The notion of capability corresponds to the idea of a teleological system.[104] The most basic specification of a capability is based on a single attribute: its *name*. However, capability specifications may entail other details, like attributes classifying capabilities of similar type and nature, for instance, a class of *technical* versus a class of *business* capabilities, or *strategic* versus *tactical* capabilities.

Linking a normalized vocabulary (i.e., standardized set of capabilities) to a wide variety of object types enables object classification that is agnostic to type-immanent attribute sets. This enables correlations between differently typed objects along standardized enterprise categories. For example, an architecture function has standardized its enterprise vocabulary based on capabilities. A capability named *sales* is associated with an application, a service, an information entity, a project, and an architecture pattern. Despite the different types and other potential differences, the application, service, information, project, and pattern now correlate and qualify as *sales-objects*. The shallowness of capability-based correlation semantics is an advantage. While the limited semantic depth prevents a differentiated view of *how* objects correlate, it indicates *that* quite disparate objects have something in common.

Architecture Function and Domain Taxonomy

Architecture functions delegate domain taxonomy responsibility to their *domain architecture discipline*, which creates and evolves taxonomies in close coordination with domain-specific stakeholders. A *domain taxonomy* establishes the common conceptual basis for a respective architecture domain. An *architecture language* includes domain taxonomies as sublanguages. Taxonomies merge with domain architecture methodologies and view models (*domain architecture methodology*) to promote their clarity and acceptance (Fig. 6.92).

---

[104] The teleological system notion is concerned with the function and (external) behavior of a system (Dietz 2006).

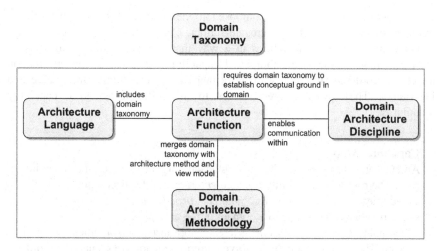

Fig. 6.92 Architecture function and domain taxonomy

Chose a neutral naming schema for your capabilities to ensure their stability over time. Avoid ephemeral terminology and aligning capability names with technical products, organization designation, or other forms of nonpermanent phenomena. Industry business models and their generalized terminology are a good starting point for a sustainable capability naming scheme.

Determine an elementary capability classification that your organization needs and ensure that all domains systematically adopt your basic classification schema. For example, introduce the dichotomy of *functional versus non-functional* as a capability classification scheme. While you classify capabilities as *functional* if they address primary needs, non-functional capabilities address your enterprise's secondary needs. Let us look at an example. A company in the financial services industry provides a *checking account balance* service in its online-banking offering. The service guarantees a defined level of protection against tampering attacks (e.g., tamper-proofing) when customers retrieve their account balances. In this example, the architecture function qualifies *check account balance* as a functional capability, while specifying the *tamper-proofing*[105] *warranty* as a non-functional capability.[106] While functional capabilities depict *what* is provided (e.g., by a service), non-functional capabilities particularly specify *how* functionality is delivered. Consider further subdivision of non-functional capabilities. For example, consider subclasses such as *security, performance, availability,* or *usability*.

Organize capabilities in a capability map. A capability map is a domain taxonomy with a composite structure (i.e., a forest of tree structures). Every capability in a map is either a leaf of the tree or a node. In the case of nodes, capabilities decompose into

---

[105] *Tamper-proofing* is a capability hindering, deterring, or detecting unauthorized access to systems.

[106] *Non-functional capability* is also known as *quality attribute*.

sub-capabilities, which in turn decompose into their own, and so on. Capabilities at the level of leaves do not disaggregate further. Capabilities at the level of nodes contextualize their sub-capabilities in a way that resolves naming collisions. A capability map augments the individual capabilities in a domain by information about their ordered structure. Capability maps make capabilities traversable and inheritable. They provide direct access to the different levels of capability granularity.

Capability Map

An enterprise has specified its capabilities and organized them in a capability map. The root-level capability is called *enterprise* and is decomposed into the capabilities *human resources, finance, procurement,* and *sales.* Each sub-capability corresponds to a domain in the enterprise.

Domain experts and architects create appropriate taxonomies for each domain. Higher-level contexts resolve naming collisions (e.g., naming multiple capabilities in the map *support desk*). For example, if the enterprise needs to know all applications that provide *support desk* capabilities, it searches for all application type objects associated with the capability "*/support desk." If the enterprise is interested in knowing all applications in the *finance* domain that provide *support desk* capabilities, it searches for all application type objects associated with the "finance/support desk" capability (Fig. 6.93).

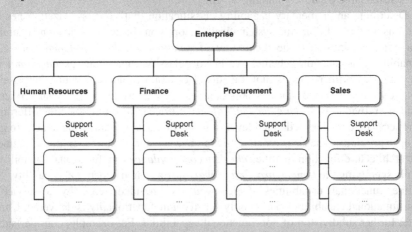

Fig. 6.93 Capability map

Solidly crafted domain taxonomies provide your function with numerous benefits. A domain taxonomy provides your architects with an overview of the crucial abstractions, concepts, dimensions, and classifications in a domain. Domain taxonomies are an excellent orientation and learning tool also for architects who are new to a field. As a normalized naming scheme, you use the capabilities defined by a domain taxonomy to relate architecture and non-architecture objects. For example, you relate applications, requirements, projects, or organizations by associating all items with the *support desk* capability.

Consider the following example. An architecture function needs to know all landscape assets related to a particular process. It has established a comprehensive information model that represents its landscape assets (*indirect correlation via rich information model*). The architecture function can navigate through the model via semantically rich linkage between specific landscape assets. However, finding all assets related (i.e., directly and indirectly) to a particular process is not a straight-forward query since there are indirections across different levels. As a complemen-tary information model, the architecture function introduced capability-based classification for all assets (*direct correlation via lightweight information model*). Capability-based classification of architecture and non-architecture assets enables the architecture function to run correlative queries with capability as the pivotal object. Establish capability-based information models for those assets that you need to rudimentarily correlate. Establish a comprehensive information model if you need to traverse asset links in a semantically rich manner (Fig. 6.94).

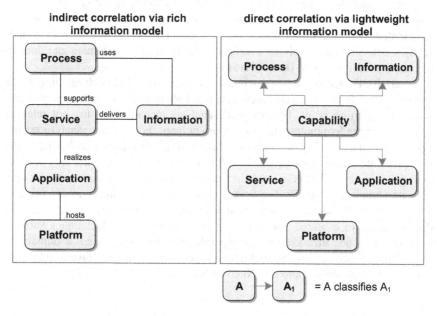

Fig. 6.94 Capability-based information model

An architecture language defines domain-agnostic architecture concepts at the lower levels of a multi-layer ontology. In contrast, domain taxonomies define domain-specific concepts at the upper levels. Therefore, make sure that the definitions of the domain taxonomy are aligned with your architecture language or based on the fundamental concepts you have defined in it (ARCHITECTURE LANGUAGE).

Align domain taxonomies with enterprise and architecture reference models. For example, align domain taxonomies with established business terminology (e.g., derived from an industry business model). Align your capability naming schema with your reference architecture asset schemas. For example, ensure that capability naming matches the naming and categorization of architecture patterns in a domain (REFERENCE ARCHITECTURE METHODOLOGY).

Distinguish and delineate domains from other domains before elaborating on them in detail. Distinguish and delineate domain taxonomies from one another, appropriately. For example, two realms, such as the *security* domain and the *human resources* domain, overlap by containing the same landscape asset (e.g., *personal master data* application). The domain taxonomies for the security and human resources domains similarly overlap. However, the security domain taxonomy may associate *personal master data* with a capability called *identity store*. In contrast, the same application in the human resources domain taxonomy is represented by a capability called *employee system*. Sharpen your domain boundaries by detecting and resolving overlaps at the level of both domain and domain taxonomy (ARCHITECTURE DEMARCATION).

Determine the scope and purpose of a domain taxonomy before developing it. For example, identify the statements architects make about a domain in their day-to-day work as a starting point. Use language analysis techniques[107] to spot relevant concepts and the terminology used to represent them. For instance, analyze textual descriptions of a domain to identify essential nouns (i.e., subjects and objects), verbs (i.e., predicates), adjectives, and adverbs (i.e., attributes) in domain stories. A subject in a sentence may point to the actors in a domain, while an object in a sentence may indicate a crucial concept. Predicates indicate activity relationships between subjects and objects, while adjectives associated with specific nouns may indicate relevant differentiation of essential concepts in a domain. Use other techniques such as generalization-specialization or analogy inference to comprehend a domain in more detail. When developing and refining a domain taxonomy, take a mile-wide rather than a mile-deep approach (NEED TO KNOW).

---

[107]Techniques for the analysis of language form, language meaning, and language in context (Wikipedia Linguistics 2020e).

6.6.3 Architecture Innovation

The world has changed at all times. However, the pace of change has increased rapidly in recent decades. An enterprise's ability to notice emerging trends, new technologies, or changing business models and to recognize novel factors that limit its space to maneuver increasingly decides over its market success. An architecture function supports the transformation of recognized innovation potential into tangible business outcomes.

> *Innovation* is commonly defined as the *carrying out of new combinations* that include "the introduction of new goods, new methods of production, the opening of new markets, the conquest of new sources of supply and the carrying out of a new organization of any industry." (Wikipedia Innovation 2020d)

Architecture innovation intends to renew the process of doing architecture and to identify or produce innovations as architecture process outcomes. Architecture innovation implies an enterprise's willingness to replace traditional ways of conducting business with *promising novel approaches* in particular *areas of enterprise interest. Area of interest* is any sphere or domain in your enterprise with the potential to benefitting the business in achieving better results (Fig. 6.95).

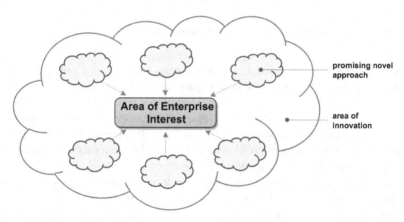

Fig. 6.95 Architecture innovation

Architecture Function and Architecture Innovation

Architecture functions pursue innovation to support their enterprises and to tangibly improve business outcomes. They embed innovation incentives in role descriptions to motivate architects stretch their minds beyond the routine thinking of a normal workday. Learning organization attitudes encourage architects in their pursuit of knowledge—creating an environment where innovation can flourish. Finally, methodologies entail steps and techniques that encourage architects to consider alternative approaches, question the question, or otherwise depart from their personal or organizational conditioning (Fig. 6.96).

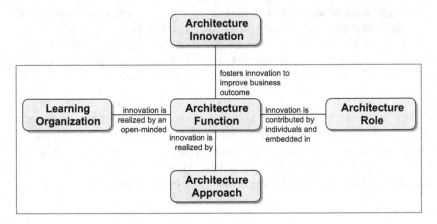

Fig. 6.96 Architecture function and architecture innovation

A promising novel approach may be brand new to the world, a new combination of existing approaches, or merely new to your business. For example, a promising novel approach can be a highly efficient method for technically transferring data between two compute nodes (*technology innovation*), a new approach to conducting business (*business innovation*), a new method for validating applications (*methodological innovation*), or an innovative design that addresses a performance concern very effectively (*architecture innovation*).

Encourage your architects to regularly explore inspiring ideas and critically challenge beliefs by embedding innovation goals and responsibilities in your role descriptions. Stimulate your architects' desire for innovation by encouraging internal and external exchange of information and ideas. For example, create an environment that encourages conference attendance and discussions with colleagues. Challenge your architects to delve into learning and teaching or architectural coaching. Regularly allow architects in your company to leave established comfort zones or to gather and share knowledge across disciplines. While targeted innovation is an invaluable source of advancement, there is a common misconception that architectural innovation is a self-sufficient playground for architects. Address such misunderstandings by making it clear in your role or mandate descriptions that in innovation, the exploration of ideas is merely a means, while the implementation of ideas is an end to drive the business forward (**ARCHITECTURE ROLE**, **ARCHITECTURE MANDATE**).

Consider personality traits such as openness, curiosity, or willingness to experiment in your recruitment policies and architecture procurement contracts. The desire to innovate is more of a personality trait than one that can be managed through incentive systems or contractual obligations. At the same time, engaging sourcing partners can be an exciting approach to broadening innovation efforts. Sourcing partners typically add to the existing specialist knowledge and experience in your enterprise and provide regular renewal of their resource pools (**ARCHITECTURE SOURCING**).

A prerequisite for innovation is the awareness of architecture functions of the technical needs or other areas of improvement in a relevant interest area. Therefore, architecture functions must understand what progress or improvement means in a particular area, and they must be able to translate inspiring ideas into business practice. Innovative progress can only be achieved if an architecture function's understanding of a business *area of interest* overlaps with its knowledge of an *area of innovation* (Fig. 6.97).

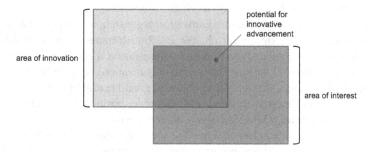

Fig. 6.97 Potential for innovative advancement

You need to understand the area of interest you want to improve and your area of expertise in architecture to innovate successfully. Let us say you are an architecture expert for storage solutions (i.e., *storage* is your area of innovation) and you work in the banking industry (i.e., *banking* is your area of interest). In this example, you need to understand the banking industry in order to suggest how current trends in the storage domain can help improve the reliability of banking products—and thus their user experience. You must also understand the area of interest from today's perspective and be able to assess its strategic plans for further growth and expansion.

From an architecture perspective, the key areas of innovation are enhancing landscape assets to improve business outcomes and optimizing the enterprise value chain to increase its efficiency. For example, an architecture function seeks to transform new technologies, platforms, and services into advanced architecture designs using proven patterns. To take another example, an architecture function improves its contributions to the enterprise value chain by evolving its methodology for designing landscape assets (LANDSCAPE ASSET).

You typically look for different types of innovations at different architecture levels. At the enterprise level, your innovation focus is on business and technological trends that are universally applicable—i.e., across all areas. A long-term planning horizon is part of the strategic perspective at the enterprise level. At the domain level, the individual domains and their relationships to other domains determine the area of interest of an architecture function. The planning horizon here is shorter than at the enterprise level—but more extensive than at the solution level (ARCHITECTURE LEVEL).

While knowing an area of interest very well is a challenge in itself, aimlessly pursuing inspirational ideas can easily become an endless endeavor. Therefore, you need to focus your attention on exploring relevant areas of innovation wisely. Make sure you do not lose sight of why you are investigating an area by immediately reviewing inspiring ideas for architectural feasibility. Anticipate both the desired and undesired effects and consequences of an idea under investigation. If the expected effects of an idea you are pursuing turn out to be desirable and relevant, continue following the idea—otherwise, drop it (NEED TO KNOW).

Consider a dedicated architecture innovation organization if your organization or industry is undergoing significant change and transformation. Organizations that provide you with a dedicated mission and whose raison d'être is innovation drive renewal more radically. Anchor innovation organizations at a higher position in organizational schemas, if possible, to combine great breadth of impact with influence and access to incentive systems—for example, position innovation organizations at enterprise level (ORGANIZATIONAL REPLICATION).

Another common misunderstanding is the misconception of innovation as purely additive and expansive. Therefore, encourage the architecture function to not only explore emerging business or technology trends but also identify innovative approaches for improved management of complexity, increased transparency for better decision-making, and smart methods to reduce the footprint of redundant or inactivated landscape assets (ARCHITECTURE CAPACITY).

Incorporate the topic of innovation into your methodology and view models. The goal is to make architects aware of the need to systematically reflect on and record inspiring ideas, new design approaches, and valuable technical considerations, for example, in the form of patterns or the updating of an architecture roadmap (YOUR OWN ARCHITECTURE METHODOLOGY).

6.7   Architecture Objective

While many patterns support the architecture function in pursuing and achieving its objectives, I have placed only two patterns in the *architecture objectives* group. The *need to know* pattern emphasizes that large gaps may exist between presumed and actual goals or between conscious and unconscious objectives. The pattern suggests ways of constructively dealing with this issue to support your architecture function in doing the right thing rightly. The *architecture mandate* pattern suggests how you meaningfully formulate a mandate for a given architecture objective such that you ensure mission accomplishment accordingly.

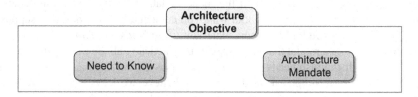

6.7.1   Need to Know

Knowing what is needed should precede any action taken in the enterprise. Thus, clarification of the expectation motivating an action should precede every architecture activity. What sounds like a trite reference to an actual self-evident fact is not an exaggerated piece of advice. It is an everyday reality that activities are performed without actors being able to identify and articulate the need that precedes their contribution. A common mistake is confusing real needs with perceived needs. Actors make serious efforts to address a need without being able to articulate it. Efforts are misinvested due to a confusion of goals and means.

A *question* is a subject or aspect in dispute or open for discussion; it is the specific point at issue. (Merriam-Webster Dictionary 2020)

Your *need to know* presupposes a reasonable cause for finding the knowledge you need. By equating *need to know* with problem, we can also say that your *need to know* corresponds to a need that you want solved. A *need to know* can always be expressed in the form of a question. If you cannot articulate your need, you do not understand it and consequently cannot formulate it in the form of a question. So note that—as long as you cannot formulate a question—no one can give you an appropriate answer. Or in other words, if you cannot formulate a problem, neither you nor anyone else can solve it.

What you may take for granted is often anything but self-evident. For example, a standard solution is selected by an organization without articulating the problem that this solution is intended to address. Instead of identifying the real problem, a perceived problem is stated. The real reason the solution is chosen may be that it pleases the leader of the organization. The (initially perceived) needs of the organization are reverse-engineered from the chosen solution and are henceforth considered the basis for procuring it. The actual needs of the organization were never seriously examined ex-ante. In another example, architects invest time and effort in sketching a model. At the same time, they cannot explain in plain language what question they want to answer with the model's data. So before you can achieve anywhere, you have to be clear about what you are actually (as opposed to supposedly) aiming for—you have to know what you *actually need to know*.

I am presenting a model that accompanies us practically all the time in life. In this conception, I distinguish needs into *conscious* versus *unconscious* and *actual* versus *supposed* needs. A supposed need is one we believe we have, when in fact we unconsciously need something else. An actual need assumes the existence of an optimum, which at the same time is unknown to us. We can only approach our actual needs through a questioning and skeptical attitude, but at the same time we can never determine that we have achieved it. While questioning the question risks infinite regression, pragmatic heuristics help you avoid philosophical rabbit holes.

Beware, the cost of the optimal answer to a supposedly meaningful question is usually much higher than for the suboptimal answer to a question that encodes your actual knowledge need. Let us distinguish between a *supposed* and an *actual* goal on the one hand and the successful or unsuccessful pursuit of the goal on the other hand. Successful goal pursuit sounds better than unsuccessful, at least at first glance. It is undoubtedly the best of all options to successfully pursue and achieve an actual goal (B). The second-best option, however, is less clear. If you think about it for a moment, there may well be situations in which you are better off with a suboptimally pursued actual goal (D) than with a successfully pursued supposed goal (A). For example, suppose you live in Basel, Switzerland, and your goal is to travel to Rome, Italy. Suppose you think (incorrectly) that you need to turn north to get to Rome as quickly as possible. So your supposed goal is to go north while your actual destination is south. Suppose you are very successful in pursuing your supposed goal. In this case, you will arrive in Helsinki, Finland, which would most likely be much less optimal than if you had traveled south—and thus perhaps, also not quite optimally, arrived in Milan[108] (Fig. 6.98).

| | | **aim** | |
		supposed	actual
pursuit	successful	A	B
of aim	unsuccessful	C	D

Fig. 6.98 Need to know

---

[108] Milan is in Italy and much closer to Rome than Helsinki.

Architecture Function and Need to Know

Architecture functions that strive to clarify their knowledge needs significantly improve their maturity. They delegate control of compliance with the *need to know* principle to their governance organization. In any case, they incorporate cues and checkpoints around the questioning process into their methodologies, view models, and platforms (Fig. 6.99).

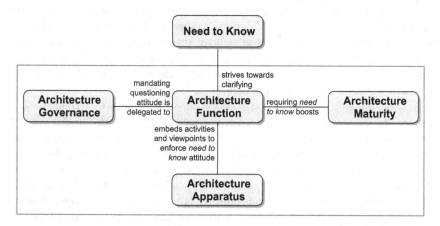

Fig. 6.99 Architecture function and need to know

Questions about architecture are often inherently complex. It is essential to avoid artificially constructed complexity (i.e., accidental complexity). For architects, therefore, pursuing actual goals and clarifying the right versus the wrong question are critical to using their limited capacities wisely. Check questions for appropriateness and avoid an intensive search for answers to unreflected questions. Write down your basic questions before searching for answers. Formulate your questions in simple terms and explain the reasons for your *need to know*. For example, if you are creating an architecture model, first write down the question or questions you want your model to answer. Be sure to phrase your question in such a way that you can determine when your model finally answers it. Formulate a definition of done.[109] Do not work out answers without first critically examining the question. Otherwise, you run the risk of putting a lot of energy into answers that turn out to be worthless (ARCHITECTURE CAPACITY).

By critically examining the question, you avoid confusing ends and means. Confusing ends and means is a phenomenon that is more common than you might think. For example, an architect designing a simple application performs all activities to the letter and meticulously creates all artifacts as suggested by an architecture

---

[109] The definition of done (DoD) is an Agile and Scrum terminology. However, it is a much broader concept for determining an exit criterion for a work product or activity. A definition of done must be created individually for each task. The DoD specifies criteria that can be held against the task's progress to recognize the achievement of the desired end state and to end the task.

method. The result is a description of the design that is impressive in its size. At the same time, a small subset of the architecture description would have been sufficient for the task at hand. How could this happen? The architecture method (actually a means) has become an end in the eyes and hands of the architect. The architect created artifacts under the impression of a rich method and lost sight of what the method's application was primarily about in the given context. Architecture methods are generic in nature. They are impressively large, are comprehensive, and attempt to cover many applications of themselves. Architecture methods are also much more tangible than a yet-to-be-developed design. In other words, architecture methods can be so impressive that architects lose sight of their real goal and purpose. As an architect, you must always keep in mind the means character of methods and immunize yourself against misunderstanding architecture methods as an end (YOUR OWN ARCHITECTURE METHODOLOGY).

You can mitigate generic method overload for your architects by creating method adapters for common and recurring types of method applications. In this context, method adapters provide your architects with a set of pre-formulated questions so they can reuse the questions they need to answer instead of developing them from scratch. For example, an architect uses one of the adapters of a solution architecture method. The selected adapter supports the application of the method in situations where sensitive information and functionality is to be offered via mobile applications—that is, situations where secure mobile applications are to be developed. In one of the generic activities described by the method's problem-solving process, architects are asked to identify significant requirements. The *sensitive mobile application adapter* lists specific requirements (both functional and non-functional) as well as constraints that mobile applications must typically meet as architecture-significant. This list of typical requirements can be directly reused by the architect. The requirements describe the recurring core of the problem of sensitive mobile applications and thus represent the questions that an architect has to answer in search of a solution (ARCHITECTURE METHODOLOGY ADAPTER).

Evaluate planned efforts in terms of their *return on investment*. State exactly *why* (rational) you are striving for *what* (purpose). Also, state *how* you intend to achieve your goal. The purpose (*what*) and rationale (*why*) should correspond to architecture or business goals, and their value should be expressed in monetary terms. Also, monetize *how* you plan to achieve your goal and consider whether *what* you want to achieve outweighs your efforts. Discuss your calculation with architecture colleagues and other disciplines and invite them to critique your *return on investment* calculation. Resist personal or even organizational reflexes to act directly until the question to be answered, the associated economic benefits, and the required efforts have been adequately clarified (ARCHITECTURE FUNDING).

Imagine that you are allowed to create and demand only one architecture policy in your enterprise. My suggestion for this guideline would be that you categorically oblige your architects to write down their *needs to know* in the form of simple questions before they begin any work. This policy kindly forces your architects to deliberate over each contribution before they engage. Such a policy can be formulated generically, is easy to implement, and will inevitably lead to more reflected output—thus ultimately to more qualitative contributions (**ARCHITECTURE POLICY**).

Architecture alternatives represent a particular form of clarifying your knowledge needs. In addition to an original question and the first attempt at an answer, there is usually a selection of alternative answers. Do not fail to consider and explore these in more depth if they seem promising at first glance. Consider requiring the search for alternative answers categorically from your architects—at least in defined situations. For example, you could require that every solution search your architects launch must always include an investigation of the *alternative of doing nothing* and an evaluation of that alternative in terms of architectural economics (**ARCHITECTURE ALTERNATIVE**).

Define a *need to know* baseline by setting an enterprise-wide focus for architecture perspectives. For example, consider *information* as a focus. Information has become a critical asset in an information-driven world. Information contained in other information is extracted using new technologies and approaches (e.g., machine learning[110]) and transformed into predictive algorithms. Yet, in many organizations, it is still the algorithm (i.e., the *application*) that receives the primary attention and is treated as the pivotal intellectual property—which puts the focus on applications. In contrast, it is the *information* that enables enterprises to achieve their goals. And yet, in many organizations, information is neglected and treated indirectly in portfolios (i.e., through applications). The entire process of using information to benefit the business has fundamentally changed. This requires a new focus on *information* as a core asset in your architecture portfolio. If the priorities are inappropriately chosen, architecture contributions will lead to unsatisfactory results (**LANDSCAPE ASSET**).

Consider alternatives to put information at the center of architectural considerations. For example, *focus on applications in new ways*. The appeal of applications as a focus is that they are well-established units of ownership, deployment, and maintenance. They are the assets that appear to end-users and provide valuable services to them. For example, end-users know the names of applications and click their icons every day to launch them. Users have learned to express their needs in terms of applications and technical functionality rather than in terms of features that applications should provide. An exciting alternative to focusing on applications is establishing the *connections between applications* and other landscape assets as the focus of the architecture function. Another alternative to application focus is splitting applications into their functional components and shifting the architecture focus to individual microservices. A microservice[111] can be compared to the fine-grained functional components of applications. However, a challenge with this shift in focus

---

[110]Machine learning algorithms create a model based on training data to make predictions or make decisions without having been explicitly (imperatively) programmed for it.

[111]Microservices are fine-grained, context-agnostic functions or function endpoints. They are requested and delivered via lightweight protocols. Applications are established as loosely coupled microservices.

is that applications provide a broader context for the functional components they host, while individual microservices lack this application context (ARCHITECTURE DEMARCATION).

Consider key perspectives other than your enterprise's *need to know* baseline, for instance, *business architecture* that focuses on business requirements, business process, business service, or enterprise capabilities. Another alternative focus could be on combinations of specific architecture domains. The goal here would be to place domain aggregates at the center of architectural considerations. Likewise, the focus could be directed to individual architecture levels and thus to the asset granularity observed at the corresponding levels (ARCHITECTURE LEVEL).

Consider *desired effects* as a *need to know* baseline and place them in the focus of your architecture function. You can shift the focus by defining policies so that the occurrence of a desired effect becomes the policy's measure—that is, that following it must produce the desired effect. Ensure that when in doubt, people do not follow a policy to the letter, but act in its spirit. This shift in focus means that an emphasis on necessary activities (i.e., means) does not obscure or mask the actually intended architecture effect (i.e., end). In the words of George Patton (Patton and Harkins 1995):

> Never tell people how to do things. Tell them what to do, and they will surprise you with their ingenuity.

Finally, note what Simon Sinek points out in his inspirational TED Talk *start with the why* (Sinek 2009). Sinek points out that people are inspired by meaning (the *why*) and that it should come first in both communication and reflection—that is, before the *how* and the *what*. Sinek calls this triad the golden circle. In the innermost circle is the *why*. This circle represents people's motives or intentions. In the next circle is the *how*, which represents people's processes or methods. Finally, in the outermost circle is the *what*, which represents the results or outcomes. For experts, the way from the outside in is acceptable—for non-experts, good reflection and communication leads from the inside out. In other words, good communication and reflection *starts with the why*.

6.7.2 Architecture Mandate

Expectations of architectural contributions are often insufficiently understood and articulated by the respective proposers. Accordingly, the architecture function makes contribution commitments without adequate clarification of what is expected. The consequences of inadequately clarified expectations and corresponding delivery commitments range from mild disappointments to significant wasted efforts. Explicit description of mandates improves expectation management and the efficiency of architecture contributions.

> A *mandate* is the authorization to act given to a representative. (Merriam-Webster Dictionary 2020)

The architecture function collaborates with other functions along the enterprise value chain. Some collaborations are lightweight, informal by nature, and part of normal day-to-day operations. Other collaborative relationships, however, require clarification of the expectations, assumptions, and commitments of all cooperating parties. Inadequately aligned cooperation inevitably leads to ambiguity about scope, objective, deliverables, timelines, or resources.

The purpose of an *architecture mandate* is to encourage and require appropriate clarification before any commitments are made. Ultimately, the purpose of mandates is precisely to precede the implementation of architecture obligations. A well-defined mandate promotes clarity of expectations on all sides by fully describing and formally agreeing on commitments. Architecture mandates are used to precisely anticipate and articulate the desired end state of an architecture activity and guide the path to its achievement (Fig. 6.100).

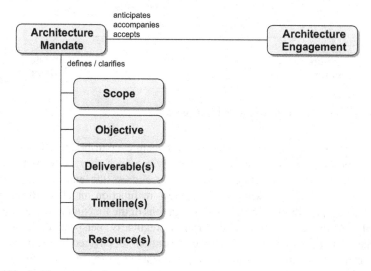

Fig. 6.100 Architecture mandate

Architecture Function and Architecture Mandate
Architecture functions use mandates to explicitly clarify and capture expectations (*need to know*) regarding their commitments with all stakeholders involved. Architecture mandates have a positive impact on the efficiency and effectiveness of architecture functions helping them to optimally deploy their capacities. They are also a central means of architecture governance to ensure that contributions are made in accordance with architecture policies. Finally, mandates are used to calibrate the appropriate use of methods and view models throughout an architecture mandate—appropriate in terms of mandate fulfillment (Fig. 6.101).

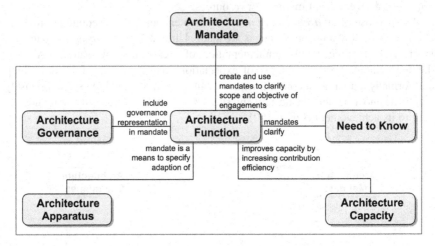

Fig. 6.101 Architecture function and architecture mandate

Mandates anticipate and accompany architecture contributions. Contributions differ in terms of scope, type, or regularity with which they are called upon. In terms of scope, an architecture mandate may address the empowerment of the architecture function as a whole. An architecture function mandate, for example, clarifies the responsibilities, rights, and obligations of the function as the architecture authority of the entire enterprise. From a regularity perspective, imagine an unplanned contribution, for example, a contribution not covered by the architecture service catalog. Accordingly, there is no pre-formulated service-level agreement for this contribution. The lack of advanced agreements on the execution of the service is compensated for by a corresponding mandate. Architecture mandates accompany the planning, creation, and discussion of agreements in which both the expectations and the necessary contributions of the associated parties are clarified. The use of mandates and corresponding processes benefits the architecture function and other corporate functions with which it collaborates. A mandate helps validate the relevance of architecture and calibrate the level of detail along an entire architecture engagement. In other words, mandates serve to continuously verify that the contributions made are delivering the expected results. They ensure that an architecture function diligently avoids both over- and underdelivery. Mandates clarify and capture questions that the architecture engagement should answer. They also define the level of detail (i.e., breadth and depth) required for engagement. For example, a mandate may specify which viewpoints are needed to answer all questions or which deliverables must be tangibly created by when (**NEED TO KNOW**).

Architecture mandates support coordination between architecture and other corporate functions. For example, a project plan references a mandate to ensure that architecture-related resources, activities, schedules, and deliverables are aligned and agreed upon between project management and architecture function. Another example where a mandate supports coordination between organizations is the link between mandates and architecture roadmaps. As long as the mandate creation process insists on including current architecture roadmap events in corresponding mandates, it ensures systematic implementation of roadmap events (**ARCHITECTURE ROADMAP METHODOLOGY**).

After an architecture mandate is initially created, it evolves through the stages of a corresponding engagement. For example, an initial mandate version is created to include the architecture function in determining alternative approaches for the design of a new service (e.g., in the *service portfolio stage*). Later (e.g., in the *service plan stage*), the same mandate is evolved to consider the costs, the risk, and the architecture's required resources. The signature field is extended accordingly so that domain and solution architects sign the mandate together with a service portfolio manager in the service portfolio stage. In the service plan stage, the same mandate requires an additional signature from a project manager. Domain and solution architect signatures are also renewed to authorize additional information and details (e.g., costs, risks, and resources) (**MANAGED ARCHITECTURE EVOLUTION**).

In the following, I outline general sections of an architecture mandate. Use these as a basis for creating your own mandate standard or to critically review your existing mandate format (Table 6.6).

Table 6.6 Architecture mandate schema

Activity	Description
Mandate scope	Definition of mandate scope (e.g., the error in a faulty application must be corrected).
	Discussions about scope often lead to a better understanding of what is expected. Also, think about what is not expected—that is, what is out of scope.
	Capture:
	• Approach of engagement
	• Architecture roles and responsibilities in the engagement
	• Architecture deliverables and by when they are expected
	• Architecture reviews and when they are scheduled
Mandate category	Define meaningful mandate categories for your environment. For example, choose *solution archetype* or the *engagement lifecycle phase* as categories to classify mandates
Mandate context	Capture details about the context of the mandated engagement. For example, record other engagements that are being performed in parallel and are related to your engagement
Mandate objective	Define the mandate's objective so that you can determine its fulfillment or progress at any time. Describe the objective in terms of a series of questions that you can answer once the mandate is fulfilled. At an early stage, you may want to ask what the cost or risk profile is of the proposed solution. In later phases, you may want to know what impact a proposed change may have on the landscape. Phrase your questions in plain English. Make sure they are clear, unambiguous, and answerable.
	Define the specific focus of the engagement. One direction might be to explore architecture alternatives that equally address a particular problem. Another focus could be to understand the requirements that are likely to influence architecture decisions (i.e., architecture-significant requirements)
Impacted and impacting architecture domains	Identify and capture domains that are likely to be affected by the mandated engagement (i.e., outbound impact). Also, capture domains that affect your engagement (i.e., inbound impact)
Mandate deliverables, timelines, milestones	Describe the deliverables, required activities, and the due dates by which you expect the mandate to be gradually completed.
	If you need more detailed mandate descriptions, you can, for example, refer to specific viewpoints in a view model appropriate to the engagement.
	Viewpoints allow you to specify the level of detail to which the mandate should elaborate solution details.
	For example, in a solution architecture mandate, you reference the viewpoints in your solution view models. For a data viewpoint in the view model, you define that an entity-relationship model must be created. For each viewpoint, you define the level of detail required to meet the mandate. For the entity-relationship model, for example, you specify that it must be implementation-ready
Mandate resources	List architectural and non-architectural resources required to execute the mandate. In the early stages, you can list roles only.

(continued)

Table 6.6 (continued)

Activity	Description
	Later, provide names and contact information for specific architects, including capacity and rate indicators
Mandate signature fields	Signatures are typically provided by domain and solution architects. Other signature fields are provided for parties that are responsible at different stages of the lifecycle.
	For example, a service portfolio manager signs a mandate in the service portfolio stage, or a project manager signs accordingly in the service architecture stage.
	Domain architects ensure that the solution architecture contributions are consistent with the plans and constraints of their domains. Solution architects confirm with their signature that an architecture mandate is feasible from a solution architecture perspective

Mandates help you specify architecture engagements in terms of their objectives, approach, deliverables, or required resources. They are not limited to specific engagements but can be applied to various engagement types. For example, you can use mandates to clarify goals, authorizations, responsibilities, or the desired maturity level of an architecture function (*organizational mandate*). You can also use mandates to set the expectations for the evolution of an architecture domain as part of the next development cycle (*domain architecture mandate*). Further examples include mandates that define the systematic development of solutions (*solution architecture mandate*) or the goals and the approach of an architecture review (e.g., verifying compliance with the organization's security policy). Once defined, architecture mandates support architects in performing the mandated engagements. Before architects perform a service in a corresponding engagement, they check with the help of the mandate whether the contribution has already achieved the desired goal. During the implementation of an architecture activity, architects use the mandate to check whether the contribution has already achieved the desired goal. Mandates, therefore, accompany architecture engagements as a kind of yardstick. This yardstick is continuously used to specifically plan and implement architectural contributions and to determine when they have been sufficiently delivered. Therefore, incorporate mandates into your methods as a calibration companion (**Your own Architecture Methodology**).

Increase the effectiveness of your mandate-aware methods by providing reusable mandate templates for frequently recurring types of architecture engagements. Extend your mandate creation process with a mandate adapter framework and deploy mandate adapters to improve the creation of concrete mandates in your enterprise. Mandate adapters also increase the accuracy of fit of specific mandates increasing the maturity of your function (**Architecture Methodology Adapter**).

The creation of mandates naturally involves effort. At the same time, conscious reflection and clarification of what is expected of the architecture function are very revealing. The unnecessary and thus avoidable effort, which results from acting without reflection, usually far outweighs the effort of consciously reflecting on the purpose and goal of an architecture contribution and mandating it accordingly. The leaner your mandate templates are, the less effort is required to create concrete mandates. So make the essential mandate sections mandatory and leave other sections optional (ARCHITECTURE CAPACITY).

Use mandates at handover points between architecture and non-architecture organizations. You can also use mandates at handoff points within the architecture organization when they cross enterprise boundaries. In particular, use architecture mandates to manage and control activities that you delegate to sourcing partners. Make mandates a legally binding contractual element with your architecture sourcing partners (ARCHITECTURE SOURCING).

Make the decommissioning of assets a standard checkpoint in all mandate templates, through which new assets can be introduced. Also, establish an adapter for decommissioning mandates, as asset removal often affects others. For this reason, decommissioning engagements deserve a similar clarified mandate as engagements through which new assets are introduced (DECOMMISSIONING REWARD).

Also make the traceability of architectures a standard checkpoint in all mandate templates. Architecture contributions and their results often suffer from monodimensionality and monocausality. Too often, architects create incomplete or isolated views of a holistic overall architecture. They do not link, for example, conditions with architecture approaches that realize these conditions. Counteract such tendencies by making architecture traversability a standard requirement in your mandate scheme (ARCHITECTURE TRACEABILITY).

Architecture Relevance

You may have noticed that this pattern tacitly assumes that architectural relevance is always given. Whenever an architecture mandate is created, this implies the relevance of corresponding contributions. At the same time, of course, it must be admitted that architectural relevance is not always given. It is therefore important to define criteria for checking architecture relevance. For example, you can apply criteria to given requirements to clarify their architectural significance.

Consider an architecture-significance checklist to standardize this activity. Differentiate criteria categories in your checklist. For example, consider a *business impact criteria* category where you review business risks, costs, or opportunities of a planned architecture contribution. Under *architecture condition*, you check the number of architecture-relevant conditions and the resulting architectural complexity to derive architecture significance. For *quantitative complexity*, determine the number of incoming and outgoing dependencies of a desired application, for example, or the number of users of a planned service, and derive architecture significance from that information. Using several criteria to determine *evolutionary complexity*, you can clarify the extent to which expected continuous accompanying changes, for example, present a planned service with additional architectural challenges. *Novelty* is another useful category to anticipate specific challenges, for example, when new technologies are used to implement innovative business model changes. Finally, consider *extent of impact* as a category. For example, a planned new application will have significant impact on many domains, multiple security zones, or even the entire enterprise (ARCHITECTURE SIGNIFICANCE) (Fig. 6.102).

Architecture-signifiance Checklist			
	Enterprise Weight	Relevance	Total
Business Impact Criteria	High		
Business Impact Criteria$_1$		☐	
Business Impact Criteria$_2$		☐	
Architecture Condition Criteria	Medium		
Architecture Condition Criteria$_1$		☐	
Architecture Condition Criteria$_2$		☐	
Quantitative Complexity Criteria	Low		
Quantative Complexity Criteria$_1$		☐	
Quantative Complexity$_2$		☐	
Evolutionary Complexity Criteria	Low		
Evolutionary Complexity Criteria$_1$		☐	
Evolutionary Complexity Criteria$_2$		☐	
Novelty Criteria	Medium		
Novelty Criteria$_1$		☐	
Novelty Criteria$_2$		☐	
Extent of Impact Criteria	High		
Extent of Impact Criteria$_1$		☐	
Extent of Impact Criteria$_2$		☐	

Fig. 6.102 Architecture relevance criteria checklist

With *enterprise weight*, you introduce a factor that goes beyond the importance of individual engagements and presents the relevance perspective of your enterprise as a whole and in relation to the architecture-significance categories. Under *relevance*, enter the architecture significance as you determined it based on the relevance criteria in each category for the engagement under consideration. Finally, under *total* you combine the enterprise weight and the engagement-specific relevance rating to determine the overall relevance of an examined engagement.

6.8   Architecture Asset

Planning, designing, implementing, and operating architecture assets are among an architecture function's primary responsibilities. The patterns in the *architecture asset* pattern group help you prepare your function to manage architecture assets. The *architecture asset* pattern introduces an abstract understanding of assets to which the other asset group patterns refer. The *architecture demarcation* pattern, on the other hand, aims to clarify boundaries, without which, for example, ownership assignments are impossible. The *landscape asset* pattern introduces the major asset types—service, application, platform, information, and technology—and explains their relationships to structural assets such as architecture domains. Finally, the *off-the-shelf solution* pattern covers assets that have been purchased as semi-finished solutions and helps your architecture function to account for them in its processes.

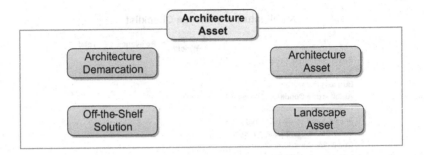

6.8.1 Architecture Demarcation

The ability to delineate an architecture asset is a prerequisite for giving it dedicated attention or assigning asset ownership to an architect. The lack of relevant demarcation criteria leads to architectural fuzziness and makes it fundamentally difficult for an architecture function to fulfill its mandate.

> *Demarcation* is a marked or perceived distinction between one area, category, etc., and another. (Merriam-Webster Dictionary 2020)

At first glance, the boundaries of architecture assets appear to be clearly defined and agreed upon with other architects, and we refer to them by name when we conduct discussions about them. For example, we refer to an application by its name to discuss a planned improvement to its design. When we agree with other architects to change the application's architecture, it is perfectly clear in our minds which asset we are talking about—that is, which asset we are changing. It also seems clear to us where the application begins and where it ends. However, when we take a second look at this question, we need to acknowledge that the application under consideration provides data or functionality to other applications or that it, in turn, obtains information from other applications. We may find that the application in question is a key component of an important business process. Any change in the application necessarily means a change in the process. So, where does the application end, and the process begin? Where does the application in question end in relation to the other application that receives data from it? As easy as it may seem at first glance to accurately draw the boundaries of an architecture asset, it becomes difficult to clearly identify the boundaries once you dig deeper.

In a small example, I illustrate the problems and effects of insufficient architecture demarcation. At first glance, only three assets are visible. Each of them has a name ($asset_1$, $asset_2$, $asset_3$) and may be listed in the company's corresponding asset portfolio. At second glance, we can see two lines, each of which connects two assets together. We must recognize that two initially independent assets that are connected together inevitably result in a new asset. Further, we must acknowledge that two initially independent assets have become part of a new whole. Neither part can be changed without fear of affecting the dependent asset. Thus, the connection between *asset₁* and *asset₂* creates *asset₁₋₂*, while the connection between *asset₃* and *asset₂* creates *asset₂₋₃*. *Asset₁* is indirectly connected to *asset₃* via *asset₂*, which is why another asset is created (*asset₁₋₂₋₃*) (Fig. 6.103).

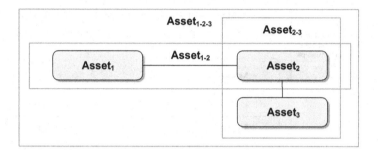

Fig. 6.103 Architecture demarcation

Architecture assets must be uniquely identifiable. To enable asset identifiability, an architecture function must define demarcation criteria so that they can be traceably applied to specific assets. Criteria can be articulated in the form of questions so that a given asset ($asset_X$) can be uniquely delineated by answering them. For example: what are the internal components of $asset_X$ (i.e., internal components are components of $asset_X$ and only of $asset_X$)? How is $asset_X$ connected to other assets (i.e., what are outbound dependencies of $asset_X$)? How are other assets connected to $asset_X$ (i.e., what are inbound dependencies of $asset_X$)? What criteria are used to delineate assets of the same asset type as $asset_X$ (**ARCHITECTURE ASSET**)?

Architecture Demarcation Example
In this example, there are three named and three unnamed assets that can be delineated. Each of the three named assets, in turn, consists of components. Asset1 comprises only one internal component (C_1) and two connecting components (C_2, C_3). Connection component C_2 within *asset₁* connects asset₁ to asset₂, while connection component C_3 is the part that reflects the connection of *asset₃* to *asset₁*. Asset₃ also has only one internal component (C_8) and one component (C_7) that connects *asset₃* to *asset₁*. Finally, *asset₂* has two internal components (C_5 and C_6), while C_4 is a component that represents the connection *asset₁* has to *asset₂*.

(continued)

In addition to the three named assets (*asset₁*, *asset₂*, *asset₃*), three other asset candidates are unnamed in this example. The relationship between *asset₁* and *asset₂* has created one of these assets, and the relationship between *asset₃* and *asset₁* created a second asset. A third unnamed asset is created from a combination of relationships between *asset₁* and *asset₂* and between *asset₁* and *asset₃* (Fig. 6.104).

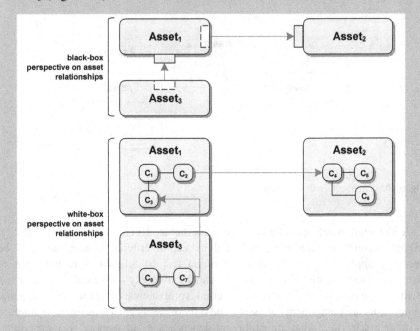

Fig. 6.104 Architecture demarcation example

Specific connection semantics depend on the types of connected assets. Internal components of landscape assets are usually assets of the same type—however, sometimes of lower granularity. For example, applications are internal components of other applications. Outbound and inbound connections, on the other hand, depend on the type of connected landscape asset. For example, an application provides its functions to a business service while using the operational functions of a technical platform. A domain architecture asset contains landscape assets and sub-domains as internal components. An architecture domain has outgoing connections to and incoming connections from other domains. For example, a technical domain supports multiple business domains. Methodological assets reference to other methodological assets. For example, a solution methodology references an assessment methodology for validating architecture designs. Methodological assets are also linked to architecture assets that are created or evolved with the methodology. A pattern is generated, for example, by the pattern methodology, or a target architecture description of a domain is developed based on the domain methodology.

The tighter[112] the connection between assets, the tighter the coupling between them, and the tighter the coupling, the more likely changes to related assets will spill over to them. You need to understand all of your asset's connections to other assets and vice versa. Only when you fully understand the architectural boundaries of your assets will you know the relationships between them in terms of their looseness and tightness. For example, if you are planning to change an asset, you need to involve architects of all closely related assets to evaluate your plan and its impact on other assets and jointly confirm its feasibility. The same applies in reverse. For example, the architect of an application that uses information from you must inform you that they are planning an application change (**ARCHITECTURE OWNERSHIP**).

Architecture functions tend to pay more attention to their well-demarcated and already named assets than to their connections. We have already seen that the innocent connection between two assets creates at least one additional asset in your landscape—one that is either recognized and named or blissfully ignored. Therefore, consider assigning ownership to architecture assets such as services, applications, or platforms and the connections between them. Establish architecture ownership of connections within your architecture function via appropriate architecture policies (**ARCHITECTURE POLICY**).

Both the number and the tightness of connections between assets are good heuristics for understanding how easy it is to change them. Note that in addition to introducing new assets as well as evolving existing ones, decommissioning assets is also a form of change. The more you have established loose asset coupling as a maxim in your company, the less impactful you will be able to decommission assets (**DECOMMISSIONING REWARD**).

Information about the various dependencies and connections between different types of assets is precious to the entire enterprise, for example, if you want to analyze the impact of a change to one asset on other assets. Another example is looking for ways to consolidate landscape assets. Asset dependencies can also provide information about reusability options or help identify redundancy hotspots. An application that provides customer information to many other applications is obviously a hub for this information. If this application is not officially authorized to provide this type of information, you have discovered redundancy to the authorized customer information application. Therefore, specifically implement the relationships between assets in your architecture platform to efficiently provide the wide range of useful queries (**YOUR OWN ARCHITECTURE PLATFORM**).

Your demarcation approach also gradually shifts and changes depending on architecture levels. You are primarily interested in cross-domain, business-relevant, or coarse-grained dependencies between assets at the enterprise level. At this level, you are also interested in dependencies between architecture methods. At the domain

---

[112]Loose coupling between components means that connected components have little or no knowledge of each other's definitions, while tight coupling is the exact opposite.

level, you focus on the inbound and outbound dependencies of a domain, while a solution-level architect is interested in the inbound and outbound connections between landscape assets (**ARCHITECTURE LEVEL**).

Architecture delineation and related issues are already included to some extent in your view models. For example, your view model defines a data viewpoint and an application viewpoint, and a placement relationship between those viewpoints. The idea is that data entities are basically offered via applications, by placing data entities on applications. In this way, your view model requires you to maintain all placement relationships between your data entities and the corresponding applications. Another typical example of a viewpoint focused on relationship information is known as a deployment viewpoint. Applications require platforms on which they are operated. The deployment viewpoint enables your architects to capture and maintain the connection (i.e., deployment connection) between an application and the platform on which it operates (**YOUR OWN ARCHITECTURE VIEW MODEL**).

6.8.2   Architecture Asset

Architects must focus their attention and, to this end, refer to architecture building blocks both terminologically and conceptually. Relative building block concepts, such as the whole and its parts, are just as important as concepts that capture different degrees of architecture significance and value or completeness and wholeness.

> A *building block* is a unit of construction or composition. (Merriam-Webster Dictionary 2020)

While the concept of *building block* allows architects to refer to entities of an essential and participatory nature, the concept of *architecture building block* adds architectural relevance as a defining characteristic. A building block abstracts what is constituent, participative, tangible, and definable to which an architecture building block adds architectural relevance.

Architecture building blocks[113] (ABBs) are the canonical building blocks for architects due to their genericity, partiality, and abstractness. Synonymous terms are *component, part, element,* or *subsystem*. Architecture building blocks help architects emphasize the architecture significance of a part in relation to a whole. Like systems,

---

[113] An architecture module (ABB) is a TOGAF concept. An ABB defines the capabilities that the relevant SBBs implement. ABBs are technology-aware and guide SBB development. An SBB (solution building block) defines the products that implement the capabilities defined by ABB. SBBs are product and vendor aware.

architecture building blocks have a purpose, properties, and relationships to other building blocks and can be viewed both teleologically[114] and ontologically.[115] Architecture building blocks do not imply a particular level of abstractness or concreteness, nor do they similarly anticipate a particular level of detail. An architecture building block may itself consist of architecture building blocks.

Before we take a closer look at the differentiation of concepts such as part and whole, building block, architecture building block, or architecture asset, *system* as a concept must be introduced. The concept of *system* is important in all sciences, with each science maintaining its specific conception of system. A general theory of systems, *systemics*, deals with the properties of systems across the sciences (Bertalanffy 2015).

Dietz distinguishes between two different system terms (Dietz 2006). The term *teleological system* deals with the function and behavior as it can be observed from the outside (i.e., external behavior). The teleological system perspective is useful for using a system. The *ontological system* view distinguishes between *aggregate* and *system*. Both concepts, aggregate and system, are collections of objects. However, in aggregates, the elements are not held together by interaction bonds, whereas in systems they are. A system, therefore, has unity and integrity which an aggregate lacks as properties.

According to Gerald Weinberg (2001), systems theory deals with the following types of problems:

[...] too complex for analysis and too organized for statistics.

By *analysis*, Weinberg means that one can formulate an algorithm in such a way that it completely solves a problem. Problems of this type can be understood and processed by machines (*organized simplicity*). *Disorganized complexity* is the segment of problems that need to be statistically understood and addressed. After all, *organized complexity* is the problem segment that systems theory deals with (Fig. 6.105).

---

[114]Teleological system concept. The term teleological system deals with a system's function and behavior as observed from the outside (external behavior). The teleological system's perspective is useful when using a system.

[115]Ontological system concept. The ontological system view deals with a system's mechanics as observed inside the system (internal behavior). It also distinguishes the concept of aggregate from the concept of system. Both concepts, aggregate and system, are collections of objects. However, in aggregates, the elements are not held together by interaction bonds, whereas in systems, they are. A system, therefore, has unity and integrity. Both properties are lacking in aggregates.

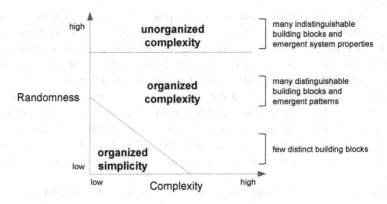

Fig. 6.105 Systems theory (adapted from Gerald Weinberg 2001)

While *complexity* is not clearly defined in the context of systems, heuristics nonetheless exist. Stefan Bente et al. (2012) suggests structural characteristics as a pragmatic approximation to the criteria of complex systems. Bente considers the criterion of *many* to be reasonable for recognizing a system as complex. For example, a system is complex if it consists of many building blocks, which have many relationships to each other, and if a system has many relationships to other systems at the same time. Another indication of complexity is whether a system's behavior is not only a function of its input but also a function of its own state. As further criteria, he suggests checking if a system can be in many states and if there are many possible state transitions.

As another viewpoint for considering complexity, Bente suggests looking at how complexity is experienced or perceived externally. In a complex system, externally observable behavior can vary widely under similar external conditions, implying that the relationship between external conditions and exhibited behavior is nonlinear.

There are general tactics for dealing with complex systems. For example, if your goal is to evolve a complex system, focus your efforts on strengthening its evolvability. At the same time, accept that the complexity of dealing with complexity—for example, the complexity of dealing with a complex application—is about the same as the complexity of the application itself. William Ashby (1964) formulates this in the *law of requisite variety*, in which he defines the variety of a system as the number of states it can assume—i.e., as a measure of the complexity of the system (Fig. 6.106):

Fig. 6.106 System complexity

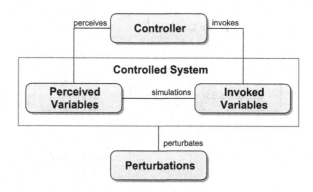

The larger the variety of actions available to a control system, the larger the variety of perturbations it is able to compensate.

IEEE[116] (2000) defines the concepts of *system*, *architecture*, and the relationships between them. IEEE leaves open the exact nature, form, or purpose of a system. Basically, anything can be viewed as a system (e.g., a technical system, a company, a service, or a system of systems). Stakeholders have interests (*concerns*) in a system. Every system has an architecture. However, architecture is immaterial, which is why architecture descriptions are needed to make system architecture tangible. Architects use architecture descriptions to understand, share, and evolve designs. Systems inhabit their environment, so the system's environment represents the various influences on the system. An architecture asset is a specific type of system. In the IEEE 2000 standard, *architecture of a system* is defined as (Fig. 6.107):

---

[116]The Institute of Electrical and Electronics Engineers (IEEE) is a professional association for electronic engineering and electrical engineering.

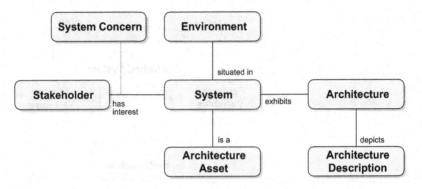

Fig. 6.107 System and architecture

[...] fundamental concepts or properties of a system in its environment embodied in its elements, relationships, and in the principles of its design and evolution.

Asset is an item of value owned. (Merriam-Webster Dictionary 2020)

Now that we have conceptually clarified building block, architecture building block, system, and system architecture, we clarify architecture asset. An *architecture asset* is a building block that is significant from an architectural point of view. At the same time, an architecture asset is a system in terms of its autonomy, completeness, and wholeness. Architecture assets are architecturally relevant, precious building blocks of decent size and possibly related to others. They have significant lifespans and therefore require adequate lifecycle management. Inappropriate management of architecture assets inevitably undermines other investments that architecture functions make to fulfill their mission and mandate.

In the context of this pattern language, I distinguish between four types of architecture assets: landscape assets, structural assets, reference assets, and methodological assets. Landscape assets are architecture assets such as services, applications, or platforms that make up architecture landscapes. Structural assets are assets, like architecture domains, that represent decent, delineated enterprise interest areas. The purpose of a structural asset is to provide structure and order. Structural assets, therefore, orderly group and arrange other assets. Reference assets have the character of an architecture-related template. Examples include architecture roadmaps, guidelines, patterns, or principles. Methodical assets are assets that guide and direct the architect in the systematic execution of activities and knowledge acquisition (Fig. 6.108).

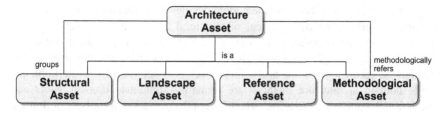

Fig. 6.108 Architecture asset types

The landscape is a defined area of management interest within an enterprise. Landscapes comprise landscape assets. The totality of all landscape parts is the enterprise landscape (i.e., enterprise domain). Service, application, platform, information, technology, but also enterprise services are landscape asset examples. Landscapes are classified according to different categories, such as the *business versus technical* dichotomy (**BUSINESS VERSUS TECHNICAL**).

Structural assets are the pivotal assets within the domain architecture discipline. Structural assets represent containers that can be used to manage landscape assets as a coherent whole. However, structural assets can also contain other structural assets and thus be part of larger container wholes themselves (**DOMAIN ARCHITECTURE DISCIPLINE**).

Methodological assets define methods, processes, and view models to carefully manage corresponding architecture assets. For example, a solution architecture method guides the creation or evolution of landscape assets such as applications or platforms. Three types of methodological assets are distinguished: methodologies for developing architectures (*architecture elaboration*), methodologies for developing and utilizing reference architectures (*reference architecture*), and methods for assessing architectures (*architecture assessment*) (Fig. 6.109).

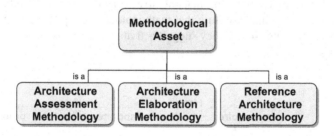

Fig. 6.109 Methodological asset

Your architecture elaboration methodologies describe the process of systematic elaboration and further development of structural and landscape assets. Domain architecture methods consider the assets they develop as order-creating containers and accordingly strongly emphasize an inventory perspective. Solution architecture methods, in contrast, view the assets they develop as solutions to given problems. While domain architecture methods are primarily applied to domain assets and solution architecture methods are primarily applied to landscape assets, a domain asset can be viewed completely validly as a solution, or a landscape asset can be viewed from an inventory perspective. This means that domain architecture methods can be applied to landscape assets and solution architecture methods can be applied to domain assets at any time (SOLUTION ARCHITECTURE METHODOLOGY, DOMAIN ARCHITECTURE METHODOLOGY).

Your reference architecture methodology explains how to systematically identify, define, propose, and approve reference objects such as architecture roadmaps, patterns, or principles (REFERENCE ARCHITECTURE METHODOLOGY).

Ensure that your architecture assessment method can be adapted to assess any asset type. Use your assessment methodology to evaluate the adequacy of the structural, landscape, and reference assets with respect to specific evaluation criteria. For example, apply your assessment methodology to a domain asset to identify systematic deficiencies or existing redundancies in the domain and respond with appropriate measures to improve the situation. As another example, you apply the assessment methodology to a platform or other landscape assets to check whether architects have correctly adopted the prescribed patterns when they developed or evolved the platform (ARCHITECTURE ASSESSMENT METHODOLOGY).

Define a general state set for your asset types. Assets are in a defined state at all times—regardless of whether they are explicitly managed. Besides, assets undergo state transitions. For example, an architecture pattern that has been proposed and accepted by an architecture committee can change its status from *proposed* to *published*. Avoid status terms that refer to state transitions, such as *planning* or *decommissioning*, and prefer terms that refer to assumed states, for example, *planned* or *decommissioned*. Finally, ensure that methodologies and platforms consistently refer to the assets states so that they suggest activities that represent state transitions (Fig. 6.110).

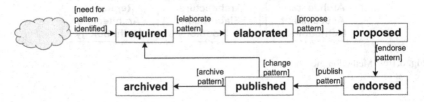

Fig. 6.110 Reference asset states

Clarify at which architecture level particular assets are primarily present as well as assets that may be visible at multiple levels simultaneously. For example, a critical application that is relevant at both the domain and enterprise levels must be visible at both architecture levels. Assets that emerge from other assets, such as architecture domains, always exist at an aggregate level. Unlike significant assets, an application that is merely relevant in a single domain might exist at solution level only (ARCHITECTURE LEVEL).

Assign an architect to each of your assets to ensure that your most valuable assets are managed carefully and responsibly. Remember to not only assign ownership to currently named assets but also consider which previously unnamed assets deserve the attention of your architecture function. Remember that every connection between two, say, landscape assets in turn creates a new asset—even if that asset may remain nameless and unmanaged (ARCHITECTURE OWNERSHIP, ARCHITECTURE DEMARCATION).

Charge your governance organization with the planning, creation, and evolution of both the methodological assets (*evaluation method, elaboration method, reference architecture method*) and the platform of your architecture function. Also, empower your governance organization with responsibility for any enterprise-wide reference assets such as enterprise-level patterns or principles (ARCHITECTURE GOVERNANCE).

Provide an architecture method for each asset type in your enterprise to systematically plan, create, and develop assets. Delegate management of asset-specific data points and attribute groups to the appropriate viewpoints in your view models. Specify in your architecture elaboration method, for example, for all assets how their data architecture should be developed. Then clarify in your architecture view model the differences in creating the data viewpoint for an application versus an information asset (YOUR OWN ARCHITECTURE METHODOLOGY, YOUR OWN ARCHITECTURE VIEW MODEL).

6.8.3   Landscape Asset

If different landscape types and their interrelationships are not sufficiently differentiated and methodically recognized, they will be inadequately identified, planned, designed, implemented, and managed over their lifecycles. Therefore, differentiating landscape asset types is as important as clarifying the key relationships that exist between them.

A *landscape* is a defined area of management interests within an enterprise.

The components of landscapes are landscape assets, while landscapes are in turn components of the enterprise landscape (*enterprise domain*).

A *landscape asset* is an architecture asset that contributes to the formation of a landscape.

Typical examples of landscape assets are *service*, *application*, *platform*, *information*, or *technology*. However, none of these (or similar) asset categories are unambiguously defined. Even standard architecture modeling languages, like ArchiMate,[117] provide modeling elements that require further specification and adaptation to enterprise contexts.

Do not despair if you cannot find *the* perfect definition for *service* or *application* right off the bat. More importantly, differentiate the types of landscape assets that are critical to managing your enterprise landscapes. As a sort of asset type nucleus, I recommend working with a set of landscape assets similar to those I propose in this pattern. Therefore, this pattern outlines several sufficiently differentiated landscape assets, the key relationships between them, and suggestions for their specific adaption.

It does not matter whether you consider the proposal of this pattern or another selection of essential landscape asset types. In either case, you must choose an appropriate approach for your specific enterprise needs. It is important to delineate landscape asset types in order to clearly distinguish them. Regardless of how you distinguish asset types, your definitions cast long shadows and have a significant impact over time. For example, your definition of the *application* concept determines how you count applications and calculate the total number of applications in your enterprise. Therefore, your application definition also determines the number of owners you need if you decide to architecturally own a particular type of landscape asset (ARCHITECTURE OWNERSHIP).

Add a *logical versus physical* dimension orthogonally to all landscape asset types. This dimension allows you to explicitly distinguish between logical architecture and physical architecture descriptions and keep them apart. At the same time, the distinction allows you to link the logical architecture representation of an application with its physical representation. The application App$_A$'s logical architecture is stored as a single entity in an architecture repository, while App$_A$'s physical architecture is scanned and kept up to date in a configuration management system[118] (CMS). By distinguishing between logical and physical architecture, both are recognized as having equal perspectives on landscape assets. This sets the stage for

---

[117] ArchiMate is an open and independent architectural modeling language that intends to support architecture analysis and description unambiguously. It is an Open Group standard.

[118] A configuration management system or database (CMS/CMDB) is a system for storing information about an organization's critical assets and the relationships between them. Assets in a CMS/CMDB are referred to as configuration items (CI). CI examples include virtual and physical compute nodes, network components, end-user devices, databases, application servers, directory services, transaction monitors, or application software components. A CMS/CMDB provides a means of understanding an organization's critical assets and their relationships at the physical instance level.

capturing, maintaining, and leveraging the relationships between logical and physical assets. Define these and other complementary dimensions in your architecture language and essential domain taxonomies (**ARCHITECTURE LANGUAGE, DOMAIN TAXONOMY**) (Fig. 6.111).

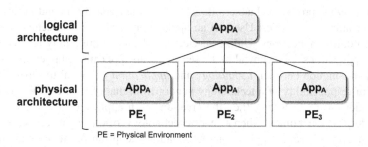

Fig. 6.111 Logical versus physical landscape assets

You are probably already working with a defined set of landscape asset types in your enterprise—a set more or less suitable and differentiated. Nevertheless, seriously compare your types with those suggested here to eliminate or at least minimize ambiguity and ensure that you have all the important landscape types actively on your organization's radar. My selection of five landscape types, including their interrelationships, is simple and compact. It gives you a solid baseline reference and can serve as a starting point to rethink the landscape types you distinguish in your enterprise: *service, application, information, platform,* and *technology* (Fig. 6.112).

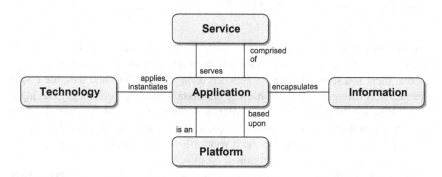

Fig. 6.112 Landscape asset types

Services are more than purely technical systems—they are socio-technical systems that provide valuable capabilities through their offerings. Services enable an intangible exchange of value (in whole or in part) between the party providing the service (i.e., service provider) and the party consuming it (i.e., service consumer). A service consumer may itself be a service.

Applications provide valuable functionality to their consumers and in this sense are comparable to services. Users of an application can be human actors, services, but also other applications. Unlike services, applications are purely technical systems. Applications are technical in the sense that an application applies technology.

This distinction between *technology* and *application* is critical to separating the scope of responsibility of a technology vendor from that of your organization. The application of a technology (i.e., the creation of an application by instantiating a technology) is the moment when a generic technology, offered by a vendor, becomes your enterprise-specific application. Applications adapt an original technology to meet the needs of an organization.

In addition, an *application* encapsulates *information*—to a certain extent, it wraps information and controls access to it. As you collect, store, change, and remove information through applications, you also use applications to find and read information.

After all, applications are platform-based. This means that *platforms* host and operate *applications*. At the same time, platforms are themselves applications, as platforms also use technologies, encapsulate information, and rely on the capabilities of other platforms.

Service

A *service* is useful labour that does not produce a tangible commodity. (Merriam-Webster Dictionary 2020)

In the broad definition of *enterprise service* in Chap. 4, I question (and eventually cancel) the tangibility criterion in Merriam-Webster's definition. However, I recognize that there is a subtle difference between intangible services and tangible goods or products. Visiting a café and ordering a croissant goes beyond simply buying a product (i.e., the croissant). The café offers a wider range of options, and the staff will advise you if you have any special requests (e.g., due to an allergy). The waiter also comes to your table to inquire about your order or facilitate the payment process and offer you various payment options.

Some service definitions do not consider the (physical) nature of the service itself or its offering as definition criteria. These definitions prefer a declarative approach to the service definition. They define a number of service attributes by which a service uniquely represents its offering (Huppertz 2012).

Regardless of which approach you choose to defining services, service-level agreements (SLA) express the service-related warranties through an interface agreement between the service provider and the relevant consumer of a service. Service-level agreements can be formal or informal; they often imply legal or warranty obligations that service providers have to consumers. Typical components of a service-level agreement are presented in Table 6.7.

Table 6.7 SLA attributes

SLA attribute	Description
Response time	Time that elapses between a received service request and a provided response
Availability	Indicates how permanently and reliably a service is expected to respond to requests
Recovery time objective (RTO)	Indication of how long it will take for a service to be restored in the event of an outage
Recovery point objective (RPO)	Commits the service to a maximum time period during which data could be lost in the event of a failure

Introduce service classification schemes that allow you to differentiate between services from an architectural perspective. For example, distinguish between services that contribute directly to the business outcome and services that only contribute indirectly. A service that contributes directly to the bottom line may serve only one domain. In contrast, a service that contributes indirectly often has architectural weight because it provides capabilities for many domains. Be careful not to confuse the terms of *technology* and *technical*. While *technology* refers to a landscape asset type, *technical* refers to the fact that an asset makes an indirect (i.e., technical) rather than a direct (i.e., business) contribution to business success (**BUSINESS VERSUS TECHNICAL**) (Fig. 6.113).

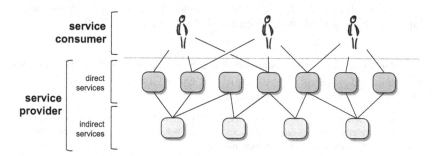

Fig. 6.113 Direct versus indirect service contributions

Consider a service classification that differentiates services based on the level of *customer involvement* and *delivery time*. A-services are personalized customization engagements with little potential for standardization (e.g., general architecture consulting). B-services also require adaptation, but unlike A-services, there is relevant standardization potential (e.g., specialized architecture consulting based on a standardized consulting method). C-services require much less customer involvement while their delivery is terribly slow. Consider, for example, the development of a data center or call center architecture. Finally, D-services are services that are both standardized and can be delivered quickly, for example, a standard service with little or no architecture involvement (Fig. 6.114).

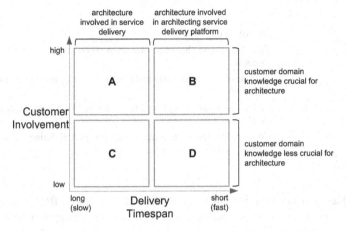

Fig. 6.114 Service dichotomy—customer involvement versus delivery time

Application and Platform

> *Application* is an act of applying. (Merriam-Webster Dictionary 2020)
>   *Application* is a program [...] that performs a particular task. (Merriam-Webster Dictionary 2020)
>   *Platform* is a vehicle [...] used for a particular purpose or to carry a usually specified kind of equipment. (Merriam-Webster Dictionary 2020)

Similar to service, many attempts have been made to define the notion of *application* and *platform*. For example, the Open Group (Open Group TOGAF 2020b) defines *application component* as:

[...] an encapsulation of application functionality aligned to implementation structure, which is modular and replaceable. It encapsulates its behavior and data, provides capabilities, and makes them available through interfaces.

The Open Group defines *application platform* as:

[...] collection of technology components of hardware and software that provide the capabilities used to support applications.

Prefer application and platform definitions that focus less on technical aspects (e.g., hardware or software) and more strongly recognize the relativity of these concepts. For example, the Open Group definition of an application platform recognizes landscape assets as platforms only if they support applications. But how about a platform that hosts other platforms or a platform that provides capabilities consumed directly by a service but does not directly support applications?

Martin Fowler takes a teleological approach to defining *application* (similar to Paul Huppertz with the definition of *service*):

> *Applications* are social constructions: a body of code that is seen by developers as a single unit, a group of functionalities that business customers see as a single unit, an initiative that those with the money see as a single budget. (Fowler 2006)

Consider heuristics as an alternative to the definitions above. Base your heuristics on the needs of your business. For example, use a questionnaire and use the number of positive responses to calibrate an *application versus platform* threshold (Table 6.8).

Table 6.8 Application definition heuristics

Question	Indication
Does the landscape asset provide cohesive capabilities that are directly (or indirectly) valuable to your business?	Directly valuable capabilities indicate an application
Is the landscape asset self-contained and does it require regular, recurring attention?	Indicates need for active asset management over its lifetime—thus indicating an *application* or *platform*, but not a *technology*
Was the landscape asset a primary result of a project, or were projects undertaken to modify or develop it?	Indicates a service, an application, or platform, but not a technology
Is the landscape asset used by clearly identifiable customers?	Indicates a service, an application, or platform, but not a technology
Is the landscape asset offered commercially?	Indicates a technology
Is the landscape asset recognized as an asset that provides critical functions in your business?	Indicates a business service, application, or platform

Information

> *Information* is the knowledge obtained from investigation, study, or instruction or the communication and reception of knowledge. (Merriam-Webster Dictionary 2020)

Despite the mantra *information is the new oil*, most companies do not even fulfill the prerequisites for exploiting the new oil. Information has no life of its own but is often perceived as an application appendage. Similar inattention to information is found in methodological frameworks—whether architectural or non-architectural.

For a very long time, active landscape asset types like *services* or *applications* have outweighed their relatively passive counterparts like *information*. Relatively new capabilities for managing and mining[119] the vast amount of data collected over a long period of time have promoted information to first-class citizens in many enterprises. Information is emancipating itself from its functional application containers.

Information is examined, terminologically differentiated, discussed, explained, and standardized in the respective sciences, methods, and, not least, industry frameworks. Richard Luke Millard (2001), for example, proposes an evolution scheme that reflects information states and state transitions toward knowledge growth (Fig. 6.115).

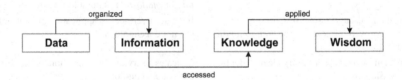

Fig. 6.115 Information evolution schema

Structured versus *unstructured* information is another essential dichotomy from an architectural perspective. While structured information conforms to a defined scheme to be stored, accessed, or manipulated, unstructured information does not conform to a rigid data schema and is examined using different methods. Architecture approaches that deal with structured and with unstructured information differ considerably.

Distinguish between *business* and *operational* information. Business information is causally related to the business and thus contributes directly to business results. Operational information, on the other hand, has a causal relationship, for example,

---

[119] Data mining is the systematic application of statistical methods to vast amounts of data with the goal of identifying cross-connections, patterns, and trends. Thus, data mining is about extracting knowledge from already existing data and not about generating new data.

with the availability of support, incident management, or problem resolution. Operational information therefore contributes indirectly to business results.

Moreover, distinguish between *master data* and *reference data* in your enterprise. Reference data is used to classify other data and rarely changes over time. Country codes, time zones, or units of measurement are examples of reference data. Master data provides context for many business transactions by representing key entities in your enterprise. Examples of master data include customer or supplier data. Both reference and master data are extremely relevant to architecture, as they are ubiquitously required by all landscape assets in your enterprise.

If information is the new oil, the information requires measures and controls to protect it from careless handling (e.g., misinterpretation, accidental loss or destruction, or leakage). Therefore, other classification schemes exist. Trust classification is used, for example, when different parties want to share information explicitly but at the same time need to restrict access to others. Typical classifiers are *secret*, *restricted*, *confidential*, *business only*, or *public*.

Also distinguish *transactional information* from *meta-information*. Transaction information is the reason your applications exist. It is inevitably created by people using your applications and entering new orders into an order management application, for example. Meta-information, on the other hand, is information about information. A company is not primarily interested in meta-information. However, they make transaction information more valuable. For example, an architecture function uses meta-information to measure and inform the performance of an information delivery process. Finally, meta-information can be used to design of highly adaptable application- or platform architectures, like generator-based architecture approaches[120] or metaprogramming.[121] However, the adaptability of such architecture approaches always pays the price of increased complexity.

Technology

> *Technology* is the study and knowledge of the practical, especially industrial, use of scientific discoveries. (Cambridge Dictionary 2020)

Technology is the last landscape asset type that is distinguished in this pattern. Think of technology as an off-the-shelf offering from a technology provider. You use the off-the-shelf portion when you apply technology in your organization. In other words, when you instantiate a technology to create an application or platform tailored to your needs. Do not limit your consideration to technology you use in your own data centers. The off-the-shelf portion of a cloud offering is no different than a software product you bought from a vendor's storefront and installed in your data center (OFF-THE-SHELF SOLUTION).

---

[120] Generator-based architecture approaches decouple solution specifications from their physical generation. They increase domain specificity and the degree of abstraction of the models that architects use to represent a solution. Generators receive architectural models as inputs and create artifacts at the source level or related physical structures as outputs.

[121] Metaprogramming is a programming technique in which computer programs treat other programs as data. A metaprogramming-based program reads, generates, transforms, or interprets another program.

Note that while there are many generic suggestions for relevant asset sets (e.g., the TOGAF content metamodel[122]), you ultimately need to identify your own meaningful set of landscape assets and implement their deliberate management in your organization.

6.8.4   Off-the-Shelf Solution

Even landscape assets that are essentially based on standard solutions (*off-the-shelf solutions*) still require architecture attention. The internal architecture of an off-the-shelf solution is acquired with the product. Hence, you do not need to elaborate the inner architecture yourself—you do not even need to know it. The architecture of adapting an off-the-shelf solution to the needs of an organization (*adaptation architecture*), on the other hand, requires the full attention of your architecture function. At the same time, architecture functions underestimate the effort associated with elaborating and evolving adaptation architectures resulting in poor evolvability, reusability, or operability of corresponding landscape assets.

> Something *off-the-shelf* is not specially designed or custom-made. (Merriam-Webster Dictionary 2020)

Off-the-shelf solutions are essentially technology assets representing semi-finished assets from a solution perspective. While an off-the-shelf solution is an immediately deployable technology, as vendors would primarily emphasize, it is not yet a solution adapted to your situation. However, the technology's immediate applicability is mistakenly equated with a solution for a particular situation. A resulting serious misunderstanding is that architecture-related efforts or interventions are superfluous when deploying off-the-shelf solutions (LANDSCAPE ASSET).

We can distinguish four different types of building blocks that technology assets usually consist of. Three of the four types of building blocks enable customization of off-the-shelf solutions to meet enterprise-specific requirements. *Modifiability hooks* enable customization of the technology asset to meet functional and non-functional requirements in a particular enterprise context. Architecture approaches that create appropriate adaptability hooks include metaprogramming[123]-based architectures.

---

[122] While metamodels specify rules needed to create corresponding models, the TOGAF content metamodel proposes a rule set for assets that TOGAF believes an architecture function should consciously manage and differentiate. TOGAF abbreviates *The Open Group Architecture Framework*, which proposes an approach to design, plan, implement, and govern enterprise architecture. It describes a generic method for developing architectures. TOGAF suggests a common vocabulary, an adaptable role model, general architecture artifacts, tooling, and a generic content metamodel.

[123] Metaprogramming is a programming technique in which computer programs treat other programs as data. A metaprogramming-based program reads, generates, transforms, or interprets another program.

Another example is architectures that enable modifications to functional and non-functional capabilities of a standard solution via inversion of control[124] approaches. *Reference and master data* similarly provide ways to embed a technology asset in a particular enterprise environment and integrate it with other assets. For example, off-the-shelf solutions provide a choice of predefined export or import formats to share data with other landscape assets in the enterprise. *Transaction data* reflects the transactions that occur over the lifetime of standard solutions. In the case of an architecture tool based on a corresponding technology asset, for example, these are the models that architects have created. The only area of technology assets that is not open to customization is their *compilation base* (Fig. 6.116).

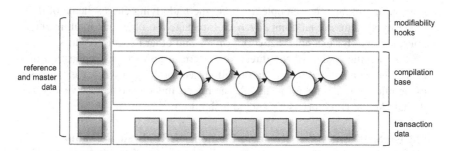

Fig. 6.116   Off-the-shelf solution

The architecture inherently inscribed in a technology asset already determines which building block types it contains and how they are architecturally arranged to implement its capabilities. The architecture inherent in a technology asset also determines what design decisions you need to make when deriving your enterprise-specific solution from a technology asset. In summary, we can say that technology assets are fundamentally always off-the-shelf solutions. At the same time, we also recognize that you need to make your own architecture-related decisions to turn technology assets into useful enterprise applications. Let us look at two examples of architecture decisions that turn a technology asset into a useful application (**ARCHITECTURE DECISION**).

> **Off-the-Shelf Directory System Example**
> Company A plans to deploy a directory system[125] and purchases a corresponding technology landscape asset, for example, Microsoft's Active

(continued)

---

[124] Inversion of control (IoC) inverts the control flow compared to the conventional control flow. In IoC, user-defined parts of a computer program receive the flow of control from a framework surrounding these parts.

[125] Directory systems assign names and attributes to network resources and their respective network addresses. Directory systems provide a shared information infrastructure for managing and finding network resources. Examples of network resources are volumes, folders, files, printers, users, or groups.

Directory.[126] A directory system is more of a technical technology asset because it offers technical capabilities.

Microsoft designed the architecture of Active Directory. Microsoft's system enables company A to install directory system copies (i.e., replicas) across many of its network compute nodes.

The directory system architecture, as designed by Microsoft, provides for company A to design a replication scheme that specifies how the directory replicas are connected. Company A can also specify which of the replicas may be written to and which may be read-only instead.

The Active Directory architecture provides company A with further customization options, for example, defining the underlying class schema of the directory system so that company A can manage the objects it is ultimately interested in—for example, network printers and other network devices.

The specific design of the directory system in terms of its replication or class schema and the directory information tree for company A are examples of significant design decisions that A's architects must make themselves, even though Active Directory is a standard technology.

Off-the-Shelf Enterprise Resource Planning (ERP) System Example
Company A is planning to introduce an ERP[127] system. ERP systems are off-the-shelf solutions offering business capabilities.

The ERP system vendor has provided in its initial architecture that companies can define a schema of logically separated tenants. The multi-tenancy[128] scheme is based on a common compilation basis and allows the parallel design, implementation, and operation of multiple logically separated tenants.

Company A defines one tenant for each of its two business units A_1 and A_2 in the ERP system. Different master data is then loaded for tenants MA_1 and MA_2. Recruitment processes are also designed differently in MA_1 and MA_2 to optimally meet the specific staffing needs of the two business units.

Both design decisions (i.e., specific multi-tenant design and recruiting process design) are decisions that company A cannot easily reverse—i.e., architectural decisions that company A makes when it converts the off-the-shelf ERP system into its application.

---

[126] Active Directory™ is a directory service developed by Microsoft for Windows domain networks and is included in Windows Server operating systems.

[127] Enterprise resource planning (ERP) is the integrated management of the most important business processes. An ERP system covers central functional areas shared by all companies, such as financial accounting, human resources, manufacturing, order fulfillment, supply chain management, or customer relationship management.

[128] Multi-tenancy design is an approach in which a single physical solution serves multiple clients (i.e., tenant). Systems adopting a multi-tenancy architecture provide physically shared resources while ensuring logically separated and tenant-specific spaces. Multi-tenant architectures are designed to provide each tenant with a dedicated share of a physical instance, where such share includes data, configuration, user administration, and tenant-specific functional as well as non-functional properties.

Accurately anticipating design decisions that have not yet been made and assessing their architecture significance is difficult or even impossible. Therefore, use heuristics to check the architecture relevance of off-the-shelf solutions. A list of simple questions supports pragmatic clarification of relevance—for example, questions like those presented in Table 6.9 (ARCHITECTURE SIGNIFICANCE).

Table 6.9   Off-the-shelf solution relevance heuristics

Question	Indication
What information and how much information is likely to be exchanged between the off-the-shelf solution and other landscape assets?	Extensive information exchange indicates higher architectural relevance, while relative information isolation of an asset under consideration indicates lower relevance
How likely are frequent or fundamental changes after the initial deployment of the considered off-the-shelf solution (e.g., frequently changing regulatory requirements)?	Anticipated frequent requirement changes necessitate increased evolvability of a solution, which raises architectural relevance for a corresponding off-the-shelf asset
How important is seamlessly embedding and monitoring the off-the-shelf solution in your enterprise's operating environment (e.g., to present expected MIBs[a] to system monitoring agents)?	The more intensive and significant the embedding and monitoring of an off-the-shelf solution is for you, the more relevant is its support by your architecture function
How seamlessly can you onboard the off-the-shelf solution onto security platforms and other security-related capabilities in your enterprise (e.g., to participate in your organization's authentication and authorization standards)?	If standard solutions can be seamlessly connected to platforms that themselves implement standards (e.g., security standards), this indicates relatively less architectural relevance than would be the case otherwise
To what extent is the off-the-shelf solution under consideration based on operational platforms in your organization (e.g., to ensure its availability, scalability, performance, or maintainability)?	If there is a tight coupling of the off-the-shelf solution to operational platforms in your organization, this tight coupling indicates increased architectural relevance
Does a technology asset's customization approach require special architectural attention (e.g., if there are no code and release management capabilities for customizations in a technology asset)?	From more complex customization approaches (e.g., interpreters[b]), you can conclude higher architecture relevance than for limited customization options such as point-and-click adaptation[c]

[a]Management information base (MIB) is a database used to manage the entities in a communication network. MIBs are also queried by monitoring agents
[b]Interpreters are built into systems to enable powerful customization hooks via which one can massively optimize the off-the-shelf capabilities of a system. Interpreters require programming skills. However, they offer programmable access to the off-the-shelf system's object model—and thus push the limits of adaptation toward the respective programmers' ambition and imagination
[c]Point-and-click adaptation is a customization approach in which typically non-experts are guided through a series of adjustment options from which they select their desired ones by simple mouse clicks or similar low-effort interventions

Establish criteria for recognizing the architecture relevance of introducing off-the-shelf solutions in your organization. Embed relevance verification based on these criteria in your methodologies and ensure that your architecture function is appropriately involved when the complexity and scale of an appropriate adaption architecture suggests increased architecture attention (YOUR OWN ARCHITECTURE METHODOLOGY, ARCHITECTURE MANDATE, ARCHITECTURE OWNERSHIP).

Note that off-the-shelf solutions exist for business and for technical capabilities. Off-the-shelf solutions that offer business capabilities primarily focus on functional optimization in the context of the corresponding business domain. Off-the-shelf solutions that offer technical capabilities, on the other hand, are often offered as shared platforms, which is why non-functional optimization (e.g., scalability, availability, security, and performance) is in their foreground. Hence, consider the business versus technical differentiation when fine-tuning your architecture contributions (BUSINESS VERSUS TECHNICAL).

6.9   Architecture Elaboration

The *architecture elaboration* patterns support an architecture function in laying the groundwork for its contributions along the enterprise value chain. The *architecture-significance* pattern introduces significance as a differentiator that distinguishes architecture-relevant from architecture-irrelevant areas of responsibility. The *architecture condition* pattern uses the significance metric to assist your architecture function focus on architecture-relevant conditions. The *architecture level* pattern points out differences in granularity and level of detail and recommends measures to adequately align your architecture function with them. While the *architecture approach* pattern introduces partial architecture or micro-architecture as concepts, the *architecture artifact* pattern addresses the tangible capture side of architecture manifestation. The *architecture alternatives* pattern alerts your architecture function of its own tunnel vision and conditioning and recommends approaches to constructively overcome them. While the *business versus technical* pattern introduces a central dichotomy to distinguish semantically rich and context-bound from context-free assets, the *baseline architecture versus target architecture* pattern differentiates states of an asset along its planning and development chronology.

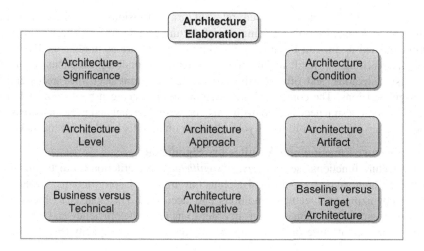

6.9.1   Architecture Significance

The lack of criteria to meaningfully distinguish between relevant and irrelevant architectural areas of interest leads to over- or under-allocation of architecture capacity and a misguided focus. Inaccurate prioritization inevitably leads to inefficiency and ineffectiveness of architecture contributions.

Significance indicates something is having or is likely to having relevant influence or effect. (Merriam-Webster Dictionary 2020)

   Architecture is the set of *significant design decisions* that shape a system, where significant is measured by cost of change. (Booch 2009)

Grady Booch proposes an architecture definition that recognizes only over time whether a measure was an architecture measure. Booch defines architecture in terms of the effects that a design decision has (*effect*), rather than the original characteristics of a decision (*cause*) (Fig. 6.117).

Fig. 6.117 Architecture definition by caused effect

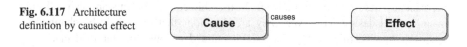

According to Booch, architecture-relevant design decisions are decisions that are difficult to change later on. Undoing an architecture decision that has been made and implemented is difficult because architecture decisions are as fundamental as they are far-reaching. Difficult in this context means that undoing decisions is labor-intensive, tedious, and often costly. Architecture-relevant decisions are essential design decisions. The concept of architectural significance can be generalized and used beyond design decisions to distinguish between relevant and irrelevant areas of architecture interest and to focus your attention on architecturally relevant issues.

Architecture Function and Architecture Significance
Architecture functions use *architecture significance* as a criterion for distinguishing between architecture-relevant and architecture-irrelevant contributions, especially for recognizing architecture conditions and decisions. The goal is to focus and prioritize architecture contributions in order to increase the efficiency and effectiveness of the architecture function—ultimately to optimize its capacity (Fig. 6.118).

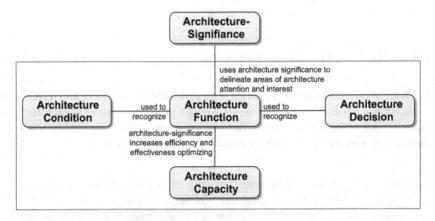

Fig. 6.118 Architecture function and architecture significance

Design decisions are the effects of *design causes*, and they represent a specific part of an overall design. The cause and effect of an architecture decision are two sides of the same architecture-significance coin. In short, we can say that an architecture cause causes an architecture decision. Analogously, non-architecture decisions are effects of non-architecture causes. Architecture decisions are the permanent parts of an overall *design*. Non-architecture decisions are also reflected in an overall design. However, they are decisions that can easily be changed or reversed. In this, they differ from architecture decisions. Similar to decisions, a distinction is made between architecture and non-architecture causes (e.g., *architecture conditions*) (Fig. 6.119).

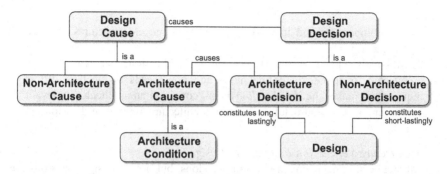

Fig. 6.119 Architecture significance of design causes and decisions

Architecture Decision Example

An insurance company developed an application for its associates. The application enables its users to capture insurance claims in detail, for example, a traffic accident reported by an insurance customer. Once a case is recorded, the application adds information from other applications to the record and follows the processing of the insurance case to its end.

The architecture team designed the application in a thin-client style.[129] Thin-client architectures are characterized by minimal installation footprint on the client computer, so most application modules reside on a central server. A suitable network connection is required between an application's thin client and its server-side components.

During the first 2 years of successful business activity, new requirements for the insurance application emerged. One of the new requirements wants to enable insurance agents to record insurance claims on-site and in dialogue with customers. However, network coverage at customer locations cannot always be guaranteed. Therefore, the insurance application must work even when there is no active Internet connection. In other words, the application must also be (at least partially) functional in offline mode.

The *offline requirement* appears innocent and small at first glance. However, this view is deceptive, and the assessment is wrong. You cannot simply convert an application design that supports operation in *online mode* into a design that allows the application to operate *offline*. An application design that hides the difference between online and offline mode from the user duplicates

(continued)

---

[129]The thin-client style is a style of architecture in which a simple (low-performance) client computer establishes a remote connection to a server-based computing environment. While some application building blocks are executed on the client side, most of the application building blocks are on the server side.

critical components and intensively replicates data and structures between client and server.

Massively changing the design of an application that was initially architected to operate in online mode and now needs to meet an offline requirement makes the initial *online model* condition an architecture-relevant condition—a condition that has led to an architecture-significant decision.

Architecture Versus Non-architecture Design

All architecture decisions are design decisions, but not all design decisions are architecture decisions. While all design decisions are important, architecture decisions are essential. Stefan Bente et al. (2012) uses the terms *Design* (with uppercase "D") and *design* (with lowercase "d") to distinguish between architecture and non-architecture design decisions. He points out that the distinction between architecture and non-architecture design decisions is more of a gray area than a sharp delineation. For example, the design decision to arrange input fields on a web form in a certain way is a design decision with a small "d." However, if there is a requirement for the form fields to dynamically adapt to the form factor of a user device (e.g., through a layout manager[130]-based design), one would possibly speak of a design decision with a capital "D" (Fig. 6.120).

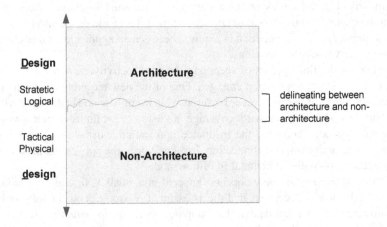

Fig. 6.120 Architecture versus non-architecture

---

[130] Layout managers are software components used to dynamically position user interface widgets, for example, optimally repositioning these in response to changing window sizes.

You cannot always clearly and unequivocally determine whether a given condition or decision is of architectural significance. At the same time, you increase the architecture function's productivity to the extent that you draw its attention to architecture-significant items and relieve it from insignificant contributions. So you need criteria that you can apply to conditions or decisions to be made to distinguish between design with a capital "D" (*architecture*) and design with a small "d" (*non-architecture*) (ARCHITECTURE CONDITION, ARCHITECTURE DECISION).

Define criteria to distinguish between architecture-significant and architecture-insignificant efforts. Hold the significance criteria against conditions or decisions to determine the extent of their significance. Ensure that your architects systematically examine conditions and decisions against the significance criteria and then base their focus and priority on the measurement outcome (Fig. 6.121).

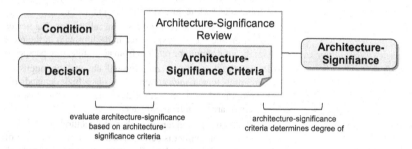

Fig. 6.121 Architecture-significance framework

Differentiate your criteria, for example, using a scale that expresses the extent to which a design decision or condition meets a significance criterion. For example, you can consider stakeholder importance to determine the significance of a condition in a more nuanced way. Different stakeholder significance levels help you define the significance of a condition more precisely. Consider further enhancing your criteria framework by introducing a *gut feeling indicator*. Such an indicator will allow your architects to express the level of gut instinct used in evaluating significance. Finally, you need concrete criteria you can apply to both design causes (*conditions*) and design *decisions* to reliably determine their level of significance.

Use this set of criteria, or questions, as a heuristic starting point to pragmatically approximate the architecture significance of conditions in your organization (Table 6.10).

Table 6.10 Architecture-significance heuristic for conditions

Question	Indication
Number of impacts caused by a given condition	Expected number of architecture decisions or architecture approaches required to address a condition. If a condition is likely to impact multiple architecture decisions simultaneously, it is more likely to be architecture-significant than conditions for which this does not apply
Stakeholder importance	Importance of the stakeholders who contributed to the condition, such as business stakeholders are more important than stakeholders representing technical concerns. A condition raised by important stakeholders tends to be more significant than conditions raised by less important stakeholders
Non-functionality	Non-functional conditions, such as availability, security, or performance conditions, often have a significant impact on the architecture. Consider all conditions affecting system quality attributes as architecture-significance candidates
Novelty	Degree to which the condition is unusual or new. The newer a condition and the less experience in dealing with it, the more significant it should be rated as from an architecture perspective
Volatility	Probability that a given condition will change continuously. Conditions that change continuously place high demands on the modifiability of a system and are therefore considered drivers of architecture significance
Degree of conflict	Conflict between a given and other architectural conditions. The degree of conflict is derived from the number of trade-offs required to resolve clashes. The more compromises are likely required to be found for a given condition, the more architecturally significant such condition is
Degree of strategic orientation	Extent to which a condition directly contributes to achieving the enterprise's strategic objectives. If a condition's estimated contribution to achieving strategic enterprise goals is high, it is to be assessed as more architecture-significant than if only few direct strategy contributions are made

Similar to the set of criteria and questions around conditions, you can use the following criteria as a heuristic starting point to approximate the significance of architecture decisions (Table 6.11).

Table 6.11 Architecture-significance heuristic for decisions

Question	Indication
Degree of risk	Degree to which a decision implies an architecture-related risk. The assessment is based on the probability of the risk in combination with its impact. If architectural risks associated with a decision are assessed as high, the architecture significance of corresponding decisions increases
Degree of change	Magnitude of change expected as a result of a decision, like the number of ripple effects caused by a decision. If an architecture decision inevitably leads to the need to make further architecture decisions, this decision is classified as architecture-significant
Degree of complexity	Estimated complexity associated with or resulting from a decision, such as the number of landscape assets and the number of their interdependencies that are collectively affected by a decision. The more building blocks are affected by a decision, the higher its architecture significance rating
Degree of supplier lock-in	Extent to which a decision results in a permanent commitment to a supplier or vendor. All decisions that result in tight lock-in are classified as architecture-significant—in particular, decisions that result in supplier lock-in that is almost impossible to reverse

Your solution architecture methodology in particular relies heavily on the concept of architecture significance, or rather, this concept permeates the entire methodology. Architecture significance is a means of assessing relevance, for example, verifying for given conditions of the problem space whether they also represent conditions of the architecture problem (i.e., whether they qualify as *architecture conditions*). Without an emphasis on architecture significance, your solution architecture methodology runs the risk of inefficiency, or ineffectiveness. Therefore, position the significance concept pivotally in your solution methodology and ensure that relevance assessments are at the beginning of each of your transformation journeys (SOLUTION ARCHITECTURE METHODOLOGY).

6.9.2 Architecture Level

Architectural considerations and contributions must consider the context in which they are created with common contextual factors coexisting with contribution-specific ones. The architecture level is a context dimension that defines the planning horizon, degree of strategic perspective, and the asset granularity for architecture contributions. Misjudging architecture levels as insignificant context variables leads to poor differentiation and over-unification of architecture contributions and perspectives.

Level is a position in a scale or rank (as of achievement, significance, or value). (Merriam-Webster Dictionary 2020)

Generally speaking, levels introduce structure, order, and sometimes hierarchy. In addition to structuring whole-part relationships, levels allow the explicit differentiation of building block granularities. The building block granularity is coarsest at the top level and becomes finer the further down the levels one progresses. In terms of building blocks, each level, in turn, represents a building block level. This means that all lower levels go into the upper level as building blocks.

Architecture Function and Architecture Level
Architecture functions associate architecture disciplines and their contributions with architecture levels, while governance organizations establish control and monitoring at and across levels. Architecture levels differentiate contributions along the dimensions of scale and granularity and are embedded in the architecture apparatus (Fig. 6.122).

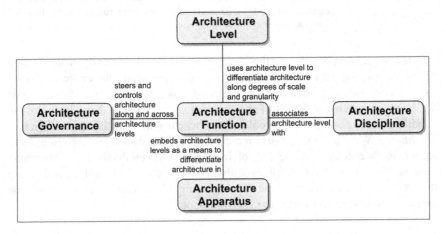

Fig. 6.122 Architecture function and architecture level

Architecture levels contextualize assets such as landscape assets or methodical assets, for example, by attributing enterprise-wide significance to a landscape asset that is visible at the enterprise level. In the case of methodological assets, such as a view model, an enterprise viewpoint is assigned a planning horizon of, say, 5 years. You define the exact number of levels required in your enterprise, with a minimum of three levels being common. Architecture levels are vertically linked so that each level (except the top and bottom levels) relates to exactly one level above and one below it. The levels enable conscious navigation between them, leading to a holistic enterprise architecture experience. Each level represents particular planning horizon, strategic perspective, and granularity of the assets it considers. In addition, levels introduce further contextual facets, for example, degree of abstraction, typical questions considered, or a specific mode of tool use. Architecture disciplines are associated with one or more levels. For example, solution and domain levels are associated with the solution architecture discipline, as both landscape assets and entire domains can be considered solutions to given problems (Fig. 6.123).

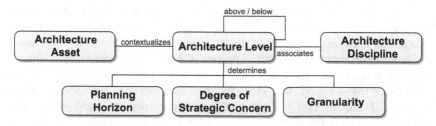

Fig. 6.123 Architecture level

Whenever architecture contributions are made, a methodology is applied, or a view model is instantiated, the level at which the activity is performed determines the planning horizon (e.g., 3 to 5 years at the enterprise level), the degree of strategic consideration (e.g., strategic at the enterprise level), or the granularity of the assets under consideration (e.g., enterprise assets at the enterprise level).

Architecture levels are a fundamental concept of order and orientation. Levels permeate virtually all patterns of this pattern language and contextualize all types of architecture assets. Introduce at least three levels (e.g., enterprise, domain, and solution level). You probably need more levels in your enterprise, and you can break down each of the three proposed levels further. Position landscape assets such as applications, platforms, or elementary information entities at the solution level. Set the planning horizon at this level to 1 year, for example. At the domain level, the main distinction is between structural assets (*domains*). Each domain manages its landscape assets, domain-specific methods, and reference assets—for example, domain-specific patterns. Domains can, in turn, be subdivided into sub-domains. This may lead to several domain levels you distinguish in your enterprise. Set the planning horizon at the domain level to 3 years, for example. The enterprise level is the level at which you consolidate domains from an enterprise perspective. You also manage enterprise-wide methods and reference assets at this level, such as enterprise-wide principles. The planning horizon at enterprise level is strategic, for example, 3 to 5 years (Fig. 6.124).

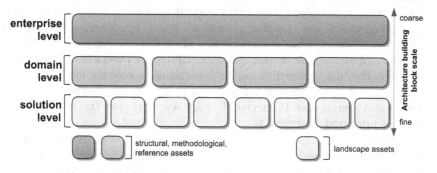

Fig. 6.124 Enterprise, domain, and solution level

Design your methods so that they take levels into account. For example, you can apply a solution architecture methodology at both the solution and domain level. You use the solution-level approach to design a landscape asset that needs to handle a solution-level problem. Similarly, use your solution architecture methodology at the domain level when you consider an entire domain as one big system—i.e., one big solution to one big problem. However, there will also be differences between the domain and solution level you will want to consider when designing your solution architecture method. For example, you will advise domain architects that they should focus on a few domain-spanning use cases when considering a domain as a large system. They should be careful not to get lost in small-scale use case deliberations (YOUR OWN ARCHITECTURE METHODOLOGY).

As an alternative to considering levels directly in your methods, you can address the consideration of levels via architecture adapters. In this case, you would design your methods to be more generic and develop one adapter per architecture level for your most important methods. Let us say you plan to apply your solution architecture method to your purchasing domain. Let us further assume you want to put a complementary focus on security. In this example, you would combine a domain-level adapter (i.e., for the solution perspective at the domain level) and a security adapter (i.e., for special focus on security) to appropriately adapt your problem-solving method (ARCHITECTURE METHODOLOGY ADAPTER, SOLUTION ARCHITECTURE METHODOLOGY).

Architecture view models, which are strongly linked to respective methods, also consider levels. While a functional viewpoint at the solution level looks at the internal building blocks of an application, the same functional viewpoint at the domain level shows the entire application as a building block. Therefore, viewpoint semantics are strongly influenced and determined by the level at which a view model is applied (YOUR OWN ARCHITECTURE VIEW MODEL).

Architecture traceability is closely linked to view models and is also fostered by levels. For example, you can get an overview of the company's most important domains at the enterprise level and understand how they are interrelated (*horizontal traceability*). You can also zoom into one of the domains at the enterprise level to get an overview of its subdomains (*vertical traceability*) or drill down into it to understand what assets it includes (ARCHITECTURE TRACEABILITY, ARCHITECTURE ASSET).

Each level is associated with at least one architecture discipline. However, it may be advantageous to use disciplines across all levels. For example, the solution architecture discipline looks at a domain as a whole from the perspective of *solving a problem*. Conversely, the domain architecture discipline views a landscape asset as a domain. The latter perspective can be instrumental in zooming into a landscape asset (e.g., application, platform, service) with an inventory or portfolio perspective (SOLUTION ARCHITECTURE DISCIPLINE, DOMAIN ARCHITECTURE DISCIPLINE, ENTERPRISE ARCHITECTURE DISCIPLINE).

Architecture levels are also crucial in organizational and governance matters. There may be only one person who assumes the role of enterprise architect. This person directs, guides, and controls multiple domain architects. A domain architect works with the enterprise architect to ensure concerted action between his and other domains. Similarly, the domain architect works with several solution architects, as they are responsible for planning and designing landscape assets in the domain. In this way, the domain architect, together with the solution architect, ensures that landscape asset planning and design are performed in a coordinated manner. The domain architecture further ensures that the domain perspective is considered in landscape designs. Architecture levels are essential to support vertical control structures and governance schemes (ORGANIZATIONAL REPLICATION, ARCHITECTURE GOVERNANCE).

6.9.3 Architecture Condition

Solutions are responses to problems in the sense that a solution absorbs the conditions representing its problem. Accordingly, a solution's architecture is shaped by absorbing architecturally relevant conditions which in turn represent forces and drivers of a problem. Inadequate architecture results are always also the result of insufficiently considered architecture conditions.

> A *condition* is a premise upon which the fulfillment of an agreement depends. (Merriam-Webster Dictionary 2020)

A solution addresses a problem by absorbing the conditions representing the problem. Conditions constrain the space to maneuver in solution endeavors. They can be divided into those that express a desire in your organization (e.g., requirements, principles), those that express uncertainty that you cannot ignore (e.g., assumptions), and those that express factors limiting the constitution of a solution (e.g., constraints).

Requirements represent the needs an organization desires to meet when solving a problem. Functional requirements are existential for a solution—they are the reason for the solution's existence. Functional requirements express *what* your organization expects from a solution, such as the ability to enter purchase orders into an order management application. While non-functional requirements are not the original reason for a solution's existence, they are usually existential, nonetheless. Non-functional requirements express *how* a solution must make its decisive contributions to be considered acceptable—for example, a performance requirement specifying the maximum acceptable response time for an order entry transaction. The term *requirement* expresses a need. The corresponding solution-related term is *capability*. While a requirement expresses a particular problem, a capability refers to the ability to address the corresponding problem. The terms capability and problem are dichotomous in that a capability absorbs a corresponding problem or sub-problem. Therefore, a functional capability refers to a solution property that addresses a related functional requirement. Accordingly, a non-functional capability refers to a solution property that addresses a respective non-functional requirement.

Similar to requirements, *principles* express a desire. In contrast, principles are much more vague and less specific to a particular solution. Requirements define what is considered concrete, tangible, and measurably useful in the face of a particular problem. Principles provide orientation by defining guardrails within which all solutions are supposed to evolve. For example, a principle requires that all solutions in a *transaction platform* domain *adopt a multi-threaded*[131] *architecture design*. To give another example, a *buy-over-build* principle defined at the enterprise level requires a particular justification for homegrown applications. In a final example, a maxim that demands all enterprise platforms to adhere to the *inversion of control*[132] principle favors architecture approaches that separate platform knowledge from business knowledge.

A *constraint* is a limiting or restrictive fact that you cannot ignore. Where requirements express a desire, constraints express facts that you cannot circumvent. For example, a constraint may be organizational in nature such as a challenging deadline for an architecture deliverable or a limited skill base in a project team that precludes the use of modern technologies.

Assumptions express relevant areas of uncertainty—*known unknowns* if you wish. An assumption is a condition that is likely, but not necessarily, to occur in the future. Assumptions can express uncertainty about something desired (e.g., requirement, principle) and uncertainty about expected limitations (i.e., constraints). Assumptions mark the fine line between conscious and unconscious uncertainty. Design decisions you based on assumptions are more likely to have to be reversed in the future. Assumptions are a good indication of reasonable investments in the evolutionary fitness of a corresponding solution. The evolutionary fitness of a solution (e.g., an application) increases by improving the extensibility or changeability of the corresponding solution. This is not about increasing the modifiability of the solution as a whole, but about targeted improvement of its changeability with respect to the capabilities and qualities whose future desired design is particularly uncertain due to an assumption.

Architecture Function and Architecture Condition

Architecture functions pay close attention to architecture conditions. They identify them in a set of overall given conditions using architecture-significance criteria. Architecture functions establish traceability between architecture conditions and approaches. They further generalize frequently recurring architecture conditions by converting them into requirement patterns (Fig. 6.125).

---

[131] Multithreading is the ability of a central processing unit to provide multiple threads of execution simultaneously. A multithreaded program contains two or more threads that run concurrently, with each thread parallelly performing a different task and making the best use of the available resources. A thread goes through different phases as part of its lifecycle. For example, a thread is born, started, run, and then dies.

[132] Inversion of Control (IoC) inverts the control flow compared to the conventional control flow. In IoC, user-defined parts of a computer program receive the flow of control from a framework surrounding these parts.

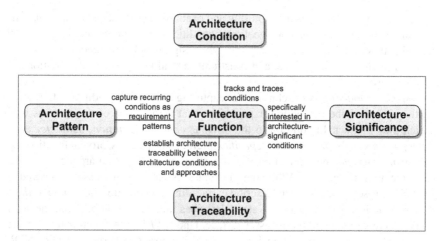

Fig. 6.125 Architecture function and architecture condition

Architecture Condition

An architecture condition is a condition that is architecture-significant and thus has an architecture impact. For example, an architecture constraint is an assertion of a fact that cannot be architecturally ignored. Examples of constraints that affect architecture are timeframe or budget (e.g., architectural superficiality due to time pressure or limited financial capacity in a project), resources (e.g., insufficient competence), or policies (e.g., compliance with technology standards) (ARCHITECTURE SIGNIFICANCE).

Architecture conditions shape the design of assets similar to how the stresses and forces of life shape the skeleton of us humans. They shape all types of assets—although the conditions differ significantly depending on asset type, for example, landscape assets such as applications, reference assets such as patterns, or structural assets such as domains (Fig. 6.126).

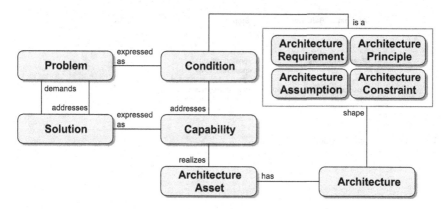

Fig. 6.126 Architecture condition

I present two techniques for capturing and examining architecture conditions, one for functional and one for non-functional conditions. Functional requirements fall into the functional condition category, while significant non-functional requirements, principles, assumptions, and constraints are all non-functional conditions.

Use Case

Use case modeling is a technique for capturing functional conditions. Use cases particularly describe behavioral expectations that actors have of the systems with which they interact. In addition to the obvious *name, description*, and *actor* attributes, a use case's *precondition specifies* prerequisites for its proper functioning. *Behavior* describes the interaction flow between an actor and an architecture asset implementing the use case. While the sunshine version of the use case is captured in the behavior section, architects describe extraordinary interaction flows under *alternative behavior*. The sequence of steps describes the interaction between the actor and an architecture asset on the asset surface. Under *NFR*, non-functional needs are associated with steps specifying *how* steps are supposed to perform. Under NFR, non-functional needs describe what additional expectations are associated with the execution of individual steps—in other words, NFRs qualify *how* steps are performed. Under *special requirements and invariants*, use case-wide or even system-wide expectations are formulated—that is, expectations that are not step specific (Fig. 6.127).

Use Case Template		
Name		
Description		
Actor Description		
Pre-conditions	- <precondition$_1$> - <precondition$_2$>	
Behavior	**Step**	**NFR**
Alternative Behavior	**Step**	**NFR**
Post-conditions	- <postcondition$_1$> - <postcondition$_2$>	
Special requirements and invariants	- <special requirement$_1$> - <special requirement$_2$>	

Fig. 6.127 Use case modeling

Automatic Teller Machine (ATM) Use Case Example

The company *Great ATMs* builds automatic teller machines (ATMs) and equips them with the appropriate software. Architects are working on a new generation of ATMs and are modeling a use case called *withdraw money*.

The use case assumes that a bank user has already been successfully authenticated and that the ATM is displaying a menu of its functions. When executing the use case, actors like bank customers initially select the ATM function they are interested in (e.g., *withdraw money, display account balance, making a bank transfer*). Then they enter the amount of money they want to withdraw. As long as the amount is within a customer's credit limit, the ATM withdraws the amount from the customer's account and dispenses the banknotes to the customer via the ATM's dispensing device.

An alternative flow of events deals with the situation in which a bank customer has entered an amount that exceeds the defined credit limit. Via its postcondition, the use case guarantees that the system has entered one of two defined states. Either the desired amount has been debited from the account and physically paid to the bank customer or the user session has ended, and the requested amount has not been debited from the account. An NFR states that steps 4 and 5 will either both complete or, if one fails, not complete at all (Fig. 6.128).

Withdraw Money Use Case	
Name	Withdraw money
Description	Bank customers can withdraw money from their account up to their credit limit.
Actor Description	Bank customer
Pre-conditions	- Successful authentication of bank customer - ATM displays menue
Behavior	1. Bank customer choses to withdraw money from his account 2. Bank customer enters desired amount 3. ATM checks whether amount is within limit 4. ATM deposits amount from account 5. ATM dispenses amount
Alternative Behavior	1. If amount was not within limit ATM makes a max amount offer 2. User accepts offered amount and proceeds XOR refuses and ends the session
Post-conditions	Bank user cancelled session XOR received amount ATM displays landing page
Special requirements and invariants	ATM information must be secured (at rest and in transit)

Fig. 6.128 Automatic teller machine (ATM) use case

Quality Attribute Scenario

As we saw above, use case modeling is a technique that architects use to specify an asset's desired functional capabilities. A quality attribute scenario supplements the use case modeling in that architects specify desired non-functional capabilities of respective assets. Note the term *quality attribute* is sometimes used as a synonym for non-functional capability. Functionality and quality attributes are orthogonal to each other. While functionality refers to *what* an asset exposes to its outside world, a quality attribute determines *how* this functionality is exposed. If we say that a functional condition specifies the desired behavior (*what*) of an asset, we would say that a non-functional condition denotes the desired behavioral attitude (*how*).

It does not matter whether the desired quality attribute has its origin in a non-functional requirement, a principle, an assumption, or a constraint. Quality attribute scenarios equally address all types of non-functional conditions as long as they can be addressed directly by the architecture design. Using quality attribute scenarios, architects specify an asset's expected response to a given stimulus.

A quality attribute scenario can specify a non-functional condition related to a particular step in a use case, an entire use case (use-case-wide condition), or even an entire asset (asset-wide condition).

Below, I give a few examples of non-functional conditions that architects might specify in the form of quality attribute scenarios. An application must scale to support 150% transaction volume at peak times (*scalability*), where 150% relates to a defined normal transaction volume of 100%. A service must respond to user-initiated transactions within 3 seconds (*performance*). A service must be 99.99% available during normal working hours (*availability*). An application must ensure that all data exchanged with other applications is securely transferred (*security*).

A quality attribute scenario enables the precise definition of a non-functional condition (i.e., the desired quality attribute). Quality attribute scenarios consist of six properties (Table 6.12, Fig. 6.129).

Table 6.12 Quality attribute scenario (QAS) properties

QAS property	Description
Stimulus	The condition that affects the asset
Stimulus source	The entity that generated the stimulus
Environment	Specifies further conditions under which the stimulus occurs
Artifact	The element that experiences stimulation
Response	The element's reaction resulting from the stimulus
Response measure	A measure by which an asset's response is assessed

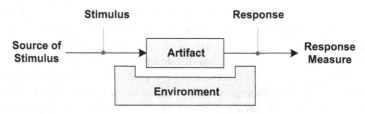

Fig. 6.129 Quality attribute scenario anatomy

Lenard Bass et al. (2003) presents attribute characterizations as collections of general scenarios, such as *availability*, *modifiability*, or *performance*.

Automatic Teller Machine (ATM) Attribute Scenario Example
The architects at *Great ATMs* are planning to equip the new ATM with a printing device. Printing bank statements is a must for the first release of the new generation of ATMs. However, it is already clear that in future sub-releases, bank customers expect to print other types of information (e.g., bank customer letters).

Therefore, a *modifiability* requirement is included and specified as a quality attribute scenario. It states that the ATM must be modifiable so that a developer can activate a new source of information for printing with no side effects and in less than three business days. The modified artifact is a source code that is changed in the development environment at design time (Fig. 6.130).

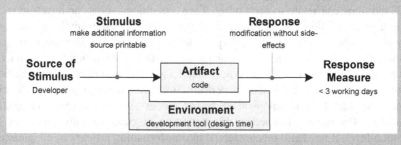

Fig. 6.130 Modifiability scenario

Regardless of technique or type of architecture condition, conditions are implemented through architecture approaches. To justify efforts, but also for impact analysis, it is essential to traverse the relationship between conditions and respective architecture approaches and thus be able to trace them forward and backward (ARCHITECTURE APPROACH, ARCHITECTURE TRACEABILITY).

Generalize use cases and quality attribute scenarios that your function deals with frequently. Develop such general descriptions as an entry point into *requirement patterns* that you make available to everyone in your enterprise. In specifying desired solutions, a significant portion of their architecture conditions fall into a relatively small number of condition types. A requirement pattern is a reusable asset in terms of a semi-final architecture condition. Requirement patterns explain their applicability, suggest ready-made use cases or quality attribute scenarios, and provide examples and considerations for instantiating the pattern in a specific situation. They provide information for the comprehensive elaboration of architecture conditions. They increase productivity and promote consistency by standardizing the process of considering, elaborating, and further evolving architecture conditions in your enterprise (ARCHITECTURE PATTERN METHODOLOGY).

Avoid fruitless debates about how to categorize a particular condition properly. For example, avoid discussing with peers whether a particular condition qualifies as functional or non-functional. What really counts instead is which of the given conditions are considered to be architecture-significant. As long as you identify all architecture-significant conditions, you are productively concentrating your capacity. If fruitless discussions nevertheless keep flaring up, differentiate the terms simply and clearly on the basis of the architecture language you have defined (ARCHITECTURE LANGUAGE).

Attention to key conditions in the context of all architecture engagements is essential—in other words, it is a mistake neither to question existing conditions nor to examine them for their architecture significance. Therefore, provide for at least an appreciation, if not questioning, of given conditions in your architecture mandate process. Furthermore, make sure that your methods and view models adequately include the examination of conditions for their significance as well as their traceability in corresponding architecture approaches (ARCHITECTURE MANDATE, YOUR OWN ARCHITECTURE METHODOLOGY, YOUR OWN ARCHITECTURE VIEW MODEL).

Conditions can relate to each other. Thus, conditions across architecture levels form a generalization-specialization relationship. To give an example, a *lease over buy over build* principle at the enterprise level affects all transformation projects without the need to formulate the principle as a dedicated condition for any individual project. Another example of vertical inheritance relationship between conditions is the domain-level requirement to perform any data exchange across application boundaries based on a canonical exchange model via the enterprise integration platform. Regardless of whether this condition is captured individually at the solution level, it must still be considered in transformation projects of all landscape assets in that domain (ARCHITECTURE LEVEL).

Finally, always remember that for the most part there are alternative ways to deal with and address any given condition. Evaluate alternative approaches to satisfy a condition—especially when you have to make architecture decisions that have far-reaching consequences. Imagine that as an architect on a project, you are considering how to temporarily persist the conversational state of user sessions to survive the failure of individual nodes in a server cluster. Among alternative ways to address this condition, each alternative has its specific advantages and disadvantages. For example, storing session states in a database is a relatively expensive operation, which can negatively impact application performance if many session state changes occur. An alternative here would be to use cluster-internal replication mechanisms, where session states are permanently synchronized between all cluster nodes via unified datagram protocol[133] (UDP). Another alternative would be to dedicate the cluster node on which the session is opened as an individual server node for the entire user session. This eliminates the need for synchronization-related data storms via datagram protocols. In any case, be attentive to conditions that lead to architecture decisions with far-reaching consequences and seriously consider the detailed evaluation of alternatives, especially here (**ARCHITECTURE ALTERNATIVE**).

6.9.4   Architecture Alternative

There are alternatives for almost every problem. However, you can only find them if you go on a search. We all act and decide under the impression of assumptions, prejudices, and conditioning that we are often unaware of. Architecture functions are no exception. They subconsciously assume that design approaches or technological foundations that were ideal yesterday are still ideal today.[134] Remaining in their own conditioning exposes architecture functions to the risk of clinging to suboptimal and outdated approaches, while more optimal ones have emerged in the meantime.

An *alternative* is an opportunity for deciding between two or more courses or propositions. (Merriam-Webster Dictionary 2020)

There is a saying coined by the French poet Alain de Lille in 1175 in the Middle Ages that translates into English as: *A thousand roads lead a man forever to Rome*:

mille vie ducunt hominem per secula Romam.

The proverb indicates that there are always alternative approaches to arriving at the same conclusion. In other words, there are always alternative ways to achieving a goal or arriving at a decision.

---

[133] The Unified Datagram Protocol (UDP) is a connectionless, unreliable, and unprotected transmission protocol. This means that once a packet is sent, there is no guarantee that it will arrive. UDP is also called *spray and pray* protocol and is used in areas where resending a lost packet would not make sense (e.g., when transmitting data that encodes audio or video information).

[134] Cognitive bias. People perceive the world under the impression of cognitive biases that lead them to draw inappropriate conclusions occasionally. Cognitive biases are systematic patterns of deviation from rationality in rationally intended judgments. Orientation approaches, which gave *Homo sapiens* an evolutionary advantage for a long time, appear in complex decision-making situations as suboptimal distortions. Clinging to something that works, or a plan once drawn up, is what psychology calls *plan continuation bias*. This subtle cognitive bias manifests itself in sticking to a tested concept, plan, or course of action, even when the conditions have changed very obviously and profoundly.

Architecture Function and Architecture Alternative

Architecture functions are looking for alternative approaches to overcome their own conditioning and find newly emerged approaches replacing older ones that have become suboptimal in the meantime. The search for alternatives takes place via architecture approaches and at all levels. Discovering and developing alternatives is an extra effort, but it pays off in the medium term through greater maturity and a positive return on investment[135] (Fig. 6.131).

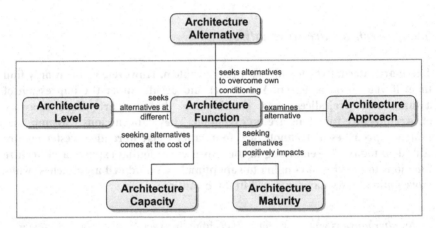

Fig. 6.131 Architecture function and architecture alternative

There are alternative ways to solve every problem, and this is no iota different in architecture. Five architects developing a design for the same problem will likely suggest five different design approaches to address the problem. Their designs may differ both slightly and seriously. Despite the considerable differences, all five designs may adequately solve the problem at hand. However, there may be relevant differences in the costs or the risk profile of each approach, differences in the technology platforms used, or the organizational consequences that arise when individual architecture alternatives are pursued. Architects examine alternatives via architecture approaches and select the most optimal one after evaluating the consequences of each approach (**ARCHITECTURE APPROACH**).

If you do not systematically consider and investigate alternative approaches, you run the risk of choosing ones that may have been optimal yesterday but are suboptimal from today's perspective. Worse, if you never rethink your previously preferred architecture approaches, you will learn nothing about technological developments or emerging patterns and styles. Ultimately, this means that expertise and experience in your function stagnate (**LEARNING ORGANIZATION**).

---

[135] Return on investment (ROI) depicts the ratio between the outcome of an investment and the associated investment over a defined period of time. The ROI indicates the performance of an investment in terms of its profitability.

Do not consider the topic of architecture alternatives just once and at the beginning of the development or from the perspective of an overall architecture. Instead, consider alternative approaches to solving problems at all stages of architecture development and at all levels of granularity. For example, first, develop alternatives for the overall architecture of a landscape asset. Once you have identified an optimal overall design from a set of alternatives, repeat considering alternative approaches for the building blocks of the overall design. Develop and regularly seek alternative approaches at all architecture levels (ARCHITECTURE LEVEL).

In the following example, the styles hub-and-spoke[136] and microservices architecture[137] are examined as possible alternative approaches at the level of the overall architecture of an application. The overall design developed so far is based on three architecture approaches (AA_1, AA_2, AA_3, and their respective relationships). For the approach AA_1, the alternatives considered relate to hosting the application. One alternative favors delegating hosting to the *cloud*, while the other alternative favors hosting the application in the enterprise data centers (on-premises). In approach AA_2, the alternatives considered deal with different technological bases. One alternative favors an *object-relational-mapping*[138] technology, while the other prefers an *OODBMS*[139] technology as the persistence approach for the application. Finally, the approach AA_3 faces a pattern decision, where two patterns are discussed as alternatives: the *pipes and filters* versus the *decorator* pattern (Fig. 6.132).

---

[136] Hub-and-spoke is an integration architecture style favoring communication via applications and a central hub over direct communication between applications.

[137] Microservices are fine-grained, context-agnostic functions or function endpoints. They are requested and delivered via lightweight protocols. Applications are established as loosely coupled microservices.

[138] Object-relational mapping (ORM) is an approach to converting data between incompatible type systems: non-scalar objects of an object-orientation paradigm and scalar values organized in tables of a relational calculus paradigm. To bridge the gap between incompatible type systems, you can either convert the object values into groups of simpler values for storage in a relational database (and convert them back when you call them up) or use only simple scalar values from the outset. Object-relational mapping prefers the first approach.

[139] Object-oriented database management systems (OODBMS) combine database with object-oriented programming language functions. An OODBMS database is one with the programming language so that the programmer can maintain consistency within an environment by having both the OODBMS and the programming language using the same presentation model.

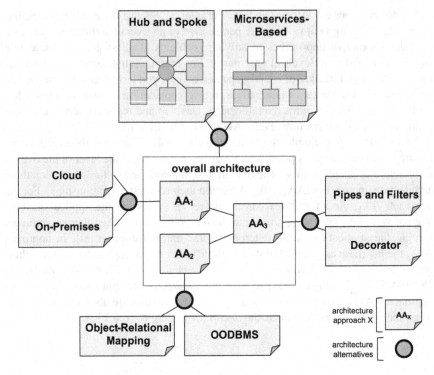

Fig. 6.132 Architecture alternatives at different levels of granularity

Regardless of granularity, as always, first understand your problem very clearly before considering alternative approaches to addressing it. In particular, you need to understand the architecturally significant conditions of the problem that must be adequately answered by each alternative architecture approach considered. As always, regardless of granularity, first clarify your problem in great detail before moving on to solution development and thus the investigation of alternative approaches. In particular, you must understand the architecture-significant conditions of the problem which need to be adequately addressed by any alternative approach being considered. Pay specific attention to aspects of the problem that may not be addressed at the solution level, but which may be useful to you in choosing one alternative over another. The speed with which a solution can be developed, risks that must be avoided, or costs that arise during the development of a solution can be conditions for which you prefer one alternative over another (**ARCHITECTURE CONDITION**).

However, before you can consider architecture alternatives, you must first find or develop them. This may prove to be the biggest challenge you face. Experienced architects have developed their own reflexes. These reflexes are automatically triggered when an architect is confronted with a problem of a known nature. The pace of socio-technological change is tremendous. This means that yesterday's ideal solution may no longer be an ideal solution today. The world, which is perceptibly and constantly changing around us, should actually convince us of the constant change. This observation suggests that careful examination of alternative approaches to familiar situations has rarely been as valuable an activity as it is in this twenty-first century.

An effective technique or systematics that an architect uses to overcome conditioning is to identify essential dimensions that span the given problem space and to abstract from the concrete problem. Shifting the focus from the concrete solution to its abstract equivalent helps architects distance themselves from the immediate and concrete search for a solution and ultimately to search for alternative solutions. At the level of generalized problem considerations, one can think more comprehensively, flexibly, and freely about alternative solutions.

Ideally, architects experiment with various abstract solution sketches that outline coarse-grained and purely logical architecture building blocks that approximate an abstract solution. For your architects, the first step is to extract the dimensions inherent in the initially identified logical building blocks. Typical dimensions to start with are the *types of landscape assets*: service, application, platform, technology, or information. Further dimensions include *actor*, *role* or *organization*, *geography*, *zone*, or *domain*. An initially identified set of dimensions almost inevitably gives rise to corresponding subdimensions. Finally, each dimension or subdimension has scaling values and categories that your architects need to capture (LANDSCAPE ASSETS).

Next, your architects extract a performance metric from architecture conditions and other optimization factors derived from the given problem and objectives. The performance metric is held against each alternative to select the most optimal one. Common criteria for performance metrics include, for example, the degree to which an alternative satisfies the given architecture conditions, or the cost, the risk, and the time associated with a solution alternative. Performance metrics are derived from your optimization objectives. Thus, there is no absolute performance metric, only relative ones.

Once dimensions have been identified and a performance metric defined, an architect derives conceivable alternatives from the mix of dimensions. Each architecture alternative represents a particular permutation of scale values of the dimensions. Ideally, the alternative candidates span a sufficiently large variant space, ensuring that they shed light on a wide range of relevant insights.

HR System Example Architects of a medium-sized company are commissioned to elaborate and propose the design of a new human resources (HR) solution. The architecture team first wants to get an overview of the HR situation. In addition, the team wants to avoid hasty decisions regarding the overall architecture approach. The team decides to develop several alternative approaches in order to counteract the danger of unthinkingly repeating its personally preferred approaches. First, the team consults the architecture conditions that have already been compiled. Next, the team abstracts the concrete problem to orientate itself neutrally about relevant problem dimensions. From experience, the architects know that *logical building blocks* are a typical problem dimension. As a second dimension, they consider *actor types*. They discuss other dimension candidates such as *geography*, *on-premises*

(continued)

versus off-premises, or *operational responsibility*—but discard them to keep the first design simple.

In the next step, the architects identify three actors and introduce three logical user interface building blocks to optimally address each group of actors (*HR super user interface, HR user interface, associate interface*). Furthermore, the architects distinguish two logical network building blocks (*client network, back-end network*), one logical *IAM platform*[140] building block, and one logical module where HR-related country regulations are made available (*HR country regulations*) (Fig. 6.133).

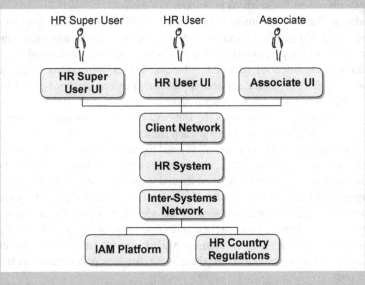

Fig. 6.133 HR system example—basic dimensions

The architects are aware that both the actor and logical building block dimensions could be further detailed. However, they refrain from these details because they only want to get an initial overview of the various alternatives.

Next, the architects derive a meaningful performance metric from the given conditions and goals of the HR system. This involves reviewing documents and holding discussions. The performance metric finally derived includes the *total cost*

(continued)

---

[140] Identity and access management (IAM) is a framework of policies and technologies that help ensure the right people in an organization have controlled access to resources they need. IAM systems identify, authenticate, and authorize not only people but also other systems. An IAM system is an enterprise platform that establishes basic preconditions for operating other systems in a company.

of ownership[141] (TCO), *secure handling of sensitive data*, and *excellent usability at the endpoints* of the HR system's user interface as measurement criteria.

To generate as colorful a spectrum of alternative approaches as possible, the architects combine additional dimensions with their initial building block sketch, for example, dimensions like *architecture style, ownership-delegation model, technology stacks utilized,* or *security architecture* approach chosen for each identified building block. This leads to the alternatives listed below, which the architects consider to be sufficiently diverse for further investigation (Fig. 6.134).

Alternative «cloud-based HR system»

User interface building blocks	General purpose http user agent
Client network	Public Internet (VPN-tunnelled)
HR system	Customized tenant from HR systems cloud-provider (pricing is based on *number of users* and *features consumed*), technology stack: vendor proprietary object API and scripting language
Inter-system network	Public Internet (VPN-tunnelled)
Architecture style	Thin client
Security architecture approach	Encrypted data at rest and in motion

Alternative «custom-developed HR system»

User interface building blocks	HTML 5 supporting http user agent
Client network	Public Internet (VPN-tunnelled)
HR system	Custom developed HR system, based on libraries from HR core services provider (pricing model is based on purchased libraries), technology stack: java EE, inhouse DB-technology, Unix OS, own data center)
Inter-system network	Private Internet (Intranet)
Architecture style	Rich internet application
Security architecture approach	Perimeter security

Fig. 6.134 HR system example—two architecture alternatives

(continued)

---

[141] Total cost of ownership (TCO) is a financial metric that helps cost bearers determine the direct and indirect costs of a product or service. The key figure is used in full cost accounting and is a long-term cost indicator.

The planned investment for the new HR system is relatively high for the company, which justifies a detailed study for each alternative. The architects give themselves 2 weeks to develop each alternative.

At the end of the 2-week period, each alternative has been studied in detail and is being benchmarked against the defined performance metrics. While both alternatives similarly address security concerns, the *cloud-based HR system* alternative outperforms the *custom-developed HR system* alternative in terms of total cost of ownership. Based on this difference, the enterprise choses the *cloud-based HR systems* alternative and discards the other one. However, when looking at the custom-developed alternative, some interesting findings emerged. These are carried over into the cloud-based alternative, so the abandoned alternative also provides value to the final overall architecture.

It is important to invest enough time exploring each architecture alternative. Relevant details must be discovered in order to measure them against the criteria of the performance metric. At the same time, any detailed exploration of alternatives involves costs. Timeboxing is a pragmatic approach to ensure that all alternatives are studied equally and that research results remain comparable. Timeboxing is particularly valuable when you want to avoid getting lost in irrelevant details and still ensure that each design alternative is given equal opportunities (ARCHITECTURE CAPACITY).

For example, architects are looking for an optimal persistence strategy for a small building block within an application. A directory service[142] or a relational database system[143] has been identified as an alternative approach. The architects have 1 week to choose a persistence approach, design, and implement the small building block. They decide to take 2 h to explore each alternative and finally decide on the more appropriate one.

The term *alternative* suggests that it is an *either-or*. However, cases in which one alternative outperforms the other in all criteria are rare. More likely, you will combine the findings from examining multiple alternatives into an architecture approach that combines the best of all the alternatives examined. The resulting approach is then pursued.

In conclusion, if you ignore everything else in this pattern and still seriously consider alternative approaches to address a given problem, the quality of your architecture contributions is already higher than that of the average architect. Value the questioning of your own preferences and the systematic search for alternative

---

[142] Directory services assign names and attributes to network resources and their respective network addresses. Directory services provide a shared information infrastructure for managing and finding network resources. Examples of network resources are volumes, folders, files, printers, users, or groups.

[143] A relational database is a database for digital data management and is based on relational calculus—a well-defined concept in mathematics. The associated database management system is called a relational database management system (i.e., RDBMS).

solutions as an important contribution to increasing the quality of your architecture function (**ARCHITECTURE MATURITY**).

Finally, the maxim in your organization to always ask for alternatives can lead to more innovation. Seeking alternatives means overcoming one's own initial reflexes and deviating, at least mentally, from the familiar paths or fundamentally allowing new perspectives. So use the regular search for alternative approaches to identify innovation potential and challenge your architects to examine the interesting insights they came across for their general innovation potential (**ARCHITECTURE INNOVATION**).

6.9.5   Architecture Approach

Some architects misunderstand the elaboration of architecture as an all-or-nothing task. They misperceive architecture as *the* design that addresses all architecture conditions in an overarching singular response rather than in a multiplicity of appropriate architecture approaches. Architects refuse to segment the entire set of conditions to address requirement fragments via suitable architecture approaches and to assemble the desired overall architecture from them. The consequences are poor economies of scale due to unused potential for parallel architecture elaboration and poor traceability between conditions and corresponding solution approaches.

> You chose an *approach* to make advances in order to create a desired result. (Merriam-Webster Dictionary 2020)

An *architecture approach* is a part of a corresponding overall architecture. Each approach addresses a subset of the conditions of an overall problem. From the perspective of the overall design, an architecture approach thus represents a partial solution. Partial solutions are combined into the overall architecture by the architect responsible for the entire solution. You plan, design, and describe individual architecture approaches based on problem-solving methods and techniques. In this respect, an architecture approach (i.e., a partial solution) is no different from an overall architecture (i.e., an overall solution). Architecture approaches can therefore also be referred to as solution design segments, micro-solutions, or micro-architectures.

Architecture Function and Architecture Approach
Architecture functions use architecture approaches to successively create solution segments of an overall solution. Architecture approaches enable an architecture function to scale development considering the *divide-et-impera*[144] principle.

---

[144]Divide et impera (Latin for divide and rule or divide and conquer) is a phrase (in Latin imperative); as a maxim *divide et impera* suggests to maintain power (i.e., to gain control, elaborate a solution, or gain orientation over an inherently complex domain) by breaking up greater concentrations of power into parts that individually have less power and thus can be better controlled or elaborated.

Architecture approaches are micro-architectures each addressing a slice of all conditions. As a micro-architecture, an architecture approach encodes decisions and is developed based on solution architecture methodologies (Fig. 6.135).

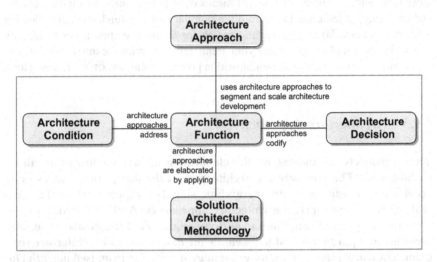

Fig. 6.135 Architecture function and architecture approach

An architecture approach is the partial manifestation of an overall solution architecture—for example, the architecture of a business platform. However, when developing an architecture approach, you need to understand its context, determine the conditions to be addressed, explore alternatives, and finally develop an appropriate design. This means that you develop each individual approach using the same solution techniques to develop the overall solution architecture (SOLUTION ARCHITECTURE METHODOLOGY).

Each architecture approach implements one or more conditions—for example, requirements, constraints, or assumptions. For a functional requirement, an architecture approach suggests a design that realizes a use case. For a non-functional requirement, constraint, or assumption, an architecture approach specifies how a corresponding quality attribute scenario is realized based on its design. Design decisions are inherently encoded in each design. In this respect, each architecture approach encodes one or more architecture decisions. An architecture function decides which design decisions need to be documented, discussed, and published separately (i.e., beyond the inherent documentation of the design decision in the form of the architecture approach) (ARCHITECTURE DECISION).

Therefore, architecture approaches provide a hinge between architecture conditions and decisions, enabling detailed traceability between them. This traceability enables architects to granularly understand the consequences (*impact analysis*) of architecture decisions on the corresponding conditions. For example, an architect can immediately determine which conditions are affected by the decision to use a replication mechanism to synchronize distributed data points. Conversely, architects can determine which design decisions are affected by an architecture condition. For example, an internationalization[145] requirement may lead to the following design decision: we manage all data for labeling user interfaces in a relational database system. In summary, an architecture approach describes how its design addresses conditions. For example, a specific approach describes how a landscape asset can resist code injection attacks using input validation. In another example, an architecture approach describes how the performance requirements of the monthly fee transaction are met through load balancing. Another architecture approach describes how the corporate data application is integrated with landscape assets based on real-time messaging (**ARCHITECTURE TRACEABILITY**) (Fig. 6.136).

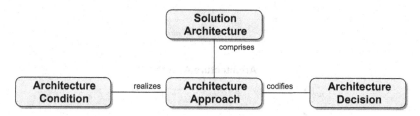

Fig. 6.136 Architecture approach

Architecture approach descriptions refer to the conditions they address. So, describe both the impact (*force*) on a corresponding asset and the desired response (*behavior*). Also, describe the architecture building blocks constituting your architecture approach—for example, applications, services, and platforms you use. Limit your descriptions to aspects that are relevant to understanding the design. *Static architecture* perspectives reflect your design's static relationships—for example, a connection between two applications. *Dynamic architecture* perspectives, on the other hand, specify the cooperative relationships in your design—for example, the exchange of messages between applications during runtime. Once you have established the static and dynamic design perspectives, they inherently include any design decisions you have made. Also consider separating out the most important or problematic *decisions* from your perspectives and describing them separately in prose (**ARCHITECTURE CONDITION**) (Fig. 6.137).

---

[145]Internationalization (I18N) describes a system's runtime capability to adapt to different languages and regional characteristics. Internationalization requires that a system can be adapted to languages, gestures, and regions without fundamental (e.g., code-level) changes.

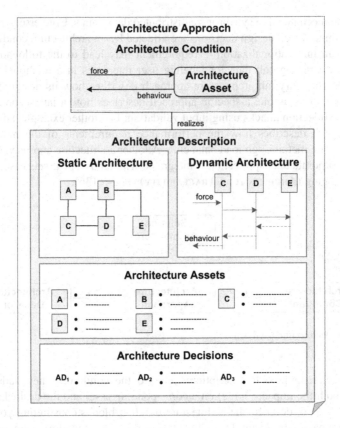

Fig. 6.137 Description of an architecture approach

Each approach represents a solution segment of the overall architecture. This means that the solution architecture as a whole is the well-ordered and interrelated set of all architecture approaches (Fig. 6.138).

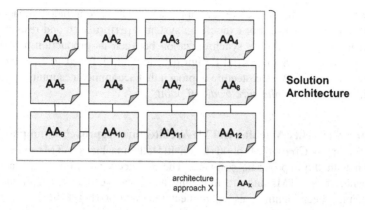

Fig. 6.138 Solution architecture as a collection of architecture approaches

A challenge in compiling the overall architecture is the previously isolated development of individual approaches. Therefore, pay special attention in your development to design approaches that realize more than a single condition. For example, a design decision to use three-factor authentication impacts security and usability requirements. Also, be aware of situations where a single condition is realized through multiple architecture approaches. An internationalization requirement is implemented by combining a database schema decision and a caching decision (Fig. 6.139).

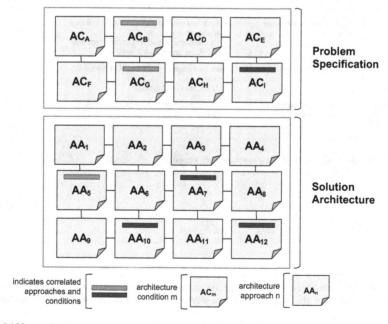

Fig. 6.139 Architecture approaches realizing architecture conditions

In particular, focus on architecture approaches that have a major impact on the desired system response. For example, a system's performance and response time depend heavily on real-time synchronization between its production and disaster recovery databases. Such crucial design decisions are referred to as *architecture sensitivity points.*[146] An architecture approach that accommodates multiple sensitivity points is called *architecture trade-off point.*[147]

Automatic Teller Machine (ATM) Architecture Approach Example

The company *Great ATMs* builds automatic teller machines (ATM) and equips them with the appropriate software. The architects are working on a new generation of ATMs and are modeling a use case called *withdraw money* which has been identified as an architecture condition (Fig. 6.140).

Withdraw Money Use Case

Name	Withdraw money
Description	Bank customers can withdraw money from their account up to their credit limit.
Actor Description	Bank customer
Pre-conditions	- Successful authentication of bank customer - ATM displays menue
Behavior	1. Bank customer choses to withdraw money from his account 2. Bank customer enters desired amount 3. ATM checks whether amount is within limit 4. ATM deposits amount from account 5. ATM dispenses amount
Alternative Behavior	1. If amount was not within limit ATM makes a max amount offer 2. User accepts offered amount and proceeds XOR refuses and ends the session
Post-conditions	Bank user cancelled session XOR received amount ATM displays landing page
Special requirements and invariants	ATM information must be secured (at rest and in transit)

Fig. 6.140 "Withdraw money" architecture approach—use case

(continued)

---

[146] Architecture sensitivity points are the system areas that are significantly affected when the system's architecture changes. They are closely monitored by an architect when reflecting on planned architecture changes.

[147] Architecture trade-off points are the basis for sensitivity points. Typical trade-offs exist between usability and security or between modifiability and performance attributes.

In a first step, the architects develop an architecture approach that addresses the use case. For this purpose, *the* architects rely on a set of building blocks. These building blocks either already exist or are logically designed in terms of their functional and non-functional properties. The architects elaborate building blocks such as *ATM* (as a facade), *screen, keyboard, cash dispenser*, and a corresponding back-end *banking application*. The architects find the basis for their component descriptions in the asset portfolio descriptions of the *Great ATMs* company (Fig. 6.141).

Architecture Approach «withdraw money» - Assets	
ATM	The ATM as a whole and the user interaction options it offers
Screen	Screen for displaying menue and use case dialogues to guide a bank customer
Keyboard	Means to send text and control signals to the ATM (e.g., to enter desired amount)
Banking Application	Application checks the credit limit of the account and debits the requested amount if below the limit
Cash Dispenser	Physically dispenses the desired amount in cash

Fig. 6.141 "Withdraw money" architecture approach—architecture assets

In the next step, architects design the static ATM architecture based on the above assets. An *ATM* consists of *user interaction devices* and interacts with a *banking application*. Screen, keyboard, and cash dispenser are variants of user interaction devices (Fig. 6.142).

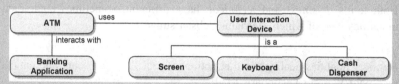

Fig. 6.142 "Withdraw money" architecture approach—static architecture

Finally, the architects describe how architecture assets collaborate to implement the *withdraw money* use case in the dynamic architecture perspective. The *ATM* uses a *screen* to display a selection menu before the *keyboard* device accepts user input such as the amount to be withdrawn. The *banking applica-*

(continued)

tion then checks the creditworthiness of the requestor. If the credit check is positive, the customer's account is reduced by the amount to be withdrawn before the banknotes are dispensed to the customer via the *cash dispenser* (Fig. 6.143).

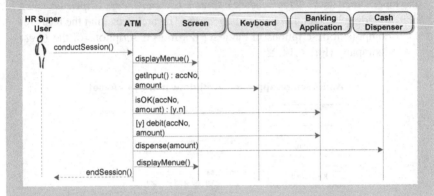

Fig. 6.143 "Withdraw money" architecture approach—dynamic architecture

6.9.6   *Business Versus Technical*

Inadequate assessment of the criticality of assets leads to disproportionate architecture-related efforts and investments. An architecture function can pay too much or too little attention to the planning, design, and operation of architecture assets. These misjudgments result from insufficiently differentiated assets—insufficiently differentiated in terms of the degree of their direct versus indirect business contributions.

Both terms, *business* and *technical*, have different, sometimes contradicting, connotations, two of which Merriam-Webster suggests.

Business qualifies dealings or transactions especially of an economic nature. (Merriam-Webster Dictionary 2020)

Technical is marked by or characteristic of mechanical specialization. (Merriam-Webster Dictionary 2020)

The distinction between *business* and *technical* corresponds to the distinction between *primary* and *secondary*. While some assets make direct business contributions, other assets make indirect (i.e., technical) ones by serving as an operating platform for the former. In other words, technical assets shoulder business assets so that the latter can make their business contributions efficiently, effectively, and reliably. A business asset that does not function adequately because its reliable operation is not guaranteed becomes dysfunctional. In this sense, business and technical assets are equally important to enable business operations.

At the same time, business assets differ from technical assets in their respective optimization goals. While business assets must precisely enable urgently needed business capabilities, ideal technical assets are expected to be deployable and reusable in the broadest possible spectrum of different contexts. Business assets must directly support the business, while technical assets must directly support business assets. Business assets are often business-specific, while technical assets are ideally business-agnostic. Business assets tend to be stateful and more semantically narrow. In contrast, technical assets tend to be stateless and less semantically constrained. The tendency toward statefulness leads to a stronger binding of business assets to their respective enterprise context. However, this binding can be mitigated by appropriate architectures. In contrast, the statelessness of technical assets increases their reuse potential. For example, database systems are technical platforms. A technical database platform is agnostic with respect to the business models that are created in it as database schemes. The same database platform can serve an accounting application, a flight simulator game, or a self-driving car as a data storage and management platform. While business assets are expected to support the right business function, we expect technical assets to run business assets reliably and securely and to be available, scalable, and performant over their lifetime.

Architecture Function and Business Versus Technical

Architecture functions use the distinction between *business* and *technical* to optimally plan, design, and operate architecture assets according to various criteria. Architecture functions consider the cross-cutting character of *business versus technical* by embedding this distinction in their methodologies and platforms (i.e., *architecture apparatus*) (Fig. 6.144).

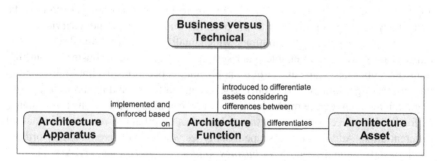

Fig. 6.144 Architecture function and business versus technical

Architecture functions introduce *business outcome qualifiers* to distinguish architecture assets that make a direct contribution (*business*) from those that make an indirect (*technical*) contribution to enable the enterprise's business operations. The *business versus technical* qualifier supports architecture functions in the optimal planning, design, and operation of applications, services, information, but also entire domains, methodologies, or reference assets (ARCHITECTURE ASSET) (Fig. 6.145).

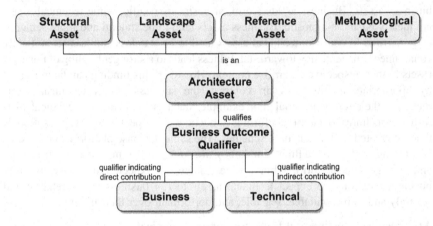

Fig. 6.145 Business versus technical

Keep the number of landscape asset types distinguished by your architecture function to a minimum to ensure you can efficiently manage the relevant landscape assets throughout their lifecycle. However, the different landscape asset types, like application, service, platform, information, or technology, do not yet indicate the immediacy of their contribution to the business outcome. Imagine a service S_1. S_1 makes no direct business contributions, which qualifies S_1 as a technical service. The only reason it exists is to enable other services that make direct business contributions. For other landscape assets (e.g., applications, platforms, technologies), structural assets (e.g., domains), reference assets (e.g., patterns), and methodology assets (e.g., domain architecture methodology), there are similar justifications for existence as for S_1. Introduce *business versus technical* as qualifiers to remedy this lack of differentiation. Add to the landscape asset types you have differentiated by orthogonally inserting the distinction of *business and technical* (LANDSCAPE ASSET).

The distinction between *business* and *technical* affects practically all viewpoints of an architecture view model and may lead to a duplication of viewpoints, especially when you combine different issues with views that have *business versus technically* connotations. The purpose of business viewpoints is to provide an abstract representation of an enterprise and the business ecosystem in which it operates. Similarly, technically connotated viewpoints provide an abstract representation of the operational vehicle by which an enterprise conducts its business. While business architecture views are capability-based and linked to business capabilities, technical architecture views are linked to technical capabilities. Constituents of business architecture viewpoints are business building blocks (e.g., *account* or *credit* in banking), business events, business actors, partners, organizations, locations, processes, rules, or guidelines. In contrast, the components of technical architecture perspectives are technical events, technical facilities (e.g., data centers), or technical actors, locations, and processes. Note that the number of architecture asset types to which you apply the *business versus technical* dichotomy doubles. While this means increased effort in the short term, it significantly sharpens your focus on otherwise hidden but decisive criteria. The clarity gained and the extent to which you can ask differentiated questions are basically worth the extra effort (**YOUR OWN ARCHITEC-TURE VIEW MODEL**) (Fig. 6.146).

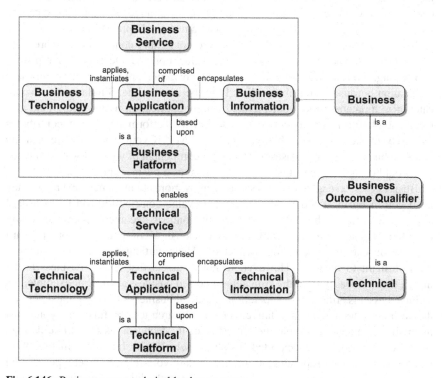

Fig. 6.146 Business versus technical landscape assets

Do not confuse the concept of *technical* with landscape assets of type *technology*. Technology refers to the off-the-shelf portion of a vendor's offering you use when applying technology in your company, for example, when you instantiate a technology to create an application or platform tailored to your needs. This means that a combination of *technical versus business* qualification with the landscape asset type *technology* is not contradictory but rather complementary. For example, when you buy an ERP[148] system from an ERP vendor, you are buying a technology. If the capabilities of the ERP technology contribute directly to the bottom line, consider the ERP technology *business technology* in your enterprise. When you apply the ERP business technology to instantiate an enterprise-specific ERP application, you get a business application. Similarly, when you buy database software from a database vendor, you are also buying a technology. If database capabilities contribute indirectly to business results, then that database software is considered a technical technology, which—admittedly—sounds a bit strange. By applying database technology in your enterprise, you instantiate a technical application.

Note that both *business and technical* are contextual concepts. They are relative—relative to your perception of business value. For example, if your enterprise is in banking, you would categorize a private banking application as a business application because it contributes directly to the bottom line. Similarly, you would categorize a database that your private banking application uses to store data as a technical platform. The database is a technical platform because it contributes indirectly to the company's bottom line. However, if your enterprise were in the software business and databases were a major component of your software products, you would categorize the same database system as a business platform.

Business assets (e.g., a business service) enjoy more attention here and now. They keep you in business today. Moreover, their value contribution can be measured directly in terms of business outcomes. In contrast, technical assets are easily misinterpreted as being relatively unimportant. As a consequence, your primary focus is on carefully managing their costs. Their particular value proposition is more difficult to measure. However, technical assets that enable business assets inherit their criticality from the criticality of hosted business assets. For example, if a technical asset is critical to the operation of critical business assets that must not fail, the technical asset must not fail either. As an architecture function, you must maintain dependencies so that the criticality of the technical assets can be derived from the criticality of the supported business assets. Establish both the methodological means and an appropriate platform to maintain your relevant asset types as well as the business outcome qualifiers. Establish your methodological means as well as a suitable platform to maintain your relevant asset in terms of their *business versus*

---

[148] Enterprise resource planning (ERP) is the integrated management of the most important business processes. An ERP system covers central functional areas shared by all companies, such as financial accounting, human resources, manufacturing, order fulfillment, supply chain management, or customer relationship management.

technical distinction (**YOUR OWN METHODOLOGY, YOUR OWN ARCHITECTURE PLATFORM**).

6.9.7   Architecture Artifact

Architecture is inherently abstract. Investments in the tangible and comprehensive formulation of architecture information are often considered superfluous—at least as overrated. Architecture artifacts in which corresponding information manifests are poorly aligned, incompatible in structure and semantics, or even contradictory. Architecture artifacts lack ownership, and lifecycle management processes are not or only insufficiently established. This leads to outdated, redundant, or contradictory and thus ultimately meaningless architecture information.

> *Artifact*, a usually simple object (such as a tool or ornament) showing human workmanship or modification as distinguished from a natural object. (Merriam-Webster Dictionary 2020)

An *architecture artifact* is an architecture manifestation. Artifacts can be more or less structured and formalized. They are means by which architects process architecture information in a tangible manner, for example, information such as architecture conditions, viewpoints, mandates, decisions, roadmaps, or calendars. The terms *architecture artifact* and *architecture work product* are used interchangeably. Think of them as physical containers for architecture information (Fig. 6.147).

Fig. 6.147 Architecture artifact and architecture information

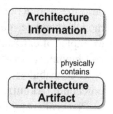

Architecture Function and Architecture Artifact

Architecture functions use artifacts to physically compile, manage, provision, and version architecture information and define and control access rights to architecture content. Architecture artifacts make design content physically traceable both horizontally and vertically (i.e., across levels). On the one hand, artifacts are incorporated or embedded in architecture methods and platforms. On the other hand, they are generated from architecture platforms (Fig. 6.148).

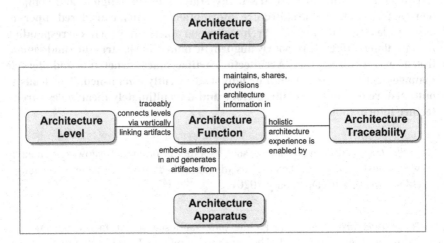

Fig. 6.148 Architecture function and architecture artifact

Some artifacts may be intended for internal use, while others are directed outward and formally link an architecture function to other enterprise disciplines. An architecture function charter is an example of an internal artifact. Function charters describe a function's vision and mission, organizational structure, engagement model, mandate, governance approach, or apparatus. Roadmaps or mandates are examples of externally facing architecture artifacts. Architecture mandates formally and bindingly capture agreements between an architecture function, its client, and other contributors. They are signed and are subject to a clearly regulated amendment procedure (ARCHITECTURE MANDATE).

Physically tangible architecture information serves various purposes. It can be accessed, sent, and exchanged between cooperating parties in a controlled and secure manner. Artifacts protect architecture content from unauthorized access by acting as a container for which access rights can be formulated and enforced. Artifacts can be signed, versioned, archived, and physically referenced from other artifacts. They are agreed upon as deliverables, whose delivery can be efficiently quantified and verified. An artifact can be fixed and represent final architecture information, or it can be dynamically or sporadically generated based on information in an architecture repository.

Architecture information—structured, unstructured, or semi-structured—is compiled into artifacts and can take various forms, including text, diagrams, lists, or matrices. For example, statements formulated in plain English take the text form. However, text can also take the form of a formal language, such as a pseudocode fragment, which expresses the algorithmic structure of an asset's capability. *Illustrations* and *diagrams* exist in a variety of visual nomenclatures and modeling languages, each with its own standardized visual symbols, such as the Unified Modeling Language[149] (UML) (Fig. 6.149).

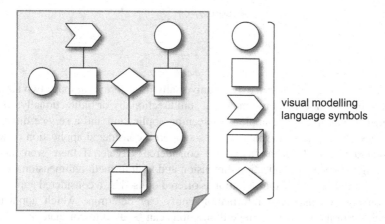

visual modelling language symbols

Fig. 6.149 Architecture information form—diagram

Lists are another common form of representing architecture information. A pattern catalog, a report on all assets in the purchasing domain, or a portfolio viewpoint in a solution architecture method are examples of artifacts that often take list form (SOLUTION ARCHITECTURE METHODOLOGY) (Fig. 6.150).

---

[149] Unified Modeling Language (UML) is a universal modeling language that provides a standard approach to modeling and visualizing system design. Note that the concept of *system* is not limited to IT system. UML supports the expression and modeling of dynamic and static perspectives, individual building blocks, and their relationships (OMG UML 2020a).

Fig. 6.150 Architecture
information form—list

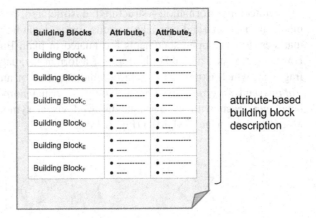

After all, *mapping* (*matrices*) is a universally used form that maps two architecturally relevant information dimensions, unidirectionally or bidirectionally, to each other. For example, the mapping between an application and a service dimension provides an overview of which services support a considered application or which applications provide capabilities to a considered service. If there were another mapping between an application dimension and an information dimension, it could give an overview of what information is offered or used by a considered application. Conversely, a considered information entity can determine which applications participate in its provision. Hinge dimensions can be used to correlate any number of mappings, enabling comprehensive queries. For example, the application dimension can be used to determine which service provisions which information entities. In addition to the very elementary *assigned-yes-or-no* semantics, assignments also enable more sophisticated mapping qualifications. For example, the mapping between application and service could qualify exactly *how* an application (X_m) supports a respective service (Y_n). For example, R_{21} could represent which capabilities and qualities, in which regions, at which service-level guarantees, application X_2 provides to service Y_1 (Fig. 6.151).

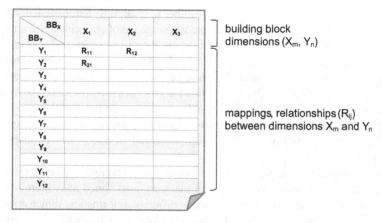

Fig. 6.151 Architecture information form—mapping

Architecture artifacts can take many different forms, for example, shapes such as whiteboard sketches, office documents, or architecture models created with specialized tools. Examples of dynamic artifacts are reports based on spontaneously retrieved data—data in an architecture repository, for example. It is quite common to combine architecture information from many sources and in various forms into an overarching architecture artifact (Fig. 6.152).

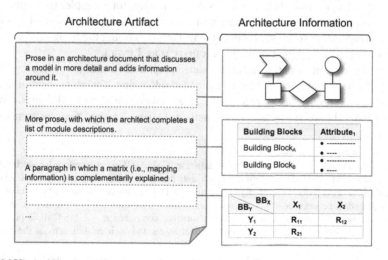

Fig. 6.152 Architecture artifact based on architecture information

The processes for creating artifacts are either manual, fully automated, or a hybrid between the two. Automated creation and maintenance of an architecture artifact or defined parts of it are based, for example, on data in transactional systems, data warehouses, configuration management bases[150] (CMS), or architecture repositories. For artifacts that participate in architecture generation processes, their human readability is not sufficient—such artifacts must also be machine-readable. An example of this is model-driven architecture[151] (MDA), where a design model is an essential input into a design generation process. An MDA generator can only generate codebases to the extent that the original model contains the corresponding information.

You enable a holistic architecture experience by relating your artifacts to each other, making them navigable. Mapping matrices, as outlined above, are common techniques to enable traceability between different information dimensions. For related artifacts, relationships can be maintained either as lightweight references or as deep copies and embeddings of one artifact in another. Embedding artifacts into each other creates redundancies. On the other hand, lightweight references are inappropriate when artifacts are subject to formal change management and must not change uncontrollably. Maintain an overview of all artifacts within your function. Such an overview shows the *types of artifacts*, their *interrelationships* (e.g., reference versus copy), their *creation* (e.g., manual, automatic, hybrid), *lifecycle management information*, and the *approach to handling physical artifacts* based on architecture platforms (ARCHITECTURE TRACEABILITY).

Complementary to topic-oriented (*horizontal*) relationships between artifacts, they are related across different levels of granularity, for example, the aggregative relationship between a domain architecture artifact outlining the design of a domain and corresponding solution architecture artifacts describing the design of landscape assets associated with that domain (ARCHITECTURE LEVEL).

Architecture information emerges and is captured in artifacts when architects apply the view models inherent in their methodologies. Therefore, certain artifact types are naturally associated with your enterprise's methodologies. When referencing between architecture methodologies, ensure that references to

---

[150] A configuration management system or database (CMS/CMDB) is a system for storing information about an organization's critical assets and the relationships between them. Assets in a CMS/CMDB are referred to as configuration items (CI). CI examples include virtual and physical compute nodes, network components, end-user devices, databases, application servers, directory services, transaction monitors, or application software components. A CMS/CMDB provides a means of understanding an organization's critical assets and their relationships at the physical instance level.

[151] Model-driven architecture (MDA) is a forward engineering approach in which executable or semi-executable artifacts are generated from abstract, human-made architectural models (e.g., class diagrams). MDA tools are used to develop, interpret, compare, align, measure, verify, or transform models and metamodels. Generator-based architecture approaches very generally decouple solution specifications from their physical generation. They increase domain specificity and the degree of abstraction of the models that architects use to represent a solution. Generators receive architecture models as inputs and create artifacts at the source level or related physical structures as outputs.

methodology-specific artifacts are complete and consistent. For example, an architecture assessment method references the view model of a solution elaboration method to explore the functional, informational, and operational design of an asset. The assessment report (i.e., an artifact of the assessment method) consistently references the solution description chapters (i.e., an artifact of the solution architecture method) (YOUR OWN ARCHITECTURE METHODOLOGY).

Formal lifecycle management of artifacts inevitably means additional effort that your function must be willing and able to stem. Therefore, carefully select the types of artifacts you impose on your organization for formal management. Distinguish different degrees of formal rigor for artifact categories to reasonably balance the capacity required to create and maintain them with their utility. For example, allow a solution design artifact to have open chapters in its draft status as long as a previously established mandate sufficiently justifies these white spots (ARCHITECTURE CAPACITY).

Clarify ownership for your artifact types to specify lifecycle management responsibility at the architecture role level. Artifacts are excellent references for your governance organization because of their tangibility and type-specific permanence. Include signature fields in all architecture artifact types to indicate personal accountability. Also, include references to artifact types in your governance and control processes to emphasize the importance of compliance and to monitor it (ARCHITECTURE OWNERSHIP, ARCHITECTURE GOVERNANCE).

Ensure that decommissioning assets (e.g., a landscape asset such as an application) retires the corresponding artifacts. Decommissioning an artifact does not mean physically destroying it but archiving it. When decommissioning, as with all other fundamental changes to artifacts, ensure that the relevant changes are propagated to all dependent artifacts. For example, if you decommission a solution architecture artifact, this is preceded by the decommissioning of a landscape asset. In this example, you need to check dependencies to other landscape assets and update their design descriptions (i.e., their corresponding artifacts) (DECOMMISSIONING REWARD).

Finally, you need to align or embed your artifacts with your architecture platform. For example, reports that are dynamically generated based on data in an architecture repository are automatically updated in response to changes at the underlying data layer. For artifacts that are not automatically generated but managed in documents, for example, your architecture platform must provide document management capabilities, such as a signature capability to route artifacts through formally controlled, multistep signature processes (YOUR OWN ARCHITECTURE PLATFORM).

6.9.8 Baseline Architecture Versus Target Architecture

Architecture is both a process (discipline component) and the result of that process (architecture artifact). While architecture artifacts capture state,

architecture processes represent state transitions. However, architecture states are diverse and are not exhaustively captured when differentiating between a current (baseline) and a future (target) state. Failure to adequately capture past states undermines architecture retrospection and learning. The consequence of underestimating current states is lack of transparency, inadequate recognition of problems, and inappropriate architecture decisions. Finally, an undifferentiated view of future states leads to suboptimal architecture planning.

State is a condition or stage in the physical being of something. (Merriam-Webster Dictionary 2020)

Architecture assets are systems, and systems have an architecture. Systems are inevitably in a state at any point in time. And this is independent of whether this state is desired, consciously assumed, or documented. Architecture frameworks, superficially, distinguish only between the two states baseline and target architecture. Mostly, however, it is important to distinguish, name, develop, and describe further architecture states (**ARCHITECTURE ASSET**) (Fig. 6.153).

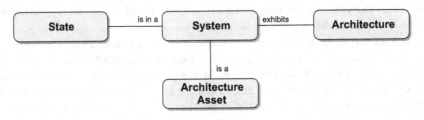

Fig. 6.153 System and state

A *baseline* is a starting point, a line serving as a basis, a usually initial set of critical observations or data used for comparison or a control. (Merriam-Webster Dictionary 2020)

A *target* is something to be affected by an action or development, a goal to be achieved. (Merriam-Webster Dictionary 2020)

Architecture Function and Baseline Architecture Versus Target Architecture
Architecture functions differentiate asset states to describe and pursue planned state transitions in a deliberate and controlled manner, for example, based on architecture roadmaps. Planned states enable simulations and what-if questions. Clearly described state transitions enable traceability of planning decisions—and thus help streamline architecture decisions. Finally, the states differentiated by an architecture function must be reflected in the architecture apparatus (i.e., methodologies, view models, and architecture platforms) (Fig. 6.154).

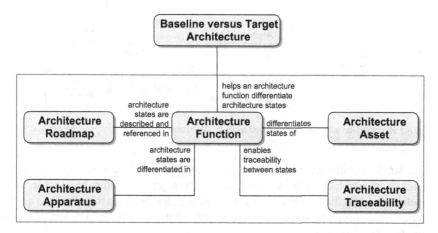

Fig. 6.154 Architecture function and baseline architecture versus target architecture

State transitions cause states to undergo state changes. While the baseline architecture reflects a current state, the target architecture represents a desired state. Baseline and target architecture thus represent different states of the same asset. Architecture states support architecture functions distinguished between the strengths, weaknesses, threats, and opportunities of a given and a planned design (Fig. 6.155).

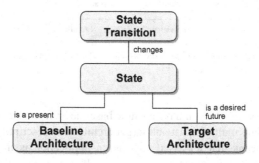

Fig. 6.155 Baseline and target architecture

Another view of baseline and target architecture and their relationship is that a target architecture describes a solution in light of an associated baseline architecture that is now perceived as problematic. As with a problem that calls for a solution, we can retroactively infer the original problem from its solution. Thus, the change in state of a target architecture with respect to its associated baseline architecture expresses the problem of the baseline that the target architecture addresses—in other words, the problem that led to striving for and planning a target architecture in the first place. In this sense, target architectures are solutions to problems inherent in their baseline architecture (Fig. 6.156).

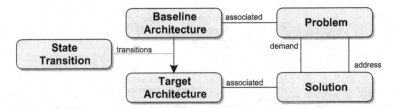

Fig. 6.156 Baseline and target associated with problem and solution

A target architecture swaps places with an associated baseline once the state transition is complete. At that moment, an asset's target architecture becomes its new baseline. Further, the former baseline architecture changes from the current to a past state—and henceforth serves as a historical view of past architecture releases (Fig. 6.157).

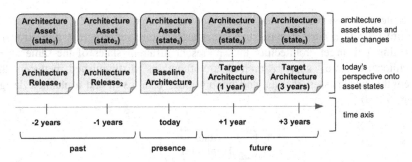

Fig. 6.157 Past, baseline, and target architecture are relative concepts

For each of your assets, you have a single baseline architecture description at any point in time, while multiple past and target architecture descriptions exist simultaneously. This means that an asset such as an application is in a single current architecture state at any given point in time. It also means that its past (e.g., *architecture release₁*, *architecture release₂*) and its planned architecture states (e.g., *target architecture (1 year)* and *target architecture (3 years)*) are captured in a corresponding set of further architecture descriptions. For example, your function can determine the difference between an asset's design description from release₂ and release₁ to analyze progress from release₁ to release₂ and establish traceability between architecture releases (ARCHITECTURE ARTIFACT, ARCHITECTURE TRACEABILITY).

Summarize the planned future architecture states for your assets in their roadmaps. Explicitly identify the issues that planned states overcome in their respective predecessor states. In parallel, maintain initial versions of architecture descriptions for future states—even if they are initially fragmentary. For example, capture early architecture visions for the *target architecture (1 year)* and *target architecture (3 years)* of an application. This way, if in doubt, you can present and discuss future visions early in the process and based on central architecture viewpoints (ARCHITECTURE ROADMAP METHODOLOGY).

Introduce *baseline architecture versus target architecture* considerations as cross-cutting perspectives in your view models, methodologies, and architecture platforms and allow for multiple future and past architecture states. However, also note that many architecture tools do not support a virtually infinite set of design states. Even architecture frameworks like TOGAF[152] or the Zachman[153] Framework address such instance-level consideration only in a very rudimentary way. In particular, it is difficult to manage several architecture states in a repository based on a database schema that does not support this concept. In such cases, choose document-based artifacts and manage a document for each design state in a document management system and connect the document management system to your architecture repository (YOUR OWN ARCHITECTURE VIEW MODEL, YOUR OWN ARCHITECTURE PLATFORM).

Managing multiple architecture states for the same asset in parallel requires a considerable architecture effort. Each architecture state managed in parallel replicates almost the complete set of artifacts for a corresponding asset in an actual implementation. Therefore, depending on the asset type, consciously select the artifacts for which you consider multi-state management to be economical (ARCHITECTURE CAPACITY, LANDSCAPE ASSET).

6.10 Architecture Apparatus

The *architecture apparatus* patterns equip your function with essential tools—methodologies and view models, reference architectures, physical platforms, and situational adapters. The *your own architecture methodology* pattern generally recommends the architecture function adapt standard methodologies to its business, while the *your own architecture view model* pattern recommends appropriate adaptation of off-the-shelf view models. The *domain architecture methodology* pattern provides you with the core design of a domain architecture methodology that your

---

[152] The Open Group Architecture Framework (TOGAF). TOGAF proposes an approach to design, plan, implement, and govern enterprise architecture. It describes a generic method for developing architectures. TOGAF suggests a common vocabulary, a generic information model, an adaptable role model, general architecture artifacts, and tooling.

[153] The Zachman Framework proposes a basic enterprise architecture schema that provides a structured approach to holistically viewing and defining an enterprise's architecture. The basic scheme distinguishes two dimensions that introduce the intersection of two classifications. While the first classification distinguishes the primitive interrogatives what, how, when, who, where, and why, the second classification is derived from the philosophical concept of reification (i.e., from the process of transforming an abstract idea into its instantiation and vice versa).

domain architects practice on an ongoing basis, while the *solution architecture methodology* pattern recommends an appropriate methodology skeleton for solution architects. The *assessment methodology* pattern introduces a methodology blueprint for examining asset designs, while the *reference architecture methodology* pattern suggests a similar approach for managing reference assets. Reference asset examples are patterns, styles, tactics, or principles. The *architecture pattern methodology* and the *architecture principle* pattern both borrow from the reference architecture methodology pattern but specify it accordingly for patterns and principles. The *architecture methodology adapter* pattern proposes a methodology and view model adapter approach to adapt all architecture methodologies and view models in a situational manner. Finally, the *your own architecture platform pattern* recommends that your function plan, build, and operate a physical tool base to improve architecture consistency and productivity.

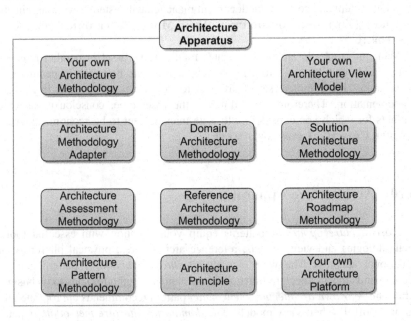

6.10.1 Your Own Architecture Methodology

Comprehensive, mature, and standardized architecture methodologies are available for many fields. An architecture methodology usually serves a particular design purpose (e.g., architecture governance, assessment, or elaboration). At the same time, methodologies are generic by design to allow a wide variety of applications. For example, standardized and off-the-shelf methodologies do not usually assume specific industries, organizational structures, company sizes, or business models. If architecture methods are used off-the-shelf (i.e., without tailoring them to the needs of the enterprise), architecture functions miss

valuable optimization opportunities. In the worst case, this means that an architect tailors an off-the-shelf methodology individually to the enterprise *and* the specific assignment.

Methodology is a body of methods, rules, and postulates employed by a discipline, a particular procedure, or set of procedures. (Merriam-Webster Dictionary 2020)

A *methodology* does not set out to provide solutions—it is therefore, not the same as a method. Instead, a methodology offers the theoretical underpinning for understanding which method, set of methods, or best practices can be applied to a specific case, for example, to calculate a specific result. (Wikipedia Methodology 2020f)

A methodology systematically directs efforts and activities toward defined objectives. It specifies the valid state and transition space for its respective field of concern. A methodology includes a method in which it outlines a systematic, step-by-step procedure. Each step in the procedure specifies what information is needed to execute the step, what information is generated by the step, and what role is responsible for performing the step. A methodology embodies the deep structure of its method and other complementary building blocks regardless of their instantiation. Methodologies facilitate discussions about the appropriateness of designs while abstracting from their material implementation aspects.

Irny Suzila Ishak (2005) understands a methodology as a basic framework or set of theoretical tools for a defined branch of knowledge:

Methodology is the systematic, theoretical analysis of the methods applied to a field of study. It comprises the theoretical analysis of the body of methods and principles associated with a branch of knowledge. Typically, it encompasses concepts such as paradigm, theoretical model, phases and quantitative or qualitative techniques.

Architecture Function and Your Own Architecture Methodology

Architecture functions derive their own methodologies from standard methodology frameworks to best fit the specific needs of their organization. Architecture functions differentiate their methodologies in terms of architecture levels and granularities. They also ensure that their methodologies differentiate between primary and secondary asset types (*business versus technical*). Furthermore, architecture functions ensure that their adapted methodologies distinguish between various architecture states (*baseline versus target architecture*). They augment their methodologies with method adapters. While an enterprise methodology considers the enterprise needs, method adapters optimally adapt methods to the concrete architecture assignments. Finally, methodologies are integrated into architecture platforms to guarantee their productive, coercive, and systematic application (Fig. 6.158).

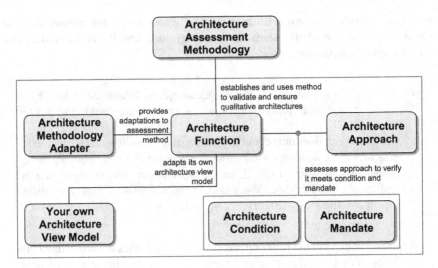

Fig. 6.158 Architecture function and your own architecture methodology

An architecture methodology increases the systematicity and repeatability of architecture governance and performance activities in an enterprise. Methodologies promote alignment, standardization, synergy, and economies of scale—ultimately, methodologies promote an attitude of repetition rather than reinvention. Architecture methodologies tangibly explain the *why*, *what*, *who*, *when*, and *how* of states and state transitions for their particular areas of responsibility.

Architecture methodology standards have been around for a long time—for example, the Open Group Architecture Framework (TOGAF[154]) (Open Group TOGAF 2009). De facto methodology standards (*architecture methodology*) are designed to be generic enough to be useful and applicable to the entire world. You customize a de facto methodology standard (*your own architecture methodology*) so that it is specifically useful for your architecture function and enterprise. Ultimately, you adapt your own methodology (*your own adapted architecture methodology*) to each concrete architecture engagement (Fig. 6.159).

---

[154]The Open Group Architecture Framework (TOGAF). TOGAF proposes an approach to design, plan, implement, and govern enterprise architecture. It describes a generic method for developing architectures. TOGAF suggests a common vocabulary, a generic in-formation model, an adaptable role model, general architecture artifacts, and tooling.

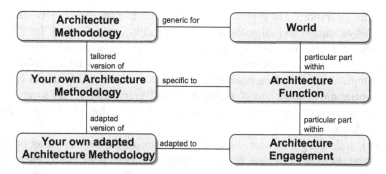

Fig. 6.159 Your own architecture methodology

Architecture methodologies are used to accompany and operationally shape engagements, such as programs or projects. Steven de Haes et al. (2020) defines respective engagements as:

> A structured set of activities concerned with the delivery of a defined capability based on an agreed schedule and budget.

Following Jan Dietz (2006), I use the term *operation* to abstract from *engagement, mission, program,* or *project* while emphasizing action orientation. An operation is a collection of activities performed by actors. Operation, regardless of implementation, can be understood as a collection of actor roles that perform *acts* that result in *facts*. While an *act* is a concrete activity, a *fact* is a concrete artifact.

Dietz distinguishes between *production acts* and *coordination acts*, with acts of production leading to *production facts* and acts of coordination leading to *coordination facts*. Actors act because they are responsible, authorized, or competent to perform acts. By performing an act of production, an actor concretely brings about changes of state in the production world. Acts of production always directly or indirectly affect facts of production. Through acts of coordination, actors commit themselves to perform acts of production. Coordination acts consist of propositional and intentional acts. While *proposition acts* anticipate something in the production world, *intention acts* refer to the production world in the form of questions, assertions, or promises (Fig. 6.160).

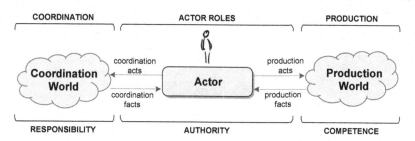

Fig. 6.160 Actor, act, fact (© 2011 Springer Science & Business Media, reprinted with permission)

Bundle operations via organizational vehicles, like projects, to control their scheduled execution and align them coherently with a specific goal, for example, operations focused on planning a change or executing a planned change. The execution of bundled operations results in a bundle of state changes in a landscape. For example, a new landscape asset is introduced, or an existing one is changed. Align operation bundles across architecture and granularity levels to coherently execute operations with a common planning horizon or strategic concern (ARCHITECTURE LEVEL).

Size is a defining characteristic of an operation, where the size of an operation depends on *the number of its acts*. The holding *cost of an operation* is defined as the cost of delaying its outcome (i.e., its intended value). The transaction cost is the cost of planning, executing, and reflecting on an operation. When an operation is small (i.e., the number of acts that comprise it is small), holding costs are comparatively low, while transaction costs tend to be high. If the size of an operation is large (i.e., the number of acts it consists of is high), holding costs are high, and transaction costs are comparatively low. That is, as the *transaction cost curve* falls (from high operation costs with a low number of acts to low operation costs with a high number of acts), the *holding cost curve* rises from low operation costs with a low number of acts to high operation costs with a high number of acts. The optimal cost balance is therefore at the intersection of the transaction and holding cost curves.

Danny Greefhorst and Erik Proper (2011) suggest that the three generic activities *assess*, *aim*, and *act* are fundamental to any architecture elaboration. An architect always investigates how best to approach (*assess*) an assessed problem (*aim*) in order to finally perform the required transformation (*act*). Ensure that your architects' thought process follows a basic argumentative logic in your architecture methodology. Emphasize reflective skepticism and relevance testing in *assess*, argumentative rigor and plausibility in *aim*, and pragmatism in *act* (Fig. 6.161).

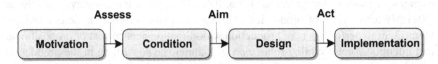

Fig. 6.161 Assess, aim, act (© 2006 Springer Science & Business Media, reprinted with permission)

Create your own architecture methodology by adapting an off-the-shelf methodology standard to your specific enterprise needs. Clarify what you need and can realistically expect to achieve with an optimal methodology. For example, clarify valid application contexts for the methodology or issues around its documentation centricity, artifact consumption and production, connectivity to architecture tools, or usability. Think of your architecture methodology as a system whose solution you must develop based on a well-developed methodology reference. Determine the architecture context and the conditions that your methodology should satisfy (NEED TO KNOW).

Augment your enterprise architecture methodology with an adapter framework so that all derived methodologies have adaptability virtually built-in. Your architects use adapters to adapt your architecture methodology to specific engagements. For example, the adapter framework of a solution elaboration methodology features three method adapters. A security-intense solution adapter describes how to adequately apply your solution methodology to solutions with extensive security requirements (*secure solutions adapter*). This adapter adds security-related viewpoints to your problem-solving method. A second adapter (*mobile application adapter*) explains the proper use of your solution method in the context of mobile application development. The adapter specifically points out that design-related precautions should be taken for mobile applications to function in offline mode. It also points out which solution viewpoints an architect should develop for this purpose. A third methodology adapter explains the optimal use of your method in the context of solutions with high modifiability requirements (*modifiability adapter*). For each specific utilization of your solution method, your architects select the adapters that best reflect a given engagement. In the case of a mobile application, for which both high security and performance requirements are formulated, a solution architect would combine all three adapters above to best adapt the problem-solving method (ARCHITECTURE METHODOLOGY ADAPTER).

Keep your customizations to a minimum to maximize the synergies of reusing standard methodology artifacts. Reuse as many assets, guidelines, templates, or role descriptions of the architecture methodology standard as possible to minimize the footprint you have to manage yourself. For example, consider simple mapping tables to connect a de facto methodology standard terminologically or conceptually to the version derived from your function. Terminological differences between the language used in your organization and the vocabulary propagated in a methodology standard are prevalent. For example, you refer to business building blocks in your enterprise as *application* while referring to technical building blocks as *infrastructure*. A de facto methodology standard may use the terms *service* and *platform*, while you refer to *application* and *infrastructure*. You may also manage more complex mappings between a de facto standard and your derived methodology. For example, while a de facto standard only distinguishes between *physical* and *logical* building blocks, you need *conceptual* as a further gradation in your own method. You can define *conceptual* by relating your definition to the *logical* conception of the de facto standard—thus maximizing your reuse effect (ARCHITECTURE LANGUAGE, DOMAIN TAXONOMY) (Fig. 6.162).

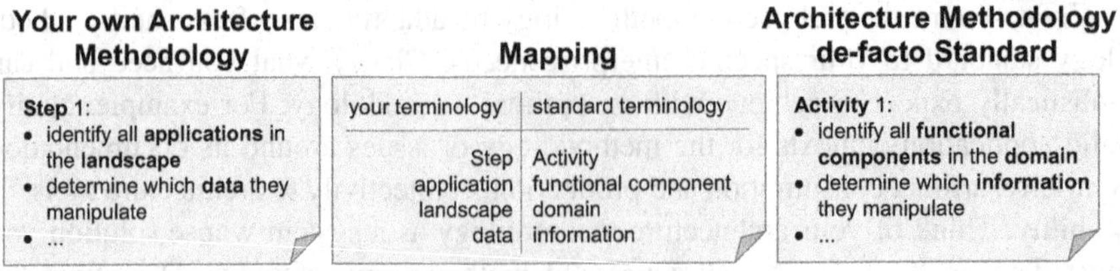

Your own Architecture Methodology	Mapping	Architecture Methodology de-facto Standard
Step 1: • identify all **applications** in the **landscape** • determine which **data** they manipulate • ...	your terminology / standard terminology Step / Activity application / functional component landscape / domain data / information	**Activity 1:** • identify all **functional components** in the **domain** • determine which **information** they manipulate • ...

Fig. 6.162 Terminological or conceptual mapping

Each adaptation step you take to a methodology standard like TOGAF, increasing your scope of responsibility, is often not only worthwhile but inevitable. You will understand most standard methodologies better if you think of them as high-level architecture heuristics rather than as immediately and very concretely applicable procedural instructions. Standard methodologies obtain a lot of information and artifacts. They are very comprehensive and often also very detailed so that at first glance they give an overwhelming overall impression. At the same time, they are generic and one-dimensional to the point of meaninglessness or arbitrariness. You misunderstand standard methodologies if you apply them in your enterprise in an unadapted way and still expect meaningful results. For example, a standard methodology does not consider your specific organizational structure, your process organization, the areas of responsibility you assign to your organizations, your geographic distribution, or the escalation relationships between your architecture governance bodies and your perform-architecture organization. An off-the-shelf methodology standard that you apply does not consider the unique characteristics of your industry, such as rigorous documentation and testing requirements in a highly regulated environment. Also, standard methodologies often overlap with each other or are incompatible. For example, the Carnegie Mellon Software Engineering Institute's standard architecture assessment methodology, the Architecture Tradeoff Analysis Method[155] [SEI ATAM], is only vaguely compatible with the Open Group TOGAF's standard (Open Group TOGAF 2009). So resist the temptation to use a comprehensive architecture method standard unadapted. Instead, invest the effort and distill the off-the-shelf standard method into a useful derivative that avoids the superfluous while still addressing your organization's unique needs (ARCHITECTURE CAPACITY).

Note that adapting a standard architecture methodology is more than adapting its original artifacts or terminological definitions. Adapting a standard methodology to your enterprise occurs at the transitions to other disciplines or other methodological frameworks. In other words, customize the inputs and outputs of the standard

---

[155] The Architecture Tradeoff Analysis Method (ATAM) is an architecture assessment and risk mitigation methodology. The process moderates between an architecture function and its stakeholders to determine business drivers (i.e., architecture conditions and goals). Then, the process extracts quality attributes from these drivers to create scenarios. Scenarios are used in conjunction with architecture approaches to understanding trade-offs, sensitivity points, risks, and non-risks.

methodology so that they meet the needs in your enterprise well. Customize what the method produces or consumes while largely reusing the internal mechanisms of the standard method. Note that you take responsibility for everything you tailor yourself. This results in your own responsibility for providing modified architecture training, customizing platforms and tools, tailoring artifacts and role models, as well as defining and maintaining your own taxonomies (LEARNING ORGANIZATION, ARCHITECTURE ROLE, ARCHITECTURE ARTIFACT, YOUR OWN ARCHITECTURE PLATFORM).

Ensure that the architecture methodologies you implement in your organization address well-chosen aspects. Be sure to include an adaptation activity in your methodologies as the first step of each engagement—the activity adapts the methodology to a given concrete context or task. Also, expect architects to articulate the need they are addressing for each step in your methodology. In other words, make sure your architects are always able to articulate the meaning, purpose, and goal of a step before they execute it. Also, introduce retrospectives as final activities in your methodologies. A retrospective motivates architects to think about improvements to a methodology immediately after it has been applied. Identified improvements flow back to the methodology owner, who incorporates them into method improvements over time.

Apply the standard methodology alignment approach described in this pattern to all method standards that exist for the various architecture disciplines. For example, architecture elaboration methodologies address the construction or evolution of landscape assets—for example, the architectural elaboration of a service or platform. Solution architects primarily use architecture elaboration methodologies to establish new or evolve existing assets. They help architects deliver solutions as answers to given problems (SOLUTION ARCHITECTURE METHODOLOGY).

In contrast to solution architecture methodologies, architecture lifecycle methodologies have a continuous character, as they accompany the entire lifecycle of corresponding assets. They accompany the phases of landscape planning, building, operation, and finally deconstruction. For example, a domain architecture methodology is typically used by domain and enterprise architects. A domain architect uses such a methodology to establish transparency for a domain. This includes maintaining the domain baseline architecture, corresponding target architecture states, and plans for transforming baselines into targets. Domain architects enhance the quality of planning investments and divestments in a domain (DOMAIN ARCHITECTURE METHODOLOGY, BASELINE ARCHITECTURE VERSUS TARGET ARCHITECTURE).

Reference architecture methodologies define and accompany the lifecycle management of reference assets, such as patterns or roadmaps. The lifecycle management of reference architectures ranges from the identification of the need for a new reference asset, its specification, validation, and publication, to monitoring and ensuring compliance with policies that relate to corresponding reference assets (ARCHITECTURE POLICY, REFERENCE ARCHITECTURE METHODOLOGY).

Finally, architecture assessment methodologies propose a systematic process for analyzing, assessing, and validating existing designs, for example, the evaluation of a proposed application modification or a design proposed to establish a new service (ARCHITECTURE ASSESSMENT METHODOLOGY).

6.10.2 Architecture Methodology Adapter

Even if an off-the-shelf architecture methodology has been tailored to the needs of an enterprise, an additional adaption step is required to adapt an architecture methodology to a concrete engagement at hand. If it remains open how this adaptation step is to be performed systematically and meaningfully, each architect must adapt the methodology and view model individually—a missed opportunity in terms of architecture standardization and productivity.

An adaptation optimizes or enables the use of a device for a situation for which it was not tailor-made. An adapter bridges an existing incompatibility between an adapted and an adapting device.

> *Adapter* is a device for connecting two parts (as of different diameters) of an apparatus. (Merriam-Webster Dictionary 2020)

In the context of methodologies, an adapter optimizes the application of a method to a specific engagement situation. A method adapter describes how a methodology is best applied by explaining which method activities should be performed and in which sequence, which method viewpoints should be developed to answer which questions, at what level of detail to operate, which additional models to specify, or which *definition of done*[156] criteria to apply.

Architecture Function and Methodology Adapter
Architecture functions define and utilize methodology adapters to guide architects in the optimal application of methodologies to specific engagement contexts. Architecture adapters guide the use of methodologies and associated view models by pointing to reference architecture assets, such as patterns (Fig. 6.163).

---

[156]The definition of done (DoD) is an Agile and Scrum terminology. However, it is a much broader concept for determining an exit criterion for a work product or activity. A definition of done must be created individually for each task. The DoD specifies criteria that can be held against the task's progress to recognize the achievement of the desired end state and to end the task.

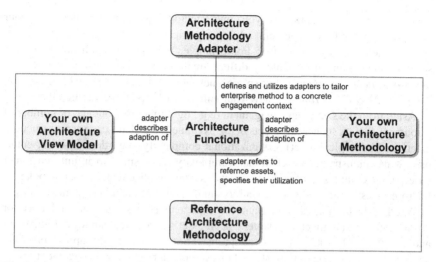

Fig. 6.163 Architecture function and methodology adapter

Once you have derived your own methodologies (*your own architecture methodology*) and view models (*your own architecture view model*) from standard methodologies (*architecture methodology and view model*), adapters support you in adapting your own methodologies and view models (*adapted architecture methodology and view model*) to specific architecture engagements (e.g., projects) (**YOUR OWN ARCHITECTURE METHODOLOGY**) (Fig. 6.164).

Fig. 6.164 Architecture
methodology adapter

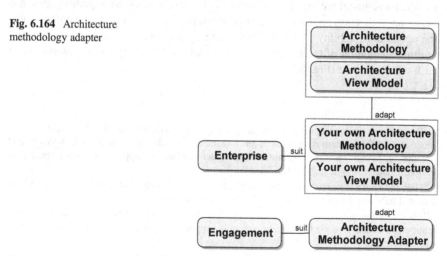

While you already optimized your own methodology and view model for your enterprise, concrete engagements differ significantly and require engagement-specific methodology adaptation. For example, the optimal application of your solution architecture methodology differs greatly when you apply it in a *2-week proof-of-concept engagement* to explore a new application, on the one hand, or in an extensive *2-year program* to renew your entire ERP[157] platform on the other.

Aside from the size of an engagement (e.g., tight timelines, budget, or number of resources), factors such as the assets being examined (e.g., landscape asset, structural asset, methodological asset), organizational complexity (e.g., domain-wide, enterprise-wide, industry-wide), customer complexity (e.g., small to infinite customer base), or the complexity of architecture styles being applied (e.g., hub-and-spoke,[158] microservices,[159] blockchain[160]) lead to significantly different engagement types.

Another factor that is important for engagement classification, and thus for consideration in architecture adapters, is an asset's investment strategy. John Ward and Joe Peppard (2002) suggest adopting various strategies to support portfolio analysis and landscape optimization. For example, a renovation engagement for an application in the *stars* segment adapts an agile evolution approach. A *stars architecture adapter* would mirror this and recommend moderate quality gates, standardization, and integration conditions. Another example is an engagement to evaluate a new service candidate in the *question marks* segment. This project must operate on a limited budget, applies an experimental development approach, and copes with low-quality gates and standard conformance constraints. Therefore, a *question marks adapter* would reflect appropriate criteria and guide architects through method applications accordingly. Finally, an engagement around a legacy platform in the *cash cows* segment weighs investments defensively, applies strict quality gates, has high standardization requirements, and at the same time is careful not to compromise the operational stability of the platform. Here, a *cash cows adapter* would guide the optimal adaptation of the architecture methodology according to the criteria of the cash cows segment (Fig. 6.165).

---

[157] Enterprise resource planning (ERP) is the integrated management of the most important business processes. An ERP system covers central functional areas shared by all companies, such as financial accounting, human resources, manufacturing, order fulfillment, supply chain management, or customer relationship management.

[158] Hub-and-spoke is an integration architecture style favoring communication via applications and a central hub over direct communication between applications.

[159] Microservices are fine-grained, context-agnostic functions or function endpoints. They are requested and delivered via lightweight protocols. Applications are established as loosely coupled microservices.

[160] Blockchain is an architecture style in which a growing list of decentrally stored records called blocks is unidirectionally linked to form a chain of blocks. A block contains a cryptographic hash of the previous block (i.e., a pointer to the previous block), a timestamp, and transaction data. By design, a blockchain is resistant to changes in its data because blocks cannot be changed retroactively without changing all subsequent blocks. Changing all blocks retroactively is made impossible by their decentralized storage.

Fig. 6.165 Investment and divestment strategy matrix

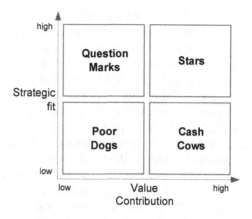

Reference architecture view models in your adapters, as they are integral parts of appropriate methodologies. Adapters are productivity tools and significantly flatten your learning curve with respect to the adequate application of a comprehensive architecture methodology and view model. For example, an adapter helps you decide which artifacts or views you should focus on and which you should rather ignore. Adapters help you determine meaningful abstraction levels or recommend context-specific *definitions of done*. For example, an adapter for security-sensitive systems (*security-intense systems adapter*) recommends how to apply your problem-solving method in security-sensitive situations. The adapter specifically suggests the viewpoints you should develop as a solution architect. For each viewpoint, the adapter describes questions you need to answer and identifies the attributes you should capture for building blocks in the viewpoints. The *security-intense systems adapter* may further recommend which combinations of viewpoints are suitable for obtaining holistic insights into emergent system properties. The adapter provides you with security-related checklists and recommends a *definition of done* that draws a reasonable line of relevance for security issues (**YOUR OWN ARCHITECTURE VIEW MODEL**) (Fig. 6.166)

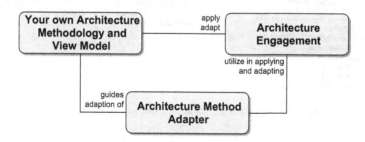

Fig. 6.166 Architecture methodology adaption

Start with a simple adapter format and create your architecture adapters tangibly, e.g., as office documents. The architecture adapter explains how you perform different methods and which viewpoints of the architecture view model you elaborate to answer which questions and how. Since adapters primarily refer to methodology artifacts (i.e., methodology outcomes), they should mirror method artifact schemes and structures. The methodology, its associated view model, and its artifact outputs remain cohesive, generic, and unchanged. Thus, the methodology continues to include all views of the architecture view model, all artifacts, all roles and responsibilities, milestones, tollgates, or checklists. Although adapters inherit the schema of generic method artifacts, they do not repeat the method content but rather supplement it with instructions that reference the method content. For example, a paragraph in an adapter document that walks through a step in a generic architecture process replicates the step's algorithmic schema but not the generic step's content. Rather, the adapter suggests criteria that help determine whether the referenced step needs to be performed at all and, if so, at what level of detail. In other words, adapters are partial copies of method artifacts—copies of their schema, not their content. Rather, adapters relate to method information by classifying, overriding, relevancy-ranking, extending, or explaining its use. In a sense, adapters overlay the generic methodologies, view models, and artifacts to explain how to interpret their content in the supported engagement context. Furthermore, adapters include a detailed description of the engagement context they support. For example, by naming the type of landscape assets (e.g., application, service, platform, information, technology), the adapter provides adaptation guidance (**ARCHITECTURE ARTIFACT**) (Fig. 6.167).

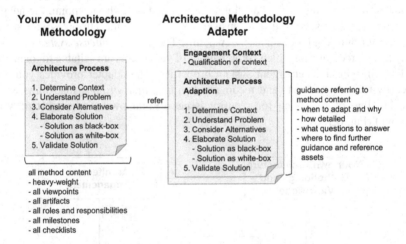

Fig. 6.167 Architecture adapter referring architecture methodology

Typically, you have one enterprise-specific architecture methodology and view model for each methodology area, for example, an assessment methodology for performing architecture assessments or a solution methodology for elaborating the solution architecture of landscape assets. Most likely, however, you have multiple architecture methodology adapters for each methodology and view model. For example, a *domain architecture assessment adapter* guides architects through the optimal assessment of entire domains, while a *solution architecture assessment adapter* guides the assessment of landscape assets. Both adapters, domain and solution architecture, explain the optimal application of the generic assessment methodology in their particular contexts.

Methodology adapters are perfectly reusable assets and contribute significantly to the productivity of an architecture function. You can add new method adapters as you observe new types of engagements in your enterprise. You can add or evolve them without compromising the existing adapters or methodologies to which they relate. Although it may not be immediately obvious, there is nothing wrong with having methodology adapters referencing more than one architecture methodology. Likewise, it can be useful to combine multiple methodology adapters—that is, to offer composites of adapters. For example, if you find that a *cloud solution adapter* is virtually always used in combination with a *security-intense system adapter*, assemble a *secure cloud* adapter (MANAGED ARCHITECTURE EVOLUTION) (Fig. 6.168).

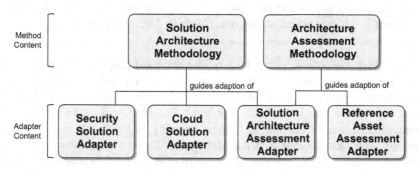

Fig. 6.168 N:M relation between adapters and methodologies

Ownership must be clearly defined for each methodology adapter. Adapters are usually associated with a single methodology. One option is to assign ownership to the owner of the referenced methodology asset. Alternatively, ownership is assigned to the realm to which an adapter proposes adaptation. For example, ownership for a *cloud solution adapter* is associated with the *cloud* domain and therefore assigned to the *cloud domain architect* (ARCHITECTURE OWNERSHIP).

An architecture methodology adapter refers to methodology, view model, or generic method artifacts and reference assets, such as patterns, styles, or principles. An adapter combines two areas of enterprise-wide guidance into one adapter artifact:

methodology and reference assets. For example, a *security-intense system adapter* references the security architecture pattern *protection from code injection attacks as* offered by the security domain (ARCHITECTURE PATTERN METHODOLOGY).

6.10.3 Your Own Architecture View Model

Architecture view models can be delineated and discussed separately from architecture methodologies, although they are virtually inevitably linked to the latter. Each architecture methodology serves a particular purpose, such as architecture assessment or elaboration. Architecture view models are equally purpose-optimized. Corresponding to the genericity of methodologies, view models are generically designed to allow for a wide variety of their instantiations. This means that, analogous to the methodologies, the unadapted use of generic view models is suboptimal. Therefore, architecture functions derive their own view models from standard models by adapting them to the specific needs of their enterprise—providing their architects with a tool to describe the architecture in a way that is appropriate for the business.

> A *model* is a description or analogy used to help visualize something that cannot be directly observed. (Merriam-Webster Dictionary 2020)

Modeling is probably one of the activities that most people primarily associate with the profession of architecture. A model is a scaled-down and abstracted representation of an object of interest. It suppresses irrelevant details in favor of those aspects relevant to the interest at hand. The purpose a model serves is the central motivation for building it. Without knowing, or being able to articulate its purpose, you cannot create a meaningful model. If you are not clear about what purpose a model serves, you should not invest effort in its elaboration. In general, you should make sure that the effort required to create and maintain a model never exceeds the expected model benefit.

Models abstract real-world phenomena for the purpose of understanding aspects relevant to answering questions of interest. They use standard modeling nomenclatures as their basic language. These languages are used to generate and explicate models. Modeling nomenclatures can be textual, graphical, iconographic, or hybrid. They are preferably formalized and strive to minimize ambiguity already at the language level. Models represent real-world phenomena. They fundamentally enable communication and collaboration and are therefore indispensable ingredients of the architecture toolbox. The influence that models have on the way we think, communicate, and perceive real-world phenomena cannot be overstated.

Models support planning by being the means to identify gaps, redundancies, or deficiencies—ultimately, they are the means to identify the right things to be done.

Models also support the design process. A model is used to prescribe how something should be done correctly—in other words, models anticipate desired states. Models support analysis, reflection, and simulation by providing a basis for performing what-if scenarios and impact analyses in a cost-effective manner. In this sense, models are a very effective means of evaluating, for example, strategic fit, cost and risk implications, reasonable remediation, or compliance with laws and regulations without physically realizing cost, risk, or noncompliance. Models also support implementation. Each model represents a phenomenon at a particular level of abstraction or from a defined perspective. The model is often related to other models that view the same phenomenon at other levels of abstraction or from other perspectives. For example, an architecture-level model is further refined by a corresponding design-level model. The combination of multiple models relating to the same phenomenon provides a condensed and descriptive anticipation of the phenomenon and thus ideally serves its realization.

The notion of *model* is almost as important as the notion of *system*. The study of a system basically amounts to building the corresponding model and studying or analyzing its behavior. This gives rise to the problem of validating a model against the modeled system—in other words, the problem of verifying whether a model adequately depicts the system it represents.

Leo Apostel (1960), in his definition of the relationship of *system* to *model*, makes it clear that nothing is a model per se. Something becomes a model when it is used to represent something else:

> Any subject using a system A that is neither directly nor indirectly interacting with system B, to obtain information about the system B, is using A as a model for B.

Models that depict the internal structure and construction of a system are white-box models. They convey a construction perspective—that is, they are used to build or change the system. This perspective corresponds to the ontological[161] conception of a system. Black-box models do not provide insight into the construction and operation of the system they model. Rather, they provide an external and behavioral perspective on a system. This perspective corresponds to the teleological[162] notion of a system (ARCHITECTURE ASSET).

There are also some uncomfortable facts about models, for example, the illusion of mathematical exactness, absoluteness, and accuracy that extensive or complicated models sometimes give. The formal nomenclatures used as model notations further reinforce this impression. Architecture models are often anything but mathematically

---

[161] Ontological system concept. The ontological system view deals with a system's mechanics as observed inside the system (internal behavior). It also distinguishes the concept of aggregate from the concept of system. Both concepts, aggregate and system, are collections of objects. However, in aggregates, the elements are not held together by interaction bonds, whereas in systems, they are. A system, therefore, has unity and integrity. Both properties are lacking in aggregates.

[162] Teleological system concept. The term teleological system deals with a system's function and behavior as observed from the outside (external behavior). The teleological system's perspective is useful when using a system.

exact. It is not uncommon for inadequate models to be vague and ambiguous to the point of being completely unusable, while at the same time being misperceived as a relevant representation of the real world.

Many modeling standards exist for a variety of modeling use cases, for example, the Unified Modelling Language[163] (UML) of the Object Management Group (OMG UML 2020a), or the architecture modeling language ArchiMate[164] (Open Group ArchiMate 2020c). Other examples include SysML[165] or the Business Process Model and Notation[166] language (BPMN) (OMG BPMN 2020b).

Architecture View Model

A *viewpoint* is a position or perspective from which something is considered or evaluated (Merriam-Webster Dictionary 2020).

View is the act of seeing, surveying, or examining, mentally (Merriam-Webster Dictionary 2020).

An *architecture view model* standardizes architecture descriptions. View models explain the *why, what, who, when,* and *how* of architecture manifestation, each related to a specific area of an overall architecture description.

Architecture Function and Your Own Architecture View Model
Architecture functions adapt their own architecture view models from off-the-shelf standards to appropriately capture the architecture of their assets and landscapes. They tightly tie view models to corresponding methodologies. View models enable traceability between viewpoints, which in turn are designed to allow relevant differentiation, for example, differentiation along architecture levels, distinctions of architecture states (*baseline architecture versus target architecture*), or asset semantics (*business versus technical*) (Fig. 6.169).

---

[163] Unified Modeling Language (UML) is a universal modeling language that provides a standard approach to modeling and visualizing system design. Note that the concept of system is not limited to IT system. UML supports the expression and modeling of dynamic and static perspectives, individual building blocks, and their relationships (OMG UML 2020a).

[164] ArchiMate is an open and independent modeling standard for enterprise architectures that supports the description, analysis, and presentation of architecture within and between architectures. It is an Open Group standard and is based on fundamental architectural concepts defined by the IEEE (i.e., IEEE 1471).

[165] SysML is a language for generic system modeling and is being further developed by the Object Management Group. It supports the specification, analysis, design, verification, and validation of a wide range of systems, including systems of systems (OMG SysML 2020).

[166] BPMN is not a general modeling language. It is specifically designed for modeling business processes.

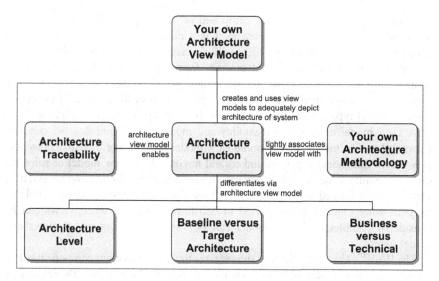

Fig. 6.169 Architecture function and your own architecture view model

View models are usually integral parts of architecture methodologies. Therefore, they are generic in nature and need to be adapted to make them specific to your architecture function and enterprise (*your own architecture view model*). Finally, architects need to adapt your own view model to their specific engagement at hand (*your own adapted architecture view model*) (**YOUR OWN ARCHITECTURE METHODOLOGY**) (Fig. 6.170).

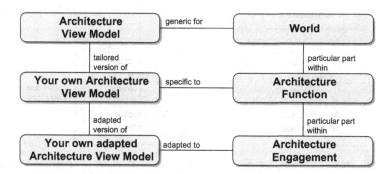

Fig. 6.170 Your own architecture view model

A view model is a systematics composed of viewpoints, types of models, and relationships between them. A viewpoint is a definition of the perspective from which a view is taken. It is a specification for constructing and using a view. A view is what you see, while a viewpoint specifies from where you look. Viewpoints are templates for the concrete views that are instantiated from them. If you think of the viewpoint as a class, then a view is a concrete instance of the associated viewpoint class. A model type defines the conventions for one type of architecture model.

A view model defines its viewpoints and model types—and thus all concrete views that will be instantiated from the view model in the future. It also defines how viewpoints and model types are linked and navigated. A view model clarifies for each viewpoint whose interests it serves, who is responsible for creating a view, how views are instantiated and evolved, how views are navigated to arrive at holistic insights, what model types are used to constitute views, or when views can be considered complete. A view model can be viewed as a system of views and model types.

The IEEE[167] Computer Society summarizes the most important components of an architecture view model in *Recommended Practice for Architecture Description of Software-Intensive Systems* (IEEE 2000) (Fig. 6.171).

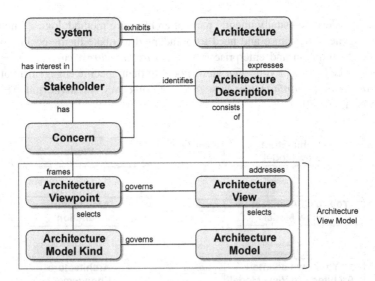

Fig. 6.171 IEEE Recommended Practice for Architecture Description of Software-Intensive Systems

---

[167]The Institute of Electrical and Electronics Engineers (IEEE) is a professional association for electronic engineering and electrical engineering.

According to the IEEE definition, a *system* is supposed to have stakeholders. *Stakeholders* are individuals, groups, or organizations that have concerns about a system of interest. A *concern* is an interest that pertains to the development, operation, or utilization of a system—for example, system functionality, performance, reliability, security, or modifiability. Every system exhibits an architecture—deliberate or not, documented or not. *Architecture* is expressed in terms of architecture descriptions. An *architecture description* comprises architecture views, where each view addresses the concerns of appropriate stakeholders. An *architecture view* consists of architecture models that relate to architecture model types. While an architecture view is a concrete subset of an architecture description, an *architecture viewpoint* is a set of conventions for constructing and using views derived from it. A viewpoint includes model types and associated modeling notations appropriate to the concerns of the viewpoint.

Consider an architecture description as a set of concrete architecture views and view models. Views and models pertain to architecture viewpoints and model types that a view model suggests as appropriate for describing architectures. There are different types of architecture view models, which, depending on their type, serve other particular purposes. View models distinguish types of viewpoints, for example, viewpoints that represent a particular selection of information, such as functional, data, and operational viewpoints. Also, consider viewpoints that emphasize architecture planning states, such as baseline versus target architecture viewpoints. While baseline viewpoints capture facts and describe the current state of an architecture, target viewpoints support architecture planning and thus capture future facts. Finally, distinguishing the semantics of primary assets is another relevant viewpoint differentiator. An example of this is the distinction between business and technical assets (BUSINESS VERSUS TECHNICAL, BASELINE ARCHITECTURE VERSUS TARGET ARCHITECTURE).

Beware that you face conflicting risks when developing architecture descriptions—and, ultimately, when developing architecture views and models. Your views and models can become so generic as to be meaningless. However, they can also become so detailed that they fail to capture the essence of architecture. Top-down architecture development risks underestimating relevant details. Obtaining comparatively narrow and monocausal designs is another common result of rigidly followed top-down elaboration approaches. Bottom-up development approaches, in turn, run the risk of obtaining partially optimal designs that are overall in an inappropriate Pareto[168] equilibrium—at the expense of a suboptimal overall architecture. Both extremes—if pursued solely—lead to imbalance, while the combination of both approaches delivers pragmatic solutions. Oscillating between top-down and bottom-up architecture elaboration leads to realistic designs. So find a

---

[168] Pareto optimum is an optimum at which no preference criterion can be better without at least one individual or preference criterion being worse off. The concept is named after Vilfredo Pareto (1848–1923), who used it to research economics.

balance between overemphasizing irrelevant details and neglecting architecturally relevant essences.

View models enable traceability between their viewpoints—that is, between concrete architecture views and models. By navigating, associating, or combining views, valuable insights emerge, and an architecture description gains plasticity. For example, understanding how functional building blocks are placed on operational building blocks allows you to simulate both the horizontal and vertical execution threads of a transaction. The functional view shows three functional building blocks (FBB$_1$–FBB$_3$) and the logical relationships among them. The operational view shows the operational building blocks (OBB$_A$–OBB$_C$) and their respective relationships. Finally, the functional and operational views are mapped to each other so that for all functional components it is captured on which operational components they are placed. This combination of both views allows the execution thread of transaction TX$_1$ to be explored by traversing the physical interaction path both horizontally and vertically (interactions *(1)* to *(12)*) (**ARCHITECTURE TRACEABILITY**) (Fig. 6.172).

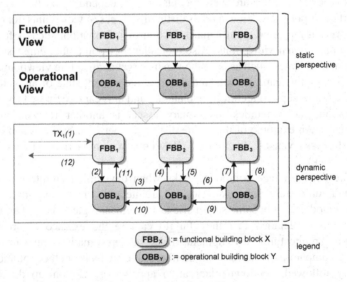

Fig. 6.172 Functional and operational viewpoint relationship

Another example of a valuable viewpoint combination is the traceability between condition viewpoints and solution viewpoints (*architecture approaches*). This combination makes it possible to understand, for a given condition, which architecture approaches address it. It is also useful in the opposite direction, for example, to understand which conditions are affected by modifying a particular architecture approach (ARCHITECTURE CONDITION, ARCHITECTURE APPROACH).

As mentioned earlier, view models are inevitably associated with methodologies and are therefore designed for a specific purpose. This means that each view model contains views that are specific to the purpose of that methodology. For example, a solution architecture view model contains state-oriented views and views that represent how a particular problem is addressed by a solution mechanism or algorithm. An architecture assessment view model, on the other hand, captures the architecture description being assessed (*solution architecture description*), the reasons for the assessment (*assessment driver*), and the solution architecture's desired state (*solution driver*). An assessment view model additionally features views that represent an assessment report. Architecture roadmap view models map relevant events to a time axis, while architecture pattern view models enable the description of individual patterns, pattern catalogs, and pattern languages (SOLUTION ARCHITECTURE METHODOLOGY, ARCHITECTURE ASSESSMENT METHODOLOGY, ARCHITECTURE ROADMAP METHODOLOGY, ARCHITECTURE PATTERN METHODOLOGY).

Three basic viewpoints and relationships between them are common to almost all architecture view models—regardless of other, specific view model purposes: functional architecture, operational architecture, and information architecture viewpoints. *Functional architecture viewpoints* encompass building blocks that carry the functional weight of a system—for example, landscape assets such as applications or services that underlie and support business processes. A functional viewpoint describes how architecture conditions (e.g., functional requirements) are realized by collaborating building blocks. It describes the functionality provided by functional components, depicts how use cases are realized, how functional components interact with each other, or on which operational building blocks they are placed.

Operational architecture viewpoints include operational building blocks. An operational building block operates either other operational building blocks, functional building blocks, or a mixture of both. An operational viewpoint conveys how functional components or other operational components are operated. It specifies operational building block details (e.g., uptime and availability, operational services offered to host functional components). The viewpoint represents how operational components cooperate to constitute an operational platform on which functional components can be placed. A technical platform such as an operating system on a physical compute node is considered an operational building block. However, a business platform may also qualify as an operational building block, for example, a business platform that provides basic business capabilities to the functional building blocks it hosts.

Information architecture viewpoints represent information building blocks. An information building block details the data, data attributes, data schema, or data context that constitutes the information. Information architecture viewpoints depict relationships between information building blocks, cardinality[169] details, or the placement of information building blocks on functional building blocks. Functional components enclose information entities to make the management, delivery, or retrieval of information functionally accessible. Information viewpoints also describe the specifics of information *at rest* and *in transit,*[170] information classifications, conversions, or canonical formats. Finally, information viewpoints also make distinctions between conceptual, logical, and physical information representation.

The three elementary viewpoints are related to each other so that you obtain a holistic understanding of the design and navigate the resulting architecture plastically. The functional building blocks are bridges into the functional requirements and depict, for example, how use cases are realized. For their own provision and thus ultimately for the realization of use cases, functional building blocks are closely linked to information building blocks (i.e., information building blocks are placed on functional ones). For the operation and hosting of functional blocks, operational blocks are needed on which functional blocks can be placed and operated. Based on such an architecture description, you can determine the contribution (direct or indirect) that each architecture building block makes to the realization of architecture conditions (Fig. 6.173).

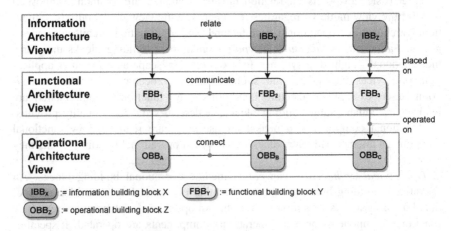

Fig. 6.173 Fundamental architecture viewpoints

---

[169] Cardinality—in mathematics, cardinality of a set is a measure of the number of elements of the set. For the directed relation A → B between the sets A and B, a cardinality δ expresses that $a \in A$ can relate to a number of elements $b \in B$, where the maximum number of relatable elements b to a is in the order of magnitude δ.

[170] Data at rest, data in use, and data in transit distinguish the three states of digital data. Data at rest refers to data permanently stored on computer data warehouses. Data at rest includes both structured and unstructured data. Data in use refers to data stored in a non-persistent state—for example, in the random access memory (RAM) of a compute node. Data in transit refers to data that flows between compute nodes over a network. A distinction is made for the data whether it flows over a public and untrusted network such as the Internet or whether it flows within the boundaries of a private network (e.g., corporate LAN).

View Model Navigation

An architecture function has adapted a standard view model and derived its own optimized solution architecture view model. The architecture function has created a simple use case (*illustration of view model navigation*) for an architecture training course.

The goal of the training is to teach new architects how the architecture view model was built and how to use it. In the training course, the use case is intentionally used as an introduction to the view model to highlight the benefits it provides. The use case is deliberately kept simple for this purpose. Its *flow of events* (*behavior*) consists only of the steps $step_1$ and $step_2$ (Fig. 6.174).

Use Case «View Model Illustrator»		
Name	Illustration of view model navigation	
Actor Description	Trainee	
Basic flow of events	**Step**	**NFR**
	Step 1	
	Step 2	

Fig. 6.174 Use case

The following *functional behavior model* is part of the functional viewpoint. Functional behavior models are dynamic models and depict cooperation relationships—in this case, the cooperation between functional building blocks. Functional behavior models are used, among other things, to represent the realization of use cases—here, the realization of the use case *illustration of view model navigation*. FBB_1 provides the capability *step$_1$* to the outside world. The functionality needed to execute $step_1$ is realized internally by FBB_1. The information IBB_X is required for the execution of the $step_1$ and is transmitted to FBB_1. The functionality required to execute $message_1$ is provided by FBB_2, where FBB_2 in turn requires FBB_3, since FBB_3 provides $message_2$ as an interface method. IBB_Y is information sent to FBB_3 via execution of $message_2$. Finally, $step_2$ (including IBB_Z) is executed based on the functionality provided by FBB_2, completing the realization of the use case (Fig. 6.175).

(continued)

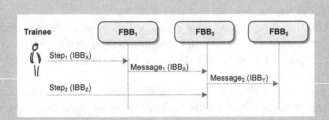

Fig. 6.175 Functional behavior model

The *functional structure model* is another model type of the functional viewpoint. It represents the behavioral capabilities of functional components. A functional structure model shows the basic and use case-independent relationships between building blocks—for example, generalization-specialization or whole-part relationships—but also other associations that are fundamental in nature (Fig. 6.176).

Fig. 6.176 Functional structure model

The *information structure model* is part of the information viewpoint. It describes the attributes and data schema for the information building blocks IBB_X, IBB_Y, and IBB_Z. It also describes their relationships and the cardinality between them. For example, the elements of information type IBB_X consist of the attributes x_1 and x_2, while an IBB_Z element is fully qualified via z_1, z_2, and z_3. The relationship between IBB_X and IBB_Y states that an IBB_X element is associated with no IBB_Y element (*0*) in the minimum case and with many (***) IBB_Y elements in the maximum case (Fig. 6.177).

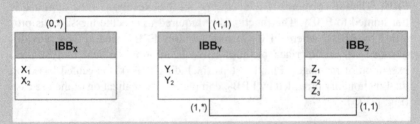

Fig. 6.177 Information structure model

(continued)

The *information placement model* is also part of an information viewpoint. It explains the placement relationships between information and function building blocks as they result from the previous use case. For example, IBB_X is partially placed on both function building blocks, FBB_1 and FBB_2, while IBB_Y is fully placed on FBB_3. Placing information on a function building block means that the information can be created, read, and changed via the corresponding function building block (Fig. 6.178).

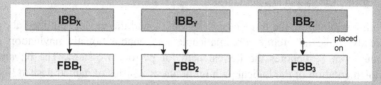

Fig. 6.178 Information placement model

The *operational structure model* is part of the operational viewpoint. It presents operational building blocks, their capabilities, and the basic relationships (*connections*) between them. For example, OBB_A is connected to OBB_B via connection$_{A-B}$ (Fig. 6.179).

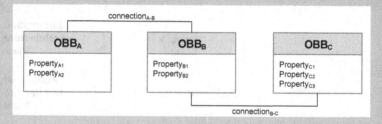

Fig. 6.179 Operational structure model

The *operational placement model* is another part of the operational viewpoint. The operational building blocks of the model are derived from the operational and communication needs that the hosted functional building blocks have. For example, FBB_1 is placed on OBB_A because OBB_A is connected to OBB_B and OBB_B operates the functional building block FBB_2. FBB_1 must send messages to FBB_2, for which the technical transmission via the operational building blocks OBB_A and OBB_B must be guaranteed (Fig. 6.180).

(continued)

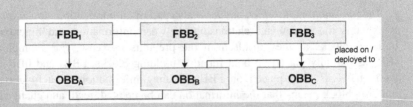

Fig. 6.180 Operational placement model

In combination, the three basic viewpoints and the models outlined above already make an architecture malleable and enable holistic navigation or simulation. S_1 denotes the logical path for performing step$_1$. The physical implementation of the logical path is shown as a series of named dashed lines ($S_{11}, S_{12}, S_{13}, S_{14}$) that illustrate the interaction between the OBB$_A$ operational building block, the operated functional building block FBB$_1$, and the IBB$_X$ information. The logical path for the execution of message$_2$ is denoted S_2 in the following. The physical realization of S_2 is again shown as a series of named dashed lines ($S_{21}, S_{22}, S_{23}, S_{24}$). The totality of relationships and mappings between the three core viewpoints allows an architect to simulate an architecture holistically already on paper (Fig. 6.181).

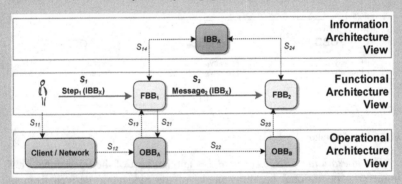

Fig. 6.181 Architecture viewpoint interplay

Other viewpoints emerge in differently oriented view models and further differentiate the viewpoints presented so far (Fig. 6.182).

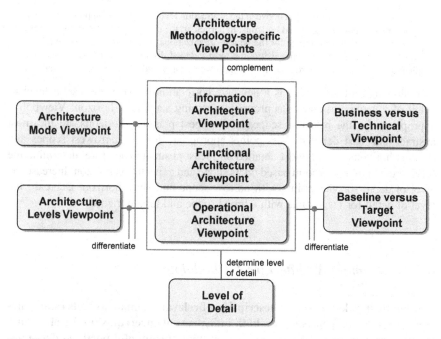

Fig. 6.182 Complementary and differentiating viewpoints

The three core viewpoints introduced above are further differentiated by additional viewpoints and integrated into an overarching view model. Thus, a *business versus technical viewpoint* cuts across all three core views to classify functional, informational, and operational components regarding their direct (*business*) versus indirect (*technical*) contribution (**BUSINESS VERSUS TECHNICAL**).

The *baseline versus target viewpoint* distinguishes all other viewpoints when chronologically different architecture states need to be delineated, for example, the current architecture situation (*baseline architecture*), the expected architecture situation in 1 year (*target architecture in 1 year*), and an anticipated architecture situation in the distant future (*target architecture in 5 years*) (**BASELINE ARCHITECTURE VERSUS TARGET ARCHITECTURE**).

The *architecture mode viewpoint* distinguishes between *design-time*, *runtime*, and *manage-time* architecture perspectives. Finally, architecture levels are distinguished via a separate viewpoint in order to explicitly differentiate between architecture representations at enterprise, domain, and solution levels (**ARCHITECTURE LEVEL**).

Finally, I have included the *level of detail* as another differentiator to tailor view models to your actual needs. As a rule of thumb, when evaluating architecture, you should take an approach that is *miles wide and inches deep*. This means aiming for broad (wide) completeness of understanding key concerns and drilling deeper only where it really makes sense. Svyatoslav Kotusev (2018) expresses this consideration as follows:

(It exists) a negative correlation between the abstraction levels of discussion points and their appropriate planning scopes and horizons. In particular, the discussion points and respective planning decisions appropriate for the widest organizational scopes and longest time horizons are the most abstract ones, while the most detailed discussion points and respective planning decisions are appropriate for the narrowest scopes and shortest time horizons.

Following Kotusev, there is a negative correlation between the useful level of detail of a viewpoint and its appropriate planning scope and horizon. Viewpoints appropriate for the broadest scopes and longest planning horizons are the most abstract and least detailed. Viewpoints appropriate for the narrowest scopes and shortest horizons are the most detailed and least abstract. Therefore, determine the level of detail of a viewpoint based on its scope and expectation horizon. Increase the level of detail for viewpoints with narrow scope and short horizon. Decrease the level of detail for viewpoints with a broad scope and long horizon.

6.10.4   Domain Architecture Methodology

Systematic development and description of relevant domain aspects establishes transparency and consistency—both indispensable prerequisites for efficiently identifying, proposing, discussing, and making meaningful portfolio decisions. In the absence of a methodical approach to domain architecture development, the architecture function's ability to make decisive contributions is undermined—especially in the planning phases of an enterprise's value chain.

A *domain architecture methodology* is a lifecycle methodology that accompanies the lifecycle of architecture assets such as services, applications, or platforms within a domain—that is, their planning, building, operational, and decommissioning phases. With a domain architecture methodology, architects create baseline and target architecture overviews as well as reference assets and they monitor compliance with domain-level policies.

A domain architecture methodology increases the systematicity, repeatability, and thus efficiency of domain architecture development. By creating holistic architecture descriptions, domain methodologies establish the basis for well-informed strategic portfolio decisions. Domain methodologies standardize the creation and evolution of domain architecture descriptions. Like architecture methodologies in general, a domain methodology includes both a development process and a view model. While the domain development process suggests activities domain architects perform, the view model suggests aspects that need to be captured.

Architecture Function and Domain Architecture Methodology
Architecture functions establish domain methodologies to define and evolve domains and to support architecture-related planning. A domain method captures

baseline and target architecture. It also captures planning events in a domain architecture roadmap. Since domains can also be viewed as large systems, or solutions to organizational problems, a domain methodology is closely associated with a solution architecture method. Other related methods and assets include reference architecture methodologies (e.g., pattern methodology), reference assets (e.g., architecture patterns, principles, styles), or assessment methods for domain architecture validation. Domain taxonomies provide a linguistic and categorical basis that underpins domain-level methods. Finally, domain architecture adapters guide the process of adapting domain methodologies (Fig. 6.183).

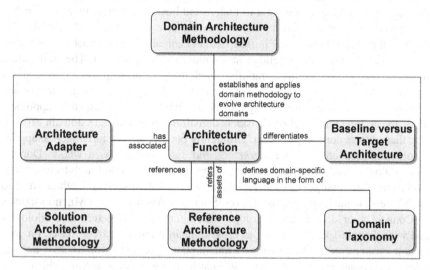

Fig. 6.183 Architecture function and domain architecture methodology

Regularly update the baseline architecture in your domain architecture descriptions. Ensure that its state can be meaningfully discussed and evaluated and that systematic deficits such as disproportionate redundancy or serious capability gaps can be identified. Also regularly relate new developments such as technological progress or business model changes to the current situation. Also, maintain domain architecture descriptions of desired (future) architecture states. Derive these from your understanding of current deficiencies and inevitable developments that will occur. Conduct planning, development, and documentation of future domain states on a regular basis. With the descriptions of baseline and target architecture, you establish a basis from which a corresponding difference results as a delta. Discuss the necessary changes, potential opportunities, costs, and risks of this delta and evaluate them strategically, tactically, and operationally. Capture decided changes as events in your domain architecture roadmaps. Ensure that planning and development based on domain descriptions are regularly performed, decided, and documented

(BASELINE ARCHITECTURE VERSUS TARGET ARCHITECTURE, ARCHITECTURE ROADMAP METHODOLOGY).

Domain methodologies guide your architects through the process of creating, evolving, and using domain architecture descriptions. An important focus of domain description is strategic portfolio decision-making in the service planning value stream. In parallel to the strategic and portfolio view of a domain, you can always think of a domain as a large system that provides a comprehensive solution to a correspondingly large problem. A solution methodology is applied at an appropriately coarse-grained level to obtain the baseline architecture of a domain and the elaboration of its target architecture. Combine your solution methodology with your domain methodology if you want to understand how a domain realizes its capabilities based on interoperating assets. For example, a *marketing and sales* domain exhibits the ability to instantly initiate market campaigns. This capability is necessary to keep pace with competitors in a rapidly evolving market. The architecture function considers the ability to rapidly launch market campaigns as a domain-level use case. It elaborates the use case's realization based on landscape assets and combines all corresponding design considerations in an architecture approach. Thus, the architecture function considers domain-level use cases as domain capabilities that address domain problems. Differently put, the architecture function applies a solution perspective to the *marketing and sales* domain as a whole. Domain methodologies can equally be applied inversely to the solution architecture level, as the *overview* and *portfolio* perspectives of a problem-solving method are also useful views at the landscape asset level (SOLUTION ARCHITECTURE METHODOLOGY).

Connect your domain methodology with reference architecture methodologies and with domain-specific as well as cross-domain reference assets. Based on concrete reference assets, like patterns, define domain-specific as well as cross-domain rules and guidelines, which serve as guardrails—guardrails within which your domain and solution architects will always operate when planning, developing, or endorsing designs. Architecture styles, patterns, or principles are examples of reference assets that you should define for control and efficiency reasons (REFERENCE ARCHITECTURE METHODOLOGY).

Note that a domain methodology is a super-methodology. Domain architecture methodologies encompass solution methodologies that view domains as coarse-grained solutions. From a solution architecture perspective, landscape assets or other domains are viewed as building blocks of the domain under consideration—building blocks that cooperate to establish capabilities at the domain level. Reference architecture methods further equip domains with reference assets. Reference assets ensure that domain development occurs within a controlled framework. Finally, architecture assessment methods validate domains throughout their lifecycle phases at defined validation checkpoints. Domains include landscape assets, reference assets, and potentially other domains. At the same time, each domain is itself an architecture asset. You should document a baseline and a target architecture description as minimal states for each of your domains. However, you will often distinguish multiple target architecture states, for example, the target architecture in 1 year versus more vaguely defined target architectures in 3 to 5 years (Fig. 6.184).

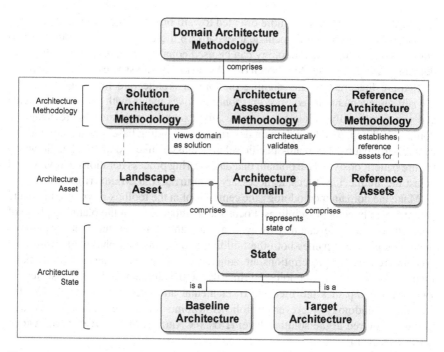

Fig. 6.184 Domain architecture methodology

Conceptualize domain architecture descriptions as compositions of various viewpoints and establish one domain architecture artifact per domain. Domain architecture descriptions are more coarse-grained than their solution design counterparts and more focused on *overview*, *portfolio*, and *inventory*. Domain descriptions emphasize the interdependencies between domain and landscape assets as domain architects seek to identify redundancies, deficiencies, consolidation potential, and other interesting cross-domain improvement opportunities. Define domain architecture artifacts as a composition of the artifacts of its building blocks. The compositional nature is evident in detailed solution descriptions of landscape assets and descriptions of architecture roadmaps or reference assets such as patterns or principles, all managed in separate artifacts. So primarily manage pointers to associated artifacts in your domain architecture descriptions. However, add domain-specific explanations to the artifact pointers to contextualize the referenced assets in relation to the referencing domain (**Architecture Artifact**).

Your architects must be able to adapt your domain methodology to concrete situations as quickly and efficiently as possible, as is the case with other methods. Provide appropriate method adapters for frequently recurring adaptations, for example, adapters that help your architects to optimally adapt the domain methodology to a business or a technical domain situation. While business domains are often oriented toward rapid functional adaptation to changes in the business model, technical domains tend to be more oriented toward broad applicability and reusability. Business or technical domain adapters absorb these fundamental differences so that the same domain methodology can be used equally optimally for both types of domains (ARCHITECTURE METHODOLOGY ADAPTER, BUSINESS VERSUS TECHNICAL).

Require the creation and signing of domain architecture mandates for larger domain engagements to equip corresponding investments with consciously made and organizationally validated decisions, for example, mandates for revising the domain roadmap, renewing domain descriptions including baseline and target architecture, or creating a domain-specific reference asset, like a domain-specific architecture pattern or style. Use domain mandates during process iterations to review and adjust the architecture focus, as necessary (ARCHITECTURE MANDATE).

Make the domain methodology the central tool in the toolbox of your domain and enterprise architecture disciplines. Focus the methodology on the planning phase of your enterprise value chain. However, at the same time, ensure that the domain methodology accompanies both the building and operational phases to ensure that domain architecture prescriptions are adhered to during these stages. Furthermore, focus your domain methodology primarily at the domain and enterprise levels, where it accompanies the lifecycle of elemental and aggregate domains. Use the domain methodology wherever portfolio viewpoints for landscape assets are meaningfully captured at the solution level (DOMAIN ARCHITECTURE DISCIPLINE, ARCHITECTURE LEVEL).

For your domain methodology, take a holistic approach to developing, capturing, and describing domain descriptions. Pay particular attention to navigability between viewpoints. In doing so, align your domain view model to efficiently support the reasoning structures and logic of your architecture function. For example, an enterprise has a set of criteria for prioritizing expenditures that particularly favors synergistic investments. A domain view model, which includes all essential landscape assets and their relationships, enables secondary contributing assets to be identified as synergistic. For example, a technology on which a platform is based—which in turn can be shared and reused—thus has great synergy potential. The traceability enabled by such view model supports synergy verification (ARCHITECTURE TRACEABILITY).

Establish a domain taxonomy for each of your domains and position it as cornerstone within your domain methodology. A domain taxonomy is a knowledge model that captures basic abstractions, concepts, categories, and relations significant to a respective domain. Capability maps are specific forms of domain taxonomies. Capability maps are singularly attributed domain taxonomies with composite structures. Domain-specific capability maps establish a normalized vocabulary for a domain, thus avoiding ambiguities and misunderstandings in a very fundamental way. Domain taxonomies or capability maps are extremely valuable, since common conceptions and categories can be used to correlate, classify, or group assets that are foreign in nature. For example, for a jointly defined marketing capability, problem- and solution-side building block types can be related to each other without being further associated in more comprehensive networked information models—e.g., marketing requirements and marketing-related architecture approaches. Domain taxonomies and capability maps lay the foundation in domain methodologies for analysis techniques such as heat mapping (**DOMAIN TAXONOMY**).

Make sure you align your methodology with the paradigm of evolutionary methods. Any understanding of a particular problem and its corresponding solution inevitably evolves over time, so any development process must consider this evolutionary nature of *context*, *problem*, and *solution*. If a reference method gives you what appears to be a strictly sequential process, then embed that process in an iterative-incremental framework. This ensures that you apply the architecture process iteratively and incrementally (**MANAGED ARCHITECTURE EVOLUTION**).

Domain architecture governance is a process group that consists of elaborating the domain architecture mandate, periodically validating domain architecture states, and ensuring strategic decisions are made in accordance with the domain's reference architecture. Elaboration of the domain architecture states includes both the evolution of a domain's baseline and the elaboration of its target architecture in light of emerging opportunities and conditions. The elaboration of a domain's reference architecture includes the evolution of its reference assets such as patterns, principles, or styles but also architecture roadmaps. Finally, domain architecture exploitation is not so much a stand-alone process. It is the continuous use of domain descriptions for versatile contributions along an enterprise value chain. The value proposition of a domain methodology is fully realized when planning, orientation, and transparency unfold as the greatest possible benefit (Fig. 6.185).

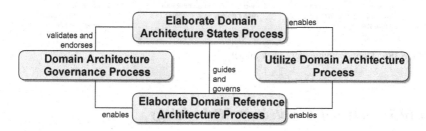

Fig. 6.185 Domain architecture processes

Periodically review a domain's architecture to ensure that current (*baseline architecture*) and planned (*target architecture*) state appropriately reflect changes in the environment. Similarly, review reference assets to systematically endorse or reject proposed state changes. Make any standard architecture assessment method compatible with your assessment process to enable your desired validation approach (**ARCHITECTURE ASSESSMENT METHODOLOGY**).

Align the domain methodology with a domain architecture view model that meets your requirements. As explained earlier, the domain methodology references your solution architecture, reference architecture, and assessment methodologies. Match your domain architecture view model accordingly to your solution architecture, reference architecture, and architecture assessment view model. Solution view models are designed to provide views of landscape assets and their relationships. Note that you instantiate your solution view model more than once. For example, one instance represents the baseline architecture of a domain, while additional instances represent the set of target architectures of the domain (**YOUR OWN ARCHITECTURE VIEW MODEL**) (Fig. 6.186).

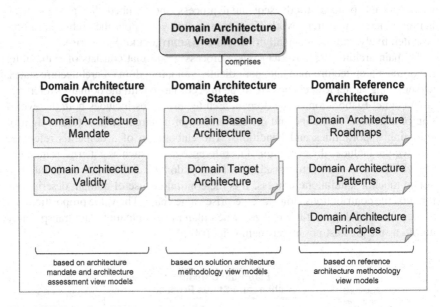

Fig. 6.186 Domain architecture view model

6.10.5   *Solution Architecture Methodology*

Systematic development and description of the solution architecture is a prerequisite for the sustainable quality and agility of enterprise solutions. Without a methodical approach to solution architecture development, architecture assets gradually lose their evolvability. In the medium term, this leads to unreliable and functionally inadequate solutions. In the long term, this leads to dysfunctionality of entire enterprise landscapes, which jeopardizes the efficient operation and performance of an enterprise value chain.

A *solution architecture methodology* guides and governs the design, development, and evolution of landscape assets such as services or applications, as

(continued)

well as structural assets such as domains. It increases the systematicity, quality, and repeatability of solution architecture development and description activities. Solution methodologies improve the quality, agility, and ultimately the sustainable evolvability of developed solutions.

Solution architecture methodologies standardize both the development and description of asset architectures. That is, each solution methodology encompasses both a development process and a view model. While a solution architecture development process defines the activities to be performed, a view model specifies what information is captured for which viewpoints to create an architecture description.

Architecture Function and Solution Architecture Methodology

Architecture functions adapt and utilize a solution methodology for the development and evolution of asset architectures. Solution view models are closely related to a solution methodology. They accompany design activities and target holistic architecture descriptions. Methodology adapters optimally tailor solution methodologies to individual engagement types. Expectations for the corresponding engagements are detailed in architecture mandates. Solution methodologies identify architecture-significant conditions, reflect on solution alternatives, develop architecture approaches, and regularly validate solution increments (Fig. 6.187).

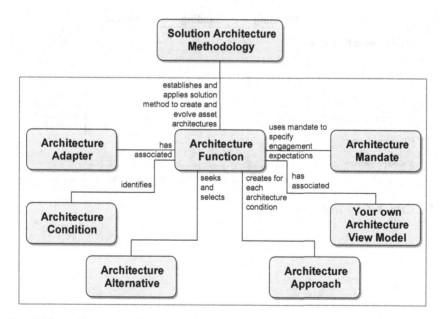

Fig. 6.187 Architecture function and solution architecture methodology

A well-designed solution methodology takes a holistic approach to developing, capturing, and describing the solution design in question. It avoids monocausal thinking and monodimensional capture of the architecture but strives to absorb the relevant dimensions of the given problem. Adaptability but also genericity and navigability of a methodology are essential for this. Furthermore, solution methodologies must consider that both problems and their solutions evolve and change over time. Thus, any meaningful methodology must address the evolutionary nature of problem-solving. Solution methodologies specify processes for solution development. Although such standard processes may seem sequential at first glance, do not be fooled by this misconception. Consider processes that do not sufficiently emphasize the iterative nature of solution development as instructions for only one iteration. In practice, this means that you stagger many applications of the waterfall-like process one after the other—i.e., you cycle through the process as part of the solution development procedure until an adequate overall design has emerged. In the first application of such a process, you begin to gain an early understanding of the given problem and develop an initial draft of a possible solution. As you proceed, you apply the linearized process again and again so that your design continually gains completeness, detail, and consistency. Thus, a solution description is developed incrementally through the repeated application of what appears to be a sequential process. Accordingly, one view of a solution view model is not completed at a time. Rather, all relevant views are also repeated again and again—and thus established incrementally (Fig. 6.188).

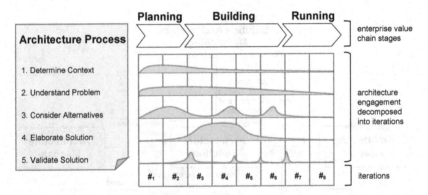

Fig. 6.188 Solution architecture evolution

Require the establishment and signing of solution architecture mandates for all architecture-relevant solution engagements to place expectations between clients and solution architects on a verifiable basis. Solution methodologies guide architects through the process of developing a solution, understanding a solution as a response to a problem. A precise clarification of solution expectations must precede any development because only what has been previously identified and named as a problem can be solved. What sounds obvious or self-evident is not necessarily always so in practice. Solution mandates are a means of clarification. They require all participants to explicitly formulate and thus become aware of the solution expectations, or expectations for a development. For this reason, solution methodologies require a sufficiently defined mandate as a necessary prerequisite. Furthermore, explicit mandates enable your solution architects to constantly check during development whether the design progress is still in line with the mandated expectations. Finally, use adapters for efficient mandate development to ensure that your architects optimally adapt your solution methodology to the respective type of engagement (ARCHITECTURE MANDATE, ARCHITECTURE METHODOLOGY ADAPTER).

Make the solution methodology a key tool in your solution architecture discipline toolbox. Focus the methodology on the building phase of your enterprise value chain. However, at the same time, ensure that the solution methodology accompanies both the planning and operations phases so that early solution designs can inform construction planning and assist in the rapid resolution of operational issues (SOLUTION ARCHITECTURE DISCIPLINE).

Consider the procedure outlined below as a rudimentary, linearized process blueprint on which you can base your own solution process. Alternatively, you can review a process already established in your organization for completeness. The approach presented here is certainly not sufficient in detail and scope, but it contains the genuinely essential ingredients of a solution process for use in your enterprise (Table 6.13).

Table 6.13 Solution architecture process

Activity	Description
Determine architecture context	Determine the enterprise context of your given problem and your envisioned solution. Understand how the enterprise context affects the proposed solution (*inbound dependencies*) and, conversely, how your solution potentially affects the context (*outbound dependencies*)
Determine and refine architecture conditions	Within the given conditions, identify those that are architecture-significant. Architecture conditions will significantly shape the design of your target architecture (ARCHITECTURE CONDITION)
Develop architecture alternatives and select alternative	Investigate and develop alternative approaches to solve the given problem. Conduct this activity based on problem-specific selection metrics. In the first iteration, initially develop alternatives for a comprehensive architecture approach at the overall solution level. Select the most appropriate alternative based on your selection metrics. In later iterations, repeat this activity in recursive descent for individual solution building blocks of the overall architecture (ARCHITECTURE ALTERNATIVE)
Elaborate solution architecture	Develop your solution design to respond to the identified architecture-significant conditions and ensure that your architecture mandate is accomplished. Establish traceability across coherent views in such a way that you create a holistically navigable design description (ARCHITECTURE TRACEABILITY)
Architecture approaches	Elaborate architecture approaches, which realize architecture-significant conditions, incrementally and add them successively to your overall design (ARCHITECTURE APPROACH)
Architecture overview	Collect building blocks such as landscape assets (e.g., services, applications, platforms, or information) that support more than a single architecture approach. Establish summary views of these building blocks and their interrelationships for convenient retrieval and discussion at any time
Architecture portfolio	Optionally create portfolio views for your key building block types (e.g., an application or service portfolio view for a specific solution)
Validate solution architecture	Perform architecture validation at the end of major progress, such as at the end of each iteration. What you specifically validate depends on where you are in your solution development. Architecture assessment methodologies guide you in systematically performing design validation (ARCHITECTURE ASSESSMENT METHODOLOGY)
Communicate architecture	Continuously communicate architecture concerns, decisions, and consequences to your key stakeholders (ARCHITECTURE LANGUAGE)

Solution processes are closely related to appropriate view models. Similar to the reference process outlined above, you can use the following view model as a reference to validate the appropriateness of your own architecture view model. At the top level, the view model decomposes into a cross-cutting and a core architecture viewpoint. We will look at the *cross-cutting architecture viewpoint* later. The *core architecture viewpoint* breaks down into context, condition, and solution viewpoints. The *context viewpoint* is elaborated by the *determine architecture context* activity, while the *condition viewpoint* is addressed by the *determine and refine architecture conditions* activity. Finally, the *elaborate solution architecture* activity is responsible for establishing or refining the *solution viewpoint* (YOUR OWN ARCHITECTURE VIEW MODEL) (Fig. 6.189).

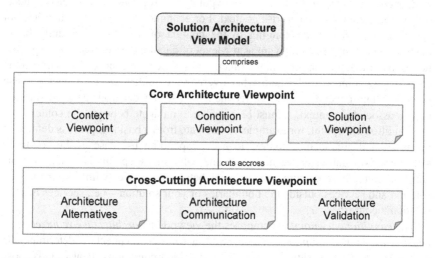

Fig. 6.189 Solution architecture view model

The *context viewpoint* is divided into the *functional architecture context*, the *operational*, and the *information architecture context*. Context viewpoints enable your solution architects to design solutions without neglecting reusability potentials or to identify existing gaps, conflicts, and overlaps between new solutions and established solution landscapes at an early stage. These views alert your architects to investigate relationships between a newly or rearchitected solution and its context, both in terms of the influence of the context on the planned solution (*inbound dependencies*) and in terms of the influence of the planned solution on its respective context (*outbound dependencies*) (Fig. 6.190).

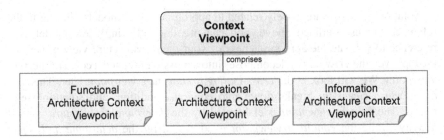

Fig. 6.190 Context viewpoint

The *context viewpoint*, like other viewpoints, evolves and continuously reflects the current state of the enterprise context. For example, an application that has not yet been recognized as belonging to the context of a solution currently being developed is identified as relevant as the level of detail increases. Once the application is identified, it is captured in the functional architecture context. You consult the context viewpoint to understand what overlaps, redundancies, deficiencies, reuse potentials, and dependencies to be reconciled exist between your targeted solution and its associated context. It must be possible to navigate between the context and the condition viewpoint, for example, to navigate from a business process defined in the functional architecture context to a corresponding use case in the condition viewpoint. Navigation between context and solution viewpoints is equally important, for example, to capture dependencies between a service within your planned solution and services outside the boundaries of your solution—i.e., services in your solution's context.

The *condition viewpoint* decomposes the viewpoints: *architecture requirements*, *constraints*, and *assumptions*. These allow a solution architect to determine the degree of architecture significance of the identified conditions. It also adds more details to the identified architecture conditions so that architects can begin to develop architecture approaches (Fig. 6.191).

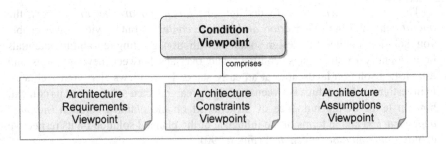

Fig. 6.191 Condition viewpoint

The *architecture requirements viewpoint* enables you to capture architecturally significant functional and non-functional requirements. Use cases are a common means of capturing details about functional requirements. Capture non-functional requirement details in the form of quality attribute scenarios[171] (QAS). Remember that, unlike architecture requirements, constraints are not the very reason a solution exists. At the same time, constraints cannot be ignored either. You capture constraints in the *architecture constraints viewpoint*. Finally, be sure to capture architecture assumptions in a meaningful way by explicitly naming areas of uncertainty or fuzziness, for example, a requirement that has been withdrawn but may soon be resubmitted. Use a minimal set of attributes to capture conditions in your architecture requirements viewpoint. In addition to technical attributes, such as a unique identifier, capture the condition type. Also, capture the stakeholders and a description of the condition. Consider differentiating the architecture significance of a condition. For example, a degree number indicates how much a condition will impact the architecture design. Also, capture indications of priority or inevitability of a condition—that is, an indicator of its relevance or criticality from a business perspective. In addition, consider providing criteria by which the successful addressing of an architecture condition can be quantified. Finally, provide a way to reference the architecture approach(es) that implements a condition through a respective pointer attribute (ARCHITECTURE CONDITION).

The *condition viewpoint* evolves in the same way as the other viewpoints. Architecture conditions that you previously captured and maintained may become obsolete or lose their significance. Similarly, if you identify a condition as architecturally significant that was not previously on your radar, you add it to the condition viewpoint. You consult the condition viewpoint whenever you need to know about the key influencing drivers that shape your design. You can also find out about conditions that form groups, for example, conditions that are collectively addressed by the same design (i.e., by the same architecture approach). Navigation must be possible between condition and solution views—for example, navigation from an architecture-significant non-functional requirement to the architecture approach that addresses it. Navigation must also be possible between conditions that are jointly addressed (*condition group*) by the same architecture approach.

The *solution viewpoint* is decomposed into *architecture approach, architecture overview*, and *architecture portfolio viewpoint*. Each of these viewpoints provides you with a different entry point into the exploration and development of a corresponding solution design. The solution viewpoints are interconnected and can be navigated accordingly (Fig. 6.192).

---

[171]Quality attribute scenarios (QAS) are quality attribute-specific requirement specifications defined based on the following attributes: source of stimulus (i.e., the entity that generates a stimulus), stimulus (i.e., a condition that must be considered when it arrives at the system), environment (i.e., the environmental conditions under which the system is currently operating, such as an overload situation), artifact (i.e., the artifact that affects the system as a whole or selected parts of it), response (i.e., the response of the system after the stimulus arrives), and response measure (i.e., a measurement metric that classifies the response of the system).

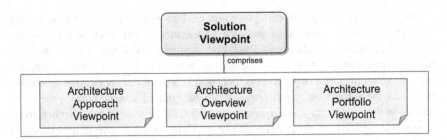

Fig. 6.192   Solution viewpoint

Architecture approach viewpoints contain architecture approaches, each of which addresses one or more conditions. For functional requirements, an architecture approach proposes a design that realizes a use case. For non-functional requirements, the architecture approach takes the quality attribute scenario (QAS) that specifies a given requirement and proposes an arrangement and interaction of building blocks that realizes the given QAS. Architecture approaches enable traceability of conditions into the corresponding architecture responses. Architecture approaches each represent a segment of the overall architecture, so they perfectly enable incremental development and elaboration (**Architecture Approach**).

You describe each of the building blocks on which an architecture approach is based in such a way that its contribution to the design becomes comprehensible. Independent of building block descriptions that may exist elsewhere (e.g., the description of an application in the application portfolio), building blocks are additionally described in such a way that their approach-specific behavior becomes comprehensible. The supplementary descriptions and the corresponding attribution depend on the respective building block type. For example, an information block that is transferred between two applications is attributed in the architecture approach as being *in transit*, while one of the applications is attributed as *sender* and the other as a *receiver*.

The *architecture overview viewpoint* represents core building blocks, assets, and relationships at the level of the entire architecture. Core building blocks (e.g., a landscape asset such as an application) contribute significantly to the various architecture approaches. Depending on their relative importance to the overall architecture, core assets bubble up and are represented in the architecture overview viewpoint. Note that the overview preserves the holistic nature of the design. It does not separate building blocks by type (e.g., applications from services or services from platforms). Instead, the overview viewpoint continues to highlight the relationships that exist between different types of assets, for example, a utilization relationship between two applications or a hosting relationship between a hosting platform and a hosted application. However, the overview presents assets and their relationships with a lower level of detail than is the case in the context of the underlying architecture approaches (Fig. 6.193).

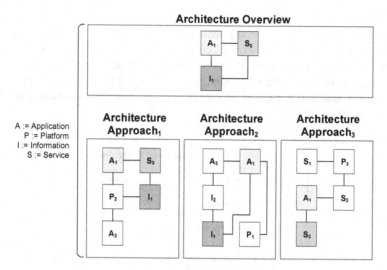

Fig. 6.193   Architecture overview

Consider further segmentation at the overview level when a solution architecture is decently large and complex. Figure 6.194 illustrates five architecture approaches, three of which address a security condition and two of which target a performance condition. Assuming that all of the building blocks in the architecture approaches shown are core building blocks, they would fit an architecture overview. In contrast to Fig. 6.193, in which all core building blocks merge into the architecture overview, here—due to the complexity of the overall architecture—the architecture overview has been divided into segments for the security and performance architecture overview. Each of the segments provides a convenient entry point for different roles. For example, a security architect might stick to the security architecture overview to gain oversight, while a performance architect might stick to the performance overview segment.

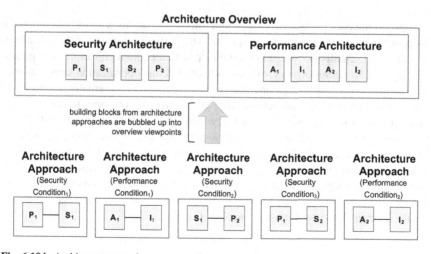

Fig. 6.194   Architecture overview segmentation

Other perspectives, sometimes very useful, give a segmented overview of an entire architecture, where the segmentation criterion is the building block type: *architecture portfolio viewpoints*. If you are interested exclusively and dedicatedly in the services that are essential to an overall architecture, consult the service portfolio viewpoint. On the other hand, if you just want to have an overview of all information assets that support an overall design, use the information portfolio viewpoint (Fig. 6.195).

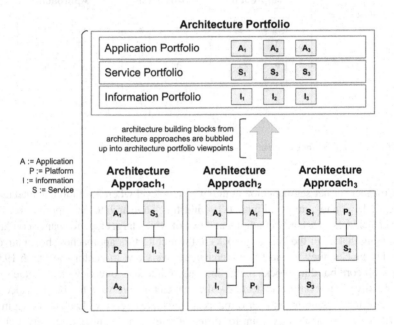

Fig. 6.195 Architecture portfolio viewpoint

Beyond the *core architecture viewpoint*, the *cross-cutting architecture viewpoint* proposes three complementary viewpoints. The particular feature of these views is that they can actually be merged or combined with all core architecture viewpoints. The *architecture alternatives viewpoint* is used to define optimization targets as well as selection criteria of design alternatives. The architecture alternatives activity of the solution development process updates this viewpoint. The *architecture communication viewpoint* indicates that not every representation of a design is suitable for adequate discussion with every stakeholder group and, if necessary, for making binding design decisions. You can take this viewpoint as an invitation to move away from formal description nomenclatures and instead use, for example, comic strips, whiteboard drawings, or the like for communication, if this seems more appropriate. Finally, the *architecture validation viewpoint* allows you to capture the validation results of regular progress monitoring (Fig. 6.196).

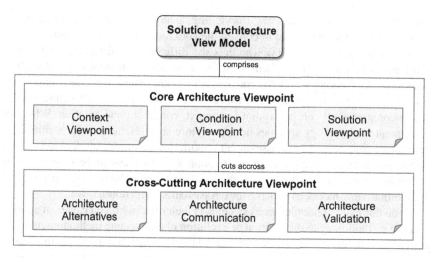

Fig. 6.196 Cross-cutting architecture viewpoint

You use the *architecture alternatives viewpoint* to define target criteria for alternatives. At least if you even consider investigating alternatives as part of your solution development, for example, criteria related to cost, risk, effort, or standards compliance. Based on the defined selection criteria, you first generate alternatives candidates. This is a creative step that depends heavily on your experience and where you should try to grow beyond your spontaneous solution reflexes. The broader you scatter to find truly alternative solution approaches, the more optimal this usually is if you want to find previously unknown but compelling solution candidates. Once you have a set of promising candidates available, roughly design each candidate's architecture approach, specifically capturing the information you need along your selection criteria. Finally, make your selection among the design alternatives and capture the reasons for your decision. The alternatives view primarily overlaps with the solution view in that it only looks for alternative solutions—not alternative contexts or problems. You use this view whenever you are interested in exploring alternative responses to a given set of architecture conditions. Remember that you can explore an alternative architecture approach not only for your overall design, but just as well explore alternatives to address individual conditions (**ARCHITECTURE ALTERNATIVE**).

The *architecture communication viewpoint* is different from the above viewpoints. It is not really a formal viewpoint but much more a reminder of the importance of communication itself. While it is a no-go for other viewpoints, it is absolutely fine to de-normalize or simplify architectural representations as long as it suits your communication goal. So always optimize your communication for the appropriate audience. This means that if you are communicating architecture to non-architects, you should use appropriate non-architecture nomenclature. For example, use whiteboard sketches, storytelling, analogies, aphorisms, comic strips, or whatever seems appropriate to convey the core messages of architecture.

The *architecture validation viewpoint* is also different from the above viewpoints. It differs in that its formal schema and other details are part of the architecture assessment methodology and the corresponding view model (i.e., the architecture assessment report). However, unlike the alternatives viewpoint, architecture validation encompasses all core viewpoints—context, condition, and solution. While an assessment methodology specifies how to capture an assessment, in an architecture description you refer to an assessment report, for example, by looking at the assessment findings at the end of an iteration as constraints to be considered in further development. For this reason, the validation viewpoint is an integral part of the solution view model (ARCHITECTURE ASSESSMENT METHODOLOGY).

If you think of methodologies as systems in their own right, you can even apply a solution methodology to the creation or evolution of architecture methodologies. For example, an architecture function plans to create an architecture roadmap method to address a practice gap that currently exists. Because the architecture function views the desired roadmap methodology as a system, it uses its own solution methodology to (a) consider the context of the roadmap method, (b) gather requirements that the new method should satisfy, and finally (c) elaborate the solution (i.e., establish the roadmap methodology) (YOUR OWN ARCHITECTURE METHODOLOGY).

6.10.6   Architecture Assessment Methodology

A systematic approach for the development of qualitative architectures suggests that a similar systematic approach to the validation of architectures exist. The lack of a methodical approach to validation leads to untested—and thus tends to be inadequate—architecture quality. A methodology for architecture validation establishes a metric that enables both quality-oriented architecture development and enterprise-wide solution comparability.

> An *assessment* is the action or an instance of making a judgment about something. (Merriam-Webster Dictionary 2020)

An *architecture assessment* validates the result of an architecture elaboration activity—that is, the adequacy of an asset with respect to a specific target design and assessment criteria. For example, an assessment evaluates the architectural appropriateness of an application with respect to the required security or performance attributes.

An *architecture assessment methodology* provides an objective, systematic, and repeatable approach to measuring asset design based on defined assessment metrics.

It provides a process for efficiently performing assessments in a flexible manner, adapted to varying validation requirements.

Architecture Function and Architecture Assessment Methodology
Architecture functions establish and leverage assessment methodologies to validate asset designs to ensure their appropriate quality and agility. Their practical focus is on validating architecture approaches against the background of given conditions (i.e., expectations for a target design) and assessment criteria. In addition to view models specifically adapted for assessments, architecture functions use methodology adapters for the tailored application of assessment methodologies. Adapters enable the alignment of an enterprise-generic assessment method to concrete assessment engagements (Fig. 6.197).

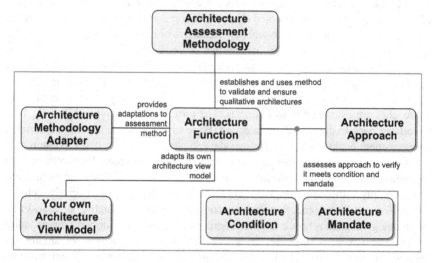

Fig. 6.197 Architecture function and architecture assessment methodology

Distinguish between three basic types of assessment scenarios—regardless of further differentiation. Support a scenario in which a new asset is introduced, and your function applies the assessment methodology to verify its initial appropriateness. Appropriateness is measured, for example, by the extent to which the asset's design meets the given conditions or the architecture mandate at hand. Note that assessment processes are iterative, so you need a definition of done[172] (DoD) in your mandates. On the one hand, an assessment DoD clarifies which areas of an architecture need to be evaluated against which assessment criteria. On the other hand,

---

[172]The definition of done (DoD) is an Agile and Scrum terminology. However, it is a much broader concept for determining an exit criterion for a work product or activity. A definition of done must be created individually for each task. The DoD specifies criteria that can be held against the task's progress to recognize the achievement of the desired end state and to end the task.

assessment DoDs specify timeframes for an evaluation, and they prescribe the required stability of analysis or refactoring recommendations. Your assessment team uses assessment DoDs throughout all activities and iterations. With a DoD, your assessment team can continuously review what areas of the assessment report need to be developed, what level of detail is required, what progress the team has already made, and what is still missing to complete the assessment report (ARCHITECTURE MANDATE).

Also, support a second scenario where an asset already exists, a modification is planned, and the proposed target design needs to be validated before the change is physically implemented. In this scenario, your architecture function uses the assessment method to validate the appropriateness of the adjusted target design and anticipate the impact on dependencies to other assets. If you do not sufficiently validate the impact of a change on existing assets, you run the risk of undesirable effects of a physically implemented change and correspondingly expensive rollbacks. Finally, support a third scenario where deficiencies or defects have been identified in an existing asset—for example, instabilities or crashes during operation. You will apply an assessment methodology to understand what caused the asset's defects and develop a design proposal to improve the situation and fix the observed defects.

In order to analyze entire designs, individual or particularly focused architecture approaches are examined in assessments. The results of the individual investigations are related back to the overall architecture. For each architecture approach examined, an assessment evaluates how it realizes desired attributes or use cases. System attributes and use cases are emergent properties of an architecture. Examples of such attributes are the concrete performance, availability, or modifiability of an architecture asset. Quality attribute scenarios[173] (QAS) are a technique for precisely defining architecture attributes and thus non-functional conditions. Finally, an assessment methodology evaluates how examined architecture approaches support corresponding attribute scenarios and thus desired system attributes. The analysis of architecture approaches enables the identification of architecture sensitivity[174] and trade-off points[175] (ARCHITECTURE APPROACH, ARCHITECTURE CONDITION) (Fig. 6.198).

---

[173] Quality attribute scenarios (QAS) are quality attribute-specific requirement specifications defined based on the following attributes: source of stimulus (i.e., the entity that generates a stimulus), stimulus (i.e., a condition that must be considered when it arrives at the system), environment (i.e., the environmental conditions under which the system is currently operating, such as an overload situation), artifact (i.e., the artifact that affects the system as a whole or selected parts of it), response (i.e., the response of the system after the stimulus arrives), and response measure (i.e., a measurement metric that classifies the response of the system).

[174] Architecture sensitivity points are the system areas that are significantly affected when the system's architecture changes. They are closely monitored by an architect when reflecting on planned architecture changes.

[175] Architecture trade-off points are the basis for sensitivity points. Typical trade-offs exist between usability and security or between modifiability and performance attributes.

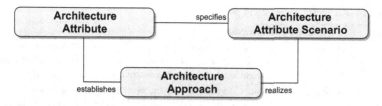

Fig. 6.198 Architecture attributes

Employ assessment methodologies to standardize the assessment process and the reporting of validation results. Assessments measure asset designs making them comparable. An assessment methodology includes an assessment process and an assessment reporting schema (i.e., view model). While the assessment process specifies the activities performed, the reporting schema suggests what information should be captured in the repeated iteration of process activities. Assessment methods guide architects through their process, considering defined assessment drivers (i.e., assessment objectives). Therefore, ensure that you clarify the objectives before conducing an assessment (NEED TO KNOW).

As with other methodologies, you should establish an assessment adapter framework with appropriate adapters to efficiently tailor your enterprise-wide assessment methodology to the wide variety of evaluation situations in your organization. Assessment adapters allow you to adapt an enterprise-wide assessment method to frequently recurring types of validation situations. For example, the different use of a generic assessment method regarding the assessment of a domain versus the assessment of an application is delegated to a *domain assessment adapter* and an *application assessment adapter*. Similar differences exist in the assessment of applications, platforms, technologies, or services. As a final example, assessing the design of a new solution (i.e., a proposed new design is assessed) is different from assessing an asset that is experiencing operational problems (i.e., an existing design is examined for a problem's root causes and measures are proposed to correct the problem). In these examples, assessment adapters significantly reduce or absorb method adaptation effort (ARCHITECTURE METHODOLOGY ADAPTER).

Use the process outlined here as a blueprint you can hold against your own assessment process to validate it and increase its fit. Of course you can also use the process blueprint to establish an outermost framework for your enterprise's own assessment process. The blueprint presented here is adopted from the Carnegie Mellon Software Engineering Institute's standard for assessing architecture, the Architecture Tradeoff Analysis Method[176] [SEI ATAM] (Table 6.14).

---

[176]The Architecture Tradeoff Analysis Method (ATAM) is an architecture assessment and risk mitigation methodology. The process moderates between an architecture function and its stakeholders to determine business drivers (i.e., architecture conditions and goals). Then, the process extracts quality attributes from these drivers to create scenarios. Scenarios are used in conjunction with architecture approaches to understand trade-offs, sensitivity points, risks, and non-risks.

Table 6.14 Architecture assessment process

Activity	Description
Determine architecture drivers	In order to evaluate the design of an asset, information about architecture drivers is needed, for example, desired quality attributes or significant architecture constraints, ranked by priority
Determine assessment drivers	Identify the reasons why the assessment is being conducted. There may be specific concerns about the architecture; it could be that the assessment is to focus on a particular part that has recently experienced operational problems. For assessments to be successful, their drivers must be understood and agreed upon at the outset. Even if there are expectations that are unlikely to be met by conducting the assessment, these should be clarified in order to appropriately manage stakeholder expectations
Determine asset architecture	Determine the architecture of the asset to be evaluated—for example, the full description or an excerpt from it to evaluate it. If no design description exists or it is outdated, this step first gathers the missing information
Elicit quality attribute scenarios	Elicit quality attribute scenarios to enable retrospective analysis of architecture approaches. Quality attribute scenarios relevant to the assessment are identified based on the architecture drivers, assessment drivers, and asset description. Each quality attribute scenario is identified and prioritized. Priorities are assessed based on two dimensions: the importance of the scenario to the success of the asset and the estimated degree of difficulty to re-implement the attribute scenario through appropriate architecture approaches. For the assessments of proposed architecture changes, it is important to capture both the quality attribute scenarios that characterize the proposed change and those not affected by the change. In refactoring assessments, the quality attribute scenarios characterize the desired architecture behavior as opposed to the identified architecture problem—i.e., the problem that architecture refactoring is intended to address
Identify architecture approaches	The basis of the assessment is the identification of architecture approaches that form the overall asset design. Once the relevant approaches are identified, they are analyzed
Analyze architecture approaches	Architecture approaches are analyzed with respect to the elicited quality attribute scenario. In particular, those approaches that are critical to achieving the prioritized quality attribute scenarios are examined. Each architecture approach is examined to understand which quality attribute scenarios are affected by the approach. Once this relationship is captured, each approach is examined to understand how well it realizes the quality attribute scenarios. This ultimately leads to the identification of architecture problems
Generate recommendations	The results of the assessment are summarized in a report that includes, at a minimum, the following: • A summary of the asset architecture (*baseline*) • Stakeholders involved in the assessment • Identified and prioritized quality attribute scenarios • Identified architecture approaches • Mapping between architecture approaches and quality attribute

(continued)

Table 6.14 (continued)

Activity	Description
	scenarios • Uncovered architecture issues (e.g., architecture sensitivity and trade-off points) • Proposed remedies for the identified problems
Deliver architecture assessment report	At the end of a completed assessment, the assessment report is communicated and delivered to the assessment stakeholders

Assessment processes go hand in hand with an assessment view model (*assessment report*). As an absolute minimum, assessment reports include the *stakeholders* involved and the architecture team that conducted the assessment (*assessment team*). Place a *summary* section prominently in the report, which summarizes both the *findings* of the assessment and the *recommendations* to address those findings. Identified findings include architectural risks, non-risks, sensitivity points, and trade-off points. In this context, an *architecture risk* is an architecturally important decision that has not yet been made, for example, deciding whether a solution should use terminal emulation[177] or client-server[178] as distribution scheme for its components. Architecture risks are also significant design decisions that have already been made but whose consequences are not yet fully understood. For example, the decision to use cloud PaaS[179] has been made, but the specific cloud platform to use has not yet been decided. An *architecture non-risk* is an architecture decision that is based on assumptions, which are often implicit in the architecture. For example, a SaaS[180] platform is used based on the assumption that no sensitive data is stored in that platform. An *architecture sensitivity point* is an architecture approach that is highly correlated with the response to a particular quality attribute. For example, the performance of an application may be highly dependent on real-time synchronization between the production and disaster recovery databases. Finally, *architecture trade-off points* are architecture approaches that are hosts to multiple sensitivity points. For example, database encryption may improve security

---

[177] A terminal emulator is a computer program that emulates a terminal within another display architecture. Terminal emulators emulate programs running on remote computers, transferring data via telnet, for example. Terminal emulator architectures minimize the emulating side's installation footprint, leaving it on the emulated side of an appropriate connection.

[178] Client-server is an architecture approach that distributes tasks and workloads between providers (i.e., servers) and requestors of a resource (i.e., clients). Both types of components (i.e., clients and servers) communicate over a network and reside on dedicated hardware. However, client-server is a communication model, which means that both client and server can also reside on the same compute node.

[179] Platform as a Service (PaaS) is a class of cloud services that provides a platform enabling customers to develop, run, and manage applications without the burden of building and maintaining the infrastructure that is normally associated with application development or hosting.

[180] Software as a Service (SaaS), similar to PaaS, is a software delivery model in which a solution is licensed on a subscription basis and customers are relieved of the burden of building and maintaining a corresponding solution themselves.

but degrade performance. The *findings* relate to the prioritized quality attribute scenarios and thus to both the *architecture* and the *assessment drivers*. The *recommendations* are in turn linked to the findings. Prioritizing the findings naturally prioritizes the recommendations, which ultimately leads to a plan and timetable. The timetable suggests when to implement the remediation actions and any dependencies between the actions. Use the assessment reporting schema outlined below as a starting point for creating or evolving your own reporting schema (YOUR OWN ARCHITECTURE VIEW MODEL) (Fig. 6.199).

Architecture Assessment Report Template	
Assessment	
Assessment Stakeholders	
Assessment Team	
Summary	
Findings	
Recommendations	
Drivers	
Architecture Drivers	
Assessment Drivers	
Asset Architecture	
Baseline Architecture	
Target Architecture	
Architecture Attribute Scenarios	
Architecture Approaches	

Fig. 6.199 Architecture assessment report schema

The design proposed to satisfy specific conditions is a common starting point for an architecture assessment. To perform an assessment, you need information about the goal of an asset architecture (*architecture drivers*). You may share this information with those involved in the assessment to establish a common understanding, such as in the form of a presentation. Specifically targeted quality attributes are common architecture drivers. They are often classified by priority, relevant technical or business constraints, or business objectives they support. Assessments conducted to analyze root causes of observed asset defects include the description of the problem to be fixed in the *architecture drivers* section.

For every assessment, there are underlying reasons to perform it. These reasons could be existing concerns about the architecture as a whole; it could be that the concerns focus only on a specific asset design area; it could also be detailed expectations and questions that stakeholders formulate regarding an assessment without narrowing down an affected area. In order to successfully conduct assessments, such drivers must be understood early and accurately. If there are expectations that are unlikely to be met by conducting an assessment, these should also be identified. Finally, all expectations are recorded in the report's *assessment drivers* section.

The *asset architecture* section of the report includes, at a minimum, the baseline architecture of the assessed asset. The baseline architectures are based on design descriptions that have been standardized by your organization via an appropriate solution methodology. The specific sections and details of the solution architecture required for an assessment will depend on the particular architecture and assessment drivers. If an assessment is to validate a proposed target architecture, a description of the desired architecture state would also be included in the asset architecture section of the report (BASELINE ARCHITECTURE VERSUS TARGET ARCHITECTURE, SOLUTION ARCHITECTURE METHODOLOGY).

Quality attribute scenarios are identified for each quality attribute and prioritized in the *quality attribute scenarios* section. Priorities are evaluated based on two dimensions: the importance of the scenario to the success of the asset design and the difficulty of accomplishing the scenario. Specifically, this section identifies quality attribute scenarios that characterize the desired behavior of the asset. For example, if it is known that there is a transactional performance requirement, there must be at least one corresponding quality attribute scenario (ARCHITECTURE CONDITION).

Identified architecture approaches are analyzed, captured, and refined in the *architecture approaches section* of the assessment report. For change assessments, particularly examine the approaches that describe the target design. Also, consider the baseline architecture approaches that will be affected by the target architecture proposal. Investigate with increased priority those architecture approaches that are critical to achieving key quality attribute scenarios that are themselves essential to the overall architecture (ARCHITECTURE APPROACH).

The purpose of conducting assessments is to obtain an objective view of an asset's architecture adequacy. However, organizational dynamics, interests, and incentives may distort your assessments. Therefore, consider delegating architecture assessments to a neutral party (ORGANIZATIONAL REPLICATION, ARCHITECTURE SOURCING).

Exploit your assessment methodology, the conduct of architecture assessments, and their objective evaluations of an asset's architectural state as a powerful governance tool. Optimize your assessment methodology so that it can be applied to assets at their various lifecycle stages. For example, distinguish between a lightweight and a heavyweight application of your assessment methodology. Additionally, reference established policies to closely align your methodology with your architecture governance framework (ARCHITECTURE GOVERNANCE, ARCHITECTURE POLICY).

Ensure that your architecture assessment method can systematically and efficiently explore both decommissioning opportunities and decommissioning impact to explicitly support the dismantling of architecture assets in your enterprise (DECOMMISSIONING REWARD).

6.10.7 Reference Architecture Methodology

Architecture is an informative, instructive, and prescriptive discipline. An architecture function establishes rules, particularly based on reference assets, to fulfill its prescriptive responsibilities. Different types of reference assets share common concepts, such as basic attribute sets, similar lifecycle management processes, and delivery vehicles such as portfolios and catalogs.

> A reference is a work containing useful facts or information, a standard for measuring or constructing. (Merriam-Webster Dictionary 2020]

The term *reference architecture* refers to something of an architectural nature that serves an orientation or prescriptive purpose. Traditionally, different types of reference architectures are distinguished. For example, architecture patterns, principles, tactics, or styles, but also architecture roadmaps can be considered reference assets, as they provide orientation about planned or desired design states.

A reduced view of the reference architecture asset concept considers reference assets exclusively as semi-finished architectures that serve as blueprints for complete architectures. An expanded understanding of the reference asset concept includes artifacts that, while not themselves semi-finished designs, provide orientation in architecture development.

Architecture Function and Reference Architecture Methodology
Architecture functions use reference architecture methodologies to govern and guide architecture development in a corridor specified by reference assets. Architecture functions use mandates to set expectations for the development of reference architecture methodologies as well as individual reference assets. Architecture mandates ensure focused and targeted reference architecture development. Also, architecture functions specify methodology adapters for reference architecture methodologies to facilitate and accelerate the reference asset development process. Reference assets are referenced both directly and indirectly by domain and solution methodologies. They are referenced indirectly, especially when they are part of policy definitions. Architecture policies that point to reference assets elevate them to architecture prescriptions whose compliance is formally verified (Fig. 6.200).

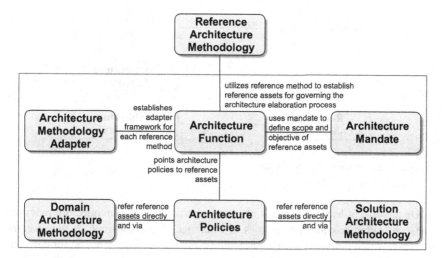

Fig. 6.200   Architecture function and reference architecture methodology

Regardless of their nature, reference assets are intended to influence design decision-making in order to significantly increase its efficiency, quality, and alignment. A key purpose of reference assets is to guide and constrain architects in performing design activities. In the process of planning, elaborating, or validating architecture, decisions are guided by reference assets. Design decisions are inherent to and constitute architecture approaches. Architecture approaches are micro-architectures that together form the overall architecture of a corresponding asset. For example, the hub-and-spoke[181] pattern guides the design decision to establish a data hub platform, so that information exchange between applications is mediated through the deployed platform. This results in minimizing the number of point-2-point exchanges that would otherwise be required. The decision is part of the *architecture integration* approach, which in turn is one among many architecture approaches of the overall architecture design (Fig. 6.201).

---

[181]Hub-and-spoke is an integration architecture style favoring communication via applications and a central hub over direct communication between applications.

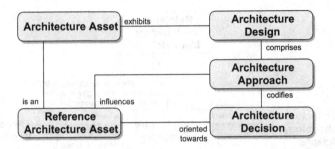

Fig. 6.201 Reference architecture asset

Distinguish at least three types of reference assets in your architecture function. These subsume possible other types of reference assets. Distinguish *architecture patterns*, which subsume architecture styles, idioms, anti-patterns, or similar concrete design orientations. Architecture patterns and their subgenera are themselves semi-finished designs. They thus provide architecture blueprints for direct adaptation. Furthermore, *architecture principles* are to be distinguished, which comprise heuristic means of orientation. Principles are not architectures themselves, but they provide basic information about the characteristics of good designs. Finally, distinguish *architecture roadmaps*, which are planning orientations. Design the generic and common foundation of a reference architecture methodology upon which you can build more specific methodologies. During the initial development phase of your reference architecture methodology, you can defer the development of more specific reference methodologies by creating methodology adapters for them. If you create an *architecture pattern methodology adapter*, an *architecture roadmap methodology* adapter, or an *architecture principle methodology adapter* at the level of your generic reference architecture methodology, you can systematically manage patterns, principles, and roadmaps without having to build their specific methodologies immediately (ARCHITECTURE METHODOLOGY ADAPTER).

Although each reference asset type serves a particular purpose and is attributed, used, and presented differently, the process of identifying, creating, endorsing, and provisioning reference assets is very similar regardless of type. All reference asset types share basic attributes, are managed similarly throughout their lifecycle, and are provided to your architects through portfolios and catalogs. Where reference asset types differ significantly, I explain this in the respective patterns—i.e., in the patterns for the architecture pattern, principle, and roadmap methodology (ARCHITECTURE PATTERN METHODOLOGY, ARCHITECTURE PRINCIPLE, ARCHITECTURE ROADMAP METHODOLOGY).

Change is the only constant; the world is constantly changing, and reference assets must reflect these changes. An architecture function constantly balances between two extremes—uniformity and diversity. While uniformity promotes economies of scale or predictability, diversity reduces an organization's monocultural tendencies as well as the associated risks (e.g., vendor lock-in). Diversity also promotes innovation. Reference architecture methodologies involve two complementary processes. The first process defines the *what*, *who*, and *how* of reference asset lifecycle management (*reference asset provider*). The second process clarifies and guides through the use and compliant application of reference assets (*reference asset consumer*) (Fig. 6.202).

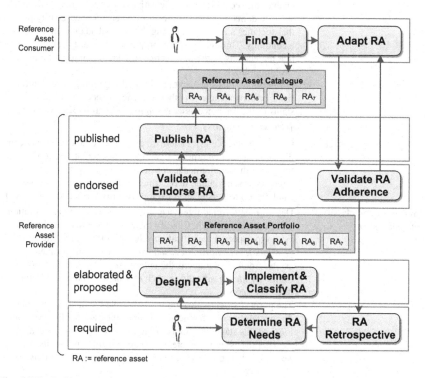

Fig. 6.202 Reference architecture methodology process

Consider the approach outlined below as a rudimentary process blueprint that you can use as a basis for your own reference architecture processes. Alternatively, you can review reference asset processes already established in your organization for appropriateness and completeness. The approach presented here is certainly not sufficient in detail and scope. It describes a generic process that you will need to adapt for different types of reference assets, for example, if you define the architecture pattern process in your pattern methodology. Finally, note that the generic reference architecture process distinguishes reference asset provider and consumer. Thus, as mentioned above, it combines two types of complementary processes: reference asset provisioning and reference asset consumption (Table 6.15).

Table 6.15 Reference architecture process

Activity	Description
Determine reference asset needs	Anyone in the enterprise should bring forward general ideas or urgent needs to adjust existing reference assets or identify new ones. For example, a new technological invention in the security domain enables the secure storage of sensitive information in the cloud. The security domain architect proposes to create a new security pattern that specifies a design describing the optimal adaptation of the new technology. Through its design proposal the security pattern ensures that the benefits of the new technology are maximized while avoiding pitfalls. Furthermore, this step captures detailed requirements, constraints, risks, or dependencies to other reference assets. At this stage, the status of the reference asset is *required* (NEED TO KNOW, ARCHITECTURE CONDITION)
Design reference asset	Generate reference asset alternatives to overcome established conditioning in your enterprise. Examine each alternative and verify its fit against the requirements, constraints, or risks present for a given reference asset. Finally, derive the most optimal reference asset candidate(s) to pursue and develop (ARCHITECTURE ALTERNATIVE)
Implement and classify reference asset	Develop the selected reference asset candidate using an evolutionary, iterative approach. Classify the reference asset based on an asset-type-specific classification scheme, for example, the *creational*, *behavioral*, or *structural* classifications for pattern assets. Another example is the *enterprise-wide*, *domain-wide*, or *solution-wide* classifications, each of which specifies a different reference scope. The purpose of classification is to improve the navigability and discoverability of reference assets once they are published in catalogs. At this stage, the status of the asset is set to *elaborated*. Register the asset in the reference asset portfolio and set its status to *proposed*. This triggers the next activity in the process (DOMAIN TAXONOMY)
Validate and endorse reference asset	Validate the appropriateness (e.g., relevance, correctness, completeness) of a newly proposed reference asset. Ensure that your assessment methodology supports validation of all reference asset types that you support in your enterprise. For example, add a *pattern assessment adapter* to your assessment methodology to enable validation of pattern-type reference assets. Formal endorsement of a reference asset sets its status to *endorsed* and triggers the next activity (ARCHITECTURE ASSESSMENT METHODOLOGY)
Publish reference asset	A newly endorsed reference asset is published in the reference asset catalogs. In the reference asset portfolio, the asset status is set to *published*. If the asset is removed from catalogs in the future, its status in the asset portfolio is reset to *endorsed*. This means that reference assets remain in the portfolio while they may not always be visible in catalogs
Find reference asset	From this step, you will switch to the reference asset usage perspective. Architects who have access to reference assets can search the appropriate catalogs to find reference assets that meet their

(continued)

Table 6.15 (continued)

Activity	Description
	guidance needs. They use reference asset classification and other asset attributes to find a set of suitable candidates
Adopt reference asset	Architects use reference assets in a variety of contexts. The range of valid usage scenarios for each asset type is explained in the associated methodology because usage scenarios are type-specific. For example, the usage scenarios for roadmap-type assets are explained in the architecture roadmap methodology pattern
Validate reference asset adherence	This activity falls within the scope of architecture governance. The governance branch of an architecture function checks whether the adoption of reference assets is performed in a compliant manner and conforms to the respective policies. Multiple validation results possible. *Not adhering* means that the design proposed for an application is not endorsed but rejected. For a roadmap-type reference asset, *not adhering* can mean that a proposed project conflicts with a planned architecture roadmap activity and that the project is asked to adjust its plan. When a proposed architecture artifact deviates from the requirements of a reference asset, the deviation must be formally tracked. It may also be accepted temporally, for example, if an architect commits to correct a deviation within an agreed-upon timeframe. *Potentially adhering* means that the validating architect lacks information for final endorsement. Finally, *adhering* means that the proposed architecture artifact is endorsed and accepted, and no further adjustments are required (ARCHITECTURE GOVERNANCE, ARCHITECTURE POLICY)
Reference asset retrospective	Finally, as with all comprehensively designed architecture processes, a retrospective is conducted. The process owner evaluates insights gained during the process regarding its optimization and, if necessary, incorporates them by adjusting the process. Retrospectives and process improvements must be performed for both sub-processes: *reference asset provisioning* and *reference asset consumption* (LEARNING ORGANIZATION)

As with other methodologies, a reference architecture methodology and a corresponding view model are inextricably linked. The view model here consists of a generic reference asset schema that comprises three main sections: *context*, *challenge*, and *constitution* (Fig. 6.203).

Reference Architecture Asset Schema	
Context	
Architecture Level(s)	
Architecture Domain(s)	
Enterprise Value Stream(s)	
Challenge (problem the Reference Asset addresses)	
RA-type specific challenge(s)	
Constitution (response to problem)	
Common attribute set	
RA-type specific attribute set	
RA content (RA-type specific)	

Fig. 6.203 Reference asset schema

The *context* section describes the circumstances under which the use of a present reference asset can be reasonably considered. Common context dimensions independent of the type of reference asset are, for example, architecture levels, architecture domains, or domain taxonomy categories, but also enterprise value streams or phases in which reference assets make their contribution. Other context facets depend on the type of reference asset. For example, differentiating architecture patterns, software design patterns,[182] requirement patterns,[183] or anti-patterns[184] are meaningful context dimensions, especially for reference assets

---

[182] Software design pattern is a relatively generic, reusable design for a frequently recurring problem in a particular context. Software design patterns typically show relationships and interactions between classes or objects without specifying the final application classes or objects involved in a design that adopts the software design pattern. Examples of software design patterns are singleton, command, composite, template method, or abstract factory class pattern.

[183] Requirement patterns generalize specific requirements or constraints. A requirement pattern is a generic, reusable, proven requirement statement intended to increase the quality and productivity of creating or validating requirements. Requirement patterns explain the questions that a requirement raises (i.e., questions that one must answer when specifying a concrete requirement). Requirement patterns point out potential pitfalls and suggest requirement variants.

[184] An anti-pattern describes a design response to a recurring design question, where the anti-pattern approach is usually ineffective and counterproductive. Anti-patterns complement the effective designs (DOs) that patterns suggest with ineffective designs (DON'Ts) that should be avoided.

of type pattern, but not for those of type roadmap (**ARCHITECTURE LEVEL, DOMAIN TAXONOMY**).

The *challenge* segment design also depends on the reference asset type. Architecture patterns, for example, summarize the problem that their proposed design addresses, while an architecture roadmap describes the questions it answers, or the decision processes it supports.

Finally, the *constitution* section consists of three subsections, with only the first section (*common attribute set*) being independent of the reference asset type. Common attributes include *asset name, owner,* or *state* to mark the lifecycle phase of an asset. Also, reference assets should have *unique identifiers* as well as *namespaces* to make them technically distinguishable. Other typical attributes are *asset description* and *rationale,* which allow users of reference asset to quickly learn about the *what* and *why* of an asset. A description of reference asset *assumptions* explicates what is a necessary prerequisite for using an asset. In contrast, a description of *implications* or consequences informs about the impacts caused by applying a reference asset. Dependency attributes (*inbound dependencies, outbound dependencies*) are beneficial for convenient navigation to the corresponding reference asset. For example, dependencies between patterns make an architect aware of related patterns. Other asset attributions can indicate *prioritization* and provide guidance on how to resolve conflicts between competing reference assets. An example of this is a situation where two architecture roadmap events conflict. A domain roadmap plans the functional extension of an application for a certain period of time. In contrast, the corresponding application roadmap plans for operational stabilization by version jump of the underlying technology for the same time period.

Manage architecture reference assets in asset portfolios. Publish architecture assets and make them widely available in catalogs. An asset portfolio is a container for architecture assets—a container that contains, for example, landscape assets such as services (*service portfolio*), applications (*application portfolio*), or information (*information portfolio*), or alternatively, a container that contains reference assets such as patterns (*architecture pattern portfolio*) or principles. Asset portfolios are cross-domain containers, i.e., containers that manage assets irrespective of their domain. A portfolio contains a whole set of assets and allows you to search asset sets based on a common schema, making architecture assets comparable and relatable. For example, you can access assets in a portfolio sorted by their cost or risk profiles. Assets are managed in portfolios throughout their lifecycle. An architecture asset is added to a portfolio long before it is officially published in a catalog. It remains available in the portfolio long after it is removed from a catalog. The final lifecycle state of an asset in a portfolio is *archived.* This distinguishes portfolios from catalogs, which contain only currently published assets (Fig. 6.204).

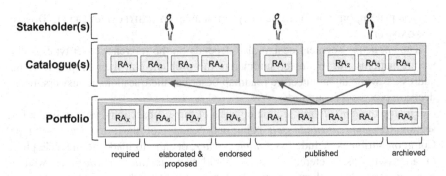

Fig. 6.204 Architecture portfolio and catalog

Make reference asset catalogs available to all architects in your function and to reference asset consumers beyond. Establish access and navigation in reference asset catalogs to best present themselves to their respective interest groups. When in doubt, serve multiple catalogs from the same portfolio. Both catalogs and portfolios provide basic container management functionality. You can publish assets to a container, remove an asset from a container, and modify the asset's attributes while it is in a container. You can also search a container and find assets that match your search criteria. Finally, you can register with containers and subscribe to specific container events, for example, the release of a new pattern in a container.

Note that there may be connections or dependencies between different architecture portfolios. Such connections result from connections at the level of architecture assets that are managed in different portfolios. Such dependencies may exist horizontally—between reference assets of the same type. For example, one architecture pattern (P_1) suggests considering other patterns (P_2 and P_3). Dependencies can also exist vertically—that is, between reference assets of different types. For example, two architecture roadmaps (R_1 and R_2) reference the same architecture pattern (P_2). Both roadmap events require that architecture pattern P_2 be adopted in their respective contexts (Fig. 6.205).

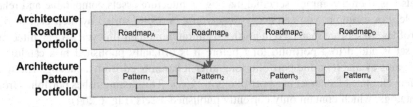

Fig. 6.205 Portfolio dependencies

Define a consistent approach to portfolio prioritization—ultimately, the prioritization of assets held in the portfolio. Base the prioritization of a reference asset on its value proposition (i.e., the value created using a reference asset), cost (i.e., the cost of employing it), strategic fit (i.e., an indication of the degree to which a particular asset supports the strategic direction and longer-term planning), cross-domain contribution (i.e., an indication of the degree to which an asset adds value to a variety of profiteers), and risk (i.e., an indication of the severity of an undesirable impact and the likelihood that it will occur). Note that asset portfolios and catalogs are used not only to record and maintain reference assets but also landscape assets. Examples of such asset portfolios include a service portfolio, an application portfolio, an information portfolio, or a platform portfolio. However, also think of requirements, such as a demand portfolio, or engagements, such as a project portfolio.

In addition to introducing new reference assets or revising existing assets on an as-needed basis, you should also regularly review existing reference assets for relevance, completeness, and correctness. Also, ensure that you appropriately solicit guidance on key reference assets (e.g., via policies). Continue to ensure compliance with reference assets where required. Leverage your architecture calendars to synchronize periodic reviews of reference asset appropriateness over time—for example, across all business domains (**ARCHITECTURE CALENDAR**).

6.10.8 Architecture Roadmap Methodology

Architecture is an informative, instructive, and prescriptive discipline—including the future planning of architecture assets. Architecture functions ensure proper planning by establishing appropriate roadmaps. An architecture roadmap is a reference asset and, similar to the other assets, must be built, evolved, and deployed. Different types of roadmaps share common concepts, such as basic attribute sets and similar lifecycle management processes. Architecture functions ensure that all architects make their decisions and perform their activities in accordance with roadmap-based planning.

> A *roadmap* is a detailed plan to guide progress toward a goal. (Merriam-Webster Dictionary 2020)

For an architecture asset, a roadmap describes both its desired future states and the events to achieving those future states. A roadmap represents a binding development plan for a particular asset. Roadmaps enable coordinated decision-making beyond the boundaries of individual organizations and assets. For example, coordination between the plans of several interrelated domains.

An *architecture roadmap* depicts planned states or anticipated future events related to architecture assets or other aspects of design interest. Roadmaps thereby support decision-making and ensure coordinated action within an architecture function. For example, an architecture function formulates a policy. The policy dictates that concrete changes to landscape assets are accepted and supported only if they relate to corresponding roadmap events. In other words, landscape changes are approved by the architecture function only if those changes are consistent with prior roadmap-based planning. Architecture functions use roadmaps to ensure the evolution of architecture assets within corridors whose boundaries are sharply and comprehensibly marked by corresponding roadmap events. Roadmaps are therefore a pivotal instrument for monitoring and controlling asset evolution.

Planned or anticipated roadmap events are always associated with architecture assets, such as applications, services, technologies, or domains. However, methodology assets, such as the roadmap methodology itself, are also considered architecture assets for which roadmaps exist. The capabilities realized by assets (i.e., asset purpose) are mentioned accordingly in roadmap event descriptions. Roadmap events trigger associated activities. Other attributes you consider for roadmap events are the rationale for an event or the associated decisions and impacts. Activities are qualified by start and end times and possibly intermediate milestones. Activities can be decomposed into sub-activities. Breaking down activities is equivalent to breaking down capabilities into sub-capabilities. Multiple roadmap activities can be bundled into single projects or programs. The outcome sought by an activity corresponds to achievements sought, which are desired end states for a corresponding architecture asset. Examples of achievements include establishing a new capability for an application, decommissioning a service, or improving the cost and risk profile of a platform asset. Events, similar to activities and achievements, are also tied to the roadmap timeline. There may be dependencies between roadmap events. These can exist both within a roadmap and across roadmaps. Finally, dependencies are differentiated into outbound and inbound dependencies (Fig. 6.206).

Fig. 6.206 Architecture roadmap components

Architecture Function and Architecture Roadmap Methodology

Architecture functions establish and use roadmap methodologies to perform development planning of architecture assets and ensure that planning impacts actions and decisions accordingly. Roadmaps are differentiated along architecture levels to equip different types of assets with planning for different planning horizons. For example, planning for architecture domains has a longer planning horizon than planning for simple applications. Roadmaps are also differentiated by how planned assets contribute to business objectives (i.e., business versus technical differentiation). Furthermore, an architecture function ensures coordinated planning and traceability between roadmaps since roadmaps replicate asset-level interdependencies. Finally, a roadmap methodology is a specialized reference architecture methodology and therefore inherits its basic features (Fig. 6.207).

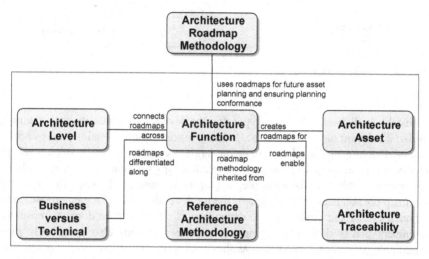

Fig. 6.207   Architecture function and architecture roadmap methodology

Ensure your roadmap methodology includes core roadmap components. First, distinguish between fundamentally different roadmap types depending on the type of assets being planned. For example, a *data center architecture* roadmap includes planned events for all data center subdomains, such as the *storage domain*, *virtualization domain*, or *data center facilities* domain. In a data center architecture roadmap, the asset is a structural asset (i.e., a domain). As another example, an *enterprise architecture* roadmap defines a plan for implementing an assessment methodology or plans for reviewing current enterprise principles in light of a recent major restructuring. In this example, the architecture assets are methodological and reference assets. Link planned events, activities, and achievements to both an architecture asset as a whole and to the specific capabilities that an asset realizes (**Architecture Asset**) (Fig. 6.208).

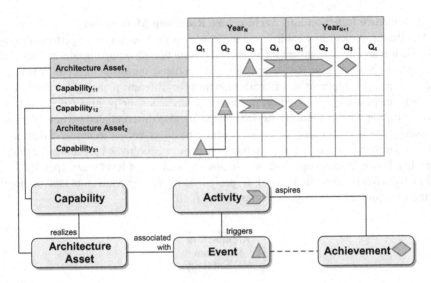

Fig. 6.208 Roadmap visualization

Establish different roadmap types for the levels of granularity and planning horizons relevant in your enterprise. In other words, establish roadmap types across essential architecture levels. Also, define aggregate relationships between levels to clarify composition and decomposition relationships for your function as a whole. *Enterprise roadmaps*, for example, aggregate domain roadmaps. An enterprise roadmap consolidates an overview of the top-level domains of the enterprise, their planned events and goals, and the dependencies between these domains, ensuring alignment across domain roadmaps. Enterprise roadmaps also specifically plan methodology and reference assets as they tend to be applied across the enterprise. Enterprise roadmaps mainly capture strategic decisions (i.e., decisions with a planning horizon of about 5 years). They support the early stages of an enterprise value chain. However, one should be aware that decisions with such a long time horizon are meant to be thought-provoking and to stimulate fruitful debates. One must be careful not to misinterpret them as certain predictions of future states. In very large companies, multiple enterprise roadmaps may coexist—for example, an enterprise roadmap for each business unit or division. A possible combination of such enterprise roadmaps into a cross-divisional roadmap would either have a low information density and thus only a vague orientation character, or it would focus on overarching aspects where coordination appears to be urgently needed (**ARCHITECTURE LEVEL**) (Fig. 6.209).

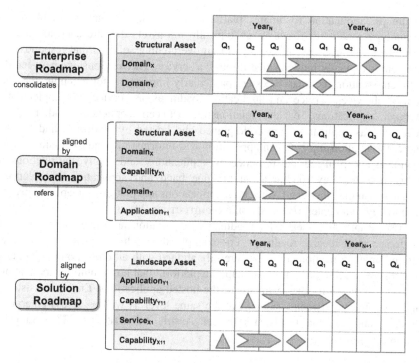

Fig. 6.209 Roadmaps at different architecture levels

Also establish roadmaps for your architecture domains. A *domain roadmap* outlines the plans for its subdomains—i.e., it works with a different planning horizon, granularity, and level of detail than enterprise-level roadmaps. Domain roadmaps relate specifically to solution roadmaps and ensure alignment with and between them. Domain roadmaps are used when making tactical decisions (i.e., decisions with a planning horizon of approximately 1–2 years). They support the portfolio decision stages in an organization's value chain. Tactical decisions are more likely to be implemented as planned in the future than strategic decisions. Nevertheless, they too are more informative and less necessarily prescriptive in nature. Domain roadmaps either encompass sub-domains or focus on the critical landscape assets of the domain and the respective relationships between them.

Finally, introduce solution roadmaps for landscape assets and overarching solutions. *Solution roadmaps* represent events, activities, and achievements for landscape assets such as services, applications, or platforms. They are utilized to guide operational decisions (i.e., decisions with a planning horizon of approximately 1–12 months) during the service planning and building stages of an enterprise value chain. Operational decisions are highly likely to be implemented exactly as planned. Solution roadmaps include one or more landscape assets that together form a respective solution. They exist for each type of landscape asset, such as service roadmaps, application roadmaps, platform roadmaps, information roadmaps, or technology roadmaps. Services are typically the assets that are used as solution culmination points. That is, the idea of an overarching solution that responds to a problem is typically implemented through a service. The relationships between the different solution roadmap types are particularly important—for example, the relationship between service and application roadmaps, as services are implemented through applications, or the relationship between application and platform roadmaps, as applications are underpinned and hosted by platforms, and furthermore, the relationship between application and information roadmaps, since information is encapsulated and provided by applications, and finally, the relationship between technology roadmaps on the one hand and application and platform roadmaps on the other hand, since both applications and platforms adapt a respective technology to an enterprise situation (ARCHITECTURE ASSET).

Also, establish a means for roadmap reconciliation and aggregation between landscape asset-specific roadmaps. For example, the roadmap of a service comprising multiple applications must be carefully aligned with all corresponding application roadmaps. Similarly, the roadmap of a platform that hosts multiple applications must be aligned with the roadmaps of the hosted applications. Ensure consistency and traceability between roadmaps at the same level as well as across enterprise, domain, and solution levels (LANDSCAPE ASSET, ARCHITECTURE TRACEABILITY) (Fig. 6.210).

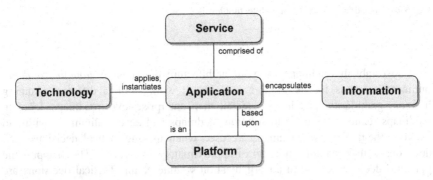

Fig. 6.210 Landscape asset types and roadmaps

Apart from the different levels at which they exist, roadmaps are also distinguished in terms of their capability connotation. For example, a solution roadmap that proposes plans for events, activities, and deliverables around a business application is called a *business application roadmap*. Similarly, a domain roadmap that proposes plans for a technical domain and relates to technical platforms is called a *technical domain roadmap* (BUSINESS VERSUS TECHNICAL).

Employ a *roadmap permutation cube* to reflect and determine the range of roadmaps managed by your architecture function. A roadmap's objective, traceability, or aggregation relationships result from its combination of architecture levels, landscape asset type, and capability connotation. The three dimensions of levels, asset type, and capability connotation form the roadmap permutation cube. For example, the business service roadmap of a single solution-level service is consolidated into a domain-level business service roadmap. The domain-level roadmap includes roadmaps of other services and ensures that the roadmaps of all services in the domain are aligned and consistent. Also, the business service roadmap of an individual service at the solution level must be linked to business or technical application roadmaps—roadmaps of applications on the basis of which this service is implemented (Fig. 6.211).

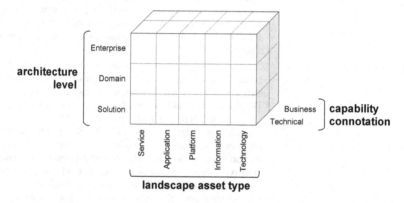

Fig. 6.211 Roadmap permutation cube

Consider the approach outlined below as a rudimentary process blueprint that you can use as the basis for your own roadmap process. Remember that architecture roadmaps are specializations of reference assets. That is, a roadmap process is derived from a reference architecture process and thus specializes the generalized process. Alternatively, you can review roadmap processes already established in your organization for their appropriateness and completeness. The approach presented here is certainly not sufficient in detail and scope. It describes a generic roadmap process that you will need to adapt for different roadmap types. For example, a domain roadmap of a top-level domain only provides events for coarse-grained sub-domains. In contrast, an application roadmap focuses on a single application and projects events for the fine-grained capabilities of that application. However, the specific roadmap processes for the different roadmap types also have common features (**REFERENCE ARCHITECTURE METHODOLOGY**) (Table 6.16).

Table 6.16 Architecture roadmap process

Activity	Description
Determine roadmap needs	Before creating a new or adjusting an existing roadmap, assess the need that justifies its evolution. For example, a new domain has been introduced in the enterprise for which a domain roadmap does not yet exist. Or, there is a need to align a business technology roadmap because the technology vendor has redefined the end date for product support. Also, consider dependencies on or to other roadmaps or reference assets, like patterns, and capture them accordingly as change requirements (NEED TO KNOW, ARCHITECTURE CONDITION)
Determine roadmap(s) or other reference asset(s)	Determine the roadmap or roadmaps that need to be adapted based on the requirements identified above. Also, consider horizontally and vertically dependent roadmaps. For example, if a new domain roadmap is required, determine the areas of the enterprise roadmap affected by the new deployment to make the appropriate updates once the domain roadmap is created
Define and classify roadmap	Classify roadmaps using the *roadmap permutation cube* categories. For each roadmap, determine at least its combination of architecture levels, landscape type, and capability semantics. The purpose of roadmap classification is to identify their stereotypical reconciliation and aggregation needs. Any additional classification will further improve the navigability and discoverability of roadmaps once they are published in appropriate catalogs. Finally, create each roadmap according to its type—that is, based on the specific roadmap definition schema of its type. For example, create the roadmap for an information entity called *customer information* based on your roadmap definition schema for business information assets (DOMAIN TAXONOMY)
Validate and endorse roadmap	Validate the appropriateness (e.g., relevance, correctness, completeness) of a newly proposed or modified roadmap and formally endorse it. The approval authority corresponds to the architecture level above the level at which a roadmap is defined. For example, a domain roadmap is validated and approved by an enterprise architect, while solution-level roadmaps are validated and accepted or rejected by domain architects (ARCHITECTURE ROLE, ARCHITECTURE GOVERNANCE, ARCHITECTURE ASSESSMENT METHODOLOGY)
Publish roadmap	Once a roadmap has received its formal confirmation, it is published in the corresponding roadmap catalog. In the roadmap portfolio, its status is set to *published*
Find roadmap	Architects find and access roadmaps via roadmap catalogs. Based on the roadmap permutation cube classification and other roadmap attributes, architects filter the set of all roadmaps to narrow down the relevant ones
Adopt and adhere to roadmap	Architects use roadmaps in two different scenarios. On the one hand, architects propose engagements in

(continued)

Table 6.16 (continued)

Activity	Description
	anticipation of upcoming roadmap events. For example, the architecture function suggests to include a necessary release update of a technical platform in a proposed project because the current release of the platform is approaching its end date according to the platform roadmap.
	On the other hand, architects use roadmaps to ensure that their decisions do not conflict with a confirmed architectural plan. An architect planning to build his service design on top of an existing information entity uses the corresponding information asset's roadmap to ensure, for example, that a plan to decommission the entity does not yet exist
Validate roadmap adherence	The architecture function ensures that decisions are made in full compliance with the roadmaps. Various validation results are possible. For example, *not adhering* means that a proposed application change is not endorsed but rejected because the proposed change conflicts with planned events on that application's roadmap. *Potentially adhering* means that the validating architect lacks information to give final approval. The result of this validation is a revision to the proposal that is compatible with a corresponding roadmap event. Finally, *adhering* means that a proposed change, e.g., to a service, is accepted because the modification is compatible with a corresponding roadmap event (ARCHITECTURE GOVERNANCE, ARCHITECTURE POLICY)
Roadmap retrospective	Finally, as with all comprehensively designed processes, a retrospective is conducted. The process owner evaluates insights gained during the process with regard to its optimization and, if necessary, incorporates them by adjusting the process (LEARNING ORGANIZATION)

Do not confuse architecture roadmaps with *project roadmaps*. While the focus of an architecture roadmap is on triggers (*event*) and achieved states (*achievement*), project roadmaps emphasize the *activities* required to accomplish a targeted achievement. However, both types of plans are closely linked. For example, there should be no project that plans or implements a service change without a corresponding event on a service architecture roadmap—an event that confirms the service change as planned and endorsed by the architecture function. Projects are vehicles to achieve a future state—by accompanying or facilitating the achievement of that state. Project roadmaps outline projects and identify architecture assets that will be effected by the execution of the project. The granularity with which a project roadmap identifies and lists touched assets can vary in coarseness. For the assets identified in the project roadmap, the planned activities are further detailed along the timeline. For example, for a platform it is indicated that it will have limited availability during a release update and that some of its guarantees may no longer be warranted. By cross-referencing project roadmaps and the timeline, planning collisions can be identified. For example, two projects are planning a critical change to an application for the same time period. In another example, one project depends on the high availability and operational stability of a platform that a second project is planning to change (Fig. 6.212).

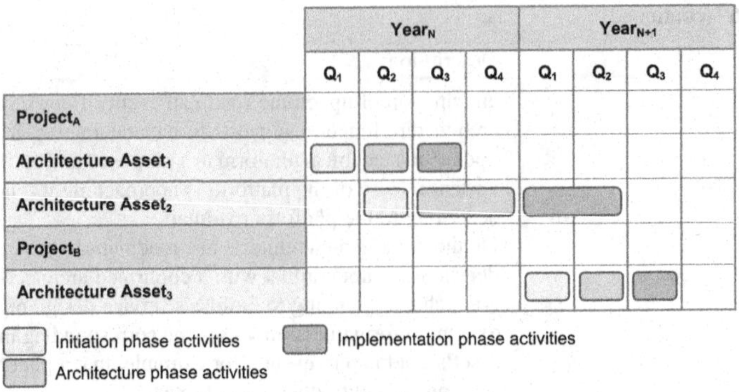

Fig. 6.212 Project roadmap

Apply portfolio management techniques when building or revising architecture roadmaps. For example, use Gartner's TIME model [Gartner TIME]. You can easily generalize Gartner's recommendations for application portfolio management to other types of landscape assets. Business value on the horizontal axis represents the relevance or importance of a landscape asset in a particular environment—such as the importance of a business application to a particular line of business. Quality on the vertical axis indicates the architecture integrity of a landscape asset and its impact on the architectural technical debt[185] of the business. High quality means that the landscape asset has architecture integrity and contributes minimally to architectural debt. The *tolerate* quadrant represents landscape assets that are not of significant importance but of good quality. While the enterprise could easily do without appropriate landscape assets, the expense of dismantling them is not worth it. Landscape assets presented in the *invest* quadrant are of both high quality and business value, justifying further investment. The *migrate* quadrant presents landscape assets that are still relevant and important but are not (anymore) optimal from an architecture perspective, so their refactoring or migration is indicated. Finally, there are landscape assets whose quality is poor, coupled with low business value. These are shown in the elimination quadrant, which means that their timely dismantling is economically justified.

Do not just consider roadmap events that represent new architecture assets or adjustments to existing ones. Rather, look to consolidate or eliminate assets at the end of their lifecycle and place appropriate events in their roadmaps. Require a decommissioning event in the roadmap of at least one landscape asset for each new landscape asset planned in your enterprise. Also, require that the decommissioning

---

[185] Architectural technical debt describes the phenomenon of inadequate system design that achieves short-term benefits at the expense of long-term gradual deterioration in system agility.

event be closely timed with the introduction of the new asset, and require responsible architects to place the event in the appropriate roadmap (DECOMMISSIONING REWARD).

6.10.9 Architecture Pattern Methodology

Design problems repeat themselves, as do their respective solutions. By generalizing both the problems and their solutions, we obtain reusable patterns of proven designs—and thus highly effective semi-finished solution assets. Architecture functions ensure the systematic identification and application of design patterns through an architecture pattern methodology. An architecture pattern is a reference asset and must be identified, developed, and provisioned in a similar manner. Different types of patterns share common concepts, such as basic attribute sets and a similar lifecycle management process.

> A *pattern* is a form or model proposed for imitation; something designed or used as a model for making things. (Merriam-Webster Dictionary 2020)

Patterns are all around us, from the people we meet to the repetitive patterns we find in nature and daily routines. Since our earliest days, we have used patterns to orient ourselves in the world around. A pattern abstracts and generalizes a concrete phenomenon such that the pattern represents the entire class of corresponding concrete phenomena. Recognizing a pattern means recognizing commonalities among concrete phenomena. As a means of abstraction, a pattern is an excellent vehicle of documenting, sharing, and communicating know-how and expertise. Patterns form a common vocabulary that enhances the uniqueness of exchanges between communicating parties. They also provide information about the potential consequences of their use. Broadly speaking, patterns can abstract and generalize anything concrete—for example, a concrete, recurring problem as well as a concrete solution to that problem.

An *architecture pattern* is a generalized and proven design for a correspondingly generalized and recurring design problem. Architecture patterns greatly increase the effectiveness and efficiency of understanding a given problem and formulating an adequate design to solve it. They are three tuples comprised of a *context*, a system of forces (*problem*) that recurs, and a response (*solution*) that resolves the forces—thus solving the problem. The problem part is associated with a surrounding situation (*context*). Contexts are often qualified along domain-specific dimensions. For example, the context sections of patterns in the *security* domain denote the *security pattern type* dimension, whose scalars are *preventive*, *detective*, and *protective*. *Context* dimensions are used to capture patterns through a pattern catalog and to search for patterns in catalogs. The *solution* part of an architecture pattern includes a design that adequately addresses the *problem* (Fig. 6.213).

Fig. 6.213 Architecture
pattern

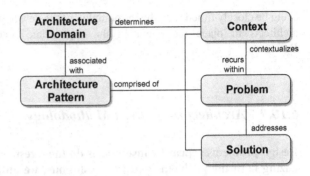

Architecture Function and Architecture Pattern

Architecture functions establish and use pattern methodologies to ensure the efficient design of qualitative enterprise solutions. Architecture patterns are particularly used by solution methodologies to provide architects with solution paths via proven designs. In addition to solution methodologies, policies refer to patterns and thereby elevate them to standards. A standard pattern is one that must be followed according to a corresponding policy. While patterns represent generic solutions to generic problems and can therefore be applied to all types of architecture assets, they are primarily applied to landscape assets. Finally, a pattern methodology is a specialized reference architecture methodology and therefore inherits its basic properties (Fig. 6.214).

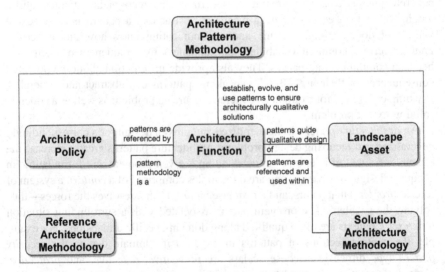

Fig. 6.214 Architecture function and architecture pattern

You create and maintain your pattern descriptions based on a pattern-specific view model. In other words, you make a structured set of attributes the basis of your pattern descriptions. In doing so, you *name* a given pattern so that it can be found intuitively by your architects. Next, you summarize the essence of the pattern in its *abstract* section. Under *context*, you describe conditions that are assumptions for appropriate pattern employment. Context descriptions are often categorical. In a *forces* section, summarize the system of forces that the pattern's solution design resolves. A system of forces usually includes architecture conditions such as modifiability, availability, or security requirements. The *solution* chapter presents the actual architecture design through which the system of forces is resolved. It is decomposed into participants, structure, collaboration, and implementation. In *participants*, the main building blocks of the pattern are described. Their structural and collaborative relationships are detailed in subsequent chapters. For example, in a domain-specific pattern, the building blocks are domain-specific landscape assets such as services, applications, or platforms. In domain-independent patterns, functional, informational, and operational components are common building block types. The *structure* chapter explains the static relationships between the building blocks in a pattern, while *collaboration* details their interactions and cooperation. For example, the collaboration chapter tells you how the pattern components must cooperate to realize a desired quality attribute, like extensibility. If variant designs of a pattern exist, they are listed under *variants*. Variants of a *proxy*[186] pattern include *virtual proxy*,[187] *caching proxy*,[188] or *protection proxy*.[189] Not all solutions presented by a pattern perfectly balance all listed forces. For example, a design that perfectly satisfies security requirements has undesirable consequences from a usability perspective. If there are implications that you want to bring to the architect's attention when considering a pattern, summarize them in the *consequences* chapter. Since patterns are not meant to describe new ideas but represent proven solutions, refer to proven uses in a chapter *known applications*. Finally, point out related patterns in a chapter *relationships to other patterns*, laying the foundation for a pattern language (**Your own Architecture View Model**) (Fig. 6.215).

---

[186] A proxy is a component that acts as an intermediary for something else. For example, a proxy can be an interface to a network connection, a large object in memory, or a file. Proxies are used to access resources that are expensive or difficult to duplicate. In other words, a proxy is an intermediary component that a service consumer invokes to access a service provider. The proxy mediates access to the service provider on behalf of the service consumer, and it mediates the service response to the service consumer on behalf of the service provider.

[187] Virtual proxy is used when a lightweight skeleton representation is beneficial instead of a complex or expensive object. For example, a virtual connection proxy facades the mounting and dismounting of expensive database connections by intermediating between database client and server.

[188] Caching proxy is a component that stores data so that future requests for that data can be served faster. The caching proxy prefers serving requests from service consumers with data from its cache memory. Data has gotten into this through previous requests. Only if the requested data is not available in the cache, the caching proxy forwards the request to a remote data store.

[189] Protection proxy is used to control access to a resource based on, for example, access rights.

Architecture Pattern Template

Name	
Abstract	
Context	
Forces	
Solution	
Participants	
Sturture	
Collaboration	
Implementation	
Variants	
Consequences	
Known Uses	
Relations to other Patterns	

Fig. 6.215 Architecture pattern description

The pattern attribute scheme presented above is used to describe all types of patterns. Models based on visual notations complement prosaic descriptions to increase the comprehensibility of patterns.

I use the proxy pattern to illustrate the attribute scheme presented above. Architects leverage the proxy pattern in the area of component interactions. While systems are generally composed of interacting building blocks, architects sometimes need to avoid components that directly access or directly depend on each other. For example, ABB_1 must not access ABB_2 without ABB_1 having sufficient access rights. At the same time, the logic for enforcing access rights should be kept separate from the responsibilities of the ABB_1 and ABB_2 components. This means that the logic for enforcing access rights should be implemented neither by building block ABB_1 nor by ABB_2 itself, but on the contrary between both building blocks. Architects faced with such situations may consider the proxy pattern (Fig. 6.216).

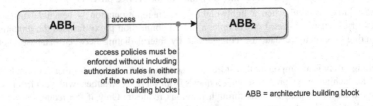

Fig. 6.216 Building block interfacing

Proxy Pattern

The *proxy pattern* has been introduced as both a software design pattern (Gamma et al. 1994) and an architecture pattern (Buschmann et al. 2007) (Fig. 6.217).

Proxy Pattern	
Name	Proxy
Abstract	
Context	A building block A must request services from another building block B.
Forces	Direct access to the service of B is not possible or inappropriate. Specific access semantics are desired. At the same time, the implementations of building blocks A and B must be agnostic to these access semantics. For example, A's authorizations must be checked each time A accesses a service from B, and a service request from A must be denied if A is not sufficiently authorized. While the overall approach is expected to systematically enforce access semantics, at the same time neither A nor B should implement these semantics themselves.
Solution	
Summary of Participants Structure Collaboration Implementation	Building block A communicates with a surrogate, the proxy, instead of directly with building block B. The proxy mimics building block B, so it is perceived as B from A's perspective. At the same time, the proxy forwards incoming requests to B. From B's point of view, the proxy thus mimics building block A. This double mimicry makes A and B virtually agnostic to additional logic that a proxy introduces into a request-response cycle between the two building blocks.
Variants	A caching proxy aims to increase runtime efficiency by caching and reusing results from previous exchanges. A virtual proxy, such as a virtual database connection, hides and optimizes the expensive operations of requesting and releasing physical building blocks (i.e., physical database connection).
Consequences	Proxies decouple building blocks and introduce additional capabilities into a request-response cycle, such as access policy enforcement. However, proxies also introduce additional indirection that can negatively impact performance and represent an additional potential point of failure.
Known Uses	
Relations to other Patterns	

Fig. 6.217 Proxy pattern

The *structure* chapter describes the static relationships between the building blocks in the design of the proxy pattern. The *Client* building block knows a component of type *Subject* that offers the parameterless operation *function*. *Subject* abstracts the two building block types *Proxy* and *RealSubject*, making them indistinguishable for *Clients*. At the same time, a relationship is established between a Proxy and an associated RealSubject (*realSubj*). In the

(continued)

proxy design, the annotation of the *function* method in *Proxy* (*realSubj.
function()*) indicates that *Proxy* objects, which have introduced their own
accountability, pass on the processing of *Client* requests to *RealSubject* objects
(Fig. 6.218).

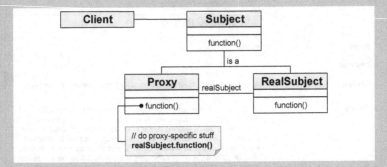

Fig. 6.218 Structure of the Proxy pattern

In the *collaboration* chapter the interactions of the building blocks are
described in detail. The interaction dynamics are illustrated in a sequence
diagram. Here, a *Client* interacts with a *Proxy* by invoking its *function*
operation. The *Proxy* fulfills the responsibility for which it is explicitly
interposed in this scenario (*do proxy-specific stuff*). Finally, *Proxy* forwards
the call to the actual *function* operation to *RealSubject* (Fig. 6.219).

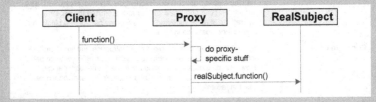

Fig. 6.219 Collaboration of participants of the Proxy pattern

Different pattern categories are distinguished (e.g., *requirement patterns,*[190] *software design patterns,*[191] or *anti-patterns*[192]), all of which are equally covered by this pattern. *Idioms*[193] are also considered patterns. These may be of particular interest to your architecture function if you want to specifically prescribe established landscape assets, such as services, applications, or platforms, in your solution designs.

Beyond the valuable contribution of patterns as solution blueprints, they also help streamline the early planning stage of an enterprise value chain. For example, a pattern that includes predictive attributes such as complexity, cost, or risk provides valuable input for estimating the consequences of a proposed change or assessing the risk of project proposals. Patterns also equip an architecture function with means to guide, measure, and control the quality of asset design. While patterns, like obligations or prohibitions, are referenced in policies, they not only indicate an architecture constraint but also provide a solution path for overcoming it. In particular, use patterns in your governance organization as a means of providing constructive design guidance (ARCHITECTURE GOVERNANCE, ARCHITECTURE POLICY).

Patterns must be formulated generically so that they can be applied not only to a particular problem but to an entire class of problems. At the same time, patterns must be applied to real-world problems that architects face in practice. For example, an architect using a pattern expects it to guide him in practically solving a problem. This means that an architect who develops a design based on a pattern must adapt the generic solution he finds in the pattern to his concrete problem. Establish adapters for the pattern methodology to support adapting your pattern method to different types of patterns. For example, architects need to utilize the pattern methodology slightly differently each time they plan and create domain patterns, architecture patterns, software design patterns, requirement patterns, or idioms. Similarly, the use of the pattern methodology is different when applying patterns. The distinction of business patterns versus technical patterns is another example of the differentiated use of your

---

[190]Requirement patterns generalize specific requirements or constraints. A requirement pattern is a generic, reusable, proven requirement statement intended to increase the quality and productivity of creating or validating requirements. Requirement patterns explain the questions that a requirement raises (i.e., questions that one must answer when specifying a concrete requirement). Requirement patterns point out potential pitfalls and suggest requirement variants.

[191]Software design pattern is a relatively generic, reusable design for a frequently recurring problem in a particular context. Software design patterns typically show relationships and interactions between classes or objects without specifying the final application classes or objects involved in a design that adopts the software design pattern. Examples of software design patterns are singleton, command, composite, template method, or abstract factory class pattern.

[192]An anti-pattern describes a design response to a recurring design question, where the anti-pattern approach is usually ineffective and counterproductive. Anti-patterns complement the effective designs (DOs) that patterns suggest with ineffective designs (DON'Ts) that should be avoided.

[193]Idioms can be understood as implementations of patterns in a specific programming language or implementation technology. An idiom still generalizes concrete solutions but is already programming language-specific. Idioms are used in detailed design to guide the implementation of a pattern's particular design aspects.

architecture pattern methodology (ARCHITECTURE METHODOLOGY ADAPTER, BUSI-NESS ARCHITECTURE VERSUS TECHNICAL ARCHITECTURE).

Consider the approach outlined below as a rudimentary process blueprint that you can use as the basis for your own pattern process. Remember that patterns are specializations of reference assets. That is, a pattern process is derived from a reference architecture process and thus specializes the generalized process. Alternatively, you can review pattern processes already established in your organization for appropriateness and completeness. The approach presented here describes a generic pattern process that you will need to adapt for different pattern types, for example, by providing adapters to customize your pattern methodology. A pattern methodology supports the systematic development, documentation, deployment, discovery, and utilization of patterns in your organization. As with other methodologies, the pattern methodology and its associated view model (*attribute schema used to describe the pattern*) are inextricably linked (REFERENCE ARCHITECTURE METHODOLOGY) (Table 6.17).

Table 6.17 Architecture pattern process

Activity	Description
Determine pattern needs	New patterns emerge from new needs (e.g., new capabilities required to support new business models). Before creating a new pattern or adjusting an existing one, determine the system of forces that will drive the pattern's development. For example, there is not yet a pattern for a new domain, even though initial solutions are already being designed in that domain, such as patterns for a new cloud or artificial intelligence domain. Also, consider dependencies on or to other patterns or reference assets when identifying new needs (e.g., references from roadmap events to patterns, relationships between patterns, and architecture principles). When pattern languages are considered as patterns of patterns, or when you manage composite patterns in your architecture function, evolution of patterns includes their continuous evolution. Thus, as new patterns are developed, the existing pattern languages must be reviewed, and the relationships between patterns may need to be adjusted (NEED TO KNOW, ARCHITECTURE CONDITION)
Determine pattern(s) or other reference asset(s)	Determine the architecture patterns that need to be created or adjusted based on the identified requirements, considering the interdependencies between them
Define and classify pattern	Classify a new pattern based on pattern categories you have defined in your organization—for example, *architecture patterns*, *design patterns*, or *analysis patterns*. Another useful pattern categorization is along their domain orientation. You derive this category from your organization's architecture domains. Another candidate for categorization is the type of landscape assets that are prevalent in particular patterns. For example, information patterns focus on information assets, application patterns place applications at the center of their consideration, and platform patterns focus on platforms. The main purpose of categorizing and classifying patterns is to improve the discoverability of a pattern once it is published in catalogs. Finally, elaborate (i.e., create or adjust) and document the pattern based on your organization's description schema and domain-specific classification language (DOMAIN TAXONOMY)
Validate and endorse pattern	Validate the appropriateness (e.g., relevance, correctness, completeness) of a newly proposed pattern and formally endorse it. Endorsement of a pattern may require more than three known uses of it. Also, any new pattern may be required to go through a community or peer-review process. The formal endorsement authority corresponds to the architecture level at which the new pattern is introduced or the level above. An enterprise-wide pattern is validated and endorsed by an enterprise architect, while a domain-specific pattern is validated by appropriate domain and/or an enterprise architects. Specify *pattern assessment adapters* for your architecture assessment methodology if you plan to use it for pattern

(continued)

Table 6.17 (continued)

Activity	Description
	assessments (ARCHITECTURE GOVERNANCE, ARCHITECTURE ASSESSMENT METHODOLOGY)
Publish pattern	Once a pattern has received its formal endorsement, it is published in the corresponding pattern catalog. In the pattern portfolio, its status is set to *published*
Find pattern	Architects find and access patterns through their catalogs. An architect uses pattern classification and other pattern attributes to narrow down suitable candidates in a pattern search
Adopt a pattern	Architects use patterns as proven designs for their concrete problems. Since a pattern suggests a generic solution design, architects still need to adapt the generic design to their concrete problem. Adopting a pattern saves architects significant time and effort and increases the likelihood of a high-quality design. Note, however, that even adopting a pattern does not guarantee that the resulting design will optimally meet all given requirements. Patterns encourage optimal designs for your solutions, but do not guarantee them—this remains the responsibility of your architects. Make sure they are aware of this. Additionally, establish appropriate quality control mechanisms to encourage the use of patterns
Validate pattern adherence	Your architecture function ensures that designs are developed with patterns in mind and that decisions are guided by patterns. Various validation outcomes are possible. For example, *non-adhering* means that a change to an established service is not endorsed, but rejected, if a security pattern has not been applied correctly. *Potentially adhering* means that the validating architect lacks information to make a final endorsement. For example, an insufficient architecture description was submitted for validation. Finally, *adhering* means that a proposed change to a service is endorsed because the service modification correctly adopts the pattern design
Pattern retrospective	Finally, as in all properly designed processes, a retrospective is conducted. The process owner evaluates insights gained during the process regarding its optimization and, if necessary, incorporates them by adjusting the process (LEARNING ORGANIZATION)

Before taking a closer look at a pattern specialty, let us look at pattern portfolios and catalogs. Pattern portfolios support the continuous evolution of patterns across all domains, pattern catalogs, as well as pattern languages. A pattern portfolio contains not only the patterns that are actively used but also those that have since been marked as obsolete. Another interesting group of patterns in a portfolio are those that are only partially elaborated. For example, a frequently recurring problem in an enterprise has been systematically captured and described, but without an ideal solution design already in place. The reason for the missing solution design could be, for example, a missing enterprise landscape capability. However, such partially clarified patterns (i.e., semi-finished patterns) already help to systematize the requirement engineering process. They are valuable input for service managers of those services that are to deliver the missing capability shortly. Semi-finished patterns are also useful in a domain roadmap. A future design pattern is displayed to provide architects a preview today of possible designs in the future.

While architecture functions typically manage a single cross-domain pattern portfolio, they may simultaneously offer multiple pattern catalogs. A pattern catalog is a collection of patterns designed to provide the architecture community with an optimal overview of actively promoted and standardized patterns.

A final category of collections that we distinguish for patterns are pattern languages. While pattern languages and catalogs both support navigation and discovery of patterns from the perspective of an interested architect, there is a distinct difference between the two. A pattern catalog provides a comparatively linear approach to navigation through a collection of patterns. It provides filtering capabilities as well as access to patterns distributed across multiple domains. In contrast, pattern languages provide further relationships and contextualized associations between patterns, making them less linear and more holistic.

The *pattern language* concept was introduced by Christopher Alexander and popularized by his famous book *A Pattern Language* in 1977 (Alexander et al. 1977). Pattern languages are organized and coherent sets of patterns, where each pattern describes a problem and the core of a corresponding solution. Pattern languages also allow each pattern to be used and combined in a variety of ways.

A pattern language is sometimes compared to a spoken language. Just as words must have grammatical and semantic relationships to each other to make a spoken language useful, design patterns must be related to each other to make up a pattern language. Pattern relationships that make up a language give an architect many additional clues. For example, each problem aspect that an architect considers at the beginning of a solution journey is related to other problem aspects. The first pattern an architect visits gives him valuable solution clues. At the same time, this first pattern points the architect to typically related problem aspects for which other patterns exist. A pattern language emphasizes the relationships that inherently exist between patterns. The main purpose of a pattern language is to help navigate patterns to raise awareness and enable architects to solve composite problems. That is, problems that cannot be solved by a single pattern alone. Moreover, a pattern language promotes the recognition of relationships between patterns belonging to different domains, thus supporting interdisciplinary architectural thinking. A pattern language inherently or explicitly brings in its own super perspective and context. In this respect, a pattern language may well be viewed as a pattern itself—a pattern composed of patterns. Moreover, a single pattern can be referenced by multiple pattern languages, which themselves serve different navigational or orientational needs.

Architects using a pattern language begin elaborating their design by finding a pattern that fits an initial part of their overall problem. Once the initial pattern is found and the first part of an overall solution design is elaborated, the pattern language points the architect to patterns that are associated with the initial pattern—thus with other potentially legitimate aspects of the given overall problem.

Navigating and viewing this initial set of associated patterns provides the architect with more useful clues for the next round of associated patterns and so on. The subset or network of patterns associated with the initial problem part can get very large very quickly. This makes pattern languages powerful tools in the study of larger problems and the design of complex solutions. Note that pattern language partitions are introduced as structures that group patterns with commonalities. In addition, pattern languages are highly scalable. Adding patterns over time does not break existing relationships, but adds to them (Fig. 6.220).

Fig. 6.220 Pattern language

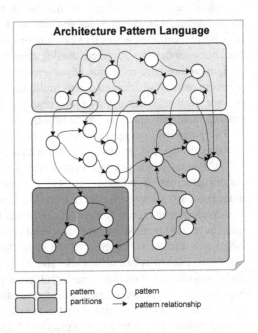

Note that the book you are holding in your hands also provides you with a pattern language. The 48 architecture function patterns found in this pattern catalog are strongly interrelated and form a semantically navigable network of patterns—in other words, a pattern language. Also, the three main chapters of this book, *context*, *challenge*, and *constitution*, provide a navigation and orientation scheme that spans all the patterns in the catalog. Thus, they provide you with a navigable perspective on this pattern catalog that will help you plan, build, and execute your architecture function—or in other words they offer you an *architecture function pattern language*.

6.10.10 Architecture Principle

Solutions are answers to problems. Architecture conditions such as architecture-specific requirements or constraints are tangible and measurable parts of problems to which solution designs concretely refer. However, there are also architecture conditions that are more categorical, fundamental, and less specific. While low specificity may seem disadvantageous at first glance, it is valuable in situations where concrete direction is lacking. Architecture principles are architecture means with less specificity, so they are particularly useful for establishing heuristic orientation. Architecture functions use principles to formulate the guardrails of a design without incurring the cost of arbitrary design.

> A *principle* is a comprehensive and fundamental law, or doctrine, a rule or code of conduct. (Merriam-Webster Dictionary 2020)
> A *principle* is a proposition or value that is a guide for behavior or evaluation. The principles of a system are understood by its users as the essential characteristics of the system, or reflecting system's designed purpose, and the effective operation or use of which would be impossible if any one of the principles was to be ignored. (Wikipedia Principle 2020g)

Etymologically, the term *principle* is borrowed from the Latin *prīncipium* meaning *beginning*, *foundation*, *first*, or *first cause*. The Open Group (2009) defines architecture principles as rules that organizations establish to coordinate cooperative action toward strategic objectives:

> General rules and guidelines [...] that support the way in which an organization sets about fulfilling its mission.

Architecture principles represent heuristics that guide architecture development without the high specificity of requirements and constraints. Architecture principles formulate categorical and normative design criteria and thus differ from principles in natural science contexts. In the latter, principles correspond to natural laws that describe the inevitable and intrinsic mechanics of a natural artifact.

Like other conditions of architecture, principles limit design freedom. Generally speaking, means that do not restrict design freedom do not contribute to design development and decision-making. Architecture principles especially support those design decisions that arise from trade-off situations. That is, situations in which making a design decision leads to both a desired and undesired effect simultaneously. For example, the design decision to introduce a *protection proxy*[194] for implementing a security requirement introduces an additional component into an

---

[194] A proxy is a component that acts as an intermediary for something else. For example, a proxy can be an interface to a network connection, a large object in memory, or a file. Proxies are used to access resources that are expensive or difficult to duplicate. In other words, a proxy is an intermediary component that a service consumer invokes to access a service provider. The proxy mediates access to the service provider on behalf of the service consumer, and it mediates the service response to the service consumer on behalf of the service provider.

overall application design. The proxy is another component that resides on the critical execution path. Thus, the proxy is a building block whose outage leads to an outage of the entire solution, which negatively affects its stability and availability. Moreover, the proxy introduces an additional hop that negatively affects application performance (Greefhorst and Proper 2011).

Architecture Function and Architecture Principle
Architecture functions employ principles to establish guardrails for architecture development. Principles particularly support design situations in which architects make trade-off decisions. They are differentiated according to their degree of validity and along architecture levels. Furthermore, principles are reference assets, which is why architecture functions adapt an architecture reference methodology for both their development and their utilization (Fig. 6.221).

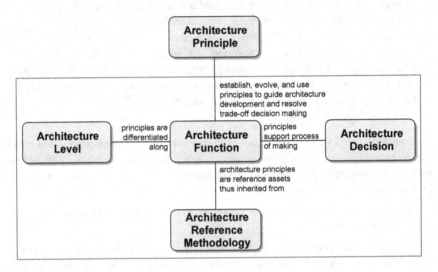

Fig. 6.221 Architecture function and architecture principle

Architecture principles fill a gap between strategic or visionary aspirations and concrete design decisions at different architecture levels. For example, universal principles are distinguished from industry principles or principles that apply to the entire enterprise (*enterprise principles*). Other typical distinctions involve principles that apply to specific architecture domains (*domain principles*) versus those that apply only to a specific solution, e.g., a service or application (*solution principles*). The categorization of principles along architecture levels specifies the scope of validity of the respective principles. For example, an architecture function defines a *buy before reuse before build principle*[195] at the enterprise level. This means all domains and solutions in the enterprise must adhere to this principle in defined situations. In contrast, a principle defined at the solution level, e.g., applied to a purchasing application, is valid only for that application (ARCHITECTURE LEVEL) (Fig. 6.222).

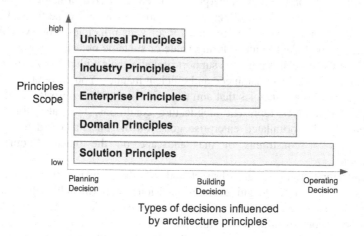

Fig. 6.222 Architecture principle categories

Architecture principles are reference assets, such as patterns or roadmaps. This means that you can derive your principles process from the generic reference architecture methodology and specialize it to your needs. Similar to the roadmap or pattern methodology, an architecture principles methodology must support the systematic development, documentation, discovery as well as utilization of principles in your enterprise (REFERENCE ARCHITECTURE METHODOLOGY).

Another categorization scheme classifies principles along the types of decisions that are influenced by it, for example, the different types of decisions along an enterprise value chain, such as planning decisions (*portfolio principles*), building decisions (*design principles*), or operational decisions (*operating principles*). Note that the quality of an architecture (i.e., the quality of all decisions of that architecture) is largely relative and can only be determined relatively, namely, relative to the adequacy with which a design satisfies its architecture conditions, such as

---

[195] *Buy before reuse before build* is a sound architecture principle embedding the concept of reuse while avoiding building new code where less expensive options exist. Stated heretically, this maxim is not so much a principle as it is almost a platitude. At the same time, it leads to serious misconceptions in its application if the following set of criteria is missing. Buy a product only if it fulfills 90% of your core requirements and is easily modifiable and maintainable to realize the remaining 10%. Buy the product also if you can adapt your business processes to the product without losses. Do not buy the product but consider reusing an existing solution or building a new one if the product does not meet the conditions formulated above.

requirements or constraints. In contrast to the relative evaluability of architecture based on requirements and constraints, principles represent absolute criteria for measuring and determining the quality of architecture decisions (**ARCHITECTURE DECISION**).

Ensure that architecture principles reflect enduring values and beliefs as well as elemental conditions of your enterprise. Therefore, derive principles from your enterprise's enduring, far-reaching, and essential goals and conditions. Use this maxim as a general relevance criterion for all your principles. For example, if a principle can be linked to an enduring value or strategic objective, the principle is relevant—otherwise, it is not. You support strategic goals with principles that aim to achieve those goals in a guaranteed and efficient manner. You account for strategic risks by articulating principles that aim to avoid risks at the enterprise level. While principles themselves represent architecture conditions, they also fill the gap between vaguely formulated enterprise goals on the one hand and the concrete requirements or constraints of the landscape on the other (**ARCHITECTURE CONDITION**).

Architecture principles are abstract and generic in nature. Therefore, unlike patterns, use principles to guide design decisions approximately rather than prescribing them specifically or very concretely. Use principles, especially in decision areas where more specific means, like patterns, do not exist to guide architecture development. At the same time, ensure that any design decisions included in your patterns are consistent with, i.e., do not contradict, your enterprise principles. Adjust your pattern methodology to refer to principles when deciding between competing patterns (i.e., for one and against all other patterns). In other words, use principles to resolve pattern trade-off decisions (**ARCHITECTURE PATTERN METHODOLOGY**).

6.10.11 Your own Architecture Platform

Comprehensive, mature, and standardized architecture platforms and tools are offered by many vendors and in numerous forms and flavors. An architecture platform may specialize in a particular area, such as architecture modeling, analysis, or artifact management. Alternatively, architecture platforms may support a broader range of design areas simultaneously. Despite the architecture activities platforms address, they are generically designed to be adapted to a variety of particular use cases and contexts. Using platforms off-the-shelf and without customization to meet your enterprise's needs leaves valuable optimization opportunities untapped. At worst, architects adapt the platform ad-hoc each time to both the enterprise and the specific task at hand. This is not only inefficient and redundant but also leads to inconsistencies in the description of the enterprise architecture.

> A *platform* is a means whereby something is achieved, performed, or fur-
> thered. (Merriam-Webster Dictionary 2020)

This pattern is so fundamental that it is related to virtually all other patterns in this
pattern language. It relates to the other patterns in that *architecture platforms* provide
the tool base for implementing all design-related means for an architecture function.
An architecture tool base aims to increase the productivity of design contributions
while ensuring consistency in the architecture description. Architecture platforms
and tools that increase the productivity of design contributions and ensure the
consistency of the architecture description have been around for some time. The
design of platforms is generic to support the widest possible range of deployment
scenarios within many different contexts—in other words, to be a valuable tool for as
many commercial customers as possible. You, therefore, need to customize architecture platforms to make them useful to your own function (Fig. 6.223).

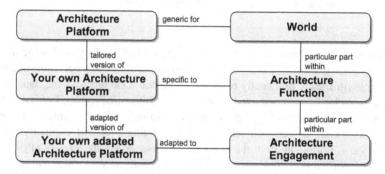

Fig. 6.223   Your own architecture platform

Architecture Function and Your Own Architecture Platform
Architecture functions establish their own platforms to provide their architects with
tools that underpin relevant architecture means. By using architecture platforms,
architecture functions pursue increased productivity as well as consistency in their
contributions. Through their physical schemas, platforms implement your architecture view models. Relevant assets are physically captured, evolved, versioned, and
archived. At the same time, architecture platforms support different levels of aggregation along architecture levels and provide horizontal as well as vertical traceability
in a sophisticated and highly flexible way (Fig. 6.224).

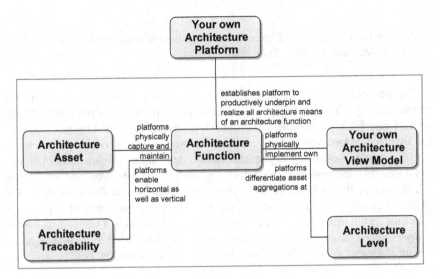

Fig. 6.224 Architecture function and your own architecture platform

You do not just have to adapt an architecture platform to your business needs before you can exploit its value potential. You usually have to meet a non-negligible set of prerequisites to practically exploit its potential. One prerequisite, banal at first glance, is to clarify what you expect from your architecture product. Formulate these expectations concretely and precisely in the form of platform requirements. When articulating them, detach yourself from any existing tool and explicitly take an outside view. Formulate both the purpose (i.e., use cases) and quality attributes of your platform. Note that what you cannot formulate in your own language as a platform expectation, you cannot formulate in the formal language of your platform. And what you cannot formulate in your platform's language, you will not be able to implement in it (NEED TO KNOW).

Another seemingly mundane but fundamental prerequisite for harnessing platform potential is the acceptance of a fact- and evidence-based architecture discipline within your organization. Make sure that the insights you hope to gain from adopting an architecture platform can be gleaned from information that you either already collect or will be able to collect within your enterprise. For example, let us say you want to use your platform to identify opportunities for application consolidation. Suppose there is fundamental organizational resistance to providing the enterprise application information you need to identify consolidation opportunities. An architecture platform will not solve this problem for you. As another example, suppose your platform enables you to automatically generate architecture artifacts based on information in an architecture repository. So the platform potentially enables you to free your architects from manually assembling artifacts. However, the platform's artifact generator needs not only the design information (*what*) you want to automatically assemble but also metadata that tells the generator *where* and *how* to insert the design information into the artifact. In this example, you need to consider the effort required to provide and maintain the required metadata before you can expect any savings from automatic artifact generation. If you ignore this prerequisite or cannot ensure detailed metadata, you will not exploit the generator potential of you platform. Be aware that an architecture platform increases the productivity of your architects and the rigidity of processing information that already exists. However, an architecture platform does not absolve you from ensuring that the information you need is available to you on a regular, sustained, sufficiently detailed, and high-quality basis. In summary, make sure that you sufficiently fulfill the prerequisites for exploiting your platform's potential (**Architecture Condition**).

Distinguish the following three aspects, or perspectives, on an architecture platform. First, you need to determine the potential (*could*) that a platform offers by itself—in other words, its off-the-shelf functional and non-functional capabilities. This gives you an idea of the maximum you can achieve with a platform under consideration. In the next step, as independently as possible from the first, determine the expectations (*want*) you have of your platform, thereby clarifying what you want to achieve with the platform. Deliberately do not limit yourself to what seems feasible at the moment but sketch a complete picture of your needs and desires. This perspective corresponds to the target architecture of your platform. Finally, determine the extent to which you meet the requirements for realizing the platform's potential (*can*). Distinguish between what seems practically feasible today and what is possible a year or 5 years from now. Consider unmet prerequisites as fundamental weaknesses in your architecture function. Review the extent to which these gaps need to be addressed. If necessary, update your architecture function roadmap accordingly (**Architecture Roadmap Methodology**) (Fig. 6.225).

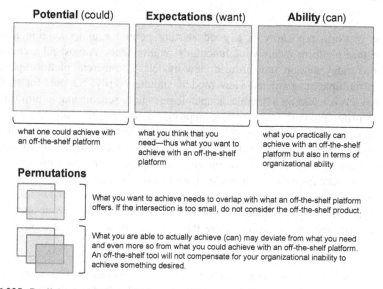

Fig. 6.225   Realizing architecture platform potential

Think of architecture platforms as systems that can be broken down into four core building blocks. The *architecture platform management* building block provides capabilities to customize, manage, maintain, and evolve the platform. The *architecture platform repository* provides capabilities for representing, storing, and manipulating design information. In contrast, the *architecture platform user experience* building block equips platform actors with means to effectively access and retrieve data stored in a repository. Finally, the *architecture platform ecosystem* represents the totality of enterprise information available. It enables seamless collaboration and information sharing between an architecture function and other enterprise disciplines (Fig. 6.226).

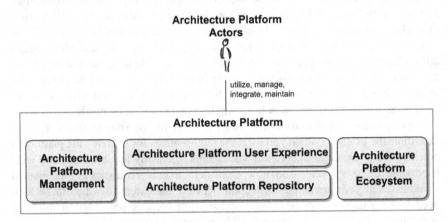

Fig. 6.226 Architecture platform building blocks

The platform repository is a good starting point for understanding how an architecture platform meets your function's requirements. Almost all architecture platforms today support standardized view models. Commercial platform products support multiple standardized view models simultaneously. Support for multiple view models is based on a flexible, adaptable repository schema that in turn is based on *metaprogramming*[196] architecture approaches. However, compare your view models with those a platform offers to determine the degree of alignment. For example, evaluate how a platform supports views such as *architecture mode* (*runtime, design-time*, or *management-time views*), *capability type* (*business versus technical capability views*), *physicality* (*conceptual, logical*, or *physical views*), or *architecture activity type* (*govern versus perform architecture views*). The assessment will help you understand how an evaluated platform meets your architecture function requirements. Finally, ensure that a platform supports the modeling and

---

[196]Metaprogramming is a programming technique in which computer programs treat other programs as data. A metaprogramming-based program reads, generates, transforms, or interprets another program.

visualization capabilities, architecture description languages, and nomenclatures that you need (**YOUR OWN ARCHITECTURE VIEW MODEL**).

Architecture platforms may not operate with the same understanding of architecture as your architecture function. For example, you view architecture as a discipline that looks at the entire enterprise as the system to be designed. In other words, you view enterprise service design, your enterprise value chain, and the architecture of landscape assets as your responsibilities. Compared to an architecture platform that sees architecture as a pure IT discipline, there is a considerable gap in this example. Such a platform would ignore the topic of business architecture, whereas business architecture is an important discipline for you. Also, assess whether a platform you are considering supports your architecture language and domain taxonomy or whether it allows for complex linguistic adaptations. For example, some platforms allow the adoption of domain-specific language[197] (DSL) (**ARCHITECTURE LANGUAGE, DOMAIN TAXONOMY**).

Ensure that your platform enables contributions across your enterprise value chain in a seamless, consistent, durable, and efficient manner. Typically, this means that your architecture platform must provide options for mutual integration with platforms from other disciplines along the enterprise value chain. For example, support for programmable integration or standardized artifact formats and exchange protocols.

Architecture platforms should meet your requirements for representing architecture assets. For example, ensure that your platform adequately represents your landscape assets (e.g., service, application, information, or platform), structural assets (e.g., domains), reference assets (e.g., architecture roadmaps, patterns, or principles), and methodology assets (e.g., reference architecture methodology or assessment methodology). Also, evaluate your platform's support for relationships between assets, for example, abstraction relationships, like generalization versus specialization, or whole-part relationships, like composition, aggregation, or association. For inter-asset relationships, you should also investigate whether an architecture platform automatically discovers connections, or auto-inverts manually maintained relationships, so that they are bidirectionally navigable. Reasonable support for asset relationships on a platform greatly improves search, navigation, and filtering capabilities. Finally, examine your platform's support for representing analog components in the physical world (e.g., data center building) and for introducing abstractions relevant to your business model perspective (e.g., customer, supplier, account, product) (**ARCHITECTURE ASSET**).

---

[197] A domain-specific language (DSL) is a formal language specialized for a particular domain, which contrasts with a general-purpose language (GPL), broadly applicable across domains. Domain-specific languages allow solutions to be expressed in the problem domain's idiom. The idea of a DSL is to enable domain experts understand, validate, modify, and often even develop solution algorithms themselves. Examples of domain-specific languages are MATLAB (i.e., an abbreviation for matrix laboratory), which allows mathematical matrix manipulations, plotting of functions and data, or SQL (i.e., an acronym for structured query language), a domain-specific language designed for manipulating data in a relational database management system.

Establishing and evolving an architecture platform is laborious. And less is often more. So take a slice-by-slice approach to building and evolving your platform. Start small and build it out incrementally. For example, ask your platform vendor for an overview of the use cases supported by their platform product. Gradually realize platform use cases along the priorities of your architecture function. Fundamentally question an architecture platform if its vendor cannot articulate the use cases, value proposition, or necessary prerequisites for realizing platform potential with crystal clarity. As with other systems that you plan to buy off-the-shelf, customize to your needs, and use over time, take steps to avoid vendor lock-in. Mitigate this risk by ensuring your platform supports standard view models (e.g., TOGAF), export and import capabilities, and a flexible metamodel. When making customizations, be mindful of whether you lose future platform compatibility as a result. Use the sophisticated customization technologies that platforms are equipped with cautiously and defensively. The more powerful a platform's customization technology is, and the more you use it for platform customizations, the more likely you are to fall into a lobster trap—getting in is easy but getting out is hopeless (MANAGED ARCHITECTURE EVOLUTION).

Ensure that your architecture platform supports not only structured information but also semi-structured and unstructured information. Also, ensure that your platform supports plain text and binary data, such as binary large objects (BLOBs). However, not all data needs to physically reside in a platform. For example, documents can be stored, maintained, and access managed in a document management system. Metadata and a reference to the document, on the other hand, are physically held in the architecture platform. Moreover, ensure a version and release mechanism for your architecture artifacts (ARCHITECTURE ARTIFACT).

An underappreciated and poorly supported concept in platforms is context. While an architecture platform may fully support the representation of an application, contextualized views of that application might not be equally supported. For example, two applications A and B exist as landscape assets in an architecture repository. Application A provides capability$_a$, capability$_b$, and capability$_c$ capabilities. In addition, A depends on B. There are also three structural assets (i.e., the domains D_1, D_2, and D_3) in the architecture repository. While each domain refers to applications A and B, both are viewed differently from each domain (i.e., in the context of each domain). Domain D_1, for example, considers application A as dependent on B and provides a capability capability$_{A1}$. In contrast to D_1, domain D_3 reduces the situation to applications B and A at the landscape asset level. If an architecture platform does not support capturing such context specifics, A and B cannot be viewed and described relatively, but only absolutely (Fig. 6.227).

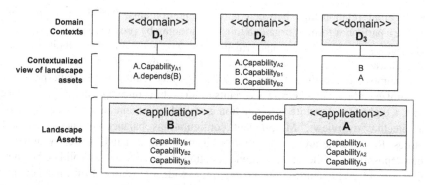

Fig. 6.227 Concept of context in an architecture platform

   Review the features a platform offers in terms of automating tasks. Pay particular
attention to automated checks, such as checking consistency and coherence criteria
for asset changes. Also, exploit automated model updates where they exist to free
your architects from manual maintenance work while minimizing the risk for
maintenance errors, for example, an automated update to an architecture description
document based on associated information in the description of an underlying
system. A platform should always tell the difference between automatically updated
information and information that has been manually modified. Another helpful
platform feature is automatic notifications, for example, notifications about redundancies that the platform has detected. Finally, your platform should support an
event chronology along a timeline based on architecture calendars. It should be
possible to create calendars for individual architecture assets. It must be also possible
to synchronize, aggregate, and query calendars, for example, to detect scheduling
collisions (**ARCHITECTURE CALENDAR**).

   The ability to manage multiple parallel architecture releases and versions (i.e.,
past, current, and future) is an important capability that not all platforms support
equally. Controlled release of an architecture description is also critical in a collaborative environment. For example, a domain architect needs to be able to describe
the future architecture of a domain (e.g., domain target architecture in 3 years). He
should also be able to hold this description next to the domain's base architecture
(*present*) and two previous architecture versions (*past*)—and thus comparing different releases to analyze deltas. At the end of an architecture development, a domain
architect should be able to transport a domain target description to a platform
production stage via a controlled process (**BASELINE ARCHITECTURE VERSUS TARGET
ARCHITECTURE**).

   A key point to consider is how well an architecture platform fits and is embedded
in your enterprise operating model. In other words: how well does your platform
support your partitioning needs (e.g., partitioning along different organizational
units, architecture boards, or individual stakeholders)? Or think about domain-
specific partitioning, partitioning along a capability map, and support for

aggregation relationships between and among domains. Architecture platforms enable a particular form of organizational partitioning by providing multi-tenancy[198] capabilities. A multi-tenant platform provides you with multiple, albeit logically separate, architecture repositories running on the same physical platform instance. For example, relatively autonomous business units within a large enterprise can customize and manage their own variants of an architecture repository. At the same time, a higher-level architecture function is tasked with maintaining enterprise-level architecture overviews. Multi-tenant configurations balance the needs of both parties. Responsible architects within a business unit can independently optimize their repositories, while an architecture function can access and consolidate business unit domain architectures into an enterprise-wide repository. Multi-tenancy and cross-tenant consolidation capabilities balance the autonomy of a business unit on the one hand and consolidated architecture overviews on the other (ORGANIZATIONAL REPLICATION).

Another common form of partitioning is vertical partitioning. Vertical partitioning allows you to represent the vertical design of your architecture function. It interlocks architecture levels to allow seamless navigation and traceability between them. Vertical partitioning supports drill-in and drill-out capabilities between architecture models at different levels of abstraction and granularity. Be aware, however, that while vertical partitioning enables holistic navigability, it also significantly increases the complexity of your metamodel design (ARCHITECTURE LEVEL, ARCHITECTURE TRACEABILITY).

Ensure reliable and up-to-date design information by connecting your platform with complementary databases, tools, and repositories. At a minimum, integrate your architecture repository with your enterprise's corresponding master and reference data sources, for example, master data such as *customers*, *products*, and *locations* or reference data such as *country* and *currency codes* that you use by default in your organization. Link identity and access management platforms to your architecture platform to control access to repository data for your architects and other stakeholders. Architecture platforms focus predominantly on a level of abstraction that represents conceptual and logical building blocks. In contrast, data representing physical reality is automatically captured by monitoring tools and managed in configuration management systems[199] (CMS). Also, link your architecture platform

---

[198] Multi-tenancy design is an approach in which a single physical solution serves multiple clients (i.e., tenant). Systems adopting a multi-tenancy architecture provide physically shared resources while ensuring logically separated and tenant-specific spaces. Multi-tenant architectures are designed to provide each tenant with a dedicated share of a physical instance, where such share includes data, configuration, user administration, and tenant-specific functional as well as non-functional properties.

[199] A configuration management system or database (CMS/CMDB) is a system for storing information about an organization's critical assets and the relationships between them. Assets in a CMS/CMDB are referred to as configuration items (CI). CI examples include virtual and physical compute nodes, network components, end-user devices, databases, application servers, directory services, transaction monitors, or application software components. A CMS/CMDB provides a means of understanding an organization's critical assets and their relationships at the physical instance level.

with configuration management systems to perform consistency checks between logical (*architecture reality*) and physical reality (*operational reality*). Landscape asset repositories such as application portfolios, service portfolios, or project portfolios are other systems you should integrate your platform with to enable portfolio-related consistency checks.

Pay full attention to platform usability. User experience largely determines the appropriateness of your architects' use of your platform and thus the relevance, completeness, and consistency of your design descriptions. When the barrier to updating architecture descriptions is low, this is directly reflected in the reliability and freshness of respective descriptions. For example, the modeling component of an architecture platform that supports a standardized and well-established modeling nomenclature will be better accepted by your architects than a modeling component that favors proprietary modeling means. Another excellent example of low hurdles is semi-structured architecture descriptions, such as hybrid wikis (Keller 2017). The less structure you enforce and the more *freestyle* you encourage, the more architects you invite to contribute their knowledge to asset descriptions on a regular basis. In this way, you inspire and harvest the intelligence of the crowd. At the same time, make sure freestyle does not come at the expense of architectural arbitrariness or lack of structure.

Your architecture function values the maintenance of design models and information because it is interested in holistic analysis. Therefore, ensure that your platform provides rich analysis, correlation, visualization, simulation, and reporting capabilities for the architecture and non-architecture community. For example, dashboards, bubble charts, and similar visualizations provide high-level overviews and are aimed at executives. In contrast, flowcharts or process models appeal to business analysts. Detailed design models like UML diagrams, on the other hand, are intended for domain and solution architects. Visualization of interrelationships (e.g., matrices) draws the attention of different stakeholder groups to overlapping areas of interest. Finally, time-bound perspectives are supported by simulations, projections, or scenario playing. Other features expected from interaction with platforms include export and import capabilities or support for different user interface channels, for example, rich and thin clients or smartphones.

Further Reading

Alexander, Christopher. 1979. *The Timeless Way of Building*. New York: Oxford University Press.
Alexander, Christopher, Sara Ishikawa, Murray Silverstein, Max Jacobson, Ingrid Fiksdahl-King, and Shlomo Angel. 1977. *A Pattern Language*. Oxford University Press.
Apostel, Leo. 1960. Towards the formal study of models in the non-formal sciences. *Synthese* 12.
Ashby, William Ross. 1964. *An Introduction to Cybernetics*. London: Methuen.
Bass, Len, Paul Clements, and Rick Kazman. 2003. *Software Architecture in Practice*. 2nd ed. New York: Addison-Wesley.
Bente, Stefan, Uwe Bombosch, and Shailendra Langade. 2012. *Collaborative Enterprise Architecture - Enriching EA with Lean, Agile, and Enterprise 2.0 Practices*. London: Elsevier.

Bertalanffy, Ludwig von. 2015. *General System Theory: Foundations, Development, Applications*. George Braziller Incorporated.

Booch, Grady. 2009. *Object-Oriented Analysis and Design with Applications*. Amsterdam: Pearson Education.

Bruch, Heike, and Bernd Vogel. 2009. *Organisationale Energie – Wie Sie das Potenzial Ihres Unternehmens ausschöpfen*. Berlin: Springer-Verlag.

Buschmann, Frank, Kevlin Henney, and Douglas C. Schmidt. 2007. *Pattern-Oriented Software Architecture Vol. 5, A Pattern Language for Distributed Computing*. New York: Wiley.

Business Architecture Guild, *A Guide to the Business Architecture Body of Knowledge® (BIZBOK® Guide) – Part 1: Introduction*, 2016.

Cambridge, *Cambridge Dictionary*, https://dictionary.cambridge.org/dictionary, 2020.

Conway, Melvin. 1968. *How Do Committees invent? Datamation*.

De Haes, Steven, Wim Van Grembergen, Anant Joshi, and Tim Huygh. 2020. *Enterprise Governance of Information Technology*. Cham: Springer.

Dictionary.Com *Dictionary*, https://www.dictionary.com/, 2020.

Dietz, Jan. 2006. *Enterprise Ontology: Theory and Methodology*. Berlin: Springer Science & Business Media.

Fehskens, Len, *What the "Architecture" in "Enterprise Architecture" ought to mean*, In: The Open Group Conference, Boston, 2008.

Fowler, Martin, *Martin Fowler's Bliki – Application Boundary*, https://martinfowler.com/bliki/ApplicationBoundary.html, 2006.

Gamma, Erich, Richard Helm, Ralph Johnson, and John Vlissides. 1994. *Design Patterns - Elements of Reusable Object-Oriented Software*. Amsterdam: Pearson Education.

Greefhorst, Danny, and Erik Proper. 2011. *Architecture Principles - The Cornerstones of Enterprise Architecture*. Berlin: Springer Science & Business Media.

Huppertz, Service-Spezifizierung – 12 Service-Attribute, http://omnitracker2.blogspot.com/2012/05/paul-g-huppertz-service-specifying-12.html, 2012

IEEE Computer Society, *IEEE Recommended Practice for Architecture Description of Software-Intensive Systems*, IEEE std. IEEE – pp. 1472–2000, New York, 2000.

Ishak, Irny Suzila, *Designing a Strategic Information System Planning Methodology for Malaysian Institutes of Higher Learning (ISP-IPTA)*, Universiti Teknologi Malaysia, Issues in Information System, Volume VI, No. 1, 2005.

IT Governance Institute, *COBIT 4.1 – Maturity Model*, http://www.isaca.org.ua/index.php/homepage/download/category/2-standards?download=6:cobit-4-1-eng, 2020.

Keith, Bonnie, Kate Vitasek, Karl Manrodt, and Jeanne Kling. 2015. *Strategic Sourcing in the New Economy – Harnessing the Potential of Sourcing Business Models for Modern Procurement*. Berlin: Springer.

Keller, Wolfgang, *IT-Unternehmensarchitektur – von der Geschäftsstrategie zur optimalen IT-Unterstützung*, dpunkt.verlag, Heidelberg, 2017.

Kim, W. Chan, and Renée Mauborgne. 2016. *Blue Ocean Strategy – How to Create Uncontested Market Space and Make the Competition Irrelevant*. Boston: Harvard Business Review Press.

Kotusev, Svyatoslav. 2018. *The Practice of Enterprise Architecture*. Melbourne: SK Publishing.

Lankhorst, Marc. 2017. *Enterprise Architecture at Work*. Berlin: Springer-Verlag.

Matthes, Florian, Ivan Monahov, Alexander Schneider, and Christopher Schulz. 2011. *EAM KPI Catalogue*. Fakultät für Informatik, Technische Universität München.

Merriam-Webster, *Merriam-Webster Dictionary*, https://www.merriam-webster.com/dictionary, 2020.

Millard, Richard Luke. 2001. *Value Stream Analysis and Mapping for Product Development*. Boston: Massachusetts Institute of Technology, Department of Aeronautics and Astronautics.

Murer, Stephan, Bruno Bonati, and Frank Furrer. 2010. *Managed Evolution – A Strategy for Very Large Information Systems*. Berlin: Springer Science & Business Media.

The Object Management Group, UML® Version 2.5, https://www.uml.org/, 2020

Patton, George Smith, and Paul Donal Harkins. 1995. *War as I Knew it*. Orlando: Houghton Mifflin Harcourt.

Pollio, Marcus Vitruvius. 2013. *De Architectura – Libri Decem*. Amsterdam: Elsevier.

Schekkerman, Jaap. 2004. *How to Survive in the Jungle of Enterprise Architecture Frameworks – Creating or Choosing an Enterprise Architecture Framework*. Victoria: Trafford Publishing.

Senge, Peter. 2010. *The Fifth Discipline – The Art & Practice of The Learning Organization*. New York: Crown.

Sinek, Simon; *Start with Why – How Great Leaders Inspire Action*, https://www.ted.com/talks/simon_sinek_how_great_leaders_inspire_action, 2009.

Tallman, Stephen. 2011. Offshoring, Outsourcing, and Strategy in the Global firm. *AIB Insights* 11: 3–7.

The Object Management Group, *UML® Version 2.5*, https://www.uml.org/, 2020a.

———, *Business Process Model and Notation*, http://www.bpmn.org/, 2020b.

The Open Group. 2009. *TOGAF™ Version 9*. Zaltbommel: Van Haren Publishing.

———, *Open Certified Architect (Open CA)*, https://www.opengroup.org/certifications/certified-architect-open-ca, 2020a.

———, *TOGAF™ Version 9 – Definitions*, https://pubs.opengroup.org/architecture/togaf9-doc/arch/chap03.html#tag_03_04, 2020b.

———, *ArchiMate®*, https://www.opengroup.org/archimate-home, 2020c.

Thucydides, *The Peloponnesian War*, Translation by R. Crawley, Random House, 1981.

Ward, John, and Joe Peppard. 2002. *Strategic Planning for Information Systems*. New York: Wiley.

Weinberg, Gerald M. 2001. *An Introduction to General Systems Thinking*. New York: Dorset House.

Wikipedia, *Ownership*, https://en.wikipedia.org/wiki/Ownership, 2020a.

———, *Policy*, https://en.wikipedia.org/wiki/Policy, 2020b.

———, Taxonomy, https://en.wikipedia.org/wiki/Taxonomy, 2020c.

———, *Innovation*, https://en.wikipedia.org/wiki/Innovation, 2020d.

———, *Linguistics*, https://en.wikipedia.org/wiki/Linguistics, 2020e.

———, *Methodology*, https://en.wikipedia.org/wiki/Methodology, 2020f.

———, *Principle*, https://en.wikipedia.org/wiki/Principle, 2020g.

———, *Time*, https://en.wikipedia.org/wiki/Time, 2021.

Withall, Stephen. 2007. *Software Requirement Patterns*. Amsterdam: Pearson Education.

Wittgenstein, Ludwig. 1998. *Tractatus logico-philosophicus*. Frankfurt am Main: Suhrkamp.

Index

A
Act, 419
Actor, 222
Adapter, 424
Aggregate, 347
Agnosticism, 290
Alternative, 385
Application, 358
Application architect, 227
Application heuristics, 359
Approach, 393
Approved provider model, 245
Architecture, 254, 256, 349, 367
Architecture act, 208, 268
Architecture alternative, 385–393
Architecture alternatives viewpoint, 460
Architecture approach, 393–400, 469
Architecture artifact, 405
Architecture assessment, 462
Architecture assessment methodology, 462
Architecture assessment process, 465
Architecture assessment report schema, 468
Architecture asset, 346–353
Architecture asset types, 351
Architecture attributes, 465
Architecture building block, 346
Architecture by maxims, 263
Architecture calendar, 286–289
Architecture capacity, 218
Architecture capacity management, 218
Architecture communication viewpoint, 460, 461
Architecture community group, 132

Architecture competence, 228
Architecture condition, 374–377, 379
Architecture decision, 299–304
Architecture decision schema, 302
Architecture demarcation, 342–346
Architecture description, 434
Architecture domain, 261
Architecture drivers, 469
Architecture evolution, 276
Architecture fact, 208, 268
Architecture function, 41, 97, 127–143
Architecture function apparatus, 103, 142
Architecture function challenge, 25
Architecture function charter, 128
Architecture function communication, 101, 137
Architecture function constitution, 25
Architecture function context, 25
Architecture function designs, 12
Architecture function elasticity, 120, 187
Architecture function engagement model, 100, 135
Architecture function evolvability, 121, 188, 348
Architecture function governance, 102, 138–140
Architecture function mission, 128
Architecture function organization, 99, 131
Architecture function pattern catalogue, 13, 47
Architecture function pattern language, 12, 23, 26, 41
Architecture function pattern ontology, 13, 49, 58
Architecture function pattern topology, 13, 25, 43

Architecture function pattern topology–
    challenge, 46
Architecture function pattern topology–
    constitution, 47
Architecture function pattern topology–context,
    45
Architecture function qualities, 184, 321
Architecture function reliability, 122, 190–191,
    435
Architecture function roadmap, 103, 140
Architecture function service, 104–117, 143
Architecture function service catalogue, 144
Architecture function usability, 119, 185, 251
Architecture function vision, 128
Architecture funding, 237–241
Architecture goals, 208, 268
Architecture governance, 234, 268
Architecture governance decision, 272
Architecture innovation, 325
Architecture KPI, 208, 209
Architecture KPI schema, 212
Architecture language, 311
Architecture level, 373–377
Architecture mandate, 334–341
Architecture mandate schema, 337
Architecture maturity, 207–218, 275, 377–380
Architecture maturity model, 208, 215, 217
Architecture methodology, 104, 136, 418
Architecture methodology adapter, 424
Architecture non-risk, 467
Architecture ontology, 312
Architecture ownership, 231–236
Architecture ownership matrix, 235
Architecture pattern, 472, 489
Architecture pattern description, 491
Architecture pattern methodology, 489
Architecture pattern process, 496
Architecture platform, 505
Architecture platform ecosystem, 508
Architecture platform management, 508
Architecture platform repository, 508
Architecture platform user experience, 508
Architecture policy, 281–286
Architecture principle, 472, 501
Architecture qualities, 118
Architecture radar chart, 215
Architecture relevance, 340
Architecture relevance criteria, 341
Architecture roadmap, 472, 479
Architecture roadmap methodology, 479
Architecture roadmap process, 485
Architecture role, 222–231
Architecture role definition, 230

Architecture role model, 226
Architecture scorecard, 213
Architecture sensitivity point, 398, 467
Architecture-significance heuristics, 372
Architecture sourcing, 241–249
Architecture sourcing model, 245
Architecture SPOC, 250
Architecture standard, 283
Architecture traceability, 304–308
Architecture trade-off point, 398, 467
Architecture validation viewpoint, 460, 462
Architecture versus non-architecture design,
    370
Architecture view model, 432
Architecture viewpoint, 435
Area of innovation, 327
Area of interest, 327
Artifact, 405
Assess architecture service, 107, 145
Assessment, 462
Assessment drivers, 469
Assessment report, 467
Asset, 350
Assumption, 378
Availability architect, 227

B
Baseline, 412
Baseline architecture versus target architecture,
    411
Basic provider model, 245
Blue ocean strategy, 276
Building block, 346
Bureaucratic organization, 65
Business, 400
Business architect, 227
Business model, 59
Business model canvas, 59
Business strategy organization, 80
Business versus domain disciplines, 291
Business versus technical, 400

C
Calendar, 286
Calendar event schema, 289
Capability, 319, 377
Capability map, 321
Capability maturity model, 216
Capacity, 218
Classical architecture, 14
COBIT maturity levels, 216

Comfortable energy, 225
Communication, 309
Communication misconceptions, 311
Competence metric, 229
Complexity, 348
Concern, 435
Condition, 377
Condition viewpoint, 456
Constraint, 378
Contact, 250
Context viewpoint, 455
Coordination act, 419
Coordination fact, 419
Core architecture group, 132
Corrosive energy, 225
Cost center, 238
Cross-cutting architecture viewpoint, 460

D
Decision, 299
Decommissioning, 294
Decommissioning reward, 295
Definition of done, 224
Delegation, 241
Delegation model, 243
Demarcation, 342
Design, 370
Design cause, 368
Design decision, 368
Determine architecture relevance *service*, 111, 160
Digital, 68
Digital business, 72
Digital enterprise, 73
Digitalization, 68
Digitalized, 68
Digital system, 68, 70
Digitization
    digitalization
        digital means, 2
Digitized, 68
Discipline, 254
Division of powers, 270
Divisional organization structure, 66
Domain, 260, 290, 318
Domain architect, 227
Domain architecture, 17
Domain architecture discipline, 260–263
Domain architecture methodology, 415, 444
Domain architecture processes, 449
Domain architecture view model, 450
Domain-organization agnosticism, 290,
    292–294
Domain roadmap, 483
Domain taxonomy, 318

E
Elaborate architecture alternatives service, 112,
    113, 163
Elaborate architecture mandate service, 115,
    174, 221
Elaborate architecture problem resolution
    service, 117, 182, 298
Elaborate domain architecture service, 108, 149
Elaborate service architecture service, 116, 178,
    271
Elasticity, 120, 187
Enterprise, 18
Enterprise alignment architecture, 19
Enterprise architect, 227
Enterprise architecture, 18, 256
Enterprise architecture discipline, 254–260
Enterprise architecture function, 20
    architecture function, 19
Enterprise business architecture, 19
Enterprise IT architecture, 19
Enterprise operating model, 41
Enterprise organization, 41, 75
Enterprise pattern catalogue, 36
Enterprise service, 75
Enterprise value chain, 75, 77
Enterprise value stage, 77
Enterprise value stream, 77
Equity partnership model, 246
Event, 287
Evolution, 121, 189, 275
Extended architecture group, 132

F
Fact, 419
Four actions framework, 276
Function
    organizational capability, 20
Functional architecture viewpoints, 437
Functional organizational structure, 66
Funding, 237

G
Goal-KPI matrix, 210
Governance, 268

I
Information, 360
Information architect, 227
Information architecture viewpoints, 438
Innovation, 325
Intention act, 419
IT service, 74

K
Knowledge model, 319

L
Landscape, 353
Landscape asset, 353–362
Landscape asset types, 355
Landscape complexity, 295
Language, 309
Learning, 204
Learning organization, 204
Level, 373
Logical domain architecture, 291
Logical versus physical, 354

M
Make-buy-outsourcing matrix, 243
Managed architecture evolution, 274–281
Managed evolution, 278
Mandate, 335
Matrix organization, 67
Maturity, 207
Meaning, 309
Mental model, 204, 206
Methodological asset, 351
Methodology, 64, 417
Mission, 98, 128
Mission statement, 99, 128
Model, 430
Modelling, 430
Multi-layered ontology, 314

N
Need to know, 329–334
Norm, 207

O
Object system, 255
Off-the-shelf solution schema, 363
Ontological system, 255, 347
Operating model, 60
Operating model canvas, 60
Operation, 419
Operational architecture viewpoints, 437
Operational planning horizon, 19
Organization, 64, 195
Organizational energy, 225
Organizational model, 65
Organizational replication, 195–513

Organizational structuring schema, 65
Organized complexity, 347
Ownership, 231

P
Pattern, 32, 489
Pattern catalogue, 36
Pattern language, 21, 36, 499
Pattern language adoption, 51
Pattern ontology, 40
Pattern topology, 40
Performance architect, 227
Performance-based model, 246
Personal mastery, 204
Phase, 77
Physical domain architecture, 291
Platform, 358, 505
Platform architect, 227
Policy, 282
Policy attribute schema, 283
Post-bureaucratic organization, 66
Preferred provider model, 245
Principle, 378, 501
Problem, 255
Problem-solution dichotomy, 264
Process model, 63
Production act, 419
Production fact, 419
Productive energy, 225
Profit center, 238
Project portfolio organization, 83, 109, 152
Project portfolio stages, 83, 109, 152
Project roadmap, 487
Propose architecture demand service, 110, 157
Proposition act, 419

Q
Quality attribute scenario, 382, 469
Question, 329

R
Reference, 470
Reference architecture, 470
Reference architecture asset, 472
Reference architecture methodology, 470
Reference architecture methodology process, 473
Reference architecture process, 473
Reference asset portfolio, 477
Reference asset schema, 476

Reliable, 122, 141
Requirement, 377
Requirement pattern, 383
Resigned phlegm, 225
Responsibility assignment matrix, 232
Roadmap, 479
Roadmap permutation cube, 485
Role, 222

S
Security architect, 227
Semiotics, 309
Service, 74, 356
Service architect, 227
Service architecture organization, 86, 99, 100
Service architecture stage, 86, 98
Service building value stream, 84, 114, 173, 266
Service delivery value stream, 91
Service demand stage, 81
Service deployment stages, 87, 114, 173
Service diagnosis organization, 90
Service diagnosis stage, 90
Service fulfillment stage, 92
Service implementation organization, 87
Service implementation stage, 87
Service measurement stage, 92
Service monitoring and detection organization, 89
Service monitoring and detection stage, 89
Service operations organization, 88
Service planning value stream, 79, 109, 152
Service plan organization, 85, 99
Service plan stage, 85, 99
Service portfolio organization, 83, 96
Service portfolio stage, 82
Service problem resolution organization, 91
Service problem resolution stage, 90
Service publishing stage, 91
Service running value stream, 88, 116, 141, 181, 266
Service strategy organization, 80
Service strategy stage, 79
Shared services model, 246
Shared vision, 204
Significance, 299, 367
Single point of contact (SPOC), 250
Socio-technical system, 74
Solution, 264
Solution architect, 227
Solution architecture, 16

Solution architecture discipline, 260–267
Solution architecture evolution, 452
Solution architecture methodology, 450
Solution architecture process, 453
Solution architecture view model, 455
Solution roadmap, 483
Solution viewpoint, 457
Sourcing business models, 245
Stage, 77
Stakeholder, 435
Standard, 283
State, 412
Strategic planning horizon, 19
System, 70, 196, 347, 431, 435
System complexity, 349
System evolution coordinate system, 279
Systems theory, 70
Systems thinking, 204

T
Tactical planning horizon, 19
Target, 412
Taxon, 319
Taxonomy, 318
Team learning, 204, 205
Technical, 400
Technical architect, 227
Technology, 361
Technology versus technical, 357
Teleological system, 255, 347
Tracing, 304

U
Usability, 119, 159
Use case, 380
Use case modeling, 380
Using system, 255

V
Validate project proposal service, 114, 169
Validate service portfolio service, 113, 166
Validate strategy service, 110, 153
Value chain, 62
Vested provider model, 246
View, 432
Viewpoint, 432
Vision, 98, 128

Printed in the United States
by Baker & Taylor Publisher Services